VOLTAIRE

VOLTAIRE

a life

IAN DAVIDSON

PEGASUS BOOKS
NEW YORK

VOLTAIRE
Pegasus Books LLC
80 Broad Street, 5th Floor
New York, NY 10004

First Pegasus Books hardcover edition 2010

Library of Congress Cataloging-in-Publication Data is available.

ISBN: 978-1-60598-119-2

10 9 8 7 6 5 4 3 2 1

Printed in the United States of America
Distributed by W. W. Norton & Company, Inc.
www.pegasusbooks.us

CONTENTS

To Jennifer

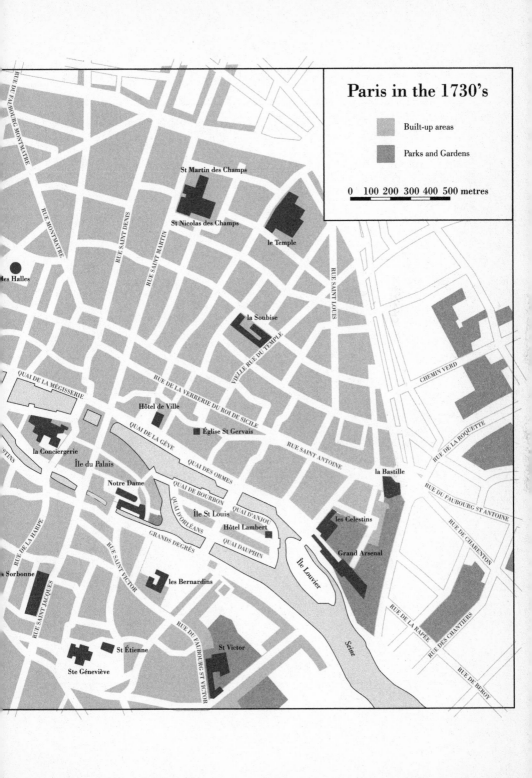

Paris in the 1730's

Built-up areas

Parks and Gardens

0   100 200 300 400 500 metres

RUE DU FAUBOURG MONTMARTRE

St Martin des Champs

RUE SAINT DENIS

RUE MONTMARTRE

RUE SAINT MARTIN

St Nicolas des Champs

le Temple

les Halles

RUE SAINT LOUIS

la Soubise

VIELLE RUE DU TEMPLE

CHEMIN VERD

QUAI DE LA MÉGISSERIE

RUE DE LA VERRERIE DU ROI DE SICILE

RUE DE LA ROQUETTE

Hôtel de Ville

QUAI DE LA GÈVE

Église St Gervais

la Concergerie

Île du Palais

RUE SAINT ANTOINE

QUAI DES ORMES

la Bastille

Notre Dame

QUAI DE BOURBON

RUE DU FAUBOURG ST ANTOINE

Île St Louis

QUAI D'ANJOU

les Celestins

RUE DE CHARENTON

Hôtel Lambert

QUAI D'ORLÉANS

GRANDS DEGRÉS

QUAI DAUPHIN

Grand Arsenal

RUE DE LA HARPE

RUE SAINT VICTOR

Île Louvier

Sorbonne

les Bernardins

RUE DE LA RAPÉE

RUE SAINT JACQUES

Seine

RUE DES CHANTIERS

St Étienne

St Victor

RUE DU FAUBOURG ST VICTOR

Ste Génevieve

RUE DE BERCY

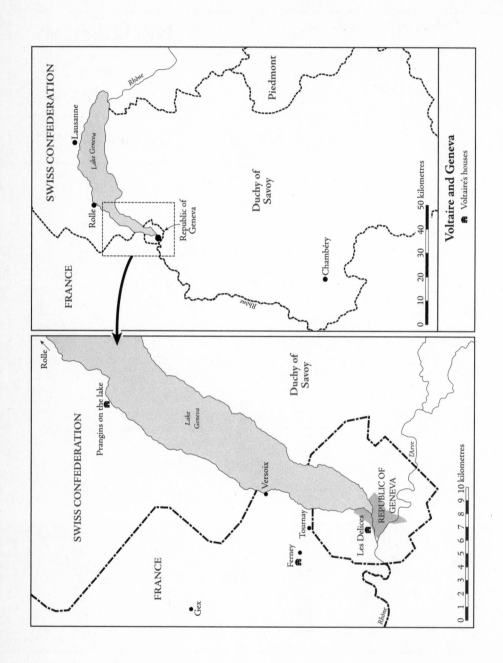

Voltaire and Geneva

⌂ Voltaire's houses

NOTE TO THE READER

Francs and livres; pounds, shillings and pence; feet and inches
Under the ancien régime the structure of the French currency was very similar, for historical reasons, to that of Britain before decimalisation in 1971. The principal currency unit in France was the livre (meaning 'pound'), and its symbol was £, a stylised form of the letter L; the franc was an equivalent term, meaning the same as livre. There were 20 sous to each livre, and 12 deniers to each sou (or sol). So the symbols for the main units of the French currency under the ancien régime were £ s. d., just as they were in England. The French currency also included the louis (a gold coin worth £24), the écu (a silver coin worth £6) and the petit écu (worth £3).

In this book, unless otherwise specified, the symbol £ should be taken to mean livre or franc.

There were analogous similarities of structure in French and English units of measurement: in France there were 12 pouces to the pied, just as there were 12 inches to the foot. But the French units were larger than the English: the pouce was 2.707 cm, and the pied was 32.5 cm, whereas the inch was 2.54 cm, and the foot 30.48 cm.

I have not attempted to make any direct translations between money values in the eighteenth century and money values today, because the attempt is hopeless: if you were to compare the price of bread then with the price of bread today, you would get one rate, but if you were to compare the prices of houses, you would get another. Theodore Besterman points out that commodity prices more than doubled between the death of Louis XIV and the French Revolution, whereas wages increased by only about 20 per cent, and yet he estimated in his biography *Voltaire* (1969) that the franc or livre of Voltaire's day was roughly equivalent to a US dollar. This kind of exchange rate conversion implies a precision that is spurious and largely misleading. Moreover, Besterman's rate seems to me wildly out of kilter; if one had to choose a single exchange rate, it would probably have to be closer to £1 = $10.

In the last resort we probably cannot get a useful answer to the question 'What would 50,000 livres be worth today?', because it is the wrong question. What we should be asking instead is: 'What would 50,000 livres have meant then?' Following this line of thought, it has been argued that in the eighteenth century a person with an annual income of 15,000 livres or more could be described as wealthy, and a person with an income of 30,000 livres or more could be described as extremely wealthy.[1] If this benchmark is even roughly valid, it implies that when Voltaire became wealthy, after 1729, he became very, very, very wealthy.

Life expectancy

On average, life expectancy was much shorter in France in the eighteenth century than it is today; but only on average. Many died in infancy, and many died of disease; but those who survived the dangers of birth and sickness and who were spared the even greater dangers attendant on poverty and malnutrition, could live long lives, comparable to those of today.

Peri-natal mortality was very high, perhaps about 50 per cent. Voltaire's mother, Marie-Marguerite Daumart, had five children, two of whom died almost immediately. Similarly, Émilie du Châtelet (Voltaire's mistress and the love of his life) had three legitimate children by her husband. The first two survived to adulthood; the third died suddenly, in infancy, only sixteen months old. Fifteen years later, in 1749, she had a fourth child, by the Marquis de Saint-Lambert; she and the child, a daughter, both died in childbirth.

Death was also common in early adulthood. Voltaire's mother died in 1701, when she was only forty-one, and Voltaire was seven; his sister, Marguerite-Catherine, died in 1726, when she was only thirty-nine.

Hygiene and medicine were both quite primitive, and one of the major killers was smallpox. Voltaire caught the disease in a major epidemic in 1723 and survived, but his close friend Nicolas de La Faluère de Génonville died of it. An even closer friend, Jean-René de Longueil, marquis de Maisons, also caught the disease at the same time as Voltaire;

in fact, Voltaire caught it while staying in Maisons's house. Maisons survived this epidemic but was infected again eight years later, in 1731, and this time he died of it.

But the survivors could live long lives. The table below shows that many of Voltaire's most prominent contemporaries, and many of his most frequent correspondents, lived into their sixties, seventies, eighties, or even nineties. The most signal exception was Étienne-Noël Damilaville, who died of throat cancer, aged forty-five.

	Dates	*Age*
André-Hercule, Cardinal de Fleury	1653–1743	90
Prosper Jolyot Crébillon	1674–1762	88
Voltaire	1694–1778	84
René-Louis de Voyer, marquis d'Argenson	1694–1757	63
Mme de Graffigny	1695–1758	63
Marc-Pierre de Voyer, comte d'Argenson	1696–1764	68
Nicolas-Claude Thieriot	1696–1772	76
Mme du Deffand	1697–1780	83
Pierre Louis Moreau de Maupertuis	1698–1759	61
Duc de Richelieu	1699–1788	89
Charles-Augustin, comte d'Argental	1700–1788	88
Jean-Robert Tronchin	1702–1788	86
François Tronchin	1704–1798	94
Jean-Frédéric Phélypeaux, comte de Maurepas	1701–1781	80
Théodore Tronchin	1709–1781	72
Louis XV	1710–1774	64
Frederick the Great	1712–1786	74
Jean-Jacques Rousseau	1712–1778	66
Denis Diderot	1713–1784	71
Jean-François, marquis de Saint-Lambert	1716–1803	87
Jean Le Rond d'Alembert	1717–1783	66
Étienne-François, duc de Choiseul	1719–1785	66
Étienne-Noël Damilaville	1723–1768	45

Footnotes and endnotes

I have tried to keep footnotes to a minimum, but occasionally there is a gobbet of information that seems to me interesting and relevant, and worth including, even though it may not fit naturally into the body of the text.

There are many endnotes, but their sole function is to provide a source or citation for information in the body of the text, usually in the form of a quotation from a letter or other document. In the ordinary course of events, therefore, the general reader can simply ignore these endnotes.

PROLOGUE

THERE IS MUCH TALK of the Enlightenment these days; and whenever one thinks of the Enlightenment, one thinks, first or last, of Voltaire. The reason for this is not because of any discovery he made or any new theory he advanced; it is because of the way he thought and the way he talked. Voltaire's voice is the voice of the Enlightenment.

Today the values of the Enlightenment, and therefore the values of our civilisation, are under attack as never before. On the one hand, we have lived through the barbarities of the Bush régime, which seemed determined to take America, and the world, a long way back, and in the process to undermine the values both of the Enlightenment and of their own founding fathers. On the other, we face an increasing threat of terrorist violence by Islamic fundamentalists, who seem determined to take the world even further back, overthrowing not merely the values of the West but also those of their own much earlier version of the Enlightenment.

The Enlightenment was not, of course, confined to one country, let alone to one man. Yet if anyone could be said to epitomise the Enlightenment, it was undoubtedly Voltaire, as his contemporaries, both his friends and above all his enemies, recognised with the greatest clarity.

Even in this context, however, Voltaire is a paradoxical figure. Today we may think of him as a pioneer of a peculiarly French Enlightenment, yet he himself never sought to be a leader of the Enlightenment, or indeed of anything. On the contrary, so intense was his personal ambition for literary success, and so great his fear of rivals, or of persecution by the authorities, that his career was marked at every step by feuds and crises; despite his celebrity, he never managed to take a philosophical view of his own ups and downs; and he certainly never took a detached interest in the works of other writers. Indeed, it was not until the appearance of the *Encyclopédie*, when he was in his late fifties, that it seems to have occurred to him that he might be part of a wider intellectual movement, let alone part of a common enterprise.

What Voltaire wanted was to be an entertainer: a writer, a poet, a playwright and a storyteller. In this he succeeded brilliantly, with a meteoric career as France's leading writer of classical verse tragedies; and in the process he became the most celebrated and the most controversial individual in Europe, for the fertility of his wit, intellect and imagination kept him permanently in the public eye; if he was a *philosophe,* he was also the first example of a truly international celebrity. In other words, he became one of Europe's first public intellectuals, independent of any patron or employer; he may even be said to have started a tradition which continues to this day in France, where the ad hoc pronouncements on events of the day by a handful of self-styled *philosophes* are treated by the media and by the ordinary public with inordinate respect.

It was Voltaire's celebrity which made him the father figure of the Enlightenment. What he needed most deeply was the freedom to write and the freedom to speak, and especially the freedom to question official doctrines; and he had two unique assets which enabled him to assert these rights, at a time when they were systematically and ferociously denied by the *ancien régime*: he was famous, and he was rich. The authorities could not effectively silence his voice, because everyone, but *everyone*, wanted to know what he was saying and writing; and they could not starve him into submission, because he had the independence of great wealth. In that sense Voltaire became a champion of the principle of freedom of speech, at least for himself; and towards the end of his very long life he went on to become the champion of justice for others.

The Enlightenment was not, of course, a uniquely French affair, although the French sometimes like to think that it was. What was unique about the Enlightenment in France was that it was characterised less by intellectual innovation than by a permanent running conflict between the emerging new movement of the *philosophes*, or free-thinkers, and the repressive apparatus of the *ancien régime*, in alliance with the deadly power of the Catholic Church.

In this conflict, which highlighted the all-too-slow death throes of the *ancien régime*, Voltaire's iconic reputation as the standard-bearer of the Enlightenment is ironic. He did not deliberately choose to confront the powers of the state, at least not for the first sixty-five years of his life, for he was not naturally equipped to play a heroic role. On the contrary, he was liable to run away at the first whiff of danger, as Condorcet wrote in one of the earliest biographies of Voltaire: 'He was often seen to expose himself to the storm, almost with temerity, but seldom to stand up to it with firmness; and these alternations of audacity and weakness have often afflicted his friends, and prepared unworthy triumphs for his cowardly enemies.'[1]

For Voltaire was not by nature a heroic warrior for the truth. He simply wanted to succeed as a playwright and poet, he wanted readers and spectators, and when they came to see his plays, he wanted to move them: the ultimate test, in his mind, was whether he could make them cry. If he came repeatedly into conflict with the authorities, it was not as a deliberate strategic choice but as the unintended consequence of his determination to write what he wanted.

Moreover, if Voltaire was the standard-bearer of the *philosophes*, he was not really a philosopher at all, at least not in the modern Anglo-Saxon sense of the term. He has given us two wonderful sardonic masterpieces, the *Lettres philosophiques* and *Candide*, but he produced no worked-through corpus of original philosophical thought to compare with Montesquieu's *De l'Esprit des Lois*, or Rousseau's *Le Contrat social*.

On the other hand, he did believe passionately in two values that are at the heart of the Enlightenment: the essential value of toleration and pluralism, in the face of the fanaticism of the régime; and the right of every man to think and say what he liked, in the face of censorship and repression.

His belief in these two core values was fixed early. He was in his twenties when he articulated his belief in toleration, with the composition of his epic poem *La Henriade*, celebrating the precarious efforts of Henri IV in the sixteenth century to make peace in the long-running wars between Catholics and Protestants. And his belief in pluralism and free speech, stimulated by early visits to the Netherlands, was crystallised by his two-year exile in England and eventually took shape in the explosive satire of the *Lettres philosophiques*.

These were, of course, precisely the values that the *ancien régime* found most threatening. At bottom, they did not care two hoots about Newton's laws of motion or Locke's views on the nature of the soul, since they knew that these were questions that were of interest to only a tiny minority of obscure intellectuals; the only thing that they really could not stand was any claim to toleration, pluralism and freedom of speech. Voltaire's pursuit of these values repeatedly got him into trouble with the authorities: he was twice locked up in the Bastille and three times sent into exile.

On the other hand, everyone (and that included everyone at court) was fascinated by Voltaire's celebrity: they wanted to see his plays, and they wanted to know what he thought and said. At the same time the authorities always regarded him as a dangerous subversive and constantly tried to muzzle him. In practice, however, they could not silence him, and in his sixties and seventies Voltaire openly challenged the powers of the state in a series of sensational campaigns on behalf of victims of scandalous miscarriages of justice.

I have written this book as the story of Voltaire's life as he lived it, up close and personal, concentrating more on the man than on his writings, for this is not what is sometimes called a critical biography. I have dwelled on some of his most memorable works – the *Lettres philosophiques*, *Candide*, and the *Dictionnaire philosophique* – as well as on his 'human rights' campaigns. But I make no pretence of analysing or assessing his oeuvre as a whole, let alone of discussing in detail all of his many plays or histories: most of his books have gone out of fashion, whereas his life and his personality remain as interesting, as entertaining and as instructive as ever.

The main difficulty, in telling this story, is that Voltaire was such an international celebrity, in his own time and since, that it has been encrusted by successive generations of angry critics and eager gossip-mongers. The angry critics, especially among the hard right and the Catholic Church, love to portray Voltaire as an atheist, which is quite simply and manifestly untrue. The eager gossip-mongers have decorated the picture with many layers of saucy tales, in which it is often difficult to distinguish uncertain fact from juicy fiction. I have tried to strip out some of the most obvious fabrications, even those which have been hallowed by long repetition and which are still regularly trotted out, straight-faced, by academics.

I have relied heavily on the work of many scholars, and especially on the monumental work of scholarship by René Pomeau and a team of collaborators, originally in five volumes, and subsequently reissued in two very thick volumes.[2] But by far my main source of information about all aspects of Voltaire's life has been his voluminous correspondence, which must surely be accounted one of the greatest collections of correspondence ever; Jules Michelet, the great nineteenth-century historian of the French Revolution, described it as 'le grand monument historique du XVIIIe siècle'.[3]

The importance of these letters, as an integral or even central part of Voltaire's oeuvre, has long been recognised. Immediately after Voltaire's death, Beaumarchais and Condorcet embarked on their project for the first complete posthumous edition of his works, and they launched a public appeal for copies of his letters, which were scattered far and wide throughout Europe; they received over 6,000, and in this so-called Kehl edition (they had to publish it on the other side of the Rhine, so as to avoid French censorship), they included some 4,500 of them. Over the next two centuries more and more of Voltaire's letters emerged: Beuchot's monumental edition of Voltaire's complete works, in the early nineteenth century, included some 7,500 of his letters, while Moland's even more monumental edition in the late nineteenth century, took the total up to over 10,000.

By now one might have thought that there could be few more surprises to come, but no. Theodore Besterman, perhaps the leading Voltaire scholar of the twentieth century, handsomely outstripped even Moland, with a new complete edition (or, as he called it, with characteristic self-importance, the Definitive Edition), which included 15,284 of Voltaire's letters, plus nearly 6,000 other letters, either to Voltaire or between third parties, making a grand total, in 51 volumes, of 21,221 letters.

Not the least significant feature of Besterman's researches was his publication of 142 letters from Voltaire to Mme Denis, which proved at last what had often been suspected, that Mme Denis, for many years Voltaire's niece and companion, was also his mistress. Immediately after Voltaire's death in 1778 Mme Denis sold the Ferney estate to the marquis de La Villette, and his library and most of his papers to Catherine the Great; but she kept back a small collection of private papers, and they remained in her family until about 1935. For the next twenty years, they disappeared; but when, in 1957, a private dealer put them on the market, Besterman persuaded the Pierpont Morgan Library of New York to buy the collection and in 1958 he published it.[4]

What makes Voltaire's correspondence so astonishing is that he writes with verve and wit about anything and everything: his anxieties about his latest play, his constipation, the reluctant death throes of an elderly lady, his latest quarrel with some literary rival, the constipation of Mme Denis, Newton's theories, the entertainment value of the scandalous stories in the Old Testament, his finances, his new theatre, his research for his latest history book, his vegetable garden, his instructions to his printer, the education of his charming adoptive daughter, the acting of the latest star at the Comédie Française or the difficulties of buying decent meat. The sheer variety and vitality of Voltaire's interests make his letters a permanent source of interest and of admiration, but it is the way he writes that ensures that he will always be read with amusement. Voltaire was not always gay; on the contrary, he was often depressed. But when he was gay, he was wonderfully entertaining, with an unmatched talent for coining free and fizzy phrases off-the-cuff. *De l'Esprit des Lois* and *Le Contrat social* are both important works, no doubt, but one cannot say that they contain many good jokes.

In the last resort the central constant in Voltaire's life was his belief in toleration and freedom of speech, and it is that which makes his life so relevant and of such compelling interest today. We may believe that the world could and should be run on rational and reasonable lines, yet we also know that it is a world of violence, torture and terrorism, where the rage of groups of fanatical Muslims is matched by the atavistic intolerance of certain fundamentalist Christian sects. These conflicts recall those of the *ancien régime* and make us think, first and last, of Voltaire, the voice of the French Enlightenment.

1

YOUTH

1694–1713

VOLTAIRE WAS BORN in 1694, in the declining years of Louis XIV. He was not, of course, called 'Voltaire' at this stage. His real name was François Marie Arouet, and it was not until 1718, when he was twenty-four and a rising literary star, that he adopted the assumed name 'Voltaire'.

His father, François Arouet, was a successful lawyer with a flourishing professional practice at the heart of Paris, right next to the law courts and the *parlement*. Voltaire was the youngest of Arouet's three surviving children: the eldest was his brother, Armand, who was nine years older, born in 1685; the second was his sister, Marguerite-Catherine, who was eight years older, and born in 1686. Voltaire cordially detested Armand, whom he later despised as a fanatical member of the revivalist Jansenist sect; but he was deeply attached to his sister, Marguerite-Catherine, and when she married, he became very fond of her two daughters.

There are two uncertainties about Voltaire's birth; at least, there were in Voltaire's mind. Officially, he was born in Paris on 21 November 1694; he was baptised at the Église St André des Arts in Paris on 22 November, and the certificate says he was born the previous day. But Voltaire disputed that this was his birthday: in later life he maintained that he had in fact been born nine months earlier, on 20 February 1694. He also believed that his real father was not François Arouet but a shadowy figure called Rochebrune, who was some kind of mousquetaire, officer and occasional poet. He did not give any evidence for either belief.

Voltaire spent much of his youth in a solitary confrontation with his father, François Arouet. His mother, Marie-Marguerite Daumart, died young, on 13 July 1701, at the age of forty-one. His detested brother Armand must have left home in 1703 or 1704, when Voltaire was nine or ten; and his much-loved sister, Marguerite-Catherine, got married (to Pierre François Mignot) in 1709, when Voltaire was fifteen. So from the middle of his adolescence until he finally left home Voltaire lived alone with his domineering father.

François Arouet must have done very well financially, because he had been able to buy a law practice (*cabinet de notaire*) in Paris at the age of twenty-six. In 1696, two years after Voltaire was born, his father sold his law practice and bought instead the more elegant position of tax collector on spices at the Court of Public Accounts (*Receveur des Épices à la Chambre des Comptes*), which went with an official apartment in La Cour Vieille du Palais, near the Sainte-Chapelle.

It was a striking story of a family on the rise. Voltaire's great-grand-father had been a country landowner in Poitou; the grandfather (also called François Arouet) had moved to Paris as a trader in silk and cloth; and Voltaire's father completed the transition by becoming a lawyer. In short, the Arouet family was climbing the professional ladder fast and efficiently, and was well on its way to making the transition from the status of mere commoners to something more elevated.

Professional advancement also brought François Arouet personal and social preferment. His clients included such noble and influential names as the families of Saint-Simon, Villars, Villeroy and Richelieu. The old duc de Richelieu condescended to be godfather to Voltaire's elder brother, Armand; and his son went to the same school as Voltaire and remained a personal friend for life. Another client was Mademoiselle Ninon de Lenclos, one of the most celebrated and most beautiful courtesans of the reign of Louis XIV; Voltaire met her once, shortly before her death, when she was very old and he was very young.

Voltaire's father also knew some of the leading literary figures of the day, including the poet and essayist Nicolas Boileau, and the famous playwright Pierre Corneille; Voltaire could even have met Boileau, who died in 1711, though not Corneille, who died ten years before Voltaire was born.

Voltaire did not get on with his father: in particular, he and his father quarrelled repeatedly over Voltaire's desire to be a writer. Arouet *père* was convinced, conventionally enough, that he had done very well in his profession, and he did his best to persuade, and then to pressure, his son into following in his footsteps. Voltaire was equally determined to be a poet and not a lawyer. This debate turned virtually the whole of Voltaire's youth and adolescence into a ceaseless struggle of wills with his father.

Voltaire did not give up, and neither did his father. Voltaire resisted repeated efforts by his father to force him to follow a career in the law; and he eventually proved his point, when at the age of twenty-four he achieved a sensational success at the Comédie Française with his first tragedy, Œdipe; that same year he changed his name to Voltaire. His father died four years later, after grudgingly conceding that his son had talent, but he still tried to carry on the argument from beyond the grave by penalising Voltaire in his will.

Voltaire has left us almost no trace of his relationship with his parents, since he very seldom refers either to his father or to his mother in his letters. During his adolescence and youth he occasionally alluded to his father, but exclusively as an authority figure who must be obeyed or appeased; there is no trace in his letters at the time of his father as a human being. His mother died when he was only seven, and he does not even mention her in any letters until fifty years after her death. Perhaps Voltaire's idea that he was illegitimate was really just a story he told himself, for archetypal and mythical reasons, as a way of diminishing his father and rationalising the absence of his mother.

In October 1704, when Voltaire was ten years old, his father sent him, as a boarder, to the Collège de Louis-le-Grand, in the rue Saint-Jacques. This was one of the oldest schools in Paris, having been founded by the Jesuits in 1563 under the name Collège de Clermont. It was a very large school, with 3,000 pupils, of whom some 500 were boarders. Throughout most of its long history it had been in conflict with the university next door, which regarded it as an unfair competitor for students, for the Jesuits had decided that education was a charity and that tuition should be free. (The boarders had to pay boarding fees.) Although this conflict had in the past periodically caused trouble for the school, by the end of the seventeenth century the Jesuits were at the height of their power and influence in France, and in 1682 Louis XIV gave the college his patronage, and with it the right to call itself the Collège de Louis-le-Grand.

François Arouet's decision to send his younger son to a Jesuit school is tantalising. The Catholic Church in France was at the time riven by an intense antagonism between two rival sects, the Jesuits and the Jansenists, and Arouet père had sent his eldest son, Armand, to a Jansenist institution. There were doctrinal and specifically religious differences between the two sects, but from a political point of view the main difference between them was that the Jesuits tended to be identified with the monarchy and the court, whereas the Jansenists tended to be identified with the milieu of the law courts and the *parlement*, if only because the lawyers of the *parlement* saw their role as one of resistance or even opposition to the monarchy. For François Arouet, a professional lawyer, to send his eldest son to a Jansenist school might have been a natural reflex; what needs explaining is why he made a different choice for his second son.

The simplest, if speculative, explanation is that this shift corresponded to the rapid advancement of his own career. Armand Arouet was born in 1685, and so was ready for school in about 1695. In the following year his father bought the lucrative position of a *receveur des épices*, but he only secured the full benefits of the situation five years later, in 1701. So when Voltaire was ready for school, in 1704, his father was in the full flower of his prosperity, and he may have thought he could raise his sights to the Collège de Louis-le-Grand, which he may have perceived (rightly) as the school most favoured by the nobility, the rich and the powerful. In short, François Arouet's decision may have been motivated simply by an upward shift in his parental ambitions.

The régime at Louis-le-Grand was strict, and the academic standards high, with a curriculum consisting mainly of Latin. When he emerged seven years later, Voltaire was utterly familiar with the great Latin authors, and for the rest of his life he could readily quote apposite chunks of Virgil, Horace or Cicero. But his education was narrow: he learned little or no history (except ancient history), little or no mathematics, little or no science and little or no modern languages. This narrowness did not prove a material handicap, since he always intended to aim for a literary career. Moreover, he later acquired fluent English and Italian, as well as a certain amount of Spanish; and he even taught himself enough mathematics to persuade himself that he could understand Newton's theories of physics. But the paradox was that his Classical education was itself one-sided, since he learned little or no Greek; so when he set out to become a writer of classical tragedies, ultimately modelled on the works of Aeschylus, Sophocles and Euripides, he had no access to the originals, except through French or Latin translations.

The school is there still; it is now called the Lycée Louis-le-Grand. It is still one of the most prestigious schools in France; it is still a very large school, of 1,800 students; and it still takes in a significant minority of boarders (339 at the last count), who pay €2,023 per year. But it is now co-educational, and the academic emphasis has shifted radically away from Latin to a pre-eminence in maths and science.

In one respect the school is unchanged: it has remained a top forcing ground for the power élite. Today admission is strictly based on intellectual competition, but in Voltaire's day it attracted pupils from many of the leading aristocratic and professional families, including some of the most glittering names of the nobility: Bourbon, Condé, Guise, Joyeuse, La Trémoïlle, Montmorency, La Tour d'Auvergne, Clermont-Tonnerre, Nemours, Noailles, Richelieu. This was the place to make contacts among the rich and the powerful, and one of the most enduring benefits of Voltaire's schooling was that it brought him a number of good friends from the élite of French society, many of whom remained friends for the rest of his life.

The friends Voltaire made at school generally came either from the nobility or from the most successful members of the upper ranks of the legal hierarchy, known as the *noblesse de robe* or *robins*. They included: the two brothers d'Argenson, the elder of whom (the marquis), later became Foreign Minister under Louis XV, the younger (the comte), minister of war; the duc de Richelieu, a great-nephew of Cardinal Richelieu, who became a leading courtier at Versailles and a marshal of the French army; and two literary friends, Pierre-Robert Le Cornier de Cideville, who became a *conseiller* at the *parlement* of Rouen; and the comte d'Argental, who became a *conseiller* at the *parlement* of Paris and remained one of Voltaire's dearest friends.

How close Voltaire was to any of these five during his school years we do not know. The elder d'Argenson was exactly the same age, and they may have been in the same class; but it seems that he was at Louis-le-Grand only during Voltaire's last two years there. The younger d'Argenson and the duc de Richelieu were two years younger than Voltaire. And d'Argental was six years younger, so he and Voltaire may not have known each other at all at school.

The only fellow-pupil of whom Voltaire has left any really vivid trace of friendship at the time of his school days, was a sixth young man, called Claude Philippe Fyot de La Marche, from a rich and powerful family linked to the *parlement* of Burgundy. Voltaire and Fyot de La Marche were in the same class and left school in the same year, 1711, but Fyot de la Marche evidently went home before the end of the school year, leaving Voltaire sad and lonely. Between May and August 1711, the seventeen-year-old Voltaire wrote him a sequence of five touchingly nostalgic letters, which are virtually the earliest letters that have come down to us.

I can assure you, without any pretence, that I really see that you are no longer here; every time that I look through the window, I see your empty room; I no longer hear your laughter in class; I miss you everywhere, and I have only the pleasure of writing to you, and of speaking about you with your other friends. I should gladly travel to Burgundy, to say what I am now writing; your departure so disoriented me, that I had neither the wit nor the strength to speak, when you came to say good-bye.[1]

The last of this series of Voltaire's letters to Fyot de La Marche throws a vivid light on one aspect of the curriculum at the Collège Louis-le-Grand: the staging of plays, directed by the Jesuits and performed by the boys.

I have delayed writing to you for two or three days, in order to tell you news of the tragedy which Father Le Jay has just put on. Heavy rain made them divide the performance into two after-dinners, which gave as much pleasure to the students as pain to Father Le Jay; two monks broke their collarbones one after the other, so neatly, that it seemed they had fallen down just to entertain us; the nuncio of His Holiness gave us eight days holiday; M. Theuenart sang; Father Le Jay lost his voice; Father Porée prayed to God for fine weather, but at the height of his prayer the skies opened; that is more or less what has happened here; all that remains, for me to enjoy the holidays, is to have the pleasure of seeing you in Paris.[2]

Voltaire's gentle mockery at the ineffectiveness of Father Porée's prayer is often cited as early evidence that he was already a sceptic about the Christian religion. Well, maybe; but almost any intelligent and highly educated adolescent is liable to question received orthodoxy, especially if it is preached in the hot-house of a high-pressure school. If a clever young man expresses mild derision at the ineffectiveness of a prayer for fine weather, it need not be taken as evidence of anything much, except that he is bold enough to express his scepticism in a letter to a friend.

The more interesting aspect of this letter to Fyot de La Marche is the light it throws on the Jesuits' practice of writing and staging plays for the boys to perform. This was no doubt in part a reflection of the importance of the theatre in high-society life in early eighteenth-century France and of the central role played in public entertainment by the Comédie Française. In turn, this early exposure to the experience of live, if amateur, theatre must have exerted a crucial influence on the formation of Voltaire's own sensibility, and may well have played a key role in encouraging him to venture into the writing of plays himself. The Jesuit fathers could not have foreseen that Voltaire would go on to be the most successful and celebrated writer of classical verse tragedies of his time.

After leaving school, Voltaire at first submitted to his father's wish that he follow a course at law school. But his heart was not in it, and he spent much of his time frequenting wits and poets, trying to become a wit and a poet himself, and above all seeking to socialise with those in high society or literary society, whom he might seek to impress and who might help him make his name. This party-going lifestyle was not at all what his father wanted to see, but Arouet clearly did not know how to deal with his recalcitrant son. At first, in the spring of 1713, he sent him out of Paris, to Caen in Normandy, but that did not last long. Then he tried to bribe him, by offering to buy him a position as a king's advocate; Voltaire turned down the offer. Then his father raised his price and offered to buy him a much more expensive position, as a *conseiller* at the *parlement* of Paris, which was equivalent to buying him an elevated place among the *noblesse de robe*. Voltaire again refused.

His father made another attempt to get Voltaire out of harm's way by sending him abroad. It so happened that Voltaire's godfather, the abbé de Châteauneuf, had a brother, Pierre-Antoine de Castagnère, marquis de Châteauneuf, who had just been appointed French ambassador to The Hague. Arouet asked him to take on Voltaire as his private secretary, the marquis obliged and Voltaire obeyed. No sooner had he arrived in The Hague, however, than he fell madly in love with a charming young woman, and she, apparently, with him. It was a most unsuitable relationship.

The mother of the girl, Madame du Noyer, was something of an adventuress, a French former Protestant who had abandoned her Protestantism and her husband in France, and was now living by her wits in The Hague, partly by editing a controversial news-sheet. She had two daughters: Anne-Marguerite, who had been twice married and twice widowed; and her younger sister, Catherine-Olympe, known as Pimpette. It was with Pimpette that Voltaire fell in love. She had already been engaged to a Protestant rebel leader from the Cévennes and abandoned by him. She had then married a self-styled baron de Winterfeldt, and borne a child by him, but he also abandoned her.[3] So though she was not in any sense an innocent, she was still only twenty-one years old, two years older than Voltaire, and it is clear from his letters to her that she must have been absolutely enchanting.

Voltaire wasted no time in declaring his love; but the ambassador wasted even less time, for as soon as he learned of the affair, he immediately forbade Voltaire to carry on his liaison with Pimpette and instructed him to return at once to Paris. 'I believe, my dear Demoiselle,' Voltaire wrote to her on 25 November 1713,

> that you love me; so prepare to use all the force of your wits on this occasion. As soon as I returned home yesterday evening, M. l'ambassadeur told me that I must leave today, and the most I could do was to persuade him to postpone it until tomorrow; but he forbade me to go out before my departure; I am absolutely compelled to leave, and to leave without seeing you. In the name of the love I have for you, send me your portrait. I shall love you always; I love your virtue as much as I love your person.[4]

Three days later, Voltaire was still in The Hague but effectively under house arrest.

> I am here a prisoner in the name of the King, but they can take away my life but not my love for you. Yes, my adorable mistress, I shall see you this evening, though I should carry my head on a scaffold … Keep away from Madame your mother, as from your cruellest enemy, what am I saying, keep away from everybody, trust nobody, keep yourself in readiness as soon as the moon shall appear, I shall leave the house incognito, I shall take a carriage, or a chaise, we shall go like the wind to Scheveningen, I shall bring ink and paper, we shall write our letters [of engagement?]. Be ready at four o'clock, I shall wait near your street. Adieu my dear heart.[5]

Two days later Voltaire was still in The Hague, and still making plans to see Pimpette.

> I shall not leave, I think, before Monday or Tuesday; it seems, my dear, that they are only postponing my departure in order to make me feel more acutely the pain of being in the same town as you, and not being able to see you. They are watching my every step; it is impossible for me to get to you by day, I shall climb out of a window at

midnight. Let me know if I can come to your door tonight. Adieu, my lovely mistress, I adore you ...[6]

Two days later Voltaire was still in The Hague, and still making plans for a secret rendezvous with his lovely mistress.

Send Lisbette at three o'clock, I shall give her a packet for you containing some men's clothes, you will get ready at her place, and if you have enough goodness to want to see a poor prisoner who adores you, you will take the trouble to come at dusk. But as they know my clothes and could therefore recognise you, I shall send you a cloak which will hide your suit and your face; I shall even hire a man's suit for greater safety.[7]

It seems, from the letter that Voltaire wrote to her two days later, that Pimpette's visit, disguised as a boy, had been wonderfully successful.

I do not know if I should call you Monsieur or Mademoiselle; by my faith you are an adorable young knight, and our doorman, who is not in love with you, thought you were a very pretty boy. Yet your appearance was as daunting as it was adorable, I was only afraid that you might draw your sword in the street, just so as to leave out none of the character of a young man; yet after all, even disguised as a young man, you are as good as a girl. I have to leave on Friday, wait patiently until I write from Paris, be always ready to leave, whatever happens I shall see you before I go: all will be well, provided that you are willing to come to France and leave your mother.[8]

Voltaire's departure was delayed yet again, and he finally left for Paris on 18 December without seeing her again.[9] But when he reached Paris, on Christmas Eve, he found that he was in such deep trouble at home that he did not dare show his face.

'Scarcely had I arrived in Paris, on Christmas Eve', he told Pimpette, 'than I learned that my father had taken out an arrest warrant [*lettre de cachet*] to have me imprisoned. I asked people to talk to him, but the most they could get out of him was to have me sent instead to the [West Indies] islands; they could not get him to change his decision to cut me out of his will.'[10] Voltaire submitted to this lesser sentence, in the only letter from him to his father which has survived: 'I consent, my father, to go to America, and even to live on bread and water, provided that, before my departure, you permit me to embrace your knees.'[11]

Within days his father had weakened. He withdrew his sentence of banishment to the French colonies, provided that Voltaire agreed to pursue a serious legal career; Voltaire did agree, and by 20 January he was telling Pimpette that he had become a boarding pupil in the office of Maître Alain, prosecutor at the Châtelet court, 'in order to learn the profession of *robin* to which my father has consigned me, and by which I hope to recover his friendship. Write to me care of Maître Alain, rue pavé Saint Bernard. Adieu, my dear; you know that I shall always love you.'[12]

But Pimpette was no longer answering his letters, and at this point, for all practical purposes, their love affair ended; shortly thereafter, Pimpette took another lover, called Guyot de Merville, a bookseller in The Hague. Voltaire was deeply upset by her betrayal; twenty-four years later he wrote: 'Guyot de Merville has never ceased to hurt me because he had the same mistress as me twenty years ago.'[13] This was not the only time Voltaire lost a mistress to another man, but it may be the only occasion when he gave open expression to such long-lasting sexual jealousy, which may be an indication of the intensity of this first love affair.

What is striking about Voltaire's love letters to Pimpette is the way his feelings seem to be reflected in his diction. In the first two letters he used the formal style of address, *vous*; in the last letters to her, Letters 15 to 21, when in practice he had ceased to see her, he again addressed her as *vous*. But in the middle of their affair, in Letters 9, 12 and 14, he oscillated, sometimes in the same letter, between the polite *vous* and the intimate *tu*; this may be related to the intensity of his emotional and sexual excitement.

These seem to be almost the only occasions in the whole of his surviving correspondence when Voltaire used the intimate *tu* form of address. The one exception is in his correspondence with Nicolas-Claude Thieriot, whom he met when they were both young legal apprentices in the office of Maître Alain in the early months of 1714, when Voltaire was twenty and Thieriot eighteen. In his first letter to Thieriot, in the enthusiasm of new-found friendship, as if to a schoolfriend or *copain*, he addresses him as *tu*. But thereafter, in a correspondence of some 500 letters, and in a friendship to which Voltaire clung for the rest of his life, despite Thieriot's repeated lapses from loyalty and decency, he always uses the more formal *vous*.

The most tantalising uncertainty on this subject is how he addressed Émilie du Châtelet, the most intimate love of his life. We know that he called her 'Émilie'. This was a quite unusual familiarity for those days, but she obviously regarded it as an endearing sign of affection, for she virtually boasted of the fact, in her letters to others. But we do not know if he addressed her as *tu*, since virtually all his letters to her were lost or destroyed.

After his letter of 10 February 1714 the correspondence of Voltaire and Pimpette apparently went dead: no further letters to her from Voltaire have survived. But he did not forget her, nor she him. Several times during the next forty years he did little acts of kindness for her; in 1736 he had a small table bought for her; in 1751 he paid off some long-standing debts which she had incurred; in 1754 he sent her a package; and in 1760, forty-six years after the end of their youthful affair, he used her name as an introduction to the husband of Mme de Pompadour. Throughout these succeeding decades he obviously remained aware of her existence and in contact with her.

Pimpette's mother carefully collected and kept Voltaire's letters to Pimpette. At the time she was violently opposed to her daughter's relationship with a young upstart, but in 1720, when he had ceased to be an upstart and had become a celebrity, she published his letters, no doubt for money.[14]

2

COMÉDIE FRANÇAISE

1714–1718

IT DID NOT TAKE VOLTAIRE long to break his promise to his father and abandon his legal apprenticeship. But he did not at first find it easy to discover how to make a literary career instead.

He went to the theatre and fell in love with Mademoiselle Duclos, the star of the Comédie Française; but she was too beautiful and too old for him (she was forty-four), he was too insignificant and too young for her (he was only twenty), and she was not interested. He tried to attract attention from potential patrons by pretending to be a smart young man about town, by developing his skills of wit and repartee or by composing and circulating well-turned verses. And he solicited invitations from the leading figures of French society, who were always on the look-out for brilliant young entertainers, either in Paris or in their country châteaux.

One of the most brilliant of the country châteaux frequented by Voltaire was that of Sceaux, home of the duc and duchesse du Maine. The duc was the illegitimate son of Louis XIV by his mistress Mme de Montespan: Louis had legitimated him and in his will had tried to ensure that du Maine would have a powerful role in the government of France. But when Louis died in 1715, the duc d'Orléans (the regent) contemptuously overturned the will, and the duc and duchesse du Maine were simply excluded. In reaction, they promoted their own extremely lavish and brilliant court at Sceaux, in some sense a rival and opposition to the official court at Versailles.

Voltaire realised quite soon that his ephemeral pirouettes were not getting him anywhere and that he would only make his way if he wrote something more substantial, which probably meant that he would have to write a play for the Comédie Française. In Voltaire's day there was only a handful of theatres in Paris. There was the Opéra, there was the Théâtre des Italiens and there were the fairground theatres. But the Comédie Française had a virtual monopoly as the only theatre authorised and supervised by the court for the staging of tragedies and serious dramas. And since theatre was the main form of public entertainment at the time, the Comédie Française had a unique position in the cultural and social life of the city. Everybody went to the theatre, and almost anybody who wanted to be a writer wanted to write for the Comédie Française.

It is not surprising, therefore, that Voltaire should have set his sights on writing a play for the Comédie Française, but it is a measure of his ambition that he should have chosen, as his first subject, one of the greatest tragic legends of Classical Greek mythology, made famous by Sophocles' play *Oedipus Tyrannus* (*Oedipus the King*).

Voltaire's biographers sometimes assert that Voltaire's choice of the Oedipus theme, the most famous story of parricide in European literature, may have been in part an expression of his own antagonistic relationship with his own father. This is very far-fetched. There is no evidence that Voltaire's relationship with his father, despite their long-running struggle, was pathologically hostile. On the contrary, he seems to have had some underlying feelings of regard and even affection for him. It is much more plausible to assume that Voltaire was drawn to the Oedipus story, partly because it is immensely powerful, but partly because it resonated strongly, in the early eighteenth century, with the sectarian controversy then raging within the Catholic Church, between Jesuits and Jansenists, over sin, grace and predestination.

The Jansenists, following the seventeenth-century Dutch theologian Cornelius Jansen, believed that man's original sin is so great that he can attain salvation only through the grace of God; and since not all men would be eligible for salvation, this doctrine ultimately amounted to a belief in predestination. The Jesuits, by contrast, believed in free will, and in the ability and duty of man to make his own efforts for salvation. In 1713 the Pope came down on the side of the Jesuits, by publishing a bull, *Unigenitus dei filius*,* which condemned the Jansenists for heresy. The doctrinal argument soon turned into a power struggle. The bull

---

* The bull was known by its opening words, in Latin, which mean 'The only-begotten son of God'.

was resisted by the French bishops and the theologians in the Sorbonne, in the name of the autonomy of the French church, and by the lawyers and magistrates in the *parlement*, who were mostly aligned with the Jansenists and who were formally contesting the legality of the *Unigenitus* bull, in terms that virtually amounted to a protest movement.

Throughout his life Voltaire was intensely interested in questions of good and evil. He may not have believed much in sin or in eternal salvation, but he was deeply allergic to ideological fanaticism, and in the debate between the Jesuits and the Jansenists he undoubtedly regarded the Jansenists as the fanatics. He may well have been additionally inclined to such a view from the fact that his elder brother, Armand, whom he cordially disliked, had been educated at a Jansenist school and had embraced an extreme, revivalist form of Jansenism.

This contemporary French controversy over sin and free will reached a peak in 1717, and it is difficult to believe that it could have failed to have a significant influence both on Voltaire in the writing of *Œdipe* and on the response to it of the Paris audience. Oedipus killed his father and married his mother. Was he guilty, even though his sins were involuntary? Could he have avoided his sins? Was it the fault of the gods? In Voltaire's version Oedipus' mother, Jocasta, criticises the role of the priests: 'Our priests are not what the foolish people imagine; their wisdom is based solely on our credulity.'[1] This pithy little maxim, with its implicit critique of the Christian church, struck a lively chord with the audience, and it has remained to this day one of the most frequently cited quotations from Voltaire.

Voltaire started work on *Œdipe* in the spring of 1715, and he made rapid progress on a first draft of it. But well before he had arrived at a final version, he conceived a second grand project, almost equally ambitious: to write a long epic poem. This was ambitious in two ways. First, France had no significant national tradition of epic poetry, so Voltaire was tacitly setting himself up against the most celebrated models of epic poetry in ancient literature; he eventually called his epic *La Henriade*, in deliberate imitation of Homer's *Iliad* and Virgil's *Aeneid*.* Second,

---

* During the composition of the epic Voltaire was at a loss for a meaningful title. At first he sometimes called it simply *Henri* or *Henri Le Grand*, or even, misguidedly, *La Ligue* – misguidedly, since the League of Catholic extremists were the enemies of Voltaire's hero. On its first appearance he gave it the title *La Ligue, ou Henri le Grand*. It was not until after publication, in February 1727 (see Letters, 201, D 308), that he adopted the title *La Henriade*. His new choice of title influenced Pope's decision to call his new satirical poem *Dunciad*, first published in 1728.

Voltaire chose as his theme what he regarded as the virtuous and heroic achievement of the French king Henri IV, in bringing about, if not a peace, at least a truce in the murderous wars of religion between Catholics and Protestants in sixteenth-century France.

This was not just a bold choice of subject, it was also politically reckless: the virtues of religious tolerance and reconciliation, which for Voltaire were exemplified by Henri IV and the truce of the Edict of Nantes in 1598, had in fact been rejected less than a century later by Louis XIV, and the persecution of French Protestants by the Catholic hierarchy of Church and state had continued in his own day under Louis XV. So for Voltaire to write an epic poem in praise of Henri IV and religious tolerance was an open and potentially seditious act of criticism of the French régime. But Voltaire never abandoned his belief in toleration, and towards the end of his life the unremitting persecution of Protestants at last provoked him into campaigning openly on behalf of some individual Protestants against the injustices of the French state.

By this time Voltaire was deeply involved in composing his first tragedy, *Œdipe*, and though he worked at it with great speed, as he did with almost all his later plays, he was not finding it easy. A serious play had to observe a whole series of formal principles of composition, ostensibly handed down from Aristotle, starting with the three unities of time, place and action. It was also expected to portray the interaction of noble characters dealing nobly with their predicaments and their emotions, and to exclude any representation of vulgar or low-life characters. As a result, French classical dramas tended to be dignified and high-minded.

Matters were not made any easier by the physical configuration of the Comédie Française theatre. At that time it was located on the left bank, in a street which was then called the rue des Fossés-Saint-Germain, and which is now called (for obvious reasons) the rue de l'Ancienne Comédie, in the 6th arrondissement. It had been built thirty years earlier, on a site previously occupied by a former royal tennis court, known as the Jeu de Paume de l'Étoile. As a result it had a long, narrow auditorium, shaped like a shoe box, with three tiers of boxes on each of the two long sides. At the time of its construction it had been considered rather a marvel, with brilliant lighting under large circular chandeliers, and with the stage (at the narrow end of the auditorium) being slightly lower than the first tier of boxes and slightly higher than the *parterre*, which was for men only, and standing-room only.

This architectural arrangement of the theatre was not necessarily kind either to the plays or to the players, and the actors could certainly not assume that the audience would be silent or attentive, let alone respectful. The elegant people in the boxes could see the people in the boxes opposite more easily than they could see the stage and were liable to show as much interest in the other spectators as in the play. The most fashionable spectators would arrive late or leave early, or both. And the male spectators jostling around in the *parterre* below them were liable to be boisterous and vocal; it was common for plays to be barracked with cat-calls and whistles, sometimes causing the action on stage to be interrupted, sometimes even causing the entire production to fail.

On the stage, the actors were constrained by the fact that a considerable proportion of the space was occupied by spectators: there were three rows of benches on either side of the stage and in full view of the auditorium, and there were more spectators standing at the back of the stage in among the scenery. These places for spectators on stage were essential to the finances of the theatre, for they were highly prized and highly priced, and usually occupied by dandies and young bloods. But the result was that the stage was a rather crowded place, which severely limited the options of the players for much movement, or indeed for much of what we would call acting.

Frequently the presence of these spectators on stage obstructed the entrances and exits of the actors, sometimes with unintended comical effects. When Voltaire wrote his tragic melodrama *Sémiramis*, thirty years later, he intended to bring the curtain down at the end of Act III with a sensational *coup de théâtre*: the appearance of a menacing ghost at the back of the stage. Unfortunately, at the first night the ghost was unable to come on, because he could not get through the crowd of spectators, and the theatre usher had to call out: 'Make way for the ghost, gentlemen, if you please!' (*Messieurs, place à l'ombre, s'il vous plaît!*).[2]

The net effect of the stage restrictions, coupled with the formal rules of composition, was that the theatre in Voltaire's day was liable to be rather static and declamatory. But in the early eighteenth century no one in France seriously challenged these formal restrictions, and Voltaire was so thoroughly convinced of their permanent and inherent rightness that he went on trying, for the next sixty years, to keep alive the kind of poetic play-writing immortalised in the previous century by Jean Racine.

By the end of 1715 Voltaire had already finished the first draft of his tragedy *Œdipe*, and he offered it to the Comédie Française. They turned it down. They did not like the fact that Voltaire had so closely imitated the model of the ancient Greek tragedies, that he had given a large role to the on-stage commentaries of a chorus representing Everyman. The actors did not want anything so anachronistic; in any case, there would have been no room for a large chorus on the stage. Worse, they did not like the fact that Voltaire, like Sophocles, had rigorously excluded any love interest – apart, that is, from the guilty and incestuous love between Oedipus and his mother, Jocasta.

Voltaire protested, but he eventually agreed to revise his play; in its final version he reduced the role of the chorus, and he invented a gratuitous love interest, in the shape of Philoctetes, a former lover of Jocasta, who loves her still. In the early months of 1717 Voltaire completed his revised text and submitted it again to the Comédie Française; and this time the actors accepted it. But it still did not get put on until November 1718, eighteen months later.

The reason for this further delay was that Voltaire, not for the last time, got into trouble with the authorities. The death of Louis XIV in 1715, and the Regency which followed it, had led to a rapid and far-reaching liberalisation of French manners and mores, precipitating dramatic changes on the political, social and cultural scene. After the long years of gloomy repression the new order of the day was boldness and experimentation, satire and mockery, and the pleasures of unrestrained enjoyment. The regent, the duc d'Orléans, turned his back on the austere and dreary grandeur of Versailles and moved the royal court to the Palais Royal, in the heart of Paris, making Paris once again the cultural and political capital of France. Parisian society rediscovered its natural high spirits, and embraced the new mood of permissiveness with enthusiasm. Plays, gambling and masked balls at the Opéra were now all the rage. The social and cultural clubs, which had been frowned on by the late king, came to life once more, notably the free-thinking, pleasure-loving and self-indulgent Society of the Temple, so-called after the former monastery of the Knights Templars; its founder, Philippe de Vendôme, revived the epicurean life of the Temple, with its little suppers and merry drinking parties, frequented by poets, libertines and aristocrats.

The liberalism of the new government had many beneficial effects. The economy recovered, and the public finances improved. But the new permissiveness was a double-edged sword. The speculative booms and busts of the new régime, which started with great excitement, ended up by causing great alarm, and some felt that the relaxed mores of the new court went much too far, often hand in hand with licentiousness. The regent was a particular object of censure, among other things for his gluttony, drunkenness, debauchery and womanising. And since freedom of thought and elegance of expression were the most prized social skills in this newly liberated and almost fevered society, it was inevitable that the wit and the mockery would sooner or later be directed, first against the government, and then against the person of the regent. The problem, for a clever young adventurer, was knowing how far it was safe to go.

Voltaire was introduced to the Temple by his godfather, the abbé de Châteauneuf, in 1708, when he was only fourteen, and he later became a regular disciple of the aged abbé de Chaulieu, one of the presiding geniuses of that epicurean and somewhat dissolute milieu. No doubt he tried his hardest to show off and shine, and he soon acquired a reputation for the sharpness of his wit, the elegance of his versification and the daring of his mockery. Inevitably he went too far, and in May 1716 he was sent into distant exile at Tulle in the Limousin, in punishment for having written some verses containing biting criticisms of the debauchery of the regent's daughter, the duchesse de Berry. Voltaire denied that he was the author of the verses in question, but he was not believed.[3] Interestingly, his father interceded on Voltaire's behalf and persuaded the authorities to commute the exile to the less remote location of Sully-sur-Loire, country château of the ducs de Sully. François Arouet argued that at Sully his son would be in the company of relatives who would teach him to behave better. This was sheer casuistry: the Sully family had been clients of Voltaire's father, but they were not relatives.

The conditions of Voltaire's punishment were not harsh. The château was fine, the countryside was beautiful, the duc de Sully was friendly and his visitors were numerous and amusing. Voltaire already knew some of them, including regular acquaintances from the Temple. In fact, the social life of the château was rather gay, and Voltaire at first made light of his exile. He wrote to the abbé de Chaulieu: 'I write to you from what would be the pleasantest place in the world, if only I were not exiled here, and in which I lack nothing to be perfectly happy, except the freedom to leave it.'[4]

One reason for Voltaire's good humour at Sully was that he acquired a mistress there, the charming young Suzanne de Livry. She was the niece of the duc's attorney-general, and she had a tender heart, lovely eyes and a breast of alabaster, according to Voltaire.[5] This was not a runaway passion, like his affair with Pimpette; at twenty-two he was now slightly more mature, and she was the same age. Moreover, she hoped that Voltaire would help her go on the stage, which he did, some years later. But it was obviously a warm relationship, which turned into a long-lasting friendship; he remained in contact with her over many years, and they met again, for the last time, in extreme old age, in 1778, the year in which they both died.

Apart from his social life, Voltaire also did some work at Sully, and it was probably there that he did most of the work on the revision of his tragedy *Œdipe*. But he soon wearied of his banishment, and he tried to wheedle the regent into forgiving him, by sending him an elegant letter in verse, in which he combined dutiful flattery with protestations of his own innocence. It did not work, and by the late summer he was beginning to complain. He wrote to a friend: 'I really wish I could go home, and sup with you, and talk about literature. I am beginning to be very bored here.'[6] Indeed, as the autumn approached, Voltaire began to fear that he would still be there after the duc left for Paris, and might even be there for the winter.[7] 'They may even leave me here long enough to become unhappy. I know my limits; I am not made to live long in one place.'[8]

After six months of this the regent relented and in October 1716 gave him permission to return to Paris. Voltaire used his freedom to complete the revised text of *Œdipe*, which he delivered to the Comédie Française in the early months of 1717. But the performance of *Œdipe* was postponed once more because by the middle of May, after seven months of liberty, Voltaire found himself once again in trouble with the authorities, this time much more seriously. Some verses started to circulate, which were recklessly censorious of the regent, and of which Voltaire was (rightly) assumed to be the author. What made these verses so explosive was that they virtually accused the regent of debauching his own daughter, and thus with having, in effect, mirrored the sin of Oedipus:

> Ce n'est point le fils, c'est le père;
> C'est la fille, et non point la mère;
> A cela près tout va des mieux.
> Ils ont déjà fait Étéocle;
> S'il vient à perdre les deux yeux,
> C'est le vrai sujet de Sophocle.

> It is not the son, it is the father:
> It is the daughter, not the mother;
> So far, so good.

They have already produced an Aeteocles
    [a son of Oedipus by his mother Jocasta];
If he were to lose both his eyes,
That would really be a story for Sophocles.

Very soon after, people started quoting another set of verses, this time in Latin, not just accusing the regent of incest but also charging him with aiming to take the crown of France, and even predicting the downfall of the kingdom. Again it was widely said, correctly, that Voltaire was the author.

Why did Voltaire take the extraordinary risk of writing, and circulating, such inflammatory verses against the regent and his administration? No doubt the explanation lay in the explosive combination of his ambition and his inexperience. He was desperate to make a name and attract attention; he discovered that he was smart enough to turn out witty verses, but he knew virtually nothing about the world of political power and he certainly did not know where to stop. He could see that the duc d'Orléans was open to criticism on many grounds, political and moral, but he completely underestimated the real power of the regency, which, like the rest of the *ancien régime*, rested on absolutism, repression and censorship.

Voltaire soon learned how naïve he had been. On 16 May 1717 he was arrested, and this time he was sent to the Bastille. The day after his arrest Voltaire wrote a very brief letter to the duc de Sully, formally declaring his innocence. But he had already admitted, to two acquaintances whom he believed to be his friends, that he was indeed the author of both sets of verses; it was only after his arrest that he discovered that they were police spies. Four days later he wrote a short note to the governor of the Bastille, consisting of nothing more than a request list of little comforts:

Two books of Homer Latin Greek,
Two handkerchiefs, two,
One small bonnet,
Two cravats
One night cap,
One small bottle of essence of cloves.

Arouet

This Thursday 21 May 1717[9]

The two books of Homer were no doubt the *Iliad* and the *Odyssey*, and presumably (since Voltaire knew little or no Greek) in a parallel translation, with the Greek original on the right-hand page and a Latin translation on the left. The essence of cloves was a form of toothpaste.

At the time of his arrest Voltaire put on a show of bluster. He declared that he was delighted to be able to spend some quiet time in the Bastille, since this would allow him to keep to his milk diet. He even boasted that he was already familiar with the place, having previously visited his friend the duc de Richelieu there. This was possible: Voltaire certainly knew Richelieu and may well have known him at school, even though there was a two-year age difference between them. Richelieu had twice been briefly imprisoned in the Bastille for youthful indiscretions, and Voltaire may have visited him there, perhaps in March or April 1716, before he himself was exiled to Sully-sur-Loire.

How did Voltaire pass his eleven months of imprisonment? The commonly repeated story is that while he was in the Bastille he wrote or at least composed some or all of the epic poem which became *La Henriade*. This is more or less the story that Voltaire later told, but it seems unlikely in the extreme that the prison authorities would have allowed paper and writing materials to any prisoner, and especially not to a prisoner who had been arrested for his crimes as a writer. Homer would have provided an inspiring paradigm for a would-be epic poet, and this was no doubt the reason why he asked the governor for the *Iliad* and the *Odyssey*; but we do not know if he ever received these books. Much later, Voltaire claimed that he had composed six cantos of the poem in his head and had written them down only after his release; but he kept only the second canto, in its memorised form, about the massacre of Saint Bartholomew, and rewrote the rest of the poem, which eventually amounted to ten cantos in all. On balance, this may seem the most likely story; it is at least consistent with the fact that *La Henriade* was not published in its final form until five years after Voltaire's release.

Voltaire found his imprisonment hard to bear. Conditions in the Bastille were harsh and oppressive, with its ten-foot walls, its 'triple locks, and grills and bolts and bars', and with poor food and no sunlight.[10] It was particularly difficult, no doubt, because he had been imprisoned, not after a trial, but on the strength of an arbitrary arrest warrant or *lettre de cachet*. This meant that his detention was of indefinite duration and could last for as long or as short a time as the regent decided. In the event, the regent relented after eleven months, and on Thursday of Easter week, 14 April 1718, Voltaire was released. But this was only a conditional discharge: he was not free to come and go as he pleased but was confined in virtual house arrest at his father's country house at Châtenay, south of Paris.

Voltaire's time in the Bastille marked a turning-point in his life: he was determined never to run such a risk again. At first, he pretended to make light of his ordeal, but he admitted to a close friend, Nicolas de La Faluère de Génonville, that he had had to learn, in this 'place of distress', to harden himself against adversity; he said that he had 'discovered in myself a courage which I had not expected, after the frivolity and errors of my youth'.[11] He was never again so reckless as directly to defy the authority or question the legitimacy of the régime.

His immediate reaction, after his release, was to make peace with the authorities. He made new protestations of his innocence, he declared his loyalty to 'such a good prince',[12] and he made repeated efforts to make his way back into the regent's favour. On 2 May, barely two weeks after his release from the Bastille, he wrote a cringing letter to the regent's secretary: 'I do not importune you to shorten the time of my exile [at Châtenay], nor to permit me to spend a single hour in Paris. The only favour I dare ask of you, is to please assure His Highness that I am as much obliged to him for my imprisonment as for my liberty, and that I have greatly benefited from the one and shall never abuse the latter.'[13] Two weeks later Voltaire wrote again, to plead to be allowed to return to Paris, just for two hours: 'I only want the honour to talk to you for a moment, and to throw myself at the feet of His Royal Highness'.[14] Over time Voltaire gradually wheedled longer and longer permissions to visit Paris, first for a day, then for a week, and then for a month. But it was not until October 1718 that his freedom of movement was fully restored to him.

Voltaire's release from the Bastille also marked the beginning of an important new chapter in his life: he gave himself a new name. In June 1718, for the first time, he signed a letter 'Arouet de Voltaire', and by the end of the year he was signing himself simply 'Voltaire', the name by which he became famous in his own time.

Names were less fixed in the eighteenth century than they are today. Condorcet, the author of one of the earliest biographies of Voltaire, pointed out that it was customary at the time, in the rich bourgeoisie, for a younger son to adopt a different name: the elder son would take his father's name, but a second son would adopt another name, often attaching to some family property. Since Voltaire's elder brother was called Armand Arouet, it would have been normal for Voltaire to choose another surname. Moreover, it was quite usual for a writer to choose a *nom de plume*. The seventeenth-century playwright Molière was really called Jean-Baptiste Poquelin: he took the name Molière when he was twenty-one, after he formed his theatre troupe. The eighteenth-century writer and philosopher Montesquieu was originally called Charles-Louis de Secondat, baron de La Brède; he added the name Montesquieu from a minor family property, and that is the name by which he became best known.

But Voltaire may also have had more emotionally loaded motives for his change of name. He may have intended it as an assertion of an identity separate from that of his father; he may have intended it as a rejection of his father; he may even have intended it as an oblique assertion of his belief that he was illegitimate. And why 'Voltaire'? He did not say. There have been many different theories, often far-fetched. Perhaps the specific choice was less significant than the more general fact, that he was making a declaration of his independence and his ambition as a writer.[15]

Œdipe was first performed at the Comédie Française on 18 November 1718, seven months after Voltaire's release from the Bastille, and almost exactly one month after he had recovered his complete freedom to live in Paris. It was an immediate and sensational success. Audiences were captivated by Voltaire's neat and fluent versification, and they applauded his political allusions, notably his attacks on 'fraudulent priests'. The play achieved an almost unprecedented run of thirty-two performances, and it went on to become a regular feature of the theatre's repertoire, in effect driving out the classic and familiar version of *Œdipe* by the great seventeenth-century tragedian Pierre Corneille. Voltaire not only had a new name: it was now the name of a new national celebrity.

Over the next sixty years, Voltaire wrote twenty-seven tragedies, of which twenty-three were performed at the Comédie Française, as well as a dozen comedies. It was a career of many ups and downs: his next two plays, *Artemire* in 1720 and *Mariamne* in 1724, were both flops, and he had to wait another six years for his next big success, with *Brutus* in 1730. But from that point on, and for the next forty years, Voltaire was France's dominant tragic playwright. His plays were performed more often than those of Corneille and Racine combined, and between 1750 and 1770 his share of the audience figures at the Comédie Française rose from 27 to 38 per cent of the total.

With *Œdipe*, Voltaire challenged the world to judge him by the highest standards, and after his play had been performed to great acclaim, some of the most respected critics did compare him with his great predecessors Corneille and Racine. At that point Voltaire lost all sense of proportion: he was so carried away by his success, and so taken in by all the flattering compliments, that he had the audacity to publish a short pamphlet explicitly comparing his *Œdipe* with those of Sophocles and Corneille; astonishingly, he had the nerve to find a string of fundamental faults with the plays of Sophocles and Corneille, but none (of course) with his own.[16]

Today *Œdipe* is no longer performed, and the cumulative effect on today's reader of Voltaire's rhyming couplets seems conventional and stilted, more formalistic than vivid or dramatic. What he was trying to do, nostalgically, was turn back the clock and revive a style of declamatory verse tragedy, full of words, posturing and noble sentiments, which had come to a peak of perfection in the work of Jean Racine half a century earlier. But in 1718, and for most of the next fifty years, what Voltaire could produce was what Parisian audiences wanted; all at once, he had been transformed from a pushy little versifier into the new literary star.

3

MONEY, AND THE SHORTAGE OF IT

1718–1722

VOLTAIRE'S SUDDEN LITERARY STARDOM brought rewards and celebrity. The regent, overlooking Voltaire's recent imprisonment, sent him a gift of 675 livres, though he turned down Voltaire's request to be allowed to dedicate the play to him. Voltaire sent a signed copy of the play to George I of England, who graciously responded by sending Voltaire a gold watch. More practically, he made some serious money from the enormous success of the play: nearly £3,000 in author's royalties. And after some delay, perhaps as late as 1721, the French court recognised the success of *Œdipe* by conferring on Voltaire an annual pension of £2,000.

Œdipe also brought Voltaire social success. He no longer had to try so hard to cadge invitations from the rich and the famous; he was now the latest literary celebrity, and he was asked out on every side. In the autumn of 1718 he struck up a warm friendship with Louis Racine, younger son of the famous playwright, and he would sometimes dine with him, followed by a visit to the Comédie Française.[1] But in the spring of 1719 he had to turn down invitations from Racine because he was inundated with so many other even more attractive invitations:

> Returning from the country [i.e., from some château], I have found a letter from you which is more flattering for me than all the praise to which you refer. You cannot believe how mortified I am not to be able to take part in the outing which you propose. For I am going immediately to Richelieu and to Sully. I can assure you that the idea of seeing you next winter will make my journeys more agreeable.[2]

In other words, Voltaire expected to be spending much of the summer in various country houses and might not be back in Paris before the winter. It was in fact from Sully, in June, that Voltaire wrote to Lord Stair, the English ambassador to France, to thank King George for the kind gift of a gold watch.[3] Later that month he wrote from the château of the duc de La Feuillade to say that he was shortly going to Vaux-Villars, the château of the duc de Villars (now called Vaux-le-Vicomte).[4] Voltaire's ambitions required him to be a social climber, and he was now climbing fast.

Voltaire's celebrity also seemed to be good for his love life. While he was in the Bastille, his mistress, Suzanne de Livry, transferred her affections to his close friend Nicolas de La Faluère de Génonville. But when Voltaire became famous as the author of *Œdipe*, she became his mistress once again, and in the spring of 1919 he persuaded the Comédie Française to cast her in the role of Jocasta, in the first revival of *Œdipe*. It was a mistake. She was too young and too inexperienced, and her provincial accent and lack of any real acting talent caused sniggering among the rest of the cast. To please Voltaire, the company went on giving her more chances, but she did not do any better, and in 1722 they dismissed her. Voltaire was quite downcast by the news. 'I am upset by the justice meted out to the little Livry girl. If everybody were as severe as the Comédie Française, very few people, it seems to me, would have a job.'[5] But Voltaire still kept in touch with her, and a couple of years later he noted that she had struck rich on the lottery, with a winning ticket which brought her an annual income of £10,000.[6]

Voltaire now fell in love with the duchesse de Villars, or thought he had done so. She was a lady in her early forties, with an elderly husband and a reputation for an active extra-marital love life. When she showed an interest in the budding young author, he thought he was being propositioned and decided to fall in love with her; he even talked about it to his acquaintances. But he soon discovered that his expectations were entirely mistaken; and since he wished to go on being invited to visit the château de Vaux-Villars, he decided to fall out of love again. 'Be reassured,' he wrote to a friend, 'that I am cured for ever of the sickness which you feared for me. You make me feel that friendship is a thousand times more valuable than love. I think there is in me something ridiculous about being in love, and I think that may be even more true of women who may love me. Well, that is over, and I give it up for ever.'[7]

Of course, Voltaire had not given up love for ever. He really liked women, and he had a number of long-lasting relationships. It is probably true that he was not an accomplished womaniser; his sex drive was not particularly strong or reliable, and his chronic ill health often got in the way of performance. On the other hand, when Voltaire says that 'friendship is a thousand times more valuable than love', he is expressing a profound truth about himself: he had a great talent for friendship, he had a deep need of it, and he worked hard all his life at keeping his friendships alive; and some of his closest and most intimate friendships were with women, or *amitiés amoureuses*.

By the middle of 1719 the money from *Œdipe* was running out, so Voltaire embarked on another play, called *Artemire*. He had no difficulty persuading the Comédie Française to put it on, which they did in February 1720, and this gave him the opportunity to strike up an amorous liaison with Adrienne Lecouvreur, the latest young star of the company. Afterwards he described himself as having been 'her admirer, her friend, her lover',[8] and he probably was one of her lovers. But the great love of Adrienne's life was really Maurice, comte de Saxe, young, glamorous and a notorious womaniser.

After *Artemire*, Adrienne Lecouvreur starred four years later in Voltaire's play *Mariamne*, and she recreated the role of Jocasta in a revival of *Œdipe* on 15 March 1730. By then, however, she was already ill with dysentery, and she died five days later, aged thirty-eight. The circumstances of her death caused Voltaire great grief and lifelong indignation. In the eyes of the Catholic Church, actors and actresses were deemed to be excommunicate, and the curé of the church of Saint-Sulpice refused to allow Adrienne a Christian burial. Her body, escorted by the police, was taken away and buried without ceremony on waste ground. Voltaire never ceased to denounce this 'Barbarity and Injustice', as he put it in his *Lettres philosophiques*, published four years later, and he mourned her death deeply and for the rest of his life.

Unfortunately, *Artemire* was such a bad play that it was hissed on its opening night, and it had to be taken off almost immediately. Voltaire was mortified and tried to suppress all trace of it; he never referred to it in any of his letters. *Œdipe* had been a great success, at least partly because he had so closely followed a great mythic legend and a great tragedian. The fate of *Artemire* showed that he still had a lot to learn about how to write a play, especially one based on an original story of his own.

With the failure of *Artemire* Voltaire was faced with the serious and urgent challenge of how to make a living. The challenge was made more difficult by the fact that, like any writer in eighteenth-century France, he had to work in the shadow of two opposing dangers: the repressive system of censorship and the lack of any copyright law.

On the one hand, no book, play or pamphlet could be published in France without the express permission of the authorities; and of course it would not secure that permission if it was deemed seditious, heretical, anti-clerical or even remotely controversial. But the censorship system was a many-headed hydra: even if the king's ministers gave permission for the publication of a book, the author could still find himself hounded by the Church, by the theologians of the Sorbonne, by the *parlement*, or even by all three separately. On the other hand, if a book *was* published and was successful, it was liable to be pirated by unscrupulous publishers and booksellers not just in France but across the continent of Europe.

The first result of the censorship system, therefore, was that since the most successful books were often the most controversial, they usually had to be published illegally, or abroad, or anonymously. But the lack of any copyright law meant that it was extremely difficult for an author to control the publication of his books and thus secure his earnings; and it was impossible for him to do so if, to avoid censorship, he was forced to publish illegally, anonymously or abroad. This dual dilemma was most acute for the most successful and the most controversial authors. Voltaire was frequently obliged to publish clandestinely or abroad, and sometimes by two competing but clandestine publishers in France, in cases where he could not get, or feared he would not get, permission. And as the years passed, and as Voltaire became more celebrated, he was increasingly forced not just to publish clandestinely but also to deny authorship, not only of books he had written and published but also of fraudulent and distorted versions produced by pirate publishers. This made it even more difficult for him to make money out of them.

An author's predicament was more straightforward for plays than for other kinds of writing, because the market for serious plays was more regimented and restricted. In the case of a serious tragedy there was only one place in Paris where it could be performed, and that was the Comédie Française; and it could only be performed with official permission. In most cases the main hurdle facing a writer was not just the formality of official censorship but the question of whether or not the actors liked a play and would agree to put it on. But even if a play was performed at the Comédie Française, the censorship authorities might still refuse to allow it to be printed. And as Voltaire had just discovered with *Artemire*, it was one thing to get a play put on and quite another to make money out of it.

Voltaire went back to working on his planned epic poem *La Henriade*, but this was an ambitious long-term project which the authorities might not approve, and which would in any case not produce any immediate income. On the other hand, he made further efforts to drum up sponsorship and support on the strength of the success of Œdipe. In 1719 he wrote a dedicatory poem which he sent to George I of England, enclosing a copy of Œdipe, and in the same year he sent another copy to Léopold, duc de Lorraine. Meanwhile, he continued to work hard at building up contacts with the rich and powerful. In 1720 he sent a flattering poem to the duc de Sully, and in 1721 an obsequious epistle to Cardinal Dubois, chief minister of the regency. But none of this bore immediate fruit, and Voltaire must have been at something of a loss how to proceed. Moreover, he must have been chronically short of money, apart from a very small allowance provided by his father.

Inevitably, therefore, he was enormously intrigued in the summer of 1719 by reports of the speculative fever then gripping Paris and the stories of fabulous fortunes reportedly being made by investors in the new banking and investment system set up by John Law, the Scottish financial entrepreneur.

To understand this, we have to go back a few years. With his interminable European wars Louis XIV had led France to the brink of financial ruin. On his death in 1715, the new men of the regency discovered that the French state was being crushed under the burden of a national debt amounting to over 3.5 billion francs, which could not even be serviced, let alone repaid. Tax revenues had been starved by poor harvests and a depressed economy. And the monarchy had only been able to continue its extravagant expenditure by issuing more and more loans.

In December 1715 the regency government devalued the internal value of the currency by 30 per cent, taking the gold louis down from 14 livres to 20 livres; in the new year, 1716, they devalued the outstanding government loans by two-thirds and cut back on the rate of interest paid on these loans; at the same time, they tried to cut back on expenditure, including deep reductions in the armed forces, and in the spring they set up a tribunal to try, punish and make a public example of those bankers, tax-farmers, contractors, brokers and discount merchants who had made their colossal fortunes at the expense of the state.

Yet these efforts at economic housekeeping were still inadequate: in 1717 the state had to make interest payments of £80m, while its tax revenues were only £165m. Now the regent at last turned for help to John Law, the Scottish financial innovator. Law believed that the French economy was hampered by its dependence on the circulation of physical gold coins, and that economic development required the establishment of a modern banking and credit system, based on a trustworthy paper currency. The regency allowed Law to set up a French central bank and passed laws making this the lynchpin of the economy; then they gave him the monopoly control of the French colonial development and trading company, through the Compagnie des Indes; and then they set up a stock market, in which anybody could invest.

For a while Law's innovations worked wonders; the stock market created enormous excitement, and a vast speculative boom. It was this speculative bubble which Voltaire heard about in the summer of 1719, as he wrote to his friend Nicolas de La Faluère de Génonville: 'Have you all gone mad in Paris? I hear no talk but of millions. Is this a reality? Is it a chimera? Is Law a god, or a cheat, or a charlatan? This is a chaos which I cannot untangle, and of which I suspect you understand nothing. Personally, the only chimeras I surrender to are those of poetry.'[9]

The boom did not last long. Some rich insiders made fortunes, or at least got out before the bottom, but when the bubble burst, most of the ordinary punters lost everything. As a result, the rise and fall of Law cast lasting discredit on the idea of paper money and prevented the establishment of a modern banking system in France for well over a century.* By luck or judgement Voltaire avoided getting sucked into the Law bubble, perhaps because he had no money to speculate with; after it burst in 1721, he continued to tread water until something should turn up.

On 1 January 1722 Voltaire's father died, at the age of seventy-one; but his death did not rescue Voltaire from his financial predicament. François Arouet died a fairly rich man: when all his assets were added up, his estate amounted to nearly £460,000. In principle it would be divided equally between his three children, which meant that Voltaire's one-third share would have amounted to nearly £153,000. But under his will Voltaire would be largely if not totally disinherited, as retribution for his insubordination and improvidence, while his one-third share would be divided equally between his siblings, Armand and Marguerite-Catherine. However, old Arouet had provided two

---

* As if by chance, the collapse of the Law bubble in France coincided with the South Sea Bubble in England, but there were two main differences. The first was that the frenzied speculation in the South Sea Company in England was much briefer, since it came and went within a matter of months in 1720. The second was that England already had a Bank of England, which had been founded in 1694; it remained quite independent of the South Sea Company, it survived unharmed after the collapse of the South Sea Bubble and it constituted a cornerstone of the development of a modern financial system in the City of London. In France the Banque de France was not founded until 1800.

significant let-out clauses, for his intentions were, as usual, not completely consistent. First, even if Voltaire did not have access to the capital of his one-third share, he would still receive the income from it. More important, Voltaire could still claim his share of his father's estate if, at the age of thirty-five, he could persuade the courts that he had shown real improvement in his respectability. A few days before his death, on 26 December 1721, Arouet drafted a codicil cancelling the exclusion of Voltaire from his will, but he died without having signed it.

Although Voltaire was virtually disinherited, he was not absolutely penniless, for there were among his father's papers some small financial assets in Voltaire's name: three shares in the Compagnie des Indes and £5,000 in bank notes. Over the next few years Voltaire made intermittent but unsuccessful attempts to challenge his father's will in the courts, but it was not until seven years later, when he finally reached the stipulated age of thirty-five, that he finally succeeded in coming into his inheritance. But by then he did not need the money.

What did Voltaire really feel about his father? There is very little to go on; he referred very seldom to him, and then only as an authority figure, almost never as a human being. One day his father went to see one of the performances of Œdipe at the Comédie Française: it seems that Arouet responded vigorously to the tragedy, giving vent to strong if grudging expressions of admiration for the play and for the worldly success that he thought it would earn Voltaire. No doubt it was Voltaire who got him the ticket. When he learned that George I of England was sending him a gold watch in recognition of the success of Œdipe, Voltaire asked that it be sent to his father: 'He will be charmed to receive a letter, as well as by the fact that a present which the king of England deigns to give me should pass through his hands.'[10] Voltaire was still hoping to please and appease his father.

Almost exactly fifty years after his father's death, in 1772, in a letter to a very old friend, Voltaire suddenly trotted out a little story about his father.

> I once had a father who was a scold. One day, after having horribly and quite wrongly scolded his gardener, and after having almost beaten him, he said to him: 'Be off with you, rascal, I hope you find another master as patient as me.' I took my father to the theatre, to see a play called The Scold [Le Grondeur, a popular play by Brueys and Palaprat], and I persuaded the actor to add these exact same words to his part; and my funny old father behaved a bit better after that.[11]

So even in extreme old age, when he was seventy-eight years old, Voltaire's father was still a very real presence to him, and a presence for whom he still felt at least some kind of wistful affection.

4

FRIENDS AND LOVERS

1722–1723

WHATEVER VOLTAIRE'S FEELINGS about his father's death, they clearly did not weigh him down. Within a matter of weeks he was launched on a delightful new love affair (with a married woman) and had made his first small-scale entry into the world of high finance.

His new mistress was Marguerite Madeleine du Moutier, the marquise de Bernières. She was thirty-five years old, charming, carefree and a bit of a glutton, and he spent many idyllic days with her, either in her husband's town house in Paris or in their country château at La Rivière-Bourdet, near Rouen. Her husband, the marquis, was a wealthy senior judge in the *parlement* of Rouen and a busy entrepreneur in the world of finance. He was not just tolerant of Voltaire's relations with his wife but remarkably friendly too, for he obligingly helped Voltaire join a financial tax-gathering scheme.

All in all, by the spring of 1722 Voltaire was bubbling with *joie de vivre* and a boundless confidence in life and love. 'I await your return with the greatest impatience', he wrote to Mme de Bernières.

> I cannot forgive your absence, except by the hope that you will prepare for us a holiday retreat where I can count on spending delicious days with you. Get your château ready for us for a long visit, and come back as soon as possible. When you went away, you left me with your husband, instead of with you. In fact, here he is now, as I write; he has just come to collect me, to take me to meet people who want to start a new company. The most important business in life, and the

only one which one ought to have, is to live happily, and if we could do that without setting up a Jewish lending-house, that would be so much pain spared.[1]

Voltaire's reference to a 'Jewish lending-house' (*une caisse de juifrerie*) is tantalising; perhaps he was just using the expression as a general metaphor for a banking house. On the other hand, he was in contact at this time with a Jewish businessman called Salomon Levi. If he was trying to borrow money from Levi, he probably failed, for shortly afterwards he wrote a report denouncing him: 'A Jew, being of no country except the one where he happens to make money, can as easily betray the king for the Emperor, as the Emperor for the king'.[2]

We do not know where Voltaire got this anti-Semitic prejudice, but there can be little doubt that it was deeply engrained, for he expressed it quite often. Yet we should distinguish between Voltaire's anti-Jewish feelings and his distaste and derision for the ancient Israelites. Some people confuse the two; but it seems reasonably clear that Voltaire's hostility towards the Israelites, and what he saw as the barbarity of their mores, their history and their religious beliefs, was really a surrogate for his hostility towards their successors and inheritors, the Christian church.

The essence of the marquis de Bernières' tax-gathering scheme was the formation of a syndicate for the collection of the salt tax, known as *la gabelle*. The details are obscure, except that it depended on a personal dispensation by the regent, with an explicit promise that Voltaire should be included in the magic circle. At one point he said that he would insist on receiving a 'hand-out from this fine business' (*un pot-de-vin de cette belle affaire*),[3] which could imply that he was to be just an intermediary to be paid off with a commission.

Voltaire seemed so confident that the operation was going to come off that he was in no hurry to return to Paris to finalise the arrangements.[4] 'These gentlemen are joking', he wrote to Mme de Bernières, 'if they imagine that the success of the affair depends on seeing me arrive in Paris on the 15th of the month rather than the 20th. I have it in writing that the regent gave his word, and I have absolutely no fear that I could be by-passed.'[5]

By now Voltaire seems to have been completely intoxicated with the world of business, especially by his new acquaintance with the Pâris brothers, the ultimate magnates of high finance. By December 1722 he was talking airily about who, in this world of financial insiders, had influence with whom, as if he himself was now a person of influence. 'Génonville cannot get anywhere with the Pâris brothers. I shall use my free time to write a letter, in verse, to the Pâris brothers, in which I shall be inspired by my friendship with them.'[6]

M. de Bernières was an energetic entrepreneur and fortune-hunter. A year later, in 1723, Voltaire wrote: 'I have seen M. de Bernières, who will make a large fortune. His latest plan [a venture into the tobacco business] is the first really sensible business project he has talked about for a long time.'[7]

Voltaire's letters at this time convey a vivid sense of his buoyant self-assurance, not just in his business venture with the marquis, but also in his worldly love affair with the marquise, which was based not on grand sentiments or hopeless passion but on frank enjoyment and pleasure in each other's company. During the spring and summer of 1722 he wrote to her several times, expressing his impatience to see her; but it was evidently a bearable kind of impatience, which did not require him to be at her side immediately. As often as not his letters were written from Villars, or from Sully, or from Richelieu, or from one of the other grand country châteaux to which he was addicted, where he was housed, fed and entertained, and from which he was always reluctant to return to Paris.[8]

To be housed and fed by other people was a real consideration for Voltaire, for though he was supposed to receive some income from his father's estate, he had not yet made any money from the salt-tax scheme, and his finances were quite pinched. With Mme de Bernières, not only did he get pleasure from her company but he could get bed and board at her country château; and in May 1723 Voltaire also rented an apartment from her in her house in Paris.[9] (By an extraordinary coincidence, it was to this very town house, on the left bank of the Seine, on the corner of the rue de Beaune and the quai des Théatins, later renamed quai Voltaire, that Voltaire was to return fifty-six years later, after many years of exile, and where he was to die.)

Voltaire was not alone in needing somewhere to live: there was also his friend Nicolas-Claude Thieriot, whom he had known since they were both legal apprentices in 1714 and who was just as impoverished. Thieriot was a born idler, but he was an amiable and civilised young man, and in their late twenties he and Voltaire forged an intimate friendship which lasted, despite repeated disappointments on Voltaire's side, for the rest of their lives.

Voltaire made repeated efforts to find Thieriot a job, or at least some kind of income. In 1724 Voltaire's friend the duc de Richelieu was appointed ambassador to Vienna, and Voltaire persuaded him to take Thieriot with him as secretary. As he pointed out to Thieriot: 'You are not rich, and a fortune based on just three or four shares in the Compagnie des Indes is very little. With this appointment a man who is clever and sensible could easily look forward to other jobs and positions which are even more advantageous.'[10] But Thieriot turned the offer down on the grounds that it was beneath him to take up a position as a wage-earning domestic servant.[11] Voltaire was quite put out by Thieriot's ingratitude.[12]

Despite his reluctance to work, Thieriot was quite good at ingratiating himself with others. Before long he worked his way into the entourage of Mme de Bernières, and he seems to have spent as much time at Mme de Bernières' country home at La Rivière-Bourdet as she would allow him. In fact, he became such a fixture there that Voltaire would sometimes write to them jointly, often with requests to Thieriot to carry out some task for him:

> And as for you, my dear Thieriot, I am in urgent need of a Virgil in Latin, and a Homer in French. Please send them care of the porter at the Hôtel Villars in Paris, so that they can be brought to me at the château de Villars. These two authors are now my two household gods, without which I should never travel. Please show as much diligence on this occasion as you can, you great idler.'[13]

Virgil and Homer had now become Voltaire's 'household gods', because they were to be his models for his epic poem *La Henriade*. In October 1721 Voltaire sent Thieriot the text of the first nine cantos of the poem. 'Please have it all copied out most precisely, for M. le Régent. You will receive further instructions from me at the château de Richelieu. I shall never forget how much I am obliged to you for taking charge of all that.'[14] Thieriot was becoming quite useful for practical help in getting his epic poem ready for the printers. In December 1722 Voltaire sent him the names of the best engravers and asked him to sort out the illustrations, and in July 1723 he sent him some money as a float towards the printing costs.[15]

If Voltaire's love affair with Mme de Bernières was enjoyable, it was not exclusive. In the spring of 1722 he set off on an extended trip to Holland in the company of another young woman, Marie Marguerite, comtesse de Rupelmonde, a lively thirty-four-year-old widow. She had been described by the duc de Saint-Simon in his *Memoirs* in the most unflattering terms: 'red as a cow, with wit and cunning, and unbeatable impudence'.[16] But Voltaire obviously enjoyed her company, and when they reached Brussels, he told Thieriot that 'they have given me all the possible honours of the city, and have taken me to the finest brothel in town.'[17] In October the couple moved on to Holland. 'I ride here every day, I play real tennis, I drink Tokay wine, and I feel so well that it astonishes me.'[18]

He asked Thieriot to send him all the news but told him to keep quiet about his travelling companion: 'Please put it about that I have come to Holland solely in order to take steps for the printing of my poem [*La Henriade*].'[19] There was enough truth in the story to make it plausible. Voltaire had hoped to publish *La Henriade* in France, but he soon saw that he was unlikely to get official permission, known as the *privilège*, because the subject-matter was so politically touchy. Henri IV was, for Voltaire, a heroic figure, and his achievement in having negotiated an end to the sixteenth-century wars of religion between Catholics and Protestants in France was a triumph of religious toleration which richly deserved to be celebrated. But Louis XIV had rejected the legacy of Henri IV and in 1685 revived the persecution of the Protestants. Since this was still the active policy of the French state, the monarchy would be unlikely to give Voltaire permission to publish an epic poem that amounted to a denunciation of French religious bigotry.

So it made sense to think about publishing his epic poem in the Netherlands, which was famous for its printing and publishing industry, as well as for its principles of political and religious tolerance. During his visit to Holland, Voltaire made contacts with potential Dutch publishers, and he wrote a long editorial letter to Thieriot, instructing him in detail on the design of the planned illustrations for the poem.

Voltaire may not have told Mme de Bernières about Mme de Rupelmonde, but he did send her, in October, in his first letter to her since leaving Paris, an enthusiastic account of the attractions of life and society in Holland.

> Your letter has added another pleasure to the life I lead in The Hague.
> I shall stay a few more days to take all necessary steps for printing my
> poem, and I shall leave when the fine weather comes to an end. There
> is nothing more agreeable than The Hague when the sun deigns
> to come out. We see nothing but fields, canals and green trees; the
> country between The Hague and Amsterdam is an earthly paradise;

I looked with admiration at this town, which is the storehouse of the universe. There were more than a thousand vessels in port.

Of the five hundred thousand people who live in Amsterdam, there is none who is idle, none who is poor, none who is a dandy, none who is insolent. We met the Pensionary [the senior political leader in Holland] going on foot, without any lackeys, amidst the common people. You see no one there who has to pay court, people do not line up to see a prince passing, there is nothing but work and modesty.

The opera house here is dreadful; on the other hand, I see every kind of clergyman, Calvinists, Arminians, Socinians, rabbis, Anabaptists, all of whom talk wonderfully well, and all of whom are wonderfully right. I am getting quite used to doing without Paris, but not to doing without you. I promise to come and see you at La Rivière, if you are still there in November.[20]

This letter is virtually a foretaste in miniature of Voltaire's later reflections on life and society in England. In Holland in 1722, as in England in 1726–1728, he was captivated by the wholly foreign but seductive experience of political liberty and religious pluralism, combined with commercial prosperity. When he said that he was 'getting quite used to doing without Paris', he was hiding half his meaning. He disliked the big city and preferred to live in the country; as he told Mme de Bernières in a letter the following year: 'I think I am in hell when I am in the cursed city of Paris.'[21] But he also meant to underline the contrast between the attractions of liberty in Holland and the repressive lack of freedom inherent in the *ancien régime* of France. Voltaire visited Holland often, and on more than one occasion in later years he gave voice to the explicit expression of the temptation of emigration.

In The Hague, Voltaire found a printer who agreed to publish *La Henriade*.[22] Yet he had not quite given up hope that he might after all be able to get permission to have the work published in France. 'I am working on my poem,' he told Thieriot, after his return home in November 1722, 'so as to soften some of those passages whose hard truths might antagonise the censors. I shall do everything I can to have the *privilège* in France. So you can spread it about that it will be printed in this country, and that the subscribers have nothing to fear.'[23]

Voltaire's hopes for *La Henriade* reached their high point a few days later when he paid a brief visit to the Château de La Source and there, for the first time, met Henry St John, Lord Bolingbroke, the English politician, now living in temporary exile in France. From the first moment

Voltaire was enormously impressed with Bolingbroke, and vice versa, as Bolingbroke wrote to Voltaire's friend Mme d'Argental: 'M. de Voltaire has passed a few days here. I was charmed both by him and by his work. I did not expect to find the author so wise, nor the poem so well constructed.'[24] Bolingbroke's enthusiasm boosted Voltaire's confidence, for within a month he told Thieriot that he had finalised the text of his epic: 'I have, I believe, completed both the poem and the commentary. I have composed an abbreviated history of the period to insert at the front of the work. I have also written an address to the king. Please pay my respects to Mme de Bernières.'[25]

Early in 1723, however, the court turned against *La Henriade*, and Voltaire was forced to accept that his poem could not be openly published in France. He also realised that he must abandon his plan of publishing it by subscription in Holland, since the costs of the edition he had planned, with lavish printing and specially commissioned illustrations, would far exceed the advertised subscription price. He wrote to Prosper Marchand, a bookseller in The Hague: 'Please let me know how many subscriptions you have taken. It is very important for me to know. Have no fear of frightening me by the smallness of the number: the fewer there are, the happier I shall be. I should actually prefer the subscribers to ask for their money back, seeing that the cost of the book will be at least 25 florins.'[26]

Instead, he decided to bring his poem out in France, in a clandestine edition, and it was at La Rivière-Bourdet, in March 1723, that he met Abraham Viret, one of a number of publishers working in Rouen. He reached agreement with him to bring out a cheap edition, with a print run of 4,000 copies; but before the edition was ready for distribution his plans were disrupted by a major national epidemic of smallpox.[27]

Smallpox was common throughout Europe in the eighteenth century, and often fatal: the number of deaths from smallpox epidemics may have averaged some 400,000 a year. According to one estimate, the fatality rate among those who contracted the disease could range from 20 to 60 per cent, while those who survived the disease were often badly disfigured with facial scars.

At the time most Western doctors did not understand the causes of the disease, or how to prevent it. Oriental physicians, on the other hand, had developed methods of inoculation which could be used to prevent the emergence of the full-blown disease, and news of their discoveries had very recently been brought to Western Europe by Lady Mary Wortley Montagu, the wife of the English ambassador to the Ottoman empire. She herself had suffered an attack of smallpox, and in Constantinople she had witnessed an inoculation procedure. She was so impressed that she had her own son inoculated, and her example caused great interest and controversy in England, to the point that in 1722 the prince of Wales had his daughters inoculated.

In France the medical establishment and the Church were opposed to inoculation on dogmatic grounds, and continued to resist it for much of the eighteenth century. When Voltaire came to write about smallpox, ten years later, in his *Lettres philosophiques*, he estimated that around 20 per cent of the population were liable to die of the disease, and that 20,000 people had died in the French epidemic of 1723.

First news of this latest outbreak reached Voltaire in July 1723, and in September he learned that his dear friend La Faluère de Génonville had caught the disease and died.[28] Five weeks later he wrote to Mme de Bernières: 'Paris is ravaged by this sickness. This is another reason for you to stay a bit longer in the country while winter approaches.'[29] Voltaire was expecting to follow his own advice, for he wrote this letter when he was visiting Jean-René de Longueil, marquis de Maisons, a wealthy and well-connected judge in the *parlement* of Paris. The 24-year-old marquis was holding a house party at his château (now known as Maisons-Laffitte), north-west of Paris, to which he had invited a large number of distinguished guests; there was to be a performance by Adrienne Lecouvreur, star at the Comédie Française, and a play-reading by Voltaire of his latest tragedy. But on 4 November smallpox broke out at the château, and the party had to be cancelled: all the planned entertainments were called off, and those guests who could, departed in haste.

The marquis de Maisons was among the victims of the epidemic, but he was not badly infected, and he soon recovered.* But Voltaire caught it much more seriously, to the point where his life seemed to be in danger. He claimed that the local doctors despaired of his recovery and made no attempt to treat the disease, and he was persuaded to make a death-bed confession to a local priest.

I had myself bled, twice, on my own authority, despite the vulgar prejudice against it. Next day, M. de Maisons had the kindness to send for M. de Gervasi, the doctor of Cardinal de Rohan; he was reluctant to come, but he came nevertheless. At first he had a very pessimistic

---

* In fact, he was so little affected that he was not effectively immunised against the disease. Eight years later, in 1731, he again went down with smallpox, and on that occasion he died of it.

opinion of my illness, but he did not abandon me for a moment. His arguments carried conviction and gave confidence to my mind, which is necessary for a patient, since hope is already the first step to a recovery. He was obliged to make me take an emetic eight times, and instead of the cordials usually given in such cases, he made me drink two hundred pints of lemonade. This prescription, which you will think extraordinary, was the only one which could save my life.

What consoled me the most was the attention of my friends, and the inexpressible kindnesses shown me by M. and Mme Maisons. I also had the pleasure of having by my side a friend, one whom one must count among the very small number of truly virtuous men: M. Thieriot, who on first hearing of my illness, came post-haste from 40 leagues away to look after me, and who has not left my side for an instant.[30]

Ten days later Voltaire was out of danger, and after another two weeks' convalescence at Maisons he was well enough, on 1 December, to be conveyed back to Paris. But the misfortunes of the marquis were not at an end.

Scarcely was I two hundred yards from the château than a part of the floor of the bedroom where I had been sleeping burst into flames; the neighbouring rooms, and the apartments downstairs, the valuable furniture with which they were ornamented, were all consumed in the fire. The loss cost nearly a hundred thousand livres, and without the help of the firemen summoned from Paris, one of the most beautiful buildings of the kingdom would have been entirely destroyed. They did not tell me of this extraordinary event when I reached home, and I only knew of it when I awoke next morning.[31]

The story as Voltaire tells it is entertaining and illuminating; what lends it extra interest is that it was written to Louis Nicolas Le Tonnelier, baron de Breteuil. We know from other references that Voltaire had been in regular contact with the Breteuil family at least as far back as 1716 and that he had visited them on at least two occasions, in 1718 and 1722. But this is the only surviving letter from him to the baron. The baron's daughter was the brilliant young Émilie, then seventeen years old; two years later she would marry and have children; eight years after that she would become Voltaire's mistress, the love of his life and his companion for the next sixteen years.

5

LA HENRIADE

1723–1726

BY THE MIDDLE OF DECEMBER 1723 Voltaire began to feel strong enough once more to take up the publication of the clandestine edition of *La Henriade*. With the help of Mme de Bernières the first batch of the edition of 4,000 copies was brought secretly from Rouen to Paris during the last weeks of December and released in the capital during the first days of January 1724.[1] It was a cheap production, ugly to look at and with so many copy-editing errors that Voltaire decided to treat it as little more than a first draft (*'la faible esquisse'*[2]); he produced a new and much enlarged version in the following year.

The official censors did their best to repress the work: 'they have cried out against it, and the official inquisition becomes more severe every day.'[3] But this first edition, despite its imperfections, was so popular that it was quickly followed by several pirate versions, and the censors were effectively swept aside. More important was the critical acclaim of the commentators: disregarding the disapproval of the court, they were unanimous in their applause, and there was a broad consensus that France had at last found an epic poet who could be compared with the great models of antiquity. Enthusiasm for Voltaire's epic was so great that at least sixty editions of the poem were published during the next half-century, and another sixty during the following forty years. In fact, the publication of *La Henriade* marked the moment when Voltaire was finally recognised by his contemporaries as France's leading poet.

Since then, critical and popular opinion has turned against *La Henriade*. What Voltaire's contemporaries saw as a great new epic seems today little more than a laboured imitation, book by book, of his Virgilian model. This is a common fate for much literature, which may in its time have been at the height of fashion but which has subsequently gone out of favour; this has certainly been the fate of much of Voltaire's writing, especially in the case of his poetic and verse compositions. But Voltaire's place in history, his seminal position in the French eighteenth century, his subsequent role as a pioneer in the French Enlightenment and his claim on the interest of later generations do not stand or fall by what we think today of *La Henriade*.

Voltaire did not dwell on the success of his epic, because he was already hard at work putting the finishing touches to his next tragedy, *Mariamne*. This new play was eagerly anticipated by a public which had been fired up by Voltaire's new celebrity, and the Comédie Française took the opportunity to double the prices of the theatre seats. Unfortunately, the première, on 6 March 1724, was such a disaster that the performance ended in uproar and could not be completed. Voltaire immediately withdrew the play and effectively suppressed it; the original text has not survived. He did not give up, however: he revised the play, and when he put it on again the following year, under the amended title of *Hérode et Mariamne*, it was a great success, both at the Comédie Française and at Versailles. After that, another five years would pass before Voltaire had another winner at the Comédie Française.

Meanwhile, his personal life was also in some confusion. Ostensibly, he and Mme de Bernières were enjoying a happy love affair, and Voltaire could live either with her at her country home at La Rivière-Bourdet or in her town house in Paris. In practice, however, their affair was starting to fade. She lived mainly in the country during the spring, summer and autumn, and he spent several weeks with her in the spring of 1723, either at La Rivière-Bourdet or in nearby Rouen, while he was organising the publication of his epic. But he went back to Paris in the summer of that year, and he did not return to La Rivière-Bourdet until September.

In Paris he made repeated efforts to carry out her request that he should rent a box for her at the Opéra, and in July 1723 he told her proudly that he had persuaded Jean-Nicolas Francini, the director of the Opéra, to let him have a small box for the coming winter season for 400 francs.[4] Throughout this time he continued to assure Mme de Bernières of his continuing devotion, as he told Thieriot in August, 1724: 'You know how much I am attached to the mistress of the house, and how much I should love to live with you'.[5]

But one reason for Voltaire's absence was that he was frequently unwell, suffering either from chronic indigestion or from recurrent infections. These bouts of illness virtually forced him to stay in Paris, 'a city which I detest',[6] but they also reduced his energy and ensured that he was not much fun to be with. In September 1724 he wrote to Mme de Bernières:

I have come back from the dead, I have had eight attacks of fever in this miserable rented room where I have taken refuge. M. le duc de Sully has offered to take me to Sully, but I should give you the preference if you are willing. I really want to get back my health and revise *Henri IV* [i.e., *La Henriade*] with you, and pass quiet days there. Tell me if you do not have a great mob there, for you know that I hate crowds as much as I love you.[7]

In the face of his sufferings Voltaire's tone became increasingly self-pitying, and his demands for reassurance from Mme de Bernières more and more plaintive. Later that month he wrote to her:

The state I am in is a thousand times worse than it was after my small-pox. I really need to be consoled by the touching reassurances you have given me of your love. Since you have the courage to love me in the state I am in now, I swear that I shall pass the rest of my life only with you. You are the only one in whom I have confidence, and by whom I am sure to be really loved.[8]

Unfortunately, he went on to make matters worse with a graphic description of his latest affliction: 'Come back to Paris as soon as possible, I beg you. You will find me with a horrible scabies which covers the whole of my body. Fortunately, I know you have enough virtue and friendship to put up with a poor leper like me. When you return, we shall not kiss, but our hearts will speak.'[9]

Unsurprisingly, she stayed in Normandy, and Voltaire remained alone and ill. He wrote to Thieriot:

I spend my time in my little apartment, I am almost always alone, and I ease my ills by doing a modest amount of work, which amuses me without being too tiring, and by enduring my sufferings with patience. Tell Mme de Bernières that she should write to me. I know that, in the end, one can get tired of a friend like me, who always needs consoling. Little by little, people are repelled by those who are unhappy. I should not be surprised if in the end Mme de Bernières's friendship for me should weaken, but tell her that I am more attached to her than even a healthy man could be, and that I promise her, this winter, good health and gaiety.[10]

Voltaire's relations with Mme de Bernières were not helped by his pitiful finances, made worse by the cost of the apartment which he was renting in her town house. It had seemed such a good idea at first, but it proved a burden for Voltaire, and a growing source of conflict between them. Voltaire still lacked a reliable income to meet his expenses: towards the end of 1723 he owed money to Abraham Viret, the Rouen printer, and to M. de Gervasi, for his smallpox treatment. To meet these debts, he was forced to sell all his furniture, but he was still so short of cash that he had to ask Mme de Bernières to lend him, for a few months, a bed and some armchairs for his rooms in her town house. Moreover, he had to spend more money converting these rooms into a self-contained apartment.[11]

In desperation, Voltaire tried to make money by gambling during a visit to the spa at Forges; and of course, he lost, 100 louis, or £2,400, which in those days was a large sum, and very large indeed for a poor man like Voltaire.[12] In August 1724 he had to ask Mme de Bernières to let him borrow some of the rooms in her part of the Paris house, since his apartment was not yet ready. 'I am obliged to spend my day with workmen who are as deceitful as courtiers; which is why I shall go willingly to Fontainebleau, since I should just as soon be deceived by ministers and ladies of the court as by my decorator and joiner.'[13]

Even when it was finished, Voltaire's apartment, overlooking the Seine, was so noisy that it was hard to live in. He wrote to Mme de Bernières: 'I am still sleeping in your apartment [i.e., not in his own], where I have put a bed. But I cannot get used to the infernal noise of the riverbank and the street. It is impossible for me to sleep there, and even more difficult to work. I hope the pleasure of living with you will overcome all that.'[14]

For a while he stuck it out, but when he fell ill from the stress, he tried to get some peace and quiet by moving to a furnished room round the corner; but because of the extra expense he soon moved back to the rue de Beaune. He told Thieriot that he looked forward to sharing the apartment with him but feared that he might not be able to endure it: 'Certainly, I do not want to leave Mme de Bernières, but it is impossible to live in her accursed house, which is as cold as the pole in winter, which stinks of dung like a stable, and where there is more noise than in hell.'[15]

He thought of escaping from the noise by going to visit some of his grand friends in their country houses, but he knew he had to stay in Paris to keep working.

> I am afraid of Fontainebleau, of Villars, and of Sully, for the sake of my health and of *Henri IV*; I would not be able to work, I would eat too much, and I would waste the precious time in pleasures and distractions which I should be spending on work, which is honourable and necessary. I think that the best plan would be to return to La Rivière, where I am left in peace, and where I should be a thousand times more comfortable than elsewhere.[16]

Voltaire also complained to Mme de Bernières about three useless servants 'whom I cannot afford to keep but whom I do not have the power to sack. You have a security guard (*suisse*) who is on your establishment, not because he wants to please you, but in order to sell bad wine to all the water carriers who come here every day, and who turns the doorway of your house into a nasty café.'[17] To make matters worse, in September, Voltaire's apartment was burgled. He wrote to Thieriot:

> I am ruined by the expenses of my apartment, and on top of that someone has stolen a large part of my furniture. Half of our books have gone missing. They took shirts, suits and some pieces of porcelain, and they may also have stolen from Mme de Bernières's apartment. That is what comes of having an imbecile part-time security guard who also runs a café, rather than a full-time porter.[18]

By the end of September 1724 Voltaire was becoming so desperate about his financial situation that he was starting to think that he might have to get a job, as he wrote to Mme de Bernières: 'My fortune has taken such a devilish turn in the Chambre des Comptes, that I shall perhaps be compelled to work to live, after having lived to work.'[19]

The 'devilish turn in the Chambre des Comptes' was an attempt to borrow some money to invest in a *rente viagère*. The principle of a *rente viagère*, or life-rent, was that the investor lent a capital sum to an individual borrower; the interest rate might be rather high, perhaps as much as 10 per cent per annum, but the capital debt would be wiped out by the death of the lender. How far Voltaire got with this particular venture is uncertain, but he admitted, in a letter to Mme de Bernières, that he had failed to raise the money. 'I have completely lost out on my 2,000 livres of *rentes viagères*, for having delayed too long in paying the loan. M. de Nicolaï has refused to make me an advance.'[20] The figures suggest that he had been trying to raise at least 20,000 livres of capital, which would have been a bold undertaking for someone without financial backing; and since Nicolaï was the First President of the Chambre des Comptes, and therefore the judge appointed to oversee the application of his father's will, it looks as if Voltaire had applied to him for part of his inheritance, and had been turned down.[21]

Voltaire's financial difficulties were made much worse by the costs of his apartment in the Bernières' house in Paris. According to the lease signed on 4 May 1723, Voltaire was due to pay, for himself and Thieriot, 600 livres a month for the apartment, plus 1,200 livres a month for his board. Voltaire may at first have thought that this was just a friendly arrangement, and he allowed his rent to fall badly behind. But he gradually discovered that the marquis intended to be paid in full, and by June 1725 it was made clear to him that he would not be welcome at La Rivière-Bourdet until he paid his arrears of rent.

Voltaire was indignant at being so brutally treated by people he had thought were his friends:

> If I cannot go to La Rivière until I have appeased the tyrant with money, it does not seem likely that I can make the journey. I do not have the means of buying the pleasure of living with Mme de Bernières and you. I have been compelled to settle with the engravers of the illustrations for *Henri IV*, who have not yet been paid, and who have agreed to accept only half of their fees until the print-run is sold. A senior judge [the marquis de Bernières] should behave more nobly. In truth, when Mme de Bernières urged me to live in her house, I did not expect that one day I would be treated this way, or that they would take advantage of my poor fortunes to hold a knife to my throat.[22]

But he was even more upset that it was Thieriot who had sent him the bad news: 'It is you who have written me this, you who, if it were not for me, would not know Mme de Bernières. Can you really suspect, as you wrote, that it was to save money that I wanted to come to La Rivière? I was only coming because I love her. Truly, you have written me a very strange letter, but one must get used to everything.'[23]

Thieriot's 'strange letter' should have told Voltaire that his dear friend was not just an idler and a scrounger but was also capable of petty treachery.

Voltaire now began to fear that his place in the affections of Mme de Bernières had been taken by the chevalier des Alleurs, a rising diplomat who had become a frequent visitor to La Rivière-Bourdet. In June he wrote to Thieriot:

> My guess is that the chevalier des Alleurs is at La Rivière, and that you are all spending a pleasant time together. Tell me how she is, if she is still very greedy, if she is enchanted with the chevalier des Alleurs, if the aforesaid chevalier is always healthy, sleeps well and has a good hard-on but says he is always ill, in fact whether they can stand seeing me in their hermitage.[24]

Voltaire even poured out his jealousy to Mme de Bernières herself.

> I envy the destiny of M. des Alleurs, who has carried to La Rivière-Bourdet his indifference and his talents; I can imagine that you have willingly forgotten everybody else in your charming solitude. A thousand compliments to M. des Alleurs. Everyone in Paris says that I have broken up with you, and all because I am not at La Rivière. The truth, however, is that I love you with all my heart as you used to love me. I am attached to you for ever with the greatest tenderness.[25]

It was at this crucial moment in the fading of his love affair with Mme de Bernières that Voltaire got entangled in the problems of a certain abbé Pierre-François Guyot Desfontaines. It was the beginning of a nightmare relationship which was to haunt him for many years to come. Desfontaines was a forty-year-old Jesuit, who had taught for a number of years in Jesuit schools but who had recently turned to journalism. In December 1724 he was arrested, charged with homosexuality and transferred to the prison of Bicêtre, the prison for sodomites: if convicted, he risked being burned at the stake.

It so happened that Desfontaines was a distant relative of the marquis de Bernières, and the marquis interceded with the duc de Bourbon on Desfontaines's behalf. Voltaire tried to help too, and through the joint efforts of Bernières and Voltaire, Desfontaines was released, in May 1725, on condition that he live in exile at La Rivière-Bourdet. Voltaire pressed for the lifting of this condition, and in June he was able to tell

Mme de Bernières that he had succeeded: 'I count on being able to bring you a new warrant (*lettre de cachet*) which will give our poor abbé Desfontaines his complete liberty.'[26]

Desfontaines duly took refuge at La Rivière-Bourdet, where Voltaire sent him a friendly message. 'I am sorry there has been an upset between you and the reverend fathers. Perhaps they will make peace with you, and let you have a living in the first peace treaty they make with you.'[27] What Voltaire did not know, and did not learn until many years later, was that after his release from Bicêtre, Desfontaines had composed a vitriolic pamphlet against Voltaire, which he showed to Thieriot. Why he wrote it is inexplicable, except as an expression of wholly irrational rage against a more fortunate benefactor. The pamphlet was suppressed, but it turned out to be the first shot in a long campaign of vilification by Desfontaines against Voltaire.

Voltaire had not given up hope of being reunited with Mme de Bernières.

> Here I am, a prisoner, for the lack of the means to pay my ransom to be able to go to La Rivière, which I had thought of as my home country. In truth, I did not think that your friendship would ever allow the imposition of such conditions on our friendship; I was hoping to spend the month of July with you at La Rivière. You have only seen me sick and lethargic; but I have recovered my gaiety. I imagined I was going to spend delicious days with you. They say you no longer love me, but I do not believe it. I love you with all my heart, and I beg you urgently to write to me often.[28]

During that summer and autumn Voltaire continued to write her wistful letters of affection mixed with regret. 'I must have been really cursed by God to have lived with you only when I had scabies and you the gout, and to be far from you when we are both well. I imagine that you have charming supper parties. Is M. des Alleurs still with you? He told me that he would stay as long as he enjoyed it. So I expect he will stay a long time.'[29]

In fact, he never again visited Mme de Bernières at La Rivière-Bourdet, and by the summer of 1725 their love affair had come to an end. Perhaps it was because he was too poor, constantly struggling to make a living; perhaps it was partly because he was too often dragged down by sickness. As he had admitted, during a sunny period of unaccustomed good health: 'I am beginning to breathe and to know good health again. Before, I was only half-alive. It seems to me that I shall love my friends much better when I cease to suffer. Now I shall only think of giving them pleasure, whereas before I could only think of my sufferings.'[30]

But probably the main reason why their affair ended was that it was not important enough to him. Voltaire was too busy making his career, and he stayed away too long and too often to keep it alive. When it was over, he was sad and lonely, no doubt, but he was not really heart-broken: his career came first.[31]

6

FROM THE COURT TO THE BASTILLE

1725–1726

VOLTAIRE DID NOT, of course, yet have a career in any dependable sense. It was seven years since his startling success with his first tragedy, *Œdipe*, and his next two plays had been flops. His epic *La Henriade* had been well received, but he could not make any real money out of a clandestine book. What he needed was the support and endorsement of the authorities, for in those days a writer had the greatest difficulty in making his way without the approval of the court.

Curiously, Voltaire showed rather little interest in the goings-on at court while the duc d'Orléans was alive. In June 1723 he told Mme de Bernières that the duc d'Orléans had ceased to do any work but had taken a new mistress;[1] but when the duke died in December, Voltaire did not even mention the fact.

In July 1724 Voltaire passed on to Mme de Bernières the latest item of court scandal.

M. de la Trémoïlle has been exiled from the court, for having frequently put his hand in the flies of His Most Christian Majesty. [Louis XV was fourteen years old, and the duc de Trémoïlle sixteen.] He had made a little plot with the Comte de Clermont by which they would make themselves masters of the king's trousers, and not allow any other courtier to share their good fortune. All this augurs well for the future of M. de la Trémoïlle, for I cannot help having a high opinion of someone who, at sixteen, wants to work on the king and control him.[2]*

The authorities at court now had to find Louis a wife. He was supposed to marry Maria-Anna-Victoria, the daughter of Philip V of Spain, but she was only four years old and was not the solution to the problem. The duc de Bourbon, who was at this time the king's chief minister, settled instead on Marie Leszczyńska, who had three recommendable advantages: she was the daughter of Stanislas Leszczyńska, the former king of Poland, so she had royal blood; her father had lost his throne and was now a virtual dependant of the French crown, so her loyalty could be counted on; and she had been born in 1703, so she was twenty-two years old and old enough to be the wife of Louis, who was fifteen. Their engagement was announced in May 1725, and the wedding fixed for September.

Voltaire immediately saw that the royal wedding festivities would provide an opportunity not to be missed. He persuaded Mme de Prie, mistress of the duc de Bourbon, to let him have an apartment in her house at Fontainebleau during the celebrations, in the hope that he would have a chance to show off his talents, and even to make contact with the new queen.

Louis XV and Marie Leszczyńska were duly married on 5 September 1725, and Voltaire gave Mme de Bernières a racy and disrespectful account of the event.

> They do everything they can to please the queen here, and the king puts himself out to do so, too. He is said to have boasted that he gave her seven sacraments during their first night, but I do not believe a word of it. Kings always deceive their peoples. The queen looks well, even though her looks are not at all pretty. But everybody here is enchanted with her virtue and her politeness. She was wearing a bit of rouge on the day of her wedding, just enough not to appear pale. She fainted for a moment in the chapel, but just for form's sake.[3]

Voltaire had prepared a little entertainment which he had hoped would be performed before the royal couple; instead they put on *Le Médecin malgré lui*, by Molière. Voltaire was not put out.

---

* Voltaire's ironic predictions of Trémoïlle's fine future were belied by events: he died of smallpox in 1741, at the age of thirty-three.

After the supper, there was a fireworks show with many rockets, but with very little imagination or variety, after which the king went off to see about making a dauphin. On the whole, it's all noise, crush, crowds and frightful tumult. I shall take great care, these first few days of confusion, not to try to get myself presented to the queen. I shall wait until the crowds have dispersed, and until her majesty has been a bit recovered from the giddiness which this holiday must have caused her. Then I shall try to get *Œdipe* and *Mariamne* performed for her. I shall dedicate both of them to her. She has already let me know that she would let me take this liberty. But nothing must be rushed.[4]

This was the first time that Voltaire made a sustained attempt to play the role of courtier, and he did not enjoy the experience. 'Ah, Madame,' he wrote to Mme de Bernières, 'I am not in my element here, madman that I am. I have found myself almost always up in the air, cursing the life of a courtier, running pointlessly after some little fortune which has seemed to appear before me, but which has fled immediately I tried to grasp it; and all that serves only to make me waste my time.'[5]

He echoed the same complaints to Thieriot:

A man who stays at court is to be condemned, or at least to be pitied. I have been received here very well, but unfortunately praise does not amount to anything, and the role of a court poet, however agreeable it may seem, trails a bit of ridicule behind him. Every day they give me hopes, which do not satisfy my hunger; you cannot believe, my dear Thieriot, how tired I am of my life as a courtier. The queen is assaulted every day with Pindaric odes, sonnets, epistles and epithalamia. I imagine that she takes these poets to be the fools of the court, and she is quite right, for it is a great madness for a man of letters to be here.[6]

In October, however, Voltaire's patience was rewarded, for two of his new plays were performed in the presence of the queen, as he told Thieriot: 'I have been very well received by the queen, she wept when we performed *Mariamne*, and she laughed at *L'Indiscret*, she spoke to me often, she called me *mon pauvre Voltaire*.'[7]

Eventually Voltaire's diligent efforts at courtly flattery seemed to pay off, as he told Mme de Bernières (and Thieriot).

The queen has just given me a personal pension of 1,500 livres, which

I was not asking for; but this is a first step towards getting those things which I do ask for. I no longer complain of life at court; I am beginning to have reasonable hopes of being able to be sometimes useful to my friends.[8]

Voltaire was rapidly disabused. The queen's pension was conveyed to him in an official warrant set out with all the proper legal solemnity, but Voltaire was so short of cash that he did not wait for the money to come through but took the warrant and sold it at a discount to the Duverney financiers. Unfortunately, the queen's gift was rescinded, the pension was never paid and Voltaire found himself in debt to Duverney for 1,500 livres.

Worse was to come. After his return to Paris a few weeks later Voltaire found himself embroiled in a public quarrel with a young aristocrat, the chevalier Guy-Auguste Rohan-Chabot. It seems that the chevalier was a rowdy young man at a loose end, with nothing better to do than cause trouble in public; and there is no doubt that it was Rohan-Chabot who picked the quarrel with Voltaire. Why he did so is unclear; perhaps it was because, being a nobleman without any personal distinction or achievement of his own, he was irritated at the spectacle of the growing literary celebrity of Voltaire, a mere commoner.

The quarrel started in the foyer of the Opéra, when Rohan-Chabot confronted Voltaire and taunted him with having changed his name: 'Monsieur de Voltaire? Monsieur Arouet? What is your real name?' Voltaire replied tartly: 'And you? Is your name Rohan or Chabot?' Two days later, this time at the Comédie Française, Rohan-Chabot again attacked Voltaire with the same sneering question, and this time Voltaire raised the stakes by retorting that the chevalier was dishonouring his name, whereas Voltaire would make his own immortal.

A few days later Rohan-Chabot sent Voltaire a dinner invitation which appeared to have come from the duc de Sully. Voltaire turned up to the dinner and was welcomed, even though he had not been expected. But during the meal a servant told him that a man had called to speak to him. Voltaire went downstairs to the street, and there he was publicly beaten by three or four lackeys, while the chevalier de Rohan-Chabot supervised the procedure from a carriage.

Voltaire was furious, but no one would support him. He appealed to the duc de Sully, whose honour must, he thought, be at stake because one of his guests had been beaten; but Sully turned a deaf ear. He appealed to Madame de Prie, mistress of the duc de Bourbon; she would not help.

He appealed to the queen; she would not help either. He appealed to all his friends at court, but none of them would help. After all, Rohan-Chabot was a nobleman from one of the greatest families in the land, but who was Voltaire? Merely a poet. In the last resort, the consensus of the people in power was that a mere commoner such as Voltaire had no right to answer a nobleman as he had done, and he had deserved what he got.

Voltaire was now beside himself with rage: if he could not have justice, he would have revenge. He acquired a pair of pistols, he took lessons in swordsmanship and pistol shooting and he prepared to challenge Rohan-Chabot to a duel. Later Voltaire denied that he had challenged Rohan-Chabot, no doubt rightly, for Rohan-Chabot virtually went into hiding to avoid any such danger. But the authorities were alerted that Voltaire was planning trouble, and on the night of 17 April 1726 the police arrested him and carried him off to the Bastille.

From the Bastille, Voltaire strenuously denounced the injustice of his imprisonment. He wrote almost immediately to the comte de Maurepas, the Secretary of State:

> I protest, very humbly, that I have been assaulted by the brave chevalier de Rohan, assisted by six cut-throats, behind whom he boldly placed himself. Since that day I have always sought to repair, not my honour, but his; but it proved too difficult. If I came to Versailles, it is quite untrue that I called out the chevalier de Rohan-Chabot, or had him called out, at the home of the Cardinal de Rohan. I ask for your permission to take my meals with the governor of the Bastille, and to be allowed to receive visitors.[9]

Voltaire never spelled out the story of his quarrel with Rohan-Chabot; he left that to others. One of the most detailed versions was written by Montesquieu, the celebrated political philosopher. His account makes clear that Rohan-Chabot was in the wrong: 'If you want to give someone a beating, you should do it yourself, not send someone else to do it (*les coups de bâton se donnent et ne s'envoient pas*).' But Montesquieu was an aristocratic prig; he disliked Voltaire as an insolent upstart, and he did not hide his belief that Voltaire had no right to insult a nobleman such as Rohan-Chabot.[10]

But what was most remarkable about Voltaire's arrest was his immediate assumption that, whatever the rights and wrongs of his quarrel with Rohan-Chabot, he could strike a deal with the authorities to ensure that he would not have to spend long in the Bastille. 'I demand with great urgency,' he wrote to Maurepas, 'the permission to go immediately to England; if there should be any doubt of my leaving, I could be sent to Calais with an official escort.'[11]

Voltaire knew that he had been arrested not for a criminal offence but merely to prevent him causing a public disturbance; no doubt he guessed that they would be glad to see the back of him.[12] It is certainly true that he had for some time been planning a visit to England. During the previous year he had reluctantly come to the conclusion that he would never receive official permission for the publication of his epic poem *La Henriade* in France, and he started wondering whether to have it published in London, in Amsterdam or in Geneva. At first he inclined towards Geneva,[13] but by October 1725 he had decided in favour of London, and he started to make plans for visiting England and for having *La Henriade* printed there. To that end, he boldly wrote to George I in person:

To George Ist, king of Great Britain and of Ireland:
Sire, I have long regarded myself as one of the subjects of your majesty. I dare to beg for your protection for one of my works. It is an epic poem, whose subject is Henri IV, the best of our kings. I have spoken in this work with freedom and with truth. You, Sire, are the protector of the one and the other; and I dare to flatter myself that you will grant me your royal protection, to have printed in your domains a work which must interest you, since it is written in praise of virtue. It is the better to learn to describe it that I urgently seek the honour to come to London to present my profound respects and the gratitude with which I have the honour to be, Sire, your Majesty's most humble and most obedient and most obliged servant, Voltaire.[14]

Voltaire had received no reply from George I or from anyone else at the English court. But the French authorities responded almost immediately to Voltaire's proffered bargain and moved to put it into effect even more rapidly than he was quite ready for. By the end of April 1726, a mere twelve days after his arrest, Voltaire was expecting to be dispatched to Calais. He wrote to Thieriot: 'They are due to take me from the Bastille to Calais tomorrow or the day after. I am impatient to see you. Come as soon as you can. This may be the last time in my life that I shall see you.'[15] On the following day he pleaded with René Hérault, the chief of police, to be allowed to receive some friends in the prison courtyard and to delay his departure by two days, so that he could settle his affairs with his man of business.[16] But by 5 May, he had been taken to Calais, though he told Hérault that he was too ill to take ship immediately.[17]

> I have arrived at Calais, sir, with gratitude for the permission which I have received to travel to England, but very respectfully afflicted that I have been exiled fifty leagues from the court, and in addition deeply conscious of your kindness, and counting always on your fairness. I am obliged, sir, to tell you that I shall not go to London until I have restored my health, which has been sufficiently brought down by the sufferings which I have endured. Yet even were I to be well enough to leave, I should certainly not do so under escort, in order not to give my enemies the chance to claim that I was banished from the kingdom. I have the permission, and not an order, to leave it, and I dare to assert that it would not be equitable for the king to banish a man from his kingdom, just because he had been assaulted. If you wish, sir, I shall inform you of my departure as soon as I can travel to England.[18]

In this letter Voltaire spells out the two distinct parts of the bargain which he thought he had struck with the French authorities. He was exiled, by which he was required to stay at least fifty leagues distant from Versailles. Quite separately, he had been given permission to travel to England, since no Frenchman could legally leave the country without permission. Voltaire's letter insisted that these two conditions were logically quite separate; in fact, he knew that they were both inseparably part of the arbitrary power of the *ancien régime*, which was why he had to go to England. If he wanted to make a life as a writer, he needed freedom to do it.

Four or five days later all delays had been exhausted, and on 9 or 10 May Voltaire embarked for England. A new chapter in his life, and in the development of the Enlightenment, was about to begin.

7

IN ENGLAND

1726–1728

VOLTAIRE LANDED AT GRAVESEND, in the Thames estuary, on 10 or 11 May 1726. But from that point on he virtually disappears into the shadows, and for months on end. The chief reason for this is that we have very few letters from him during his exile: none for the first three months, only five in the next four months, and none at all again in the four months after that. For the whole of 1727 we have only eight letters, and in the next year there is another gap, which lasts for six months from August 1728 until some time after his return to France.

So though we know that Voltaire was in England for about two and a half years, we do not have any continuous chronological trace of his life and how he passed it. It is almost as if he had walked through a door and allowed it to swing closed behind him.

One of the possible reasons for the lack of letters during his exile may be that he was unhappy, or lonely, or at a loss, or in low spirits. This is what he told Thieriot, in one of his first letters from England, five months after his arrival there: 'I was without a penny, sick to death of a violent ague, a stranger, alone, helpless, in the midst of a city, wherein I was known to nobody. I could not make bold to see our ambassador in so wretched a condition. I had never undergone such distress; but I am born to run through all the misfortunes of life.'[1]

This letter could have been describing a short-term crisis of arrival, but nowadays we might also conclude that he had fallen into some kind of depression. There is some evidence that Voltaire may have suffered chronic or at least recurrent bouts of depression at several different points of his life.

As for the shock of arrival, that was real enough. In France he had parleyed his way, through his gift with words and in a society which he had known all his life, to a precarious but recognisable identity as a rising poet. In England he did not speak or understand the language, and he was reduced to silence, impotence and obscurity.

To make matters worse, he was penniless. Before leaving France he had assembled as much money as he could scrape together and had sent it, in the form of a letter of credit, to a London banker, Anthony Mendes da Costa; but when he reached London, he found that Mendes da Costa had gone bankrupt. 'I had about me', he told Thieriot later, 'only some bills of exchange upon a Jew called Medina* for the sum of about eight or nine thousand French livres, reckoning all. At my coming to London, I found my damned Jew was broken.'[2]

In theory, Voltaire was not without friends and contacts. He had letters of introduction to a number of prominent members of London society, some of which had been provided by Henry St John, Lord Bolingbroke, the Tory politician with whom Voltaire had become friendly when Bolingbroke had been living in exile in France. But in his state of destitution he did not dare use his letters of introduction, nor did he care to intrude on Bolingbroke, who was living in his country house at Dawley, near Uxbridge.

How Voltaire got through his first few days in London is not clear. It was John da Costa, father of Anthony Mendes da Costa, who broke the news to Voltaire that his son had gone bankrupt, and it is possible that he may have given him a small amount of cash to tide him over. Voltaire also received an advance from someone else, probably from John Brinsden, Bolingbroke's secretary and man of business. But he was really rescued by a young man of his own age, whom he had met in Paris the previous year and who offered him asylum.

This was Everard Fawkener, a successful young member of a prominent merchant family which specialised in trading in wool and silk with the Middle East. When Voltaire met him in Paris, in 1725, he was on his way home from Aleppo, where he had spent nine years managing the family trading office and building up his own fortune. On his return to England, Fawkener had established himself in a large and comfortable house in what was then the village of Wandsworth, south

---

* Voltaire seems to have written the name Medina by mistake for Mendes da Costa.

of London, and he invited Voltaire to stay. Voltaire accepted gratefully, and he lived as a guest of Fawkener in Wandsworth most of the
summer and autumn, from June to October that year. During his retirement he started to study the English language, in conversation and with
Fawkener's books; if he was depressed, this was probably the most acute
period, when he had the least energy and needed the maximum security.

In July, Voltaire returned secretly to France, for what proved to be a
very short trip. Afterwards he said that he had gone to France to search
out the chevalier de Rohan-Chabot; but if so, he did not find him, and he
did not dare stay long enough to have a realistic chance of finding him.
Perhaps he also hoped to raise some money to live on. But it is obvious
that a secret trip back to France, so soon after his sentence of exile, was
an act of folly, fraught with danger from the French secret police, and
not entirely rational. It is difficult to avoid the suspicion that this double
journey may have been really a desperate and activist form of escapism,
betraying Voltaire's uncertainty whether he had the resilience to make
a go of his stay in England.

On his return from France he knew that he had to go on living in
England, but he was uncertain and apprehensive how to deal with the
challenges he faced.

I confess, my dear Thieriot, that I made a little journey to Paris a short
while ago. I was only looking for one man, but his instinct for cowardice hid him from me, as if he had guessed that I was on his track. In
the end the fear of being discovered made me leave more precipitately
than I had arrived. I am still very uncertain whether I shall retire to
London [that is, leave Wandsworth for the hurly-burly of the capital].
I know that it is a place where the arts are all honoured and rewarded,
and where, though there are social differences, the only difference
between men is based on merit. It is a country where people think
freely and nobly, without being held back by any servile fear.

If I were to follow my inclination, it is there [i.e., in London] that
I should settle, just with the idea of learning to think. But I do not
know if my modest fortune, much upset by so much travel, my poor
health, more uncertain than ever, and my taste for the deepest retirement, will allow me to throw myself into the hubbub of Whitehall
and London. There are only two things I can do with my life, one is to
risk it with honour just as soon as I am able to do so, and the other is to
end it in the obscurity of a retirement which suits my way of thinking,
my misfortunes, and my knowledge of men.[3]

Considering the extreme boldness with which Voltaire had previously thrown himself into his worldly ambitions in France, it is striking that he was now experiencing such a deep loss of confidence in this foreign country. While he hesitated, he embarked on an intensive course of study to become competent in English.

In October, Voltaire's recovering mood received a real blow, when he heard of the early and unexpected death, at the age of thirty-nine, of his elder sister, Marguerite-Catherine, to whom he was deeply attached. But by then his depression must already have lifted significantly, for he had started going out more, meeting people and making fairly frequent visits to the theatre in the centre of London. 'I have only just received your letter,' he wrote to Mme de Bernières.

I could not get it sooner, in the deep solitude to which I have withdrawn. I have just come to London for a moment, and I am returning immediately to my lair. I am most unhappy [about his sister's death]: it would have been better for her to live and for me to die. It was an error of fate, and I suffer painfully from her loss. I forgive you for having been to the opera with the chevalier de Rohan, provided you are embarrassed about it. Let me hope that my absence will not have entirely effaced your memory of me. Love me, at least for reasons of generosity, even if you can no longer love me by inclination.[4]

Not surprisingly, he never wrote to her again.

He also wrote a long letter to Thieriot, recounting the circumstances of his arrival in England; and it is striking that, five months after his arrival there, he felt able to write it in English:

I intend to send you two or three poems of Mr Pope, the best poet of England and at present of all the world. I hope you are acquainted enough with the English tongue to be sensible of all the charms of his works. For my part I look on his poem called the 'Essay upon Criticism' as superior to the 'Art of Poetry' of Horace.

My star, that always pours on me some kind refreshment, sent to me an English gentleman unknown to me, [probably John Brinsden, Bolingbroke's man of business], who forced me to receive some money that I wanted. Another London citizen that I had seen but once in Paris [Everard Fawkener] carried me to his own country house, wherein I lead an obscure and charming life since that time, without going to London, and quite given over to the pleasures of indolence and friendship. The true and generous affection of this man, who soothes the bitterness of my life, brings me to love you more and more. I have seen often my lord and my lady Bolingbroke. I have found their affection still the same, even increased in proportion of my unhappiness. They offered me all, their money, their house; but I refused all, because they are lords, and I have accepted all from Mr Fawkener because he is a single gentleman.

All that I wish for is to see you one day in London, drawing up the strong spirit of this unaccountable nation. You will translate their thoughts better when you live among them. You will see a nation fond of their liberty, learned, witty, despising life and death, a nation of philosophers, not but that there are some fools in England, every country has its madmen.

One day I will acquaint you with the character of this strange people, but 'tis time to put an end to my English talkativeness.

I have written so much about the death of my sister, that I had almost forgotten to speak to you of her. You know my heart and my way of thinking. I have wept for her death, and I would be with her. Life is but a dream full of starts of folly, and of fancied and true miseries. Death awakes us from this painful dream and gives us, either a better existence, or no existence at all.[5]

Considering that Voltaire had been in England for barely five months, and had been studying English intensively for less time than that, this letter shows that he had attained an impressive command of the language. This was not quite his first attempt at writing in English: that was in a letter which he had written two or three weeks earlier, to the poet Alexander Pope, commiserating with him over an accident which had happened to him while driving in his carriage. At that point Voltaire had not yet met Pope but wanted to do so, and since he knew that Pope did not speak French, he wrote the letter in English. Sure enough, he did meet Pope soon afterwards. But it is remarkable that in this second letter in English, to Thieriot, Voltaire already felt confident enough of his sense of the English language, to express a judgement on the poetry of Pope and to compare it favourably with that of Horace.

Moreover, the whole tone of the letter shows that his mood has really lifted; he is no longer complaining of being miserable and penniless but is really enjoying his 'obscure and charming life, quite given over to the pleasures of indolence and friendship'. He is now not merely beginning to take some serious notice of England and the English, but is already finding the subject so interesting that he is thinking of writing a book about it.

It is important to remember that this was not why he came to England: his main purpose was to have the freedom to publish *La Henriade*. He did in fact publish this epic poem in England, a year and a half later and with great success, in a sumptuous subscription edition; and it added to his glowing literary reputation as a poet. But it was the book which he eventually constructed out of his observations and reflections on England that was the first of his works to give him immortality.

Not surprisingly, it is already clear from this letter to Thieriot that his interest in England is essentially political and social: he says 'one day I will acquaint you with the character of this strange people', and he describes the English as 'fond of their liberty, learned, witty', and 'a nation of philosophers'. But he never intended to write just another travel guide, as he wrote a year later: 'I will leave to others the care of describing with accuracy, [St] Paul's church, the Monument, Westminster, Stonehenge etc.'[6]

But if Voltaire already knew what kind of book it would *not* be, it would take him several years to work out what kind of book it would be. What finally emerged after seven years of gestation was a book which masqueraded as an ironic, pseudo-journalistic description of England, its mores and its institutions, but which was in reality a wickedly satirical back-handed attack on the *ancien régime* of France, an attack which continued to reverberate for another half-century, until the French Revolution and beyond.

Voltaire's English was somewhat idiosyncratic, but there is no doubt that he could write it fluently, idiomatically and with panache; it was a skill he retained for the rest of his life. By the following year his confidence in his facility in English was so great that he started to think of becoming an English writer; and by the end of that year, 1727, he had composed a short pamphlet in the form of a pair of essays: the *Essay upon the Civil Wars of France* and the *Essay upon Epick Poetry*. The purpose of the pamphlet was to drum up interest in his forthcoming publication of the new edition of his *La Henriade*; and since he was hoping to attract English customers, he had to write it directly in English.

But if Voltaire was vain enough to boast to Thieriot of his fluency in English, he did not explain how he had acquired it. He even virtually claimed that he was leading 'an obscure and charming life ... without going to London'. In fact, Voltaire was by now starting to go out and about, and his social life was becoming so active at about this time, October or November 1726, that he moved from Wandsworth to London. He saw a lot of Lord Bolingbroke and his family, who had moved back to London from their country house at Dawley, and he even wrote letters using Bolingbroke's house in Pall Mall as his address; but it seems that he did not live with the Bolingbrokes but took furnished lodgings. It was partly through Bolingbroke that Voltaire met Pope and through him a number of other writers, including Jonathan Swift the satirist, William Congreve the playwright, Edward Young the playwright and James Thomson, poet and author of *The Seasons*.

Pope was in some ways a pivotal figure among Voltaire's literary acquaintances. The two men had known one another by reputation before Voltaire arrived in England, for Bolingbroke had talked about Pope to Voltaire in France; in 1724 Voltaire sent Pope a copy of *La Henriade*, and Pope commented on it favourably: 'I esteem him for that honest principled spirit of true religion which shines through the whole; and from whence (unknown as I am to M. de Voltaire) I conclude him at once a free-thinker and a lover of quiet; no bigot but yet no heretic.'[7] When they met, Voltaire was obviously deeply impressed.

Mr Voltaire has often told his friends, that he never observed in himself such a succession of opposite passions as he experienced upon his first interview with Mr Pope. When he first entered the room and perceived our poor melancholy English poet, naturally deformed, and wasted as he was with sickness and study, he could not help regarding him with the utmost compassion. But when Pope began to speak, and to reason upon moral obligations, and dress the most delicate sentiments in the most charming diction, Voltaire's pity began to be changed into admiration, and at last even into envy. It is not uncommon with him to assert, that no man ever pleased him so much in serious conversation, nor any whose sentiments mended so much upon recollection.

This comes from Oliver Goldsmith's *Memoirs of M. de Voltaire*, which is one of the more frequently quoted sources of anecdotes about Voltaire. Unfortunately, everything Goldsmith says about Voltaire's stay in England is at best second-hand, since he was not born until 1728, the year Voltaire returned to France.

Voltaire's acquaintance with Pope is often associated with a famously scandalous anecdote. Voltaire was invited to dinner at Pope's home in Twickenham, where he proceeded to complain loudly about his poor health. Pope's mother asked him how his constitution came to be so bad at his age. 'Oh,' said he, 'those damned Jesuits, when I was a boy, buggered me to such a degree that I shall never get over it as long as I live.'

Voltaire had no doubt become accustomed, in regency France, to a libertine freedom of language far in excess of what was acceptable in England. Yet he was a sensitive and a subtle man, and it is difficult to believe that he could have deliberately come out with a remark that he must have known would be offensive, especially in a Catholic household, and even more so in front of an old lady. Some scholars claim to believe in the authenticity of the tale, even though it is at best third-hand, and not published until forty years later.[8]

When Voltaire finally produced his English edition of *La Henriade*, Pope was one of the few distinguished men of letters who did not subscribe. On the other hand, we know that Pope showed great interest in Voltaire's epic and that it inspired the choice of the title of his own poem the *Dunciad*, which came out the following year. Perhaps the simple explanation is that Pope was a Catholic and Voltaire an unbeliever.

One of the reasons that Voltaire moved from Wandsworth to London at the end of 1726 was that he had started going quite frequently to the theatre. What he heard and saw there made a profound impression on him, and on his sense of the power of the English language. For if he thought the English people were strange, few things were stranger to him than the English theatre, especially as exemplified in the plays of Shakespeare, which he found wild and uncouth and yet totally compelling.

Shakespeare did not follow any of the rules attributed to Aristotle, and his plays were virtually unknown in France. So when Voltaire went to see his first Shakespeare play in London, in 1726, he must have found the experience disorienting or even deeply shocking. He had grown up with the assumption, unquestioned in France, that a play must be dignified, noble and stately; but now he suddenly discovered an English theatre, especially an English Elizabethan theatre, which obeyed none of the expected rules: the three unities were disregarded, the tragedies might include comic scenes or characters, noble characters appeared alongside peasants or artisans and there was a great deal of physical action on stage.

But if Voltaire was dismayed by the contrast with the formal dignity and urbanity of the French stage, he also discovered that this was a kind of drama which could be raw, vigorous and astonishingly powerful. Against his will, he was deeply impressed by at least some aspects of English theatre.

In fact, we can pick up the trace of one of Voltaire's experiences in the theatre in the letter to Thieriot quoted on page 62. When he says that 'Life is but a dream full of starts of folly, and of fancied and true miseries. Death awakes us from this painful dream, and gives us, either a better existence, or no existence at all', we know at once that he is quoting, erratically but unmistakably, the celebrated soliloquy in *Hamlet* 'To be or not to be'.

Voltaire saw a number of Shakespeare's tragedies in his time in England. During the 1726–27 season, the Drury Lane Theatre put on *Othello, Hamlet, Macbeth* and *King Lear*, and the Lincoln's Inn Fields Theatre put on *Hamlet, Macbeth, King Lear, Henry IV, Henry VIII, Richard III* and *Julius Caesar*. Voltaire must have seen *Hamlet, Othello* and *Julius Caesar*, because he later referred to them in the *Lettres philosophiques*, and he later drew heavily on *Julius Caesar* for a tragedy of his own, *La Mort de César*; he may also have seen *Henry IV* and *Richard III*.

Considering how difficult Shakespeare's language can be, even to the English, it is a tribute to Voltaire's theatrical intelligence, as well as to his progress in learning English, that he was able to respond to Shakespeare on stage. He did not now, or ever, whole-heartedly approve of Shakespeare, but he was obviously deeply moved by some of the scenes he saw. When he came to write his book about England, the *Letters concerning the English Nation*, he included a chapter 'On Tragedy', and this is part of what he wrote about Shakespeare. 'Shakespeare boasted a strong, fruitful genius: he was natural and sublime, but had not so much as a single spark of good taste, or knew one rule of the drama. There are such beautiful, such noble, such dreadful scenes in this writer's monstrous farces, to which the name of tragedy is given, that they have always been exhibited with great success.'[9] For good measure, he went on to give the full text of Hamlet's soliloquy, in English, followed by his own translation into French.

Voltaire's experience of Shakespeare was intensified, and the linguistic difficulties eased, by the fact that he secured the special privilege of being able to follow the plays in the text while the performances were going on. Having got to know Pope, Voltaire also met a number of his writer friends, including the playwright John Gay, author of *The Beggar's Opera*, with whom he struck up a warm friendship. Gay introduced Voltaire to Colley Cibber, a leading actor, playwright and poet, and Cibber in turn introduced him to William Chetwood, the prompter at the Drury Lane Theatre. Chetwood later recalled Voltaire's visits:

This noted author, about twenty years past, resided in London. His acquaintance with the Laureate* brought him frequently to the theatre, where (he confessed) he improved in the English orthography more in a week than he should otherwise have done by laboured study in a month. I furnished him every evening with the play of the night, which he took with him into the Orchestre (his accustomed seat).† In four or five months, he not only conversed in elegant English, but wrote it with exact propriety.[10]

Chetwood's high opinion of Voltaire's spoken English was echoed by others. John Gay said of him in November 1726 that 'he hath been here about half a year, and begins to speak English very well',[11] which suggests remarkable progress, especially considering that Voltaire could not pronounce the English 'th', a weakness which he blamed on the fact that he was missing some teeth.

Much later, Oliver Goldsmith, in his *Memoirs of M. de Voltaire*, praised Voltaire's 'proficiency in our language, laws and government, and [his] thorough insight into our national character'. Goldsmith never met Voltaire, however.

Voltaire's command of English was apparently good enough to speak in public and even to calm an angry crowd. One day in the street Voltaire was being jostled or even threatened by a crowd, which had taken against him because they realised that he was French, and thus a traditional enemy. According to the story, Voltaire climbed onto a milestone and harangued the crowd in English to such good effect that he brought them round to his side. Some scholars go on to argue that Voltaire was inspired by the example of Mark Antony's rabble-rousing speech to the crowd in Shakespeare's *Julius Caesar*. It is a good story; it may even be true; René Pomeau retails it as if it were true, but its sourcing is terribly flimsy.[12]

Voltaire was particularly taken with Swift, and he obviously had a much more immediate personal rapport with him than with Pope. He was so entertained by Swift's *Gulliver's Travels*, which had just been published, that he sent a copy to Thieriot in the hope that he would translate it into French. 'He is the Rabelais of England, as I already told you, but a Rabelais without his confusion, and the book would be very amusing by itself, for the remarkable inventions of which it is full, the lightness of its

---

* Colley Cibber was made poet laureate, amid much controversy, in 1730.
† The Orchestre was a small section of the auditorium, also known as the Music Room, which was set aside for special guests.

style etc., not to mention the fact that it is a satire on the human race.'[13] Swift was much older than Voltaire, nearly sixty to Voltaire's thirty-two, but their shared inclination for mockery, paradox and irreverence virtually guaranteed that they would get on well together. In the spring of 1727 Swift planned a visit to France, and Voltaire wrote several letters of introduction for him. Swift changed his mind and did not go, but Voltaire remained in contact with him after Swift returned to Dublin.

Voltaire's chief contacts with the political world, when he came to England, had been with the Tories, largely because of his connection with Bolingbroke. But his socialising in the winter season of 1726–27 now brought him into contact with the Whig government and the court. On 27 January 1727 Voltaire was introduced to George I, as well as to the king's daughter-in-law Caroline, princess of Wales, who gave him permission to dedicate to her his new edition of *La Henriade*; and in May he received from the king, through the offices of Robert Walpole, the Whig Prime Minister, a gift of £200. Some have suggested that this £200 gift was really a political pay-off, implying that Voltaire had now been persuaded to transfer his allegiance from Bolingbroke and his Tory friends, who were currently in opposition, to Robert Walpole and the Whigs, who were currently in government. Some even claimed that Voltaire had become a government spy. This seems quite absurd; Voltaire was an outsider without influence, and the gift of £200 was almost certainly nothing more than a casual piece of royal largesse to a young and promising young poet from France. In any case, the main source for the spy story was not published until forty years after Voltaire left England.

During the early spring of 1727 Voltaire seems to have had second thoughts about whether to stay in England. He wrote to Jean-Frédéric Phélypeaux, comte de Maurepas, the Secretary of State, asking permission to return to France, and after some delay Maurepas replied that he could return, but only for three months. We do not know why Voltaire was thinking of leaving England, even before his grand edition of *La Henriade* had been published, but we do know that he did not take up Maurepas's grudging offer. What decided him may well have been the news, in June 1727, of the unexpected death of George I: with George II on the throne, Voltaire could now dedicate *La Henriade* not to Princess Caroline, the princess of Wales, but to Queen Caroline.

Voltaire now cut back on his casual socialising and settled down to make sure that his grand new edition of *La Henriade* would come out successfully and profitably. He returned in May to Wandsworth, but this time he did not stay with Everard Fawkener, but took lodgings in the home of a local scarlet-dyer, who may have been professionally connected with Fawkener's textile-trading business. This new edition was going to be elaborate and expensive, priced at 3 guineas a copy, so the first part of his task was to launch a marketing operation. In the spring he opened the subscription lists, and during the next few months he made sales visits to all the important people he knew or could get introductions to, in the hope of signing up customers. But to spread his net wider than the select group of people he could meet in person, he resolved to produce the equivalent of what today would be an advertising pamphlet; and to be effective in England, this advertising pamphlet had to be written in English. So Voltaire started taking intensive English lessons from the headmaster of a local Quaker school, John Kuweidt, and from his assistant Edward Higginson.

The lessons were successful. Voltaire made such progress in English that he was able to write his *Essay upon the Civil Wars of France,* together with the *Essay upon Epick Poetry,* directly in English, and it came out at the beginning of December that year, 1727. In itself this was a remarkable achievement for a man who had known no English when he arrived eighteen months earlier. Voltaire sent a copy of his *Essays* to Swift in Dublin, and asked him to help find Irish subscribers to *La Henriade.* It seems that Swift obliged, for when the poem came out, in March 1728, Voltaire told Swift that he had sent a consignment of volumes to Ireland care of the Lord Lieutenant, and he asked Swift to take one of them for himself.[14]

These English lessons, and the conversations that went with them, had another result which was at least as significant: they aroused Voltaire's intense interest in the values and mores of the English Quakers and what they believed. Voltaire had already met one of the leaders of the Quaker community, Andrew Pitt, a retired Merchant Taylor, at his home in Hampstead, perhaps twice; and he may even have been taken by Pitt to a Friends' Meeting. But the combined effect of his talks with Pitt and his much more extended lessons and conversations with Kuweidt and Higginson inspired Voltaire to make Quakerism the subject of the opening chapters of his book on England, the *Letters concerning the English Nation.*

Voltaire constructed his opening chapter as a fictional encounter between himself and a nameless Quaker gentleman, and his seeming purpose was to make fun of the Quaker's simplicity, plain-speaking and non-conformity, in contrast with his own Parisian urbanity and worldliness. But as the chapter unfolds, the reader gradually comes to see that Voltaire's real purpose is to display the Quaker's honesty, sincerity and good sense, however odd and unconventional they may seem on the surface, and to contrast them with his own silly foppishness as a fashionable Parisian dandy.

> I never in my life saw a more noble or a more engaging aspect than his. He was dressed like those of his persuasion, in a plain coat, without pleats in the sides, or buttons on the pockets and sleeves. He did not uncover himself when I appeared, and advanced towards me without once stooping his body; but there appeared more politeness in the open, humane air of his countenance, than in the custom of drawing one leg behind the other, and taking that from the head which is made to cover it. 'Friend,' says he to me, 'I perceive thou art a stranger, but if I can do anything for thee, only tell me.' 'Sir', says I to him, bending forwards, and advancing as is usual with us, one leg towards him; 'I flatter myself that my just curiosity will not give you the least offence, and that you'll do me the honour to inform me of the particulars of your religion.'
>
> 'My dear Sir', says I, 'were you ever baptised?' 'I never was,' replied the Quaker, 'nor any of my brethren.' 'Zounds,' says I to him, 'you are not Christians then.' 'Friend,' replies the old man in a soft tone of voice, 'swear not; we are Christians, but we are not of opinion that the sprinkling of water on a child's head makes him a Christian.' 'Heavens,' says I, shocked at his impiety, 'you have then forgot that Christ was baptised by Saint John.' 'Friend,' then replies the mild Quaker once again, 'swear not. Christ indeed was baptised by John, but he himself never baptised anyone. We are the disciples of Christ, not of John.'[15]

It appears that this passage is an echo of a real conversation which had taken place between Voltaire and Edward Higginson, on the subject of baptism and its place in Christianity. According to an account ostensibly attributed to Higginson, but published much later, Voltaire at first refused to believe his claim that Saint Paul had said that he was sent by Christ not to baptise but to preach the gospel; and Voltaire was persuaded of the fact only when Higginson showed him the text of Saint Paul's Letter to the Corinthians in the original Greek of the New Testament. The story goes on that Voltaire chanced not long after to have a debate on this very question with other friends elsewhere in London, took a bet with them, jumped on a horse, rode hell for leather to Wandsworth, found Higginson, noted the chapter and verse of Corinthians, rode back across London, and won his bet.

It is a nice story, and it is regularly quoted by Voltaire's biographers. Some of it may well be broadly true, at least in spirit, but it is obviously too good to be quite true. The main problem with the story, apart from the fact that the Higginson account was not published until 1833, well over a hundred years after the events in question, and many years after the death of all the participants, is that Voltaire did not read Greek.

During the summer and autumn of 1727 Voltaire went on a sales tour of a whole series of grand houses soliciting subscriptions to his epic poem. The two *Essays* came out in early December, priced at 1s 6d, and the grand quarto edition of the epic poem in March 1728. At 3 guineas this was a really expensive item, and at first Voltaire expected subscribers to pay half of it in advance at the booksellers Woodman and Lyon in Covent Garden; towards the end of the year he merely asked that people should send in their names and addresses, with payment on publication. In the hope of sweeping in a few more of those readers who could not afford 3 guineas, he also issued two smaller editions in octavo, priced much more reasonably at 4 shillings.

By the end he had mustered 343 subscribers, starting with the queen as the dedicatee, and including members of the court and the aristocracy, members of the Whig government, members of the Tory opposition, members of the diplomatic corps, leading figures in finance and business, as well as writers and playwrights. It was an impressive catch for a young Frenchman who had so recently arrived in the country; some of the subscribers bought several copies – Bolingbroke bought twenty – so the total number of copies subscribed for was 475.

Soon after publication Voltaire returned to Wandsworth, and from this point on he recedes once more into the shadows. In March he protested at the publication of two pirate editions of the *La Henriade* in England; in other words, it did not take long for other people to start trying to steal his work. In May he wrote to Thieriot to ask him to go to the French police chief, to prevent the abbé Desfontaines from publishing another pirate edition in France, and in June he wrote to criticise Desfontaines's very poor translation of his *Essay upon Epick Poetry*. Evidently Thieriot did nothing, for in August Voltaire himself wrote to the chief of police to ask him to suppress pirate editions of his poem and told Thieriot that he was working on revisions of the poem, and a new version of the *Essays*.

But that was the last letter Voltaire wrote from England, and after August he effectively disappears from view. Towards the end of the year, probably in October or November, he returned to France, but there is such a total absence of hard information about the time or the circumstances of his departure, from him or anyone else, that it must have been either surreptitious or precipitate or both.

There is some suggestion that Voltaire's final weeks or months in England may have been overshadowed by some kind of cloud, possibly some kind of scandal. But if his stay ended badly, the adverse comments of his critics are composed more of gossip and innuendo than of hard facts. On the other hand, there seems to be a common theme in some of the backbiting that Voltaire had got into trouble, or had behaved badly, about money.

The central question is, what did he live on while he was in England? He was almost penniless when he arrived in 1726. He received some financial help from Bolingbroke, and probably from Everard Fawkener as well; he certainly received a grant of £200 from King George. Moreover, he seems to have remained on cordial terms with the Mendes da Costa banking family, for even though their son Anthony had gone broke, they subscribed collectively for several copies of Voltaire's *La Henriade*, so perhaps they helped him out financially as well.

But this still leaves two rather large financial question marks over Voltaire's two and a half years in England. He does not appear to have earned any money of his own until the publication of the *Essays* in December 1727 and *La Henriade* in March 1728. The subscriptions to *La Henriade* should have brought a total revenue of 475 copies at 3 guineas each, or a total of 1,425 guineas, and the smaller octavo editions should have brought in some more. But the production costs of *La Henriade* were substantial, for it was lavishly produced, and André Rousseau thinks they may have absorbed much of the gross revenue. But what did he live on until then? And what did he do with the net profit from *La Henriade*?

One story is that Voltaire had a quarrel with an unnamed bookseller about money; this is not unlikely, especially if the bookseller was producing a pirate edition of his poem; but the story comes from the abbé Desfontaines, who was not in England at the time and whose evidence is in any case not to be trusted where Voltaire was concerned. The *Grub-Street Journal* published a letter from a Quaker alleging that Voltaire 'had an excellent knack of multiplying a small sum to a greater by way of erasement', in short that he made money by fraud. The force of this letter is lessened, however, by the fact that it was published five years after Voltaire left England. Thomas Gray, the poet, went further: 'If Voltaire had stayed longer in England, he would have been hanged for forging banknotes.'[16] The accusation seems absurd, if taken literally; if, on the other hand, it was meant figuratively, to imply that Voltaire may have resorted to controversial or discreditable expedients in his money dealings, it is not absolutely inconsistent with what we know of Voltaire's money dealings on some other occasions; but it still does not tell us what Voltaire was supposed to have done.

The most obvious possibility is that he may have borrowed money to cover his living expenses in 1726 and 1727 but failed to repay his debts in 1728, when he was flush with the profits from *La Henriade*. This is only a guess, but it could be consistent with the implications of the criticisms of Gray and others, and with what appears to have been Voltaire's sudden and unexplained exit from England in late 1728.

Some accounts suggest that the faults were not all on one side, and that if Voltaire left England suddenly and in silence, it may at least in part have been because he felt ill used by the English and disillusioned by England. There seems to have been some kind of quarrel between Voltaire and Lord Peterborough, who had in effect been one of Voltaire's patrons; what the quarrel was about is unclear, but a later comment by Peterborough about Voltaire's attitude – 'the country and people of England are in disgrace at present' – implies that Voltaire was very angry about something when he left England.

Whatever the rights and wrongs, it is clear that Voltaire's departure from England took place in circumstances of some disorder. Neither then nor later did Voltaire ever give any account of the circumstances surrounding his departure from England, which may suggest that they were discreditable or painful or both. All we know for sure is that when Voltaire arrived back in France, he was in a very low state.

8

RETURN TO FRANCE

1729–1733

WHATEVER THE REASONS that prompted Voltaire to leave England so hurriedly, his homecoming was miserable and distressing. When he landed in Dieppe, towards the end of 1728, he was either ill or very depressed or both; and since his sentence of exile had still not been lifted, he could not return to Paris. So he went to ground, and stayed there for several months in the winter of 1728–29, masquerading as a travelling Englishman, feeling unwell and wretched, and waiting until he felt better.

Much of this time he lived in the house of an apothecary in Dieppe, called Jacques Féret, from whom he took lessons in pharmacy and medicine, in the hope of finding a cure for his malaise. But he did not break his silence to his friends until February 1729, when he wrote a letter to Thieriot complaining of his ill health.

I have suffered many ills, and I know by sad experience that sickness is the worst of all. To have a high temperature or a bout of smallpox is nothing; but to be weighed down with weaknesses for years on end, to see all one's appetites evaporate, to have enough life to want to enjoy it but too little strength to do so, to become useless and unbearable to oneself, to die bit by bit, that is what I have suffered, and which has been more painful than all my other trials. If you are in this state of inertia, you will not find any remedy in medicine, for I searched in vain. I only found it in nature. If I am still alive after all that I have suffered and after the griefs which poisoned the little blood that was left in my sad machine, I owe it solely to exercise and diet.[1]

Voltaire seems to be describing some kind of psychosomatic affliction. He was often physically ill and also something of a hypochondriac, much given to complaining of his digestion and other problems; but here he does not even attempt to explain this weakness as a physical ailment. This is something different in kind, more deep-seated, more chronic and perhaps more psychological. When he says that it lasted 'for years on end', he is surely exaggerating; yet in this winter of 1728–29 it seems to have gone on for months.

If Voltaire was suffering from depression, he may have experienced something similar on other occasions, for example in 1724, when his affair with Mme de Bernières had faded and he was ill, lonely and miserable by himself in Paris, and barely able to work; or again in 1726, shortly after his arrival in England, when he went to ground and ceased to communicate with his friends.

Whatever its causes, Voltaire's malaise gradually lifted. In March he summoned the energy and the courage to move much closer to Paris, in defiance of the sentence of exile, and he holed up, still incognito, in the house of a wig-maker in Saint Germain-en-Laye, just outside the capital; and from there he made a couple of secret one-night forays to Paris. For a young man who had left France three years earlier as a rising literary celebrity it was an ignominious return, and a dire omen of his future relationship with the régime.

In April 1729 Voltaire received permission once more to live openly in Paris, though he still had to stay away from the court at Versailles. In Paris he made contact with some old friends, among them Charles Marie de La Condamine, a young and brilliant mathematician. La Condamine had recently spotted a loophole in the state lottery system, and he now devised a plan by which he and Voltaire, and other friends, could all make their fortunes.*

The French state financed its activities partly by taxation, partly by issuing government loans, normally issued as bonds in the name of the Hôtel de Ville. But the state's expenditure chronically outran its income, and the authorities regularly had to resort to desperate expedients. One of these was to cut the rate of interest paid on state loans; this is what they had done in 1716, and they did it again in 1727.[2]

By reducing the rate of interest, however, the authorities also reduced the attractiveness of government loans; the market value of the

---

* In 1735 La Condamine led a ground-breaking scientific expedition to Peru, to test (and confirm) Newton's hypothesis that the earth is flattened at the poles.

outstanding bonds had fallen steeply, and this made it difficult for the government to raise money by issuing new loans. So in 1728 Michel Le Pelletier Desforts, the finance minister, tried to restore the perceived value of government bonds by launching a state lottery. Holders of the bonds would be entitled to buy lottery tickets, and if they won, their bond would be repaid not at its devalued market price but at its official face value; to promote ticket sales, the government would also provide a large prize, of £500,000 each month, later raised to £600,000 a month, for the holders of the winning tickets. Unfortunately, Le Pelletier Desforts had not done his arithmetic properly: the prize money was much larger than the total value of all the possible ticket sales, so anyone who could corner the market for lottery tickets was bound to make a lot of money.

And that was what La Condamine and Voltaire did, in conjunction with a number of other friends; every month, for over a year, they shared out £500,000 or £600,000 in prize money, and by the end of the year Voltaire's share of the takings may have amounted to around £500,000. When Le Pelletier Desforts realised what was going on, he tried to change the rules of the lottery, but the courts ruled that this would be illegal.

Voltaire was now a seriously rich man. Even as the lottery operation was in full swing, he discovered a new scam in which he could reinvest some of the money. In September 1729 he heard that the duc de Lorraine was planning a share issue in a new company which seemed likely to be very profitable, and he determined to stag it.

Two friends bundled me at midnight, without any supper, into a post chaise; and after rushing along for two days and two nights, we reached Lorraine, which is a country with very little trade, very disagreeable, and with few people. These sad impressions of poverty did not seem to augur well for the share issue.[3]

Voltaire found, to his dismay, when he got to the issuing house, that the share issue could be sold only to citizens of Lorraine. But after some enquiries he claimed that his legal name, Arouet, was directly related to a certain Haroué, a gentleman at the court of Lorraine, and he persuaded the officials to accept his bona fide as a citizen of Lorraine. 'After my pressing requests, they let me subscribe for fifty shares, which were delivered to me a week later. I immediately took advantage of the popularity of these new shares, and tripled my money.'[4]

A third wave of good fortune was still to come. Seven years earlier

Voltaire's father had died, almost cutting Voltaire out of his will. But there was a let-out clause: Voltaire could recover his share of the inheritance if, after the age of thirty-five, he could persuade the courts that he was of good conduct. He reached the critical age in 1729, the year of his return to Paris, and he applied to Jean-Aymard de Nicolaï, First President of the Chambre des Comptes, to restore his rights. This was the same President Nicolaï who in 1725 had refused to let Voltaire have an advance of £20,000 against his future inheritance. Now, on 1 March 1730, Nicolaï allowed that Voltaire had met the conditions for receiving his legacy, declaring that Voltaire 'so far from dissipating his property, has on the contrary increased it.'[5] Voltaire could now receive the £153,000 which was his share of his father's estate.

Voltaire treated his new-found wealth as a serious matter deserving serious attention, because it would not come again. He always had one or more men of business to help manage his finances, and he signed up with the best bankers and the sharpest lawyers; but he also took, throughout an exceptionally busy and creative working life, a close personal interest in his money and how it was doing.

During the early years he invested heavily with the Pâris-Duverney brothers, who had a large and hugely profitable business providing supplies to the French army: fodder for the horses, cloth for the uniforms and food for the men. He invested in the wheat trade between North Africa, Spain and Italy. And after a while he invested in the immensely lucrative, if risky, trade between France and the French colonies, through a trading firm based in the port of Cadiz; the risks became apparent some years later, in the Seven Years' War, when the English started sinking French merchant ships in large numbers.

As the years passed, he scaled back his investment in risky ventures and put his money more and more into personal life-loans or *rentes viagères*, and because a *rente viagère* expired with the death of the lender, an elderly lender could command a high rate of interest, often as much as 10 per cent per annum. To begin with, he lent money to French dukes and noblemen: the prince de Guise, the duc de Bouillon, the duc de Villars, his 'friend' the duc de Richelieu; at one point Richelieu owed him interest of £4,000 a year. Late in life, when he was once more out of favour with the French court, he lent money to German dukes and princes, because he thought it might be safer. But on one point the German dukes were exactly like the French dukes: they were extremely unreliable payers, and Voltaire was continuously having to chase them up for their huge arrears of interest, running back years or even decades.

Some people find it incongruous, even distasteful, that Voltaire, one of the pioneers of the Enlightenment and human rights, should have paid so much attention to the question of his finances. This criticism seems to me illogical and silly. In eighteenth-century France it was difficult for a writer to earn a decent living by writing, especially if he wanted to be independent of the powers of the state; and by 1729, when he was thirty-five years old, Voltaire had not really succeeded in doing so, even though he was now a rising literary star. From time to time he had earned a significant chunk of money, as from his first tragedy *Œdipe*, and perhaps from the profits of the English edition of *La Henriade*; but on the whole, he had not made any kind of serious living by his pen, and he had spent long periods in poverty or near poverty. Even when he later became one of the most celebrated writers in the whole of Europe, he still did not make any commensurate income from his writing, largely because of the twin curses of censorship and the lack of any copyright law.

If Voltaire had not acquired the independence that came with money, he could not have gone on to do those things for which he deserves to be remembered. He would never have been in a position to speak up for tolerance or to wage his later battles against injustice; and the more vocal Voltaire became as a spokesman for the Enlightenment, in the face of the fierce disapproval of the authorities, the more necessary it was for him to have the independence of money. If there is a valid criticism of Voltaire's attitude to money, it is that he was liable to fret, excessively and obsessively, over whether enough was coming in or too much was going out; excessively, because there was always more coming in than going out.

Voltaire had returned to France with a number of works in progress in his baggage which he had started in England but which were still unfinished. There was the beginning of a *Histoire de Charles XII*, the king of Sweden, who had become a legendary titan of European warfare in Voltaire's lifetime, and who had died on the battlefield barely ten years earlier; there was the beginning of a tragedy about the early Roman republic, entitled *Brutus*, which he had started to draft in English prose while in England; and there was the beginning of a book about England, which eventually became the *Letters concerning the English Nation*, or in its French version, the *Lettres philosophiques*.

What is striking about these projects, is how new they were, how political and how strongly influenced by Voltaire's experiences in England. Voltaire had made his name as a poet and playwright; now, with the *Histoire de Charles XII*, he was setting out to write a book of modern history. It was also his first long work in prose, and thus his first attempt to develop a prose voice which could carry a long book. It was to be followed by several more substantial history books, most notably *Le Siècle de Louis XIV, Le Précis du siècle de Louis XV*, and the *Essai sur les mœurs*. And all of them, because of their political connotations, got him into trouble.

His first three tragedies, *Œdipe*, *Artemire* and *Mariamne*, had centred on the conflicts and emotions of individual characters; his new tragedy, *Brutus*, was a political drama about the conflict between liberty and tyranny. Voltaire followed it up with another tragedy on the same theme, *La Mort de César*, this time focused on the murder of Julius Caesar by the republicans Brutus and Cassius.*

And then there was Voltaire's book about England, *Letters concerning the English Nation*, which was quite new in form and substance, and so inherently controversial that Voltaire spent five years trying to work out how to write it. Its gestation was so long and so difficult, and its consequences so momentous for Voltaire and the Enlightenment movement, that it needs a separate chapter.

In comparison, the composition of Voltaire's *Histoire de Charles XII* was a comparatively straightforward affair: he started researching it in England, in 1728; he worked intensively on it in 1729, he finished it in 1730 and he published a first version in early 1731.

Charles XII of Sweden was born in Stockholm in 1682, only twelve years before Voltaire. In 1700 he set out on a whirlwind campaign, defeating the Danes, defeating the Poles, laying waste in Ukraine and at first defeating Peter the Great of Russia. He was a great conqueror, a soldier of genius and superhuman courage, and the story as told by Voltaire is a rattling good read; and it can sometimes be found in print (in paperback) in France.[6]

The central focus of Charles's military campaign was the struggle for control of Poland. Augustus II, elector of Saxony, had been elected king of Poland in 1697, but in 1704 Charles removed him from his throne and replaced him with Stanislas Leszczyński, the Polish governor of Poznan. Charles went on to create havoc in Russia and Ukraine, but his triumphs came to an end with his defeat at the hands of Peter the Great at Pultava in 1709. The Russians quickly deposed Stanislas from the

---

* The hero of *Brutus* was Lucius Junius Brutus, first Consul of the Roman Republic after the overthrow of King Tarquin, in 509 BC, 465 years before the murder of Julius Caesar.

throne of Poland and restored Augustus II. Charles went on fighting the Russians, but in vain, and he was killed, at the siege of Fredrikshald in 1718.

Voltaire was obviously attracted to the heroic image of Charles as the fearless warrior, but what was particularly interesting, from the point of view of Voltaire as an apprentice historian, was that many of the main characters in the story were still alive, and he contacted a number of them, including Maurice, comte de Saxe, one of the many illegitimate sons of Augustus II and an even greater womaniser than his notorious father. In fact, Voltaire almost certainly already knew Maurice, since he was now living in Paris, and they were in some sense rivals for the favours and affections of Adrienne Lecouvreur, star of the Comédie Française. By the time she fell ill and died, in 1730, Maurice was making a brilliant career in the French army, and he ended up a marshal of France.

No doubt all this helped Voltaire to write such a vivid and compelling narrative. The disadvantage, when the book was published in 1731, was that not all the characters in Voltaire's story enjoyed the way he told it. Augustus II, in particular, objected to the unflattering terms in which Voltaire described the manner of his ousting from the Polish throne in 1704, and since he was now back on the throne, he was in a position to make a diplomatic fuss; the book had to be abruptly withdrawn and reissued in a revised form a year later.[7]

The revised edition of the *Histoire de Charles XII*, which appeared in 1732, was not the end of the story. Voltaire was seldom able to believe that he had said his last word on any subject, and in the case of his history books he was particularly liable to have second thoughts, and then third thoughts, and then more thoughts, with new editions, revised editions, new additions and frequently expanded editions. The *Histoire de Charles XII* very much conformed to this pattern, partly because it was such a popular success, and he produced a new edition in 1733, a revised edition in 1738, another revised edition in 1739 and more editions with revisions or alterations in 1748, 1751, 1756 and 1768. No one can say that Voltaire was lazy.

The irony is that history went on repeating itself and intruded directly into Voltaire's own life. Stanislas Leszczyński had been deposed in 1709; but after the death of Augustus II in 1733, he again claimed the throne, thus precipitating the War of the Polish Succession. When he finally abdicated, in January 1736, he was given, in compensation, the life-tenancy of the duchy of Lorraine. Voltaire and his mistress, Émilie du Châtelet, were frequent visitors to his court at Lunéville, and it was there that Émilie died in childbirth.

But if history was now Voltaire's new intellectual hobby, his central ambition on his return to France was to build on his reputation as France's leading writer of tragedies, starting with *Brutus*, a story of the double conflict between tyranny and liberty, and between father and son. In England he had drafted some of it in English prose, but when he returned to France, he reverted to rhyming French couplets. At its first run in December 1730 the play had a disappointing public reception; yet it remained in the repertoire and became popular much later, for political reasons, during the French Revolution.

Voltaire's next tragedy, *La Mort de César*, another play about liberty and tyranny, was directly inspired by Shakespeare's *Julius Caesar*, which he had seen performed in London. In order to observe the three unities, he confined the action to the events immediately surrounding the assassination of Caesar and left out the second half of Shakespeare's story, portraying the final disarray of the republicans. Voltaire finished writing it in 1731, but the actors at the Comédie Française did not like it, perhaps because it was in three acts rather than five, but probably because Voltaire had not included any love interest; either way, they did not perform it until 1743, and then without much success.

Voltaire's next effort, called *Ériphyle*, fared even worse. He had hoped to produce a play which would induce 'terror' in the audience, with ghosts and phantoms, but the result was an unsatisfactory farrago of bits of *Hamlet*, bits of *Oedipus* and bits of *Macbeth*, and friends advised him against it. It had an unsatisfactory première at the Comédie Française on 17 March 1732, after which he did his best to revise it, but he did not have it printed and quite soon put it to one side.

In short, Voltaire was having real difficulty in creating a tragedy that worked. But he did not give up, and later that spring he dashed off an exotic, romantic melodrama called *Zaïre*. He described his intentions in a long letter published in the *Mercure de France*:

> *Zaïre* is the first play in which I dared abandon myself to all the sensibility of my heart, the only romantic tragedy which I have written. I had thought that love was not a fit subject for the tragic theatre. But the public has changed its tastes. It needs tenderness and sentiment; and that is what the actors act best. So I had to submit to the values of our day, and at last start to talk of love.[8]

Voltaire wrote it at great speed, claiming afterwards that he wrote it in twenty-two days flat; and this time his inspiration struck lucky.[9] The play is a tangled tale of a Muslim sultan and a beautiful Christian prisoner called Zaïre, with whom he falls in love. They are going to get married but she has to convert to Islam, and then there are her brother, her father and several complications owing to recognitions and misunderstandings and mistaken identity. The play ends with the sultan, in a jealous rage, stabbing Zaïre to death and then, realising his mistake, turning the knife on himself. It had a hesitant start at the Comédie Française, on 13 August 1732, but after a few revisions by Voltaire it surged to a huge triumph, with a run of thirty-one performances, and it became one of his most popular plays. It was translated into several European languages, and it became a popular success at the Drury Lane Theatre in London two years later.

Despite his new prosperity, Voltaire continued to live fairly modestly, without a fixed home of his own. In 1730 he lived for a while in rooms in the rue Vaugirard, near the Porte Saint Michel. His landlady was a notorious and noisy drunk, and Voltaire appealed repeatedly for help against her to René Hérault, the chief of police.

The woman Travers continues to make a public scandal, getting drunk every day, beating her neighbours, uttering oaths in which the name of God is mixed up with the most infamous words, exposing herself quite naked and showing what modesty cannot describe, threatening to set fire to the neighbours' houses, and keeping the neighbourhood in perpetual alarms. The local inhabitants hope that you will put a stop to this scandal.[10]

In the spring of 1731 Voltaire went to stay in Rouen, in Normandy. He was trying to write his tragedy *La Mort de César*, and finding it hard going. It seems he was ill much of the time, but he also took bizarre steps to remain in hiding, and even to pretend, quite gratuitously and misleadingly, that he was going to England. This puzzling behaviour has prompted speculation whether, on top of his illness, which may well have been real, he was also going through another bout of depression. On the other hand, he later said that he had been very happy during his time in Normandy. It is a conundrum.

In Rouen he lived at first in a modest inn, recommended by his friend Pierre-Robert Le Cornier de Cideville, a senior official at the *parlement*. But since he was also working on the publication of the new (and revised) edition of his *Histoire de Charles XII*, he soon found that it was more convenient to move in with the publisher, Claude-François Jore, one of the leading printers there.

In July 1731 Voltaire moved back to Paris, but he was soon complaining of the terrible noise of the town. He wrote to another Rouen friend, Jean-Baptiste-Nicolas Formont: 'I regard my stay in Rouen as one of the happiest events of my life. But life in Paris is beginning to horrify me. It is impossible to think in the middle of the din of this accursed city.'[11] In August he looked for ways of getting out of town, and he got an invitation from the prince and princesse de Guise to visit them at Arcueil, their country home south of Paris. There he made himself so welcome that they invited him back, and he gratefully accepted their offer of a house in which he could spend September. He wrote to Cideville: 'I have been very ill, my dear friend, so ill that I could not write to you. I shall pass the month of September, all alone, at Arcueil, in the house which the prince de Guise has the kindness to lend me.'[12]

Voltaire's plan was to spend September at Arcueil, working on his new play. But in fact he did not stay there more than a week or so, for he was soon called back to Paris on the news that his friend Jean-René de Longueil, marquis de Maisons, had come down with smallpox. Eight years earlier, in the smallpox epidemic of 1723, Voltaire and Maisons had both caught the disease at the same time, when Voltaire was visiting Maisons at his home just outside Paris. At the time both recovered, but Maisons's infection was not sufficient to immunise him, for in 1731 he again went down with it, and he died on 13 September. Voltaire wrote to Cideville:

> My dear friend, the death of M. de Maisons has left me in a despair which has brought me close to senselessness. I have lost my friend, my support, my father. He died in my arms, not by ignorance, but by the negligence of the doctors. So long as I live, I shall never be consoled for his loss. What can you say of doctors who left him in danger at six o'clock in the morning, and then made an appointment to visit him at noon? They are guilty of his death.[13]

Voltaire had never before expressed such extreme grief at the loss of a loved one, except perhaps after the death of his elder sister. His description of Maisons as 'my father', is a striking testimony of the intensity of his sorrow, not least because Maisons was only thirty-two years old when he died, five years younger than Voltaire.

In the autumn of 1731 Voltaire's life started to look up. First, his revised edition of the *Histoire de Charles XII* had just come out, to great acclaim. In fact, it was so successful that it was soon followed by a number of pirate editions. 'I was a fool to print so few copies of that book', Voltaire told Thieriot in the spring of 1732. 'They have made here four editions of it. The fourth edition was sent to me this very morning.'[14]

Voltaire soon had another reason for cheerfulness: after three years of a nomadic existence he had at last found a home in Paris which was friendly and hospitable, and where he could come to rest. This new home, a town house in the rue des Bons Enfants, overlooking the Palais Royal, belonged to the comtesse de Fontaine-Martel, a seventy-year-old widow, who had long been a merry libertine of flexible virtue and who now took in lodgers, not for their money but for their company.

Voltaire first learned about the Fontaine-Martel establishment from his friend Thieriot in early December 1731, for Thieriot had just taken up residence there. By the end of the month Voltaire had persuaded Mme de Fontaine-Martel to let him have a room in the attic.[15] This was where Voltaire was to live for the next year, and it was the unaccustomed stability which he found there that made it possible for him to work through the worst difficulties of his book on England: within twelve months he would have finished it.

Voltaire was particularly attracted by the fact that the Fontaine-Martel house was a convivial establishment, in which she would often invite her lodgers to eat and drink together, at suppers which were apparently long and gay. The overriding rule of Mme de Fontaine-Martel (the 'baronne', as Voltaire called her behind her back) was that she intended to be the only woman of the house: she would admit single men, but she would not give house-room to men with mistresses, and she did not really like to take in young men, who might be tempted to take mistresses. 'I think', Voltaire told his friend Cideville, 'that she only accepted me in her house because I am thirty-six years old,* and my health is not strong enough to have a love affair. She does not want her friends to have mistresses. The best entry ticket is to be impotent. She is always afraid that someone will cut her throat and take her money to give to an opera singer.'[16]

Evidently she did not know that Thieriot, despite his ambiguous sexual orientation, was courting a certain Mademoiselle Marie Sallé,

---

* In fact he was thirty-eight.

who was indeed a dancer at the Opéra. But by the time Voltaire wrote this letter, Thieriot had already left the house and set off for England in pursuit of the lovely Mlle Sallé. Voltaire did not have a mistress and had not had one for quite a long time, but he liked the convivial customs of the house because he could call on the other lodgers to take part in amateur dramatics and give private performances to try out his latest plays. As he told Formont: 'At Mme de Fontaine-Martel's we put on plays fairly frequently. Yesterday we rehearsed the new version of *Ériphyle*. Sometimes we are fed well, though fairly often rather badly.'[17] In fact, Voltaire seems to have become the dominant figure in the household; he later told Cideville that he had been the 'master' of the house and that he had had the disposal of £40,000 of Mme de Fontaine-Martel's income just for spending on his entertainment.[18] It seems hard to believe that he had really been able to spend £40,000, for that would have been a colossal sum; perhaps all he really meant was that her total income was £40,000, and that he had the free use of a large part of it.

The irony was that throughout the spring of 1732 Voltaire kept revising his play *Ériphyle*, and he kept persuading his friends and fellow-lodgers to perform the latest versions *chez* Mme de Fontaine-Martel, but he never managed to turn it into a satisfactory tragedy. When he dashed off *Zaïre*, however, in June of that year, it went almost immediately into rehearsal at the Comédie Française. The first performance was terrible, as he told Formont: 'The actors performed badly, the promenade was in a tumult, and I had left in a few careless passages which were picked on with such ferocity that the show was lost.'[19] But it recovered, and Voltaire was soon boasting of its success to his friends Cideville and Formont.

My dear, kind critics, I wish you could have witnessed the success of *Zaïre*. Never has a play been so well acted as *Zaïre* was, at its fourth performance. I appeared in a box, and all the audience below applauded. I blushed, I hid myself, but I should be a fraud if I did not admit that I was really moved. It is pleasant not to be despised in one's own country.[20]

Voltaire was obviously intoxicated by this triumph, his first really big stage success since *Œdipe* fourteen years earlier, in 1718. No doubt this was why, at a gambling session *chez* Mme de Fontaine-Martel in September, he was so carried away by the return of literary glory that he bet heavily on a mindless game of chance called biribi (a bit like lotto or bingo), and lost a packet. Voltaire was normally pretty wary of the dangers of gambling: on this occasion, however, he told Cideville, he had lost 12,000 francs.[21] His loss was not a disaster, of course, because he was now rich. But in any case the continuing popularity of *Zaïre* still kept him buoyed up; it was performed at court in October, and it was put on again at the Comédie Française in November for another run until the new year. In December he told Jore, the Rouen printer, to publish the play but not to print more than 2,500 copies of it.[22]

In January Voltaire persuaded his fellow-lodgers to put on a private performance of *Zaïre* at the home of Mme de Fontaine-Martel; Voltaire himself played the part of the aged father, and to such pathetic effect, he later told Cideville, that the audience all wept.[23] This was Voltaire's litmus test for a successful tragedy: did it make the audience cry? Throughout his life Voltaire remained addicted to amateur dramatics, and he himself usually preferred to take the parts of pathetic old gentlemen.

Unfortunately, Voltaire's carefree, sociable home life in the rue des Bons Enfants was soon cut short: barely a fortnight later Mme de Fontaine-Martel fell ill and died. Voltaire described her end, in a letter to Formont:

> I cannot imagine how I have borne up under all the burdens which have weighed down on me during the past two weeks. They were calling for *Zaïre* on one side, the baronne was dying on the other, I had to appeal to the Lord Privy Seal, and I had to send out for her last rites. I looked after the patient at night, and I looked after the house-keeping during the day. Just imagine, it was I who had to tell the poor woman that she had to go. She would not listen to any talk of the ceremonies for her departure; but I was honour-bound to make sure she died according to the rules. I brought her a priest who was half Jansenist, half politician, who made a show of giving her confession, and who came again to give her the rest. When this comic turn from Saint-Eustache asked her out loud if she was convinced that her God, her creator, was in the Eucharist, she replied 'Ah, yes!', in a voice which would have made me burst out laughing in other, less lugubrious circumstances.
>
> I did everything I could to persuade the dying woman to leave something to her servants, and above all to a young woman of quality whom she had taken as her companion. But the baronne was inflexible, and was absolutely determined to relieve the whole household of

any temptation to regret her departure. Three years ago she made a will to disinherit her daughter as far as she could. As for me, I have a problem of looking for a new lodging, and of recovering my furniture which had become confused with that of the baronne.[24]

A month later, in February 1733, Voltaire was still sorting out his affairs in the rue des Bons Enfants, and he decided that he would stay there until Easter, but then he would move near Saint-Gervais. This was, he told Thieriot, 'a less agreeable neighbourhood, but I must move there for personal reasons'.[25]

Saint-Gervais was the remaining portal or façade of what had once been a Gothic church, just to the east of the Hôtel de Ville. It was an unfashionable neighbourhood, and much less attractive than the area round the Palais Royal: the better class of Parisians had already started moving west. When Voltaire said that this was 'a less agreeable neighbourhood', he was understating his real feelings, as he admitted to Cideville shortly after moving there. 'I am at last opposite this fine portal, in the ugliest neighbourhood of Paris, in the ugliest house, and more deafened by the sound of church bells than a sacristan.'[26]

Voltaire's 'personal reasons' for moving to Saint-Gervais were that he had now decided to move in with his man of business, a certain Demoulin, and Demoulin lived in the rue de Longpont, just opposite the portal of Saint-Gervais. Voltaire was starting to lend money in life-rents, or *rentes viagères*, and one of the first people he lent money to was the duc de Richelieu. But Voltaire was still rather new to the game of moneylending, and since Richelieu was in some sense a friend of his, he was at first reluctant to lend money in his own name. So he provided Demoulin with the money, and Demoulin became the ostensible provider of the loan to Richelieu. This was obviously a risky procedure. Demoulin was already known to Voltaire, for he was the brother-in-law of a certain Germain Dubreuil, a former employee of Voltaire's father. Even so, it made prudential sense for Voltaire to keep a close eye on Demoulin, which is why he decided to go and live in his house.

He moved there in May 1733. And it was while he was moving in that he first met Émilie du Châtelet, who was to become the love of his life.

9

LETTRES PHILOSOPHIQUES

1731–1733

THE BOOK WHICH VOLTAIRE WROTE after his experiences in England is undoubtedly one of his masterpieces, and one of the most widely read texts of the French Enlightenment. In appearance it was quite unassuming: a conversational entertainment, brief and apparently innocent and carefree; in form it was almost a travelogue, less than 200 pages long; in practice it was a vibrant manifesto for the new Enlightenment. This was the *Lettres philosophiques*, or in its English version the *Letters concerning the English Nation*.

The marquis de Condorcet, Voltaire's friend and biographer, and editor of the first posthumous edition of his collected works, said of it: 'This work was for us the start of a revolution.'[1] Gustave Lanson, the first modern editor of the *Lettres philosophiques*, described it memorably as 'the first bomb thrown at the *Ancien Régime*'. Voltaire had discovered a new and unforgettable voice, the voice of *la philosophie*, a voice which would echo round Europe for the rest of the century and beyond.

And yet we know very little about its composition, starting with the question of when and where Voltaire wrote it, whether in England or in France. It was in October 1726, not long after he arrived in England, that he first told Thieriot that he was thinking of writing some such book. But the book itself did not appear until almost seven years later, and when it did, Voltaire repeatedly asserted that the *Letters* had been mainly written in 1728, that is, before he left England.[2]

Was this true? We do not know. Some of the chapters were certainly written in France, several years after his return from England: at least the chapters on Newton and Locke, as well as the chapter on Pascal, which was a late afterthought. On the other hand, it seems quite likely that Voltaire did start work on the book in England. He was certainly thinking about it while he was in England; he must have taken notes of his experiences and observations; and some of the scenes in the book, as it finally appeared, are so vivid and so detailed that it is difficult to believe they were not written down close to the time.

Which leads to a second question: if he wrote some of it in England, in what language did he write it? For the first two centuries after publication it was assumed that the book Voltaire actually wrote was the *Lettres philosophiques*, and that the *Letters concerning the English Nation* was the work of an English translator, a certain John Lockman, working from Voltaire's French original.

But in 1967 a scholar named Harcourt Brown argued that Voltaire must have written at least some of the chapters of the book directly in English. He observed that there are many striking differences between the French and the English versions, and that the English version is often more expressive and idiosyncratic than the French. In Letter XXI, for example, the French version characterises the French writer Rabelais rather flatly as 'notre curé de Meudon', whereas the English version is bolder and describes him as 'our giggling rural vicar'. Harcourt Brown believed that no self-respecting translator would have gone so far and so often beyond the 'original' French, so he concluded that some parts at least of the book must have been written by Voltaire in English. In the end, he thought that Voltaire probably wrote about two-thirds of the *Letters* directly in English.[3]

The proposition is certainly consistent with the fact that, by the time he left England, Voltaire's command of English had become very fluent; he had spent two years surrounded by English conversation and English books; he had written the two *Essays* in English and published them in England; he was drafting, in English prose, the first act of his new tragedy *Brutus*; and the two private notebooks he kept during the years he was in England were both written almost entirely in English.[4]*

So it is not surprising that Harcourt Brown's thesis became the new consensus view. But thirty years later, in 2001, another scholar, J. Patrick

---

*In April, 1728, he wrote (in English) to a friend, saying ' I think and write like a free Englishman'. *Letters* 215, 11 April, 1728. And five years later, in November 1733, he said in a letter to a friend: 'If, like me, you had spent two years in England, I am sure that you would have been so impressed by the energy of their language, that you would have written something in English.' *Letters*, 454, 20 November, 1733.

Lee, argued once more that the whole of the English version could easily have been the work of a translator as experienced and talented as John Lockman. He produced examples of Lockman's translations of other writers, which were just as free and individual as his 'translations' of Voltaire. And since there was no positive evidence that Voltaire did write any of the chapters originally in English, Lee concluded that he had written them all originally in French, and that the English version was the work of the translator.[5]

As argument, this is pretty feeble stuff. Harcourt Brown may have failed to prove that Voltaire did write some of the *Letters concerning the English Nation* in English; Lee certainly failed to prove that he did not. Neither has any positive evidence either way.

The idea that Voltaire may have written some of the book in English, while he was in England, is quite appealing, especially for those passages which reproduce English dialogue. The opening scene in the first chapter, depicting a meeting between himself and a Quaker gentleman, consists largely of dialogue. We know that Voltaire really did meet several Quakers, that he talked with them at length and that these conversations took place in English. The opening scene in the book may have been based on one or more of these real conversations. But to imagine that Voltaire had some such conversation, in English, and then went home and wrote down a record of this conversation, *in French*, leaving it to some later translator to turn it back into English, defies all credibility.

Voltaire knew the book was going to be immensely controversial in France. It was precisely for that reason that he determined that the English-language version should come out in England about a year before the French version came out in France, in order to ensure that at least this version would appear uncensored. Are we to believe that Voltaire, with his impressive command of idiomatic English, could have simply entrusted to someone else the drafting of the English text of a book as important as *Letters concerning the English Nation*, without playing a substantial part in it? The idea is simply bizarre.

One of the most puzzling questions about this book is that we know almost nothing about the thought processes which went into its composition, except right at the very end, just before Voltaire completed it. In this respect the *Lettres philosophiques* is unlike almost any of his other works.

When he was writing a tragedy, for example, it is usually fairly easy to track the process, for he never stopped talking about it. He would write constant letters to his friends, telling them how he was getting on, asking their advice, sending them copies, informing them of his latest revisions, reporting on the reactions from the actors and so on. In 1731, Voltaire wrote forty-one letters, most of which were to his friends Thieriot, Cideville and Formont, and most of which were directly or indirectly about his writings; there are ten references to his latest edition of *Charles XII*, and ten references to his latest revisions of his play *Ériphyle*. In 1732 he wrote seventy-six letters, and there were eighteen references to *Ériphyle* and five to *Charles XII*, plus five to his new tragedy *Zaïre*.

None of this happened in the case of the *Lettres philosophiques*. In October 1726 Voltaire wrote to Thieriot: 'One day I will acquaint you with the character of this strange people.'[6] But he never did: for over five years there is complete silence from him on the subject until 21 November 1731, when he wrote to Formont: 'I must ask your advice on how I should finish my *Letters on the English*.'[7] If he did ask Formont's advice, there is no trace of it in his letters.

In 1732 he wrote four letters in which he talked of writing the book, but in none of them did he say anything about its content. In September he told Formont: 'I shall finish those *Lettres Anglaises*, which you know; it will only take a month.' But he said nothing about the substance of the book, and in fact it took him four months.[8]

One possible explanation for his silence is that he was trying to write a wholly innovative type of book, without any obvious precedent or model. His friends could advise him on a tragedy because they were familiar with the tragic model and they knew how it was supposed to go. But here he was exploring new territory, and they could not help. Moreover, Voltaire knew that any description of England and English society would be seen by the régime in France as an implied commentary on France and French society, and he may not have cared to put his thoughts and his value judgements in writing, for fear of the censors.

In the end Voltaire's solution to his problem was to finesse it, by adopting the tone of voice of a sophisticated traveller, slightly astonished at the characteristics of this 'strange people', as if he intended to deride their ever-so-foreign peculiarities. But he could not resist the temptation to put the knife in, with serious comments which are clearly meant, quite often explicitly, as a criticism of France.

Voltaire constructed his book as a series of chapters surveying different aspects of English society: religion, government, trade, finance, the theatre, the arts, the sciences. And he opened it, provocatively, with four chapters about the Quakers, as if to make fun of their idiosyncratic attitudes and values, and he went on to direct more mockery at the Church of England and the Presbyterians.

But the underlying point of this opening section of seven chapters is to emphasise the advantages which England enjoyed from its relative freedom and religious tolerance. Voltaire conveys this point tellingly, by making a direct connection between England's religious tolerance and its freedom of trade. 'Take', he says at the end of the chapter on the Presbyterians,

> a view of the Royal Exchange in London, a place more venerable than many courts of justice, where the representatives of all nations meet for the benefit of mankind. There the Jew, the Mahometan, and the Christian transact together as tho' they all professed the same religion, and give the name of Infidel to none but bankrupts. There the Presbyterian confides in the Anabaptist, and the Churchman depends on the Quaker's word. At the breaking up of this pacific and free assembly, some withdraw to the synagogue, and others to take a glass.
>
> If one religion only were allowed in England, the government would very possibly become arbitrary; if there were but two, the people would cut one another's throats; but as there are such a multitude, they all live happy and in peace.[9]

No Frenchman could possibly mistake Voltaire's meaning: in France there *was* only one religion permitted, and the government *was* arbitrary; and in the wars of religion in the sixteenth century, there had been two rival cults, Catholics and Protestants, and they had indeed cut one another's throats.

But if Voltaire's delays in writing the book were initially due to its innovatory character and to his fear of censorship, his difficulties became much greater when he tried to address the subjects of English science and English philosophy. If he was going to write about English science, he had to write about Isaac Newton. In England he had been astonished to discover that Newton had apparently turned the world of science upside down; he was enchanted by the vivid anecdote of Newton and the apple, which he was one of the first to relate, and which he used on three different occasions;[10] and he was deeply impressed to observe that, when Newton died in 1727, he was buried with every public honour in Westminster Abbey. It all made a wonderful parable about different aspects of English society: intellectual liberty, scientific adventurousness, the autonomy of the scientific community, the role of the Royal

Society, the respect of civic society and so on. Voltaire obviously had to write about Isaac Newton and his revolutionary theory of gravity. There was just one problem: he simply did not have the mathematics to understand it.

But there was an even deeper reason for hesitation: fear of the reaction in France. He could perhaps pretend that some of the characteristics of English society could be dismissed as outlandish, exotic, peculiar or just foreign, without any necessary relevance to France; the English were, as he said, a 'strange people'. But when he came to English science and English philosophy, these evasions would be impossible. If Newton's scientific theories were true, they must be true in France as well as in England; and if Locke's philosophical theories were true, they must be true in France as well as in England. But in France it was the theories of Descartes which were held to be the true orthodoxy, both in science and in philosophy; they were incompatible with the theories of Newton and Locke, but they were endorsed by the establishment and the Catholic Church. If Newton and Locke were right, then Descartes must be wrong. So if Voltaire was to write positively about Newton and Locke, he would be in conflict with the French intellectual, political and theocratic establishment.

On the scientific and mathematical front, help reached Voltaire in the nick of time. Newton and his theory about gravity may not have been accepted by the French establishment, but among up-to-date young scientists in France his work was already well known, and one of these scientists was Pierre Louis Moreau de Maupertuis, a 34-year-old mathematician from Saint Malo, who had known about Newton for some years. Voltaire was overjoyed when he learned, in the autumn of 1732, that Maupertuis was just about to bring out a book, in French, which would explain Newton's theory of gravity. This was his *Discours sur les différentes figures des astres* (Discourse on the Movement of the Stars), which came out in October that year.

Even before the book appeared, Voltaire wrote in haste to Maupertuis to ask him for advice about Newton.

I appeal to you in my state of doubt. It is about the great principle of attraction of Mr Newton. I enclose a short memorandum on the subject. I beg your pardon for my importunity, but I ask you urgently to give me a moment of your time to enlighten me. I await your reply, to know whether I should or should not believe in attraction. My faith will depend on you, and if I am as persuaded of the truth of this theory as I am of your merit, I shall certainly be the staunchest Newtonian in the world.

Voltaire's 'short memorandum' was a two-page summary, with an accompanying sketch-map, of what he understood of Newton's theory of gravity.

If the power which causes bodies to gravitate to earth, is the same as that which keeps the celestial bodies in their orbits, and if this power acts according to the inverse ratio of the squares of the distances, Newton's theory of attraction must be accepted; and one must regard this power of gravity, or attraction (whatever its cause), as the principal force on which the machinery of the universe depends.[11]

Voltaire kept up a rapid-fire succession of interrogatory letters to Maupertuis during the next few weeks, badgering him for more and more explanations of Newton's theories: four more letters in November, and three in December. In his second letter, Voltaire claimed to be completely converted to Newtonism, and astonished at Newton's revolutionary discoveries.

The more I glimpse of this philosophy, the more I admire it. With every step that we take, we see that the whole of the universe is organised according to mathematical laws which are eternal and necessary. Who would have thought, fifty years ago, that the same power could cause the movement of the stars and the weight of gravity? Who could have suspected the refraction and the other properties of light discovered by Newton? He is our Christopher Columbus; he has led us to a New World.[12]

At the same time, however, Voltaire confessed 'with pain' how little he really understood. And in his third letter to Maupertuis he was assailed, like any new religious convert, by fresh doubts: 'Ah, I have just had a frightful uncertainty, and all my faith is shaken. If you do not have pity on me, all Grace will leave me!' This anguished if self-mocking introduction was followed by another tortured attempt to grapple, with the aid of a scribbled sketch, with what he understood of the orbit of the moon: 'If the line bD is really fifteen feet, I am proud to be a believer. But the moon cannot be supposed to fall to the point D in one minute.'[13] Three days later Voltaire was completely reassured, and a week later he had received Maupertuis's book and had read three-quarters of it, 'with as much pleasure as a girl reads a novel, or a convert the Scriptures'.[14]

By the beginning of December Voltaire had become so much more confident of his grasp on Newton's theories that he sent Maupertuis a preliminary draft on the subject. Maupertuis sent back some comments, and on 15 December Voltaire felt able to send Maupertuis a series of chapters, which he had now revised, and which he proposed to include in his English letters. 'You have become accustomed to give me lessons. Permit me then, Sir, to submit to your judgement a few letters which I once wrote from England, and which they want to have printed in London. I have recently corrected them, but they seem to me to stand in great need of being reviewed by your eyes.'[15] Once again, Voltaire was claiming, as he was to do many times, that he had written at least some of these letters long ago, at another time and in another place. A week later Voltaire sent Maupertuis a final letter of thanks for his help.[16]

If Voltaire felt relieved that he had at last dealt with Newton's theories, he knew that those of John Locke would be much more difficult to write about safely. Newton's theory of gravity was undoubtedly in conflict with Descartes's notion that the universe was made up of invisible vortices or *tourbillons*. But though the French Church was committed to Descartes as a matter of doctrine, the scientific and mathematical arguments on either side were way above the head of most ordinary Frenchmen, and above the head of most ordinary churchmen as well; so perhaps the Church would not make too much of a fuss if Voltaire wrote favourably about Newton. 'I am at last determined to bring out my English Letters', Voltaire told Formont in early December 1732, 'and that is why I had to re-read Newton; for it is not permitted to speak of such a great man without knowing him. I have entirely re-cast the letters in which I spoke of him, and I have dared to give a little précis of all his philosophy.'

But he was quite worried about how to treat Locke.

I have been obliged to change everything that I had written on the subject of Mr Locke, because, after all, I want to go on living in France, and I am not allowed to be as philosophical as an Englishman. I must disguise in Paris what I could say in London as loud as I liked. This unfortunate but necessary circumspection has made me strike out several fairly amusing passages on the Quakers and the Presbyterians.[17]

The problem posed by Locke was that he was much easier to under-stand than Newton, and in theological terms much more obviously in conflict with Descartes. Descartes was a dualist, who distrusted the senses and believed that there is a total separation between mind and matter. The essence of the individual person is his soul: *cogito ergo sum* ('I think, therefore I am'). The theological importance of this idea, from the point of view of the Catholic Church, was that it made it much easier to maintain that the soul was immortal, even if the body was not. One of the corollaries of Descartes's dualism was that he also believed that we are born with innate ideas.

Locke disputed Descartes's claim that we are born with innate ideas, and he argued that the only hard information that we can acquire is through our senses. What made this view particularly controversial or even scandalous in the French Catholic Church of the time, was that it appeared to be in conflict, not just with Descartes but with Christian Revelation. Locke was not anti-Christian, at least not in public; on the contrary, he wrote a book on the *Reasonableness of Christianity*, and he did not rule out the possibility of Revelation from God. But he claimed that the only information we can receive about *this* world, comes through our senses. This might seem to raise questions about the nature of the soul and its immortality, and could therefore seem inflammatory to the French Church; Voltaire was acutely aware of the dangers.

'There is only one letter about Mr Locke,' he told Formont in December.

> The only philosophical question which I treat in it is the trifling ques-tion of the immateriality of the soul; but the thing is too important to be treated seriously. I have had to lighten it up, so as not to offend, head on, our masters the theologians, people who see the spirituality of the soul so clearly that they would like to burn, if they could, the bodies of those who question it.[18]

The result was a hilarious essay in which Voltaire treated received doctrine on the question of the soul with withering ridicule.

> Before his time several great philosophers had declared, in the most positive terms, what the soul of man is; but as these absolutely knew nothing about it, they might very well be allowed to differ entirely in opinion from one another. Mr Locke has displayed the human soul in the same manner as an excellent Anatomist explains the Springs of the

human Body. He everywhere takes the Light of Physics for his guide. He sometimes presumes to speak affirmatively, but then he presumes also to doubt. I shall leave, says he, to those who know more of this Matter than myself, the examining whether the soul exists before or after the Organisation of our Bodies. 'We shall, perhaps, never be capable of knowing, whether a Being, purely material, thinks or not.' This sage assertion was, by more divines than one, looked upon as a scandalous Declaration that the Soul is material and mortal. It was loudly claimed, that Mr Locke intended to destroy religion; nevertheless Religion had nothing to do in the Affair, it being a question purely Philosophical, altogether independent of Faith and Revelation.[19]

By January 1733 Voltaire's English *Letters* were effectively finished, for better or for worse, but he still worried that he would not be allowed to publish in France. He showed the text to Charles d'Orléans, abbé de Rothelin, an influential figure in the literary world, in the hope of getting a steer on what would get past the censors; but he did not like the advice he got. 'M. l'abbé de Rothelin', he told Cideville, 'has suggested to me that, if I soften certain passages, I might be able to get tacit permission to publish; but I do not know if I shall decide to spoil my work just to get their approval.'[20]

By the end of January, Voltaire had sent the text of the English *Letters* to Thieriot, who was still in England, for publication in London. But he was still hesitating whether to have it printed in France, 'and run the risk of taking on the inquisition which persecutes literature here.'[21] A month later he decided to go ahead with the printing of the English edition. He wrote to Thieriot:

I have spent two months getting bored with Descartes, and banging my head against Newton, to finish the *Letters*. If these *Letters* have pleased you, then that gives me pleasure. Do not let your friendship be alarmed over the printing of this work. The English think that the authorities put half the French nation into the Bastille and the rest into beggary, and any author who is a bit bold into the pillory. It is not quite true. At least, I do not think that I have anything to fear. M. l'abbé de Rothelin, who likes me and whom I have consulted, and who is certainly as difficult as anyone, has told me that he would give his approval to all the *Letters*, with the single exception of that on Mr Locke. I confess that I do not understand this exception. But the theologians know more than I, and we must take them at their word. All

I conclude from this, is that you must print the *Letters* immediately, since they can be of some use to you, and are of no danger to me. I am even preparing to bring out a little edition in Paris, just as soon as you have started yours in England.[22]

Five weeks later, on 1 April 1733, he gave Thieriot the go-ahead for publication of the London edition, on condition that the book should not appear to have been published by Voltaire.[23]

By this time Claude-François Jore, Voltaire's printer in Rouen, had embarked on typesetting the French edition; but he was sworn to secrecy, and in any case, Voltaire had agreed with Thieriot that the *Letters* would not come out in France until well after their publication in England.[24]

By 21 April 1733 printing of the London edition had already started, with a planned print run of 3,000 copies, and in July it was on sale. In August Voltaire commented to Formont: 'The *Letters* philosophical, political, critical, poetical, heretical and diabolical are selling well in London; but then the English are heretics cursed by God, who are always ready to approve the works of the devil.'[25] But behind Voltaire's devil-may-care tone there still lurked great anxiety that he had gone too far.

'I do not think', he wrote to Formont, 'that our *English Letters* will easily frighten the bigots. For, in truth, my dear metaphysician, is there any reasonable being who, provided his spirit has not been corrupted in these reverend little houses of theology, could possibly complain about Mr Locke? Who will dare to say that *it is impossible for matter to think*?'[26]

Unfortunately, there were plenty of people in France who would say precisely that.

Just as the English edition was coming out, Voltaire's nerve began to fail, and he told Thieriot to hold up publication until further instructions; but by then it was too late. Now, for the first time, he started to express the depth of his anxieties. He wrote to Cideville: 'As I see the danger approaching, I am beginning to tremble a bit, and I begin to think that I have been too bold in what, in London, will seem simple and ordinary.'[27] Three weeks later he was on the edge of panic: 'In my last letter', he told Thieriot, 'I told you that I was not too worried if the *Letters* come out. But now I am obliged to tell you that I think I am lost if they appear.'[28]

Nine months later, in April 1734, when Voltaire was at a country-house party in Burgundy for the wedding of his friend the duc de Richelieu, the French edition of what Voltaire was still calling his *Lettres anglaises* came out, in chaotic and unplanned circumstances, and the long-expected storm finally broke.

VOLTAIRE AND ÉMILIE

1733–1734

IT WAS ALMOST EXACTLY A YEAR before the publication of the *Lettres philosophiques*, in the spring of 1733, that Voltaire met Émilie du Châtelet. He was thirty-nine years old and unattached; she was twenty-seven, married and the mother of three children; and they were both looking for love.

Apart from his episodic liaison with the actress Adrienne Lecouvreur, in 1729–30, Voltaire had had no significant love in his life for several years. His affair with Mme de Bernières had expired at least eight years earlier, in 1725, and during the previous year (1732) he had been compelled to submit to Mme de Fontaine-Martel's rule of celibacy. He could have been in danger of turning into a reluctant bachelor.

Émilie du Châtelet would change all that. She was a young woman of noble birth, striking appearance, impressive intellect and great panache of manner, and she was intent on having a good time. She loved gadding about with her friends, going to parties and to the theatre, to dances and to the Opéra, or even slumming in low-life bars. She was also very much in the market for love. She had already had two rather public affairs, but they were over, and she was free.

Émilie's first meeting with Voltaire may have been at the Opéra, some time in the second half of April 1733, at a performance of a new work by François Augustin Paradis de Moncrif, *L'Empire de l'amour*. Voltaire was worn out by the upheaval of his removal, he was not feeling very well and he was quite reluctant to go; but since he was a good friend of Moncrif, he agreed to put in an appearance. Émilie, on the other hand, always loved going out, and there she met Voltaire; they liked each other; and they became lovers quite soon after.*

Voltaire had long known Émilie and her family, he had corresponded with her father and he had stayed at the family home; but he had not seen her at all recently. In later life he claimed that he had known her since birth, but this was a typical Voltaire exaggeration; when he visited the family in 1716, she was nine or ten years old. When they met again in the spring of 1733, he may not have seen her for at least ten years.[1]

In appearance, Émilie was probably more striking than beautiful, clever and amusing, lively rather than lovely; but though she was unmistakably an intellectual, she also liked being feminine, she enjoyed dressing up and she loved showing off in public. There is a celebrated description of her by Mme du Deffand, the leading society hostess, which reeks of disapproval and hostility.

Imagine a tall, dried-up woman, no arse, no hips, a narrow chest, two little tits sticking out ever so far, big arms, big legs, enormous feet, a very small head, a sharp face, a pointed nose, two little sea-green eyes, a dark complexion; a flat mouth, teeth sparse and extremely spoiled. That is what the lovely Émilie looks like, and she is so pleased with her appearance that she spares no effort to show it off: curls, pompons, jewels, glass ornaments, all in great profusion; but since she wants to be more beautiful than nature made her, and more magnificent than her poor fortune, she is often obliged to go without stockings, shirts, handkerchiefs or other little articles.

Born without talents, without memory, without taste, without imagination, she became a geometer so as to seem above other women, not thinking that oddness does not confer superiority. Her knowledge of science presents a difficult problem: she speaks about it in front of people who do not understand it. Beautiful, magnificent, educated, all that remained was for her to become a princess; and so she did, not by the grace of God, not by the grace of the king, but by her own. People think of her as a princess of the theatre, and have almost forgotten that she is a woman of good birth.[2]

It is a vivid picture, especially in its malice, and it is the more

---

* Besterman and Badinter say it was the duchesse de Saint-Pierre who introduced them at the Opéra, on or after 14 April; but Pomeau says it was Dumas d'Aigueberre, also at the Opéra, at the end of April or beginning of May 1733, and that is what Voltaire implied, in a letter written sixteen years later, after the death of Émilie. *Letters*, 2520, D 4046, 26 October 1749.

remarkable in that Mme du Deffand and Émilie were distant cousins. It implies that Émilie was ugly and unattractive, but this was simply untrue. Contemporary portraits show that she was a fine-looking woman, even if not a model of slinky feminine beauty, and contemporary accounts make clear that she was lively, amusing, and attractive. Mme du Deffand's pen-portrait demonstrates that Émilie's real fault was not that she was ugly but that she was too intellectual, and too unconventional.

Good society disapproved of Émilie all the more because, as Mme du Deffand said, she was a woman of high position: she was a member of the nobility by birth, and her marriage to the marquis du Châtelet gave her even higher status, including the *droit du tabouret*, the privilege of sitting (on a stool) in the presence of the queen. Émilie was acutely conscious of her rights and always insisted on her social position in the aristocracy; she moved in the circles round the queen, and her friends came from the highest ranks of society: the duchesse de Saint-Pierre, the duchesse de Richelieu, the duchesse de Boufflers. The reproach of Mme du Deffand was that Émilie insisted on her rank when it suited her and stepped beyond it when it amused her. In short, she did not know how to behave.

The irony, of course, is that Mme du Deffand, as the hostess of the leading literary salon of the day, was herself something of an intellectual; but she saw her own role as an enabler, in the background, not as a performer on the stage. Émilie, by contrast, was an ambitious intellectual in her own right, and she would, within a very few years, make good her aspiration to be taken seriously in the field of maths and sciences. For a woman to have such ambitions made her an oddity in the eyes of good society.

Émilie was born on 17 December 1706, the fifth child of Louis Nicolas Le Tonnelier, baron de Breteuil, a one-time courtier and head of diplomatic protocol at Versailles. He was an educated and enlightened man, and he was also quite unconventional: he decided that Émilie would not be palmed off with the minimal convent schooling usually considered sufficient for a well-bred girl, but would receive serious tuition at home. Under the care of her father she had the free run of his substantial library, and she received a wide-ranging education. Voltaire said of her later that in her youth she had learned several languages; she knew by heart the finest passages of Horace, Virgil and Lucretius, she was familiar with the works of Cicero and she had started a translation of the *Æneid*; she had learned Italian and English, and had read Milton and Locke in the original. Above all, she had developed an extraordinary natural talent for mathematics and science, and these subjects became the centre of a devouring intellectual interest for the rest of her life.[3]

When Voltaire met her, Émilie was married but living a largely independent life. In 1725, when she was nineteen, she had married Florent-Claude, marquis du Châtelet-Lomont, an amiable man and a career army officer of an ancient and noble family from Lorraine, but of limited intellectual or cultural interests. Shortly after their marriage they moved to the château of Semur-en-Auxois in Burgundy, where the marquis was governor and commander of the local regiment. In 1726 she had her first child, a girl; and in 1727 her second, a boy.* Her husband's military career frequently took him away from home for prolonged periods, and in 1728 he happened to be with the army, so Émilie moved from Semur to live in her husband's house in Paris.†

Émilie considered that she had now done an important part of her marital duty by her husband and was free to pursue her own life. This did not mean there was any breakdown in her marriage; on the contrary, she remained permanently on friendly terms with her husband and was consistently respectful of his status and family welfare. But from now on they lived mostly separate lives, he at the army and she in Paris. He recognised that it was not in her nature to play the role of the dutiful wife at home, that her intellectual interests were far beyond his own and that she needed to be free to pursue her own life, interests and amusements; he always respected her independence.

In Paris, Émilie launched herself with obsessive excitement into a love affair with the comte de Guébriant. He was a fine talker and a lovely dancer; he was also the most notorious womaniser and serial seducer in France. Émilie seems to have imagined that his seduction must be the prelude to an all-consuming passion on both sides, and she pursued him relentlessly. He had a quite different view of sexual conquest and was not ready to respond to her invasive emotional demands.

---

* The daughter, Françoise-Gabrielle-Pauline, was born in Paris on 30 June 1726. In 1743 she married Alfonse Caraffa Despina, duc de Montenero-Caraffa. She died in 1754. The son, Louis-Marie-Florent, was born in Semur on 20 November 1727. He caught smallpox in April 1745; see *Letters*, 1908, 1910, 1911. He became an army officer, and later ambassador to Vienna and London. He succeeded his father as marquis, and was then made a duke, but was executed during the Revolution in 1794.

† Pomeau says that her husband's house was in the rue Traversière-St-Honoré, not far from the Palais Royal (Pomeau et al., *Voltaire en son temps*, vol. I, p. 243). He does not comment on the fact that it was in this same street that the marquis du Châtelet later rented a house in 1745.

At last, she tried to blackmail him by staging a melodramatic suicide scene, but the ploy failed and he disappeared out of her life for good.

Next, Émilie had an affair with another celebrated womaniser, Louis-François-Armand de Vignerot du Plessis, the duc de Richelieu, nephew of the great Cardinal Richelieu; Émilie knew him well, for he was the younger brother of a close friend, Catherine de Richelieu. This time she was more reasonable in her demands, and after a short while their love affair faded and turned into an intimate and long-lasting friendship.

If the marquis du Châtelet knew about Émilie's affairs, he did nothing to put a stop to them. But when he came home from his regiment, in 1732, he summoned Émilie to join him at Semur. She obeyed and soon became pregnant once more; and when the marquis returned to the wars in January 1733, Émilie returned to Paris to have her baby there.

The child, a boy, was born on 11 April 1733, and as soon as Émilie's health allowed, she resumed her hectic life of social amusement. So when Voltaire and Émilie met, it was a matter of weeks, at most, after she had given birth to her third child.

Émilie was attracted to Voltaire; but Voltaire, starved of love, was completely bowled over by this remarkable woman, so lively, so amusing and so clever. In fact, she may have been the first woman intellectual that he had ever encountered, an aspect of her personality which was to prove an important part of the attraction which bound them together. Very early in their relationship, and while he was in the throes of moving in to his new home in the rue de Longpont, he wrote her a letter which hints eloquently at this imbalance between them. 'I am in all the horrors of moving house, in fear of being hissed [at the Comédie Française] and in the pains of a stomach-ache. I have more desire to see you, than you have to console me. Farewell.'[4] This is the first letter from Voltaire to Émilie that we have; very few have survived, since most were destroyed after her death by her husband, with Voltaire's acquiescence.

Voltaire soon confided in Cideville that Émilie was 'a very lovable woman'.[5] At first he and Émilie kept quiet about their relationship and did not publicly admit it until the following year. But to close friends they were more explicit. He told Mme de Saint-Pierre that he had 'found happiness', a claim that he must have known would get back to Émilie.[6] In August he referred to her, for the first time, as 'la divine Émilie', a variant of a phrase that he would later use many times in the years to come.[7] And yet his sexual performance often fell short, as he admitted to Cideville: 'I have too little passion, but my mistress pardons me, and I love her all the more tenderly; I am happier than I deserve.'[8] In December he told Cideville that he had been ill for two weeks, and therefore 'dead to all pleasure'.[9]

The disequilibrium in their relationship, in which Voltaire loved and needed Émilie more than she loved and needed him, continued for quite a long time, perhaps three years; later this imbalance was completely reversed.

Early on, Voltaire made a serious tactical mistake: he introduced Émilie to Pierre Louis Moreau de Maupertuis, the fashionable young scientist and mathematician. Maupertuis had given him crucial help in grappling with Newton's theory of gravity and attraction; now, having discovered the depth of Émilie's interest in maths and science, Voltaire thought he would give her pleasure, and help her intellectually, by putting her in contact with the celebrated scientist. In September he invited Maupertuis to come to meet Émilie: 'If you were kind enough to. come today to the home of Mme du Châtelet, you would overwhelm me with joy'.[10] Maupertuis duly came and agreed to help Émilie with her studies in mathematics. Early in 1734 she became his student and, almost immediately, his mistress as well.

Émilie may not have been aware that Maupertuis had a reputation as a serial seducer, but she was once again carried away by an overpowering and one-sided romantic infatuation. She pursued him high and low, she bombarded him with letters and invitations, she sought him out in cafés and even at the door of the Académie Française; her letters to him managed to combine, to a comical degree, the possessive complaints of the infatuated lover with the anxious submissiveness of the earnest student. She wrote to him in January 1734: 'I do not want to reproach you, Sir, for not having come back here the other evening, and I realise that I must not abuse your kindness. I have studied hard, and I hope that you will be a little less displeased with me than the last time; if you want to test me tomorrow, I shall be infinitely obliged to you.'[11]

Later that month she wrote again: 'I have been leading a completely disorganised life these days. I am dying; my soul needs to see you, as much as my body needs rest. Come anyway, alone or in company, you will give me extreme pleasure, and I shall wait for you.' And again:

I sent to find you at the Académie Française and at your home, Sir, to tell you that I would be spending this evening at home. I did spend it at home, with binomials and trinomials; but I can no longer study, if you do not set me a task, for which I have an extreme desire. I shall not go out tomorrow before six o'clock; if you could come here around four o'clock, we could study for a couple of hours.[12]

Émilie's infatuation with Maupertuis was so unrestrained that she wrote to him nine times during the month of January 1734 alone.

Voltaire minded enough to write her a little poem of mild reproach.[13] But he consoled himself with the thought that Maupertuis's book on Newton had sold only 200 copies, and he hoped that he would do better with his *Letters concerning the English Nation*, as of course he did: literally, about a hundred times better.[14]

Voltaire was now working extremely hard. In 1732 he had finished two plays which failed, *Ériphyle* and *La Mort de César*, and one which triumphed, *Zaïre*. In addition, he had started researching a major new history project about the seventeenth century, which eventually emerged as *Le Siècle de Louis XIV* ('The Century of Louis XIV'). He wrote a new play, *Adelaïde de Guesclin*, which was ready for performance the following year. He completed the revision of his *Histoire de Charles XII*. He wrote an opera, *Tanis et Zélide*, which was never publicly performed, but then Voltaire was not in the least musical: 'I was stupid enough to write an opera', he wrote to a friend; 'it is a talent which I lack.'[15]

He also started writing a long essay on cultural taste, under the title *Le Temple du goût,* in which he set out his canon of the great writers and the lesser writers, both of the present and the past. In it he enumerated the virtues but above all the faults of other writers; when it came out in 1733, it caused so much offence to living writers, who objected to being marked down by Voltaire, that he had to revise it and produce a second edition. In short, Voltaire was far too busy to have much time for jealousy of Émilie's affair with Maupertuis.

What was particularly preoccupying Voltaire in 1733, and even more in 1734, were the arrangements for publishing his English *Letters* in its various forms. The printing of the two editions in England, by a bookseller named Davis, under the local supervision of Thieriot, was fairly straightforward. The English-language version, the *Letters concerning the English Nation*, was set in the spring of 1733 and published in August in a print-run of 2,000 copies. As Voltaire told Formont, the English *Letters* 'are being sold in London with great success'.[16] The French version of this 'English' edition, *Lettres écrites de Londres sur les anglais et autres sujets*, was set at about the same time, with a print-run of 1,500 copies in September 1733 but not due to be released until March the following year, 1734.

Publishing the book in France was much more problematical. Knowing that he would not get official permission to publish, Voltaire resolved to bring out an unofficial or clandestine edition; and he contacted Claude-François Jore, who had already published his *Histoire de Charles XII*. Since this French version of Voltaire's English book would be illegal, and since the book was bound to be immensely controversial, the operation was fraught with danger for both writer and publisher, so Voltaire offered to pay all the publishing costs, for a print-run of 2,500 copies, giving Jore in effect all the revenue of the edition. The only condition was that Jore must not bring out his edition before the appearance of both the English editions, that is, not before the spring of 1734; and Voltaire tried to reinforce this condition by lending Jore £1,500.[17]

Unfortunately, the French authorities soon heard that a French edition was being put together in Rouen. Voltaire urged his Rouen friends Formont and Cideville to make sure that the Jore edition was kept safe 'under twenty keys'.[18] But he now decided to make a back-up arrangement, by passing a copy of the book to a Paris publisher called François Josse; he may have meant this as an insurance policy, but he should have foreseen that Josse would almost certainly bring out a pirate edition of his own.

This French edition was slightly different from the English one in one important respect: to the twenty-four letters of the English edition, Voltaire decided to add a twenty-fifth, on the *Pensées* of Blaise Pascal, the seventeenth-century mathematician and philosopher. He first started thinking of this in June 1733, when he wrote to Formont: 'I have been re-reading the *Lettres anglaises*, and in fact, what is best about this little work, is what deals with philosophy. Would you advise me to add a few little detached reflections on the *Pensées* of Pascal? I have long wanted to do battle with this giant.'[19] One month later, Voltaire had written this twenty-fifth chapter and sent it off to Jore.[20] By this time the English edition was already coming off the press, so that it was too late to include the Pascal letter.

Why Voltaire added this twenty-fifth letter remains unclear, since it had nothing to do with England; but it now made sense to change the title of his book for the French edition. Until now he had always referred to the book as the *Lettres anglaises*; he only started calling it *Lettres philosophiques* after the French edition was published in the spring of 1734.

The situation was now tailor-made for the convulsive publication, in the spring of 1734, of three competing editions of Voltaire's book, for the appearance of the French version of the English edition would almost inevitably precipitate the publication of not just one but two rival versions of the French edition of the *Lettres philosophiques*, from Jore and Josse. Voltaire seems to have thought he could control this process.

At the beginning of April, Voltaire and Émilie du Châtelet set off for Burgundy, to attend the marriage of the duc de Richelieu and the young Marie-Élisabeth de Guise, daughter of the prince and princesse de Guise. 'My dear friend,' Voltaire told Cideville,

> I am leaving to be the witness of a marriage which I brought about. I had long had the idea of marrying M. le duc de Richelieu to Mlle de Guise. I conducted this affair, like an intrigue in a comedy. The dénouement will take place at Montjeu near Autun. Poets are much more likely to write epithalamia [wedding poems] than marriage contracts, and yet it was I who made this contract, and I shall probably not write any verses.[21]

Pomeau seems to think that the intrigue to which Voltaire refers was romantic, as if Voltaire had engineered the love affair between Richelieu and Marie-Élisabeth de Guise; and that this intrigue was conducted jointly by Voltaire and Émilie. In fact, the intrigue was crudely financial, and it was conducted solely by Voltaire: the marriage took place only because Voltaire provided the money for the bride's dowry.[22]

Richelieu wished to marry Marie-Élisabeth, the young and charming daughter of the prince et princesse de Guise, and he expected her to come with a dowry; but the Guise family, though of the highest aristocratic lineage, were rather impoverished. Voltaire knew both sides well, and he was able to resolve the problem by lending her father £25,000; this loan enabled them to provide the dowry for Richelieu, and Voltaire became the witness, or best man, at the wedding.[23]

The marriage took place on 7 April 1734 at Montjeu, near Autun in Burgundy, where the Guise family had a country house. The wedding party was still going on two weeks later, when word reached Voltaire, on 24 April, that the *Lettres philosophiques* had started appearing in Paris. He was appalled. He wrote to Cideville:

> I was here quite calm, my charming friend, enjoying the fruit of my little negotiation between M. de Richelieu and Mlle de Guise, when

the most frightful news came to disturb my rest. Those cursed *Lettres anglaises* have suddenly come out without anyone having consulted me, or given me the least warning. I would not wish to suspect Jore of having played this trick on me, for on the smallest suspicion he would surely be put in the Bastille for the rest of his life. Please tell me what you know.[24]

Evidently, Voltaire did not know, at this point, whether it was Jore or Josse who had released the French version of the *Lettres philosophiques* in France.

On the same day he wrote a wretched, cringing letter to Cardinal André-Hercule Fleury, the king's chief minister, protesting his blamelessness:

For over a year, I have spared neither effort nor money to suppress the work which Mr Thieriot has finally published despite me. I protest, Monseigneur, that so far from having played any part in the publication of this book, I shall take action in my own name with the utmost rigour (if you will permit it), against the bookseller who is releasing it to the French public. I am scarcely recovered from a mortal sickness, and the pain of displeasing you would finally deprive me of my most unhappy life.[25]

He also wrote anxious letters of protestation to Maurepas, the Secretary of State, and to René Hérault, the chief of police.

In vain. On 3 May Maurepas issued a warrant for Voltaire's arrest, and for his imprisonment in the château of Auxonne. Jore was arrested and put in the Bastille, though only for fourteen days. And the *parlement* in Paris, in a move reminiscent of the Inquisition, condemned the *Lettres philosophiques* and decreed that they be publicly lacerated and burned on the steps of the Palais de Justice.

An urgent message warning of the arrest warrant was sent to Voltaire by his close friend the comte d'Argental, and he got away just in time.[26] His friends at Montjeu told the police that he had gone, for health reasons, to the spa at Plombières-les-Bains in the Vosges. In fact, he had fled to the remote and dilapidated country château owned by Émilie's husband at Cirey-sur-Blaise, in the region of the Champagne, to the east of Paris. There he trembled with anxiety and waited for Émilie to join him. He had to wait five months before she did so.

11

ÉMILIE COMES AND GOES

1734–1735

VOLTAIRE WAS ALONE WHEN he reached the Château de Cirey, and quite frightened, and he sent off a flurry of letters to protest his innocence and appeal for news. He tried to conceal his whereabouts, and sometimes gave a false address; he told his friends to write to him care of Demoulin near Saint-Gervais in Paris.

He poured out his anxieties to the comte d'Argental, the friend who had sent him the warning.

> More trouble, another letter. That *lettre de cachet* [arrest warrant] makes me want to write a thousand more letters in response. What is the position, I beg you, please tell me? Is it my book which is to be burned, or me? Do they want me to retract like Saint Augustine? Do they want me to go to the devil? Burn this envelope, and do not say where the letter came from.[1]

D'Argental was one of Voltaire's closest friends, not least because they shared a passion for the theatre. They wrote to one another with great frequency, especially on matters connected to the theatre, and their correspondence includes over 1,200 letters from Voltaire, though far fewer from d'Argental to Voltaire. D'Argental had been in love with a number of actresses, including (like Voltaire) Adrienne Lecouvreur; history does not relate with what success. He maintained close relations with the Comédie Française, and he became Voltaire's main adviser on his writing, and an unofficial but influential intermediary between Voltaire and the theatre company.

Voltaire also wrote to Mme du Deffand, the society hostess, to ask her to intervene with Maurepas, the Secretary of State.

Truly, Madame, when I had the honour to write to you, and to beg you to get your friends to speak to M. de Maurepas, it was in the hope that he would help me. I was in London when I wrote all that [the English *Letters*], and the Englishmen who saw my manuscript thought it was very moderate. It was two years ago that I gave Thieriot the regrettable permission to print those trifles, and at that time I was thinking of leaving France for good. Since then, I have changed my mind; unfortunately these letters are appearing in France just at a time when I have the greatest desire to stay here.[2]

To Maurepas himself, Voltaire wrote a pathetic appeal, snivelling with feeble excuses:

It is certain that I had nothing to do with the book which has flooded the market, that it is full of passages which have been added to the original, that I disavow it, that I will take legal steps against the publisher, that I am being made very ill with all this, and that a high temperature, an attack of dysentery and a *lettre de cachet* are quite capable of sending me to debate with Pascal in the other world. I have done all that I humanly could to prevent the publication of this scandalous work. Over six months ago I received a fine letter from M. le Cardinal Fleury, in which he assured me that no steps would be taken against me without giving me a hearing. If they want to burn my book, but leave me unharmed, I accept the deal. I was in London when I wrote those trifles, and that was six years ago; I was not thinking of France.[3]

Voltaire may have hoped that the French authorities could be mollified if he could persuade them that the *Lettres philosophiques* had all been written long ago and in an eccentric foreign country. But his claim that he 'was not thinking about France' was manifestly misleading, for the book was littered with constant cross-references to France, many of them disobliging or even derisory.

Take the chapter on trade, for example, where Voltaire describes with admiration the respected status in English society of merchants and traders, and contrasts it with the absurd and servile position of courtiers at Versailles.

In France the title of Marquis is given gratis to anyone who will accept of it; and whosoever arrives at Paris from the midst of the most remote Provinces with money in his purse, and a Name terminating in *-ac* or *–ille*, may strut about, and cry 'Such a man as I!', and may look down upon a Trader with sovereign Contempt; while the Trader on the other side, by thus often hearing his Profession treated so disdainfully, is Fool enough to blush at it. However, I cannot say which is most useful to a Nation; a Lord, powdered in the tip of the Mode, who knows exactly at what a Clock the King rises and goes to bed, and who gives himself Airs of Grandeur and State, at the same time that he is acting the Slave in the Antechamber of a prime Minister; or a Merchant who enriches his country, and contributes to the Felicity of the World.[4]

Voltaire's vulnerability was made much worse, when Claude-François Jore, the printer who had released the French edition of the *Lettres philosophiques*, denounced Voltaire as the author. 'While he was in prison', Voltaire told Cideville,

I never stopped writing to magistrates and ministers to assure them of his innocence; but he, on the contrary, told the chief of police that it was I who had caused the publication of the edition which has been circulating. On the basis of his deposition they went and overturned everything in my house in Paris, and they took away a little cupboard in which were my papers and all my fortune. They took it to the police chief, but it fell open on the way, and was pillaged.[5]

In the course of their investigations the police also discovered the second French pirate edition, produced by René and François Josse, and Voltaire, in a desperate attempt to curry favour with the authorities, wrote to René Hérault, the chief of police, to denounce Josse as the publisher.[6] His convoluted explanations did him no good.

Voltaire now heard that Richelieu had been wounded in a duel, and he left Cirey at once to be with him. After his wedding party at Montjeu, Richelieu had rejoined the French army, where he was serving as a colonel at the siege of Phillipsburg, in the War of the Polish Succession (1733–38). There he had been insulted by a fellow officer, Jacques Henri de Lorraine, prince de Lixin, a cousin of Richelieu's new wife. Lixin had sneered that Richelieu's ancestry was not nearly good enough for him to marry a member of the Guise family, and Richelieu had picked up the challenge. They fought, and Richelieu was slightly wounded; but he killed Lixin.

Voltaire spent a month with Richelieu at Phillipsburg and made friends with the marquis du Châtelet, who was serving in the army under Richelieu. Whether or not du Châtelet already knew about Voltaire's relations with his wife is unclear, but he proved extremely friendly. He gave Voltaire permission not just to stay at Cirey but also to do whatever was necessary to make it more habitable. As Voltaire had already discovered, the château was seriously dilapidated, cold, draughty and uncomfortable, and the marquis did not have enough money to keep it in good repair.

When Voltaire returned to Cirey, he embarked on a far-reaching programme of improvements; and he also started to make friends with some of the local gentry, notably the young and charming comtesse de La Neuville and the not-so-young but still charming Anne Paulin du Raget de Champbonin, the wife of a cavalry officer, whom he affectionately called his 'gros chat' ('fat cat'). They became an important part of his social life, but he was soon so busy doing up the building and landscaping the garden that he could not visit them as often as he wanted. In August he wrote to Mme de Neuville to complain about how overworked he was. 'Terraces, sheds, hedges, long alleys, have all torn me away from the pleasure of paying my respects to you. Just imagine all the things I have to do, surrounded by masons, and covered with plaster.'[7]

For the first time Voltaire was starting to create a home of his own. What was lacking was Émilie to share it with him, and her continued absence raised acute questions about her real feelings for him. For after the wedding at Montjeu, Émilie had gone back to Paris, ostensibly to intervene on Voltaire's behalf with the authorities at court but really, as he knew, to see Maupertuis again.

After Voltaire's sudden departure from Montjeu, Émilie wrote to Maupertuis, openly admitting the ambivalent state of her affections: 'Your friendship, Sir, was the delight of my life in my happiest times, that is to say, when I saw you often. You may judge how much more necessary it is to me in a time of unhappiness. I have just lost Voltaire. His departure fills me with pain, and I do not know if he will return to a country where he is treated so badly.'[8] A month later Émilie wrote again from Montjeu to tell Maupertuis that she would soon be returning to Paris, and that she counted on him to give her lessons again. 'I have gone back to geometry, but I have learned nothing. I know how much I should lose if I did not take advantage of your kindness to overlook my weakness, and to teach me such sublime truths.'[9]

In Paris that summer Émilie and Maupertuis evidently saw one another quite often. She wrote to him from Versailles:

> I think that you disliked our outing to the country so much that you did not even say goodbye to me. So you have been at fault with me in every way, and I am at fault in writing to you, so our flirtation is complete. I shall get to Paris on Saturday around nine o'clock. If you are kind, you will come and have supper with me. You owe me that at least, to make good all your faults. When I have not seen you for several days, my wits desert me.[10]

By August Voltaire was complaining openly of Émilie's infidelity. 'Please note', he told Mme de La Neuville,

> that my pleasures take second place to my duties. Every day I expect the arrival of workmen, and I am the one who must urge them on. I write their names every day in a large account book; and until I have someone who can take over, I cannot give up. You are on very good terms with Mme du Châtelet, but you will be on even better terms when she returns to her château. Please keep up the good will that I enjoy at La Neuville. As for that of my wife, I trust to providence and to the patience of a cuckold.[11]

What Voltaire did not know was that Émilie had just received a tragic blow when her third child, a baby boy only sixteen months old, fell ill and died. She was devastated, and it was to Maupertuis that she turned for comfort. 'My son died last night, Sir; I am, I admit to you, extremely afflicted. As you may imagine, I shall not be going out. If you wish to come and console me, you will find me alone. I have had my door barred, but I feel that there is no time when I would not find extreme pleasure in seeing you.'[12]

In general Émilie gave little sign of maternal feelings for her children, but she obviously felt deep grief at this boy's death, as she told another friend: 'I have suffered one of the griefs attached to the state of motherhood: I have lost my youngest son. I have been much more distressed by this than I would have expected. I was very troubled by his illness.'[13]

Not long after the death of her baby Émilie's thoughts turned once more to Voltaire, and in September she decided to rejoin him. It must have been a sudden, nervous decision, for she turned up in October, without warning, but with great enthusiasm and enormous quantities of luggage. Voltaire could hardly contain his joy. 'Mme du Châtelet is here,' he told Mme de Champbonin.

She arrived from Paris yesterday evening. She came just as I was opening a letter from her, saying that she would not come at all soon. She is surrounded with two hundred packages, which arrived at the same time. We have beds without curtains, bedrooms without windows, cabinets made of chinoiserie but no armchairs, and charming phaetons but no horses to pull them. In the middle of all this disorder Mme du Châtelet laughs and is charming. She arrived in a sort of cart for two, shaken about and bruised, without having slept, but very well despite this. We are having some old tapestries pieced together. We are looking for some curtains, we are having some doors made, and all this so as to be able to entertain you.[14]

Émilie's arrival put Voltaire in such a euphoric and triumphant frame of mind that he wrote to Maupertuis to invite him to come and stay.[15] When Maupertuis answered, it was to Émilie, to say that he could not come. Émilie's reply to him shows that she was nothing like as elated as Voltaire and was certainly not yet committed to staying with him for good.

At last, Sir, you have remembered me, I received a letter from you when I had given up hope of one. I am here in a most profound solitude, which suits me pretty well: I share my time between M. Locke and the masons. I am doing up my hermitage in the sweet hope of spending some philosophical years with you; but I must live in town for some time yet, if I am to lose my taste for it.[16]

It is a brutal letter. She makes no mention of Voltaire, least of all any suggestion that she was glad to be with him; she seems to claim that she is renovating the Château de Cirey in order to share it with Maupertuis, but she does not say that it is Voltaire who is paying for it; and she implies that she has not given up living in Paris. The most charitable interpretation is that Émilie was a woman of turbulent and changeable emotions, but it is hard to be sure whether she was being deliberately duplicitous or simply keeping her options open.

115

Over the next few weeks Voltaire repeatedly insisted to Mme de Champbonin on 'the pleasure of living with Mme du Châtelet', whom he described as 'the most lovable mistress of the most decrepit château in the world'.[17] Yet there were battles of wills between them over the improvements to the château, in which Émilie consistently and wilfully over-rode Voltaire's previous plans. 'Mme du Châtelet has become an architect and landscape gardener,' he told Mme de La Neuville.

She has windows made in places where I had made doors. She changes staircases into fireplaces, and fireplaces into staircases. She gets them to plant lime trees where I had planned elms; if I laid out a kitchen garden, she would make a flower bed. All this work will be keeping her busy for a few more days. I trust that I shall soon have the honour of acting as her coachman to drive her to La Neuville, after having acted as her apprentice gardener here.[18]

Their efforts to make Cirey really comfortable made slow progress, and Voltaire admitted obliquely to Mme de Champbonin that all was not well between him and Émilie.

Charming lady, there is some goblin who is keeping us away from you. I know you will be sorry that this adorable person, whom you love so much, cannot come to visit you. Comfort yourself, but do not count on her arrival. She is like love, which does not come when one wants it to. Cirey is not at all in a state for receiving visitors. What surprises me is that the lady of the place can live here. Until today she has stayed here, because of her enthusiasm for building works; today she is kept here by necessity, for she has a bad toothache.[19]

In December 1734, very shortly after he wrote this letter, Émilie abruptly went back to Paris again, as suddenly as she had arrived two months earlier, leaving Voltaire alone once more. It may be that she was not ready for life in unfamiliar proximity with Voltaire, in the solitude of the country, in winter, in an uncomfortable house, which was still in the turmoil of building work. No doubt she missed the urban pleasures of the city, for when she got back to Paris she immediately reverted to her hectic party-going life. As Formont wrote to Cideville: 'I have seen Émilie, who is truly of unusual merit. But the extreme dissipation of her life prevents me from meeting her very often.'[20]

Above all, Émilie wanted to see Maupertuis again. She reached home, in late December, and she wrote to him on Christmas Eve. 'I want to celebrate the birth of Christ with you; see if you can come and drink his health; I shall expect you between eight and nine; we shall go to midnight Mass together, and listen to carols played on the organ.'[21]

Meanwhile, Voltaire's friends were trying to persuade the authorities to pardon him for publishing the *Lettres philosophiques*, and in the end it was agreed that Voltaire might be permitted to return to Paris if he made a public recantation disowning the *Lettres philosophiques* and promised to behave better in future. In January a text was submitted to Cardinal de Fleury, and at the beginning of March 1735 René Hérault, the chief of police, wrote to Voltaire to tell him the good news.

His Eminence, and the Keeper of the Seals, have instructed me to tell you, Sir, that you can return to Paris whenever you judge it good. This return will be on condition that you will occupy yourself with subjects which will give no grounds for forming against you the same complaints as in the past. The more talent you have, Sir, the more you should be aware that you have enemies and envious people. Close their mouths for ever by behaving as a wise man who has already reached a certain age.[22]

Voltaire's amnesty was wholly conditional: the warrant against him was not revoked, and he could be arrested at any time.

After Émilie's departure Voltaire hesitated for three months while he wondered what to do. In March he decided to return to Paris and have it out with her. He got there at the end of March 1735, and at first things went well between them: they wrote a joint letter to his friend Cideville, in which Émilie expressed her 'joy' at Voltaire's return, and her 'extreme pleasure at seeing him again'.[23]

Barely a month later, however, Voltaire abruptly left Paris again, in dismay and disarray. And he went not to Cirey (for he could hardly go there now, while Émilie was undecided) but to the court of Lorraine at Lunéville, and he went there in company with Émilie's friend Marie-Élisabeth de Guise, duchesse de Richelieu. Before leaving Paris, he wrote an incoherent farewell to Formont: 'I am leaving, my dear friend; I have not seen the ballet *The Graces*. I should be going to Rouen, but I am going to Lorraine, tomorrow. Everything in Paris is on the way out, and so am I.'[24] And he wrote an even more disjointed farewell to Cideville: 'No priests in the homes of our Émilies, my dear friend! Ah, if only we could live together! Ah, destiny, destiny! I am leaving. I shall love you always.'[25] Voltaire must have delivered an ultimatum to Émilie: he would not continue their relationship except on different terms.

Émilie was a wilful young woman, and she was not used to being forced to make choices. Now she hesitated while she tried to sort out her own feelings. For two weeks she wrote to no one, not even to Maupertuis. Finally she concluded that she did, after all, love Voltaire enough to accept his terms, and she set out her reasons, not to Maupertuis, but to her friend and former lover the duc de Richelieu.

These letters tell us a great deal both about what Émilie was really like and about the life she planned to live with Voltaire. But what is most extraordinary about them is the frankness with which she lays out not just her feelings towards Voltaire, her reasons for choosing him and her planned strategy for keeping him, but also her feelings towards Richelieu himself. In one sense these are not just letters about her love for Voltaire, they are also love letters to Richelieu as well; in another they constitute an extended eulogy for the universal and over-riding importance in human affairs of love and friendship.

In the first letter to Richelieu, on 21 May 1735, Émilie launched straight into the question of love and friendship.

Happiness only comes with these two feelings. But what can I say about happiness? All that is mine is either at Lunéville [where Voltaire was] or at Strasbourg [where Richelieu was, with the army]. I am wasting my life, far from everything I love, in this great city, which in the last twenty-four hours has become a desert.

You know my heart, and you know how preoccupied it is. I congratulate myself on loving, in you, the friend of my lover. He does not forgive me for having once had, for you, some passing feelings, however slight they may have been; but surely the nature of my friendship for you must repair this fault. For me, friendship is not a calm and insipid feeling, and the extreme happiness of passing my life with someone I adore will not prevent me from trembling with anxiety for you.[26]

Émilie wrote again to Richelieu two days later.

I cannot delay any longer without replying to your letter, without telling you the extreme pleasure it gave me. I find in your wit all the charm, and in your company all the appeal, that everyone finds; but you are a unique man, incomparable, you know how to combine every virtue, delicious friendship, intoxication of love, you feel everything.

Voltaire seems to be having a wonderfully amusing time in Lorraine, and I am delighted; I am not like the dog in a manger. If you see M. du Châtelet, as I expect you do, speak to him of me with esteem and friendship. Tell him about Voltaire, but simply, with interest and friendship, and try above all to suggest that he must be mad to be jealous of a wife who is respected and who behaves well; that could be essential for me. He has great respect for your judgement, and will easily agree with you on that.[27]

It was not until eight days later, however, that Émilie really started to open up her thoughts about a future life with Voltaire.

I hope to leave Paris on 20 June. I cannot tell you the pleasure it will give me to abandon it; my only regrets, at Cirey, will be missing Mme de Richelieu and you. The more I think about Voltaire's situation, and about my own, the more I think that my decision is necessary. First of all, I believe that all those people who really love passionately would live in the country, if that were possible; but I also believe that it is only in the country that I can get a bridle on his imagination; in Paris I should lose him sooner or later, or at least I should pass my life in fear of losing him, and in complaining to him.

I love him enough, I admit to you, to be ready to sacrifice all the pleasures and amusements that I could find in Paris, for the sake of the happiness of living with him without alarms, and for the pleasure of getting him away, despite himself, from his imprudences.[28]

Émilie's attempts to control Voltaire's imagination or, as she put it, to put a bridle on him were to prove a source of serious and growing tension in their relationship. She wrote again on 15 June 1735:

I take friendship as the most serious thing in my life, and I love you truly, so I was worried and upset by your silence. I said to myself, we must love our friends with their defects and all. M. de Richelieu is frivolous and inconstant; I must love him as he is. I felt that my heart was not satisfied on these terms. I love you sad, gay, lively, obstructive; I want my friendship to increase your pleasures, diminish your pains and share them.

Do not forget to be eloquent to my husband, and prepare to love me still, even if I am unhappy. To avoid unhappiness completely, I am going to spend the happiest three months of my life; I shall leave in four days. My mind is weighed down by it, but my heart swims with joy.[29]

At the end of June 1735 Émilie returned to Cirey, and Voltaire joined her from Lunéville. This time he did not give way to unrestrained expressions of joy; he must have been quite wary of her. But slowly he and Émilie settled into a routine, in which their time was divided between large-scale renovations to the house, visits to neighbouring friends and serious studying and writing. Gradually Voltaire became happier in his work, and in his new life with Émilie. 'I am enjoying', he told Thieriot, 'in the purest peace, and in the freedom of being totally busy, the pleasure of friendship and study with a unique woman, who reads Ovid and Euclid, and who has the imagination of the one, and the precision of the other.'[30]

While he had been alone at Cirey, waiting for Émilie to make up her mind, Voltaire's main occupation had been finishing two tragedies, *Alzire* and *La Mort de César*, and researching his planned history of the seventeenth century in France. After her return he knew that he would have to take more account of her scientific interests, but he was not ready to subordinate his intellectual agenda to hers. He told his friend Cideville that his first intellectual priority was still literature and history, not science.

> Metaphysics, a bit of geometry, and physics, each get a certain amount of my time, but I study them without any great intensity, and therefore with a fair amount of indifference. My main occupation at present is *Le Siècle de Louis XIV*, of which I spoke to you a few years ago. This is my life's work. I am calm, happy and busy, though I miss you in my happiness.[31]

This was exactly what Émilie wanted to prevent. She thought that Voltaire's history of Louis XIV would be bound to antagonise the court of Louis XV, and of course she was right. This disagreement emerged in a letter from Voltaire to Richelieu a few weeks later: 'History is a necessary science for people of your position, and is much more use to society, more amusing and less tiring than all the abstract sciences. That is what I have to say about history, which you like, and which Mme du Châtelet despises too much. She treats Tacitus as if he were a neighbourhood gossip, retailing the local news.' Voltaire was determined not to let Émilie hobble his history project: in July 1735 he was pestering his friends for anecdotes to use in his history; in August he started writing it, and by September he had already written thirty years of it.[32]

By November, however, Voltaire was no longer asserting his intellectual independence so defiantly. 'Sometimes', he told Thieriot, 'we read a few cantos of my *Jeanne la Pucelle*, or one of my tragedies, or a chapter of *Le Siècle de Louis XIV*. From there we return to Newton and to Locke.'[33] It is a striking change of tone, and the reasons for it become clear a few lines further on, when he speaks of his love and admiration for Émilie:

> What she has done for me, in the face of the undeserved persecution which I have suffered, and the manner in which she has helped me, would bind me to her chariot for ever, if the extraordinary enlightenment of her spirit, and her superiority over all other women, had not already chained me to her. You know how much I value friendship; so you may judge the infinite attachment that I must have for a person who makes me forget the whole world, by whom I am enlightened every day and to whom I owe everything.[34]

But the seclusion of Cirey did not protect Voltaire from the envy and hostility of the outside world. In July 1735 he was attacked in a vicious pen-portrait, published anonymously in Paris:

> You ask me, Sir, for a portrait of M. de V., whom you say you do not know except through his works. M. de V. is shorter in stature than great men, that is to say, a bit more than mediocre. He is thin, of a dry character, a spare face, witty and caustic in manner, eyes sparkling and sharp. All the fire which you find in his works you will also find in his actions. He has a fervour which comes and goes, which dazzles and sparkles. Gay by nature, but serious by discipline, open but without frankness, political but without subtlety, sociable but without friends. He loves grandeur but despises the great; he is at ease with them, but constrained with his equals. He starts with politeness, continues with coolness and finishes with disgust. He loves the court but is bored there, sensitive but without attachments, voluptuous without passion. His mind is straight, his heart is unjust, he can think anything, and he mocks at everything. Vain to excess, he works less for the sake of

reputation than for money, for which he hungers and thirsts. He was made to have pleasure, but he wants to amass a fortune.

A poet from birth, his verses cost him nothing, and this facility harms him; nothing that he publishes is really finished. An easy writer, ingenious, elegant, after poetry his talent would be for history, if only he did not rationalise so much. It has long been said, that to become a writer without passion, one would have to have neither religion nor fatherland. On these terms, M. de V. is advancing with great strides towards perfection. M. de V. is always in rebellion against his own country and praises to excess whatever is a thousand leagues away. As for religion, we can see that he is undecided. M. de V. knows a lot of literature, foreign and French, with that complicated erudition which is so fashionable these days. Politician, physicist, geometer, he is anything he wants to be, but always superficial and incapable of any depth. To sum it up in one word, M. de V. wants to be an extraordinary man, and he certainly is.[35]

Voltaire appeared to shrug off this particular attack, though he rejected some of the specific criticisms. 'I have seen the portrait which has been made of me. It is not, I think, at all like me. I have more faults and fewer talents than are attributed to me; but I am sure I do not deserve the reproach of avarice and insensibility which is levelled at me.'[36]

Voltaire's envious critics have frequently accused him of avarice, but the facts do not support them. Undoubtedly he wanted money, but to imply that he only wrote to make money is the opposite of the truth. Not merely had he found it difficult to make a living from his pen in the past, but he had now virtually given up the attempt; in 1735 he even stopped claiming his author's rights from the Comédie Française. Moreover, if he was assiduous in managing his income, he was also generous in spending it.

The description of Voltaire as 'gay by nature ... sociable but without friends' is completely untrue: he was, on the contrary, rather depressive by nature, but he had an insatiable appetite for making friends, as well as enormous diligence and loyalty in keeping friendships alive.

Nevertheless, it is this pen-portrait, with its barbs and its sneers and its innuendos, and its biased mixture of truths, half-truths and falsehoods which has proved decisive in blackening and distorting the character of Voltaire. If the popular imagination today has any image of Voltaire and of who he was, it has been crucially influenced by the malicious caricature conveyed in this bilious pen-portrait.

If Voltaire was dismayed by this attack, he did not let it distract him. He pressed on with his work on *Le Siècle de Louis XIV*, which was now his main occupation, and he welcomed the arrival into the Cirey household of Michel Linant, a chubby-faced young abbé and would-be writer.

Voltaire had been trying to help Linant for nearly four years. At first he believed that he was a potentially talented poet or dramatist; soon he realised that he was bone idle; in time he concluded that he was so ignorant and ill educated that he would never amount to anything, but still he went on helping him.

As for our Linant, he has written one scene in two years, and it is not worth anything. I do not know what he imagined when he came to lodge with me. He really behaves as if he were my son, and he costs me a lot. And yet he has complained to three or four other people that he does not have enough pocket money for his little pleasures. He thinks that I took him in as a reward for his merit, whereas he is completely useless to me. He sleeps, he eats and he goes, all powdered up, to the stalls at the Comédie Française: that is his life.[37]

Voltaire's generosity to Linant is just one example among many of his endearing instinct for helping young writers, despite their faults. Voltaire never married, and he never had children. But the fact that he should have described Linant as behaving 'as if he were my son', may be more than a simple slip.

Eventually Voltaire concluded that the only way to help Linant was to get Émilie to take him on as a tutor for her son, even though he was under-educated; and in August 1735 Linant arrived. 'It will be up to her to teach Latin to the tutor, and he will pass on to the son what he has learned from the mother. I hope that, under her supervision, Linant will finally write some kind of good tragedy, unless she decides to turn him into a geometer and a metaphysician.'[38] If Voltaire really thought Émilie could turn Linant into a geometer, there was no limit to his admiration. 'There is nothing in the whole of this century which is as admirable as Émilie. She reads Virgil, Pope and algebra as easily as one reads a novel. I cannot get over the facility with which she reads the essays of Pope *On Man*.'[39]

Émilie's husband was proving extremely benevolent. He had already given Voltaire his personal permission to live at Cirey; now he persuaded the authorities to accept the fact that Voltaire was legally living there.[40] And in September he came home from the war, acquiescing without fuss in his role as the third member of the *ménage à trois*. In practical terms he lived a life quite independent from that of Voltaire and Émilie: they spent their time in study and earnest conversation, often working late into the night, while he busied himself during the day with the affairs of the estate; and whereas they had an eccentric timetable, rising late for coffee in the middle of the morning, with no other regular meal until supper late in the evening, he observed a much more conventional schedule, taking his lunch at noon and his supper at 8 p.m., in company with his son and his son's tutor.[41] His attitude towards the two lovers was always friendly and helpful; from time to time he would make visits to Paris, and sometimes he would carry out errands on Voltaire's behalf.[42]

But Émilie was not enjoying the situation as much as Voltaire, because even now she still had not finally given up Maupertuis. In August she wrote to him: 'I spend my life with masons, carpenters, carders of wool, cutters of stone. I no longer think, I am not worthy of writing to you today, but I cannot prevent myself. I absolutely must tell you how much I miss you in my solitude, and how little I miss the rest of Paris.'[43]

A little later that month Émilie was called to make a flying visit to her mother, who had fallen ill at her home in Créteil, just outside Paris, and she wrote from there to Maupertuis: 'They told me that my mother was very unwell. Fortunately she is out of danger, and I shall go home on Sunday. If you love me a little, you will come and see me. By whatever means, I must see you. I shall spend a few hours in Paris on Friday. If you wait for me at the café Gradot, I will collect you between five and six.'[44] Maupertuis ignored her appeal: 'I only spent six hours in Paris. One of the consolations of such a disagreeable journey was my hope of seeing you, and it was cruelly disappointed.'[45]

A few days later Émilie was back at Cirey but still not quite reconciled to the choice she had made, as she told Richelieu: 'Your absence makes me feel that I have yet something to demand of the gods, and that to be perfectly happy I should have to live between you and your friend [Voltaire]: my heart dares to desire it.'[46]

Émilie and Voltaire invited Richelieu to come and visit them at Cirey on his way home from the war, even though they warned him that the house was not yet entirely comfortable for receiving visitors. Voltaire foresaw that such a visit from Émilie's former lover would be a risky event: he expected that Richelieu would be looking for sex after his enforced celibacy at the front, and he asked him not to try anything on with Émilie: 'Tired of campaigning, avid for young cunts, and for firm, round arses, your passing kindness will seize the first woman you meet, peasant or tart; but if you have any pity for your neighbour, spare the beauty whom my heart adores.'[47]

It was not until five months later, towards the end of November, that Richelieu finally came to Cirey for a brief visit; and when he did, he completely disregarded Voltaire's plea. Émilie wrote to him very shortly after he left:

I should never have said what I admitted to you; but I could not deny myself the sweetness of letting you see that I have always been fair to you, and that I have always felt your true worth. The friendship of a heart like yours seems to me the most beautiful gift of the gods, and I should never be consoled if I was not sure of your friendship for me, even in the midst of the violent feelings which carry away my soul. I have given up everything in order to live with the only person who has ever been able to fill my heart and my mind; but I should abandon everything in the world, apart from him, to enjoy with you the joys of friendship.

The only thing which makes me bitter is that you should have thought me capable of an indignity which must have excited your indignation and contempt. It is frightful that there should have been times in your life when you had these feelings for me. Blush for your injustice, and see how a heart like mine is incapable of perfidy. Think of what you must put right with me, and that you cannot do too much to console me for having been suspected of a crime by him in whose heart I would have thought to have found justice.[48]

Exactly what happened at this emotional scene can only be guessed at, except that Émilie must have said something quite strong about the warmth and depth of her feelings for Richelieu. She may have intended it as an expression of innocent friendship; he evidently interpreted it as something different and made a pass at her; worse still, and to her later shame, she responded to his advances, more than she had intended but not as much as he wanted.

This encounter underlines the fact not merely that Émilie was an intensely emotional person but also that she could be recklessly imprudent in the way that she expressed her feelings. Whether this was because her feelings were so strong that she could not contain them or because she did not realise that her emotional gestures were liable to be misinterpreted is hard to say. We may speculate whether Émilie, as an extremely intelligent person with a highly developed bent for mathematics, may not have suffered from some attenuated form of autism in emotional matters. But in any case the upper-middle classes in France were now increasingly liberated, while the rules of the game were still unclear, especially when it came to questions of friendship between men and women.

In this respect Richelieu and Voltaire were very different. Richelieu was a highly accomplished and civilised man, but in his dealings with women, like many men of his age and class, he was something of a sexual caveman. Émilie was a new type of liberated woman; but most of the rest of the world did not know how to deal with her on her terms, and Richelieu clearly thought he did not need to. Many years later Voltaire wrote: 'We must fuck the ladies, and respect them.'[49] It is not clear that Richelieu would have subscribed to the second half of that sentence.

Voltaire was more modern in his attitudes: he was very good at friendship, including with women, and throughout his life, he had a number of *amitiés amoureuses* ('loving friendships') with women, which obviously had quasi-sexual overtones but did not necessarily involve a full physical relationship. This was partly because he was not, for all kinds of reasons, sexually macho by nature, but partly because he had come, under the influence of his relationship with Émilie, to have great respect for women. As he said in a letter the following year: 'Women can do everything we do; the only difference between them and us, is that they are just more amiable'.[50]

Émilie's emotional scene with Richelieu seems to have shocked her profoundly, for she did not write to him again for another three years. But she never ceased to love him, and when, five years later, her love affair with Voltaire started going wrong, it was to Richelieu that she turned.

1 2

THE INTELLECTUAL
LOVE-NEST

1735–1738

THE MÉNAGE OF VOLTAIRE AND ÉMILIE at Cirey was an extraordinary and exotic phenomenon, which gripped the imagination of France at the time, and it has exerted its fascination on succeeding generations ever since.

Paris society was agog with curiosity for news, gossip or even plain rumour about the life of the two lovers at Cirey. The most controversial writer of the age was setting up house with a brilliant and passionate woman, in a remote country château, not just with the acquiescence but even with the amiable support of her husband. Moreover, Voltaire and Émilie were said to be living a life of extravagant luxury or even shocking decadence. Voltaire did nothing to discourage these reports: he had spared no expense in improving the château de Cirey, he told Thieriot, and he felt no shame in living a life as agreeable as possible, 'not without some champagne, and some excellent food, for we are very voluptuous philosophers'.[1]

Voltaire was even working on a satirical poem which boasted of the extreme luxury of the life he was sharing with Émilie. He was partly inspired by Alexander Pope's *Essay on Man*, which had just been published (1734), but even more by Bernard Mandeville's much older book *The Fable of the Bees* (1714), which he and Émilie had been studying together and which she was translating into French.

Mandeville's thesis, by analogy with the beehive, was that the prosperity and health of society were dependent on the egotism of the people in it: the pursuit by individuals of their own selfish interests are in fact of benefit to society and turn private vices into public virtues. In his poem *Le Mondain*, Voltaire applied Mandeville's thesis to his own luxurious life with Émilie in their self-indulgent love nest at Cirey: 'The Earthly paradise is where I am,' he wrote, and he made matters worse by including a gratuitous sneer at the myth of Adam and Eve in the Garden of Eden, in which he transformed the Christian ideal of purity and lost innocence into an image of uncouthness and primitive savagery.[2]

Voltaire tried to keep the poem secret, but vanity got the better of him. In the summer of 1736 Émilie sent a copy to Cideville, though she warned him that it was not 'public', but by October, Voltaire knew that the poem was in general circulation.[3]

In fact, the fevered image of Cirey as a place of unbridled sensuality and decadence was much exaggerated. Voltaire made it as comfortable as he could, but the comfort was essentially confined to the separate apartments used by Émilie and Voltaire; the rest of the house was cold and draughty.

The late-night suppers enjoyed by the two lovers and their occasional local visitors were lavish and amusing events and were sometimes followed by improvised entertainments, including musical and dramatic performances; Voltaire was addicted to amateur dramatics, especially of his own plays, and Émilie was an enthusiastic singer of opera roles.[4] But their days, and indeed much of their nights, were spent in concentrated intellectual and artistic endeavour; they went to bed late, they got up late and they had no regular meal between coffee around eleven o'clock in the morning and supper around eleven o'clock at night. The time in between they spent partly reading, studying and writing in their separate rooms and partly meeting for intense discussions of the books they had read, from Pope to Locke to Virgil, from Newton to the Bible.

As for their love affair, Émilie's erratic on-again-off-again behaviour had its inevitable repercussions on Voltaire's own feelings. He had been ecstatic when she first joined him at Cirey in the autumn of 1734; he was wary when she re-joined him, after their showdown in Paris, in the summer of 1735; and it probably took another year, until well after Émilie's crisis encounter with Richelieu, for Voltaire fully to recover complete confidence in Émilie and her love for him.

The ups and downs of their emotional relationship were reflected in the shifts in Voltaire's intellectual interests. At first he refused to acquiesce in Émilie's agenda of scientific enquiry; by the end of 1735 he again started rhapsodising about Émilie and his love for her; and by the middle of 1736 he was spontaneously engaged, quite independently of Émilie, though obviously very much under her influence, in his own programme of scientific study.

Yet despite Émilie's efforts to rein him in, Voltaire would keep writing things which got him into trouble with the French authorities; sometimes he ran away for safety, and when he reached some more liberal country (at first it was usually the Netherlands), he enjoyed the feeling of freedom so much that he was reluctant to return. The first of his absences came in December 1735. Voltaire was working on a long satirical poem called *Jeanne la Pucelle* ('Jeanne the Maid'), which derided the traditional idealisation of Jeanne d'Arc: its bawdy narrative turned on a succession of picaresque episodes in which Jeanne's virginity was constantly threatened by lustful monks or licentious soldiers, but she was always saved in the nick of time, just before she could succumb to their immoral advances.

Voltaire had started writing this poem in 1730, and he went on revising and extending it for at least thirty years. But because of the scandalous and lubricious overtones of *La Pucelle*, and because any derision of France's national heroine was bound to cause offence, Voltaire did his best to keep it under wraps. But rumours about it regularly spread, and many people, including Frederick of Prussia, repeatedly tried to get hold of a copy. In December 1735 Voltaire heard a rumour that parts of the poem had got out and were now circulating in Paris. He wrote to Thieriot: 'I have just been warned that several cantos of *La Pucelle* are making the rounds in Paris. Please tell me if it is true. If someone has betrayed me, it can only be a certain Dubreuil, brother-in-law of Demoulin, who made a copy of the work six months ago. It is vital that I should be warned; for I may have to go and die in a foreign country.'[5]

Demoulin was Voltaire's man of business in Paris, and Voltaire had been a lodger in Demoulin's apartment in the rue de Longpont since 1733. Since Demoulin had access to Voltaire's rooms, he could easily have taken some of his documents. Voltaire feared that the leak of *La Pucelle* could lead to more persecution by the French authorities, and he decided to run away to some place of safety. On 28 December 1735 he wrote to Thieriot: 'I am presently at the French frontier with a post-chaise, some riding horses and some friends, ready to reach a place to stay in freedom.'[6] Voltaire's choice of the word 'freedom' (*liberté*), rather than the word 'safety' (*sécurité*), is no doubt significant. Quite soon, however, he seems to have realised that this was a false alarm, for he did not go very far, and he was back at Cirey on 2 January 1736. A few weeks later he sent Thieriot a copy of the latest version of *La Pucelle*.[7]

Voltaire now concluded that he could no longer rely on Demoulin as his man of business. In February 1736 he commented to Thieriot: 'Demoulin is a devious fellow, and I should give him a good dressing down. But I must take care, because he has my finances in his hands.'[8] Ten days later Voltaire appointed a new man of business, the abbé Bonaventure Moussinot. The terms of Voltaire's instructions give an idea of how rich he had become:

I should like, in the greatest confidence, to have a certain amount of cash on deposit with a discreet and trustworthy notary, which he could invest in the short term, and which I could get my hands on immediately, in case of need. I think everything ought to be in your name; you could just give me a note of acknowledgement under your personal signature. The deposit will be, little by little, about fifty thousand francs, within two years, and perhaps more.[9]

Two weeks later Voltaire changed the plan.

My dear Abbé, I should a thousand times prefer your safe deposit box to that of any notary. Just see whether you could take charge of the money of an unbeliever. I shall give you drafts to enable you to draw on other sources of money; and Demoulin will give you some too, and will bring it to you. Everything will be in the greatest confidence.[10]

Voltaire soon found Moussinot so useful and so helpful that in no time he was calling on him for all kinds of services, treating him not just as his banker and financial representative but as a general factotum and mail-order supplier. In April he asked him to send a collection of books, including some tomes from the Académie des Sciences, and a consignment of oranges and lemons.[11] A week later the oranges and lemons arrived but were found to be rotten.[12]

In the spring of 1736 Voltaire's earlier manoeuvrings over the publication of the *Lettres philosophiques* started to catch up with him. Jore, the Rouen bookseller who had published the clandestine French edition, wrote Voltaire an innocent-seeming letter, asking him to help him clear his name: the authorities, he said, had offered to give him back his printer's licence provided he told them the whole truth about the publication of the book. Suspecting nothing, Voltaire provided him with a detailed if not entirely honest account: yes, he had originally instructed Jore to publish the book but then, learning of the hostility of the authorities, had ordered him not to publish it after all; and he had lent Jore £1,500 to tide him over. He implied that Jore had followed his latest instructions and not published the book; he therefore denounced François and René Josse as the real publishers of this criminal edition.[13]

Armed with this letter, Jore now proceeded to blackmail Voltaire. Since Voltaire acknowledged that the Rouen edition had not been published, Jore demanded that Voltaire reimburse him for the printing costs, for which he claimed the colossal sum of £22,000. If Voltaire refused, Jore would use Voltaire's letter to incriminate him as the author of the *Lettres philosophiques*.

Alarmed by this unexpected attack, Voltaire hurried to Paris to try to negotiate a deal with Jore. But when he tried to buy Jore off with a small bribe, Jore immediately retaliated by publishing a memorandum denouncing Voltaire; and it seems that he enlisted Voltaire's old enemy the abbé Desfontaines to help him draft the memorandum in as damaging terms as he could.[14]

When a government minister asked Richelieu for his comments, Richelieu made matters worse by adopting an impatient and contemptuous tone. Voltaire complained to his friend d'Argental:

> M. de Richelieu, tired of all the trouble caused by this book, said: 'The affair is finished, what does it matter whether it was Jore or Josse who printed this f****** book, let Voltaire go f*** himself, and let's talk no more about it'. What was the consequence of this flippant manner of treating a serious question? They must have assumed that even my protectors were convinced of my guilt, and a guilt moreover of a most criminal kind.[15]

Meantime, Voltaire was at last discovering the depth of Demoulin's treachery. For whether or not he had filched a copy of *La Pucelle*, he had certainly stolen a substantial amount of Voltaire's money, which he was supposed to be looking after, as well as other documents written by Voltaire. When Voltaire tried to force Demoulin to give back the money, amounting to some £23,700, Demoulin retaliated with a menace of blackmail, threatening to publish the documents which he had stolen, which he claimed would expose Voltaire to the risk of criminal prosecution.[16]

For the next ten weeks Voltaire dragged out his quarrel with Jore, appealing noisily to all and sundry. By the end of June the authorities were completely fed up with this agitation, and René Hérault, the chief of police, ruled that Voltaire must give a charitable donation of £500 to the poor.[17] After this inglorious conclusion to a degrading quarrel, Voltaire hurried home.*

His return to Cirey, in the middle of July 1736, seems to have marked the start of a new honeymoon in his relations with Émilie, not only emotionally but also intellectually. It was only now that he began to show a serious personal interest in science; it is as if, after a full year of life with Émilie, he had finally succumbed to the enchantment of her personality and her dazzling mind. As he admitted to a friend in July that year: 'My occupations are rather taking me away from poetry. I am studying the philosophy of Newton under the eyes of Émilie who is, to my taste, even more admirable than Newton.'[18]

Voltaire also embarked on his own line of scientific enquiry, quite independently of Émilie. The Académie des Sciences was offering a prize for an essay on the subject of 'The Nature of Fire and its Propagation', and Voltaire resolved to submit an entry of his own. Significantly, he did not discuss it with Émilie; it was only afterwards that he discovered that she too had been working on the same subject and that they had each submitted competing entries to the Académie des Sciences.[19]

In September Voltaire was studying gravity, as well as the optics of Descartes, and in September he told Thieriot: 'We are studying Newton with great intensity. You pleasure lovers, you only like the opera; you should like opera *and* Newton. That is Émilie's way.'[20] At first these studies were all conducted with second-hand sources; it was not until the end of September that he finally received a copy of Newton's *Principia Mathematica*. 'I have finally received the parcel sent by M. du Châtelet. It contained a copy of Newton. The first thing I did was to kneel down before it, as was only right.'[21]

Voltaire's scientific pursuits were often inspired by those of Émilie, either working away in his study, while she worked in hers, or else in joint study together. They embarked on scientific research together, they ordered large quantities of scientific equipment and they conducted experiments in heat and optics. Émilie embarked on a survey of the current state of knowledge in the field of physics (*Les Institutions de Physique*), which came out in 1740; she wrote a commentary on, and then a translation of, Isaac Newton's *Principia Mathematica*. On his side, Voltaire told a friend: 'I am even thinking of soon publishing a little

---

* Voltaire and Hérault had been at school together twenty-five years earlier. Voltaire made no overt attempt to trade on this relationship, and in fact he did not allude to it at all until some time after the dispute had been settled (*Letters*, 931, 21 February 1738).

work which will enable everyone to understand this philosophy, which is much talked about but little known.'[22] This was the first mention of what would turn out to be Voltaire's popular account of Newton's scientific discoveries, which he called *Les Éléments de la philosophie de Newton*.

But while Voltaire was busy studying Newton and fire, and doing business with Moussinot, and researching the history of the seventeenth century, and doing up the château de Cirey, and living and loving with Émilie, a long-fuse bombshell landed on his desk, in the shape of a letter of flattery and seduction from Frederick, crown prince of Prussia.

> Sir, although I do not have the satisfaction of knowing you personally, you are none the less known to me by your works. They are treasures of wit, if one can express oneself so, and pieces worked with so much taste, and delicacy, and art, that their beauties seem fresh each time one reads them.[23]

He went on in the same shameless vein for several more pages before revealing the real purpose of his letter: he wanted Voltaire to send him everything he had written, including unpublished works, which he promised to treat in the greatest confidence; and he wanted Voltaire to visit him in Berlin.

Frederick was a young man in his early twenties, who was living in constant conflict with his father. Frederick William was a boor and a bully, with two obsessions in life: the efficient administration of his kingdom, provided it did not cost any money, and building up a highly drilled and fiercely disciplined army of six-foot grenadiers, provided that they were not used for any fighting. In his personal life Frederick William was a man of a violent temper, all too ready to lay about him with kicks or blows from his cane on all and sundry, including women and children, and including his own family.

His son Frederick was quite the opposite, an aesthete and an intellectual and a musician, whose only desire was to live a life entirely different from that of his father. In fact, at the age of eighteen, he had made a half-hearted attempt to run away; and his father, in reprisal, had imprisoned him and compelled him to watch, from the window of his prison cell, the beheading of a friend who had been implicated in his plan of escape. After his release from prison, two years later, Frederick submitted to his father's will and made no further attempts to run away; but he was still determined to model his own life on the ideals of *la philosophie*, and that meant seeking sustenance from every form of French civilisation. And that, in turn, meant trying to recruit all the leading intellectuals of the day, starting with Voltaire.

Voltaire was deeply flattered by the crown prince's approach, and he replied, at almost as great length, in a letter just as full of obsequious sycophancy and courtly grimaces. He did not foresee that the philosophical young aesthete in Berlin would quite soon also turn out to be a master of war and *realpolitik* and would make the fullest possible use of those well-drilled grenadiers whom his father had kept on the parade ground.

> Monseigneur, one would have to be insensible not to be infinitely touched by the letter which Your Royal Highness has deigned to honour me: my self-esteem has been all too flattered by it, but the love of humanity, which I have always had in my heart and which, I dare to say, makes my character, has given me a pleasure a thousand times purer, when I have seen that there is, in the world, a prince who thinks like a man, a philosophical prince who will make men happy.[24]

Meanwhile, Voltaire was adding yet another protégé to the Cirey household, or rather, a protégée of a protégé. In 1735 Voltaire had persuaded Émilie to take on young Michel Linant as tutor to her son, even though he was quite uneducated and had poor handwriting. It had not worked out well, for almost immediately Linant had started complaining about how bored he was.[25] Émilie had wanted to fire him on the spot, but Voltaire calmed her down.[26]

Linant now tried to get Voltaire to find a job for his sister. 'I finally persuaded Mme du Châtelet to take her in, despite her repugnance for the idea. I dare say the girl has just as much repugnance to be a servant as Mme du Châtelet has to be served by a chambermaid who is also the sister of her son's tutor. But these are just the little discomforts one must put up with.' As a tutor, Linant was a superior kind of servant, since he took his meals with the marquis and his son; his sister, as a chambermaid, would be just a servant and would therefore eat with the other servants below stairs.

In October Voltaire was becoming quite enthusiastic about his study of Newton.

> I am currently engaged in trying to calculate how much the sun weighs. This is a different sort of madness. What does it matter, you will ask me, provided we can enjoy the sun. Oh yes, it really matters,

even to us muddle-heads, for it is connected to the great principle of gravitation. Newton, my dear sir, is the greatest man who ever was, but so much the greatest that the giants of antiquity were, in comparison, like children playing games with marbles.[27]

But Voltaire's Newton studies had to be fitted into the time left over after more pressing practical tasks, starting with the renovation and furnishing of the château: 'As for reading Newton, well, building terraces fifty feet long, building courtyards with balustrades, installing baths made of porcelain, decorating our apartments in yellow and silver, it all takes up so much time.'[28] And some of Voltaire's time was taken up with ordering supplies from Moussinot: a case of books and candles, as well as a miniature portrait of himself, to be set in a ring, plus some paper, pens and a bed-cover.[29] Later that month he asked for 'two very large shoe buckles set with diamonds, some garters set with diamonds, and two little prints of my little face', and he wondered whether to get the painter Boucher to come to Cirey to decorate some tapestries: 'the whole thing might not cost more than £10,000.'[30]

A fortnight later Voltaire had another lavish and carefree shopping list for Moussinot:

As for the carpet, it must be about eleven feet by eleven, or ten by eleven, or eleven by twelve. If we can trim and adjust it, as you suggest, just send it to Cirey, together with the brilliant buckles, and a pen-knife. I am having second thoughts about the tapestry, for £35,000 is a bit much. As for the carpet, they have just brought me one from Chaumont, which will do nicely. So instead of the carpet, please send round to the perfumer named Provost, in the rue Saint-Antoine, and buy an enormous pot of make-up cream, the kind he usually supplies for Mme du Châtelet; but in the name of God, do not get it from anywhere except Provost.[31]

Towards the end of November Voltaire heard that far more copies of *Le Mondain* were in circulation than he intended, some of them illicit or pirate copies, and it was all stirring up trouble in Paris. At first, he tried to make light of it,[32] but by early December he was so frightened that he prepared to flee abroad for safety. At four o'clock in the morning on 9 December 1736 he wrote to d'Argental from a staging post not far from Cirey, where he was waiting with Émilie for new horses.

Your friend [i.e., Émilie] was at first astonished to learn that a work as innocent as *Le Mondain* should have been used as a pretext by some of my enemies to persecute me. But she could not bear the idea that I should stay any longer in a country in which I am treated so inhumanly. For myself, I should leave with inexpressible joy, I should go and visit the prince of Prussia, I should live abroad, I should be free and I should be the happiest man in the world. But your friend is here with me, and she is weeping. My heart is full of pain; but I shall wait for you to tell me what to do.[33]

D'Argental told him to go. But Voltaire's hint that he was going to visit Frederick in Berlin was just talk; his real plan was to go to the Netherlands, to supervise a new complete edition of his works, free from the censorship and dangers of persecution of France.[34] While he was away, Émilie wrote a blizzard of letters to d'Argental in a frenzy of anxiety for Voltaire's health and safety. 'My guardian angel, I have at last received news of your friend; he has arrived without accident, and in good health. Yet when I see the ground covered with snow, when I think of the climate where he is going, and of his extreme sensitivity to the cold, I am ready to die of grief.'

She begged d'Argental not to let him go on to visit Frederick: 'I absolutely do not want him to go to Prussia, and I beg you on my knees to prevent it. He would be lost in that country, months would pass before I could have any news, and I should be dead with anxiety before he came home. In Holland, it is almost as if he were in France, I could see him from one week to another, I should have news of him.' Moreover, she added, 'The crown prince is not yet king, and until he is, there would be no safety. His father is suspicious and cruel, and he is quite capable of having Voltaire arrested and handed over to the Keeper of the Seals in France. In one word, no Prussia, I beg of you.'[35]

From the Low Countries Voltaire assiduously kept up his new correspondence with Frederick, but in the end he respected Émilie's fears and d'Argental's prudent advice and politely turned aside an invitation to visit Berlin. As he told d'Argental: 'You advised me to leave, and I left; you advised me not to go to Prussia, and I did not go.'[36]

At first Voltaire tried to outbid Frederick in mutual flattery. 'You think like Trajan, you write like Pliny, and you speak French like our finest writers. What a difference there is between men! Louis XIV was a great king, but he did not think as humanely as you, Monseigneur, nor did he express himself as well. He did not even know how to spell.'[37]

But after receiving a couple more letters from Frederick all Voltaire's courtly reflexes could no longer contain his impatience with the inadequacy of the crown prince's French: 'You say that *Caesar est supra gramaticam,* and that is true. A prince need not be a purist. But a prince should not write and spell like a woman.'[38]

Voltaire was delighted with his reception in the Netherlands, and he admitted to Thieriot that he had received a warmer welcome there than he had ever known in France. In fact, it was in the Low Countries that he started writing the book which became the *Éléments de la philosophie de Newton*. But the attractions of life in a free country made such a deep appeal to him that towards the end of his stay it burst out in a letter to Cideville. 'Do not believe that France is the only place one can live. It is a country made for young women and voluptuaries, it is the country of madrigals and pompons, but you must look elsewhere for reason, for talents, etc. Pierre Bayle could not live anywhere except in a free country.'[39]*

After two months' absence Voltaire decided to go home to Émilie: 'Friendship recalls me,' he told Frederick, and he reached Cirey again shortly before the end of February 1737.[40] But after his return to Cirey he poured out the depth of his passion for freedom in a letter to d'Argental on 1 March 1737:

> I will confess to you, that if a friendship stronger than every other sentiment had not recalled me, I should have willingly spent the rest of my days in a country in which my enemies cannot hurt me, and where caprice, superstition and the authority of a minister are not to be feared. A man of letters must live in a free country, or submit to live the life of a fearful slave, whom the other jealous slaves never cease to denounce to their master. In France I can expect nothing but persecution, and that will be my only reward. It is not likely that I shall ever return to Paris, to expose myself to the furies of superstition and envy. I shall live at Cirey, or in a free country.[41]

Voltaire's first preoccupation, after his return to Cirey, was to sort out his finances. Much of his income came from personal loans to eminent individuals, and in the middle of March 1737 he wrote to Moussinot

---

* Pierre Bayle was a seventeenth-century forerunner of the Enlightenment, whose *Dictionnaire historique et critique* (1695–97) was one of the most distinguished predecessors of the *Encyclopédie* edited by d'Alembert and Diderot. At the age of thirty-four, he left France for Rotterdam in 1681, and he died there in exile in 1706, aged fifty-nine.

pointing out that many of them were far behind in paying the interest they owed: the marquis de Lézeau, three years behind, totalling £6,900; the comte de Goësbriand, five years behind, totalling £2,160; the prince de Guise, three years behind, totalling £7,500; the duc de Villars, one year behind; the Président d'Auneuil, one year behind; the marquis d'Estaing, one year behind; and the duc de Richelieu, nearly one year behind.

In fact, Voltaire and Moussinot had some difficulty in sorting out exactly how much money was outstanding from Voltaire's debtors, especially from Richelieu. Moussinot told Voltaire that Richelieu had paid back £43,200 of the principal of his debt, but Voltaire protested that the principal owed was in fact £46,417, plus arrears of interest amounting to £4,641, bringing the total debt to £51,058. Either way, Richelieu's substantial repayment meant that Voltaire suddenly had a large inflow of cash. He told Moussinot that he should spend part of it on pictures, but not more than £4,000 or £5,000, or even £6,000; and that he should invest half of the rest in bonds issued by the tax farmers, which would produce interest at 6 or 7 per cent, and place the other half in cash on deposit with Charles-François Michel, General Tax Collector at Montauban, whose probity, said Voltaire, was well known.

In the event, Voltaire placed £20,000 with Michel in the form of a *rente viagère*, and another £20,000 in a short-term deposit at an interest rate of 5 per cent.[42] Unfortunately Voltaire's confidence in Michel turned out to be misplaced: four years later, in 1741, Michel went bankrupt, and Voltaire lost his deposit.[43]

In the meantime Voltaire sent Moussinot several shopping lists. In one of them he asked him to buy three brooms for cleaning the floor, some high-quality scissors and two ladies' vanity cases, 'not those sold on the quai de Gesvres, but those sold in the rue Saint-Honoré'.[44] Meanwhile Émilie had quite separately ordered a dressing case from the silversmith Hébert, in the rue Saint-Honoré; this was going to be very expensive, so Voltaire asked Moussinot to pay the jeweller a deposit of £1,200 as an advance on the cost of the silver.[45] Voltaire admitted a few days later that 'Hébert is expensive, but he does have taste, and taste costs money; give him the £1,200, and tell him that if he wants a further advance of £1,200, he will have that as well.'[46]

Meanwhile, Voltaire continued to write more flirtatious letters to Frederick. 'You were made to be my king, and it is to my king that I write. Every day I thank heaven that you exist.'[47] Or again: 'You are quite unlike all other princes: from them we ask for benefits and honours; but from you, we only ask that you be enlightened.' Voltaire also threw out a mordant judgement about metaphysics: 'The whole of metaphysics, to my taste, contains just two things: first, what is known by all men of good sense; and second, what they will never know.'[48]

In the spring of 1737 Voltaire tired of these distractions and turned again to his scientific research. In May he finished a first draft of the *Éléments de la philosophie de Newton*, and he told the physicist Henri Pitot that even the French authorities now wanted the book to come out in France.

> I had arranged to publish the book in Holland, but I have since heard that the government would like it to come out in Paris. It is being waited for with even more curiosity than it deserves, for the public is really looking forward to having a good laugh at the spectacle of the author of *La Henriade* trying his luck as a physicist.[49]

Meanwhile Voltaire also stepped up his research into *The Nature of Fire and its Propagation*, and he sent Moussinot a series of shopping lists of specialised scientific equipment: a large concave mirror and a large burning lens, convex on both sides, as well as some glass retorts and crucibles.[50] Then the components for making thermometers and barometers: glass tubes, mountings, some mercury (separately) and some instructions on how to get the mercury into the glass tubes and then to seal them hermetically. 'This cannot be difficult', he added, optimistically, 'but we need to find out from someone who really knows.'[51] Next, 'a good air pump, a good reflecting telescope, which is very rare, a perfect Copernicus sphere and a very large burning lens, but not a burning mirror.'[52]

Voltaire's investigations did not always run smoothly.[53] Moussinot sent him thirty-one volumes of publications from the Academy, but it seemed that they must have been from the wrong Academy:

> I see by the delivery note on the box you sent, that it contains 31 volumes from the Académie. I think it is inconceivable that the Académie des Sciences could have produced so many volumes in the ten years that they have been offering prizes. I think you must unfortunately have mistaken the Académie Française for the Académie des Sciences. It's like the man who asked for 18 swans (*cygnes*) to put on his canal, and instead received 18 monkeys (*singes*); I seem to have received 31 monkeys, instead of the 8 or 9 swans that I needed.[54]

Voltaire soon realised that he would not be able to make much progress until he had a real laboratory to work in, and in July he instructed Moussinot to find him a laboratory assistant, for whom he would provide a room, a laboratory, a table and a small salary.[55] In September the laboratory assistant duly arrived at Cirey, but he seems to have kept himself to himself. 'I have hardly mentioned the assistant you sent me, since I scarcely see him except at Mass. He likes solitude, so perhaps he is happy. But I shall not be able to do any work on chemistry until the laboratory which I am building is finished.'[56] A week later the assistant, having surveyed the situation, returned to Paris to order all the equipment necessary, to be paid for by Moussinot.[57]

Meanwhile Émilie had got rid of Linant and his sister. 'I discovered some letters written by his sister, whom I had, out of the kindness of my heart, taken on as my chambermaid, in which she spoke of me in the most insulting terms. I do not know if her brother was her accomplice, but either way I cannot keep either of them.'[58]

Voltaire regretted their departure. 'I believe the sister was more guilty than the brother, but I am no longer allowed to communicate with him.'[59] Nevertheless, he continued to keep in touch with Linant indirectly, and sometimes he sent him small amounts of money. Towards the end of 1738 Linant actually wrote to Voltaire to thank him for the money; but Voltaire was grieved to learn that Linant had been heard making spiteful remarks about the Cirey household.[60] Eight years later, in 1746, Voltaire was still trying to help Linant indirectly.[61]

Voltaire could not hide his disappointment when he learned, in May the following year, that he had failed to win the prize of the Académie des Sciences. 'I am far from complaining,' he told Henri Pitot, 'and I consider it a great honour to have been allowed to compete. But I am quite upset, all the same, that I did not get the prize, for it would have been a great feather in my cap. Tell me frankly, could I get the Académie to print my essay?'[62]

Voltaire does not seem to have known that Émilie, too, had submitted an essay to the competition, for it was not until a month later that he made any mention of it: 'As for the memorandum on fire which Mme du Châtelet composed, it is full of things which would honour the greatest physicists.'[63] Happily, the Académie des Sciences agreed to print both his essay and Émilie's, even though neither of them had won prizes.[64]

Voltaire's popularizing study on Newton's theories (*Les Éléments de la philosophie de Newton*) had a much rougher ride. In the summer of 1737 the French authorities expressed interest in seeing it published in

France, and Voltaire duly submitted a copy of the manuscript. But in January 1738 the Chancellor decided that the book was still too controversial and refused permission. 'Perhaps', Voltaire told Thieriot, ironically, 'I ought to be grateful to him; for I should only have made new enemies, so I shall keep the truths of Newton to myself.'[65]

As a result, *Les Éléments de la philosophie de Newton* came out in Holland, but only on the basis of an incomplete and defective manuscript. Voltaire remained deeply dissatisfied by this new experience of the arbitrariness of French censorship, and he made a new approach to get it published officially in France.[66] He was turned down and had to be satisfied with a revised but still unofficial French edition (produced by Laurent-François Prault), with a title-page pretending that it had been published in London.[67]

Voltaire had by now largely lost interest in any original scientific research or what he had called, in a moment of disillusionment, 'the sterile truths of physics'.[68] 'It is six months since I gave up all sorts of natural philosophy,' he told Maupertuis; 'instead, I have gone back to poetry.'[69] He continued to equip his laboratory with lavish consignments of scientific equipment ordered from Paris, and he hired a laboratory assistant to help him.[70] But in reality the publication of his essay on fire marked virtually the end of Voltaire's personal engagement with science.

If the years 1736–38 were the high point of Voltaire's engagement with science, they were also, and partly for that reason, the high point of his intellectual and emotional convergence with Émilie. After 1738 there was a gradual divergence between them, at first intellectually and then emotionally, leading to tensions, rows and an increasingly frenzied life. If 1735 was the first year of their real happiness together at Cirey, 1738 may have been the last. It was a happiness which lasted less than four years.

ORDEAL OF
MME DE GRAFFIGNY

1738–1739

IN 1737, BEFORE THE END of his honeymoon with Émilie, a new interest came into Voltaire's life, in the shape of a zesty young woman of twenty-five called Marie-Louise Mignot. Though not exactly beautiful, a contemporary portrait suggests that she was good-looking and attractive, and she seems to have been gay and sociable, and fond of music and theatre; she was also very feminine. Voltaire knew her well, for she was his niece, the eldest daughter of his much-loved sister Marguerite-Catherine.

Her father was Pierre-François Mignot, who had married Voltaire's sister in 1709. She had borne him four children, two girls and then two boys, but she had died in 1726, aged only thirty-nine, when Voltaire was in England, a loss which caused him great grief.

When Pierre-François Mignot died in 1737, Voltaire immediately wrote to Marie-Louise; and after a tearful opening paragraph of condolence he moved briskly on to practical questions.

> I do not understand how your uncle [i.e., Voltaire's elder brother, Armand] can tell you that you have no option but to go into a convent. That, it seems to me, is the one thing you should not do. It is obvious that you will each inherit £80,000, and with that you could make a home for yourself, either by yourself or with your sister; separately you would be poor, but together you would be rich.
>
> If you wanted to spend some time in the country next spring, Mme du Châtelet can offer you her château, where you would find excellent

food, very attractive rooms, some music and a good harpsichord, a pretty theatre with fairly good actors, plenty of good books of every kind and an uncle who loves you tenderly, and who would have loved you even if you had been strangers. I embrace you, my dear nieces.[1]

Voltaire was obviously very attracted by the idea of having Marie-Louise near him, for he returned to the idea a week later. 'You should go and see my nieces,' he told Thieriot. 'There is an elder niece who is a student of Rameau, and has a delightful personality. I should really like to have her come and stay; and her sister as well. You could suggest the idea to them. They would not regret the journey.'[2]

A month later, in December 1737, Voltaire proposed that Marie-Louise should marry young Louis-François-Toussaint de Champbonin, son of Mme de Champbonin, a close friend and neighbour of the Cirey household. 'She would be mistress of a rather pretty château,' he told Thieriot, 'which they would do up for her. She would spend part of the year with Mme du Châtelet, and she would sometimes come with us to Paris. In fact, I should be her father.'[3]

But Marie-Louise decided against young Champbonin, and Voltaire was quite put out: if his proposal had been taken up, he said, he would have given her a dowry producing £8,000 a year.[4] Even so, in the new year he sent her a bag of money containing £1,000, plus £400 for her younger sister.[5] Six weeks later she married Nicolas-Charles Denis, a supply officer to the French army (*commissaire ordinaire des guerres*), based at Landau near the Rhine, to the north of Strasbourg. After the wedding Marie-Louise and her husband set off for Landau, and on the way they paid a brief visit to Voltaire and Émilie at Cirey. Voltaire saw little of the newly married couple, since he was ill during most of their stay, but Marie-Louise (or Mme Denis, as she now was) gave an eloquent account of their visit in a letter to Thieriot, after her arrival at Landau:

> I think I shall get quite used to the life I lead here. I have a very fine house, and 400 officers at my disposition, of whom I shall select a dozen of the most agreeable, who will frequently come to supper at our house.
>
> M. de Voltaire is of very delicate health; he was ill all the brief time I stayed at Cirey. Mme du Châtelet has put on a lot of weight, but she has a lovely face, and is in very good health.
>
> As for my uncle, I am in despair for him. I think he is lost to all his friends. He is shackled so fast to her that I think it is impossible

for him to break his chains. They live in a solitude that is frightening for humanity. Cirey is four leagues from any habitation, in a countryside where one sees nothing but mountains and neglected fields, they are abandoned by their friends and hardly ever have anyone from Paris.

Such is the life led by the greatest genius of our century, in truth, with a woman of great wit, who is very pretty and who employs every imaginable art to seduce him. There are no pompons which she does not adorn herself with, no passages from the best philosophers which she does not quote, just to please him, for she spares no effort. He appears more enchanted by it than ever.[6]

This striking little vignette of the ménage at Cirey shows that Mme Denis was a woman of sharp and observant mind, quick to make judgements but not malicious. She obviously thought that Voltaire and Émilie were still very fascinated with each other and still very much in love, and she was disarmingly impressed by Émilie's attractiveness ('*fort jolie*') and feminine wiles. Mme Denis was evidently a worldly woman, with a strong preference for a social life, no inclination for intellectual isolation and, above all, an eye to the main chance. Her comments on Voltaire were ostensibly framed to express a disinterested concern for him as 'the greatest genius of our century', but it is hard to avoid the suspicion that she was quite worried on her own account, that Émilie had ensnared her rich uncle.

Later Mme Denis would become an increasingly important figure in Voltaire's life, but now she disappeared off the scene for quite a long time, while his life remained calmly centred on Émilie and his work.

In June he reported that he was expecting a large new consignment of scientific instruments,[7] and he sent out copies of the new edition of *Les Éléments de Newton* to various friends. In July he suggested to Frederick that Maupertuis would be a good man to set up an Academy in Berlin,[8] a suggestion that Frederick duly followed after he became king. He continued to fret about his finances, and he referred for the first time to a disputed property near Liège called Ham and Beringhem, which belonged to relatives of Émilie and which was later to become the subject of a long-running and fruitless court case in Brussels. He continued to debate the pros and cons of Descartes and Newton with Maupertuis and others, he revised his play *Mérope* and he continued to work quite intensely on *Le Siècle de Louis XIV*. He revised some of his earlier works, *La Henriade*, *Brutus*, *Œdipe* and the history of Charles

XII, and he made arrangements to have his portrait copied and distributed to friends.[9]

In short, it seems that Voltaire, at the age of forty-four, was settling into a steady routine of industrious and comfortable success, in a harmonious life with Émilie. That autumn Voltaire summed up his life in a letter to the abbé Olivet, a schoolmaster whom he had known as a boy at the Collège Louis-le-Grand:

> I pass my life with a lady who employs 300 workmen, who understands Newton, Virgil and Tasso, and yet who is not above playing at piquet. I know that people are surprised that, having started with poetry, I then moved on to history, and ended up with natural philosophy. But after I have spent three months among the thorns of mathematics, I am only too happy to return to the flowers of poetry.[10]

The harmony of the ménage was soon disrupted by the arrival of Françoise d'Happencourt, Mme de Graffigny, whose visit was to set off the most violent emotional storm at Cirey of which we have any knowledge. Mme de Graffigny was a lady from Lorraine, a member of the old nobility but now in distressed circumstances. In 1712, at the age of seventeen, she had married an army officer called François Huguet; as part of the marriage settlement he had received a dowry of £40,000 and a property at Graffigny, which he adopted as his name. He proved both a waster and a man of violence, and after six years she left him; in 1723 she secured a formal separation from him. She was now effectively on her own, almost without resources and living precariously as a hanger-on at the ducal court of Lorraine.

Her situation became still more difficult in 1736, after the end of the War of the Polish Succession. As part of the settlement of the Treaty of Vienna, Francis Stephen, the duc de Lorraine, was forced to give up the duchy, and it was handed over to Stanislas Leszczyński, the former king of Poland and also, conveniently, Louis XV's father-in-law. As a result, all the nobles and officials attached to the court of the previous duke were forced out and obliged to leave Lunéville, starting in 1737.

Voltaire already knew Mme de Graffigny slightly, for he had met her in 1735, when he had visited Lunéville in the company of the duchesse de Richelieu. Mme de Graffigny was also distantly related to Émilie's husband, whose family came from Lorraine. With the change of régime at Lunéville, Mme de Graffigny lost her place at court and had nowhere to go. Mme de Richelieu offered to give her refuge in

Paris, and Émilie invited her to stay in Cirey on her way there. Both ladies simply assumed that she could pay for the journey; in reality Mme de Graffigny had almost no spending money and was forced to rely on the help of friends, first in order to get to Cirey and then in order to leave on the onward journey to Paris. After many tribulations she arrived at Cirey on 3 December 1738.

> Cirey, Thursday, 4 December 1738
>
> I arrived at two in the morning, after dying of fear, on roads ruined by the devil, thinking to be overturned at any moment, stumbling in the mud, because the postillions said that, if I did not get down, they would overturn me. You can imagine my state.
>
> Finally, I did arrive. The Nymph [Mme du Châtelet] received me very kindly. I stayed a moment in her room, then I went up to mine to clean myself up. A moment later, in came your Idol [Voltaire], a little candlestick in his hand like a monk, who gave me a thousand caresses. He seemed very pleased to see me; he kissed my hands ten times, and he asked me with great interest for my news. At last he left me, so that I could write to you.
>
> At first, she talked, without further ceremony, about her court case [about the property at Ham and Beringhem]. Her gabble astonished me; she speaks extremely fast; but she talks like an angel, I could tell that. She had a cotton dress, a large black apron and her hair, very long, pinned up behind, up to the top of her head, and curled, like they do for little children. It suits her very well. As for your Idol, I don't know if he was powdered specially for me, but he was all got up as if he were in Paris. The Old Fellow [the marquis du Châtelet] leaves for Brussels tomorrow; so there will be just the three of us, and no one will be sorry.[11]

This letter, like all the letters Mme de Graffigny wrote from Cirey, was addressed to François-Étienne Devaux, one of her closest confidants, whom she nicknamed 'Pan-Pan'. He was a 26-year-old friend from Lorraine, and he and she were both mad about literature and the theatre; what is remarkable about their correspondence is that Mme de Graffigny was able to gossip to Pan-Pan about anything and everything, in the most unbuttoned and intimate manner. He was not her lover, just a very close friend; her lover was another young man, also from Lorraine, a 30-year-old cavalry officer, named Léopold Desmarest.

Mme de Graffigny stayed at Cirey for just over two months, from

3 December 1738 to 12 February 1739. In that time she wrote thirty-one letters to Devaux, many of them long and all of them breathless. She did not have much idea of grammar or spelling, but her letters are striking in their immediacy, and they convey the most extended and vivid picture of life at Cirey that has come down to us.

Friday, December 5, 1738

I was writing to you yesterday right up until supper time. They came to call me, and led me to an apartment which I soon realised was that of Voltaire. He came to greet me. No one else had arrived, but I just had time to look about me. We sat down. What didn't we talk of! Poetry, science, and all in a light-hearted tone, and full of kindness. The supper was not copious, but special, quite proper, with lots of silverware. I had, opposite me, five spheres and all the machinery of physics, for it is in the little gallery that they take their only meal.

Voltaire was next to me, just as polite, just as attentive, as he was amiable and scholarly; the old gentleman was on the other side, so that my left ear was charmed and my right very slightly bored, since he said very little, and he withdrew as soon as we got up from table.

Mme de Graffigny continued her letter the next day, describing the apartments of Voltaire and Émilie in great detail:

Today I went down to coffee at eleven o'clock, which they take in the gallery, and which lasted an hour and a half. Voltaire went off to write, and the châtelaine and I went to her apartment. She told me all about the court case [the property at Ham and Beringhem], from the very beginning, about eighty years ago, until the present day. What is strange is that, though this took more than an hour and a half, she spoke so well that I was not at all bored.

The post came, but there was nothing for me; so I came upstairs to write to you and to describe my room. It is like a barn, it is so high and so wide. All the winds whistle through the thousand cracks around the window, and which I should like to stuff up, if God gives me life. There is a vast fireplace, but though it burns a great quantity of wood, the room remains very cold. The window gives little light and little view, since an arid mountain shuts it out. Such is my room, which I really hate. In fact, everything in the house is disgusting, apart from the apartments of the lady and Voltaire. Now here is what I have to read this evening: *Mérope* and the *History of Louis XIV*, which the old lady [Émilie] does not want him to finish, so she keeps it under lock and key; he had to beg her to let me borrow it; and the *Life of Molière*. He told me that, if I was very good, he would let me have something else, which he would tell me about another time.[12]

After a few days Mme de Graffigny gradually became clearer about the daily routine.

From half-past ten until half-past eleven they call everybody to coffee, which we take in Voltaire's gallery. That lasts until midday, or one o'clock, depending on whether we started earlier or later. At the midday bell all the so-called coachmen go for dinner, including the master of the château. We stay behind, Voltaire, the lady and I; he then makes a deep bow, and we all return to our rooms. Around four o'clock there is sometimes tea, and we meet again. I seldom go, even when they call me; but it does not happen every day. At nine o'clock we have supper, and we stay together until midnight. The master of the château joins us at table, but he does not eat, but sleeps, and so says nothing, and withdraws when they clear the table.[13]

Apart from the two meals, coffee at 11 a.m., and supper at 9 p.m., and occasionally tea at 4 p.m., and any shared entertainment after supper, Mme de Graffigny was generally expected to spend the whole day in her room. Sometimes she was visited by Mme de Champbonin, a friend and neighbour, but they would meet in Mme de Graffigny's room, not in the public rooms of the château. Mostly she spent her days reading, as often as not books by Voltaire, or writing to Pan-Pan.

After coffee I came upstairs, because I could not resist *Le Siècle de Louis XIV*. He says it is the work of which he is most satisfied, but she keeps it locked away, so that he shall not finish it. He said yesterday that he will surely finish it, though probably not as long as he is at Cirey. She turns his head with her geometry, that is all she likes. It is astonishing that she shuts out history, and stories. But just as I was starting to read it, they sent for me to go downstairs. I found that the lady was going to bed, because she was not feeling very well; she said that, since she could not work, Voltaire would read to us from *Mérope*.
But when Voltaire appeared, the lady took it into her head that he must put on a different jacket. It is true that the one he was wearing did not look good, but he was well powdered and wearing fine lace.

He gave good reasons for disagreeing, saying that he would catch a cold, but finally he had the good humour to send his *valet de chambre* to fetch another jacket. But he could not find one, and Voltaire thought that that would be the end of it.

Not at all, her persecution started all over again; and Voltaire began to get upset, he spoke to her sharply in English and then he walked out. A moment later she sent to fetch him, he sent word that he had the colic, and that was the end of *Mérope*. I got up and said I would go to see him; I found him in a very good humour, and he seemed to have forgotten that he had the colic. Then the lady sent for us, and he returned with me but got into a huff as soon as he entered the room, and sat in a corner and said nothing. Soon after, the old gentleman left the room, and the two sulkers started talking together in English. This was the first sign of love between them that I have seen, for they usually behave with surprising restraint. She makes his life a bit hard. To me, she was at first rather cold, but she has become more human.

The next day Émilie proposed going for a ride in their barouche, but Mme de Graffigny was frightened by the liveliness of the horses and stayed behind; instead she and Mme de Champbonin went to explore Émilie's apartment.

O, what enchantment! An antechamber as big as your bed, the bathroom itself entirely done up in tiles of faïence, a dressing room of the same size, a small sofa, charming little armchairs and finally her bedroom, with mirrors, and amusing books on the side-table. If I had an apartment like that, I should wake up at night just to look at it.[14]

In the evenings Voltaire would frequently read aloud, sometimes from *La Pucelle d'Orléans*, his bawdy satire about Jeanne d'Arc. He tried to keep it confidential, but many people had heard about it, and all of them wanted to get hold of it. Three years earlier Voltaire had panicked when he heard that parts of it were circulating freely in Paris, but now he must have thought that he was in safe company at Cirey, for he read aloud from the poem ('*Jeanne*', as Mme de Graffigny referred to it) on four successive days. One of these readings was interrupted by a lovers' tiff between Voltaire and Émilie.

Yesterday after supper there was a charming scene. Voltaire was sulking over a glass of Rhine wine, which the lady was trying to stop him drinking; so he refused to read *Jeanne* to us as he had promised, and he was in an ill humour. We tried to bring him round by joking about it, and even the lady could not hold out against him. It turned into a charming scene, which lasted a long time, but which finished by him reading a canto of *Jeanne*.[15]

From time to time the daily round at Cirey was interrupted by bursts of social entertainment, especially with amateur performances of plays, as often as not plays by Voltaire himself, in which the parts were all taken by members of the household. Not long after Mme de Graffigny's arrival at Cirey they put on two of Voltaire's comedies, *L'Enfant prodigue*, followed by *Le Grand Boursoufle*. There were too few people in the household to take all the parts, so Émilie sent for her twelve-year-old daughter Françoise-Gabrielle-Pauline from the convent where she was being educated, to play one of the supporting roles.

The little young lady arrived yesterday evening; they sent for her to play Marte. She is not pretty, but she speaks like her mother, and with the greatest wit. She is learning Latin, she likes reading, and she learned her part in the carriage on her way here from the convent, which is only four leagues away.[16]

Monday evening, 22 December 1738
After supper, la Belle Dame asked me if I had had any children, so from question to question, though I held them off, they made me tell them my life story, of which they knew nothing. [After her marriage in 1717, Mme de Graffigny had had three children in quick succession, but they all died in early infancy.] O, what kind hearts! La Belle Dame laughed to stop herself crying, but Voltaire, like any human being who is not ashamed to appear so, broke down in tears. This scene revived my happiness at being with people who think, for I feel they do so with tenderness as well.[17]

Over the next week Pan-Pan must have become increasingly perplexed by what he was hearing from Mme de Graffigny. Her letters were as long and as breathless as ever, and she continued to tell him about what she was reading; but she became less and less communicative about social life at Cirey. She virtually ceased to regale him with stories about the gay social evenings after supper, and he may even have started to worry that something was wrong.

He must have been even more puzzled by the letter she wrote to him on 1 January 1739.

> I have received your letter, in which you speak of a canto of *Jeanne*, and which you say you find charming. I do not recall anything of that kind, and I beg you to send back the sheet of paper in which I spoke of it. I really must have this letter. Do not make any argument on that point, it would be quite useless.
>
> It seems to me that we were already too much in agreement, that you would never speak about anything that could happen here, for you to raise any question about it now. I must therefore repeat, once more, that I can make no exception. In God's name, keep quiet.[18]

What her letter did not say was that two days earlier, on 29 December, Mme du Châtelet had burst into Mme de Graffigny's room in the middle of the night and had denounced her furiously as a thief and a traitor. She accused her of having made a copy of one of the cantos of *Jeanne* and sent it to her friend Pan-Pan Devaux in Paris. As the tirade went on, Mme de Graffigny began to realise that Mme du Châtelet had been opening her letters, since she was brandishing what she claimed was one of them in her face.

Mme de Graffigny indignantly denied having done any such thing, which is why she asked Pan-Pan to send her back her letter, in the belief that it would exonerate her. More than two weeks were to pass before Mme de Graffigny could bring herself to describe that midnight scene of confrontation; even then she did not know the full story.

It is unlikely that Mme de Graffigny did in fact copy out the text of a canto of *Jeanne*, or even that she ever had a text in her hand. On the other hand, it is quite probable that she did write a summary of what she remembered from Voltaire's reading; but it is only probable, because part of the key letter, number 65, dated 19 or 20 December, is missing, as we shall see later.

On 8 January she told Pan-Pan that his letter had been opened, and badly resealed, and she retracted her earlier request that he should send her a copy of *Voltairomanie*: 'Do not send me the satire which I asked for in my last letter but one, I do not want it.'[19]

Two days later she was still trying to get evidence which would exculpate her in the eyes of Mme du Châtelet. 'I must repeat, I only replied very shortly to your letter in which you said: "The canto of *Jeanne* is charming" – that was your phrase. But since it seems ambiguous, I must absolutely insist that you send me back the page of my letter which contains the canto of *Jeanne*.'[20]

On 12 January Maupertuis came to stay for a few days. Mme de Graffigny had supper with him three times and found him very agreeable and gay. 'I have read his *Journey to Lapland*; I've never read anything better written, so far as I can understand it, for towards the end it is all calculations and observations about which I understand nothing.'[21]

Although Mme de Graffigny was gradually recovering her strength, she was clearly miserable. It sounds as if she was being ostracised by Émilie and Voltaire, and desperate to leave; but she could not leave, because she was penniless.[22] She heard that the butler sometimes played at backgammon, and two days later she played with him; but she did not enjoy it.[23]

Finally, on 19 January 1739, the dam broke: Mme de Graffigny decided at last to tell what had happened to her.

> Until now, my dear friend, I have not dared let out of my head the frightful experience which I have been through. I was so ill that I thought I would die; but now I am better. Desmarest is coming, and I shall give him my letter to post in Paris, or I shall entrust it to the maître d'hôtel, who feels as I do the ill-will of the people here.

Now Mme de Graffigny poured out the story in dramatic detail. She started writing this letter on 19 January, and went on adding to it until her departure from Cirey some three weeks later, on 11 February.

> On 29 December supper went as usual, without much conversation, and I saw no advance warning of the storm which they were preparing for me. I withdrew to my room, to seal a letter. Half an hour later I was visited by you know who [Voltaire]. I was extremely surprised, for he never came to my room, but I was even more surprised when he said that he was lost, and that his life was in my hands. 'Well, my God, how can that be?' I said. 'Because', he said, 'there are a hundred copies of a canto of *Jeanne* which are circulating in Lunéville. I shall have to go for safety to Holland, or to the ends of the earth, I don't know where. You must write to Pan-Pan, so that he can help to have them withdrawn. Is he enough of an honest man to do it?' I said I was terribly sorry that such a thing should have happened while I was at Cirey. He got up in a great fury and said: 'No wriggling, Madame: it is you who sent it to him.'

I assured him that I had never seen a line of his verse, nor written any down. I was in despair. Voltaire insisted that you had given copies to everybody, and that Mme du Châtelet had the proof of this in her pocket. Finally he said: 'Come, come, just write to him and tell him to send back the original and the copies.' I started to write, but when he read the letter, his cries and shouts increased, he wept, he said he was lost, he said he could see that I did not wish to repair the damage that I had done. This scene lasted more than an hour, but it was nothing compared with what was to come.

For now the lady arrived like a fury, crying out loud and saying much the same as Voltaire. She pulled from her pocket one of your letters, and thrusting it almost into my face, she said: 'Here, here is the proof of your infamy. You are the most unworthy creature, a monster whom I received in my home, not out of friendship, but because you had nowhere to go. And now you have had the infamy to betray me, to assassinate me, to steal from my desk a manuscript in order to copy it.'

I replied only: 'Ah, madame, I am too unhappy for you to treat me so unjustly.' Then Voltaire took hold of her and pulled her away from me, for she was screaming all that in my face, and with such gestures that I expected her to hit me at any moment. She then walked up and down the room, crying out and making exclamations about my infamy.

For a long time I could not speak, but at last I asked them for your letter. They shouted that I would not get it. 'Well, at least show it to me', I said, 'so that I can see the evidence against me.' Well, it was that unfortunate phrase of yours 'The canto of *Jeanne* is charming'. Now I could see what had happened, and I explained it to them. Right away Voltaire believed me, and asked my pardon. This scene lasted until five in the morning. The old shrew would not give way. Voltaire spoke to her at length in English and implied to me that she was sorry for what she had said. But they made me write to you, to get you to send back my letter, in order to clear my name completely. All this time I never stopped trembling. I wrote the letter with extreme difficulty, I gave it to them and they left the room.

I was in a state of despair until midday: no home of my own, insulted in a house which I could not leave, not a penny to have myself taken to the nearest village, where I would sleep better on a bed of straw, and condemned to go on seeing such unworthy people.

That evening, around eight o'clock, the old shrew came to see me, with all her attendants, and after a brief bow, said in a dry tone: 'Madame, I am sorry for what happened last night', and then turned to Mme de Champbonin to talk of other things.

What you should have said, was: 'The *scheme* of *Jeanne* is charming', not 'the canto'. If you had wanted to recapitulate all our little secrets, you could not have done better. They also denounced me for what I had written about the plan for *Le Siècle de Louis XIV*, and for the extract from the *Life of Molière*, in fact for everything.

I have been in hell, always feeling ill, and only leaving my room at nine o'clock at night, when I could. The suppers were torture, no one said a word, and from time to time the old shrew threw a look of fury at me.

This went on, they kept it up, until we received that letter of mine, when you sent it back. I went downstairs, and right away she made a long apology, but still in the most acid tone. She said that her coldness came from her embarrassment at such a violent scene, but that if I was willing, life could return to normal. I answered, not what I felt, but what the circumstance required. I was calmer, because I thought, from their expressions, that they were not dissatisfied with my letter. They gave it me back a week later. I called in Mme de Champbonin, and I asked her if she wanted to see it. 'Certainly not', she said; so I threw it on to the fire in her presence.

Voltaire seems to have believed me completely. He wept more than once, seeing me so unwell, repeating over and over that he was really sad to be the cause of my miserable state. He often went so far as to say that Mme du Châtelet was a terrible woman, who had no flexibility in her heart, though her heart was good. Besides, he was always considerate to me, and he was made uncomfortable by her unfriendliness at table, he would speak to her in English to get her to behave differently. But he seems to have more shame than her, for he never admitted that she had been deliberately opening my letters; his embarrassment makes me think that he did not know that she was still doing it.

The irony of the situation was that Émilie's denunciation of Mme de Graffigny, for the alleged theft of a canto of *La Pucelle d'Orléans*, was in fact a fortuitous by-product of a surveillance operation which she had carried out with an entirely different object in mind. Three months earlier, in October 1738, Voltaire had released a pamphlet violently attacking his enemy the abbé Desfontaines, called *Le Préservatif*. It revealed, for the first time, that Desfontaines had once been imprisoned for sodomy and had been released partly through the efforts of Voltaire. Desfontaines was so enraged by this revelation that he counter-attacked with a vitriolic attack on Voltaire, entitled *Voltairomanie*. Émilie learned about *Voltairomanie* in the middle of December and expected that a copy of it would be sent to Cirey, but she was determined, if at all possible, to prevent Voltaire seeing it.

That was why she was secretly opening all the letters and packets reaching Cirey; and that is how she came to read the letter from Pan-Pan, in which he said that he had been charmed by the canto from *Jeanne*.[24] Émilie did not yet know that Voltaire had already received a copy of *Voltairomanie* and was drafting his own counter-attack. But she was still opening letters arriving at Cirey, and still full of intense anxiety that Voltaire might commit some imprudence.[25]

After a while Émilie started to become more friendly towards Mme de Graffigny.

> Yesterday and today, when we were expecting Desmarest, Mme du Châtelet and I went for a ride in a calèche, on the road by which he should come. She wanted to be alone with me, apparently to give me a better opinion of her. But she does not touch me. She had a bath yesterday, to prepare for Desmarest's arrival, which naturally led them to have their supper in the bathroom and light up this little apartment. In fact, they are like people who begin to realise how badly they have behaved and who are afraid that word of it will spread abroad. Yesterday, she went as far as to say that she would let me borrow one of the metaphysical works, provided I kept it a secret from Voltaire.[26]

When Desmarest at last arrived, on 1 February, Émilie and Voltaire started to put on a better show.

> I have hardly talked to him, because we spent all day in the room of Mme du Châtelet, who stayed in bed even though she was not ill. Today she sang to the accompaniment of the harpsichord, in a little while we shall play *Boursoufle* [by Voltaire], in which Desmarest will read a part. He has decided that we must leave on Ash Wednesday. Between now and then we shall perform *Zaïre* [by Voltaire], *L'Enfant prodigue* [by Voltaire], and *L'Esprit de Contradiction* [a comedy by Dufresny].[27]

The days passed with still more entertainments. 'We dined by candlelight today, and we shall soon have supper, at midnight. Our time is divided between music and rehearsals every day, with just time to learn our roles.'[28] The social life at Cirey was now becoming hectic:

We are performing *L'Enfant prodigue* today, and another play in three acts, for which we have still to rehearse. We rehearsed *Zaïre* until three o'clock this morning, and we shall perform it tomorrow with *Sérénade* [a comedy by Regnard]. We have to do our hair, fit our costumes or hear an opera sung. Yesterday evening, we added it up, and in the previous twenty-four hours we had either rehearsed or performed thirty-three acts, whether tragedy, opera or comedy. We have just come from the thirteenth act which we have performed today; after supper, Mme du Châtelet will sing an entire opera.[29]

On Monday 11 February, at midday, Émilie proposed that she and Mme de Graffigny should sing together, which they did for two hours. Then they sang an opera together; then Mme du Châtelet proposed taking Mme de Graffigny for a ride, from which they returned at four o'clock. They rehearsed *L'Enfant prodigue* until six o'clock, and then started singing again, two acts of an opera, until seven.

At nine o'clock, we started performing *L'Enfant prodigue*, followed by *Boursoufle*. We finished the play at one in the morning, and then we had supper. At half-past two everyone was falling asleep; but Mme du Châtelet proposed that I should accompany her singing two operas; which I did. In short, we sang two and a half operas, from beginning to end, until seven o'clock in the morning. She finally allowed me to go to bed, after we had both laughed immoderately at the absurdity of having spent the night singing operas.[30]

On Tuesday they performed *Zaïre*. Voltaire did not know his part and got very bad-tempered with his valet, either for prompting him too much or for not prompting him enough. 'Mme du Châtelet's performance was sickening, without any soul, all on the same tone, and reciting the verses line by line. And yet, despite all that, I have never wept so much at a tragedy.'

The most bizarre and poignant note, in the midst of all this frenzied acting and singing and laughing and talking, was that Émilie started to flirt openly with Desmarest. 'She was throwing all kinds of knowing glances at him, on the last evening without any restraint, as if she were a stupid young girl. Voltaire was furious, and rebuked both of them as much as he could.' Yet Émilie's flirtation with Desmarest does not seem to have spoiled Mme de Graffigny's enjoyment. 'Never in all my life have I spent days so pleasant as the last six at Cirey. The voluptuous disorder which reigns in this house makes it seem like an earthly paradise. What a lovely and charming life!'[31]

At eight o'clock in the morning of Ash Wednesday Mme de Graffigny and Desmarest set off from Cirey, and by Sunday they were in Paris. The duchesse de Richelieu renewed her offer to take her in, and though at first Mme de Graffigny recoiled, for fear of losing her freedom, in practice she could not afford to cold-shoulder someone as influential as Mme de Richelieu.

When Voltaire and Émilie went to Paris later that year (1739), they occasionally met Mme de Graffigny at social occasions, quite often at the home of Mme de Richelieu. Ostensibly Émilie and Mme de Graffigny went through the motions of well-bred friendship, and would apparently enjoy spending time together; in reality Mme de Graffigny never forgave Émilie for the humiliation she had endured at Cirey, and her comments about her, in letters to Pan-Pan, remained incurably waspish.

Thereafter Mme de Graffigny ceased to play any significant role in the life of Voltaire and Émilie. For several years she lived a precarious existence in Paris on the edge of the literary world. However, she struck gold, first in 1747 with a highly successful novel called *Lettres d'une péruvienne*, and then three years later with a successful comedy entitled *Cénie*. On the strength of these successes she became a celebrated figure, and the hostess of a noted literary salon. Voltaire, as was his habit, continued to keep in touch with her from time to time; in 1758, when her latest play had flopped, he wrote to console her. She died later that year, aged sixty-three.

What is most curious about Mme de Graffigny's visit is that Voltaire, in his letters, makes only one mention of her visit to Cirey, after she had been there for a month, and then only to say that hers was a sad situation which would make him weep; he does not say why, and he makes no mention of a monumental midnight row about the supposed filching of part of *La Pucelle*. Does this raise a question over Mme de Graffigny's credibility? Not really. She wrote her letters from day to day, on the spur of the moment, and the midnight drama came to her as a complete surprise; it is most unlikely that she made the whole thing up.[32]

The most plausible explanation is that virtually the only thing which concerned Voltaire or Émilie at the time was his feud with Desfontaines. Émilie was obviously in a state of extreme tension over *Voltairomanie* and how Voltaire might react to it – so extreme that she was even prepared to commit the ultimate solecism of opening visitors' letters. When she opened a letter which seemed to suggest, to her inflamed imagination, that Mme de Graffigny had copied one or more cantos of *La Pucelle d'Orléans*, she was already primed to explode, and explode she did.

Mme de Graffigny's account of life in the Cirey household throws a brilliant light both on the relationship between Voltaire and Émilie and on the frictions between them; and it seems to lie at the watershed between the years of happiness and the years of disintegration. The squabbles over whether Voltaire should have a glass of wine or change his jacket were obviously trivial in themselves. But the underlying thread in these petty incidents, as well as in Émilie's efforts to prevent Voltaire from working on *Le Siècle de Louis XIV*, is that there was an ongoing battle of wills between them, in which she was repeatedly trying to control him.

This battle seems to have reached a new intensity, first over *Voltairomanie* and Émilie's determination to stop at nothing to prevent Voltaire seeing it, and then in the midnight explosion over *La Pucelle d'Orléans*. These incidents were omens that all was really not well between Voltaire and Émilie, advance symptoms of a parting of the ways.

1 4

ÉMILIE'S COURT CASE

1739–1740

VOLTAIRE'S BATTLE WITH DESFONTAINES over *Le Préservatif* and *Voltairomanie* became a complete obsession in the early weeks of 1739: in the single month of January 1739 he wrote fifty-seven letters, of which thirty-eight were wholly or partly devoted to this quarrel. But what particularly upset Voltaire was the suspicion that his old friend Thieriot was betraying him in this quarrel and taking sides with Desfontaines, and that perhaps he had always taken sides with Desfontaines.

After his imprisonment in the Bicêtre prison for sodomy in 1724, and his rescue by Voltaire and others, Desfontaines had drafted a vicious denunciation of Voltaire. This pamphlet was never published, because Thieriot had persuaded him to throw it in the fire. But why had Desfontaines shown Thieriot the draft of a pamphlet attacking Voltaire; had Thieriot been complicit in the drafting of it?[1] It is possible that Thieriot may have been gay, and thus may have had a special but unavowed relationship with Desfontaines, though Voltaire never mentions the idea in his letters. But if Thieriot was a friend of Desfontaines, Voltaire was now afraid that Thieriot might, as Frederick's literary agent in Paris, use his position to enlist Frederick's support in favour of Desfontaines, at Voltaire's expense. Sure enough, Thieriot did send Frederick a copy of *Voltairomanie*.[2]

In early February Voltaire was set on bringing a court case against Desfontaines, until d'Argental persuaded him to desist.[3] Desfontaines was determined to escalate the dispute, however, as Voltaire told d'Argental. 'Desfontaines has got in first, and has obtained permission to denounce me as the author of the *Lettres philosophiques*. I have dropped my own court case, as you instructed, but now I am afraid of being brought to court by the very villain who is persecuting me.'[4] Voltaire now appealed directly to René Hérault, the chief of police, and he deluged him with documents supporting his side of the argument.[5] It seems like a re-run of Voltaire's public dispute with Jore three years earlier, and with a similar dénouement: Hérault decided to stop the quarrel by bringing pressure on both men to disown their contentious pamphlets. In early April Desfontaines agreed to do so; Voltaire held out for another three weeks.[6]

If Voltaire finally conceded a draw in his battle with Desfontaines, it was partly because Émilie had decided to take up a long-running dispute over the inheritance of the family properties at Ham and Beringhem, not far from Liège. To do that, she had to take the issue to court in Brussels, and she believed that she could press her claim most effectively if she went there in person. She planned to leave for Brussels in early May 1739.

Just why Émilie had decided to involve herself in an old inheritance dispute which had been rumbling on for at least sixty years remains unclear. One theory is that she had set her sights on a splendid house in Paris which was up for sale, and she thought that a victory in the Brussels court case would help her raise the money. The house in question was the Hôtel Lambert, on the quai d'Anjou on the Île Saint Louis. It had been built in 1642 by the distinguished architect Le Vau for Jean-Baptiste Lambert; in 1732 Lambert's heir, Jean-Baptiste Lambert de Thorigny, had sold it to Claude Dupin, a chief tax inspector (*receveur des finances*). Now Dupin was looking for a buyer.

Voltaire first mentioned the idea of buying the Hôtel Lambert in October 1738: 'I am not really keen on the Palais Lambert, for it is in Paris. If Mme du Châtelet wants to buy it, it will cost her less than you think. But it is all the same to me. I do not think that this purchase will upset her finances too much.'[7] Émilie, by contrast, was really eager, as she told d'Argental in the New Year: 'M. du Châtelet will go to Paris around 15 January, and I hope he will conclude the business of the house of the late Président Lambert, which I really want to buy: it seems to me a fine and worthy morsel to place in my estate, and it would be very agreeable to be able to look forward to passing part of my life near you.'[8]

By April the marquis had indeed bought the Hôtel Lambert, as Voltaire told Frederick:

It seems that when we return from the Low Countries we shall think of settling in Paris. Mme du Châtelet has just bought a house built by one of the greatest architects of France; it is a house made for a sovereign and a philosopher. Fortunately, it is in a part of town which is far from everybody (*éloigné de tout*); that is why we got it for 200,000 francs, when it cost 2 million to build and decorate.[9]

Some scholars find it difficult to believe that M. du Châtelet could have bought this very distinguished *hôtel particulier* for as little as £200,000. In fact, it appears that when Claude Dupin bought the house from the Lambert family, he paid as little as £140,000 for it; and though Voltaire says that Mme du Châtelet paid £200,000, one source claims that she only paid £180,000.[10] Considering the expense originally lavished on the house, these prices imply either that it was in a very dilapidated state or else that the address was simply too unfashionable. Voltaire says that it was 'far from everybody'; today the Île Saint Louis is immensely chic, but in those days it was much further east than the most fashionable neighbourhoods, such as around the Palais Royal.

In fact, Voltaire and Émilie never really lived in the Hôtel Lambert. For the first three years it remained empty; perhaps Émilie did not have the money to do it up and was hoping that her Brussels court case would provide it. According to one account, Émilie and Voltaire did briefly move in, in the summer of 1742; but if so, it must have been very brief, for Voltaire does not mention it. Two years later Émilie rented it out, and a year after that she sold it again.[11]

In short, the Hôtel Lambert was a phantom home, which came and went, leaving no trace in their lives. In the meantime, whenever Émilie and Voltaire visited Paris in the next few years, they would stay in other people's houses, or she might stay with the duc and duchesse de Richelieu while Voltaire would stay in a hotel or take rented rooms.

The personal implications for Voltaire and Émilie, both of her decision to buy the Hôtel Lambert and of her decision to fight a court case in Brussels, were similar and far from phantom: the idyll of Cirey was over, she was tiring of her secluded life in the country, alone with Voltaire, and she wanted to return to the bright lights. In May 1735 she had told Richelieu that the country was the only place for people in love and that she did not want to live in Paris, for fear of losing Voltaire. Four years later these arguments no longer applied.

Émilie's court case kept dragging them to the Low Countries for prolonged periods during the next three years. In the spring of 1739 they

161

went to Brussels and stayed there for three months; but from Brussels they went not to Cirey but to Paris. At the end of the year they went back to Brussels for a new stage of the court case and stayed there for much of 1740. At the beginning of 1741 they were once more in Brussels, and they stayed in the Low Countries until September. During their periods of servitude to the processes of the court case, they lived a very social life in Brussels; during periods of remission they sometimes returned to the calm of Cirey, but more frequently they would hurry to the even more hectic social round in Paris. This frenetic ricocheting between Brussels, Cirey and Paris ended only in 1742, when Émilie finally accepted that she had lost her court case. If Voltaire and Émilie did briefly move into the Hôtel Lambert in 1742, this might have been a final, once-off fling, before selling the house again.

Voltaire almost always accompanied Émilie on her legal pilgrimages, and when he was in Brussels, he tried to work, though he found it difficult without his library. In May 1739, as they prepared to set off for Brussels for the first time, Voltaire gathered some books to take with him, including a couple in Greek. He told Thieriot: 'The Demosthenes has arrived, and I shall take it with me, even if I can scarcely understand it. I read Euclid more easily, because it is mainly in the present tense or in participles, and in any case the sense of the argument is always in unanswerable axioms.'[12] Voltaire could still not read literary Greek with any ease, but after his long apprenticeship with Newton he had become competent enough in mathematics to understand Euclid, even in the original.

From Brussels they went to look at the disputed properties, and Voltaire's first impressions were not favourable. 'Here we are in a barbarous country,' he wrote to Mme de Champbonin.

> If Mme du Châtelet stays here long, she will be able to call herself the queen of the savages. Tomorrow we are going to the superb château of Ham, where we are not sure of finding any beds, nor even any doors or windows. They say that there is a gang of thieves round about here; but in that case, they must be thieves in a state of penitence, since there is nobody worth stealing from but us.
>
> P.S. We have just come back from the château of Ham. It is less ornamental than Cirey, and there are fewer baths or rooms decorated in blue and gold; but it is habitable and it has some fine avenues. Mme du Châtelet is working really hard on her case; and if success depends on wit and work, she will be very rich. Unfortunately it all depends on other people, who do not have as much wit as she does.[13]

By August Voltaire was already tiring of his new shuttlecock life. 'My dear fat cat (*gros chat*)', he complained to Mme de Champbonin,

> here we are at Cambrai, travelling by slow stages. If you ask me why we are going to Paris, I can only speak for myself: I am going there, because I am going with Émilie. But why is Émilie going there? I do not really know. She claims that it is necessary, and I am bound to believe her and to follow her. We still hope to see Cirey again before we take up residence in the Palace at the tip of the island [Île Saint Louis]; but it will be a long time before we see Cirey and Champbonin again, alas! We have bought some furniture in Brussels, and it feels like the flight from Babylon. I have not much enjoyed my stay in that country; I ruined myself in expenditure; and to cap it all, the customs seized some pictures which I had bought.[14]

It seems that the customs officers had confiscated Voltaire's pictures at the frontier because he had declared their value far below their true worth.

In Paris he complained again to Mme de Champbonin that nothing seemed to arrest the hectic social life he was forced to lead.

> My dear friend, Paris is a deep chasm, in which one loses all rest and contemplation. I do not live: I am carried, dragged, far from home, as in a whirlwind. I come, and I go; I have supper one day at one end of the town, only to have supper at the other end on the next. We have to fly to the Opéra, then to the Comédie, we have to go and see sights as if we were tourists, we embrace a hundred people in a single day, we make and accept a hundred appointments, without a moment to ourselves, without any time to write, to think or even to sleep. From this continual tempest, from this round of visits, from this deafening chaos, we shall probably leave at the beginning of October, to plead our sad case [in Brussels], after having been bounced around here quite gaily, but too violently.[15]

Voltaire and Émilie left Paris a few weeks later, in November 1739, but even before they reached Brussels he was once more in trouble with the French authorities. After many years of work, he had made so much progress on his history of *The Century of Louis XIV* (*Le Siècle de Louis XIV*) that he now felt able to publish a reasoned outline, together with the first two chapters. The work was immediately seized by the authorities, and on 4 December 1739 it was condemned by the Paris *parlement* to be burned by the public executioner. Voltaire's history was written in praise of the reign of Louis XIV, so it was automatically assumed at Versailles to imply a disparaging judgement of the reign of Louis XV.

In 1739 Voltaire reverted to his enthusiasm for classical verse tragedy. His last effort in this genre, *Alzire*, had been put on with great success at the beginning of 1736, and it long remained one of the most popular works in the repertoire of the Comédie Française. In his new tragedy, which he called *Zulime*, Voltaire tried to repeat the recipe: an exotic location, but this time a Muslim country of North Africa, and a tale of fathers and daughters, of lovers and husbands, of cultural conflict and divided loyalties, and above all of romantic love, licit and illicit, culminating in murder and suicide.

Voltaire made it quite clear, in a letter to d'Argental on 6 January 1739, that he was making a deliberate choice in favour of literature and against science. 'I am making a tragedy, and you are the only one who knows. I do not answer for how it will go, but I have an excessive desire to make you weep. I shall write some verses; farewell Euclid, for three months, farewell physics, welcome to tender feelings and to harmonious verses.'[16]

Voltaire's work on *Zulime* followed a pattern which he was to repeat many times: he dashed off a first draft at almost unbelievable speed and then spent many months revising and rewriting it in the light of criticisms and advice from friends, mainly from d'Argental. By 26 January he had finished the tragedy in draft form, but he soon admitted that he had perhaps written it too fast. 'The extraordinary, and perhaps misguided, effort which I made to compose it in eight days, I owe to your recommendation that I should write something really interesting. Tell me what you think, and I shall correct in eight weeks the errors I committed in eight days.'[17] By the autumn, however, Voltaire admitted that *Zulime* was 'really rather feeble; I have gone cold on this work, and almost lost any idea how it should go.'[18] It was eventually put on at the Comédie Française, on 9 June 1740, but the public did not like it, and a week later Voltaire denied that *Zulime* was anything to do with him. 'The play which you mention, is by one of my friends; I helped him slightly with it. It is quite untrue that it is by me, and I hope you will say so to others.'[19]

This staging of *Zulime* was doubly unfortunate for Voltaire, for it provoked a rift between him and the duc de Richelieu. At the time Richelieu's wife was seriously ill, probably with tuberculosis, and Richelieu felt that it was unfriendly of Voltaire to have put on his play at such a gruelling time. '*Zulime*, my respectable friend,' Voltaire told d'Argental,

> has been destined to bring me great sorrow. You know that Mme de Richelieu is on her death-bed, perhaps she has already died as I write. You are aware how much I shall miss her, I counted on her kindness, and I dare to say that I count on the friendship of M. le duc de Richelieu. But I have learned that M. de Richelieu is very angry with me for having allowed *Zulime* to be put on in such cruel circumstances. I have done everything humanly possible to have it withdrawn. Perhaps you are in a position to persuade M. de Richelieu of my innocence. It is very hard to be thought insensitive, when in fact one's heart is bleeding.[20]

Mme de Richelieu died five weeks later, on 2 August 1740.

Meanwhile Émilie was still pressing on with her scientific studies, most notably by completing and publishing in 1740 her first major scientific work, which she called *Les Institutions de physique*. She pretended that this was just a semi-private venture, intended for the education of her son; in fact it was a serious attempt to survey the whole of the state of knowledge of physics at the time, an extraordinarily demanding undertaking in itself, not least for a woman trying to break into a field dominated by men.

To help her in this daunting task she relied heavily on a series of leading intellectuals in the field, starting with Maupertuis, but then going on to Jean Bernoulli, a prominent mathematician from Switzerland, who was also a friend of Maupertuis, and then to Johann Samuel Kœnig, a young mathematician from Germany who had been a pupil of Bernoulli. Kœnig was a feisty and aggressive young man; he gave Émilie a great deal of detailed help in the writing of *Les Institutions de physique*, but he managed to quarrel violently with her, and he even put about the wholly unfounded claim that it was he who had written her book.[21] Several years later, in Berlin, he quarrelled even more spectacularly with Maupertuis, with explosive consequences for Voltaire.

The divergence in the intellectual interests of Voltaire and Émilie was a growing source of friction between them, and both of them began to look elsewhere for personal warmth, reassurance and consolation. When Voltaire started to flirt, increasingly seriously, with Frederick of Prussia, Émilie looked back, once again, to her former love affair with the duc de Richelieu.

Voltaire's correspondence with Frederick of Prussia, which had started in September 1736, in response to Frederick's first letter to him, continued erratically for the next three years, at a rate of about one letter a month. Most of Voltaire's letters to Frederick ring the changes on various forms of sycophancy; yet he was not a natural courtier, and his true thoughts kept poking through the smarmy surface.

In October 1737 he assured Frederick of his adulation:

> You are like the God of Abraham: to see you face to face is a happiness which is not given to us. And you have done the French language the honour of knowing it so well; though there are always a few small commas, a few dots on the 'i's, which need inserting, but I shall take care, if you approve, of those small details.[22]

In January 1738 Voltaire flattered Frederick for his superb command of French, but then delicately pointed out a handful of spelling errors which demonstrated that Frederick's knowledge of French was in fact quite crude: *ause* for *ose*, *tres* for *traits*, *matein* for *matin*. Voltaire could not quite contain his patronising contempt for such barbarisms: 'These comments are of a kind that you might hear even from the doorman at the Académie Française; but then I have no others to make.'[23] A week later Voltaire was ecstatic, but also offensively condescending, over an ode which Frederick had written and then revised: 'Now for the ode. It is infinitely superior to what it was before, and I could not get over my surprise that anyone should have been able to write odes so well in the depths of Germany.' Voltaire concluded this letter with a few more points about the defects in Frederick's French grammar.[24]

On philosophical subjects too Voltaire could not help correcting Frederick's views. In March 1738 he expressed his deep gratitude for Frederick's opinions on fate and free will, but he nevertheless felt obliged to add a few philosophical scruples about these opinions, which continued for four more pages.[25]

More intriguing are those letters to Frederick in which Voltaire grappled, sometimes obliquely, with political issues. In the course of his researches for *Le Siècle de Louis XIV* Voltaire had become increasingly taken with the idea of the great enlightened statesman who could be counted on to do good things for his country. Louis XIV was, of course, the supreme example of such a statesman: 'What king has rendered more services to humanity than Louis XIV? He did not do everything he could have done, because he was only a man, but he did more than any other, because he was a great man.'[26]

Voltaire also became interested in Peter the Great, on the grounds that he too was a great and enlightened man, who had done great things for Russia. 'Your Royal Highness', he wrote, in April 1737, 'does me the honour to tell me in your last letter, that you regard the late czar as the greatest man of the last century, and that your admiration for him does not blind you to his cruelties. We can admire the king, even if we cannot like the man.'[27] Voltaire knew rather little about Russian history, and when Frederick sent him some historical memoirs to fill in the gaps, Voltaire felt obliged to make excuses for Peter: 'I accept that he was a barbarian; but after all, he was a barbarian who had done good to men; he founded cities, he built canals, he taught the people about naval affairs, and he even introduced society to an unsociable people.'[28] After some more reading Voltaire became convinced that Peter's record was much blacker:

> What Your Royal Highness has told me about czar Peter, completely changes my ideas. Is it possible that one man could combine such horrors, with reforms which would have honoured Alexander? What, to be the governor of these people and yet also murder them? To be a public executioner, an abominable executioner, and at the same time a legislator? Oh Prince, who honours the human race by your heart and by your spirit, please deign to explain this conundrum.[29]

Voltaire never lost his interest in the Russia of Peter the Great, and many years later he would write a book about it. But this was the last time he mentioned the subject to Frederick: perhaps he sensed that, on political questions, Frederick and he might be on dangerously different sides of the fence.

Frederick was not interested in Voltaire's political views, though he obviously thought that Voltaire could be useful to him in a subordinate editorial role, and he now recruited him to supervise the publication of a political pamphlet, which he called *L'Anti-Machiavel* (*The Anti-Machiavelli*). The thesis of this work was that Machiavelli's view of politics was far too cynical: instead, Frederick argued for a benevolent ideal of rational statesmanship, in which the king has a duty to maintain the health and prosperity of his subjects. It is not clear whether Frederick genuinely believed in his liberal thesis, for he seemed ambivalent about the book. He was determined that it could not appear under his name, and at the last minute, just as Voltaire had got the text ready for publication, he demanded that it be taken off the market. Voltaire made further editorial changes, and in the end it was salvaged. When it was published, shortly after Frederick became king, it became a best-seller; though this version contained so much material introduced by Voltaire that Frederick claimed not to recognise it.

For Émilie, Voltaire's dealings with Frederick of Prussia were freighted with threats and dangers. She knew that Frederick was trying to lure Voltaire away from her to Berlin, as an ornament to his 'enlightened' court; she feared that Frederick, as a representative of a foreign power, might succeed in getting Voltaire into all sorts of dangerous deep waters; above all she feared that she and Frederick were engaged in a struggle for possession of Voltaire, and that she might lose.

In the summer of 1740 her anxieties became more acute. During the previous three years Voltaire and Frederick had exchanged letters at a moderately sedate rhythm: Voltaire wrote twelve letters to Frederick in 1737, fifteen in 1738, and sixteen in 1739. But after 31 May 1740, when his father, King Frederick William, died, and Frederick, now aged twenty-eight, ascended the throne of Prussia as Frederick II, their correspondence accelerated: Voltaire wrote to Frederick five times in July 1740 and seven times in October, with a total of twenty-eight letters in the last seven months of the year.

In June Voltaire was already boasting of his familiarity with Frederick: 'Hardly had he ascended the throne, than he thought of writing me the most friendly letter, in which he ordered me always to write to him as a man, and never as a king.'[30] It was no accident that it was to René-Louis d'Argenson that he passed on this piece of testimony, for d'Argenson was not just an old schoolfriend: he was also an influential figure at the French court and a future Foreign Minister of France. It was obviously risky for a French subject to be in direct correspondence with a foreign king, and since Frederick was constantly urging Voltaire to visit him in Berlin, it was essential that he keep his lines clear with the French authorities.

Émilie did her best to ingratiate herself with Frederick by sending him her *Institutions de physique*; but Frederick was not prepared to make any concession to *la divine Émilie*. He openly sneered to Voltaire about her book: 'When I read your *Métaphysique* [Voltaire's new preface to his *Les Éléments de Newton*], I cry out, I admire it, and truly believe. But when I read *Les Institutions de physique* of the marquise, I do not know if I have been deceived or if I am deceiving myself.'[31]

On 10 July Voltaire offered to visit Frederick, but in company with Émilie:

I have heard that you were due to visit France. If that were so, we could receive Your Humanity (as one says) at Cirey on your way home. But if circumstances were to prevent your journey, could Mme du Châtelet accompany me to Clèves? You will understand that Mme du Châtelet would come with her husband, but if that should cause the slightest problem, do not hesitate to say so.[32]

Frederick did not care for the idea. At the end of July he sent Voltaire a long letter of seduction, concluding with a poem which ended in an unmistakable sexual innuendo: 'I shall kiss a hundred times that mouth, so eloquent in seriousness and fun, whose touching voice covers the range from tragedy to comedy, always enchanting and always more charming.'[33] It sounds as if Frederick was making an overtly homosexual overture to Voltaire; but was Frederick really homosexual? It is sometimes claimed that Frederick's supposed homosexuality was just a malicious canard, deliberately spread about by Voltaire to discredit Frederick. On the other hand, it seems clear that Frederick was in some sense gay, and that women were not welcome at his court. On 5 August he coldly ruled out any visit by Émilie. 'To speak frankly on the subject of her travels, it is Voltaire, it is you, it is my friend, whom I desire to see; and the divine Émilie, with all her divinity, is only an accessory to the Apollo of Newtonianism.'[34]

For several more weeks Voltaire and Frederick continued their negotiations about the supposed visit of Frederick. 'Sire: my king is at Clèves: a small house awaits him in Brussels, and a palace which is almost worthy of him in Paris [presumably, the Hôtel Lambert], while I await my master here.'[35] For Voltaire to describe Frederick, a foreign king, as 'my king' and as 'my master' was reckless and possibly treasonable; a Frenchman could have only one king and one master, and that was Louis XV.

Within a few days Frederick fell ill with a high temperature, and he gave up any plan to visit Brussels. 'My dear Voltaire, I must submit to my fever; however much I may desire to visit Antwerp and Brussels, I am not in a state to undertake the journey. Please make my excuses to the marquise. Next Sunday, however, I shall be at a little place near Clèves, where I can have you completely at my ease.'[36]

Voltaire did not wait to be asked twice, and on the following Sunday, 11 September 1740, he duly presented himself at the Château de Moyland near Clèves, where he spent the next four days in close company with Frederick. It was many years later, in the *Mémoires* which he wrote in 1759, that Voltaire described this first meeting with Frederick.

I was led into the apartment of His Majesty. There were only four bare walls. I saw in a cupboard, in the light of a candle, a little truckle-bed barely two and a half feet wide, on which there was a small man wearing a dressing gown of thick blue cloth: it was the king, and he was sweating and trembling under a nasty blanket, in a violent fever. I made my bow, and began my acquaintance with him, by taking his pulse, as if I were his chief doctor. The crisis passed, he dressed and sat down at the table. Algarotti,* Maupertuis, and the king's minister, and I, were all at supper, and we spoke deeply about the immortality of the soul, about freedom and about the androgynous figures in Plato.[37]

Voltaire was obviously thrilled by this meeting, as he made clear to d'Argental:

We are just about to leave. M. de Maupertuis is going with the king to Berlin. He, M. Algarotti and I, unworthy, have passed three charming days with a king who thinks like a man, who lives like an ordinary citizen and who forgets entirely his Majesty, for the sake of the gentle pleasures of friendship. He lacks only one thing to be perfect. I am tired of so much pleasure, and I shall go back to Brussels via Holland.[38]

Voltaire does not specify Frederick's one defect. Was it his homosexuality? It is not clear. And yet there was obviously a level of intensity and excitement in his relationship with Frederick, especially after his visit to Moyland, which generated considerable emotional tension between him and Émilie, amounting to something close to sexual jealousy. For when Voltaire left Clèves, despite what he told d'Argental, he did not go home to Émilie in Brussels but went directly to The Hague, in order to pursue the editing and publication of the revised text of Frederick's *Anti-Machiavel*, and he stayed there for several more weeks, until early November.

In late September Émilie had learned that her mother had fallen ill, and she hurried to Paris to be at her bedside. In fact, her mother was dying; but after she died, Émilie did not return immediately to Brussels but went on to Fontainebleau, where the French court was in session.

---

* Francesco Algarotti was a young intellectual from Venice who had visited Cirey, and who had written a popularisation of Newton, entitled *Newtonism for the Ladies (Il Neutonianismo per le dame)*. He was gay, and was ecstatically at home at Frederick's court.

Émilie spent several weeks at Fontainebleau, where she did her best to see if she could bring about some kind of reconciliation between Voltaire and the French court. In this she seems to have been rather successful, or so she told Voltaire. He was still in The Hague, and he immediately wrote a letter of thanks to Cardinal André-Hercule de Fleury, Louis XV's chief minister. 'I learn with the greatest gratitude the renewal of your kindness for me. I have always been most tenderly attached to Your Eminence.'[39]

By now, however, events in the outside world were starting to move very fast, with the death of Charles VI, the Austrian emperor, and the threat of another European war looming on the horizon. Charles had two daughters, but no male heir. According to received law and precedent, he could not be succeeded by a woman; but he believed he had got round this problem, many years earlier, by negotiating an international agreement, known as the Pragmatic Sanction, which would allow Maria Theresa, his eldest daughter, to inherit the Habsburg titles and her husband to become emperor. But when Charles died, on 20 October 1740, it turned out that this agreement did not after all command sufficient international assent. The Elector of Saxony and the Elector of Bavaria both claimed the succession for themselves; but the most serious objection came from King Frederick, ostensibly on the grounds that the Pragmatic Sanction had been negotiated long before he came to the throne, in reality because he did not accept the status quo in Europe and was determined to carve out a bigger place in Europe for Prussia.

The succession to the Austrian throne was now in doubt, and Europe was poised for the question to be settled by force; and it was Frederick who started the process, later that year, when he was ready.

Moreover, Voltaire now started to complain, to Frederick no less, about the burden of Émilie's possessiveness.

I shall soon absolutely have to return to Brussels [from The Hague] for Mme du Châtelet's court case, and thus to leave Marcus Aurelius for chicanery; but what man, Sire, is master of his actions? Have you not also an immense burden to bear, which often prevents you from satisfying your preferences, in order to fulfil your sacred duties?[40]

In November Voltaire thought he would visit Frederick in Berlin, and he wrote to Cardinal Fleury to tell him so. 'I cannot resist the repeated orders of His Majesty, the King of Prussia. I am going, for a few days, to pay my court to a monarch who takes as his model your manner of thinking. I flatter myself that Your Eminence will approve my zeal.'[41] The cardinal, now eighty-seven years old, duly agreed: 'I can only approve the journey that you are going to make. I did not know that the *Anti-Machiavel*, which Mme du Châtelet gave me, came from you. Whoever is the author of this work, if he is not a prince, he should be.'[42]

Voltaire did not wait for permission. By the time Fleury wrote his letter, Voltaire was already on his way from The Hague to Berlin. And it is symptomatic of the deterioration in the relationship between him and Émilie that he did not consult her as to whether she approved of his going; he simply went. His journey took him almost a fortnight; he arrived in Berlin on 19 November; and he stayed there for twelve days.

Émilie was still in Paris, and she responded to this fait accompli by writing a letter of deep bitterness to Richelieu.

I have been cruelly paid back for everything which I did for M. de Voltaire at Fontainebleau. I brought the most difficult issues to a decent settlement, I secured for him an honourable right of return to his own country [i.e., Paris], I restored him to the favour of the Ministry, I opened for him the way into the Académie, in short I gave him back in three weeks everything that he had done his best to lose in the previous six years. Do you know how he paid me back for so much effort and so much faith? By leaving for Berlin: he sent me the news in the driest way, knowing that it would pierce my heart, and he abandoned me to a pain which has no equal, which others cannot conceive of, and which only your heart can understand.[43]

Voltaire tells us virtually nothing of how he passed the time during his stay in Berlin. Towards the end of November, however, he told Frederick that he must return to Émilie, on the grounds that she was ill (even though she was in fact in perfectly good health, as Frederick suspected). Voltaire set off on 1 December, but before leaving Berlin, he wrote Frederick a slightly nauseating farewell note, partly in verse, in which he complained of the burdens of his duty towards Émilie. 'I leave you, it is true; but my broken heart will always fly again to you. For the past four years you have been my mistress, but a love which goes back ten years must take precedence; I am fulfilling a sacred duty. Yes, I am going to the knees of an adored object, but I am leaving behind what I really love.'[44] It is hard to imagine what meaning Voltaire thought he was attaching to the word 'mistress'; in a letter to Maupertuis, written on the same day, he described Frederick as a harlot (*putain*), and in a letter to Frederick himself, written only a few days later, he quite explicitly distanced himself from the 'Grecian' (i.e., homosexual) *mœurs* prevalent at Frederick's court.[45]

He dawdled on the way back to Brussels, visiting friends and acquaintances on the way, and took a month to arrive back in Brussels at the beginning of January 1741. On the way he wrote to Frederick, to complain once again of the weight of his duty to Émilie: 'My soul is not consumed by some silly love, and I have not left your adorable court just to sigh like a fool at the knees of a woman. Love is often ridiculous, but pure friendship has rights greater than those of the orders of kings. That is my pain and my conscience.'[46] Voltaire seems to be telling Frederick that he no longer loves Émilie.

When Émilie complained to his friends of his over-long absence, Voltaire became quite defensive. He told d'Argental: 'She was at Fontainebleau, she had to spend some time in Paris, and if it had not been for various mishaps on my return journey, flooded rivers and contrary winds, I should have been back in Brussels before her.'[47] But the story he told to another friend a few weeks later was closer to the truth: 'As soon as I heard that she was back in Brussels, I immediately took my leave of the king of Prussia.'[48]

It is perhaps not surprising that Émilie should have looked for consolation with Richelieu. She clearly had an unresolved relationship with him, an affair which had turned to friendship, but without quite leaving love behind. After their intense emotional encounter, in late 1735, she did not write to him for three years. Then, out of the blue, in 1738 or 1739 she wrote him a letter which was almost a new declaration of love.

I do not know a problem which is more difficult to solve than you. However that may be, I have made up my mind to love you, and to tell you so. I do not know what good my virtuous behaviour will do me, since I am just as much deprived of your company. You write to me as though I were your enemy; but I still prefer your letters, however strange they may be, to your silence. Will you always be in Toulouse? [Richelieu was currently governor of the Languedoc.] Farewell. M. de Voltaire is with me [i.e., in the room with her]. It is more than three years since I mentioned your name to him. He does not know that I am writing to you. Farewell.[49]

By telling Richelieu that she had not mentioned his name to Voltaire for more than three years, she clearly meant him to understand that this letter was an important emotional overture. Did she mean it to be just a reconciliation after several years of silence, or did she mean much more?

For the next eighteen months she left the question hanging in the air. But in the autumn of 1740 she went on a visit to Fontainebleau (but without Voltaire, for he was in The Hague), and there she saw Richelieu again; and they seem to have had another emotional encounter, which went well beyond a simple reconciliation between friends. It was not until late December, however, that she finally put her feelings in writing to him.

> Your friendship is the only consolation which remains to me. I do not know why I admitted what I said to you at Fontainebleau. I said it because it is true, and because I feel I owe you an accounting of all that my heart feels. It is this same certainty which makes me tell you, without fear and without remorse, all the movements of my heart for you. No doubt, the feeling I have for you must be incomprehensible to anyone else, but it takes nothing away from the frenzied passion which now gives me such pain.[50]

In some ways this emotional scene between Émilie and Richelieu, in Fontainebleau in the autumn of 1740, was a re-run of their encounter five years earlier, at Cirey, in December 1735. On both occasions there seems to have been an uncontrolled swelling up of Émilie's feelings of love for Richelieu, feelings which in principle she had already twice renounced. This time, however, there was one telling difference: she did not tell him afterwards that she was sorry for what she had said.

On 13 December 1740, while Voltaire was on his way home, Frederick invaded Silesia, at the time part of the Austrian domain, and thus started what became known as the War of the Austrian Succession. Voltaire was appalled to discover that his enlightened idol was in fact another wager of wars. 'If I flew to the empire [of Frederick], it was to the soft sound of his lyre; but the trumpets of war have driven me away. You have opened, with a bold hand, the horrible temple of Janus [i.e., war]; I return in great confusion to the chapel of Émilie.'[51]

But the chapel of Émilie was no longer what it had been. Their love affair had entered a period of stress and alienation, and while there were no doubt many contributory factors, the most immediate was Voltaire's infatuation with Frederick. He pursued this flirtation for at least another ten years, apparently oblivious to the underlying realities and the consequences for his love affair with Émilie.

15

MISSION TO POTSDAM

1741–1743

BY THE END OF 1740 Voltaire and Émilie were increasingly at odds
with one another, divergent in their interests and pulling in different
directions. To the outside world this divergence may not have been
immediately apparent. They continued to live together (at least most
of the time), they travelled together and they remained in some sense
an iconic example of a celebrity couple. But in fact their love affair
was deteriorating, and in the years from 1741 to 1743 the process is
unmistakable.

It was Voltaire who tired of Émilie, not she of him. We need not
draw any far-reaching conclusions from the fact that, towards the end
of 1740, he was complaining to Frederick of the burden of Émilie's
demands. She obviously was a very demanding woman, and she insistently tried to stop him doing things he wanted to do. But something
more must have happened in the next six months which caused Voltaire
to go cold on Émilie.

What this was we do not know for sure, but it seems entirely possible that it was in the spring of 1741 that Voltaire started to lust after his
29-year-old niece Marie-Louise, the wife of Nicolas-Charles Denis. This
is not the conventional wisdom, at least in terms of timing. We know
that Marie-Louise became Voltaire's mistress in or about 1745, and most
scholars tend to believe that Voltaire first made sexual overtures to her
in 1744, after the death of her husband. Yet if he was starting to tire of
Émilie towards the end of 1740, it could well be because he was starting to
find Marie-Louise very attractive long before the death of her husband.

That is speculation. What is fact is that, in the middle of 1741, he told one of his closest friends, with sadness and regret, that his love for Émilie had turned to friendship. Evidently, he had crossed some kind of watershed, and perhaps that watershed was called Mme Denis.

Voltaire's turning away from Émilie was a source of great and lasting grief to her. Despite their divergence, it is clear that she clung to the idea of their love for at least another four years, when she wrote a long and moving lament, under the brave but misleading title Discourse on Happiness (*Discours sur le bonheur*).

Voltaire was at this time working on a new tragedy called *Mahomet* or, to give its complete title, *Le Fanatisme ou Mahomet le Prophète* (Fanaticism, or Mahomet the Prophet). This was another tangled tale, in an exotic location, of mistaken identities, illicit love, the discovery of long-lost fathers and children, and all culminating in murder and suicide. What made this story especially controversial was Voltaire's depiction of Mahomet, the founder of Islam, as an impostor and a fanatic: not merely was he the prophet of a new religion which he knew to be wholly false, but his purpose was to enslave the Arabs and conquer the world.

Voltaire had hoped that *Mahomet* would have its first performance at the Comédie Française, with the help of Jeanne-Françoise Quinault, one of the most influential actors in the company. But in 1741 he learned that she was unwell, and he realised that the staging of his tragedy at the Comédie Française might be at risk.[1]

By coincidence, Voltaire was in contact at this time with an energetic actor-manager called Jean-Baptiste La Noue, who was, among other things, the main moving spirit of the theatre in Lille. In the summer of 1740, after succeeding to the Prussian throne, Frederick had started actively seeking to attract all kinds of talent to his court, including theatre talent, and Voltaire suggested to La Noue that he might be able to get a valuable position in Potsdam. In October Frederick agreed to invite La Noue and his company to Berlin, but both sides started by making unrealistic demands: Frederick wanted a binding contract for five years, La Noue a down payment of 40,000 écus, and soon the negotiations were deadlocked.

The impasse turned to Voltaire's advantage. By now he saw that Mlle Quinault would probably be too ill to supervise the production of *Mahomet* in Paris, and he thought that La Noue could provide an alternative. In January 1741 he and Émilie went to Lille to see an opera, as well as the performance of a play written by La Noue; but his real objective was to sound out the possibility of La Noue staging *Mahomet* in Lille. In March he went back to Lille once more, to meet La Noue and to read through with him the text of *Mahomet*. By the end of the month he learned not just that Mlle Quinault was still unwell but also that she had decided, in protest at their working conditions, to leave the company. He sent her a letter of regret, but in fact he had already arranged for the play to be put on in Lille, and it was performed there in April 1741.[2]

Cumulatively, then, Voltaire went to Lille three times in the early months of 1741. On the first and third of these occasions he went with Émilie; on the second he may have gone alone. On each occasion, no doubt, he spent several days there, and on each occasion no doubt he (and Émilie) stayed at the home of M. and Mme Denis. Three occasions to spend time in the company of his charming niece: it is unlikely that this sequence was purely fortuitous.

Mahomet was finally staged in Lille on 25 April 1741, and it was a great success, as Voltaire exulted to d'Argental:

> The people of the town were so keen that we could not refuse to put on four performances, one of which was at the home of the local governor, for the benefit of the clergy, who absolutely insisted on seeing the founder of a religion. You will perhaps think that I am blaspheming when I say that La Noue, despite his monkey appearance, played the role of Mahomet much better than Dufresne would have done.[3]

The provincial clerics of Lille, it seems, were quite ready to be entertained by a spectacle depicting the superstitions of an alien religion in a bad light. But when the play was staged in Paris a year later, it was denounced by the Jansenist fundamentalists as an attack on all revealed religion, and thus as an indirect attack on the Catholic Church, and Voltaire was forced to withdraw it after only three performances.

Three months after the première of *Mahomet*, in July 1741, Voltaire told Cideville that his sexual love for Émilie had changed to friendship.

> We die twice over, I see that:
> To cease to love and to be lovable
> Is an unbearable death;
> In comparison, to cease to live is nothing.
>
> Yet from the heavens, friendship deigns
> To descend to rescue me;

It is steadier, just as tender,
Even if it is less lively than love.

This friendship is, however, a charming consolation. Farewell, my
charming friend. I shall bury myself in work, which, after friendship,
is a great consolation.[4]

Voltaire had already expressed an analogous thought some months
earlier in a letter to Frederick; but in that case he may have thought to
ingratiate himself to Frederick by minimising his feelings for Émilie,
whereas he could have had no such ulterior purpose in writing to Cideville. We should assume that on this occasion he was telling the painful
truth and needed to confide in one of his oldest friends.

Shortly before the première of *Mahomet*, the War of the Austrian
Succession had moved up a decisive notch, with the battle of Mollwitz.
When Frederick invaded Silesia in December 1740, he thought he had
made a painless conquest; his troops settled down quietly into winter
quarters and did virtually nothing more. In the spring, however, the
Austrians resolved to challenge him in the field, and on 10 April 1741
they forced a battle against him at Mollwitz in Silesia (now Małujowice
in Poland). The two armies were initially fairly evenly matched in
numbers, with about 20,000 men each, and both sides suffered heavy
casualties. At first, Frederick was so taken completely off guard by the
Austrian cavalry charges that he fled the field when it seemed that the
battle was lost; but in the event the Prussians proved to be better trained,
and Frederick's general, the 77-year-old Field Marshal Kurt Christoph
Graf von Schwerin, won a decisive victory.

Afterwards Frederick vowed that he would never again leave his
troops on the battlefield (he never did) and that his strategy would in
future always be offensive. His victory virtually ensured that Prussia
would hold on to Silesia, and that outcome was made even more likely
by the reaction of the French; two months later, on 4 June 1741, they
entered into an alliance with Prussia in which they guaranteed that
Prussia would keep Silesia.

One of the casualties of the battle of Mollwitz, in a metaphorical
sense, was Pierre Louis Moreau de Maupertuis, the French mathematician who had already played such an important part in the lives of both
Voltaire and Émilie. Like Voltaire, Maupertuis had for some time been
courted by Frederick, who hoped to lure him as a distinguished ornament to his court at Potsdam; and like Voltaire, Maupertuis was strongly

tempted. He was one of Frederick's guests at the château de Moyland in September 1740, and after that meeting, when Voltaire went home to Émilie, Maupertuis followed Frederick to Berlin.

When Frederick led his army against the Austrians in April 1741, Maupertuis went with him, thinking this would improve his image with the king. Unfortunately, Frederick did not provide him with a horse, and the donkey Maupertuis acquired for 2 ducats could not keep up with the king's entourage.[5] He failed to witness the battle of Mollwitz, for he got lost in the countryside two days before and was captured by the Austrians. Voltaire cackled with glee when he heard the story from the marquis de Valori, the French ambassador to the Prussian court.

'Sir,' he wrote to Valori,

> you were born to enchant society, since you have taken the trouble to copy out the whole of the newspaper article about poor Maupertuis. I have just read it to Mme du Châtelet, and we were moved to tears. I recall that he had had a blue coat made for him; he must have worn it in Silesia, and this cursed coat may have been the cause of his death, for they must have taken him for a Prussian. It is a great loss for France, but we must not despair; perhaps he is taken prisoner, perhaps he is only wounded.
>
> P.S. I have just learned, Sir, that Maupertuis is at this moment in Vienna, and in good health. He was robbed by some peasants in that cursed black forest, where he was doing penitence, like some Don Quixote. They stripped him quite naked, but a few hussars, one of whom spoke French, had pity on him, which is unusual for a hussar, and they gave him a dirty shirt, and took him before Count Wilhelm Reinhard von Neipperg [the Austrian commander in chief]. Neipperg lent him 50 louis, with which he set off immediately for Vienna, as a prisoner, on his honour; for they did not want him to go back to the king, after he had seen the Austrian army. So he went to Vienna, where he met the princess of Liechtenstein, and they fêted him in Vienna as they would have in Berlin.[6]

Maupertuis was in a foul mood when he returned to Paris. The Austrians had let him go, but he feared that his mishap had made him a laughing stock, and he believed that Voltaire, in particular, had been spreading derisive gossip about him. Voltaire played the mock-faced innocent: 'I have been told that you complained to Berlin about expressions which I used in speaking about you. I do not recall ever having used any expressions, other than 'worthy supporter of Newton', or 'master in the art of thinking'. If these are the expressions which have shocked you, I must warn you that I shall not change my ways.'[7]

Voltaire's laboured irony enraged Maupertuis even further, but he was also out of humour with Frederick because he felt that he had been invited to Berlin on false pretences: he thought that Frederick had been offering to make him the head of a new Academy of Science and Letters at Berlin, but the offer did not materialise.* Voltaire was delighted. 'M. de Maupertuis', he wrote to a scientist friend in June, 'must have reached Paris by now. They say he is discontented: he did not found an Academy as he hoped, he wasted a lot of money, he lost his bags at the battle of Mollwitz, and he has not been compensated as he had hoped.'[8]

After exactly one year, on 11 June 1742, Frederick simply abandoned his alliance with France and made a separate peace treaty with Austria, under which Prussia would keep Silesia. The French found themselves looking foolish and on the wrong side of everyone, but Voltaire, apparently oblivious of the dangers, immediately wrote to Frederick to congratulate him:

> Your Majesty has made a very good treaty, very good for you, no doubt. Whether it is also good for us French is much debated. Half the world cries out that you have abandoned our people. But a few philosophical followers of the abbé Saint-Pierre [author of a celebrated work on a *Plan for Perpetual Peace*] bless you amidst the tumult, and I am one of these philosophers, for I believe that you will force all the powers of Europe to make peace. Have you ceased to be our ally, Sire? Ah, but you will be the ally of the human race.[9]

To Voltaire's consternation, a copy of this letter got out and quickly did the rounds of French society, where it provoked great indignation at Voltaire's lack of patriotism. This scandal made Voltaire acutely aware that his identification with a foreign monarch, especially one who was no longer an ally of France, was jeopardising his position in Paris and making it increasingly difficult for him to gain acceptance by the French establishment. The acceptance that he most wanted, the ultimate test of public recognition, was membership of the Académie Française: his friend Richelieu had been a member since 1720, Montesquieu since 1728

---

* Frederick finally made good on his offer in the summer of 1745, when he made Maupertuis the head of the Royal Academy of Sciences and Belles-Lettres in Berlin (*Letters*, 1955 and 1956, June 1745).

and his friend Moncrif since 1733; Voltaire was now forty-eight years old, and his writings and his celebrity should by now have entitled him to expect membership as well.

His first step was to try to mend fences with the French court, and he now tried to persuade them that he was still a loyal Frenchman and that they could make use of his connection with Frederick in ways that would be useful to France. In August 1742 he wrote to Cardinal Fleury, chief minister of Louis XV, to tell him that he had received a new invitation from Frederick and that he intended to visit him, provided Fleury gave his agreement. Frederick now renewed his invitation, and Voltaire, without waiting for permission, set off almost immediately to meet Frederick at Aix-la Chapelle.

On his return to Brussels ten days later he wrote Fleury a long report which he hoped would persuade the French authorities of his good faith and of his value as a source of diplomatic intelligence.

I shall now give you an account of my journey to Aix-la-Chapelle, hoping to fulfil the duties of a subject and of a good citizen, without failing in my gratitude to the king of Prussia.

I was lodged in a room near his apartment, and he came to visit me two days running, on each of which he spent fours hours in my room, with that kindness and familiarity which you know is part of his character. He did not doubt that I would accept the propositions which he has always made, that I should settle at his court, and on this assumption he spoke with all the greater freedom. He asked me, first, if it was true that the French people were still so hostile to him, if the king was, if you were. I replied that the French people had indeed felt great indignation at such an unexpected change of policy, but that it was not my place to know the feelings of the king.

Then he deigned to speak at length of the reasons which induced him to seek peace. He repeated several times that he hoped to see Bohemia in the hands of the emperor; but that he himself only wished to keep Silesia.

There is no doubt that his ideas about France are as false as his ideas about Austria seem to be true. He asked me if it was true that France has exhausted its money and its manpower and is totally discouraged. I had the honour to reply that there are still eleven hundred and fifty million of currency in circulation, that army recruitment has never been so easy and that the nation has never been in such good heart.[10]

Fleury's reply suggests that Voltaire's efforts to ingratiate himself had paid off: 'Your words are golden, Sir, and I can willingly confirm everything you have said, since I think like you, and you have entered perfectly into the spirit of the king. I had the honour to read him your letter, with which he was very pleased.'[11]

In November Voltaire and Émilie hurried back to Paris, for Voltaire had heard that there was a vacancy at the Académie Française. As soon as he arrived, he put his name forward; but he did so demurely, almost *sotto voce*, as if he did not really expect to get in. He certainly did not mention the fact in writing to any of his friends.

The Académie Française, then as now, was a self-perpetuating club at the heart of the French élite. Membership was limited to just forty academicians, and a vacancy could only be filled by the vote of the remaining thirty-nine members. But membership was such a coveted public distinction that any would-be candidate needed to get support not merely among the existing members but also among their friends and allies in Parisian society, notably in the literary and social salons. And of course, a candidate needed at least the tacit approval of the court.

In this first attempt on the central citadel of French culture Voltaire was defeated by a rival playwright, Pierre Carlet de Marivaux, a successful author of witty, worldly comedies. Voltaire's handicap was his controversial reputation as a pioneer of the Enlightenment and a sceptic about Christianity, for the Académie Française was an increasingly conservative microcosm of the French power élite, dominated by the hierarchy of the Catholic Church. In the early days, after its foundation in 1635 by Cardinal Richelieu, the Académie Française had been relatively secular, and membership had even been based in theory on intellectual or literary merit: in 1650 the members had included just one bishop and four abbés. By the reign of Louis XV, however, it had become much more religious. In 1730 there were two cardinals, one archbishop, two bishops and eight abbés; and in this year of 1742 there were three cardinals (including Fleury, the king's chief minister), one archbishop, four bishops and eleven abbés, making a total of nineteen fully paid-up representatives of the Catholic Church, or just under half the total membership of the Académie Française. When Marivaux was unanimously elected in December 1742, the result was at least as much a vote against Voltaire the unbeliever as a vote for Marivaux.

No doubt Voltaire was disappointed, but not for long, for he was heavily engaged in the final preparations for the staging of his latest tragedy, *Mérope*. This was a story, set in ancient Greece, of a murderous tyrant, Polyphonte, and of a long-lost son whose life is saved by his mother's love. *Mérope* was an immediate and an enormous success. On the first night, on 20 February 1743, Voltaire was called on stage to take applause (a first in the history of the French theatre), and it went on to be one of the most frequently performed plays in the repertoire of the Comédie Française, with a total of 340 performances over the years, the same number as *Œdipe*, but fewer than *Zaïre* (488) or *Tancrède* (383).

Voltaire had a second chance of membership in the Académie Française, with the death in January 1743 of Cardinal Fleury. In the French political context this was a major turning-point: Fleury had been at the heart of the *ancien régime* for the past twenty-seven years, and for seventeen of those years, since his promotion to chief minister in 1726, he had been, for all practical purposes, the government of France. Now, after his death, Louis XV started, for the first time, at the age of thirty-three, to rule in his own name.

This time Voltaire resolved not to be coy about his candidacy to the Académie Française but to tackle the key power brokers directly. He lobbied Jean-Frédéric Phélypeaux, comte de Maurepas, the Secretary of State, and an increasingly powerful figure at court, to see whether the king would have any objection. Just as significantly, he wrote to three prominent churchmen in the Académie to argue that he was of impeccable character and a good Christian.

'I can say before God, who hears me,' he wrote to Jean-François Boyer, the former bishop of Mirepoix, one of the king's closest ecclesiastical advisers and one of Voltaire's fiercest critics, 'that I am a good citizen and a true Catholic. I say it solely because that is what I have always been at heart. I have not written a single page which does not breathe humanity, and I have written many which are sanctified by religion.'[12] He wrote in similar terms to the abbé Vaux de Giry, the tutor of the dauphin, and to Jean-Joseph Languet de Gergy, the archbishop of Sens.[13]

When these letters got out, they caused dismay among Voltaire's enlightened friends and derision elsewhere. Frederick was delighted to be able to send Voltaire an ode of mockery.

What? Does effective grace work after all,
Indoctrinated by Mirepoix,
And sprinkled with holy water?
Will you become a hermit,
And in a saintly nasal tone,
Will you mutter some prayer,

And yawning, read your breviary?

That is what I assume, on the basis of the letter you wrote to the bishop of Sens, and what I learn from all the letters that have come from Paris. You can imagine my surprise, and the astonishment of a philosophical spirit, when it sees the servant of truth bending the knee before the idol of superstition.[14]

Voltaire was embarrassed but undeterred. He claimed to his friends that his campaign was making good progress, and he implied that his meeting with Maurepas had been successful: 'The king', he wrote to Moncrif, 'has given his permission for me to join the Académie, supposing they want me.'[15]

But in his *Mémoires,* written many years later, he gave a very different account of his interview with Maurepas. 'I went to find this minister, and I said to him: "A place in the Académie is not a very important affair, but if one's name were put forward, it would be sad to be excluded. I ask you to tell me frankly: would you oppose me?" He considered a moment, and then he said to me: "Yes, and I shall crush you."'[16] Some scholars claim that such brutality was quite out of character for Maurepas, but in any case Maurepas simply blocked Voltaire's candidacy. When it looked as though Voltaire might be elected by default, Maurepas instructed Paul de Luynes, bishop of Bayeux, to put his name forward. Luynes did as he was told, and on 22 March 1743, he was duly elected to the Académie Française by unanimity. If Voltaire was the problem, the answer had to be a bishop.[17]

Voltaire was quite resentful that this honour had again been snatched away from him by Church and state. 'I know nothing about this Académie,' he told d'Argental; 'All I know is that it is really cruel that powerful men should have got together to deprive me of the only reward I asked for, after thirty years of work.'[18] But he took comfort from the continuing success of *Mérope.*

I cannot appear at the theatre without being applauded. This popularity has slightly consoled me for the persecution that I suffered at the hands of the bishop of Mirepoix. The Académie, the king and the public had all designated me to have the honour of succeeding M. le cardinal de Fleury, but M. de Mirepoix did not want it, and he found a bishop to take the place that had been destined for me.[19]

In later years the Catholic Church's hold on the Académie Française weakened slightly, but it remained the citadel of the French power élite; in 1760 the membership still included two cardinals, one archbishop, two bishops and seven abbés, or twelve seats out of forty. Even in the twentieth century, the Académie Française included seven cardinals, of whom the most recent was elected in 1995, and five self-styled dukes, of whom the most recent was elected in 1972. By the early twenty-first century some of these ultra-conservative anomalies were beginning to die out. The last self-styled duke among the *immortels*, René de la Croix de Castries, duc de Castries, died in 1986, and the last cardinal, Aaron-Jean-Marie Lustiger, former archbishop of Paris, died in 2007. By 2009, 220 years after the Revolution, the Académie Française had only one solitary bishop, Claude Dagens, bishop of Angoulême – but he had been elected in 2008.

Voltaire now conceived the extraordinary idea that he might be able to rebuild his own position in Paris if he were to offer his services as a diplomatic intermediary between France and Prussia. It was a fantastic notion. In France he had long been a controversial figure and a disturber of the peace; Émilie made repeated efforts to appease the authorities, and each time she had some superficial success, but Voltaire remained, by nature and by choice, an outsider and a challenger of the status quo, and he was not really trusted by the French government.

Nevertheless, in the spring of 1743 Voltaire managed to persuade them to give him a try as an unofficial go-between, though they tried to disguise his mission by pretending that he was in disgrace and was virtually going into exile. In early June Voltaire travelled to The Hague, and from the residence of the French ambassador he wrote a letter in code to the French Foreign Minister, Jean-Jacques Amelot de Chaillou: 'I am obliged to use this code, to have the honour to tell you that the king of Prussia has given me the order to meet him at Aix-la-Chapelle.'[20]*

Voltaire's story, in his dealings with Frederick, was that he had been totally alienated by his failure to get into the Académie Française, and he wrote several letters to Frederick complaining of his ill-treatment by Boyer, the former bishop of Mirepoix. 'This evil Mirepoix is as hard, as fanatical, as imperious, as Cardinal Fleury was gentle, conciliatory and polite. We must despair at seeing Boyer in a position once held by Fénelon and Bossuet; he is a born persecutor.'[21]

---

* The diplomatic code used by Voltaire was based on a numeric system replacing words by numbers. But Voltaire's security awareness was minimal, for he frequently lapsed from the numeric code to plain French.

But he also wrote to d'Argenson to emphasise his loyalty as a Frenchman:

The little upsets which I suffered in France do not at all diminish my zeal for the king and for my country. I shall not conceal from you that His Majesty the king of Prussia has just written to me from Magdeburg, and has asked me to meet him at Aix-la-Chapelle at the beginning of August. He absolutely wants to take me from there to Berlin, and he speaks to me with the greatest indignation of the persecutions which I have endured.[22]

Ten days later he sent d'Argenson details of the military forces of the Dutch and their order of battle: 'You can be sure that the Dutch will not do you any harm.'[23]

Later that month Voltaire wrote to Amelot de Chaillou, the French Foreign Minister, to tell him that Frederick had secretly borrowed 400,000 florins in Amsterdam at 3½ per cent.

It must be supposed that his financial resources are less than people think, or that he wants to write off other debts. In either case, I ask you, Monseigneur, if you do not think that this prince would gladly accept a subsidy. Rest assured that I shall make him no such proposition, but I ask whether you will permit me to let him glimpse the idea that France might give him some subsidies. He has done me the honour to write to me three times since I have been at The Hague, to urge me to settle at his court, and to forget France for ever.[24]

What is most striking from these letters is the amateurishness of Voltaire's enterprise. He was supposed to be promoting a rapprochement between France and Frederick, but he did not really know how to set about it, and he did not have clear instructions from the French government. Moreover, Voltaire's ostensible cover story was in tatters almost immediately. He was supposed to be leaving France in disgrace, but he had scarcely arrived in The Hague before the word was out among the gossips of Paris society that he had in fact been sent on a mission. Moreover, Maurepas undermined the French government's own story by writing a letter to Émilie to insist that Voltaire had left France without the king's permission and that he must return without delay.

Neither Voltaire nor the French government seems to have addressed the inherent ambiguity in his mission. If he was seeking credibility with

Frederick by claiming to be deeply alienated from France, why was he trying to bring about a rapprochement between France and Prussia? If he was leaving France in disgrace, if not virtual exile, why was the French government anxious for him to return so soon? Obviously Frederick was never taken in by Voltaire's manoeuvres, but it is surprising that Voltaire should ever have ventured into this curious game in the first place.

Towards the end of August 1743 Voltaire was on his way to Berlin, and soon boasting of the successful start of his visit. 'Today,' he wrote to the French Foreign Minister, 'after a dinner full of gaiety and enjoyment, the king of Prussia came to my room. "Sire," I said to him, "you know that the interests of Your Majesty and of France are destined to be always united." "But how can I believe," said the king of Prussia, "that France intends to tie itself firmly to me?"'[25] A week later the marquis de Valori, the French ambassador at Berlin, reported to Amelot de Chaillou that Voltaire had been received by Frederick 'with all the grace that one can imagine, such as no private person has ever received, nor even, I dare say, any prince'.[26]

Frederick openly mocked Voltaire's transparent manoeuvrings.

It seems to me, my dear Voltaire, that you have not yet decided what role you want to play. I will not say any more about it, for I must seem suspect in anything I could say to you. The picture of France which you give me is painted in lovely colours, but, say what you will, an army which runs away three years running, and which is beaten wherever it appears, is surely not a troop of Caesars nor of Alexanders.[27]*

Three weeks later Voltaire discovered that Frederick had tried to discredit him in France by deliberately circulating parts of those letters in which Voltaire had made critical remarks about Boyer, the former bishop of Mirepoix. 'He thought', Voltaire wrote to Amelot de Chaillou,

that if I were to quarrel irreparably with Boyer, I should be forced to accept his invitation, which I have always refused, to live at the court of Prussia. Being unable to win me over in any other way, he thought to get hold of me by destroying my position in France. I swear that I

---

* The French army had just been soundly beaten at Dettingen by an alliance army led in person by George II of England, a battle celebrated by Handel in his *Dettingen Te Deum*.

would rather live in a Swiss village than enjoy the favours of a king who was capable of putting treachery in the place of friendship.[28]

Seven years later Voltaire would eagerly seek the favours of the Prussian king, and four years after that he would embrace a life of involuntary exile in (or near) a Swiss village.

Émilie was now becoming increasingly agitated at Voltaire's long absence, and above all at his long silence. 'I have only now received a letter from him,' she wrote to d'Argental.

It is just four lines long, and he does not say anything about coming home. How much I have to reproach him with! And how far his heart is from mine! I shall go to Brussels, and wait for him there, and I shall return with him to Paris. I count on you to make him see how barbarous it would be for him to subject me any longer to such pain. But if I see him again, all my ills will be cured.[29]

Émilie did not wait for her letter to have any effect but sent a messenger to Germany to urge Voltaire to return.

Voltaire gave in to her pressure, but without enthusiasm, and in the middle of October he told Maupertuis that he was being summoned home 'by a more powerful sovereign, named Mme du Châtelet';[30] to Frederick he pretended that he was only going to be away for a short time and that he would return to Berlin 'as soon as I have sorted out my affairs'.[31] Frederick bade him an apparently fond farewell and reassured him that he would always be welcome. 'I want my capital to become the temple of great men. Come, my dear Voltaire, and dictate anything that would please you. Choose an apartment or a house, settle for yourself what you need for your comfort and more. You will always be free, and entirely master of your fate; I do not claim to bind you except by friendship.'[32]

Voltaire was not yet ready to take up Frederick's offer, though he must have been tempted by these promises of comfort and freedom. But he was not keen to return to Émilie either, and on his way back to Brussels he wrote a letter to d'Argental on 4 November 1743, in which he poured out his anger and resentment at Émilie's harassment.

My dear and respectable friend, what a horrid amount of fuss about nothing [*horriblement du bruit pour une omelette*]. I could not be less guilty, nor more vexed. I have not missed a single post chaise, and it is not my fault if they are so unreliable on the side roads of Germany. I was a whole month without hearing any news from your friend [Émilie], but though it pained me, I was not angry, I did not believe I was being betrayed, and I did not set about stirring up the whole of Germany. I must admit that I was very upset by all the fuss that has been made [by Émilie]. I trust that you will see me soon, and that you will teach your friend [Émilie] not to make storms in a sky as calm as ours.

P.S. 6 November: I have arrived in Brussels, where I am overjoyed in the happiness of seeing your friend [Émilie] (who is in much better health than I am), and I shall be perfectly happy when both of us shall have the consolation of embracing you.[33]

D'Argental must have been struck by the tone of this letter, not just because Voltaire pointedly avoided mentioning Émilie's name but also because this was the first time that Voltaire had ever expressed sustained anger at Émilie. Occasionally, in the past, he had made passing little utterances of impatience, but never such a prolonged burst of annoyance and resentment.

Perhaps Voltaire got over his irritation when he got back to Brussels, and perhaps he really was glad to see Émilie again. That is certainly what he claimed, a week later, in a letter to Mme de Champbonin.

My dear friend, my body has travelled, but my heart always stayed with Mme du Châtelet, and with you. Unexpected circumstances dragged me to Berlin against my wishes. But nothing which could encourage *amour-propre*, interest or ambition has ever tempted me. To be free and to be loved, is something that the kings of earth do not have. It was a disagreeable journey, but my return has been the height of happiness. I have never found your friend so lovable.[34]

Yet in reality, all was not well between Voltaire and Émilie. The next day they set off for Paris, and they stopped on the way at Lille, where they stayed once more with M. and Mme Denis. From there Émilie wrote to d'Argental a letter of despair at the end of love.

Your friend has told you himself of his arrival, and of the end of my unhappiness. I always had some hope that he, whose side you always took, despite his apparent faults, was not in fact guilty. And he is not, for he loves me, and you can easily feel that there are no faults which love does not wipe out. Finally, love brought him back to me, and I only want to see my happiness. He has begged me to repair his reputation in your sight, but if he loves me as he swears, I think that I shall not have a heavy task.

Ah, be sure to tell him, my dear friend, when you see him, how unhappy I am in his absence, tell him that people must never be separated if they love each other. There is always a loss of love in an absence of five months, the heart loses the habit of loving, one grows hard among those horrid Germans, especially at the court of a king who does not know how to love.

We are on our way to Paris.[35]

This letter marks the beginning of Émilie's terrible realisation that Voltaire has fallen out of love with her. Pomeau interprets it as an advance warning from Émilie to d'Argental that she is falling out of love for Voltaire.[36] This is obviously wrong, for it is not what the letter says. Superficially the letter is ambiguous, for it starts by saying that Voltaire still loves her. But the sequence of thought is unmistakable: at first she says that he loves her; then she says that he *swears* that he loves her; but she ends by saying that 'the heart loses the habit of loving ... among those horrid Germans'. By the end of the letter it is clear that Émilie knows she has lost Voltaire.

In any case, we know that Émilie never fell out of love with Voltaire. We also know that Voltaire did fall out of love with Émilie and soon took another mistress. That mistress was Mme Denis. The most significant fact about this letter is that it was written from the home of Mme Denis, and the most plausible explanation for its content, as well as for its timing, is that Émilie must suddenly have realised, in the presence of Voltaire and Mme Denis, not just that Voltaire was no longer attracted to her but also how much he was attracted to Mme Denis.

In public, Voltaire and Émilie remained a virtual couple for another four years. But in private, they never recovered the love they had once had.

16

VOLTAIRE AT COURT AGAIN

1744–1746

VOLTAIRE AND ÉMILIE REACHED PARIS in a state of high tension. It seems that they quarrelled loudly and often, and long into the night, and their unhappiness became a subject of common gossip. On one occasion, it is said, Voltaire insisted on eating his supper by himself at a small table; when Émilie came in and demanded that they sit together at a larger table, he refused.

It was the beginning of a long period of conflict and disintegration. They stayed together, but increasingly unhappy and dislocated. Voltaire cast about to find new purposes in life: Paris, Prussia, Versailles, the court. Eventually he settled on the pursuit of official recognition, and membership of the Académie Française, but the centre of his problem was that he was unhappy with Émilie while still committed to her, and yet groping after a relationship with his niece Mme Denis.

After they got to Paris, it was said that Voltaire had an affair with Jeanne Gaussin, one of the leading actresses at the Comédie Française. She was thirty-three years old, apparently very luscious and languorous, a moving performer on stage, and allegedly free with her favours off it. Hard facts are elusive; Besterman believes that a contemporary police report, alleging Voltaire's ostensible affair with Mlle Gaussin, in fact confused it with his real love affair with Mme Denis.

Although Voltaire's affair with Mme Denis was serious and sustained, it did not break his commitment to Émilie, or hers to him. Even after he had lost interest in her sexually, and despite their unhappiness together and the growing divergence between them, Voltaire and

Émilie never did break up as a couple until her death five years later.

They quarrelled frequently about money, and about her financial extravagance. Émilie started gambling heavily again; she lost, she got into debt and she was permanently penniless. She borrowed money from Voltaire and from others; sometimes she failed to keep up the payments, and one of her creditors, the ultra-rich tax farmer Helvetius, threatened to have her furniture seized and sold. Voltaire became increasingly angry over her financial recklessness, and he started insisting on an explicit separation of accounts between them, including a split accounting for the costs of the house which the marquis had rented in the rue du Faubourg St Honoré. In January 1744 Émilie wrote him a pitiful letter, abjectly pleading with him to bail her out once more.

> *Dear Lover,* *
> It is only to one's friends that one appeals in case of need. Please forgive me for preferring to write than to speak to you, but the fact is, *dear lover,* that I am in extreme need of 50 louis to cover the month of April, and twelve and a half louis that I owe for gambling, and so as not to be absolutely penniless. I shall not draw it until the last day of the month.
>
> I have sent £500 to M. du Châtelet for kitting out his son.† I shall pay you back in rental for the house, or else, if you prefer, here is the note from M. du Châtelet which, luckily, I did not tear up. He will not be surprised that I could not pay him. Keep it, and lend me the money, and we shall make a new account, or else I shall not spend it; that would be better for me and for you.
>
> You will be doing me a great favour; I hope you can do it, for I am sure that, if you can, you will.[1]

Voltaire was angry with Émilie not just over her financial irresponsibility but also over her frenzied and dissolute social life, which was wearing him down. Significantly, it was to Mme Denis that he poured out his woes.

> For the last three months, my dear niece, they have not let me get to bed before four o'clock in the morning. I get up very late, and when I

---

* Émilie writes '*Dear Lover*' in English.
† Louis-Marie-Florent was, of course, also her own son; she refers to him as 'his son' because he was following in his father's footsteps as an army officer: he was sixteen years old, and he had just joined the army as an officer cadet.

do I feel very unwell. I rush around Paris, and I seem to find myself, I know not how, over-burdened in the midst of idleness; and though I am always running after the phantom of pleasure, the reality eludes me.

Always ill, always busy with nothing, much ashamed and weary of my life, I write to you while I am shaving, and dictating my letter with a horrible colic, some medicine in my body, and a hundred follies in my head.[2]

In February, Voltaire started taking an interest in the case of the young Charles Edward Stuart, exiled grandson of James II of England, and a pretender to the English throne. The French government seemed to believe that, if they provided him with a fleet and landed him in England, he could overthrow George II. 'The scheme in favour of the pretender', Voltaire told Podewils, the Prussian ambassador in The Hague, 'seems very serious and very well organised. There are eighty large vessels at Dunkirk, which the king is paying for at the rate of 1,400 francs per month, and which can carry 9,000 men. I beg you not to tell anybody of this news, except the king your master.'[3] In the event, a violent storm wrecked the French fleet in May, and the operation was abandoned. The Young Pretender had to wait another year to raise a much smaller fleet of his own.

Voltaire was still trying hard to get back into favour at court, and he wrote frequently to Amelot de Chaillou, the Foreign Minister, to ply him with scraps of information which he had picked up on his recent visits to Berlin and The Hague. This political seduction campaign collapsed ignominiously in April, when Amelot was dismissed without warning.

In any case Voltaire and Émilie now had to return to Cirey, for her husband had returned home on leave, after four years' absence with his regiment, and he was calling for her to rejoin him. But scarcely had they reached Cirey when Voltaire learned from Mme Denis that her husband had just died. He immediately wrote her a letter of condolence, in which he moved rapidly and daringly to proposition her.

My dear niece, as I write, I wet the paper with my tears; if my deplorable health permitted, and if I could leave at once by the post-chaise, I should certainly come to weep with you. I count on coming to embrace you in October. It is one of my sorrows not to be able to pass the rest of the days of my life with you. Life is a dream, and a sad dream, but live for your friends, and for me, who loves you tenderly.[4]

Six days later he returned to the charge: 'May it please God that we should live together. It would be the consolation of my life, and I would try to make it yours too.'[5]

Meanwhile, Richelieu had come up with a new scheme to get Voltaire back into favour at court. Recently promoted First Gentleman of the King's Chamber, Richelieu had control over court entertainments, and he now commissioned a comedy-ballet for the planned marriage of the French dauphin to the infanta of Spain, to be called *La Princesse de Navarre*: Voltaire would write the libretto, and the celebrated composer Jean-Philippe Rameau the music.

Voltaire found this commission an uphill struggle, for he knew nothing about music or comedy-ballets and he had no inspiration. 'You have given me a terrible task,' he told Richelieu. 'I should much rather have written a tragedy than a work in this style. The difficulty is almost insurmountable, but I trust that in the end hard work will save me. I have only a certain measure of talent, and I confess that I have put in this prologue everything which the nature of the subject suggests to my very feeble ability.'[6]

Worse, Voltaire did not get on with Rameau. 'I have received three letters from Rameau which are fairly mad,' he told d'Argental, 'but I have not answered any of them.'[7] And five days later: 'You have not said whether you have had the misfortune to pass on to this strange Rameau fellow all the verses which are destined for his triple crotchets.'[8] Voltaire's reference to 'triple crotchets' was just an expression of the most philistine derision: he knew nothing about crotchets, single, double or triple.

Voltaire was getting desperate. 'Why', he asked d'Argental, 'have they given this entertainment to Rameau? What a strange man! He has gone mad, as you may judge by the criticisms which he has made. You should let Richelieu know that Rameau is not at all cut out for this kind of entertainment in music. I predict that it will be impossible for me to work with Rameau: he is good to listen to, but not to live with.'[9]

Eventually the work was finished, and by the end of August Voltaire decided to return to Paris. The staging was scheduled for the following February, and he needed to be in Paris for the rehearsals; and since the performance was to take place at Versailles, he also wanted to be on the spot there, to be noticed. In fact, Voltaire the outsider was now set on becoming a courtier; by this route, he hoped, he would finally be admitted to the Académie Française.

His pursuit of courtly promotion required unending subservience and obsequiousness, and ceaseless running after powerful people, and he found the process arduous and degrading, as he told his friend Cideville:

> Pity a poor devil who has become the king's fool at the age of fifty. I hurry from Paris to Versailles, and I write verses in a post-chaise. I rush to Paris for a rehearsal, and back to Versailles for a stage-setting. I must praise the king highly, Madame la dauphine subtly, and the royal family sweetly, I must please the court, and not displease the town.[10]

Armand Arouet, Voltaire's elder brother, died three days before the première of *La Princesse de Navarre,* and Voltaire discovered that Armand had effectively cut him out of his will. He could not have been surprised.

February 1741 was marked by the arrival on the scene at Versailles of a young woman who would become immensely influential at court, and a powerful friend of Voltaire. This was Jeanne-Antoinette Poisson, a beautiful and talented 23-year-old, who had been taken up by Charles-François Le Normant, a rich *fermier général*. He had married her off to an insignificant nephew, given her the château d'Étioles and assiduously groomed her to attract attention at court; and it was at the première of *La Princesse de Navarre* that Jeanne-Antoinette Poisson made her first public appearance at Versailles, as a member of the audience. Within three months she became the king's new mistress and received from him the title of marquise de Pompadour.

Voltaire had met her before, since she had been introduced by Le Normant into the most refined circles of society, and he reminisced about her arrival in his co-called *Mémoires*, published many years later.

> The girl was well brought up, well behaved, agreeable, full of graces and talents, born with good sense and a good heart. I knew her quite well: she even took me into her confidence about her love. She admitted to me that she had always had a secret premonition that she would be loved by the king and that she felt a violent inclination for him.
>
> This idea, which could have seemed fantastic for someone in her position, was based on the fact that she had often been taken to the king's hunts in the forest of Sénars. They took her out in a pretty carriage, and the king noticed her, and sent her some venison. Le Normant often exclaimed that 'The daughter of Mme Poisson is a choice morsel for a king'. Finally, when she had held the king in her

arms, she told me that she believed firmly in her destiny; and she was right. I spent several months with her at Étioles, while the king was away at the wars.

This brought me better recompense than I had ever received for my writings or for my services. I concluded that, to make the smallest way in the world, it was better to say four words to the mistress of a king than to write a hundred books.[11]

Voltaire did not think much of *La Princesse de Navarre*, which he described afterwards as a 'fairground farce'.[12] But the performance at Versailles on 25 February 1745 went off splendidly. Voltaire complained that the audience at this courtly performance had been even rowdier than the vulgar groundlings at the Comédie Française, but everyone liked the show, including the king.[13]

After his triumph Voltaire wrote to the marquis d'Argenson, an old friend from school, and now the new Foreign Minister, to ask for his reward.

The position of Gentleman in Ordinary of the King's Chamber does not do very much, and is just an honorific title; so they could also throw in the little position of King's Historian [*historiographe du roi*] as well, and instead of the pension that normally goes with this historiography, I only ask for a grant of £400. All this seems to me really modest; try and get M. de Maurepas to put it through.[14]

Getting the king to deliver was not easy, however, as Voltaire explained to Mme Denis.

I was counting, my dear child, on seeing you after the show at Versailles, but the ticklishness of court procedure decided otherwise. They told me that I must run at full gallop [*à bride abattue*] after the king, and place myself at a certain moment in a certain corner, to thank him, I do not yet quite know for what, for I had asked for several things, and they told me he had granted all of them.

So they presented me to His Very Gracious Majesty, who received me very graciously, and I thanked him very humbly; but getting him to sign a commission is much more difficult than thanking him. They tell me that I must not let up until everything has been signed, sealed and delivered [*bien cimenté, scellé et consommé*]; but I should much prefer to come and embrace you.[15]

In fact, the king had already granted what Voltaire had asked for, though only in two instalments. 'The king', Voltaire told Mme Denis two days later, 'has granted me the *expectation* of a position as Gentleman in Ordinary, but the *appointment* of the position of King's Historian, together with a salary of £2,000 a year for life, and free entrance to his chamber. He deigned to speak to me with the most touching kindness.'[16] For the position of Gentleman in Ordinary of the King's Chamber, Voltaire had to wait another eighteen months: it was formally conferred on him on 22 December 1746.[17] Even then Voltaire jumped the gun: he first signed himself 'Voltaire, Gentleman in Ordinary of the King's Chamber', five weeks early, on 14 November 1746, but discreetly, in a letter to an Italian friend, written in Italian.[18]

Voltaire was now becoming increasingly outspoken about the stresses in his relationship with Émilie. In February 1745 he replied to an invitation from d'Argental with brutal frankness: 'I must warn you that Mme du Châtelet insists on being included in the party. I am like the Jesuits, I never walk alone. You can well understand that since I am a mere accident, and Mme du Châtelet a being in her own right, I cannot separate myself from her without being destroyed.'[19] Sometimes Voltaire and Émilie went their separate ways. In April he told d'Argental: 'Here I am, all alone in my Faubourg [St Honoré]. Mme du Châtelet is playing at cavagnole* in Versailles; as for me, I do not know what I am doing in Paris. I fear that I cannot call on you today, and that I shall not have a good day [*passer très mal mon temps*].'[20]

Sometimes Voltaire managed to spend time with Mme Denis.

My dearest, who would ever have thought that there would be demand for 7,500 tickets for this ballet by Rameau? Here are three tickets for three ladies; but you must come before three o'clock. Tell the coachman to take the last gate in the last courtyard on the right hand side, beside the chapel. Then, go down a little staircase, which will lead you to my little room, number 144, near the most stinking shit-hole in Versailles [*vicino al più puzzolente cacatoio di Versailles*]. I embrace you a thousand times. I hope to dine with you on Wednesday. Farewell, I shall escort you into the theatre and will try to find a place for your coachman.[21]†

---

* A mindless gambling game, similar to biribi, lotto, or bingo.
† This letter, like much of the correspondence at the height of their affair, was written in Italian. The sanitary arrangements at Versailles were deplorable: a year later, Voltaire had to write to Charles-François de Tournehem, supervisor of the royal buildings (and uncle of Mme

In April, Mme Denis failed to turn up for a theatrical event at the palace of Versailles, and Voltaire was quite desolate. 'How are you, my dear child? Why did you not come yesterday? I do not yet know when I shall leave my inconvenient dwelling in Versailles, for my unhappy Faubourg [in Paris]; wherever I am, I am far from you, and I am dismayed.'[22] In June, Voltaire invited Mme Denis and her sister to a fireworks party on the banks of the Seine; his invitation made it plain that Émilie was not invited.[23]

And yet there was no question of Voltaire leaving Émilie. When her son Louis-Marie-Florent fell ill with smallpox at his military base outside Paris, she hurried at once to be at his bedside, and Voltaire went with her. After they got there, they found they were not welcome in the town: 'Mme du Châtelet has done very well to go and see her son,' he told Mme Denis, 'but here they treat us as if we were carriers of the plague, just because we have been in a bedroom of a sick man. The Governor [*Intendant*] of Châlons is as frightened of this disease as a young girl, and he will not receive us; but the bishop is bolder, for he has given us magnificent lodgings and good food, and has taken us about with him.'[24] After they returned to Paris at the end of the month, however, they were forbidden to go near the court, for fear of contagion: 'I must submit to the prejudice which bans me from Versailles for forty days, just because I have seen a sick man forty leagues away.'[25]

Voltaire's domestic preoccupations were soon interrupted by spectacular new developments in the War of the Austrian Succession. In April the French army laid siege to the city of Tournai, an Austrian possession some 85 kilometres south-west of Brussels. When the Anglo-Dutch-Austrian army of the 'Pragmatic Alliance', led by the duke of Cumberland, moved up to relieve the city, Marshal Maurice de Saxe, commander of the French army, determined to force the issue in a decisive battle.

At this time Maurice de Saxe was very sick, and Voltaire went to see him in Paris shortly before he left for the front. He asked him how he could manage in his weakened state, but the marshal brushed off the question: 'It is not a question of living, but of leaving (*Il ne s'agit pas de vivre, mais de partir*).' Even when Saxe reached the army, he was still so weak that he could not ride.[26]

In May Louis XV set off from Paris to join the French army, in

---

de Pompadour) to ask him to put a door on the public privies at the bottom of his staircase, and to divert a gutter so as to sluice them out. See *Letters* 2142, 14 June, 1746.

the expectation of a major battle, of which Voltaire later left a graphic account in his *Précis du Siècle de Louis XV*:

> The king arrived at Douai on 6 May, and from there he went to reconnoitre the terrain where the battle was due to be fought. The whole army, seeing the king, cried out with acclamations of joy. Never did the king show so much gaiety as on the night before the battle. He was the first to be woken on the day of the battle; and at four o'clock in the morning, he himself woke the comte d'Argenson, Minister of War,* who immediately sent to ask the marshal de Saxe for his latest orders. They found the marshal in a wicker litter which he used as a bed, and in which he had himself carried about when his exhaustion prevented him from staying in the saddle.[27]

The battle of Fontenoy, on 11 May 1745, was a bloody affair, but it claims its place as an event of legend, with one of the most memorable anecdotes of formalistic chivalry in the history of warfare. The English Guards found themselves opposite the French Guards, and Captain Sir Charles Hay, of the 1st Foot Guards, is supposed to have taunted the French, shouting out: 'Gentlemen of the French Guards, fire! (*Messieurs des gardes françaises, tirez*).' The count of Auteroche, then lieutenant of the French Grenadiers, replied loudly: 'Gentlemen, we never fire first, fire yourselves!' Voltaire does not say who fired first, but his narrative goes on to suggest that the French gesture of military courtesy, however noble, was ill judged, since the English guards had an advanced system of rolling fire, by which one battalion fired while another one reloaded, and were able to cause many casualties.[28]

At the outset the two armies were fairly evenly matched in numbers, with about 50,000 men each. According to Voltaire, the allies lost 9,000 men, compared with fewer than 4,000 for the French, and the French won a decisive victory; they went on to take Tournai and numerous other towns in Flanders, including Bruges, Ghent and Ostend. Moreover, the French victory inspired the Young Pretender to try a second rising against the English crown and forced Cumberland to withdraw his troops to England to deal with it.[29]

For Voltaire this was a good opportunity to improve his credit as a

---

* There were two d'Argenson brothers, both friends of Voltaire. This was Marc Pierre de Voyer, comte d'Argenson, the younger brother, who was Minister of War from 1743 to 1757. His elder brother, René Louis de Voyer, marquis d'Argenson, was Foreign Minister from 1744 to 1747.

loyal courtier. Within days he dashed off a narrative victory ode describing the battle in detail, which went down well with the king, and which he allowed Voltaire to dedicate to him. This *Poème de Fontenoy* was in great popular demand, running through five editions in ten days, a fact that Voltaire asked the marquis d'Argenson to draw to the king's attention. 'Please do not overlook this little courtly manoeuvre, I beg you.'[30]

As more and more details about the battle of Fontenoy filtered back to Paris, Voltaire made multiple corrections and alterations in successive editions, and steadily expanded the poem from about a hundred lines in length to 350. His critics scoffed that this was no way to compose a poem, but Voltaire just went on pumping out new editions of his poem for all he was worth. He sent copies off 'to I don't know how many crowned heads', and he sent the latest edition to Empress Élisabeth of Russia, together with copies of *La Henriade* and *Les Éléments de la philosophie de Newton*.[31] In June he persuaded the authorities to have his poem officially printed at the Imprimerie Royale, and in July he asked that the print run be doubled to 1,200 copies.[32]

Émilie, meanwhile, was immersing herself ever more deeply in a translation of Newton's *Principia mathematica*, which Voltaire called 'the deep and sacred horrors of Newton'.[33] She was finding it hard going, as she admitted to her mathematician friend Jean Bernoulli: 'The Latin of M. Newton is one of the difficulties.'[34] But she pressed on, and by the following May Voltaire told Maupertuis (now thoroughly established in Prussia at the head of the new Royal Academy in Berlin) that she was having it printed.[35]

Voltaire's *Poème* did wonders for his standing at court, and Richelieu commissioned Voltaire and Rameau to write another work for Versailles, an allegorical opera, which Voltaire called *Le Temple de la gloire,* and which he evidently intended as a morality play, in praise of peace and justice, for the political edification of Louis XV. This time Voltaire made much less fuss about the difficulties of collaborating with Rameau, and when it was first performed, on 27 November 1745, Louis XV seems to have enjoyed Rameau's music; he said nothing about Voltaire's libretto.

Richelieu now had the idea that Voltaire could capitalise on his success with *La Princesse de Navarre* by rewriting it in a shorter and more easily performable version. Voltaire was reluctant to take on such a chore, however, so Richelieu gave the task to the young Jean-Jacques Rousseau, who had recently arrived in Paris and was trying to make his way as an aspiring musician.

Rousseau was an admirer of Voltaire; he later claimed, in his *Confessions*, that it was his reading of Voltaire's *Lettres philosophiques* which had persuaded him of the virtues of study and hard work; and he was glad of the opportunity offered to show his respect to the great celebrity. Many years later, when Voltaire was living in exile and Rousseau had become famous as an irascible eccentric, they were to quarrel interminably, and their bitter wrangling echoed round Europe. But at this stage Voltaire wrote Rousseau a warm letter of thanks for getting him off the hook.

> I am sorry that you should be employing your talents on a work which does not deserve it. A few months ago, M. le duc de Richelieu absolutely ordered me to do, in the twinkling of an eye, a small and bad sketch of a few insipid scenes. I obeyed with the greatest exactitude, I did it quickly, and I did it badly. I sent this miserable sketch to M. le duc de Richelieu, assuming either that he would not use it or that I could correct it later. Fortunately, it is now in your hands, and you are completely in charge. I hope that I shall soon have the honour of expressing my thanks in person.[36]

Voltaire himself was already on a new tack, for he had decided to build on the success of the *Poème de Fontenoy*, by taking advantage of his new position as King's Historian, and to write a history of the king's recent military campaigns. He quickly set about gathering research materials for this work of instant history, and in September 1745 he wrote to Jean Moreau de Séchelles, governor of Hainault in the Low Countries, seeking evidence and anecdotes about people and events in his area. But he did not want to restrict himself to patriotic French sources: he also set about making enquiries among people on the other side, and he wrote (in English) to the secretary of the duke of Cumberland.

> Sir, My duty is to write the history of the late campaigns. And my king and my country will approve me the more, the greater justice I'll render to the English. Tho' our nations are enemies at present, yet they ought forever to entertain a mutual esteem for one another; my intention is to relate what the duke of Cumberland has done worthy of himself and his name, and to enregister the most particular and noble actions of yr chiefs and officers which deserve to be recorded. If you are so kind as to send me some memoirs, I'll make use of 'em.[37]

By return of post, he discovered to his great surprise that Cumberland's secretary was his old friend Everard Fawkener, who had looked after him when he was in England nearly twenty years earlier. Fawkener had been knighted in 1735, and in 1737 was sent as English ambassador to the Ottoman empire, where he had stayed until 1744. Voltaire had known of Fawkener's diplomatic posting to Constantinople, and he had written to him there at least twice.[38] What he had not known was that Fawkener had returned to England and had joined the service of the duke of Cumberland.

> My dear and honourable friend, How could I guess that your Musulman person had shifted from Galata to Flanders, and was passed from the seraglio to the closet of the Duke of Cumberland? Had I thought it was my dear Sir Everard who was secretary to that great prince, I had certainly taken a journey to Flanders. You would have procur'd to me the honour to see your noble master. I would have learned more in two or three conversations with you, than I could do by letters, since you are so loath to write. Pray, dear Sir, be not so neglectful; a secretary must be used to write. I send you the poem you speak of: you will see with what respect I have spoken of the Duke of Cumberland, and what just praises I have bestowed on your noble nation. Help me to do more justice to both; I entreat you to send me the London magazines of these last three years.[39]

Fawkener responded with a long letter, but when Voltaire consulted the marquis d'Argenson on whether he should travel to Flanders to talk to Fawkener, he was sharply rebuked and immediately backed off. 'Honestly, Monseigneur, I merely told you that Fawkener had *pacific sentiments*, but I draw no conclusion. If you do not think that such a journey could be useful, let us speak no more about it. In any case, I should much rather work on my history here in peace, than run about looking for news.'[40]

Five months later, in March 1746, he gave the king a short first draft of his history, covering events up to the taking of the city of Ghent,[41] but he never completed the project as originally planned. He had intended to call it the *Histoire de la guerre de 1741*, but the title proved misleading, because the War of the Austrian Succession went on and on, year after year, and did not end until 1748. In the late 1740s Voltaire decided to fold his researches into a much larger parallel undertaking, a history of the first half of the French eighteenth century, which finally appeared in 1768 as his *Précis du siècle de Louis XV*.

All the while, of course, Voltaire was still working on *Le Siècle de Louis XIV*, which he had embarked on over a dozen years earlier, in 1732, and which he eventually published, in its first version, in 1752. In addition he was also working on an even more ambitious project, which he called *Essai sur les mœurs*, and which was an innovative history of civilisations: he had started work on it in 1741 and finally published the complete text in 1756.

In the autumn of 1745 Voltaire stepped up his courtship of Mme Denis. He had written to her regularly during the year, and in August he had told her: 'I shall love you always, whether I am well or ill.'[42] Most scholars believe Mme Denis probably became Voltaire's mistress towards the end of 1745 or early in 1746; Besterman implies that it happened significantly earlier, which would be consistent with the fact that his alienation from Émilie, and his interest in Mme Denis, had both been going on for at least two years.[43]

In November 1745 he invited Mme Denis to a dress rehearsal of *Le Temple de la gloire*, and two weeks later to a full performance of the opera; he did not invite Émilie to either event.[44] Later in November he was calling her *mia carissima*, and by December his overtures to her were openly sexual. 'The court, the world, the great ones, they all bore me. I shall not be happy until I can live with you. I kiss you a thousand times. My soul kisses yours, my prick and my heart are in love with you. I kiss your sweet arse, and all your enchanting person.'[45]

Voltaire's next letter to Mme Denis, written in late December 1745, shows that she positively welcomed his overtures. 'You have written me an enchanting letter, which I kissed. By God, I cannot believe that you do not have a lover. How do you manage? You, not make love? You tell me that my letter brought pleasure to all your senses. Mine respond to yours; I could not read your caressing words without feeling enflamed right to my heart. I kiss you a thousand times.'[46] These two letters strongly suggest that, with so much encouragement, he must surely have made her his mistress very shortly after the second, if not after the first.

It was a difficult courtship, for all kinds of practical reasons, starting with his need to keep it secret from Émilie. On one occasion he had to break off a letter quite suddenly: 'Tomorrow I shall come to you. But no more now: I am with the lady, who is watching me.'[47] On another, he saw an opportunity to escape from Émilie's vigilance: 'My dear, the lady du Châtelet will dine today with the duchess of Modena; and I with my dear muse, whom I love more than life itself.'[48]

In March 1746 a new vacancy occurred at the Académie Française, with the death of the lawyer and litterateur Jean Bouhier. At first Voltaire pretended to his friend d'Argental that he could not make the effort to campaign for the place. 'Voltaire learned yesterday of the death of Président Bouhier. People have spoken to Voltaire of the possibility of his taking this place. But Voltaire is ill, Voltaire is scarcely able to move about, and is certainly not in a state to go knocking on doors.'[49] Knocking on doors, and paying formal and flattering visits to influential members of the Académie Française were all part of the campaigning ritual required for serious candidates. Whether Voltaire was really ill or just pretending, he soon started knocking on doors in earnest. He wrote to several members of the Académie Française to ask for their support, and he wrote a grovelling letter of entreaty to the marquis d'Argenson, pathetically begging for an interview.

> I should like to have a little word with you. I came yesterday, but they refused me admittance. I sent a message this morning, and they said that you were seeing only ambassadors, and I am not one. But if in my capacity as the oldest and most devoted of your servants, I could have the honour of seeing you for a little moment today, or tomorrow, or the day after, please have the kindness to tell my *valet de chambre*. Could I for example see you after the opera in your little box, or as you leave your little box? I await your orders, adorable minister.[50]

What position d'Argenson took on this occasion is uncertain: the begging tone of Voltaire's letter implies that d'Argenson was cold-shouldering him. But Voltaire had the crucial support of Mme de Pompadour, the king's new mistress, and on 25 April 1746, on his third attempt, Voltaire was finally elected to the Académie Française. Voltaire claimed to Mme Denis that he had been elected unanimously, but in fact only twenty-nine members were present for the election, and some of them voted against him.[51] Voltaire may have won international celebrity as a writer and secured some slight reconciliation with the court, but he was still a highly controversial figure, detested by conservatives. As Montesquieu implied in a typically caustic remark, the establishment did not really want Voltaire in the Académie Française, but they could not decently keep him out.[52]

As 1746 wore on, it became clear that Mme de Pompadour was becoming increasingly powerful and that the marquis d'Argenson was at odds with her. When a second vacancy occurred at the Académie

Française in 1746, d'Argenson supported the candidacy of a certain abbé de La Ville, whereas Mme de Pompadour supported the historian Charles Pinot Duclos. Voltaire promised d'Argenson that he would support La Ville against Duclos, and at the election he voted for him.[53] But d'Argenson paid for his imprudence: after a third vacancy at the Académie Française, later that year, Duclos was finally elected; and shortly after that, d'Argenson lost his job as foreign minister. Duclos went on to become one of the leaders of the Enlightenment movement at the Académie Française, and in 1755 he was promoted permanent secretary of the Académie (*secrétaire perpétuel*); and he never quite forgave Voltaire for having voted against him.

But Voltaire had got what he wanted. He had set out to become a courtier, and he had achieved virtually everything he had come to Versailles for: he was a *gentilhomme ordinaire du roi*; he was *historiographe du roi* with a regular salary; and he was now a member of the Académie Française. Above all, he had the patronage of the most powerful woman in France.

END OF A RELATIONSHIP

1746–1747

VOLTAIRE HAD ACHIEVED the worldly success he had come to Versailles for, but it brought him no happiness. On the contrary, his election to the Académie Française marked the beginning of the most miserable period in his life.

After his election, he wrote a letter of triumph to Maupertuis in Berlin, who had been elected to the Académie three years earlier: 'Here I am, at last, your colleague in this Académie Française, where they elected me unanimously, and not even the bishop of Mirepoix raised the slightest opposition. I sometimes see your friend La Condamine, who comes to have his *café au lait* with us, on the way to *his* Académie [des Sciences].'[1] Voltaire was exaggerating once more: he had not been elected unanimously. More noteworthy is the fact that this was probably the last really cheerful letter he wrote for several years.

His love affair with Émilie du Châtelet was disintegrating in growing agitation, but he could neither leave her nor love her. He was embarked on a new love affair, with his niece Mme Denis, but it was a one-sided relationship, to which he could not give the commitment it required and from which he could not get the love he needed. He was working hard on the researches for his histories but not writing much, or at least not publishing much of a creative kind. He was dragged about by the demands of Émilie and by her social gallivanting, and he was got down by chronic ill health. In public he had arrived, with professional celebrity and courtly honours; but in personal terms he was all at sea, and he was becoming increasingly desolate.

He was still indissolubly attached to Émilie; they continued to live together in the same house in Paris (when he was not holed up in his little apartment at Versailles) or at Cirey, and they continued to go around together in public. But all the joy and most of the love had gone out of their love affair, and when Émilie rattled around from Fontainebleau to Versailles, from Cirey to Lunéville, or from plays and salons in Paris to house parties in the country châteaux of the nobility, Voltaire often trailed unwillingly in her wake. It is commonly assumed that by now they had long ceased to sleep together.

Voltaire's affair with Mme Denis was obviously a refuge from the frenzy and the friction of life with Émilie. He was strongly drawn to her sexually, as we can see from some of his letters to her, and he repeatedly told her that he loved her, or wished to kiss her a thousand times; it also seems clear that he enjoyed her company, for her gaiety and her sociability, and for her companionship; one of the most constant themes of his letters to her was his desire to spend some peaceful time with her:

My dear child, your letter consoles me for the misfortune that I have to be at Versailles. I am really foolish and unhappy not to be living with you quietly and inconspicuously, far from kings, courtesans and passers-by. There is no reason and no happiness, except for those who live with their friends. Oh how weary I am, not to be living with you in the same house![2]

In practice, however, his new affair with Mme Denis was beset with difficulties, starting with Voltaire's admitted shortcomings as a lover. On one occasion at the beginning of their affair he wrote to her: 'I blush with shame to be so philosophical in ideas, and such a poor performer as a man.' Ten months later he wrote: 'I ask your permission to come with my limpness. It would be better to have a hard-on, but whether I have a hard-on or not, I shall always love you.'[3]

Some of Voltaire's letters to Mme Denis have become notorious for the explicitness of his sexual intentions, but they are a tiny minority. Voltaire wrote to her frequently, but most of his letters during the first two years of their affair, between 1746 and 1748, are short practical notes, and their cumulative effect is to underline the difficulties of the relationship.

The most obvious problem was in his repeated attacks of ill health. Voltaire was frequently unwell throughout his life, but it seems that his chronic ill health was particularly acute during the first two years of his affair with Mme Denis. He frequently made appointments to see her, which he then had to cancel. Sometimes this was because he was doing his duty at court; sometimes it was because he was immersed in research for his history books; sometimes it was because of his continuing commitment to Émilie; but most frequently it was because he was unwell.

> I wanted to come and see you today, but the return of my cruel pains prevented me. If I have a small ray of good health tomorrow, I shall not fail to come and spend a few moments with you.[4]

> I shall see you tomorrow, my dear. I was hoping to come to you today. And if my health allows, I shall see you in an hour. But in any case, I shall tell you tomorrow how much I love you.[5]

As a result, the overall effect of Voltaire's letters to Mme Denis, when taken together, is not at all erotic: there is no doubt that Voltaire was strongly attracted to Mme Denis, that he wanted to make love to her, and that he desperately wanted to spend intimate time with her; but one is much more deeply impressed by the underlying tone of sadness, weakness, frustration and pessimism.

> The day before yesterday I returned to Paris, and I was ill when I got here. Today I have been painfully unwell, I wanted to go out and come and see you, but I could not. That is how my unhappy life is organised, or rather disorganised. I think of you, and I shall love you until my death, for as long as the time which remains to me, if any.[6]

> My dear, I had not slept, I was dead with fatigue, when you sent to me; and now my cruel fate forces me to go to Versailles. Oh, when will you be my neighbour! I hope to see you in a few days. Farewell, I am disgusted with this world, but more entranced than ever by you.[7]

Voltaire's self-pitying complaints cannot have helped make Mme Denis love him more, especially on those other, and all too frequent, ccasions when he made it plain that he could not see her because he was gadding about, however unwillingly, with Émilie.

> My dear friend, I shall stay a few days longer at Versailles. My only sorrow is that I shall spend a month without you. I shall go in a few days to the château d'Anet, and from there I shall go to take the waters at Passy. Life is a torment without you, and without good health.[8]

But Voltaire's relationship with Mme Denis was limited not just by his continuing commitment to Émilie but also by his determination to keep it secret: Mme Denis was his niece, which meant that a sexual relationship between them would be regarded by the state and the Catholic Church as incestuous. Once the marquis du Châtelet had accepted Émilie's relationship with Voltaire, they lived almost openly as a couple, but Voltaire never acknowledged in public the sexual nature of his relationship with Mme Denis. The truth, though often suspected, may not have been known to any of Voltaire's friends beyond the comte d'Argental, and was not finally confirmed until Theodore Besterman published Voltaire's love letters to Mme Denis, two centuries after the event.

Even apart from the need for secrecy, it was an unbalanced affair, between an ageing man and a much younger woman: he needed her much more than she needed him, as he must have known. Voltaire was now fifty-two, and chronically unwell, whereas Mme Denis was only thirty-four, and still full of *joie de vivre*. She seems not to have been at all downcast by his frequent absences; on the contrary, she consoled herself by having a gay social life with her own friends, and indeed with other much younger and perhaps more attractive men, some of whom had been introduced to her by Voltaire and some of whom she took as lovers.

One of these was Jean-François Marmontel, a young (22-year-old) would-be writer from the southern province of the Cantal. Voltaire introduced him to Mme Denis, and in the spring of 1746 he twice invited her and Marmontel to take part in readings of his poem *La Pucelle*. At some point not long after, Mme Denis became Marmontel's mistress.[9]

And then there was François-Thomas-Marie de Baculard d'Arnaud, another of Voltaire's young literary protégés, who was also a rival for the favours of Mme Denis. In 1747 she wrote to him:

> Your verses are almost as delightful as you are, I am enchanted with them, and I thank you a thousand times. I am sorry to say, my dear heart, that I believe Voltaire is coming to supper here this evening. He will be busy with that woman [Émilie], but I cannot avoid inviting him, since a friend of his, the marquis d'Argens, is coming. Farewell, I feel that if God does not help me, I shall love you to madness.[10]

A little later she wrote to him again: 'Your letter is charming. As for me, I am dying to see you, and am upset that I am not in Paris.'[11] The following year she wrote to say: 'Farewell, I love you with all my heart, but I do not want a lover.'[12] Whether this meant that he had been her lover and was now being let go is unclear, but there is no doubt that Mme Denis had had, at the very least, an extended flirtation with him.

Evidently Mme Denis had a liberated attitude to love, sex and friendship, and did not treat her relationship with Voltaire as requiring any special emotional or sexual faithfulness. Even if she regarded him with affection, as she may well have done, she can have seen no grounds for offering him exclusive fidelity when he was so often unavailable, and still committed to Émilie. We do not know whether, at this stage, she made any protest at the one-sided nature of their affair; but we do know that, in later years, she bargained strenuously with Voltaire on the terms of their relationship.

Over the years Mme Denis has had a bad press, on the grounds that she was worldly, materialistic and self-centred; some people would describe her as a hard little number. On the other hand, she was pretty and sexy, lively and sociable, fond of music and the theatre, and good fun to be with. In later years she became stout, though still flirtatious and still lively and sociable, and in his late middle age her talents and her virtues suited Voltaire very well. But the plain fact was that she was never in love with Voltaire; and she cannot be blamed for that.

In any case, it would seem that Voltaire's frequent bouts of ill health were exacerbated by non-physical symptoms, such as sleeplessness,[13] unhappiness,[14] or a need for 'consolation' from Mme Denis.[15] At some point in 1746 (many of his letters to her are undated) he told her that he was suffering from 'anguish of soul, waste of time, wanting so much, working a bit, but doing nothing'.[16] It sounds as though Voltaire was going through a bad patch psychologically, in addition to his physical ailments.

If so, this may help to explain why he wrote very little during the years 1746–48. No doubt he continued to work on accumulating material for his three major history works, Le Siècle de Louis XIV, Le Précis du siècle de Louis XV, and the Essai sur les mœurs, for by habit and inclination he was relentlessly hard-working. But he wrote very little creatively during these years. In 1746 he started work on a new tragedy, Sémiramis, but he found it hard going, and it was not performed until the middle of 1748. The only other significant work he wrote during this time was the pessimistic little story Zadig, which he was working on in 1747 and which he published in September 1748. This was an important new development in his œuvre, the first of a series of philosophical contes, of which Voltaire eventually wrote about fifty-six, and which culminated more than a decade later in his masterpiece *Candide*. And the point of *Zadig*, rather like that of *Candide*, is that it was the story of a character whose life is buffeted by the storms of fate, which can raise him to the peak of success or cast him down to the abyss of misery, which make no moral sense and over which he has no control. It is a story redolent of *mal de vivre*, a phrase that, incidentally, may have been coined by Maupertuis.

Moreover, Voltaire almost goes underground during the years 1746–48. He continued to write roughly as many letters as he had before, but they give no real clue about his life. A large proportion of them are very short letters to Mme Denis, either asserting his love for her in minimalist terms or making appointments to see her or complaining of his ill health and unhappiness; they tell us almost nothing beyond these narrow subjects, and most of the rest are formalistic or impersonal, which are equally un-illuminating about Voltaire's real life. If we try to find out what Voltaire was doing or thinking or feeling during these years, by looking through the prism of the letters, we see almost nothing: he virtually disappears from view.

Cumulatively, these symptoms may suggest that Voltaire could have been suffering from chronic depression, just as he had been in 1726 when he first arrived in England, and again in 1729 after his return to France. Perhaps he was going through a dip of disillusionment after his intense efforts to become a success at court: he had made it, but at what cost, and for what purpose? He may also have been suffering from discouragement over the difficulty he was having in making a go of his new affair with Mme Denis.

But a contributory explanation for Voltaire's 'anguish of soul', could be that he was suffering a long-delayed reaction at the loss of his love for Émilie and at the pain this was causing both of them. It was several years since his original passion for Émilie had faded, but Émilie had persisted in turning a blind eye to it. Only now was she facing up to the fact that she had lost Voltaire for good; and the realisation was plunging her into deep sadness, or quite possibly into a depression of her own.

Characteristically, she tried to exorcise her pain by writing about it, in an extended essay, which she called *Discours sur le bonheur* ('Discourse on Happiness'). This question of happiness was one of the major 'philosophical' preoccupations of society in eighteenth-century France. No doubt this was one of the indirect consequences of the advance of the Enlightenment and rationalism and of the slow retreat of religious belief: if people were starting to believe less strongly in the Christian afterlife, and in the rewards and punishments that went with it, they were bound to be more interested in this life and how it could be lived. Mathematicians and physicists might be professionally interested in the philosophy of Newton, philosophers might be professionally interested in the philosophy of Locke, but everybody was interested in happiness and everybody wrote about it.

It has been calculated that happiness was the subject of over fifty weighty treatises in France in the eighteenth century;[17] but in fact the question of happiness bubbles up everywhere you look in the writings of the French eighteenth century. Montesquieu, Rousseau, Diderot, Helvetius, d'Holbach and Marmontel were among those who wrote about it repeatedly and at length; Voltaire never stopped discussing it with Mme du Deffand; and even Maupertuis, though a professional mathematician, could not resist plunging into the happiness debate as well.

So when Émilie du Châtelet wrote her essay *Discours sur le bonheur*, she was ostensibly making her own contribution to a constant subject of conversation that was going on all around her. Like her fellow-intellectuals, she tried to analyse the sources and ingredients of happiness, and to describe the essential ways of getting it or keeping it; and like many of them, she considered some of the various factors that can contribute to happiness, such as work, or love, or virtue. But the real purpose of her essay was to analyse the causes of her own *un*happiness and to try to prescribe for herself a cure. She concluded that the essential ingredient of real happiness was passionate love, but that if love fails, as it had in her case, there was no other resort but work, by which she meant intellectual work (*l'étude*). She does not mention Voltaire by name, but she leaves no doubt that she is writing about him and her love for him, and about how much she suffered when she lost him.

> The more our happiness depends on ourselves, the surer it is; and yet passion, which can give us greater pleasure and make us happiest, makes our happiness dependent on others: it is clear that I am talking of love.
>
> This passion is perhaps the only one which can make us want to live, and make us thank the author of nature, whoever he is, for having given us our life. If this mutual desire (*goût*), which is a sixth sense, and the finest, the most delicate, the most precious of all, can bring together two souls equally sensitive to happiness, to pleasure, everything is said, one needs nothing more to be happy; all that one needs is health.

I have received from God, it is true, one of those tender and unchanging souls, which do not know how to disguise or moderate their passions, which do not know any weakening or indifference (*dégoût*) and whose tenacity can endure anything, even the certainty of no longer being loved. But I was happy for ten years, with the love of him who had conquered my soul; and these ten years I spent face to face with him without a moment of disgust or weariness.

When age, illness, perhaps also the ease of pleasure had diminished his desire for me, I went for a long time without perceiving it. I loved for two, I was passing my entire life with him, and my heart, free from any suspicion, enjoyed the pleasure of loving and the illusion of thinking myself loved.

It is true that I have lost that happy state, and that it has not been without costing me many tears. It needs terrible blows to break such chains; the wound in my heart bled for a long time; I have had ground for complaint, and I forgave everything. I have had enough justice to realize that my heart was perhaps the only one, in this world, which could have such immutability as to deny the power of time. But the certainty of the impossibility of a revival of his desire and his passion, which I know is not natural, has gradually brought my heart to the peaceful sentiment of friendship; and this sentiment, combined with my passion for study, has made me fairly happy.

The great secret, to make sure that love does not make us unhappy, is to try never to be in the wrong with your lover, never to show him urgency when he cools off, but always to be one degree cooler than he is; it will not bring him back, but nothing will bring him back; there is nothing to be done but to forget someone who stops loving us.[18]

Émilie's *Discours sur le bonheur* is a heart-rending work, which will doubtless be read long after her translation of Newton has been forgotten. At the time she kept it secret, and it was not discovered until after her death. It seems that she finished writing it in 1747, so it is quite likely that she started drafting it in 1746.

Émilie probably did not show it to Voltaire, and he may not have known that she was writing it. But he cannot have been unaware of her emotional state of mind. If he was depressed in 1746 and 1747, it may have been partly a reflection of Emily's mood when she was writing her *Discours sur le bonheur*.

One symptom of Voltaire's evasiveness at this time is not just that we do not know what he was thinking or feeling, but that there are large stretches of time where we cannot tell, from his letters, what he was doing. As a result, many writers seek to fill in the blanks by drawing on the so-called *Mémoires* of Sebastien Longchamp, which provide some of the most frequently quoted anecdotes about this period of Voltaire's life.

The difficulty with these *Mémoires* is not just that they came out long after Longchamp's death, but that Longchamp almost certainly did not write them in the form in which they were published; and we do not really know how much of a part he did play in their composition. Sebastien Longchamp was a domestic servant who became Voltaire's secretary in 1746, when he was about twenty-eight years old. He had previously been the *valet de chambre* to the wife of the governor of Brussels. His sister was employed as Émilie's femme de chambre, and in January 1746 Émilie took him on as her *valet de chambre*. Later that year he became Voltaire's secretary, and he remained in Voltaire's employment, either at Cirey or in Paris, for about five years.

After Longchamp left Voltaire's employment in 1751, aged thirty-two or thirty-three, he disappeared from the scene. Thirty years later a certain abbé Jacques Joseph Marie Decroix, an enthusiastic student of the works of Voltaire, tracked down Longchamp and went to see him. Between 1781 and 1787 Decroix conducted a number of interviews with him, and wrote down his recollections of his time with Voltaire. It seems that these interviews were based largely on what Longchamp could remember of past events; he does not appear to have kept much of a written record at the time.

In about 1790 Longchamp died, at the age of seventy-two. Thirty-six years later, in 1826, Decroix published what he called the *Mémoires* of Longchamp, and he himself died in that same year. In short, the book was concocted by Decroix and may have been largely written by him; any connection between the events in Longchamp's life in the 1740s and the book published in the late 1820s is quite tenuous. Moreover, Decroix admitted, in his capacity as the 'editor' of the book, that Longchamp had added, from memory, things which he only knew through other people, and that there were possible 'inexactitudes' or 'errors', or 'exaggerations' in the text. So even Decroix doubted whether the *Mémoires* of Longchamp could be trusted as evidence of fact.

Moreover, Longchamp was personally dishonest. After Voltaire dismissed him in 1751, he took with him a number of Voltaire's papers. He was made to give most of them up quite soon thereafter, but he hung onto one of Voltaire's more important philosophical works, then unpublished, the *Traité de métaphysique* and did not surrender it until after Voltaire's death in 1778. In fact, Longchamp may have started purloining Voltaire's papers even before he went to work for him, as Voltaire told Frederick in September 1746: 'A secretary, whom Mme du Châtelet regrettably gave me, had taken the trouble to transcribe several of my letters, and several of hers, and indeed several of yours, and had placed them with a dealer in Brussels called Desvignes.'[19] This secretary, according to Frédéric Deloffre, must be Longchamp.[20]

Here is an often quoted passage, from Chapter 2 of the *Mémoires*, which describes one of Longchamp's earliest encounters with Mme du Châtelet as her *valet de chambre*:

The next day, while I was waiting for her to wake, I heard the sound of her bell. I entered her bedroom at the same time as her chamber-maid; she told her to draw the curtains, and got out of bed. While my sister was preparing a chemise, Madame, who was standing opposite me, suddenly let drop the chemise she was wearing, and remained naked like a marble statue. I was silent, and did not dare lift my eyes to look at her.

When I was alone with my sister, I asked her if Mme du Châtelet always changed her chemise like that in front of everybody. She said, No; but that she was not embarrassed to do it in front of her servants.

A few days later, at a moment when she was in her bath, she rang the bell; I hastened into her room; my sister, occupied elsewhere, was not there. Mme du Châtelet told me to take a kettle which was in front of the fire, and to pour some water into the bath, because it was getting cold. As I came closer, I saw that she was naked, and that they had not put in any bath essence, for the water was entirely transparent. Madame spread her legs, so that I could pour the boiling water more conveniently without hurting her. As I began this task, my eyes fell on what I did not seek to see; ashamed, and turning away my head as much as possible, my hand shook and poured the water anyhow. 'Take care', she said brusquely, in a louder voice, 'or you will scald me.' I was obliged to keep my eyes on my work, and to stay there longer than I should have wished. This incident seemed to me even stranger than that of the chemise.[21]

These incidents may have occurred, or they may not; but they are entirely plausible. A disdainful disregard for servants, and the lordly assumption of an invisible but uncrossable barrier between them and the master-class, was an integral part of the ethos of the French aristocracy at that time. But you only have to read this passage once to know that its primary purpose is not information but titillation: this is a salacious serving up of What the Butler Saw. The flaw in the *Mémoires* is not just to do with possible errors of fact; it is about the moral intentions behind the whole concoction.

Nevertheless, because there is often no alternative source, the juicy but unreliable little anecdotes in the Longchamp *Mémoires* are regularly quoted at length by Voltaire biographers, occasionally with a cough of embarrassment but often with unscrupulous enthusiasm.

There is one episode in 1747 for which we do not have to depend on Longchamp. This was a visit that Voltaire and Émilie paid to the duchesse du Maine at her summer residence in the château d'Anet, near Dreux, and on this occasion we have a sizzling contemporary account, in a series of letters from Mme de Staal, at the château, to Mme du Deffand, in Paris.

Mme du Châtelet and Voltaire, who were expected today, appeared last night at midnight, like two ghosts. We were just getting up from table, but these ghosts were famished: they had to have supper and, moreover, some beds, which had not been prepared. The concierge was already in bed but got up in haste. Voltaire found a place to lie; but as for the lady, her bed was not suitable, and we have to find her another room today. As for her bed, she made it herself, for lack of available servants, and she found a defect in the mattress which, I think, offended her very precise mind more than her indelicate body.

Our ghosts did not show themselves all day long, but yesterday they put in an appearance at ten o'clock in the evening. I do not suppose that we shall see more of them today; the one is writing about high matters, the other is writing a commentary on Newton; they do not want either to play or to walk; they are completely useless in society, where their learned writings are of no relevance. Much worse, this evening's apparition launched into a vehement denunciation of the choice of tables for playing *cavagnole*, and in a tone which for us is quite unheard of.[22]

Mme de Staal was the companion of Mme du Maine, and though she was a baronne (by marriage), she was of quite modest social origins. It would seem that Émilie, who was noble in her own right, had treated her like a servant, and Mme de Staal was smarting at it. Five days later Mme de Staal gave Mme du Deffand another instalment on the unsociable conduct of Voltaire and Émilie at the château.

Mme du Châtelet yesterday moved to a third room: she could no longer stand the one she had chosen; it was too noisy, and there was smoke but no fire (which seems symptomatic of her). As for the noise, it is not at night that it upsets her, she told me, but during the day, at the height of her work, and it disturbs her ideas. She is currently making a review of her principles: it is an exercise that she repeats each year, without which they might escape her, and perhaps go so far that she might never find any of them again. She prefers this occupation to any amusement, and persists in not showing herself before nightfall. Voltaire has given us some gallant verses, which go some way to repairing the poor impression of their extraordinary behaviour.[23]

During the following week Voltaire and Émilie redeemed themselves somewhat in the eyes of Mme de Staal, for he got the house guests to stage his comedy *Le Grand Boursoufle*, which Mme de Staal greatly enjoyed; she was particularly full of admiration for the acting of Mme du Châtelet, with one reservation:

She could not submit to the simplicity of costume which her rôle required, but preferred the interest of her own appearance to that of the play; this caused a disagreement between her and Voltaire, but she is the sovereign and he the slave. I am sorry that they have gone, even though I was quite irritated by the various acts of wilfulness which she imposed on me.[24]

Three days later, after the departure of Voltaire and Émilie, Mme de Staal sent Mme du Deffand an epilogue of their visit.

We shall keep a good room for you: it is the one which Mme du Châtelet, after an exact survey of the whole house, took for herself. There will be a little less furniture in it, for she had devastated all the other rooms which she had used so as to furnish this one. We found it now had six or seven tables: she needed them of every size, immense ones to spread out her papers, solid ones for her dressing case and lighter ones for her pompons and her jewels. But this fine array did not save her from an accident, in which, after a night of writing, an ink bottle was spilt over her papers; what was spoiled was her algebra, which is difficult to get cleaned up.[25]

On his return to Paris, Voltaire wrote to Mme Denis to tell her that he had been ill at Anet, but that he hoped to recover his strength with her. 'My heart and my prick* send you the most tender good wishes. This evening I shall surely see you.'[26] In September Voltaire and Émilie went to take the waters at Passy, the recently developed spa just outside Paris. But the waters did him no good: he told Mme Denis afterwards, that he felt a hundred times worse than before, and that in a few days he was to be 'dragged off' to Fontainebleau.[27]

Longchamp had now become Voltaire's secretary, and his account of their visit to Fontainebleau contains one of the most celebrated anecdotes in his *Mémoires*. He relates how, every evening, Émilie would join the gamblers in the queen's entourage, and every evening she would lose heavily. At first she lost all the money she had with her, amounting to 400 louis; Voltaire lent her 200 louis more, and she lost that; a servant brought her another 200 louis from Paris, and she lost that. At last Voltaire, alarmed at the scale of her losses, tried to warn her that she was obviously playing with cheats. He said it in an undertone, and in English, but someone heard him and repeated his words. To accuse the queen's entourage of cheating was obviously a dangerous insult. Voltaire and Émilie at once left the room and decided to return immediately to Paris; they roused their coachman in the middle of the night and left Fontainebleau before daybreak.

Voltaire was evidently worried that he might pay heavily for his overheard remark. So before reaching Paris he left the carriage and wrote a letter to Mme du Maine at Sceaux, telling her of his predicament and asking her to give him asylum, so as to hide from his enemies. She immediately invited him to stay.

> He waited until nightfall to travel to Sceaux, where he was taken to a secret staircase, which led to a private apartment. It was from this retreat that he came down every night, to see Madame la duchesse du Maine, after she had gone to bed and all her servants had retired. A single footman, who was in the know, put up a little table close to her bed, and brought a supper for M. de Voltaire. The princess took great pleasure in seeing him and talking with him. He amused her with the playfulness of his conversation, and she told him many old anecdotes about the court which he did not know. Sometimes, after the meal, he would read a story or a little novel, which he had written

---

* As so often, Voltaire wrote to Mme Denis in Italian. In her copy of this letter she heavily crossed out the Italian word for 'prick' (*cazzo*), replacing it with the word *spirito*.

during the day to amuse her. That is how he wrote *Babouc*, *Memnon*, *Micromégas* and *Zadig,* of which he wrote a few chapters every day. Two months passed in this way, before M. de Voltaire dared leave the apartment in daylight. But at last Madame du Châtelet managed to pacify the gamblers who felt that they had been insulted by M. de Voltaire's remarks.[28]

There are other picturesque ingredients in Longchamp's story: when Émilie and Voltaire were travelling back to Paris, the axle of their carriage broke. A wheelwright was called, but they had no money to pay him; but they were rescued by a gentleman who happened to be passing, and who happened to be a friend of theirs, and he paid the wheelwright.

There are obvious questions about the accuracy of Longchamp's story: he places the incident in 1746, when we know it took place in 1747; and Voltaire's seclusion at Sceaux did not last two months, and probably no more than ten days. Moreover, Longchamp was not present at the gambling session, nor in the carriage when the axle broke, nor when Voltaire made his way to Sceaux by night, and he does not say who gave him these details. And if you summarise all the melodramatic ingredients of the story – the sensational overheard remark, the dramatic escape by night, the broken axle, the providential but nameless wheelwright, the providential but nameless friend, more travel by night, the secret staircase, the secret room, the midnight conversations – it is hard to avoid the suspicion that they are far too much like the cobbled-together fragments of an adventure story for children.

It is possible that Voltaire was working on *Zadig* in his seclusion at Sceaux, partly as a pastime, partly so as to have something to read aloud for the entertainment of the duchesse du Maine – just as, eleven years later, he composed some or all of *Candide* during a visit to Schwetzingen and read some of it aloud to the Elector-Palatine. Whether Voltaire actually wrote any of *Zadig* during this particular visit to Sceaux is unclear, though the pessimism-fatalism of the story of *Zadig* may well have been partly inspired by his own depressed mood at the time, whereas eleven years later Voltaire was in a much more cheerful frame of mind, and the apparent pessimism of *Candide* was lightened by an astonishingly innovative gaiety.

In December 1747 the royal court staged a performance of Voltaire's comedy *L'Enfant prodigue* in the king's private theatre, and it went so well that Mme de Pompadour persuaded the king to invite Voltaire to

Versailles. Voltaire sought to thank Mme de Pompadour by writing her a flattering little ode.

> Pompadour, you embellish
> The court, Parnassus, and Cythera.
> Charm of every heart, treasure of a single mortal,
> Let such a lovely destiny prove eternal!
> Let your precious days be marked by feasts!
> Let the peace of our fields return with Louis!
> May you both be without enemies,
> And both keep all your conquests![29]

But he had overstepped the mark. Everyone knew that Mme de Pompadour was the king's mistress, but it was unwise to underline the fact so publicly. The king did not mind, nor did Mme de Pompadour; but the queen was offended, and Voltaire decided to make himself scarce. He later denied that he had been sent into exile, but he evidently thought he would be safer if he disappeared for a while from public view. In mid-January 1748 Voltaire and Émilie left Paris to spend some time at the court of Stanislas, at Lunéville in Lorraine. It was the beginning of the last act of their life together.[30]

18

DEATH OF ÉMILIE

1748–1749

THE COURT OF STANISLAS LESZCZYŃSKI at Lunéville, in the duchy of Lorraine, was a place of frivolity and amusement. Stanislas was a former king of Poland; in fact, he had twice been king of Poland, and on both occasions he had been installed by the Swedes and driven out by the Russians and the Austrians. After his second eviction, in 1737, he was given the duchy of Lorraine, but only as a precarious life-tenancy: his daughter Maria Leszczyńska had married Louis XV in 1725, and part of the deal was that, when Stanislas died, Lorraine would become an integral part of France.

In practice, Lorraine was already virtually subject to the French government, and Stanislas, now seventy years old, had no political power and no political ambition; the only purposes of his court were social and cultural. Since he was a civilised man, this suited him rather well, and his court laid on a non-stop succession of parties and plays, operas and suppers, where everybody had a good time.

Émilie had long been familiar with the court at Lunéville. Her husband came from an ancient line of Lorraine nobility, and Cirey was not far away; and now she hoped that Stanislas would give her husband command of the military forces in the duchy. But her real reason for going to Lunéville was to look for entertainment, and perhaps also for a little flirtation.

One of the consequences of a court without politics or policy was that the social life was dominated by women, since there was very little in the way of business to keep their men there. Most of the men were in the army in one way or another, which meant that if they were not campaigning in the field, they were probably tied to routine military duties in barracks at Nancy, which was not far from Lunéville but far enough to be tiresome. The few men around were highly prized by the women, with the result that, in the intervals between the parties and the plays, the main preoccupations of the court were flirtation, love-affairs and sex. As Voltaire commented acidly, in a letter to Mme de Champbonin, his dear friend at Cirey: 'Here we know very little of the disposition of the armies in the field: *lansquenet** [a card game] and love are the main business of this court.'[1]

The key figure at this flirtatious court was Marie-Françoise-Catherine de Beauvau, marquise de Boufflers, a fascinating and charming woman in her mid-thirties, whose talents included painting and playing the harp. She was also adept at playing the game of love, and she had several lovers at the court, some of them simultaneously. She was not in love with any of them; for her, the point of the game was not love but pleasure, flirtation and power.

One of her first lovers was said to be François-Étienne Devaux, Mme de Graffigny's penfriend, nicknamed 'Pan-Pan'. Another was Antoine-Marie de Chaumont, marquis de La Galaizière, the Chancellor at the court of Lorraine, and virtually the prime minister of the duchy. But she also became the mistress of duke Stanislas himself. In 1747 she also took on a young salon-soldier and minor poet, Jean-François, marquis de Saint-Lambert. And finally, or at least in addition, in 1748 she took on another handsome young lover, the vicomte Adhémar de Marsanne.

Voltaire did not enjoy the social whirl at the court of Lorraine. 'Well, here I am at Lunéville!', he wrote to d'Argental on 1 February 1748, shortly after they had arrived. 'But why? Mme du Châtelet sends you the most tender compliments; but I do not know if she intends to stay here the whole of the month of February. I am just a little planet in her orbit, I follow her hither and yon, and even though I lead a most pleasant and convenient life here, I should be delighted if I could return to pay my respects to you.'[2]

Émilie, however, was thoroughly enjoying herself. She took a leading part in an opera called *Issé,* by Antoine de La Motte, in which she appeared in three performances, lavishly decked out with diamonds; and Stanislas laid on, in Voltaire's honour, a performance of his tragedy

---

* *Lansquenet* was a card game reputedly introduced into France in the sixteenth century by German mercenary soldiers, known in a Frenchified version of the German word *Landsknecht*.

Mérope, at which everybody wept profusely. But Voltaire wanted to be gone: 'I do not know if she intends to pass her whole life here,' he complained to d'Argental; 'as for me, I prefer a calm life and the charms of friendship to any of these fêtes, and I would much rather return to your court.'[3]

Five weeks later, Voltaire was still trying to leave. 'My dear child,' he wrote to Mme Denis,

> I no longer know when I shall be able to come home. I have already sent off my little packages, and by now they must already be in Paris; but we are being kept back in Lunéville by the sickness of Mme de Boufflers. She has had a temperature for a week now, and we cannot leave her; but here I am, without a dressing gown, without shirts and, worst of all, without books. Perhaps we shall leave in three or four days, or perhaps in fifteen. I am completely uncertain of my fate.[4]

But Émilie was determined not to leave, because she had now fallen head over heels in love with Jean-François, marquis de Saint-Lambert. Very soon after their arrival she started making eyes at him; he responded; she fell into his arms; he told her that he loved her; and she swept him up into a passionate love affair.

Saint-Lambert was available because Mme de Boufflers had just transferred her favours from him to Adhémar de Marsanne; and since he was a callow young man, he may have assumed that a fling with Émilie du Châtelet would be just another turn on the Lunéville roundabout, without meaning or consequence. If so, he reckoned without Émilie's fiery and passionate temperament and her desperate craving for love and sexual fulfilment. He found himself the object of her ardent and all-devouring infatuation, to which he was incapable of responding. Throughout their love affair, which lasted another eighteen months, Émilie never ceased to reiterate the consuming intensity of her love for him, just as she never ceased to reproach him for his lukewarm indifference.

Under the assault of her impassioned demands for love, Saint-Lambert was reduced to questioning her sincerity. She was indignant:

> What do you mean by saying that I have become accustomed to mistake simple attraction for true love (*prendre des engouements pour des passions*)? I swear to you that for the past fifteen years I have been attracted to only one man (*je ne me suis connue qu'un goût*), that my

heart has never felt anything which it had to refuse or resist, and that you are the only one who has made me feel that my heart was still capable of love.[5]

At first Voltaire may not have realised what was going on, for Émilie pretended that she needed to stay at Lunéville in order to lobby for her husband's military promotion. But he soon found out. 'I have just had', she told Saint-Lambert, 'a fairly emotional scene with M. de Voltaire about you, which ended with me denying everything. I hope that tomorrow he will think no more about it.'[6] But of course Voltaire did go on thinking about it. 'M. de Voltaire is in the greatest fury, I am afraid he will explode; he told me this morning that he could easily see that I had had no fire in my grate last night, and he left in the greatest anger.'[7] Since the grate was cold, Voltaire guessed that she had spent the night not in her own apartment, but with Saint-Lambert.

Despite Voltaire's anger, Émilie continued to pursue Saint-Lambert. After three months she could no longer resist Voltaire's desire to return to Paris, in order to supervise rehearsals for his new tragedy *Sémiramis*, and they set off at the end of April. They stopped at Cirey on the way, but they stayed there not just a day or two, as Voltaire had hoped,[8] but for more than ten days; Émilie could not bear to be without Saint-Lambert and summoned him to come to Cirey, and then went herself to spend a day or two with him at Nancy. It is hard to see how she could have crammed these frenzied comings and goings into so short a time, but the evidence of her letters is compelling.

> All my distrust of your weakness of character, all my resistance to love, have been unable to save me from the love you have inspired in me. I no longer seek to combat it, I realise the uselessness of it, the time I spent with you at Nancy has increased it so much that I myself am astonished. In fact, I am afraid I love you too much; come to Cirey to prove me wrong.[9]

Voltaire and Émilie finally reached Paris in the middle of May, but Émilie was already making plans for a new life with Saint-Lambert: 'As for me, here is my plan,' she wrote to him from the rue Traversière:

> To rejoin you in July, to get M. de Voltaire to believe that it is necessary to my fortune to go to Cirey, where you will come and see me, and then to pass the whole of the rest of my life with you, either at

Lunéville or at Cirey, and to forget the rest of the world for you. You have not told me whether people know about your trip to Cirey; but what do I care? Do not tell me anything, except that you love me, tell me that over and over without end, for you will never say it enough for my happiness.[10]

Almost immediately Émilie dragged Voltaire back to Lorraine again, cutting short their visit to Paris after only six weeks. As a result, Voltaire did not manage to see much, if anything, of Mme Denis during this visit. From Lunéville he had repeatedly told her how much he loved her and how much he wanted to be with her;[11] but once arrived in Paris, his life seems to have been taken over by preparations for *Sémiramis* or by duties at the court at Versailles. He wrote six letters to Mme Denis during this period, but most of them are full of complaints about his health and his work, and one of them tells her that he cannot see her; in none of them is there any trace of a meeting between them.[12]

Mme Denis was so put out by Voltaire's neglect that, after Voltaire and Émilie returned to Lorraine at the end of June, she told him that she was thinking of getting married again. She did not give any details of her future husband, except to say that he was an army major based in Lille, and we may suspect that her real purpose was to provoke a response from Voltaire. Perhaps she had learned of Émilie's affair with Saint-Lambert and thought that this was her chance to detach Voltaire from Émilie.

At first no suspicions seem to have crossed Voltaire's mind, and he became quite anxious. 'Is it really impossible for us to live together? Can I not take the place of your Lille major?' And he added, for good measure, in Italian: 'I throw myself at your knees and plant kisses on all your beauties, your round breasts, your enchanting arse, on all of you, who have so often given me a hard-on and plunged me in a river of delight.'[13]

Mme Denis was unmoved by Voltaire's sexual intonation, however, and she kept him in suspense over the spectral Lille major for another four months. Voltaire kept rising to the bait. 'My dear child, your Lille major upsets me. What decision will you take? All I know is that I should be greatly pained if you left Paris, and I had no consolation. My ill health makes me desperate. But the idea of losing you wipes me out.'[14]

Émilie, meanwhile, was tirelessly pursuing her passion for Saint-Lambert and, with the help of Mme de Boufflers, secured optimum living arrangements to make it easy for them to see each other. Mme de Boufflers was glad to promote Émilie's affair with Saint-Lambert because she was fully occupied with her new lover, Adhémar de Marsanne. The court of Lorraine now moved to Stanislas' summer residence at Commercy, some 20 miles west of Nancy, and Voltaire and Émilie were lodged in one of the wings of the château, with Voltaire on the second floor and Émilie in a ground-floor apartment with a door and windows giving onto the main courtyard. 'I am writing to you from the room of Mme de Boufflers, who is looking after you,' she told Saint-Lambert.. 'You will have an apartment near the chapel and the library, they are putting a bed there, and you can go there this evening. I beg you, make sure that you go there this evening, if you do not want me to be the unhappiest creature in this world. I shall not leave you, I adore you.'[15]

And yet Saint-Lambert was still not in love with her. 'What hurts me most,' she told him, 'is that though I love you passionately, I am not making you happy. Your letters are like your conversation, half tender and half detached, and it seems that you reproach yourself for loving me. But I cannot help feeling, at every moment, that I miss you, that without you everything else is unbearable, and that everything bores me, including solitude.'[16]

At the end of August, Mme de Boufflers went to take the waters at Plombières; Émilie went with her, and so did Adhémar de Marsanne. So Voltaire was free to return briefly to Paris, where he arrived on 30 August, just one day too late to see the première of *Sémiramis* at the Comédie Française. The play was rather ridiculed by the critics, and though Voltaire blamed the shortcomings of the play on the actors,[17] he recognised that the appearance of the ghost had been ludicrous: the actor was manifestly 'as plump as a monk', and looked rather less like a ghost than like the porter of the mausoleum.[18] 'At future performances', he wrote to d'Argental, 'please make sure that the ghost appears in darkness, and that it is not played by a chubby boy with his face showing. It is easy to make it dark, if they put out the candles in the wings and lower a frame round the chandeliers'.[19]

During this trip to Paris, Voltaire made much greater efforts to see Mme Denis than he had before. 'Yes, my dear, I shall see you this evening.' 'I hope to see you tomorrow, and to dine with you.' 'I have had a thousand appointments, and I have been ill. But nothing will stop me from coming to see you in a few hours' time.'[20] By the time Voltaire left Paris for Lunéville once more, on 10 September, he seems to have been reassured that he had little immediate reason to worry about the story of her major. 'My dear child,' he wrote to her cheerfully at the end of the month, 'my health has been getting better, and the more it does, the more I miss you. Tell me your news about the army citadel at Lille, and about your new comedy *La Femme à la mode*.'[21]

Early in October, however, Voltaire became quite agitated when he learned that there were plans to stage a parody of *Sémiramis*, both in Paris and at the court. At the time parodies of serious plays were common, especially by the acting troupe at the Théâtre des Italiens, and were in effect a back-hand form of compliment to the success of popular plays; several of Voltaire's own plays had already been parodied in the past, and others would be later. But on this occasion Voltaire was so conscious that aspects of *Sémiramis* were inherently open to mockery that he was intensely anxious to prevent the play being further ridiculed, and he wrote to everybody he knew to stop the parody being staged.

Voltaire was particularly upset that the proposed parody had been passed by Crébillon, the official theatre censor. Prosper Jolyot Crébillon was an elderly and long-established poet and playwright who had become a stumbling block in Voltaire's path: as royal censor, he insisted on changes to Voltaire's *Temple du goût* in 1733, he stopped the performance of *Mahomet* in 1742, and he stopped the performance of *La Mort de César* in 1743. Voltaire had come to think of Crébillon as a troublesome and unfriendly rival, and when Crébillon's tragedy *Catilina* was performed in December 1748, Voltaire was delighted to claim that it had been a flop; from now on Crébillon would be a permanent butt of Voltaire's bile.

To prevent the parody of *Sémiramis*, Voltaire wrote to all and sundry, to the chief of police (twice), to Maurepas, the Secretary of State, to Mme de Pompadour and even to the queen.[22] Mme de Pompadour was helpful, but Maurepas was not. Mme de Pompadour promised that, when *Sémiramis* was put on at Fontainebleau at the end of the month, it would not be coupled with a performance of the parody; but Maurepas decided that the parody could be performed in Paris, and that the best that could be done for Voltaire was to delay the satire until after the first run of his play. 'But since this first run can already be said to have finished,' Voltaire complained to d'Argental, 'we can conclude from the letter of M. de Maurepas that the Théâtre des Italiens is already entitled to hold me up to ridicule.'[23] In the event the planned parody was not, after all, performed; Voltaire's intense lobbying may have paid off, but it had cost him some four months of anxiety and agitation.

During the autumn Voltaire repeatedly urged Émilie that they should return to Paris, but she could not bear to leave Saint-Lambert, and in December he told Mme Denis despondently that he would not be seeing her in Paris before January: 'I shall not be leaving here much before Christmas. I confess that I feel great sadness to be far from you for so long, but that is what has been decided, and I must submit to my fate. I shall be going to Cirey for a few days, and then at Christmas at last I shall leave for Paris.'[24]

In fact, Émilie had already told d'Argental that she intended to spend Christmas at Cirey and return to Paris at the beginning of January; and her letter makes it clear that this was her personal decision, not one shared with Voltaire.[25] They reached Cirey on 24 December 1748, and almost immediately she broke the bad news: she was pregnant by Saint-Lambert, and she needed to stay on at Cirey to work out what to do about it. Voltaire now had to tell Mme Denis that there was another postponement of their return to Paris, though he did not tell her the real reason.[26]

Émilie's discovery of her pregnancy must have been a major shock, not least because she was now forty-two years old, and childbirth at her age was in those days quite dangerous. Almost immediately she and Voltaire agreed that there was only one possible course of action: they had to legitimise the pregnancy by getting the world, and her husband, to believe that he was the father of the child.

Émilie had not had sexual relations with the marquis for some years, so she and Voltaire resolved to stage a scenario for a marital reconciliation, virtually in public, and they invited him to Cirey, ostensibly to discuss family business. He was happy to be invited, pleased when they fêted him in a convivial atmosphere, more than delighted when Émilie went through the motions of seducing him, and rapturous when Émilie told him, later in January, that she was pregnant. 'M. du Châtelet is not as upset as I am over my pregnancy', she told Saint-Lambert; 'he tells me that he hopes I will give him a son.'[27]

Though Mme Denis did not know about Émilie's pregnancy, she now started to raise the stakes over her marriage plans. In October she had stopped writing about her 'Lille major', but in December she started hinting that she had another husband in view, though she did not say who it was. 'You have written to me about a more suitable affair than that of the army citadel at Lille,' he wrote to her in late December: 'Please tell me more. What is this affair of which you write so mysteriously?'[28]

For a short while Mme Denis still kept Voltaire on tenterhooks, but Voltaire soon suspected that he was being had. 'My dear child, I have just received your letter of the 2nd. A lieutenant-general! An envoy of the king to Italy! My dear child, there is no way you could turn that down. Marry your lieutenant-general, I beg you on my knees. Of course, this is not what I had dreamed of; quite the contrary.'[29]

A few days later Mme Denis named her lieutenant-general, but now she seemed to be hesitating between him and the duc de Richelieu. 'You have said no more about M. de La Caseique; I thought from your recent letter that you were just about to take his name. For myself, I should be upset but full of joy for you. But this affair seems to me more feasible, according to what you tell me, than that with the maréchal de Richelieu.'[30]

In her letter Mme Denis must have hinted at a relationship with the duc de Richelieu, and conceivably at the possibility of marriage with him, since his second wife, Marie-Élisabeth de Guise, had died in 1740. Voltaire knew that Richelieu had affairs with many women, and he described him, three months later, as a 'great deceiver of women' (*un grand trompeur de femmes*);[31] but he evidently thought that, for Mme Denis, Richelieu was well out of reach. We do know, however, that Richelieu did at some point have an affair with Mme Denis, and it may have been now.[32]

A few days later Mme Denis seems to have abandoned her tantalising stories of imminent marriage, for she now confronted Voltaire with questions that he had long been avoiding. Though we do not have the text of her letter, we can guess, in the light of his answer, that one of them must have gone to the heart of their relationship: was he prepared to give up Émilie?

No, Voltaire told her, he was not. 'Have I not opened my heart to you? Do you not know that I have a duty to the public not to make a scandal, which they would turn to ridicule? That I have felt duty bound to remain loyal, and to respect a liaison which has lasted twenty years?'[33]

Voltaire's explanations to Mme Denis of his feelings and reasons are painfully minimalist. He has often told Mme Denis that he loves her, but here he says nothing about how he will translate it into action. He says nothing about loving Émilie, but he makes it plain that he will not leave her; he implies that he is only staying with her out of long-standing loyalty. He tells Mme Denis nothing about Émilie's pregnancy, but he says that he will not leave her for fear of causing a scandal. But the word Voltaire uses for scandal, *éclat*, is ambiguous in its implications. Was he just referring to the scandal that he would incur if he left Émilie in the lurch, after sixteen (not twenty) years of partnership? Was he referring to the scandal that he would incur if he left Émilie in the lurch when she was pregnant? Or was he, as some scholars think, obliquely referring to the question of possibly marrying Mme Denis?

The idea seems absurd. Mme Denis was his niece, and marriage with her would be incestuous and illegal. And yet it was not absolutely impossible, in the eighteenth century, for a man to marry his niece, if he got the right papal dispensation. Charles-Marie de La Condamine, the mathematician and physicist and one of Voltaire's friends, married his niece in 1756; and the financier Jean Pâris de Montmartel also married his niece. Voltaire investigated the question in some detail. He claimed that there may have been about forty such marriages every year; and he estimated that the cost of the papal dispensation would have been some 120,000 francs ('once you include the small expenses'), though he went on to say: 'I have always heard it said that it cost M. de Montmartel only 80,000 francs.'[34]

If Voltaire was so interested in the question of marriage between uncles and nieces and what it entailed, the implication must be that at some stage he gave real consideration to the idea of marriage with Mme Denis. The essays in which he set out his research on the subject were not published until much later, but the question could well have started to interest him at the height of his love affair with Mme Denis, especially if we are to judge by the frequency with which Voltaire told her, at that period, how much he wanted to live with her.

Whether Voltaire ever talked openly about marriage to Mme Denis is not known, but after this letter from him, Mme Denis stopped writing about her prospects of marriage to other men. For the moment he had called her bluff.

And yet Voltaire's position was tantalisingly enigmatic and riddled with contradictions. He was staying with Émilie, even though she was passionately in love with Saint-Lambert and was carrying Saint-Lambert's child; would he stay with her after the birth of a baby fathered by Saint-Lambert? It seems almost inconceivable, but Voltaire does not say. For the moment he could get no further than to say that he intended to stay with Émilie.

And yet he could not wait to get away from her; for in the middle of the crisis over her pregnancy he now started making plans to visit Frederick – a project that he knew Émilie would detest – and to go there in the weeks immediately before she was due to give birth. Over the previous five years his correspondence with Frederick had virtually gone into hibernation, but in 1749 his interest sprang to life once more. That year, he wrote fifteen letters to the Prussian king, and in January 1749 Voltaire openly asked Frederick for an invitation. 'Do you deign to wish, Sire, that I should have the happiness of coming to pay my respects to you? The king, my master, has relieved me of all my duties at court. It would be sweet to come and fall at your feet at the beginning of summer.'[35]

If the king had relieved him of all his duties as a Gentleman in Ordinary at the court, it was no doubt because of his extended absences in Lorraine. Later in the spring of 1749 Voltaire was given permission to sell his position as Gentleman in Ordinary, while keeping the right to use the title; and he did so on 27 May, for £60,000.[36]* But the point that Voltaire was making to Frederick was clear enough: he was free from his duties at Versailles, he was no longer a servant of the French king and he was now available; and he spent much of the next year negotiating with Frederick the terms of a visit to Potsdam.

Meanwhile, Voltaire and Émilie were still lingering at Cirey, and they had to explain it to their friends. 'I have some essential tasks at Cirey,' Émilie told d'Argental, 'which would become very tiresome if I did not do them: there is a master blacksmith who is leaving, and another who is taking over, some woods which need looking after, and some legal arguments which must be settled, and all that, even if I do not waste a minute, cannot be finished before the end of the month.'[37] D'Argental could not possibly have believed this absurd story, especially when Voltaire explained in another letter that Émilie was making use of her time at Cirey to get back to her scientific work. 'She has just finished a preface on Newton, and it is a masterpiece. There is nobody at the Académie des Sciences who could have done it better.'[38]

At the end of January Voltaire and Émilie returned to Paris, and Émilie tried to go on working at her translation of Newton's *Principia*; but she was so distracted that for several weeks she was unable to concentrate.[39] Instead, she spent most of her time in solitude, writing impassioned, reproachful and despairing love letters to Saint-Lambert in Lorraine.

> I cannot help it, I cannot help re-reading your last two letters, and I cannot find in them all the love which I desire, and which my love deserves. I regard the loss of your heart as the only unhappiness which I fear, but it is your heart, such as I imagine it, that I adore; it can make

---

* Besterman says £53,000 (Besterman, *Voltaire*, p. 279), Pomeau £60,000 (Pomeau et al., *Voltaire en son temps*, vol. I, p. 592).

my happiness, but if you give it to me worn out and cold, I shall not be happy. I love you with an extreme ardour, which makes everything else seem insipid, but if you love me so feebly, of what use are my feelings? I spend my life in monologues with you: this is my 23rd letter to you, and I have only received two in return.[40]

Bring back your heart to me, though I know all too well that desire cannot be brought back; perhaps study, care for my health, which really needs care, distance, even dissipation, can help me. I shall try it at least. I know that I must madden you with my letters, I hope I can undertake not to write to you until you have decided my fate.[41]

Needless to say, she went on writing to him and reproaching him for his failure to love her. 'I spend my life weeping over your faithlessness, but hiding my tears from those who could hurt me. You make me die of pain, me and that which should be most dear to you; you could end everything with a word, but you withhold it. That word is that you love me; but if you no longer love me, do not ever say so.'[42]

Meanwhile, Voltaire was stepping up his overtures to Frederick for a visit to Prussia.

You have a prodigious genius, and your genius is cultivated. But if, in the happy leisure which you have secured with so much glory, you wished to go on occupying yourself with literature, if your passion for great souls should last, as I hope, if you wanted to perfect yourself in all the delicacies of our language and of our poetry, to which you do so much honour, you ought to have the goodness to work with me for two hours a day for six weeks or two months.[43]

In Paris, Voltaire made contact with Denis Diderot, who was still making his way as a young and comparatively unknown writer. In June 1749 Diderot sent Voltaire a copy of his latest book, *Lettre sur les aveugles à l'usage de ceux qui voient* (Letter on the blind for the benefit of those who can see). This was a philosophical work, in the form of a dialogue, which took the example of a man born blind, to argue against the existence of God.

Voltaire thanked him for his 'ingenious and profound book', and sent him in return a copy of his own *Éléments de la Philosophie de Newton*.

I have read with extreme pleasure your book. But I confess that I am not at all of the opinion of the man who denies the existence of God just because he is born blind. I may be mistaken, but in his place I should have recognised a most intelligent being, who had given me so many other senses besides sight, and I should have suspected the existence of an infinitely capable craftsman. It must be most impertinent to pretend to guess what he is, and why he has made everything which exists, but it seems to me very bold to deny his existence. I should desire most passionately to talk with you.[44]

In fact, they did not meet at this time, though they corresponded by letter a few years later, when Voltaire was contributing to the *Encyclopédie*. But this first exchange of letters underlines one of the key differences between Voltaire and some of the younger intellectuals of the Enlightenment. Voltaire had always been, and would remain, a Deist, who believed in some kind of benevolent God, though not the God of Christianity, whereas Diderot, like a growing number of the *philosophes*, inclined towards atheism, and it got him and them into trouble. In fact, the *Lettre sur les aveugles* caused such a scandal that on 24 July Diderot was imprisoned for three months in the Château de Vincennes. Voltaire was quite upset by the news. 'What barbarian is now persecuting that poor Diderot,' he exclaimed to d'Argental; 'I really hate a country where the sanctimonious hypocrites can shut up a philosopher.' By chance, the governor of the Vincennes prison was a cousin of Émilie, and she wrote to ask him to soften Diderot's treatment as far as he could.[45]

Émilie was now distraught to learn, through an inadvertent remark dropped by her husband, that Mme de Boufflers, wearying of Adhémar de Marsanne, had taken up with Saint-Lambert again. 'M. du Châtelet, with a naïveté which pierced me with a thousand dagger blows of which he was quite unaware, told me things which I would give half of my life to forget. What, would you leave me, without cause, without any reason, would you abandon me in the state I am in, would you make me die of pain! Would you betray me for someone who has inflicted such insults on you, and whose heart is so little made for yours, would you sacrifice me for her favours!'[46]

Yet Émilie did not give up her plan to have her baby in Lorraine. Stanislas readily invited her to come to Lunéville for her lying-in, but the support of Mme de Boufflers would be even more important, and Émilie asked for her help. And even though Mme de Boufflers was now sleeping with Saint-Lambert, she was not in the least in love with him, and she was perfectly prepared to be a sympathetic and helpful friend to Émilie.

Mme de Boufflers really consoled me; she came to see me at midday, and we did not part until eight o'clock in the evening, and honestly the time did not drag. All the time, truly almost all the time, we talked about you, she enchanted my heart, and I love her a thousand times better. She said that you love me passionately, and that you never stopped saying it. On the strength of that, I want to give myself up to your love and her friendship, and I feel that whatever either of you do to me, I shall always love both of you. You can already see how confident I am by the way I speak of her, but I love her madly, I have such a natural feeling for her, that if ever she were to put her mind to it, I could love her with an extreme tenderness. Mme de Boufflers is perhaps not capable of loving as much as I am, at least I hope not, for I should be quite upset if, having so many other advantages over me, she did not leave me that one. But I immediately grasped that she has a fancy for you, and you a bit for her.[47]

In June, Émilie began to panic that she was falling behind in her translation of Newton, despite the fact that she was getting regular help from a brilliant young mathematician called Alexis-Claude Clairault. 'The date I can leave depends not on me,' she told Saint-Lambert,

but on Clairault and on the difficulty of what I am doing; I am sac-rificing everything to it, including my appearance. I get up at nine o'clock, sometimes at eight; I work until three, when I take my coffee, I go back to work at four, and I stop at ten to eat a bite alone. I chat until midnight with M. de Voltaire, who joins me at my supper, and I start work again at midnight, until five in the morning. I used to go out in the evening, for I thought the daytime would be enough for work, but now I have made it a rule never to go out to supper, so as to be able to finish my work. My health is holding up marvellously, I am staying sober, and I am drowning in barley water, it keeps me going, my child moves a lot, and is as well as I am, or so I hope.[48]

By now her time was running out, and three weeks later Émilie and Voltaire set off for Lunéville, stopping on the way for a few days at Cirey. Three weeks later they arrived at Lunéville, and at the end of July Voltaire told Frederick that he would now come to Potsdam in the second half of September.[49]

In Lunéville, Émilie sought out distractions to take her mind off her anxieties over her forthcoming delivery: she went to parties, she gambled (and lost) and she tried to work on her translation of Newton. But above all, she continued to harry Saint-Lambert with demands for his love. She gave a reception, to which Saint-Lambert was invited and to which he came, but the next day she reproached him bitterly for not having paid her enough attention.

> My God, how impatient I got with all those who stayed behind after you left! My heart had so many things to say to you! But you treated me really cruelly, you did not look at me even once. I know that I ought to be grateful for it, that it was just decency and discretion, but for all that, I felt the loss of it; I am accustomed, at every single moment of my life, to see in your charming eyes that you are looking after me, that you love me. I did not want to love you to such excess, but now that I know you better, I feel that I can never love you enough.[50]

Towards the end of August, within a week or so of her due date, she wrote to him in despair: 'When I am with you, I endure my state with patience, and often I do not notice it; but when I miss you, everything seems black. I went today to my little house on foot, and my belly is so terribly swollen, I have such a pain in my back, I am so sad this evening, that I should not be astonished if I were to give birth tonight, though I should be in despair.'[51]

Voltaire, meanwhile, was leading his own solitary life. He had become largely reconciled to Saint-Lambert,[52] and he even commended to d'Argental the first draft of a long descriptive poem by Saint Lambert called The Seasons (Les Saisons), whose verses he said were very 'agreeable'. But he had soon tired of the narrow social round at the Lunéville court, and he even tried to avoid turning up at meal times; he claimed that his ill health required him to eat in his rooms. 'The poor state of my health,' he wrote to the major-domo,

> does not allow me, either to stay long at court, or to eat at the tables to which one must go at fixed times. I can assure you that, in Berlin, I have not been obliged to beg for bread, wine and a candle. The dignity of the king should not allow you to refuse these little attentions to an officer of the court of France, who has the honour to come to pay his respects to the king of Poland.[53]

In his isolation Voltaire seems to have become slightly unbalanced, for he now launched into a frenzied campaign of rivalry against Prosper

Jolyot Crébillon, the elderly poet and playwright, who had in the past trodden on Voltaire's toes. Nine months earlier, Crébillon's *Catilina* had been performed at the Comédie Française; now, out of the blue, Voltaire became possessed with anger over all the faults he saw in *Catilina*, and he resolved to write a Roman tragedy of his own, just to show up Crébillon. On 12 August he sent a first draft of the new work to d'Argental: 'Read it, just read what I am sending you! You will be astonished, as I am myself. In eight days, yes in eight days, not nine, my *Catilina* was written. It is all scribbled, and I am completely exhausted. We can take eight weeks to revise what I have written in eight days. But believe me, believe me, this is a real tragedy.'[54]

Voltaire soon renamed his tragedy *Rome sauvée*, in order to avoid any too close association with the *Catilina* of his hated rival, and he tried to enlist all his friends and allies in his campaign against Crébillon. 'I know that I am waging war,' he told d'Argental, 'and I want to wage it openly. Far from me to propose ambushes by night: arm yourselves, I beg you, for pitched battles, and gather my troops.'[55] Voltaire was notorious for his literary feuds, some of which became poisonously personal; in this case the ferocity of his campaign seems almost deranged, since Crébillon was now an old man and no longer a serious rival: most of his successful plays dated back thirty or forty years, well before Voltaire ever came on the scene. It is almost as if Voltaire had become unhinged by the stress of Émilie's pregnancy.

Voltaire also sought to enlist the support of Mme de Pompadour, his most highly placed friend at court. But she would have none of it: she was a supporter of Crébillon as well as of Voltaire, and she advised him not to get carried away. More ominously, she warned Voltaire not to go to Berlin: 'Farewell, and keep well; but do not think of going to find the king of Prussia, however great a king he may be, and however sublime his spirit. One should not want to leave our master when one knows his admirable qualities. For my own part, I should never forgive you.'[56]

Voltaire was in no mood to heed her warning. He had already written to Frederick, not just underlining his determination to go to Berlin but even virtually begging him to give him a Prussian decoration:

The king [Louis XV] cannot prevent me from running to thank you. No one can hold me back. Let me add that I ask you for a mark of your esteem, which would show Lunéville and the people on the road to Berlin that you deign to love me. Permit me to say that the position which I hold with the king my master is not merely compatible with the honour which I dare ask of you, but makes me deserve it all the more. In fact, I am speaking of the Order of Merit. I am preparing to leave in October.[57]

On the night of 3 September, Émilie's labour began. Despite her fears, it proved remarkably easy, and she was delivered quite soon of a baby girl. Voltaire immediately wrote in great joy to all his friends, starting with d'Argental: 'Last night Mme du Châtelet, while scribbling her *Newton*, felt a little need, she called her femme de chambre, who scarcely had time to hold out her apron and catch in it a little girl, which they put in its cradle. The mother arranged her papers, and went back to bed, and now, as I write, they are all sleeping like little dormice.'[58]

The good news did not last long. Within a few days Émilie developed a fever, no doubt from an infection. Doctors were called, but during the night of 9 September 1749 Émilie du Châtelet died. Her baby daughter died soon after.

Voltaire was devastated and instantly regretted the light-hearted gaiety with which he had recounted the story of her easy delivery.[59] 'Oh, my dear friend,' he wrote to d'Argental,

I have no one but you left on this earth. What a frightful blow! I told you of the happiest and most remarkable delivery. A terrible death followed it! And to add to the pain, I must stay another day in this abominable Lunéville, which caused her death. I shall go to Cirey with M. du Châtelet. From there I shall return to weep in your arms for the rest of my unhappy life. Pity me, my dear and admirable friend. Write to me at Cirey.[60]

He wrote the same day to Mme Denis: 'My dear child, I have just lost a friend of twenty years. As you know, I had long ceased to regard Mme du Châtelet as a woman, and I am sure that you share my grief. I am not abandoning M. du Châtelet in the pain which we both share. We must go to Cirey, to deal with important papers. From Cirey I shall return to Paris, to embrace you, and find in you my only consolation, and the sole hope of my life.'[61]

Émilie's exuberance and extravagance in life were reflected in the debts that she left on her death: £165,000, including over £5,000 due to various tradesmen, from butchers and builders to jewellers and dressmakers. Scholars puzzle how the marquis du Châtelet could have paid off these debts, but the broad arithmetic may not be too difficult. We do not really know how he had financed the purchase of the Hôtel Lambert in 1739, but we do know that by 1749 he had sold it, so that particular slate may have been wiped clean.[62] In Brussels, Émilie had failed to win her lawsuit claiming the inheritance of the estates of Ham and Beringhem, but in 1747 Voltaire had helped negotiate a fall-back settlement, by which the marquis would receive £200,000.[63] The defendants were painfully slow to hand over the cash, but by 1749 it seems that they had done so; at the time of Émilie's death, therefore, the marquis should have been well in credit.[64]

After Émilie's funeral Voltaire and the marquis left Lunéville and went together to Cirey to tidy up their respective affairs, personal and financial. They had to make a detailed inventory, so that Voltaire could remove his furniture and other property; and it seems that they destroyed all the letters between Voltaire and Émilie that they could find. For Voltaire it was a gruelling process. 'I do not know', he told d'Argental, 'how many days we shall stay in this house, which friendship had made beautiful, and which for me has become an object of horror. I am doing my duty with her husband and her son. I am in a frightful state.'[65] To Mme Denis he wrote: 'I spend my days here in tears. Cirey is like a magician's palace: everything that it once was, has now vanished, and it is nothing more than a horrible desert.'[66]

Six days later Voltaire left the Château de Cirey for the last time, having packed up all his belongings in twenty-five large packing-cases, containing furniture, books and scientific instruments, and sent them off to Paris loaded on two large carts. He himself dawdled on the way, stopping for several days each at Châlons and Reims, for he dreaded arriving in Paris and having to answer upsetting questions about Émilie's miserable death. From Reims (where he hired a new secretary),[67] he told Mme Denis that he had no desire to return to the house in the rue Traversière: 'The house where I lived with that unfortunate woman is hateful to me, and I do not want it for anything. M. du Châtelet is quite right to rent it out. There is another house, in the rue Saint Honoré, which I may buy: you and I would be very comfortable there.'[68] In the first instance, however, he had to return to the rue Traversière, for he had nowhere else to go, and that was where he went when he arrived in Paris, on 12 October; and within a few days he agreed to take over the lease of the whole house from M. du Châtelet.[69]

It was a painful homecoming. When he reached the house in the rue Traversière, he was ill and desolate with grief. During the day he saw nobody, and at night, according to Longchamp, he would wander from room to room, like a lost spirit, calling for Émilie by name.

To some of his correspondents he tried to minimise his sense of loss and downplayed his personal relationship with Émilie by emphasising instead her great scientific achievements. 'I have lost a friend of twenty-five years,' he told Frederick, 'a great man whose only fault was to be a woman, and whom all Paris regrets and honours.'[70]

To his young protégé François-Thomas-Marie de Baculard d'Arnaud, he revealed more of his feelings:

> My dear child, a woman who translated and explained Newton, who made a translation of Virgil, without ever letting on, in her conversation, that she had done these prodigies, a woman who never spoke ill of anybody and never told a lie, an attentive friend, and courageous in friendship, in a word a very great man whom ordinary women did not know except through her diamonds and her playing of cavagnole – that is what I cannot help weeping for, for the rest of my life.[71]

But it was to his closest friend, d'Argental, that he expressed more of the depth of his grief. 'I shall be obliged to stay in our house,' he told d'Argental.

> I can even admit that a house which she lived in, even if it fills me with pain, is not at all disagreeable. I do not fear my pain, and I am not running away from what speaks to me of her. The places which she made beautiful are dear to me. I have not lost a mistress, I have lost half of myself, a soul for whom mine was always made. Everywhere I love to rediscover the idea of her. I love to talk of her to her husband and her son.[72]

VOLTAIRE IN PRUSSIA

1750–1753

THE DEATH OF ÉMILIE DU CHÂTELET was a traumatic loss for Voltaire, and one from which he probably never fully recovered. But it also opened the door to a vital new phase in his life, in which he gradually became the acknowledged patriarch of the French Enlightenment. And the catalyst for this transition was his prolonged stay at the court of Frederick the Great, from the summer of 1750 to the spring of 1753.

Émilie had done her best to keep Voltaire away from Potsdam and to rein in his intellectual and creative life, and to some extent she had succeeded: it is striking how little Voltaire produced during the last four years of their life together. With her death he regained his freedom not just to go to Prussia but also to think and to write what he wanted. It was only after her death, and in the relative calm and solitude of Frederick's court, that Voltaire was finally able to finish *Le Siècle de Louis XIV*.

But Voltaire's stay in Berlin was life-changing in a more fundamental way as well, for it was while he was there that he perceived, really for the first time, that he was part of a much broader movement of like-minded intellectuals. Of course, Voltaire was already a pioneering figure of the French Enlightenment, most dramatically in his *Lettres philosophiques*, and yet he was in some ways an outdated and isolated figure. He was so concentrated on the pursuit of his own ambitions, intellectual and social, on his rivalries with other writers and on his running conflicts with the establishment authorities that he was not really aware that his own struggles for freedom of expression were part of a wider movement. In fact, he was not really interested in the thought-processes of his contemporaries.

Jean-Jacques Rousseau, born in 1712 (and therefore eighteen years younger than Voltaire), was a rising member of the younger generation. He had already been briefly in contact with Voltaire in 1745, over his adaptation of Voltaire's musical drama *La Princesse de Navarre*. Yet when, in 1750, he sent Voltaire a copy of his prize essay on the effect of literature on morals, known as the first *Discours*, which started his career as a major figure of the Enlightenment, Voltaire was quite dismissive: 'I am hardly in a position to read prize essays which schoolboys compose for the Académie de Dijon.'[1]

Denis Diderot was another young leading intellectual, a year younger than Rousseau, who was to become famous as the leading editor of the *Encyclopédie*. In 1749 he sent Voltaire a copy of his latest philosophical work, *Lettre sur les aveugles à l'usage de ceux qui voient*, and Voltaire thanked him politely, but with a summary put-down. Voltaire was mildly concerned when he heard that Diderot had been locked up in the prison at Vincennes, but he did not write to him at the time, nor indeed for many years, and he showed no interest in what Diderot was writing.

Of course, Rousseau and Diderot were young and unknown, yet Voltaire did not show similar indifference to other more purely literary young writers, such as Baculard d'Arnaud or Michel Linant, who were just as young, just as unknown and much less significant.

Montesquieu, by contrast, was five years older than Voltaire and a long-established intellectual from an earlier generation. His important political essay *De l'Esprit des Lois* (The Spirit of the Laws), attracted a lot of attention when it was published in 1748, but Voltaire did not mention it until three years later, and then only to sneer. 'I could have wished that his book had been as methodical and as truthful as it is full of wit and large maxims; but, such as it is, it seems to me useful. Mme du Deffand was right to call it "Witty remarks about the laws" ("*de l'esprit sur les lois*").'[2] Voltaire never communicated with Montesquieu, but then Montesquieu was a minor aristocrat and a narrow-minded snob, and he looked down on Voltaire as a pushy upstart.

Jean Le Rond d'Alembert was a brilliant young mathematician, who had already been admitted to the Académie des Sciences in 1741, at the age of twenty-four. Voltaire certainly knew him in Paris, and since d'Alembert was a firm convert to the theories of Newton, he should have been a natural ally of Voltaire and Émilie. But there is no trace of any real intellectual contact between them, and when d'Alembert sent

Voltaire a copy of his latest book, in 1746, Voltaire thanked him politely, but showed no particular interest and simply allowed the correspondence to drop.[3]

D'Alembert later became one of Voltaire's closest friends and allies, and the factor that changed their relationship was the *Encyclopédie*, that massive collective monument to the French Enlightenment, which was jointly edited by d'Alembert and Diderot and to which many of France's leading intellectuals contributed, including Rousseau and Montesquieu. This *Encyclopédie* or *Dictionnaire raisonné des sciences, des arts et des métiers* (Analytical Dictionary of Sciences, Arts and Crafts) had started out in 1745 as a project by André Le Breton, the king's printer, for a translation of the English *Cyclopaedia* of Ephraim Chambers, published in 1728. Within a couple of years, however, it had evolved into a plan for a wholly original and independent encyclopaedia in French, to chart the state of knowledge of the modern world.

The prospectus, published in 1750, promised a work of eight volumes of text and two volumes of plates, and it invited subscriptions of £60 down, followed by £280 on delivery; non-subscribers would be charged £25 per volume of text and £172 for the two volumes of plates. Over the years the project swelled inordinately: when it reached completion in 1772, there were seventeen volumes of text and eleven volumes of plates.

Most people tend to think of it as 'Diderot's *Encyclopédie*', with reason, for he was involved in the editing of it from start to finish, whereas d'Alembert gave up less than half-way through. Since then, Diderot's name has remained better known as a writer, philosopher and art critic, but at the time it was d'Alembert who was the more prominent intellectual, and it was he who wrote the 86-page introduction or *Discours préliminaire*, setting out the scope and terms of reference of this vast new enterprise.

When the first volume of the *Encyclopédie* was published, in 1751, Voltaire was immediately enthusiastic. Yet in 1748 and 1749, when d'Alembert and Diderot were working hard on drafting their plan for the *Encyclopédie*, Voltaire does not seem to have been aware that any such enterprise was under way. Nor does he seem to have known about the prospectus for the *Encyclopédie*, when it came out in 1750. Was this because he was not interested? Was it because they thought he was too grand and celebrated to be interested? Was he too busy with his own career? It is hard to say; the fact remains that he was not part of the gestation of the most spectacular expression of the French Enlightenment.

In time Voltaire became an eager contributor to later volumes of the

Encyclopédie, and his main interlocutor there was d'Alembert. Naturally, Voltaire's habitual quirks of character remained unreformed: even though he greatly admired Diderot's work as editor of the *Encyclopédie*, he felt little interest or sympathy for him as a writer and none at all for Rousseau, with whom he later quarrelled memorably and irretrievably. Nevertheless, it was the *Encyclopédie* which seems to have persuaded Voltaire to end his intellectual isolation and made him realise that he could have friends and allies on the intellectual scene, not just rivals and enemies.

After the death of Émilie, Voltaire at first backed off his earlier plans to visit Frederick. 'I am very far from going to Prussia,' he told his friend Baculard d'Arnaud, and to Frederick he wrote: 'I can hardly bring myself to leave my house. The state I have been in this last month does not leave me much hope that I shall ever see you again.'[4]

Instead, it was to Mme Denis that he turned. On the day of Émilie's death he told her that he would return to Paris 'to embrace you, and find in you my only consolation and the sole hope of my life'.[5] Writing from Cirey, two weeks later, he told her:

> I spend my days here in tears, in sorting the papers which remind me of her. I do not regret a mistress, far from it. I regret a friend and a great man [*un ami et un grand homme*], and my regrets will surely last as long as my life. You will bring happiness to this life, beset by so many griefs; and I shall consecrate it entirely to you. I do not and cannot think about any of those activities which used to delight me, and I cannot stand my own writings; but I shall love yours as if they were my grandchildren. My heart, my life, is yours, to dispose of as you will.[6]

Voltaire returned to Paris in the middle of October, and by the end of the month he had persuaded Mme Denis to come and live with him.[7] In early January 1750, when he fell ill in Versailles, she went out there to nurse him,[8] and on 10 January she moved in with him in the house in the rue Traversière.[9]

He may have told Mme Denis that he had lost all interest in his own writings, but in Paris his interest recovered almost immediately, and he pushed forward with two new tragedies, *Rome sauvée* and *Oreste*, which he had written in direct competition with plays by his despised rival the playwright and censor Prosper Jolyot Crébillon. Neither did well: the première of *Oreste,* on 12 January 1750, went badly and was taken off after only five more performances; *Rome sauvée* was turned down by the actors and not performed at the Comédie Française until 1752.

Six months after the death of Émilie, Voltaire decided, apparently quite suddenly, to go to Prussia.[10] This may have been partly a reaction to the relative failure of his last three plays; he felt that he was not appreciated in France, and hoped that he would be better valued in Prussia. 'I left France', he told Richelieu later, 'because I found more consideration and more freedom elsewhere.'[11] In addition, no doubt, he was still suffering acutely from the loss of Émilie; he simply had to leave.

At first, Voltaire conceived his project of going to Berlin with the greatest enthusiasm. 'Frederick the Great', he told his young friend Baculard d'Arnaud in May, 'is the only person in the whole world who could make me undertake such a journey. For him I would leave my home, my affairs and Mme Denis.'[12] This sounds like a conscious decision to embark on a new life and to abandon the past, including Mme Denis. In fact, Voltaire does not seem to have made any coherent long-term plan for the future: he went without Mme Denis, but once he got there he tried to persuade her to join him; yet he told his friends in Paris that he had only intended to stay in Prussia for six weeks.[13]

Voltaire could not resist haggling with Frederick over his travelling expenses.

> I am rich, even very rich, for a man of letters. Nevertheless, it is impossible for me to make an extraordinary expenditure. I do not want to be a burden on you. But I cannot get a good travelling carriage, nor take with me the first aid necessary for a sick man, nor provide for my household in my absence, etc., for less than four thousand German marks. You only have to say a word, Sire, to the correspondent of some bank resident in Paris, and four days later I shall leave.[14]

Voltaire may have thought he was driving a shrewd bargain; he was really bargaining away some of his independence. But Frederick did not quibble, and five days later he instructed his Berlin bankers to send Voltaire £16,000. 'One cannot pay too dearly for pleasure', he told Voltaire; 'I consider that I made a very good bargain'.[15]

Before Voltaire could leave for Prussia, however, he had to get permission for his journey, and he went to court to seek it in person from the king. Louis did give permission, but with the greatest coldness, and ostentatiously turned his back on him. It was only now that Voltaire started to understand that he was taking an irrevocable step, and he had a attack of panic. 'Why am I here?', he wrote to d'Argental. 'Why should I go on? Why did I leave you, my dear angels? Forgive my journey. Do not scold me, I already have remorse enough.'[16]

It was a difficult journey, which took over three weeks, partly because of the terrible state of the roads. Voltaire was deeply struck by 'the vast, sad, sterile and detestable countryside of Westphalia', and even more by the poverty of the peasants.[17] But when he reached Potsdam, he was eager to claim to d'Argental that Frederick's Prussia was admirably civilised and up-to-date:

> Here I am at last, in a place which was once so savage, and which has now been embellished by the arts and ennobled by military glory. A hundred and fifty thousand victorious soldiers, opera, comedy, philosophy, poetry, a philosophical hero who is also a poet, grandeur and grace, grenadiers and muses, trumpets and violins, society and freedom! Who would believe it? And yet it is all too true.[18]

Voltaire already knew some of the people at Frederick's court. François-Thomas-Marie de Baculard d'Arnaud, the ambitious young writer and his one-time protégé, had recently arrived. Frederick had astutely played on Voltaire's anxieties by circulating a little poem which compared d'Arnaud to the rising sun and Voltaire to the setting, 'declining in decadence'. Within a few weeks Voltaire persuaded Frederick to dismiss him.[19]

Then there was Francesco Algarotti, an agreeable young Venetian intellectual who had visited Voltaire and Émilie at Cirey many years earlier, and who had written his own popularisation of Newton's theories, called *Neutonianismo per le dame* (Newtonism for the Ladies). Frederick had made him a count (*Graf*) in 1740 and a chamberlain in 1747.* Voltaire and Algarotti had always got on well, and in Prussia they spent a lot of time together.

But the most resonant figure at Frederick's court, from Voltaire's point of view, was of course Pierre Louis Moreau de Maupertuis, the mathematician who had tutored Voltaire (and Émilie) on Newton's theories and who was now the head of Frederick's Berlin Academy.[20] In the early days Voltaire had put up, without protest, with Émilie's infidelity with Maupertuis; appropriately enough, it was an explosive conflict

---

* 'Chamberlain' at Frederick's court seems to have been a loose appellation, similar to the position of 'Gentleman in Ordinary' at Versailles. While Voltaire was in Prussia, he was one of several chamberlains.

with Maupertuis twenty years later that finally brought Voltaire's stay in Prussia to an end.

And then there was Mme Charlotte-Sophie Bentinck, a lively and attractive young woman of the north German nobility who had very recently arrived. She was a talented woman who painted and sang and played the harpsichord; she was also highly educated, in French and in German, and she charmed all who got to know her, including Voltaire. But until people got to know her, she had to overcome a scandalous reputation in good society, for she had left her husband and children for another man, who was himself married and by whom she had more children.

She was born in 1715, the only daughter of Anthon von Altenburg, in Varel, in Ost Frisen, between Wilhelmshaven and Bremerhaven; when she arrived in Berlin in 1750, therefore, she was thirty-five. The family estates in north Germany and the Netherlands were crippled with enormous debts, and in 1733, when she was eighteen, her father had married her off for financial reasons to Willem Bentinck, a wealthy Dutchman who lived in The Hague and had close connections with the prince of Orange.

She had two sons by Willem Bentinck, but it was an unhappy marriage: not only did she not love him, but she was already in love with her 34-year-old cousin, Count Albrecht-Wolfgang zu Schaumburg-Lippe, and he with her. By 1737, at the latest, she and Wolfgang were lovers. Wolfgang was already married and had two legitimate sons of his own. But over the next few years Sophie had three sons by him, and she became, in disregard of his austere and devout wife, a familiar figure at his château of Bückeburg.*

In 1739, after the death of her father, she sought a legal separation from her husband, and in 1740 he conceded it, but on draconian terms: she lost all rights over their children, and from then on Bentinck never stopped trying to strip her of her estates and her livelihood. These estates had feudal and financial links with different courts of Europe, so that her personal dispute with Bentinck became a diplomatic and political tangle involving governments in the four corners of the continent. Wolfgang died unexpectedly in 1748, and Charlotte-Sophie spent many years lobbying one court after another, seeking help against the vindictiveness of her husband: when she came to Berlin in the summer

---

* Albrecht-Wolfgang zu Schaumburg-Lippe was also a friend of Frederick's and in 1738 had helped arrange Frederick's initiation as a freemason. See Giles MacDonogh, *Frederick the Great* (Weidenfeld & Nicolson, London 1999), pp. 113–4.

of 1750, it was to seek the political and diplomatic help of Frederick the Great. And that was after two years in Copenhagen; later she moved to Vienna, and later still to Hamburg.

So when she arrived, alone, in Berlin, she was feared not just as a trouble-maker but as a dangerously attractive independent woman.

Voltaire and Mme Bentinck already knew one another, for Voltaire had met her in 1740, when they were both visitors at the château of Bückeburg, the home of her lover, Wolfgang. She had long admired Voltaire, and had read a number of his books, including the *Lettres philosophiques* and *Les Éléments de Newton*. 'Even before you knew me', she told him many years later, 'you taught me to think.'[21] In Berlin, Mme Bentinck quickly became Voltaire's closest, possibly his only, real friend, during his stay in Prussia. Whenever he was in Berlin, he would write to her or see her almost daily, but even when he was in Potsdam, he would write to her with great frequency. Over the two-and-a-half years that he was in Prussia, he sent her over 250 letters or notes, which means that on average he wrote to her about twice a week.

Voltaire professed to be delighted with his new life at Potsdam, boasting to d'Argental of the brilliance of the public spectacles, and even more of his privileged relationship with Frederick:

Add to that the complete freedom which I enjoy here, the kindness and the attentions of the conqueror of Silesia, who carries the full weight of government from five in the morning until dinner time, who gives the whole of the rest of the day to literature, who deigns to work with me for three hours at a stretch, who at supper is the most agreeable of men and the bond and charm of society. After all that, what could I possibly miss, except your company?[22]

In reality, he was not at all happy to be there. He may have been impressed by the Prussian court, but there is not the smallest hint, in his letters, of any recurrence of that tremor of exhilaration which in 1740–43 had marked his earlier encounters and conversations with Frederick. On the contrary, there creeps in, between the lines, an undertone of regret, disappointment, resignation and remorse.

This note emerges even in his very first letter from Potsdam, to d'Argental. 'I had to see Solomon [i.e., Frederick] in all his glory; but to live, I have to be with you and the abbé Chauvelin.* Tell him how much

---

* The abbé Henri-Philippe de Chauvelin, a canon of Notre-Dame, was theatre-mad and, like d'Argental and Thibouville, was among Voltaire's close intermediaries with the Comédie Française.

I miss him, even when I am listening to Frederick the Great. Farewell, my angels; Frederick the Great takes my time and my soul.'[23]

The sense of sadness comes through even more strongly a month later.

My dear angels, if I were to tell you that we have had a firework display reminiscent of those at the Pont Neuf, and that every day there are parties, you would be only moderately interested. In any case, my heart is overflowing, and more rent by my decision than dazzled by our fêtes; I really feel that the rest of my days will be poisoned, in spite of my new freedom, in spite of the ease of a calm life, and in spite of the kindnesses of the king. I ask you, please, to encourage Mme Denis to come and settle with me here in Berlin, in a good house, where she will live in the greatest opulence. There is no going back. I can no longer live in France after having wanted to leave it. For the past month I have been tortured by the thought, and it has made me ill. A decision like mine has its costs, no doubt of it. You can be quite sure that it is you who are rending my soul; but when I talk to you, you will approve of me. Do not condemn me before having heard me out. My eyes are wet with tears as I write, Adieu.[24]

It may be that Voltaire was depressed after his arrival in Prussia. Frederick seems to have believed that he may have tried to commit suicide, with an overdose of opium.[25] We know that Voltaire did regularly take opium for his physical ailments; we do not know whether he tried to commit suicide.[26] But it seems clear that he was in very low spirits.

Voltaire tried to finesse his position in Prussia by claiming to the French authorities that he was still a patriotic Frenchman and a loyal subject of Louis XV. 'I flatter myself', he wrote to the French Foreign Minister, Louis-Philoxène de Puisieux, 'that the king will be pleased to see that I still serve him in the person of the king of Prussia, that he will continue to regard me as one of his most faithful subjects, and that he will deign to let me keep all the rights and privileges of his subject and his servant.'[27]

He also wrote to the marquis de Saint-Florentin, Secretary of State in the king's household, in the hope of salvaging something of his position at the French court.

I accept that I may not be able to keep the position of King's Historian. And yet I beg you to consider that the salary which has been linked to this position, was in fact given to me thirty years ago. I trust that His Majesty will deign to consider that I only attached myself to the king of Prussia after I had asked permission, and that I only decided to do so because I was convinced that to be at the court in Berlin was still to belong to the king [of France] and to be his subject for a second time.[28]

Voltaire's pleas were coldly ignored, and he began to panic that he might be in real danger if he put himself into Frederick's power. Frederick did his best to alleviate his fears: 'Just because you retire to my house, can it be said that this house will become your prison? I am your friend: will it be said that I shall be your tyrant? I am firmly persuaded that you will be very happy here as long as I live.'[29] Reassured, Voltaire asked the French authorities for a general authorisation to be allowed to live indefinitely in Prussia, 'and to receive from the king of Prussia all the marks of favour and distinction with which the king wishes to honour him'.[30] His request was granted, and Frederick appointed him a chamberlain of the court, with a salary of £20,000, and the decoration of the Order of Merit. Without seriously planning it, Voltaire had migrated from the status of an honoured visitor to that of a servant of the Prussian king.

Voltaire's friends continued to regret and disapprove of his decision to move to Prussia. 'You know how much your departure grieved me,' d'Argental wrote to him. 'You depend on the caprices of a single man, and that man is a king. You have looked for liberty, and you have submitted to the greatest constraints. We really miss you, and we very much want you to come home. You have made a big mistake, and you cannot repair it too soon.'[31] Voltaire responded defensively, either apologising for having left France, or else blaming his 'persecutors' in France for having driven him out. 'How could I forget the barbarous manner in which I have been treated in my own country? If you remember, they took *Le Mondain*, which was just the most innocent pleasantry, as a pretext to drive me into exile. You will say that that was fifteen years ago. No, my angels, it is like yesterday.'[32]

Despite his new position at Frederick's court, Voltaire talked as if he was still free to come and go as he pleased. 'When I see you in Paris', he told d'Argental in August, 'you will approve of me, and feel sorry for me. I do not yet know if I shall spend the winter here, or if I shall make a long journey abroad. Whatever happens, I shall probably not be in Paris before March.'[33] In September he told Saint-Florentin that he would be coming to Paris in November, and he asked him in the meantime to delay any decisions affecting his positions at court.

During the autumn Voltaire repeatedly postponed his plans to return to France, either because of the mud on the roads or because of the frost or because of his heavy work schedule,[34] and by January he dropped them altogether: 'The climate here is killing me', he told d'Argental,

> and you are killing me with your reproaches, with your hardness, with your injustice. You are blaming me for the seasons, for my poor health, for business affairs which hold me back, and for a new edition of my works, the whole of which I must correct. I have been delayed from month to month, from week to week. I know I am in the wrong, my dear and admirable friend, I have come to die 300 leagues from home. A hero may be a great man, but however great, he cannot replace a friend. I am in the wrong.[35]

What Voltaire did not tell his friends was that he had got embroiled in a demeaning financial scandal, made all the worse by its political overtones. This was the Hirschel affair, which involved some murky transactions with a Jewish businessman called Abraham Hirschel. It damaged Voltaire's relationship with Frederick for several months and left a lasting shadow on his reputation.

Abraham Hirschel was a businessman in Berlin, whose business seems to have involved money and jewellery. In September, Voltaire lent Hirschel 4,430 écus, equivalent to 26,580 francs. Why? We do not know. In November, Voltaire asked Hirschel to bring some diamonds, which he needed for the costumes of a performance of *Rome sauvée*.[36]

Two weeks later Voltaire gave Hirschel a letter of credit for £40,000, drawn on his Paris lawyer, Guillaume-Claude Laleu. It seems that he was intending to speculate in Treasury bonds issued by the Saxon state. On the open market these bonds were trading at a large discount, sometimes as low as 35 per cent below their face value; but under the terms of the Treaty of Dresden, which in 1745 had brought peace between Prussia and Saxony, it was agreed that Prussian citizens could redeem their holdings of these Saxon bonds at par. For Voltaire to get Hirschel to buy quantities of these bonds and cash them in at a profit was obviously fraudulent in intention, and even illegal, since Voltaire was not a Prussian citizen. (In this respect, the operation was similar to one with which Voltaire had first made his fortune just over twenty years earlier:

on that occasion he had gained access to a share offering issued in Lorraine by falsely pretending to be a citizen of Lorraine; he sold the shares again immediately, and made a large return on the deal.)[37]

Voltaire realised immediately that his operation with Hirschel was extremely dangerous. Next day he decided to back out and wrote to Laleu to countermand the letter of credit. But word of the operation was out, and Voltaire was teetering on the edge of disgrace. The French ambassador told Paris that the affair was damaging Voltaire's standing at the Prussian court. 'M. de Voltaire's great reputation seems to me to have taken a terrible tumble. I am told that the Prussian king is furious with him. Voltaire is really unfortunate to have so much wit, and so little judgement.'[38]

Afterwards Voltaire protested his innocence to Frederick, but in terms that virtually admitted his guilt. 'Why did they tell you that I had bought Saxon Treasury bonds for 80,000 écus, whereas I never asked for a single one, and after being publicly solicited by the Jew Hirschel to take some like everybody else, and having made enquiries on the nature of these instruments, I immediately revoked my letter of credit on 24 November, and forbade Hirschel to buy a single one for me.'[39] No doubt the initiative had come from Hirschel, since Voltaire, as a newcomer, would probably never have heard of these Saxon Treasury bonds. But Voltaire's reference to his letter of credit shows, by implication, that he had at first intended to go along with the scam.

In the event, Hirschel failed to buy any Saxon Treasury bonds. But the cancelled letter of credit was bound to be returned by Laleu to Hirschel, and Voltaire demanded that Hirschel hand it over, since he was afraid that Hirschel might try to cash it at a discount on the open market. When Hirschel failed to produce the letter, on 1 January 1751, Voltaire issued a formal complaint against him, and the case was sent for trial. The court case was complicated by claims and counter-claims over the value of the diamonds which Hirschel had supplied; but on the central issue it ended six weeks later, on 18 February 1751, with a legal victory for Voltaire but a moral defeat: Hirschel was ordered to hand over the letter of credit, but Voltaire's honour was seriously compromised.

Voltaire was kept going, amid all this turbulence, by the support of Mme Bentinck, with whom he had soon developed confident and friendly relations. By November 1750 Voltaire was starting to advise her on her legal case, and on the best tactics for approaching Frederick.[40] In return, she promoted the idea of a new Academy of Arts and Letters in Berlin, of which Voltaire would of course be president. Since there was already an all-purpose Academy of Science and Letters in Berlin, headed by Maupertuis, the implication of Mme Bentinck's plan was that Maupertuis's institution would be reduced in scope and restricted to the sciences.[41] Voltaire was at first suitably flattered by the idea, but he soon drew back, claiming coyly that he had no public ambitions – 'What! Me be President!' – and the idea faded.[42]

Voltaire was soon so attached to Mme Bentinck that in November he declared his 'tender attachment' to her, and in January his 'tender devotion'.[43] In January he also said that he would like to spend his life with her, and that he 'dared to believe that you have a bit of friendship for me', declaring that she was one of 'most beautiful souls in the world'.[44] In some oblique ways she may even have reminded him of Émilie; he certainly hoped that they would be brought closer together by their shared consciousness of loss. 'The similarities between your destiny and mine, concerns me more than you think. Our star brought us together, so that we could console one another.'[45]

So how close did their friendship become? Theodore Besterman says that 'she almost certainly became his mistress', but he offers no evidence and is almost certainly wrong.[46] No doubt Voltaire would have liked to make Sophie his mistress, for she was very attractive, full of vitality and charm. She may not have been beautiful, but she was a woman of great presence and great intelligence, a good listener and a good talker, and she loved to sing, to dance, to ride and to laugh. She was also very fond of Voltaire.

But the letters that he wrote to her strongly suggest that their friendship, though warm and confident, did not extend to sexual intimacy, because Sophie did not want it to. Voltaire pressed his case and was turned down. 'You have assured me most positively', he wrote to her in August 1751, 'that you have no love for me; but you cannot prevent me from taking the deepest interest in everything that concerns you.'[47] Later that month he returned to the attack: 'It is in vain that you tell me that you do not love me. I shall tell you boldly, that I take the liberty of loving you with all my heart.'[48] For a year Voltaire went on pressing his suit, but it was no use; Voltaire was asking for more than she was willing to give, and he had to content himself with a loving friendship, or *amitié amoureuse*.

Sophie was much younger than Voltaire and full of gusto, and she may have had love affairs with other men in Berlin – with Prince Henri, younger brother of Frederick (to Frederick's irritation), and even, most poignantly, with Wilhelm zu Schaumburg-Lippe, the younger (legitimate) son of her dead lover Wolfgang, now in his late twenties – but not with Voltaire. Nevertheless, she and Voltaire remained close friends for life: the last letter she wrote to Voltaire was in 1778, just weeks before his death.

So what about Mme Denis? Where did she fit in? At the beginning Voltaire talked often to his friends of persuading her to come to Prussia; but she never went, perhaps just because she was reluctant to leave Paris. But we are largely in the dark about Voltaire's relationship with Mme Denis during this period, because none of the letters he ostensibly wrote to her is quite genuine. His stay in Prussia ended in a public humiliation at the hands of Frederick, and when he returned to France he decided to get his own back. He took back from Mme Denis all the letters that he had sent her from Potsdam, and rewrote them to dramatise his side of the story. It was not until late in the twentieth century that scholars finally realised that these letters had been cooked by Voltaire and that they cannot be taken literally. In the meantime, however, they have given us apocryphal stories which are now irreversibly part of the Voltaire legend.

One of the best-known anecdotes about Voltaire's stay in Prussia comes from a letter to Mme Denis, ostensibly dated September 1751, in which he relates a remark reportedly made about him by Frederick: 'I shall need him for another year at most; we shall squeeze the orange, and then throw away the peel.'[49] In another letter, apparently dated July 1752, he says that Maupertuis 'is putting it about that, when the king sent me his verses for me to correct them, I responded: "Will he never weary of sending me his dirty linen to launder?"'[50]

Is there any truth in these stories? It is hard to say. Voltaire must frequently have been irritated by the tedium of sub-editing Frederick's inadequate prose and verse, but he is unlikely to have expressed his irritation in the presence of Maupertuis; Voltaire's purpose in recounting this anecdote may have been to paint Maupertuis as a malicious gossip. The story about the orange peel is even more dubious. Frederick undoubtedly lured Voltaire to Potsdam in order to make use of him, but there is no evidence that he ever planned to get rid of him; on the contrary, he did not want Voltaire to go and in the end only released him when Voltaire forced his hand.

After the Hirschel scandal erupted, Frederick refused to see Voltaire, and Voltaire did his best to keep out of the way. In January 1751 he asked to be allowed to move out of the royal château at Potsdam to the Marquisat, a more distant summer house near the Brandenburger Tor.

While the trial was under way, Frederick refused to listen to his request; when it was over, he wrote Voltaire a fierce letter of rebuke.

I was really glad to welcome you here; I admired your wit, your talents and your knowledge; and I must have thought that a man of your age would be tired of quarrelling with other writers, and would be coming here for refuge in a calm harbour.

But you have had the worst possible affair with the Jew; the affair of the Saxon bonds is so well known in Saxony that I have received grievous complaints. And you have interfered in the affairs of Mme Bentinck, even though it was none of your business.

I must warn you, that if you have a passion for intrigues and cabals, you have come to the wrong place. If you can resolve to live philosophically, I shall be glad to see you; but if you give yourself up to all the storms of your passions, you will give me no pleasure by coming here [i.e., Potsdam], and you can just stay in Berlin.[51]

At first Voltaire tried to defend himself, and it was not until two days later that he adopted a sufficiently grovelling tone.

All things carefully considered, I made a serious error in bringing a case against a Jew, and I ask pardon of your majesty, of your philosophy and of your goodness. Do with me as you will. Have pity on brother Voltaire, for brother Voltaire is a good man, he is not on bad terms with anybody, and he takes the liberty of loving Your Majesty with all his heart. I learn that Your Majesty permits me to move to the Marquisat for the spring. I offer him the most humble thanks.[52]

He apologised even more deeply the next day.

Your Majesty is absolutely right, and I am almost irreparably wrong. I have never corrected my cursed habit of getting involved in public affairs. Be sure that I am in a state of despair, and that I have never felt such deep and bitter pain. I have lost my only reason for coming here, I have been deprived of the conversations which enlightened and revived me, and I have displeased the only man whom I wanted to please.[53]

By the end of March 1751 Voltaire moved out of the hurly-burly of the court and into the relative isolation of the Marquisat, and his life became much calmer. He did his minimal duty to Frederick, which involved reviewing and revising the king's efforts in French prose and verse or having supper with him; but most of the time he spent on his own, working on *Le Siècle de Louis XIV*. 'I am so busy with this *Siècle*', he told d'Argental, 'that I have given up writing any verse.'[54]

Voltaire was also dealing with two new complete editions of his works: one to be published by Georg Conrad Walther, a bookseller and printer in Dresden,[55] the other by Michel Lambert in Paris.[56] Voltaire was particularly anxious about the Lambert edition, because he feared that it would get him into trouble with the French authorities. 'People may say', he told d'Argental, 'that I only decided to move abroad in order to print things which are too free, and which cannot be published in France, even with tacit authority. I will admit that I would not like to reappear in France until these storms had subsided.'[57] But he was also worried that the Lambert edition would be a slapdash affair, as he told Georg Walther: 'The editions which have come out in France, my dear Walther, are very poor, according to what I hear; I have not yet seen them. I should like you to put them out of business by bringing out a good and correct edition, which you would prepare with great care. I should like it to be in duodecimo, in no more than seven or eight volumes, in a small and clear typeface.'[58]

By the summer of 1751 Voltaire was starting to sound really rather cheerful again. 'Life here is very sweet and very free,' he told Mme du Deffand, 'and its calmness is good for my health. Just imagine how pleasant it is to be free, at the home of a king, to think, to write, to say anything one wants.'[59] Moreover, he was also starting to feel better: 'After having been ill last winter', he told Mme Fontaine, younger sister of Mme Denis,

> I have started to eat dinner, and supper, and even breakfast. People tell me that I am looking better, and seem younger. Of course, I know that is not true. But I have never enjoyed a happier and a more tranquil life. Just imagine, an admirable château, whose master leaves me complete freedom, handsome gardens, good food, a bit of work, good company and delicious suppers with a philosophical king.[60]

The only real defect in his new life was that he could not see Mme Bentinck as easily or as often as he would like: she lived in Berlin, whereas he was mainly required to be in Potsdam, and the regulations made it difficult for unauthorised visitors to get close to the royal palace at Potsdam. Nevertheless, they did manage to meet, sometimes in Berlin, sometimes at the Marquisat, when Frederick was away. 'I have many things to say to you, Madame,' he wrote to her in June 1751. 'Come and eat a bustard at the Marquisat at one o'clock, and there we shall talk, far from the noisy world.'[61]

A year after his arrival in Prussia, Voltaire was still justifying himself defensively to his friends. 'You ask why I am in Prussia,' he wrote to Richelieu.

> I came in order to pay my court to the king of Prussia, planning then to go and see Italy, and to go home after having my *Le Siècle de Louis XIV* printed in Holland. It never occurred to me that the [French] king or Mme de Pompadour took any notice of me or could be in the least offended. I said to myself, what can it matter to a king of France, whether there is an atom like me more or less? In France I was harassed, knocked about, persecuted for thirty years by other writers and by bigots. Here I am tranquil, I lead a life which is entirely suitable for my poor health, I have all my time to myself, no duties to carry out, the king always lets me take dinner in my room, and often supper too.[62]

Sometimes Voltaire had to accompany Frederick on visits to Berlin, especially for the traditional year-end social season. But quite often, when Frederick was touring the country or reviewing his troops, Voltaire would be left in peace: sometimes, indeed, too much in peace. 'I wanted to consult Your Majesty,' he wrote to Frederick. 'I went up to your ante-chambers to try to find someone through whom I could get permission to speak to you, but I found no one, and I had to leave empty-handed.'[63] On another occasion he complained of the brusqueness of Frederick's soldiers: 'I am absolutely alone from morning to night,' he told Frederick. 'My only consolation is the necessary pleasure of taking the air. I wanted to work and walk in your garden in Potsdam; I believe that is allowed. I went there, all absent-minded, and I found great devils of grenadiers who stuck their bayonets in my belly, and who shouted at me: "Out!", "Sacrament!" and "Der König!" ("The King!"). I fled.'[64]

In the autumn of 1751 Voltaire started to think about going home. His play *Mahomet*, which had been hounded off the Paris stage in 1742, was now being revived there, and he heard that *Rome sauvée* was likely to be staged the following spring. It looked as though he might be coming back into favour. 'I should willingly give up the golden keys, the cross and the 20,000 francs in salary, which you hold against me,' he told Richelieu.

> I should give it all up for the honour of living among you, and to be with my niece and my friends again. But you will admit that I would need to be at least morally certain of being well received in my homeland.
>
> How then will I be received if I come home? Could you not have the kindness to point out to Mme de Pompadour that I am on the same side as her? If she is offended by my desertion, if she regards me as a refugee, I ought to stay where I am so well off; but if she thinks that I could be counted among those who, in literature, can be of some use; if she wishes me to return, could you not tell her that you know of my attachment to her; that she alone could make me leave the king of Prussia; and that I only left France because I was persecuted by those who hate her?
>
> These are not conditions which I am posing. I am not an exile asking to be recalled, and I am not an important man who wants to be ransomed; I am just your ancient servant, who desires passionately to live among you in a suitable and honourable manner.[65]

In fact, he was not really ready to leave just yet, because he was too busy with *Le Siècle de Louis XIV*. But by the end of December 1751 he had handed over the finished text to C. F. Henning, the king's printer at Berlin, to be published, in two volumes, with a print run of 3,000 copies; Voltaire kept back 500 copies to be distributed to friends in England and 100 copies to give away as presents. Almost immediately it was pirated far and wide and attracted a vast amount of comment and criticism.[66] But Voltaire claimed that this was just a trial edition, full of errors and omissions, and when he heard, in May 1752, that there was a new pirate version of his *Le Siècle de Louis XIV*, he urged Walther to rush out a revised edition, a quarter as long again as the first.[67] In the preface to this 'second' edition he pointed out that there had already been seven others, in less than ten months.[68]

By the spring of 1752 Voltaire was getting really comfortable in Potsdam. 'I am a funny kind of chamberlain,' he told Mme Fontaine, his younger niece. 'I have no other function than to walk from my room to the apartment of a philosophical king, to have supper with him; and when I am more unwell than usual, I have supper by myself. There is no example of a sweeter and more convenient life.'[69] 'I have absolutely nothing to do for the king of Prussia,' he told another Parisian friend. 'My days, occupied with agreeable studies, end with suppers which are even more agreeable, and which restore my strength for the next day. Our meals are of the most extreme frugality, our conversations of the most extreme liberty.'[70]

It was only now, when he was so comfortable in Potsdam, that Voltaire first became fully aware of the impact that the *Encyclopédie* was having. He had already commented warmly, in December 1751, on d'Alembert's prefatory *Discours* setting out the aims of the *Encyclopédie*, and he wrote d'Alembert a paean of praise after the second volume appeared in January 1752: 'You and M. Diderot, you are making a work which will be the glory of France. Paris is full of scribblers; but as for philosophers, I know of none to compare with you and him.'[71]

But it was not until the summer of 1752, when he learned of the persecution of one of the minor contributors to the *Encyclopédie*, that he grasped how much was at stake. The abbé Jean Martin de Prades was a brilliant young theologian, who in November 1751 successfully defended his thesis for a doctorate in theology. But in January 1752 the Sorbonne condemned his thesis as heretical, the *parlement* condemned it to be burned and a warrant was issued for his arrest. The abbé de Prades had to flee for his life, and he eventually made his way to Potsdam. When Voltaire heard of his trials, he offered to take him in.

> Everything that M. d'Alembert and others have told about you, has redoubled our desire to help you. The king is almost never in Berlin; he lives in the palace of Potsdam. I am lodged in the palace with two worthy young people who work with me.* His Majesty has permitted me, in consideration of my poor health, to have dinner in my room; sometimes I have supper there too. They serve me a meal which is quite enough for three; I also have a small apartment in the town where there is nothing but the bare minimum: a canvas bed, two chairs, two tables, a mean little entresol and a room for a cook, who gives me food when the king is not at Potsdam. I almost never go to Berlin.

---

* The 'two worthy young people who work with me' were his two secretaries, Joseph du Fresne de Francheville and Cosimo Alessandro Collini. Francheville's father was a member of the Berlin Academy and the first editor of *Le Siècle de Louis XIV*; Voltaire had a room in Francheville's house and took on his son as a secretary in March 1752. Cosimo Alessandro Collini was a young Florentine of education and good family who was in Berlin when Voltaire arrived; Voltaire took him on as secretary in April 1752.

Consider, sir, if you would do me the kindness to accept, I cannot call it the apartment, but the hovel which I have at Potsdam. My cook could make you soup, if you were to fall ill. We should dine together with the two friends I have with me, and it would cost me hardly anything to supplement the food the king supplies. In that way you would be spared finding rent, which must be dear, and the need to look for your dinner in the German inns. In any case, do not scruple to accept my miserable offer, for the lodging is very small and mean; but at least it is among Frenchmen. In any case, we should all live together.[72]

Prades reached Berlin in August, and Voltaire helped him get a position as one of Frederick's secretaries.

The completion of *Le Siècle de Louis XIV* had left Voltaire with time on his hands, and he used some of it to write (but above all not publish) some scandalous free-thinking 'philosophical' works: the *Sermon des cinquante*, which was a ferocious attack on Christianity, and the *Poème sur la loi naturelle*, which argued for a universal Deist religion and for equality for all before the law.[73] Both of these were partly inspired by the publication of the *Encyclopédie*. He also started to work, with the active encouragement of Frederick, on his own philosophical (i.e., anti-Christian) dictionary, for which he drafted a few tentative articles, and which eventually came to fruition a dozen years later as his *Dictionnaire philosophique*.[74]

Voltaire's speculative philosophising was abruptly interrupted in the summer of 1752 by the explosion of a real-life human drama at the heart of Frederick's cultural establishment. This started out as an intellectual argument, on a question of scientific theory, between Maupertuis, in his capacity as president of the Academy of Berlin, and Johann Samuel Kœnig, professor of natural law in The Hague, and an associate member of the Berlin Academy. It soon escalated into a classic academic quarrel, in which intellectual questions were wholly submerged in an all-out struggle of power and pride.

This quarrel had been brewing for some time before Voltaire became aware of it. In 1749 Maupertuis had enunciated the proposition that nature operates according to a principle of 'least action', meaning that any event in nature takes place with the minimum expenditure of energy; by extension, Maupertuis claimed that this principle proved the existence of God, by means of an algebraic formula.

In 1751 Kœnig published a paper taking issue with Maupertuis and claiming that the principle of 'least action' had been enunciated long before by Gottfried Leibniz (1646–1716), citing as evidence letters written by Leibniz. Maupertuis erupted in rage, and when Kœnig failed to produce the original letters from Leibniz, Maupertuis convened a plenary session of the Berlin Academy to try Kœnig on a charge of forgery.

Since Maupertuis had total power over all aspects of the Academy, notably the salaries of the members, most of them meekly did what he wanted, and on 13 April 1752 they found Kœnig guilty; those who disagreed simply stayed away. Kœnig resigned from the Academy, but he published an 'Appeal to the Public', setting out his case and complaining of the injustice of Maupertuis's actions.

When Voltaire learned of the quarrel between Maupertuis and Kœnig, he quickly came to the conclusion that Maupertuis's proceedings were monstrous and unjust. 'He may be unwell,' he told Mme Bentinck, 'but he should not be allowed to try to persecute Kœnig, who is in the right, or to launch the Academy on measures which are ridiculous and odious. It would be better to be dead than to act in ways so impertinent and so tyrannical. I detest tyrants.'[75]

Voltaire already knew both men well, since Kœnig had succeeded Maupertuis as Émilie's maths tutor, and he needed no encouragement to take sides. He had always thought the diminutive Maupertuis a slightly absurd figure,* and when he reached Prussia, he also found him 'unfriendly' and 'a hard and ferocious person'.[76] Maupertuis may have been jealous of Voltaire's privileges as a member of the inner circle at Frederick's little suppers, but Voltaire soon came to the conclusion that Maupertuis's position as the head of the Academy had gone to his head. He exercised his powers in a wholly authoritarian way, and he had taken to the bottle, to the point that Frederick noticed, and repeatedly advised him to abstain. 'He has ruined his health with strong liquor', Voltaire told the mathematician La Condamine; 'he has lost friends even more by excessive pride, and he has made enemies in Paris, in Berlin and in Holland.'[77] It was a situation that was tailor-made for Voltaire's high-octane talent for wounding polemic and irresistible satire.

Voltaire now embarked on a campaign to denounce and ridicule Maupertuis, starting with an open letter for publication in a Dutch intellectual journal called *La Bibliothèque Raisonnée*. 'M. Moreau Maupertuis has claimed, in his *Essai de cosmologie*, that the only proof of the existence of God is the formula AR + nRB, which must be a minimum.†

---

* He was less than 5 feet tall, according to Voltaire. See Voltaire, *Histoire du Docteur Akakia*, in *Mélanges*, (Edition de la Pléiade), p. 289.

† In fact, Maupertuis's formula was slightly different but just as risible: m.AR + n.RB.

He affirms that in all possible cases action must be a minimum, which has been shown to be false; and he says that it was he who discovered this law of the minimum, which is equally false.' Voltaire's letter went on to denounce the Academy's forgery trial, which he said was as incompetent as it was unjust, and he concluded: 'Master Maupertuis has been shown, before the intellectual world of Europe, to be guilty not just of plagiarism and error, but of abuse of power, for having persecuted an honest man whose only crime was to have disagreed with him.'[78]

When Frederick learned of Voltaire's attack, he leaped to Maupertuis's defence and charged into the controversy with an open letter of his own, in which he praised Maupertuis as 'a man of rare merit' and scorned Kœnig as a mediocrity and Voltaire as a second-rate scribbler. Ostensibly, the letter was anonymous, but when it provoked fierce criticism, Frederick had it reissued on paper adorned with his royal arms.

This was a mistake. Frederick may have thought that his personal intervention would strengthen Maupertuis's position and cow most of his critics; but in fact, by engaging personally in the controversy, as if he were any street pamphleteer, he was putting himself on the same level as Voltaire, and forcing Voltaire to choose between submission and escalation. Voltaire chose escalation. From this moment Voltaire's feud with Maupertuis was subsumed into a struggle with Frederick, and the argument was no longer about an abstruse scientific theory, about which Voltaire cared nothing, but about principles of justice and freedom of expression, on which he had decided views.

As Voltaire later wrote, in one of his doctored letters to Mme Denis:

> The king of Prussia, without having read a word of Kœnig's reply, without listening to or consulting anyone, has just written a brochure against Kœnig, against me and against all who wanted to justify the innocence of this professor so cruelly condemned. The journalists of Germany, who did not imagine that a victorious king could have produced it, spoke openly of it as the essay of a schoolboy who knew nothing of the question. Then the brochure was reprinted, this time with a Prussian eagle, a crown and a sceptre on the title page. Everybody shrugged their shoulders and lowered their eyes: no one dared speak. I do not have a sceptre; but I do have a pen.[79]

Having chosen escalation, Voltaire was forced to shift the battle onto a new terrain: the field of public opinion. This was a life-changing moment for him, and for the Enlightenment in general. Voltaire could not directly challenge Frederick's authority, for he was a contracted servant of Frederick's court, and in theory Frederick could easily punish him; but he could challenge Frederick indirectly, in the wider world. It was to prove a precedent for much greater battles later on.

Voltaire's first response to Frederick's pamphlet was to publish a pamphlet of his own and to write Kœnig an open letter for publication, in which he ridiculed some of Maupertuis's more eccentric speculative ideas.

> I have been brought a volume which Maupertuis has just had printed, and I can only be sorry for him. This is a man who claims that, to understand the nature of the soul, we must go to the other side of the world and dissect the brains of 12-foot giants; he proposes that we should dig a hole to the centre of the earth; and he says that it is as easy to see the future as the past. His whole book is full of such ideas from one end to the other. They say that your adversary is presently very ill.[80]

But Voltaire did not stop there. In November he raised the stakes again by publishing *Diatribe of Dr Akakia,* a wickedly satirical pamphlet, only a few pages long, which poked more fun at Maupertuis. The point of the joke was that the pamphlet was cast as a fictional psychiatric report by a 'Doctor Akakia' ('Doctor Harmless') on some ludicrous ideas being put about by a 'native of Saint Malo' (Maupertuis's birthplace), but which were being falsely attributed to the great President of the Berlin Academy.

> He has made some profound meditations on the art of prolonging life. First, he agrees with all sensible people – and we congratulate him on it – that our forefathers lived to be eight or nine hundred years old. Then, having found that maturity is not the prime of life but the moment of death, he proposes to delay this moment, in the same way as one preserves eggs, by preventing them from hatching. It is a fine secret, and we advise him to ensure the honour of this secret in some hen-house. We can see that, if these letters were by some President, they could only be by a President of Bedlam, and that they are obviously by a young man who has assumed the name of a sage respected throughout Europe, and who has consented to be called a 'Great Man'.[81]

Few copies of the first edition of the *Diatribe* were printed, and none survived, for Frederick had them all seized and privately burned. He made Voltaire sign a promise never again to write against anyone, and he reassured Maupertuis that all was now well: 'I have taken care of Akakia,' he told him. He spoke too soon. A Dutch printer had got hold of the *Diatribe* and in December brought out a new edition, which quickly spread to Berlin and caused a sensation. Frederick again seized all the copies he could, and this time he had them publicly burned by the state executioner. Voltaire was now in disgrace, and virtually banished from frequenting the court; so much for Voltaire's illusion that Frederick was Europe's great enlightened monarch. 'I was enthusiastic about him for sixteen years,' he told a friend, 'but he has cured me of this long illness.'[82]

The *Akakia* pamphlet was now in the public domain and could not be suppressed. In January Voltaire boasted that 6,000 copies had been sold in Paris in one day, and he proceeded regularly to update it, by adding more sections.[83] Maupertuis was now a very sick man, and in April 1753 he sent Voltaire a letter threatening him with physical violence; Voltaire made sure that it was published in the Leipzig newspaper. Maupertuis left Berlin on 29 April 1753, never to return; he travelled in France for a while, and finally took refuge in Basel, where he died in 1759, aged sixty-one.

Having won the moral argument, Voltaire had to leave Prussia as soon as possible. A few months earlier he had already taken some preparatory steps to place his fortune beyond the reach of the Prussian authorities: he approached Charles Eugene, duke of Württemberg, whom he knew to be in need of money, and offered to lend him 40,000 écus at an interest rate of 10 per cent. By December the arrangements were finalised, and on 31 January he negotiated a second contract with Württemberg for another 4,000 écus.[84] All that now remained was to get Frederick's permission to go.

On 1 January 1753 Voltaire tried to resign from the king's service by sending back his chamberlain's key and the cross of the Order of Merit. But Frederick refused to accept his resignation and immediately sent back the key and the cross. Voltaire again insisted; Frederick still resisted; and they remained deadlocked for over two months. 'Everyone', Voltaire told d'Argental, 'tells me to leave, but when one has been ill in bed for a month, and when one does not have permission to leave, then getting oneself carried past 100,000 bayonets is not as easy as you might think.'[85] Nevertheless, at the end of February, Voltaire started moving out; he returned all the books he had borrowed from the royal library; he had all his possessions packed up; and he took rooms, at his own expense, with Collini, his secretary, in a country house in Stralau, a suburb in the outskirts of Berlin. But he still did not have permission to leave Prussia.

On 9 March 1753 Frederick finally relented and gave Voltaire leave to return to France; in theory, he would return when his health was better. 'You do not need the pretext of having to visit Plombières: you can leave my service when you want. But, before leaving, you must return to me your contract of employment, the key, the cross and the volume of poetry which I entrusted to you.'[86] Voltaire asked for a final audience, which was granted, and he spent the next nine days in Potsdam. Finally, on 26 March, early in the morning, in a heavily laden carriage, with Collini beside him, Voltaire left Potsdam for good.

20

HUMILIATION AT FRANKFURT

1750–1753

VOLTAIRE DAWDLED on his journey home. He visited Leipzig, Gotha and Kassel on the way, and spent a month being fêted by the duke and duchess of Saxe-Gotha, so that it was not until 31 May 1753 that he reached Frankfurt.

The next morning, just as Voltaire was getting ready to set off again, he was confronted in his hotel by Baron Franz von Freytag, the local representative (*résident*) of the Prussian authorities. Freytag told him that he had orders to require him to hand over a book of poems by King Frederick, and he made it clear that until this happened he would place him under virtual house arrest. Voltaire explained that this book of poems, which had been given him by the king, was in a large trunk following on behind. Freytag was not satisfied, and insisted on going through all Voltaire's belongings. At the end of this humiliating process, which lasted from nine in the morning till five in the afternoon, Freytag took away an unopened package, a poem by Voltaire, two packets of personal papers, the Chamberlain's key and the cross and ribbon of the Order of Merit. Voltaire promised not to leave until his trunk had arrived; Freytag promised that Voltaire would be free to go as soon as he received the book of poems.

Voltaire now settled down to wait, and he wrote several letters, including two to his friend d'Argental; but he did not mention the fact that he was under arrest.[1] He must have assumed that this tiresome contretemps would soon be over. It was not until five days later that he started appealing to influential friends and contacts across Europe for help against Freytag.

Meanwhile Mme Denis had come from Paris to accompany Voltaire on his journey home. Her original plan had been to join him in Strasbourg, but when she heard of his troubles, she travelled on to Frankfurt; she got there on 9 June 1753 and was herself placed under house arrest.

On Sunday 17 June Voltaire's trunk arrived, and he expected that he would now be allowed to go. But Freytag refused to open the trunk without fresh instructions from Frederick. Voltaire now panicked: taking only his manuscripts and his money box, and accompanied only by Collini, he left the hotel and attempted to leave the city by a public coach. The alarm was raised, and they were stopped at the city gates and taken into custody. This time it was no longer a question of house arrest: they were taken to a tavern and locked up in separate rooms under armed guard. Mme Denis was still in her room at the Lion d'Or hotel; Herr Dorn, Freytag's secretary, went there to fetch her and dragged her to the tavern under armed escort. Dorn then installed himself in her garret bedroom for the night, had dinner sent up, drank many bottles of wine and was only dissuaded from forcing himself on her by her cries for help.

The next day, Thursday 21 June, Freytag received new instructions from Potsdam: he was to release Voltaire and his companions and allow them to leave in peace, provided Voltaire gave a written promise to return Frederick's book of poems. Freytag did not reveal these instructions, nor did he carry them out. Collini and Mme Denis were released from their rooms but kept under house arrest; Voltaire remained locked up. Voltaire and his party were still under arrest two weeks later, when, on 5 July, a fresh letter came from Frederick in response to the widespread public outcry at Voltaire's arrest. He rebuked Freytag for having arrested Mme Denis and ordered the immediate release of Voltaire and his companions. Freytag disregarded the orders; and it was not until 7 July that Voltaire and Collini were allowed to make a hurried departure from Frankfurt. Mme Denis left the following day, for Paris.

Before Voltaire left, Dorn confiscated his money box, containing cash, letters of credit and jewels. It was not until many weeks later, on 13 September, that Voltaire got any of his money back: just 1,000 francs.

Voltaire did not go straight home to France, however. Perhaps this was because he was waiting to learn whether he would be welcome in France, for he may have heard that he was in disgrace in Versailles for having accepted a position at the court of Frederick. Meanwhile, he decided to enjoy himself: he spent three weeks at Mainz, where he stayed with the worldly prince–bishop, and two weeks at Schwetzingen near Mannheim, summer home of the Elector-Palatine, where he was entertained with a constant round of parties and theatre performances.

On 5 August 1753 Voltaire wrote to Mme Denis in Paris:

It's been some time since I wrote to you. But it's not entirely my fault, my dear child. I was ill at Mainz, but every day, every hour, I planned on leaving, as soon as I should have the strength. From Mainz I went to Mannheim, and fell ill again. But it was an indispensable duty for me to pay my respects to their Electoral Highnesses, and thank them for the extreme kindnesses with which they have honoured me. All that I lack is the health to enjoy all the pleasures on offer. Comédie-Française, Comédie-Italienne, Italian grand opera, opera buffa, ballets, plenty of food, conversation, politeness, grandeur, simplicity, that's the Mannheim court for you.[2]

Six days later, on 11 August 1753 he wrote to her again:

I am still, my dear child, the Elector-Palatine's patient. His country-side is delicious, his company even more. There is everything here, and nothing in excess. They have put on for me *Alzire* and *Nanine* [two of Voltaire's plays]. The troupe of actors is fairly good. You will admit that one cannot entertain an author better than by putting on his own works. I shall leave tomorrow; or the day after.

P.S. They are keeping me here until Tuesday: they are putting on for me *Zaïre* and *L'Indiscret* [another two of Voltaire's plays].[3]

Voltaire also took advantage of his visit to do a little business. The Elector-Palatine was ruining himself with his extravagance, so he borrowed 100,000 francs from Voltaire. It was to be the first of many such transactions, until the closing years of Voltaire's life.

On 15 August 1753 Voltaire reached Strasbourg, where he lingered for several months, anxiously waiting for news from Mme Denis in Paris. The first news was very exciting, for she told him, after her return to Paris, that she was pregnant; evidently their brief reunion in Frankfurt, after a separation of two and a half years, had reawakened their sexual fires. Perhaps it was in response to this news that he returned later that month to the erotic charge, with a letter from Strasbourg: 'Me not love you! My child, I shall adore you until the tomb. I wish I could be the only one to have the happiness of fucking you, and I wish now that I had never had any other favours but yours, and had never discharged except with you. I have a hard-on as I write, and I kiss a thousand times your lovely tits and your lovely arse.'[4]

Besterman dismisses the story of Mme Denis's pregnancy as pure fiction: 'She even pretended to be pregnant by Voltaire, and Voltaire pretended to believe her.' In fact, it is obvious that Voltaire did believe her, for he repeatedly asked her for news of her pregnancy and her health, with concern and delighted anticipation at the prospect of a child. 'I really hope that your suspicions about Mme Daurade [his code-name for Mme Denis] are true. Is it true that she is pregnant? I should really like a little Daurade, but tell the mother to look after herself.'[5]

A month later Mme Denis told him that she had had a miscarriage, and Voltaire was deeply upset. 'The misadventure of Mme Daurade pierces my heart', he replied. 'One instant has destroyed everything'.[6] And a week later: 'You cannot believe how deeply I regret what Mme Daurade had promised me. I am afraid that it is an irreparable loss.'[7]

Voltaire never married and never had children, and until now he had never shown any desire for children. After 1753, however, there seems to have been a real transformation in his attitude towards home, family and children. When he moved to Geneva, he delighted in gathering round him members of Mme Denis's family, and there were several episodes over the next few years strongly indicating Voltaire's desire for children in the house.

In January 1754 Voltaire learned that he was condemned to exile. Mme Denis had seen Mme de Pompadour, she told him, and she had told her that the king would not allow Voltaire to return. Voltaire described the news as 'an overpowering thunderbolt ... the bomb which has fallen on my head has upset my plans and my hopes'.[8]

What was most perplexing was the vagueness of the sentence. Exile was usually expressed in specific terms, such as exile of so many leagues from Paris or to a particular place or for so many months or years. In this case there was only an oral message from Mme de Pompadour, without specifics, and without any reference to a formal document or decree. In fact, there was no formal decree, and we may speculate whether the decision to exile Voltaire had been made not by the king but by Mme de Pompadour herself. After all, it was she who, in 1749, had warned Voltaire in the most personal terms not to think of going to Prussia: 'For my own part, I should never forgive you.'[9]

Voltaire spent most of the rest of that year hanging about near the French frontier, trying to decide what to do and where to go. He asked Mme Denis to find out if he would be allowed to live near Auxerre (in northern Burgundy) or elsewhere. 'Having received no positive order, I suppose that I can choose my own exile.'[10] And the next question was whether Mme Denis would be prepared to share his exile with him, or whether she would stay in the bright lights of Paris society. In some ways Paris was an attractive option for her, since she knew that Voltaire would continue to support her in considerable comfort. But the question of how much comfort was and remained a regular subject of disagreement between them. When she drew 4,800 livres from his banker over the space of about ten days, Voltaire complained of her extravagance. She reacted violently to his reproaches, accusing him of avarice: 'The love of money torments you. Avarice stabs you. In your heart you are the worst of men.'[11]

Her attack seems to have led to some kind of showdown on the question of money, for in March 1754 Voltaire set out an account of the state of his finances, which, he said, 'would enable me to live with Mme Denis in a manner which would be agreeable to her'.[12] Mme Denis was persuaded, and early in April she indicated that she was thinking of spending her life with him.[13] He replied: 'Your letter of 6 April overwhelms me with joy.'[14] Finally, in late July 1754, Mme Denis joined him in Colmar, and she and Voltaire were now set on a life together.

It is not easy to form a confident picture of the nature of the evolving personal relationship between them. In the 1740s they had obviously had a strong sexual encounter. After 1754 the question becomes more difficult, but in day-to-day terms they seem to have negotiated a strong quasi-marital partnership, in which she managed the household, he managed the income, she spent it freely, she managed the entertainment of local society, and they both managed the amateur dramatics. We know nothing about the nature of the later sexual relationship between them, if any.

Voltaire's stay in Prussia and his humiliating exit from it marked a fundamental watershed in his life. The sentence of rejection was a great shock; he viewed the uncertain prospect of permanent disgrace, and banishment from his friends and the rest of the world, with deep anxiety. Yet against all expectations, the years of exile turned out to be the most productive years in his life, and time and again, over the next twenty-five years, he would declare that he was really happy. His happiness dated from his involuntary retirement; to his great surprise he found that he really liked the new life better than the old.

21

SENTENCE OF EXILE

1754–1755

FOR SEVERAL MONTHS VOLTAIRE did not know where to go. He thought of moving somewhere just a few leagues outside Paris; he enquired about the property laws in Lausanne; he wondered about Lyon, or Burgundy, or even Bayreuth or Gotha.

One important consideration was that, since he was still writing prolifically, he wanted to live in a place where he could supervise the output of a respectable local publisher. This led him to consider Geneva, since it was the home of the brothers Gabriel and Philibert Cramer, well-known and politically prominent printers and publishers. In August 1754 Philibert Cramer travelled to Colmar especially to see Voltaire and offered to publish a complete edition of his works.[1] After Voltaire moved to Geneva, he established a friendly and trusting professional relationship with the Cramers, which was to last for most of the rest of his life until, in the winter of 1775–76, they gave up their printing business.

It was on a trip to Lyon, in December 1754, that he decided to move to Geneva. His friend the duc de Richelieu was travelling from Paris to the Languedoc, where he was governor, and he summoned Voltaire to meet him on the way. When Voltaire arrived at the Palais Royal inn in Lyon on 15 November, he was sick and out of sorts: 'It is a bit of a bad joke', he grumbled, 'for a sick man to have to travel 100 leagues just to have a chat with M. le maréchal de Richelieu. He never made any of his mistresses travel so far, though he always led them a fine dance.'[2]

The turning-point in Voltaire's visit to Lyon was his meeting with Jean-Robert Tronchin, a prominent local banker and a member of one of

Geneva's leading patrician families. They obviously hit it off splendidly, for Voltaire immediately opened an account with him and instructed his man of business in Paris to deposit £50,000 with the firm of Tronchin and Camp in Lyon. (Ami Camp was a cousin of Jean-Robert Tronchin and his junior partner.) Jean-Robert Tronchin was now Voltaire's main banker and financial adviser; Voltaire referred to him as 'my friend and perfectly honest man'.[3]

On 10 December 1754 Voltaire and Mme Denis left Lyon for Geneva, where they met several other members of the Tronchin 'tribe', all leading members of Geneva's oligarchy. On the first night he stayed with Jean-Robert's younger brother François, one of Geneva's leading politicians and a fellow theatre enthusiast, who hosted a select dinner for him and Mme Denis. The next day he was invited to dinner by Théodore Tronchin, a cousin of Jean-Robert and one of the most celebrated doctors in Europe. In fact, Voltaire already knew both François and Théodore: he had met François in 1722, at the Comédie Française in Paris, and Théodore in the winter of 1736, in Amsterdam.*[4]

It was the charm and sheer usefulness of the various Tronchins that finally clinched Voltaire's choice of Geneva. 'Good heavens,' he wrote, 'how delightful all the Tronchins are; we are very glad to have got to know them. We were wonderfully received in Geneva; they were even kind enough to keep open the city gates for us until 6.30 p.m., which they normally never do.'[5] To Théodore he wrote:

> I do not know how I can thank all who bear the name of Tronchin, and especially you, Sir, who have been willing to help me with so many kindnesses. As soon as my stomach has recovered and I have some horses, I shall come to tell you how much you have attached me to you. Permit me to enclose a little note for that member of the Tronchin tribe who gave me indigestion with a good supper, whereas you were giving me good advice.[6]

Voltaire was particularly pleased at the idea of having a famous (and friendly) doctor within easy reach, since his chronic ill health was as bad as ever. In 1754 he described his pitiful condition: 'white hair, colic, some hydropsy, and scurvy'.[7] The following year he had a new problem:

---

* Théodore Tronchin trained as a doctor in Leyden in 1730, and he practised medicine in Amsterdam until 1754. In that year he returned to Geneva, not long before Voltaire's arrival (*Letters*, 830, 832, 837). Voltaire could even have met Théodore in England, for Théodore had been a student at Cambridge and a houseman in a London hospital from 1726 to 1728.

'It is rare that milk is suitable to somewhat dried-up temperaments like ours. It so happens that our stomachs make bad cheese which stays in our poor bodies, and which becomes an unbearable weight. It then goes to the head. The cursed animal functions don't work, and one is in a deplorable state.'[8]

The most regularly recurring complaint of Voltaire (and of Mme Denis) was constipation, and Voltaire, Mme Denis and Théodore Tronchin each had different ideas on how to deal with it. Voltaire preferred rhubarb, and he asked Jean-Robert Tronchin to send him some: 'I beg you, Sir, to send half a pound of the best rhubarb that Chinese Tartary ever produced.'[9] But Théodore did not approve of rhubarb. A month later Voltaire wrote again to Jean-Robert: 'Mme Denis and I send you again all our thanks. Everything you have sent has been approved, except the rhubarb. Your cousin the doctor gives such a strong preference to cassia that it is quite impossible to speak of rhubarb in his presence.'[10]

In December 1755 Voltaire wrote to Théodore Tronchin: 'Mme Denis is unwilling to purge herself without your instructions; but that is what she needs, for though she is doing well in the dining department, she is doing badly in the cloakroom department; and for her constipation and her swelling she requires a certain very agreeable and very efficacious medicine that you have prescribed for her. As for my particular case, I am faithful to cassia, manna and oil.' (He did not dare mention rhubarb.)[11]

Voltaire did not stay long in the city of Geneva, for he had heard from his younger niece that the baron de Prangins, in Paris, was offering to lend him his château on the north shore of Lac Léman (Lake Geneva), at least until Voltaire should have found a longer-term solution. Voltaire was quite relieved, and by mid-December 1754 he and Mme Denis were installed in the château de Prangins, which he described as 'the most beautiful situation in the world, a magnificent château, with trout which weigh 10 pounds, and I who weigh scarcely more, seeing that I am more skeletal and more moribund than ever.'[12]

Mme Denis quickly set about getting furniture and clothes, and hired some servants, including an excellent cook. One of the new servants was a fifteen-year-old local boy, Jean-Louis Wagnière, whom Voltaire took on to help Collini; he had good handwriting and a taste for literature, and Voltaire gave him Latin lessons. When Collini left Voltaire's service in 1756, Wagnière took over as Voltaire's principal secretary, and he stayed with him for the rest of his life.

Voltaire soon found the château de Prangins too large, and too cold in the fierce winter winds, and he looked for a warmer home of his own. It did not take long. 'A few days ago', he told Jean-Robert,

> I saw a country house near Geneva, which belongs to a M. Mallet: it is the palace of a philosopher, with the gardens of Epicurus; it is a delicious retreat; and I think it would suit you one day. You know how difficult it is for a foreigner, and for a good Catholic like me, to acquire property in the land of the people of God [i.e., protestant Geneva]. Your brother has suggested that I could be your concierge until my death. You would buy the estate with money which I would provide. I have offered 80,000 French livres; we could go as high as 90,000. On my death you could reimburse 50,000–60,000 livres to Mme Denis, my niece.[13]

In other words, the Tronchins were cooking up a plan to help Voltaire get round the law which banned Catholics from owning property in Geneva. Jean-Robert would be the front-man in buying the house, with money put up by Voltaire; when Voltaire gave up the property, or died, it would revert to Jean-Robert, in exchange for a partial reimbursement of the original purchase loan.

Within a couple of weeks, Voltaire agreed to pay £87,200 for the house, which was called Saint-Jean, and which he promptly renamed Les Délices; in the meantime, he had already taken a lease on another country house, called Montriond, just outside Lausanne, which was less rigidly Calvinist, less autocratic and more worldly than Geneva, and therefore more relaxed about Voltaire's theatrical activities. Thereafter Voltaire tended to split his time, summer and winter, between Geneva and Lausanne.

Early in March 1755 Voltaire acquired possession of Les Délices, but even before moving in, he decided that he must make substantial changes to it. Les Délices was a pretty house, he told Thieriot, 'whose gardens are comparable to the most beautiful near Paris. The great misfortune of this house, however, is that it was apparently built by a man who thought only of himself, and who completely forgot about any convenient little apartments for his friends. I shall immediately rectify this abominable defect.' He added that the excellent cook whom he had had at Prangins, was unfortunately staying there. 'I don't really mind; but Mme Denis, who is very greedy, is making a capital fuss out of it.'[14]

Immediately after moving into Les Délices, Voltaire rushed into a hectic programme for the improvement and remodelling of the house and garden: 'It will undoubtedly be very agreeable to live in this house', he told d'Argental, 'for it is charming, convenient, spacious and surrounded by delicious gardens; but I shall live without you, and that is really living in exile. Our place is costing us a lot of money and a lot of trouble. I speak to no one except masons, carpenters, gardeners. I am having my vines and trees pruned. I am busy making a chicken run.'[15]

Voltaire's correspondence with Jean-Robert now became quite intense, not just as his banker but also as his supplier of everything from wine and seeds and trees and medicines to horses and paint and soft furnishings. He wrote to him pretty well every week, sometimes several times a week; and sometimes he wrote to him from his bed, for he was frequently unwell.

> I have abused your kindness on the question of wine. I have found some very good stuff at Versoix which I could not help buying; it is excellent and ready to drink; it is the best Burgundy, and I shall use it to supplement the two barrels of Beaujolais which you are kindly sending me. I suppose the Beaujolais is rather for laying down. We cannot yet receive anyone: the house is full of workmen of every kind. I am building a small extra wing; I am putting up grills, I am knocking down walls, I am embellishing a house which one day you will be tempted to live in.[16]

Over the next few months Voltaire's shopping lists poured out in an absolute torrent. In March:

> Many thanks for the lavender; I promise to have it planted in all the borders of your kitchen garden. I have already planted 250 trees; I have created some avenues for you, and I am building you a little wing. Monsieur your brother has just brought me some seeds; it was the nicest present you could give me. At this moment I am sowing your Egyptian onions; even the Israelites did not like them more than me. Please send me everything you can in the way of flowers and vegetables. The garden was completely bare; we must start from scratch; I am founding a second Carthage. I embrace you tenderly.[17]

In April it was 'artichoke bulbs, and as much as possible of lavender, thyme, rosemary, mint, basil, rue, strawberry bushes, pinks, *thadicée,* balm, tarragon, *sariette,* burnet, sage, and hyssop to cleanse our sins etc.,

etc., etc.'[18] Later that month he ordered 'six number 4 pins, six number 18 pins, a dozen number 9, and a dozen number 14; and then you will send me a dozen times to the devil'.[19] In May he ordered quantities of carpets, and eight wing armchairs plus another sixteen ordinary arm-chairs, plus 'a good little barrel of green oil, which really smells of olives'.[20] Later that month he told Jean-Robert: 'Our Délices will have the finest chicken run in the world. When will you come to eat your chickens and your eggs?'[21] In August he asked Jean-Robert to 'have the goodness to send me a beautiful backgammon board, for we must amuse our griefs. Letters only serve to poison our lives; in fact the only good letters are letters of credit.'[22]

All this improvement was costing a lot of money. In April he said that he had on the strength 'two master gardeners, twenty workmen and twelve servants'; later the number of gardeners rose to four.[23] In August he told Jean-Robert that his 'so-called Délices has already cost me more than 120,000 livres',[24] i.e., more than 30,000 livres on top of the purchase price. A few days later the figure went up to 40,000 livres.[25]

He was undeterred. In October he asked Jean-Robert to send various components for a carriage which he was having built, plus '50 pounds of the best Marseille coffee, and about 50 bottles of that good red and white Muscat wine which you let us have once before'.[26] He explained later that the carriage would be lined to keep out the drafts, but the ornamentation would be kept simple, in deference to Geneva's sumptu-ary laws, which banned the use of gold and silver in decoration except in the case of buttons and uniform braid.[27]

This question of the carriage decoration was symptomatic of the potential friction between the austere principles of the Geneva repub-lic and Voltaire's very different lifestyle. In principle, citizens were not allowed to travel in coaches unless they were sick or going on a journey, and no one was supposed to have a carriage pulled by as many as four horses. But Voltaire's establishment at Les Délices towards the end of 1755 included a good cook, many servants and four horses in the stables; by the following spring it had expanded to six horses, four carriages, a coachman, a postillion, two servants, a valet, a French cook, a scullery boy and a secretary. Voltaire was unrepentant: 'My dear colleague,' he wrote to François Tronchin, 'it is true that I have the insolence to have six horses. Mme Denis claims that six horses are necessary. Personally, I should like to have twelve of them, to come and embrace you sooner.'[28] Voltaire's flippant disregard of the local mores caused irritation among conservative Genevans.

A more serious source of potential conflict between Voltaire and the Genevans was his love of theatre and amateur dramatics. No public theatre was permitted inside the city, but since Voltaire was determined not to go without theatrical entertainment, he had to put on performances at home. Even before work was finished on the house and gardens he wrote to Henri-Louis Lekain, the leading actor of the Comédie Française, to urge him to visit:

> If you have the courage to come here, you must also have the courage to be ill housed and ill bedded; my Délices is upside down. You will see me acting as a mason, as a carpenter and as a gardener; only you can restore me to my original trade [as a playwright]. You can easily travel from Lyon to Geneva by the public vehicles. My house is exactly at the gates of Geneva, and I shall send a carriage which will pick you up on the road.[29]

Lekain did come to stay with Voltaire that spring, over the Easter holidays, when the Paris theatres were closed; and he created a local sensation when he appeared before the upper crust of Geneva society in a performance of Voltaire's tragedy *Zaïre*. 'We brought tears to the eyes of almost the complete Geneva Council,' wrote Voltaire; 'I have never seen so many tears; never have the Calvinists been so tender.'[30]

After his visit to Voltaire, Lekain wanted to stop off at Lyon on his way home, in order to put on some freelance performances there and earn a bit extra to supplement his meagre earnings from the Comédie Française, which amounted to barely 2,000 livres a year.[31] But first he had to get permission from the duc de Richelieu, for the actors at the Comédie Française were not free agents: if they wanted to travel, or to act anywhere else but at the Comédie Française or the court at Versailles, they had to get permission from the court, represented in rotation by one of the six First Gentlemen of the King's Chamber. This year it was Richelieu who was duty officer, and on this occasion he did give Lekain his permission.[32]

In principle the Geneva protestants disapproved of Voltaire's theatrical entertainments, even at home. In the spring of 1755 Voltaire was working on his latest tragedy, *L'Orphelin de la Chine* (The Orphan of China), and when he finished it, he sent Collini to Paris to deliver the text to his friend d'Argental. Collini would not mind making an extra copy of the play, he told him, even though he must by now be tired of making copies and even though 'he is very busy with a pretty

Italian girl whom he has taken to Paris'.[33] In August the play was a great success at the Comédie Française, and Voltaire started rehearsals for his own staging of the play at Les Délices, with the theatre-mad François Tronchin reading the lead part rather well.

But he soon heard echoes of disapproval from the Protestant clergy in Geneva, and he had second thoughts: 'I think we shall not put it on,' he told Collini. 'It seemed to me that our plan was upsetting the priests, and since I did not want to upset anyone, I decided that I would not perform it. Come home when you are tired of pleasures, of women, and of Paris.'[34] Collini was evidently still enjoying pleasures, women and Paris, for he did not come home for another month. But Voltaire's cancellation of his production of *L'Orphelin de la Chine* was just a tactical withdrawal, not a strategic retreat; he and Mme Denis now decided that they would build a proper, small theatre of their own at Les Délices.

In August 1755, five months after moving in, he took stock and started to realise just how much he was enjoying himself. 'You would find my retreat charming in summer,' he told Thieriot. 'In winter one must not leave the fireside; but then, all places are the same when it freezes. But on fine days I know nothing to compare with my situation. I did not know this new pleasure, nor that of sowing, planting and building. I would like to have you in this little corner of the earth, where I am very happy.'[35]

Voltaire was obviously getting great fun from doing up Les Délices.

> Mr Loup must get in some large gravel, which must be spread and rolled from the paving of the courtyard right up to the grill which leads to the paths to the vines. The gardeners should already have made two square lawns, on the right and left of this sandy path, while leaving three feet to be sanded at the two extremities of these lawns, as I had ordered. The servants must be sure to shake the chestnut trees, to bring down the cockchafers, and feed them to the chickens.[36]*

One of the most regular visitors from Paris was Marie-Élisabeth Fontaine, the younger widowed sister of Mme Denis. Voltaire was

---

* The word Voltaire uses for 'lawn' in this letter is *boulingrin*, a Frenchified transliteration of 'bowling green'; it has been an officially recognised French word since 1663. Then, as now, French garden designers preferred gravel to grass; but when they used grass, the implied reference was England. The irony is that the French play *boules*, which does not need grass, but not bowls, which does.

obviously very fond of her, and never happier than when he could gather all his family round him. He particularly admired her drawings, for which she evidently had some talent, and felt concern at her regular bouts of ill health. But there is a curious question mark over Voltaire's feelings for her. In January he wrote to discuss the symptoms of her ill-health, for which he had asked Théodore Tronchin to prescribe some suitable treatment; and he concluded his letter: 'Adieu, my dear niece, try to come and see us, with bouncy tits and a big arse (*avec des tétons rebondis et un gros cul*)'.[37] In March he wrote again about her health, and declared that Théodore Tronchin will be 'unworthy of his reputation, if he does not give you an arse and tits'.[38] Voltaire does not use this kind of language in writing to any other woman, except of course to Mme Denis, but the suggestiveness of the words fairly leaps off the page.

On 8 June Marie-Élisabeth came to stay at Les Délices, with her lover and future husband, the marquis de Florian, and immediately found fault with the arrangements. Voltaire wrote to Jean-Robert in mock dismay.

> Mme Fontaine rightly finds my house ill-furnished. 'Oh Heavens!', she says, 'No bidets!' She is not yet accustomed to the severe and unclean customs of the city of Calvin. Please be so good, my dear correspondent, as to add to your deliveries three bidets with all the fittings. Such importunate requests! Candelabra with silver hatching, coffee, sugar, candles, gilt nails, and now bidets![39]

The candelabra were for a present for Théodore. The following year Voltaire ordered for his winter home at Lausanne two more of these 'arse-washers called bidets, with which a lady can wash herself without showing her backside to anyone'.[40]

Mme Fontaine's arrival at Les Délices was followed almost immediately by the sacking of Collini. A servant girl had found in his room a letter that contained mocking references to Mme Denis, in which he described her as 'the louche working-woman'. The letter was shown to Mme Denis, and she demanded, and got, Collini's immediate dismissal. He left Geneva four days later, on 12 June, and was succeeded by his assistant, Jean-Louis Wagnière.

Voltaire's home soon became the place that almost everyone wanted to visit. Opinion in Geneva was deeply divided about Voltaire. Conservatives wished that he had gone to live elsewhere; the more worldly and cultivated laymen were fascinated by his brilliance, intrigued by his provocative liberalism and seduced by his lavish hospitality. Even the clergy were split; the most austere were hostile, yet Voltaire counted quite a few pastors as friends and frequent visitors. Lausanne was more open-minded than Geneva, with its own theatre for amateur dramatics; and some of the Lausanne pastors even took part in Voltaire's theatrical entertainments. In March 1757 he wrote to Jacob Vernes, one of the most enlightened Protestant pastors in Geneva: 'Yesterday we were honoured with the presence of twelve preachers, who brought with them all their novices. Moreover, we had two preachers who played the violin very well in the orchestra. Piety is not at all the enemy of honest pleasures.'[41]

His visitors came not only from Geneva and Lausanne but from far and wide. In April he told Richelieu that he was visited every day by Englishmen: 'I have never seen them so polite. I think they owe it all to you', (a sly allusion to the fact that Richelieu had just inflicted a serious naval defeat on the English at Minorca, at the start of the Seven Years' War).[42] In September he wrote to d'Argental : 'I haven't a moment to myself. I have to spend time with the processions of the curious who come from Lyon, from Geneva, from Savoy, from Switzerland, and even from Paris. Almost every day, I have seven or eight people to have dinner with me'.[43]* As Voltaire implied, many of his visitors were strangers, who just invited themselves.

In the spring of 1757 he put on the tragedy *Fanime* in his little theatre at Montriond: 'I have never seen so many tears. We have about 200 spectators, who are quite the equal of the people in the stalls in Paris, for they listen only to their hearts, have much wit, and have nothing to do with cabals.'[44]

In short, Voltaire was having a wonderful time in his new home. He moaned and groaned and complained about his health, but it was mostly an act, pure façade. Quite unexpectedly, he was enjoying a new kind of happiness.

---

* Geneva at this time was an independent republic; it had links to Switzerland, which included Berne, Zurich and Lausanne, but was not part of it. Geneva did not become part of Switzerland until 1815.

2 2

ENCYCLOPÉDIE

1753–1759

IT WAS NOT LONG after his return from Prussia that Voltaire became involved in the *Encyclopédie*. The first three volumes had already been published, in 1751–53, while he was away in Potsdam; in May 1754, while he was hanging around anxiously in Alsace, Jean Le Rond d'Alembert got in touch with him and asked if he would like to contribute. Voltaire immediately agreed, and his participation in the project was announced in the fourth volume of the *Encyclopédie*, which came out later that year.

This *Encyclopédie*, or *Dictionnaire Raisonné des Sciences, des Arts et des Métiers*, set out to chart the state of knowledge of the modern world and is often associated with the notion of *philosophie* or *les philosophes*. However, the word *philosophie* in the French Enlightenment context does not necessarily imply a fully worked-out system of ideas. What the *philosophes* mostly had in common was a belief in rationality and science, and varying degrees of scepticism about religion. Some of the *philosophes* were atheists, while others, such as Voltaire, were not; but there was so pervasive an air of scepticism about religion throughout the work, in the interstices between down-to-earth articles about the arts and sciences, that eventually it got the *Encyclopédie* into trouble with the French establishment.[1]

Voltaire and d'Alembert quickly established a close working rapport, and d'Alembert became not just Voltaire's main contact with the *Encyclopédie* and his closest ally against the forces of darkness but also one of his warmest friends. Voltaire may have felt a special personal bond with his young colleague, since d'Alembert was illegitimate, just as Voltaire suspected that he too may have been illegitimate. As was the custom with illegitimate children at the time, part of d'Alembert's surname, Le Rond, came from the name of the church, Saint-Jean-Le-Rond, where he had been abandoned in infancy, while d'Alembert, like Voltaire, was an assumed name.

The irony is that d'Alembert was in reality of quite distinguished birth: his mother was the celebrated courtesan Claudine Alexandrine Guérin, marquise de Tencin, and his father was the chevalier Louis-Camus Destouches-Canon, a lieutenant-general in the French artillery. His mother's elder sister, Marie Angélique Guérin de Tencin, had married Augustin de Ferriol, and was the mother of Pont de Veyle and d'Argental. In effect, therefore, d'Alembert was the illegitimate cousin of d'Argental.

As soon as Voltaire agreed to contribute to the *Encyclopédie*, d'Alembert assigned him twenty-five articles, and Voltaire set to work with a will, though he warned the Cramers, his publishers, that these tasks would delay his other writing. Voltaire's attitude to the *Encyclopédie* was always deeply serious but not solemn: he described it as 'a great and immortal edifice', but he was surprisingly unassuming about his own role, as if he was just a workaday jobbing journalist, and he accepted without demur that his own contributions were liable to be edited, altered or even rejected. He complained that the editors seemed to want articles that were much too wordy, whereas he would prefer entries as succinct as possible, with short definitions and a few examples. 'I'm sorry that they want such long articles. But I shall make the article "Literature" as boringly useless as they could wish. If I were on the spot, I would willingly be an artisan in their workshop.'[2]

Characteristically, he could not resist making little jokes about his articles. Towards the end of 1755 he wrote to d'Alembert:

> I shall send you my ideas, and you will rectify them as you see fit. I should gladly take on 'History', and I think I could include fairly interesting things in it. As for 'Fornication', I am all the more entitled to develop this subject in that I am, unfortunately, entirely disinterested. By the way, there is another 'F' which has a certain merit, but I do not think it is up to me to speak of it.'[3]*

The cheerful serenity of Voltaire's Geneva retirement was briefly

---

* *Foutre* ('fuck') was presumably what he meant.

disturbed towards the end of 1755 by the shocking news of a massive earthquake at Lisbon, which on 1 November destroyed the city and killed around 30,000 people. This was one of the most violent earthquakes of modern history, and it set off a major debate across Europe about the problem of evil: if God was good, how could He permit such a catastrophe?

Voltaire learned of the earthquake with certainty on 23 November 1755, and at first he thought there had been 100,000 casualties. By the first week of December he had written a commentary on the event, in the form of a *Poème sur le Désastre de Lisbonne*, consisting of a preface and 234 alexandrine verses. Many people had expected that he would use the earthquake as a pretext for an anti-religious diatribe and would attack those pietists who claimed that the disaster was God's punishment for man's wickedness. In fact, he devoted only six lines to the question of religion; the main burden of his *Poème* was an attack on the philosophy of Gottfried Wilhelm Leibniz (1646–1716), who had argued that, since God was good, this must be the best of all possible worlds. This idea, subsequently simplified and popularised by Alexander Pope in the phrase 'Whatever is, is right', had become fashionable under the neologism 'Optimism'.

The day after he learned the news, Voltaire wrote to Jean-Robert Tronchin: 'There, Sir, was a really cruel physical event. One would be quite embarrassed to guess how the laws of movement [i.e., of physics] can bring about such frightful disasters in the *best of all possible worlds*.' And to another friend, a Protestant pastor in Berne, he wrote: 'You know about the horrible events at Lisbon, Seville and Cadiz. There you have a terrible argument against *Optimism*.' Here we can hear a pre-echo of Voltaire's later satirical tale *Candide*, in which he repeatedly ridiculed the 'Optimism' of Dr Pangloss, a caricature of Leibniz.[4]

Voltaire could not remain solemn for long. 'You will have heard', he told Jean-Robert,

> that we too have been honoured with a small earthquake. It cost us a broken bottle of Muscat wine which fell from a table. We were lucky to get off so lightly. But while waiting for the end of the world, I am again forced to importune you, Sir, for some of the knick-knacks of this life. Our saddler had forgotten to ask you for ten yards of large braid, similar to the sample I enclose. And the insatiable Mme Denis swears that you will not refuse her 4,000 gilt nails for the armchairs. It seems to me that we need rather a lot of things to live in a land of heretics.[5]

As he told Thieriot, not even the Lisbon earthquake could spoil Voltaire's new-found contentment. 'If I live in opulence, it is only for other people, for thus I defy ill fortune and enjoy a very pleasant and very free situation, which I owe only to myself. When I have spoken, in verse, about the sufferings of my fellow human beings, it was purely out of generosity; for apart from my failing health, I am so happy that I am ashamed of it.'[6]

In the summer of 1756 d'Alembert came to visit Voltaire at Les Délices. He wanted to cement relations with his celebrated contributor, but he also wanted to research and write an article for the *Encyclopédie* about Geneva. It turned out to be a momentous event, a turning-point both in the battle between the *philosophes* of the Enlightenment and the forces of obscurantism and in Voltaire's relations with the Geneva authorities.

D'Alembert arrived on 10 August 1756 and stayed for three weeks. He met many people in Geneva, including some open-minded Protestant pastors; and of course he was also heavily briefed by Voltaire himself. When his article 'Genève' appeared the following year, in volume VII of the *Encyclopédie* (November 1757), it caused a major scandal. For although d'Alembert's article was in general laudatory of Geneva's political and social arrangements, he managed to detonate two explosive controversies: first by urging the Genevans to give up their Calvinist ban on theatres and theatre-going; and second by expressing the opinion that, while Geneva's Protestants may have believed in God, many of them did not believe in the divinity of Jesus Christ. The clear and scandalous implication was that the Genevans were not really Christians at all, but just Socinian heretics or even Deists. Genevan society found d'Alembert's opinions offensive, and they blamed Voltaire for stirring up subversive trouble; they were all the more incensed in that some of them suspected Voltaire of being an atheist.

In Paris the representatives of the *ancien régime* were even more outraged than the Genevans, since they took d'Alembert's article to be an attack not just on Genevan Protestantism but on Christianity in general; by extension, they concluded that the article was confirmation that the *Encyclopédie,* under the cloak of science and rationalism, was really part of a campaign against true religion. From this moment on there was a deep and unbridgeable rift between the *ancien régime* and the *philosophes* of the *Encyclopédie*.

In November 1756, however, the explosion was still a year away, and Voltaire, comfortably unaware in his lakeside retreat, was still living life to the full. He tried to interest Richelieu in the idea of a battlefield tank but failed. He ordered more supplies from Jean-Robert Tronchin: wine, candles, sugar, coffee, paper and two wheeled stoves, because two of the fireplaces at Les Délices smoked; then Beaujolais, lavender water, Parmesan cheese, 6 pounds of chocolate and two dish warmers; then lots and lots of sugar. He agreed that Jean-Robert should pay him an interest rate of 4 per cent on his savings account balance of £400,000; for running expenses he should keep a current account balance of £20,000.[7]

All this while, he was busily writing and sending d'Alembert contributions for the *Encyclopédie* and still trying to persuade d'Alembert of the virtues of brevity and succinctness: 'I see how difficult it is to be both short and full, to discern nuances, to say nothing too much, but leave nothing out. The most general complaint is the length of the monologues; we need method, truth, definitions, examples; one would wish each article to be treated like those written by you and M. Diderot.'[8]

At the turn of the year, however, Voltaire's happy and industrious little retreat was disturbed by news of two violent events, one in France, the other in England. On 5 January 1757 Robert François Damiens, a lowly servant in the Paris *parlement*, attacked Louis XV in an open courtyard in Versailles with a penknife; and on 27 January the English admiral John Byng was condemned to death by court martial for having been defeated by the French in the first naval engagement of the Seven Years' War.

Damiens's attack on the king took place in the courtyard of the palace of Versailles, just as the king was about to get into his carriage to go to the Trianon. It was winter, around six o'clock in the evening, already dark and very cold. The king was accompanied by the dauphin, and surrounded by a number of senior officers; all were wearing heavy greatcoats. Damiens managed to squeeze through the surrounding officers and guards, and he drew a spring-knife with two blades. He lunged at the king with the small pen-knife blade, inflicting a minor superficial wound. Damiens put the knife back in his pocket and just stood there. The king felt the blow and turned round. He saw this unknown man, who was conspicuous because he was still wearing his hat, and said: 'This is the man who struck me. Arrest him, but do him no harm.'[9]

When Voltaire heard of the attack eight days later, he immediately assumed that it had been inspired by some fanatical Catholic sect. He wrote to a friend: 'Did you think to see such crimes in our enlightened

time? Was it Jansenism which produced this monster? Or Molinism?*
I thought these two sects were just ridiculous, yet like the others they
spill the most sacred blood.'[10]

Voltaire was obviously leaping to conclusions, on the basis of little
or no evidence. His excuse was that Henri III and Henri IV had both
been assassinated by religious fanatics, and Voltaire was always ultra-
conscious of the fact that the assassination of Henri IV had put paid to
his efforts to end the long-drawn-out wars of religion between Catholics
and Protestants in France.

By now Voltaire was referring to Damiens as 'a mad dog', 'a criminal
idiot' and 'a crazy monster'. Three days later Mme Denis wrote, more
sinisterly: 'It is highly desirable that they make this monster talk. He
is certainly a mad fanatic, but if he has accomplices, it is essential to
know who they are.' In other words, she (and perhaps Voltaire as well)
expected and wanted Damiens to be tortured.[11]

Torture was systematically used in the French judicial system to
secure confessions and/or to discover the names of accomplices, and
inevitably Damiens was tortured. He revealed nothing comprehensible
about his motives; he said the strangest things about the king, God and
the *parlement;* in all likelihood he had no rational motives. He revealed
nothing about his accomplices; almost certainly he had none. In fact, he
was probably deranged. As Voltaire said: 'All his replies were those of
a madman, like his actions.' Nevertheless, Damiens was condemned to
die a regicide's death.[12]

Voltaire described the execution, which took place on 28 March
1757, in his *Histoire du parlement de Paris*, published in 1769, though he
did not, of course, witness it himself.

> After the reading out of the sentence, in the presence of five princes
> of the blood, twenty-two dukes and peers, twelve senior judges, seven
> honorary judges, four senior lawyers [*maîtres des requêtes*], and nine-
> teen judges of the Grand Chamber, he was put to the question [i.e.,
> torture] by wedges forced between the knees and two planks tied
> together.
> The prisoner was placed, around five o'clock, on a scaffold eight

---

* Jansenism was a revivalist and ascetic Catholic sect, deriving from the teachings of the
Dutch theologian Cornelius Jansenius (1585–1638). Molinism was a Jesuit sect derived
from the teachings of the Spanish Jesuit Luis Molina (1536–1600). These two sects were in
permanent conflict with each other in France at this time, ostensibly over their differing
teachings on divine grace, in reality as a struggle for influence in the *ancien régime*.

and a half feet square. They tied him with heavy cords held by iron rings which immobilised his arms and his thighs. They started by burning his hand in a brazier filled with burning sulphur. Then they took red-hot pincers and tore at his flesh on his arms, his thighs and his chest. They poured molten lead and pitch and boiling oil on all his wounds. These tortures dragged from him the most frightful screams.

Four vigorous horses, whipped on by four executioners' assistants, pulled with cords on the bleeding and flaming wounds of the patient; these pullings lasted an hour. His limbs stretched but did not part. The executioners finally cut some muscles. His limbs parted one after the other. Damiens, having lost two legs and an arm, was still breathing, and did not expire until his other arm was separated from his bleeding trunk. The limbs and the trunk were thrown on a pyre ten feet from the scaffold.[13]

Under the *ancien régime* in France it was widely assumed, at least until the latter part of the eighteenth century, that the purpose of state punishment was to inflict physical pain on convicted criminals; in the case of extreme crimes such as regicide and parricide, the maximum possible pain; to inflict it with maximum publicity in a public ceremony; and to envelop it with the presumption that the pain was expiation inflicted in the name of God.

What Voltaire thought about these general assumptions we do not know, for until now he never expressed any opinion; he may not even have thought about the subject. And yet, faced with the specifics of the Damiens affair, his reactions were clearly inadequate. He saw clearly that Damiens was in some sense deranged, but he did not discuss whether such a man could be responsible for his acts; he merely pigeon-holed him as a dangerous religious fanatic and a threat to law and order. He expressed no revulsion at the obscene tortures inflicted on Damiens in the name of the protection of the monarchy; his concern, at that moment, was only with the stability of the state.

Voltaire's reaction to the case of the execution of the English admiral John Byng was entirely different, more rational and, above all, more personal, for he had known Byng personally in 1726–28, when he was in exile in England. At that time Byng had been a young navy captain, while his father, Admiral George Byng, whom Voltaire also knew, was First Lord of the Admiralty, with the title Viscount Torrington.[14]

Thirty years on, in 1756, John Byng had reached the rank of admiral and had been sent with a poorly equipped squadron to relieve the

English-held fortress of Port Mahon on the island of Minorca, which was being threatened with a blockade by a French fleet. Voltaire followed events closely, not least because the commander of the French blockading force was his friend Richelieu. 'Take Port Mahon, my hero, I've got money on it. Do you know that a mad Englishman is offering odds of twenty to one that you will be taken prisoner to England in less than four months? I am sending an order to London, to lay out 20 guineas against this extravagant fellow, and I hope to make £400 sterling, with which I shall give a fine fireworks display.' Voltaire won his bet: Byng did not reach Minorca until 19 May and was defeated by the French fleet on 20 May. Minorca fell to Richelieu on 28 June.[15]

On his return to England, Byng was relieved of his command, imprisoned at Greenwich and charged with cowardice. Voltaire asked Richelieu about the circumstances, to see whether he could get Byng exonerated, and Richelieu assured him that Byng was not at fault. Voltaire transcribed his testimony and sent it to Byng in England: 'All the manoeuvres of admiral Byng were admirable, according to comments of all our sailors. There has never been a more glaring injustice than that which is threatening Admiral Byng.' In the event, Byng was acquitted of cowardice or disaffection but found guilty of neglect of duty and condemned to death. On 14 March he was shot by a firing squad in Portsmouth harbour on the deck of HMS *Monarque*. Before he died, he wrote Voltaire a letter of thanks, in which he described Richelieu as 'so generous a soldier'.[16]

Historically, the fall of Minorca was the exception that proved the rule: from now on the English did much better and the French much worse, and by the end of the Seven Years' War England had secured a major consolidation and expansion of its empire, in India and North America, mainly at the expense of France. Moreover, England's gain was Voltaire's loss, for Voltaire had been earning vast profits from his investments in French overseas trade via the brothers Gilly at Cadiz, notably in the Compagnie des Indes. In 1756 these investments earned him over £34,893; but in 1757 he complained ceaselessly about the losses of French ships to the English, and his income from Cadiz fell to £14,752. In 1758 it got worse: no receipts until April, and then only for £600.[17]

The executions of Byng and Damiens were obviously two very different events, but together they constituted a moment that was to mark the beginning of a fundamental change in Voltaire's outlook on life and death. In the case of John Byng, Voltaire had been moved by the claims of friendship and of justice, and he immortalised his death for ever in one of the most memorable pages of *Candide*, which he wrote the following year, and published in 1759.

As they talked, they docked in Portsmouth; a multitude of people covered the shore, and looked attentively at a fairly large man who was on his knees, his eyes blindfolded, on the deck of one of the vessels of the fleet; four soldiers, posted opposite this man, each fired three balls into his skull as peacefully as possible, and all the audience went home extremely satisfied. 'What is all this?', said Candide, 'and what devil is at work?' He asked who was the large man, who had just been killed with such ceremony. 'It is an admiral', they replied. 'But why kill this admiral?' 'It is' they told him, 'because he has not had enough people killed; he gave battle to a French admiral, and people thought he had not got close enough to him.' 'But,' said Candide, 'the French admiral was just as far from the English admiral, as he was from him.' 'That is incontestable', they replied; 'but in this country it is good to kill an admiral from time to time to encourage the others (*pour encourager les autres*).'[18]

In the case of Damiens we may be disappointed by Voltaire's reactions; nevertheless, Damiens's execution marked him profoundly and was to recur repeatedly in his later writings. By the time he wrote his account, he had already for several years been personally engaged in a number of individual campaigns against miscarriages of justice and was deeply immersed in a general rethinking of his attitudes on crime, punishment and human rights. So if the dominant theme in the later years of his life became his concern for the defence of human rights, that process started some time after January 1757. And if the civilised world has moved on from the barbaric notions of physical punishment so characteristic of that period, it is to a significant extent because Voltaire changed his mind, and ours.

But that was later. In the early months of 1757 Voltaire was busier than ever, and the visitors kept coming to see him in his winter home at Montriond, outside Lausanne:

Zaïre has been better performed here, all things considered, than in Paris. It drew tears from all those Swiss eyes. Mme Denis may not have such beautiful eyes as Gaussin [an actress at the Comédie Française], but she acts better. People come from 30 leagues around to hear us. We eat hazel grouse, and capercaillies, and trout which weigh

20 pounds, and when the trees have resumed their green livery, we shall return to Les Délices. Don't you feel sorry for us?[19]

In February 1757 the Empress Elisabeth Petrovna of Russia invited Voltaire to write a history of the reign of Peter the Great, and he quickly agreed; but he proposed to rewrite the terms of the commission, for he did not want to write much about wars, or about Peter's private life. Above all, he did not want to go too deeply into why Peter's son, the Tsarevitch Alexis, was murdered in 1718, and by whom, and he would therefore rather make no reference to it.[20]

> You know, Sir, that my principal object is to recount everything that Peter I did which was beneficial for his country, and to paint those happy beginnings which are being perfected every day in the reign of his august daughter. It seems to me important not to call this work the *History* or *Life of Peter I*. Such a title would necessarily commit the historian to leave nothing out. He is then forced to tell odious truths, or if he does not, he dishonours himself without doing honour to his employers.[21]

Voltaire's instinct to bow and scrape to despots, even allegedly enlightened despots, remained with him for ever. Just as he did not want to tell 'odious truths' about Peter, so later, in the reign of Catherine the Great, he would not want to go too deeply into why her husband, Peter III, was murdered in 1762, and by whom; nor into why the imprisoned ex-Emperor Ivan VI was murdered in 1764, and by whom.

In the spring of 1757 Voltaire's relations with the Geneva authorities started to go downhill. In a letter to Thieriot, Voltaire had referred to the 'wicked soul' (*l'âme atroce*) of Jean Calvin: wicked, because in 1553 he had caused a dissenting preacher, Michel Servet, to be burned at the stake. Unfortunately this phrase found its way into the public prints, as Voltaire's pungent phrases so often did, and the Geneva authorities were furious.[22]

Matters became even more heated in December of that year, after the appearance of volume VII of the *Encyclopédie*; in the article 'Genève', d'Alembert not only accused the Genevan Protestants of being Deists, and therefore heretics, but he also reiterated Voltaire's phrase about Calvin's 'wicked soul', and even attributed it to Voltaire by name. The Geneva clerical authorities demanded that d'Alembert withdraw his article (he refused), and they set about refuting d'Alembert's thesis, by appointing a commission, with Théodore Tronchin as its secretary, to draft a Protestant declaration of faith. Voltaire wrote to d'Alembert to express his rage: 'Papist fanatics, Calvinist fanatics, all are moulded from the same sh…, and soaked in corrupted blood' (*tous sont pétris de la même m…*). But when the commission finally reported, its declaration lacked any clear-cut assertion that the Protestants believed in the divinity of Jesus; as Voltaire dryly commented, even the heretic Michel Servet could have signed it.[23]

In France the court at Versailles now turned irrevocably against the *Encyclopédie* and rescinded the previous official authorisation for its publication. This caused a deep and permanent rift between its two editors. D'Alembert resigned from the editorship of the *Encyclopédie*, on the grounds that it was impossible to continue work under the harassment of official persecution, but Diderot soldiered on alone and eventually brought the great project to completion. Voltaire instinctively sided with d'Alembert against the censorious state, and at first demanded that all the *philosophes* associated with the *Encyclopédie* should either go on strike together, to assert their solidarity, or else move their operations to Lausanne, where he would finance them. But Diderot was determined both to continue and to stay in Paris, and d'Alembert was determined to stop.

Voltaire himself veered erratically from one side to another: at first he announced that he was cutting all connection with the *Encyclopédie* and demanded that his articles and letters be returned to him, then he resumed contact; but by the summer of 1758 he had ceased to be a contributor. Yet he never ceased to lament that the *philosophes* were weakened by their divisions.

It was now that he started writing his story *Candide*. He may have started thinking about it at the end of 1757, at the height of the crisis over 'Genève'. He was certainly writing it in the summer of 1758, during a visit to the Elector-Palatine at Schwetzingen, a visit for which, such are the curious contradictions of despotism, the king of France provided him with a passport. Voltaire's main reason for visiting the Elector-Palatine was to lend him £130,000, at a suitably rewarding rate of interest; Voltaire had already lent the Elector-Palatine £100,000 in 1753, so he clearly believed that this was a valuable financial relationship. During the three weeks he spent in Schwetzingen, it seems that he regularly read aloud, to the Elector-Palatine, the latest extracts from his work in progress. Voltaire also sent *Candide*, chapter by chapter, to the duc de La Vallière, the king's Grand Falconer and one of Voltaire's most loyal admirers, as well as a familiar of Louis XV and Mme de Pompadour.

The work was published under a pseudonym on 15 January 1759, in three places simultaneously, for Voltaire knew it would scandalise: in Geneva (by the brothers Cramer), in Paris (supervised by La Vallière in person), and in Amsterdam. Ostensibly, the tale was represented as having been written by a certain Mr Le Docteur Ralph and translated from the German, but Voltaire's authorship was soon exposed, for it could only be by him; and yet the world was astonished that this seasoned, familiar, rather old-fashioned 65-year-old writer could have produced this youthful new voice. The authorities immediately tried to suppress the book by seizing printed copies: the French in Paris on 25 February 1759 and the Genevan authorities on 26 February. Voltaire continued to deny that he had anything to do with the book. He wrote to Jean-Robert in early March: 'As I find that this work is very contrary to the decisions of the Sorbonne, I maintain that I have no part in it. I am still building an even more beautiful château than that of M. the Baron of Thunder-ten-tronckh. It is ruining me, but I hope that the Bulgars won't come.'[24]*

The repressive efforts of the authorities were overwhelmed by the popular success of the work, which was instantaneous and Europe-wide. On 10 March 1759 Voltaire told Cramer that 6,000 copies had been sold in Paris,[25] which implies that there must have been two or three immediate reprints, since print runs in those days were rarely more than two or three thousand. In the whole of 1759, there were over twenty editions and re-editions of the work: six or seven in Paris, two in Lyon, one in Avignon, one in Liège, one in London (in French), plus three translations into English and one into Italian. All told, *Candide* sold at least 20,000 copies in 1759 alone, and perhaps as many as 30,000. This, in eighteenth-century terms, made it a massive best-seller.

It is easy to see why *Candide* was so popular with ordinary readers at the time of publication and so unpopular with the authorities. It is a highly entertaining little tale, at once so pessimistic and so gay, which through the medium of a knowingly unrealistic and picaresque international travel adventure makes sceptical fun of the pretensions of all the institutions of church and state, starting with the theologians, metaphysicians, Jesuits and inquisitors. Its most central theme is the contrast between the blind 'Optimism' of Dr Pangloss (who repeatedly claims, like Leibniz, that this is the best of all possible worlds), and the many horrors, natural and man-made, of real life.

---

* In *Candide* the Château of Thunder-ten-tronckh was over-run by the invading Bulgars. Voltaire's 'Bulgars', were in fact code for the Prussians, in an allusion to Frederick's homosexuality: 'Bulgars' = bougres = buggers.

Voltaire wrote some fifty other short tales and fictions, but by common consent it is *Candide* that is his masterpiece. Voltaire designed it to be not just iconoclastic but short, light, rapid and humorous, and therefore readable and entertaining. It marks a striking moment of departure from his courtly and literary voice, his plays, his poems and his histories, aimed at the restricted audience of the educated establishment. His invention of a popular voice, aimed at public opinion in a broader sense, undoubtedly added to his popular credibility when he came to engage in his later human rights cases.

There are several famous tags from *Candide*, starting with *'pour encourager les autres',* quoted earlier in relation to Admiral Byng, but perhaps the most famous is the sign-off line at the end of the book: 'That was well said', replied Candide, 'but we must cultivate our garden'.[26] The phrase is usually understood as a metaphor, as if to say that we should concentrate our attention and our efforts on simple, local things where we have some chance of doing good. But Voltaire also meant it literally. He had discovered for himself the pleasures and the virtues of gardening and planting and sowing and building in the home he created at Les Délices, and he would re-enact them, with greater enthusiasm and on a much larger scale, in the new home that he was to create at Ferney.

1. Voltaire in 1732, when he was thirty-eight. He had recently returned from exile in England, but he had not yet met Émilie du Châtelet, nor written the *Lettres Philosophiques*.

2. A view of central Paris in 1739, showing the Tuileries on the right bank of the Seine, and the quai des Théatins (since renamed quai Voltaire), on the left. Voltaire died in the Hôtel Villette, on the eastern corner of the rue de Beaune and the quai des Théatins.

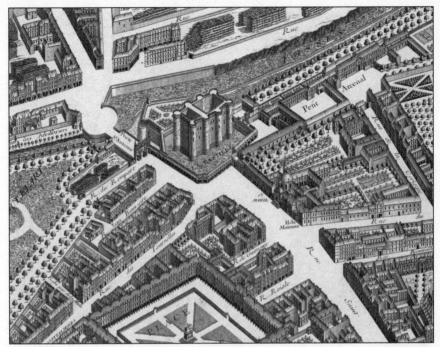

3a. The Bastille prison in eastern Paris. Voltaire was twice imprisoned there; for eleven months in 1717–18, for writing libellous verses about the Regent; and again, very briefly, in 1726, before his exile to England.

3b. The château de Cirey in Champagne, mid-way between Paris and Lorraine, where Voltaire lived in quasi-exile with his mistress, Émilie du Châtelet, from 1734 to 1749.

4. Émilie du Châtelet, Voltaire's mistress, was an aristocrat and an intellectual. She was a keen student of mathematics and physics, and her translation of Newton's *Principia* remained the standard version in France until the twentieth century.

5a. The abbé Pierre Desfontaines was a literary journalist, who became one of the bitterest of Voltaire's many rivals and enemies. He was arrested for sodomy in 1725, and Voltaire helped rescue him from prison; in return, Desfontaines feuded relentlessly against Voltaire until his death in 1745.

5b. Frederick the Great of Prussia. He started cultivating Voltaire, as Europe's most celebrated intellectual, in 1736. In 1750 he lured Voltaire to take up a position as a resident courtier at Potsdam, where he stayed until they quarrelled memorably in 1753.

6a. A view of Geneva, as seen from Voltaire's home at Les Délices, just outside the city.

6b. Les Délices was Voltaire's main home for the first ten years of his exile, from 1755 to 1765. He devoted enormous energy to improving the house and, especially, the garden. '*Il faut cultiver notre jardin.*'

7a. The Calas family in prison. In 1765, Mme Calas, seated with her two daughters, is told by her son Pierre of the rehabilitation of her late husband, executed three years earlier. Standing behind Pierre is his friend Gaubert Lavaysse. Standing at the back is Jeanne Viguière, the servant of the Calas family.

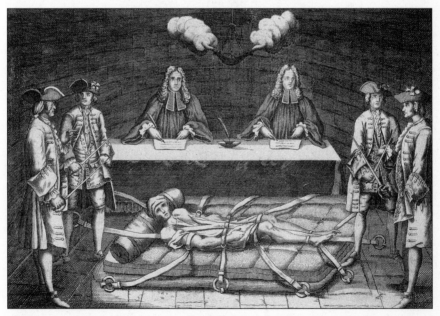

7b. In 1757 Robert Damiens attacked king Louis XV with a pen-knife. His torture and public execution, by methods of barbarous cruelty, marked a key moment in Voltaire's attitude to penal reform.

Ja.ˢ Taylor sculp.

8. Voltaire in winter. Voltaire was susceptible to the
cold, and often wore a bonnet on top of his wig; in
winter he often suffered from partial snow blindness.

9a. The château de Ferney. After years of friction with the Geneva authorities, Voltaire decided to move away from Geneva, and bought the estate and château of Ferney, just across the border inside France.

9b. Voltaire's room at Ferney, depicted in the 1780s, after his death. The pictures on the walls were of his friends and acquaintances.

10. Jean Le Rond d'Alembert, one of Voltaire's closest allies among the younger *philosophes* in his campaigns against *L'Infâme*. He was a distinguished mathematician and scientist; with Diderot, he was one of the founding editors of the *Encyclopédie*.

11a. Charles Augustin de Ferriol, comte d'Argental, seen here in a caricature portrait, was one of Voltaire's closest friends, and a fellow fanatic about the theatre.

11b. Jean Antoine Nicolas de Caritat, marquis de Condorcet, was a mathematician, a young friend and pupil of d'Alembert, and an admirer of Voltaire. After Voltaire's death, he became the chief editor of the first complete posthumous edition of Voltaire's works, as well as the author of the first biography of Voltaire.

12. In 1770, Jean Baptiste Pigalle was commissioned to make a statue of Voltaire, to be financed by public subscription. Pigalle decided to sculpt Voltaire naked; the result was so controversial, that for nearly 200 years the statue remained hidden out of sight. It was not exhibited, in the Louvre, until 1962.

13a. Voltaire and Mme Denis. Mme Denis (Marie Louise Mignot) was the elder daughter of Voltaire's sister Marguerite-Catherine, and therefore Voltaire's niece. She became his mistress in 1745, and his constant companion from 1754 onwards. Their relationship remained a secret known only to d'Argental.

13b. Father Antoine Adam was a Jesuit priest whom Voltaire befriended at Ferney. In 1759, he took Adam into his household, and for the next seventeen years he served as Voltaire's personal almoner, saying mass, making conversation, and playing chess.

14. On his return to Paris in 1778, in his last weeks of life, when he was eighty-four, Voltaire sat once for the sculptor Jean Antoine Houdon, who made several busts and statues of him. Several, like this one, are in the Louvre; there is also a seated Voltaire in the upstairs bar of the Comédie Française.

15. One of the high points of Voltaire's return to Paris in 1778, was the performance at the Comédie Française of his latest tragedy, *Irène*. After the performance on 30 March, the company crowned a bust of Voltaire, and saluted him in his box (on the left).

16. Many of the most vivid and informal images of Voltaire were those made by Jean Huber, a Geneva artist and frequent visitor to Ferney, who became famous for his portraits of Voltaire.

FERNEY

1758–1761

AFTER THE CRISIS over the *Encyclopédie* and the article 'Genève', Voltaire concluded that he could no longer live entirely at ease in Geneva. He did not want to give up Les Délices, but he needed to find somewhere else, since the house really belonged to Jean-Robert Tronchin, and Voltaire's position depended crucially on his being on good terms with the Tronchin clan and the rest of the Geneva oligarchy.

At first he explored the idea of moving to Lorraine, which was closer to Paris. Stanislas Leszczyński would undoubtedly have liked to have him as an ornament of his court in Lunéville; but Lorraine was virtually dependent on the French crown, and Louis XV made it clear that he was opposed to the idea, so it was dropped.

It was only now, five years after his return from Prussia, that Voltaire finally accepted that his exile from Paris was likely to be permanent; and it was only now, therefore, that he started to look for somewhere permanent that would really belong to him. In the autumn of 1758 he found the new home he was looking for. Or rather, he found two new homes: the château de Ferney and the château de Tournay, two estates virtually adjoining one another, just outside the territory of Geneva, and across the frontier into France. He decided to take them both, but without giving up Les Délices.

He found Ferney in October, and buying it was quick and trouble-free. It was for sale freehold, and Voltaire rapidly reached agreement on a price of £130,000. The total cost would eventually be much greater, partly because he went on to buy other parcels and enclaves of land to round out the estate, but mainly because the château was old, ill maintained and inconvenient, and he decided substantially to rebuild it. All told, he reckoned, in a letter to Jean-Robert in December, that the overall cost would be £333,000. Final signature on the contract was delayed until early February 1759, but well before then Voltaire had moved in and started improving the estate.[1]

Buying the château de Tournay, which Voltaire had found the previous September 1758, turned out to be a tiresome haggle with its formalistic and disputatious owner. Charles de Brosses was a senior judge at the *parlement* of Dijon and a moderately distinguished writer; but as Voltaire soon discovered, he was also by nature incurably pernickety and difficult, and his insistence on driving a hard bargain verged on the dishonest. The root of the problem was that de Brosses was only offering a life-tenancy in Tournay, and while he imposed various obligations and restrictions on Voltaire's use of the estate, he also made promises, explicit or implied, which he did not fulfil. Some people have suggested that de Brosses's combative character had something to do with the fact that he was a very short man: when defending his doctoral thesis, he had had to stand on a stool to be able to look over the edge of the pulpit.[2]

During the weeks of bargaining de Brosses drove up the price from £30,000 to £35,000 and imposed the extra condition that Voltaire should spend £12,000 in repairs. The final haggle was over the *chaîne du marché*, the symbolic present which the purchaser of a property was expected to give to the wife of the seller. Voltaire offered to give Mme de Brosses a sowing plough (*charrue à semoir*), an ultra-modern combine agricultural tool, which in one operation turned the earth, sowed the seeds, covered the furrow and harrowed it; it was Voltaire's latest passion in his enthusiasm for cultivating his new fields and gardens. No doubt his offer was tongue-in-cheek, or so de Brosses thought, for he turned it down and settled for £500 in cash; but his hard bargaining left a nasty taste. As Voltaire wrote to de Brosses in January: 'I read and I re-read your contract, and the more I re-read it, the more I see that you have dictated your law as a conqueror. But that is all right. I like to improve the places where I live, and what I am doing will benefit you and please me.'[3]

Voltaire's resigned acceptance of the onerous contract soon turned to fury. De Brosses had told him that Tournay was exempt from various heavy taxes, and Voltaire claimed that de Brosses had given him such a promise in writing.[4] But once the contract was signed, de Brosses told Voltaire that the tax exemption was personal to him and therefore could not be passed over. For the next six months Voltaire raged at de Brosses over what he saw as his double-dealing.[5] In May 1759 he wrote to de Brosses: 'I have embellished Tournay, I have improved the land; but I shall burn everything, if the least of my rights were stolen from me. I am not reasonable when I am vexed. It was only on this condition, that I should enjoy all the tax exemptions, that I settled with you. You know it, you guaranteed it in writing'.[6] But after a while he accepted that de Brosses was impervious and immovable. So he turned to Versailles and tirelessly lobbied his court contacts, until eventually his friend the little duc de Choiseul (who was effectively Prime Minister) got him the tax exemptions he was demanding – but only for Ferney, not for Tournay.[7]

Unfortunately this was only the first of several quarrels with de Brosses over the terms of Voltaire's tenancy. One of the bitterest was over five loads of firewood. Voltaire claimed that de Brosses had agreed that he could take a dozen loads of firewood from the estate, free of charge. Then it emerged that de Brosses had a previous standing arrangement with Charles Baudy, a local café owner, by which Baudy sold firewood on behalf of de Brosses. Baudy demanded that Voltaire pay him for fourteen loads of wood. The total sum at stake was trivial, somewhere between £50 and £150, but Voltaire resisted the claim, and de Brosses persisted in pressing it, and the quarrel dragged on venomously for another two and a half years. Voltaire's critics maintain that this episode shows Voltaire in a poor light, cheap and mean-minded; but de Brosses behaved much worse, with ill will and bad faith, and that cannot be said of Voltaire.

De Brosses must have thought that he had driven a wonderful bargain when he sold Voltaire the Tournay life-tenancy. But many years later, when de Brosses wanted to get himself elected to the Académie Française, Voltaire had his revenge. He told the other members that, if de Brosses were elected, he himself would resign and would bring a court case against de Brosses, to expose and punish him for his disgraceful behaviour over the Tourney lease. De Brosses was rejected.[8]

The acquisition of Ferney and Tournay brought with it a profound transformation of Voltaire's feelings and attitudes about the world and his place in it, as a result of his new responsibilities as a landed proprietor. Until this moment Voltaire had shown no interest in the well-being of the lower orders; his only concerns had been his own comfort and convenience, the cultivation of the powerful and the pursuit of his very hard-working and very successful literary career. Now, all at once, he started to talk and think very differently, as we can see from a letter written on 18 November, just as he was about to take possession of his new estates.

> This area was very depopulated, very miserable, without industry, without resources. My land is excellent, and yet I have found 100 *arpents* [roughly 50 hectares] belonging to my inhabitants which remain uncultivated. The [previous] tenant farmer had not sown half of his fields. It is seven years since the curé celebrated any marriages, and no children have been born, since we only have Jesuits in the neighbourhood and no Franciscans. The most dreadful calamity is the rapacity of the tax farmers and the brutality of their employees. Poor people who have scarcely even any black bread to eat are arrested every day, stripped and imprisoned, for having put on this bread a bit of salt which they have bought near their cottages. Half the inhabitants die of poverty, and the other half rot in prison cells. One's heart is torn when one witnesses so much misery. I only bought the Ferney estate in order to do a bit of good.[9]*

These are sentiments that Voltaire had never expressed before, but he soon acted on them. Within weeks he was starting what became a long-running campaign on behalf of the poor peasants, to protect them against a violent and rapacious local curé who was using the law courts to extort massive arrears of tithes, and who employed thugs to beat up his parishioners.[10]

In September the following year (1759) Voltaire wrote to his old friend Thieriot: 'I must visit my smallholdings, I must look after my peasants and my cattle when they are ill, I must find husbands for the girls, and I must improve fields abandoned since the Flood. I see all round me the most frightful misery, in the midst of a smiling countryside. I put on a show of trying to remedy a bit of the evil that had been done over the centuries. When one is in a position to do a bit of good to a half-league of country, that is rather honourable.' And to de Brosses he wrote in November: 'Most of my income goes to relieve many unhappy people, both at Tournay and at Ferney. The misery was horrible in all this region, and the fields were not sown. Now they are, thank God.' And at the end of that year he embarked on a campaign to buy off the tax farmers' stranglehold on salt and tobacco for the whole of the

---

* The reference to Franciscans is a typical Voltaire joke: he implies that the Franciscans were liable to father children on local girls, but not the Jesuits. The reference to 'a bit of salt' alludes to the salt trade, which was strictly controlled and heavily taxed.

province, centred on the local town of Gex. In fact, this was to be the start of a series of campaigns whose ultimate aim was to buy off the tax farmers entirely from the province.[11]

Voltaire's sudden and unexpected movement of compassion for the peasants of Ferney and Tournay in November 1758 was not just a passing whim or a literary indulgence; it was his acceptance of a whole new personal moral dimension that he had not acknowledged before. In 1755 Voltaire had been appalled by the Lisbon earthquake and by its implications for the problem of evil; but his dismay at that distant event was more philosophical than concrete or deeply felt. It was only now, after looking closely at his new estates of Ferney and Tournay, that he began to feel that the problem of evil was not some large and dramatic catastrophe in a faraway country but was here and now, in the everyday sufferings of the poor and downtrodden. Moreover, he realised that he now had a personal responsibility for trying to alleviate it on his own estates, as well as the means to do so. This was a key moment in Voltaire's evolution; his new sense of responsibility remained with him for the rest of his life and informed his attitude both towards his own estates and towards events in the wider world.

Voltaire's first step was to make long overdue improvements to his estates. The château de Tournay, Voltaire told d'Argental, 'is a hovel made for the owls, a garden with nothing but snails and moles, vines without grapes, fields without wheat, and cow-sheds without cows'. But, he reassured de Brosses: 'Don't worry about your château or your forest; I am building more than I am destroying; I am planting more than I am pulling up; I am becoming a patriarch.' And a couple of weeks later he told him: 'I already have twenty workers who are repairing the broken-down vines; we shall repair your château right away; your forest was in a frightful state, I shall put it right, everything is settled. Let me have 4,000 vine stocks, or rather 5,000.' And this was just in December 1758, almost before the ink was quite dry on the contract. In January he wrote again to de Brosses: 'Send me the vine stocks. They will be planted with the same dispatch as your staircase had been shifted, as the fields have been repaired, the hedges restored, the ditches cleaned and widened, and the field beyond the forest ploughed for the first time in its life. I shall populate the country of Gex with partridges; I should like to populate it with people.'[12]

Voltaire's enthusiasm for cultivating his garden was whole-hearted and practical: he personally got engaged and got his hands dirty. He visited the cowsheds and examined the beasts: 'I love my bulls', he said,

'I stroke them, and they make eyes at me.' To walk about the farm he had some clogs made, and he set aside a particular field for himself, which he personally supervised.[13]

By April 1759 he regularly had eighty or a hundred people working for him, and by May he was bringing in extra families from Switzerland, since he did not have enough farm hands to cultivate the fields; in July he said that he had 'eighty persons and eighteen horses to feed'. In April he announced that he was 'a great partisan' of the new sowing plough which he had just acquired, and which had five blades and five seed drills, and he was looking into a new and more convenient grape press. Not content with all this hectic activity, in which he was very much his own master of works, Voltaire continued to add to his landholdings. In May he told Jean-Robert Tronchin that he was buying two parcels of land between Tournay and Ferney, but he added in mock humility: 'I must end this letter, for fear of having to tell you about more land that I am buying.' In August, he again acquired several small pieces of land.[14]

In May 1759 Voltaire started thinking about horse-breeding. He wrote to Jean-Robert:

As for the mares which I had the honour to ask you for, I should explain my policy. I use all my horses (except for two that are privileged) for pulling either a carriage, or a cart, or a plough. I choose my mares the way one should choose a wife, not too beautiful nor too ugly, but capable of bearing children; and I want my mares to bear children, since my serving women do not; so if you find two creatures which would suit my seraglio, black and young like Solomon's mistress, you would do me great pleasure if you would send them at your convenience, especially if they are not too dear.[15]

Two weeks later he told Jean-Robert that he had just come across a good mare and had bought her. 'You won't guess who she's for: she's for me. I want to ride. I now have a little horse which is scarcely bigger than a donkey, and which will help the circulation of the blood.'[16] Voltaire was obviously quite excited by his new horse, for he wrote again a few days later: 'Do you want to know, my dear correspondent, the size of my pony?* Imagine a lovely she-donkey, like Balaam's ass, and from that you can measure the height of the prophet's arse.'[17] Voltaire was only 5

---

* The word Voltaire uses for his pony was *haquenée*, a Frenchified transliteration of the English word 'hackney', which itself comes from the London borough of Hackney, long celebrated for its horses. *Haquenée* has been an officially recognised French word since 1360.

foot 6 inches tall, and skeletal into the bargain, so he did not need a big horse to carry him.*

The Château of Ferney needed substantial rebuilding, and Voltaire threw himself into it with gusto. In July 1759 he wrote to d'Argental: 'You will come and see the little château that I am building. You will be enchanted with it, it's of the Doric order, it will last for a thousand years. I shall put on the frieze *Voltaire fecit*. Posterity will take me for a famous architect.'[18] Three weeks later Voltaire said the façade was Ionic,[19] while others described it as Palladian. Voltaire had little taste in visual aesthetics: for the interior decoration of his home he ordered pictures by the square yard.

By the autumn of 1759 the heavy building work was largely complete at both Ferney and Tournay. In October Voltaire wrote to Jean-Robert to ask for some wine:

Have you no nectar from Beaujolais, really tasty, full of sap? Three barrels would do nicely. I have already had some fruit from the trees I planted at Les Délices less than three years ago. Everything is going well. We are making some new bedrooms in the outhouses. Tourney has become an agreeable château, Ferney is built, and people even say that it is really handsome. But nothing will compare with the garden at Les Délices when the terrace was finished. Won't you come and see our little kingdom next year? You will see the happiest of men.[20]

Naturally, all this was costing a lot of money. In May, in a letter to Jean-Robert, he reckoned up his finances: 'The little patriarch from Gex province can see, my dear correspondent, that he now has more bulls, cows and sheep, than you have bags of his money.' He worked out his outgoings at £286,150 and went on: 'In these circumstances, I do not see how I could ask you for another 32,000 livres to round out my estates. It seems to me that I should have nothing left, or almost nothing.'[21] A week later he promised Jean-Robert that he would go on an economy drive. 'Your advice will be followed. No more orders for 16 or 17 thousand livres; I shall prune everything, even my orders for uniform braid. Everything which was to have been crimson will now be green instead, and the decorations will be smaller, and especially

---

* Voltaire himself says he was 5 foot 2 inches tall. But the foot and the inch used by the French in the eighteenth century were slightly larger than the English equivalents: a French foot (*pied de roi*) was 32.4 cm, rather than the 30.5 cm of an English foot, and an inch 2.7 cm rather than 2.54 cm. So in today's terms Voltaire was just over 5 foot 6 inches tall.

cheaper.'[22] In August he moaned to Jean-Robert that he was much less wealthy than before:

My dear correspondent, we are no longer as great a seigneur as we used to be. We used to reckon by 500,000 livres; but now we are reduced to reckoning by 200,000, and thanks to the Ionic façade of my château, to the water basins, to the fountains, to the land which costs a lot and brings in little, and to the sixty-plus people I have to feed every day, you may expect that soon we shall be reduced to reckoning in 50,000 écus.[23]

It is not clear whether Voltaire was really worried about his finances, or whether he was just making a half-lamenting, half-exulting joke about the sheer scale of his spending. Over the years he went through quite frequent cycles of money worries, but on this occasion his money anxieties, whether real or not, soon evaporated, for in September he wrote to Jean-Robert: 'Despite the cost-cutting rules, I admit that if I found two pretty silver sauce boats ready-made, I should take them. But do not think you have to send any gold, for we have some. In fact, we are overflowing with it.'[24] A few days later Voltaire wrote again to Jean-Robert: 'Having visited my cashbox and my wallet, I have the boldness to send you £14,062 10s, instead of the weakness to ask you for £12,000. You see that I am adding to the loot instead of taking from it.'[25] In fact, Voltaire's deposit account with Jean-Robert amounted to £500,000.[26]

You might think that Voltaire would be fully occupied by his hectic programme of improving his new estates: not a bit of it. In June 1759 he was suddenly inspired to write a new tragedy, *Tancrède*, and he boasted to d'Argental that, as with his earlier tragedy *Zaïre*, he had written it in three weeks flat: 'We have witnesses', he declared proudly.[27] What inspired him, at least in part, was the news from Paris that there had been a revolutionary change at the Comédie Française. For many years the management of the theatre had sold tickets for seats actually placed on the stage. These seats severely restricted the space for the actors and for stage action, but they brought in extra revenue and the theatre could not afford to get rid of them. In April of that year, however, the comte de Lauraguais persuaded the Comédie Française to remove the seats, in exchange for a gift of £30,000 in compensation. Voltaire wrote to d'Argental: 'I am overcome with feelings of the noblest zeal when I learn that the white-powdered wigs and the red heels will no longer mingle with Augustus and Cleopatra. For in that case the Paris theatre will change its appearance. Tragedies will no longer be conversations in five acts, at the end of which one learns that there had been a bit of blood spilled. People will want pomp, spectacle, noise.'[28]

Voltaire's new play, *Tancrède,* was a patriotic and tearful melodrama of medieval chivalry, and naturally Voltaire wanted to see it performed. Even before the structural work at Tournay was complete, he planned a private theatre inside the château. It would be a miniature affair, in a gallery, and it would only be able to hold 100 spectators, but Voltaire was quite excited about it. 'My little Punch-and-Judy theatre will not cost much,' he told Jean-Robert; 'I shall make the theatre all by myself. It's not my fault if the generous Président de Brosses does not have a gallery which is longer and wider. I am sorry that the height from floor to ceiling in my theatre is only eight foot, but all we have to do is act well, and then one forgets where one is. These are performances between friends. It is as if one were reading beside the fire.'[29]

By October 1759 his 'green and gold' theatre was already in use.[30] After a performance of *Tancrède*, Voltaire wrote to d'Argental:

My Punch-and-Judy theatre is very small, I admit, but yesterday, my divine angel, nine of us were quite comfortable in a semi-circle on stage. Moreover, we had lances and bucklers, and we had shiny green batons for pilasters. A troupe of violin scrapers and Saxon horn blowers made up the orchestra. How handsomely we were dressed! Madame Denis gave a superior performance. All in all, I only wish that the play could be played as well in Paris as in my hovel at Tournay.[31]

In November he boasted that he had put on three performances of *Tancrède* and one of *Mérope*, with spectators from Geneva, Switzerland and the country round about.[32]

Tancrède was performed in Paris at the Comédie Française the following year, on 3 September 1760, and it was a great popular success; but it was Voltaire's last really successful play, for his neo-classical verse formulae belonged to an earlier age and were increasingly out of tune with changing French tastes.

While the building work was going on at Ferney and Tournay, Voltaire moved between his three homes, but he still lived mainly at Les Délices. 'God has given me, barely a quarter of a league from Les Délices, a château where I have transformed the great hall into a theatre. We can get there on foot. We have supper there; and the next day we go to Ferney, which is a fine estate.'[33]

In April 1759 he wrote to Gabriel Cramer, his publisher, to urge him to be especially diligent over some proofs, 'for, as the man said (*comme disait l'autre*), I spew the luke-warm out of my mouth* ... Dictated in the middle of my ruins, on a step-ladder in the attic of our palace for bats, in the midst of the masons who prevent me from sleeping, and who are ruining me.'[34]

Voltaire's theatre at Tournay soon became a popular draw.[35] In September 1760 he wrote: 'Tomorrow we are performing *Alzire* at Tournay, and then *Tancrède* and then *Mahomet*; we have spectators who come over 100 leagues to see us, including the duc de Villars.'[36] The duke was an excellent actor, according to Voltaire, though he only performed in private. 'M. le duc de Villars is getting dressed to play Genghis Khan behind closed doors; La Denis is primping herself; these are two great actors, I might say. My bonnet is being adjusted.'[37] A week later: 'We have to put on a play twice a week. In our little hole we have had forty-nine persons to supper, and all of them talked at once. It rather interrupts the continuity of my studies.'[38] What really interrupted Voltaire's studies was that his library was in a part of the house now occupied by the visiting duc de Villars.[39]

In the spring of 1760 the internal decoration and furnishing of Ferney were complete, and he told d'Alembert that he had decided to make it his main home. 'Write to me by the post, and address it boldly: "To Voltaire, gentleman in ordinary of the King, at the château of Ferney, via Geneva"; for it is at Ferney that I shall live in a few weeks. We have Tournay for putting on plays, and Les Délices will be the third string to our bow. Philosophers should always have two or three underground holes, against the dogs which run after them.'[40] Voltaire and Mme Denis moved definitively to Ferney in December that year (1760).

Despite the success of the little theatre at Tournay, within twelve months Voltaire decided to build a bigger one, this time at the château de Ferney. As he wrote to his younger niece, Mme Fontaine, in the autumn of 1760: 'The Tournay theatre will in future be at Ferney. I shall build an auditorium despite the hardness of the times [i.e., the Seven Years' War]. But if I damn myself by building theatres, I am earning salvation by building a church; I must hear Mass there with you, after which we shall perform some new plays.'[41] By October of the following year, 1761,

---

* Whenever Voltaire used the expression 'comme disait l'autre', it is almost always an oblique introduction to a quotation from the Bible, as here. Voltaire is quoting from Revelation, 3:16: 'So then, because thou art luke-warm and neither cold nor hot, I will spew thee out of my mouth.'

the new church and the new theatre at Ferney had both been built.[42] The theatre was constructed in a large barn close to the château, with seating for 300 spectators; the church bore the inscription: *Deo erexit Voltaire* ('Voltaire built it for God'), in which Voltaire's name was carved on a much larger scale than the word for God.[43] Voltaire kept Les Délices for several more years, but from now on he lived mainly at Ferney, and would do so for the next eighteen years.

His happiness continued. In September 1759 he wrote to a friend: 'Four years ago I was getting ready for death, but now I find I am stronger than I have ever been, building, planting, versifying and writing the history of the Russian empire.'[44] In October 1759 he wrote to Mme du Deffand, the Parisian literary hostess: 'To have pleasure, you need a bit of passion, a great and interesting purpose, a determined desire to learn, which occupies the soul continuously. It is difficult to find, and does not come without effort.'[45]

He pursued the same theme the following April, 1760, in another letter to Mme du Deffand:

I have never been less dead than I am at present. I haven't a free moment. The bulls, the cows, the sheep, the pastures, the buildings, the gardens, all take up my mornings; the afternoons are for study; and after supper, we rehearse the plays which we perform in my little gallery theatre. This way of life makes me want to live. When you get down to it, I am a decent fellow, and my priests, my vassals and my neighbours all approve of me.[46]

That autumn he wrote to Mme Fontaine:

I am quite amazed to find that I have been happy here for the past five years. I have made a little sovereign state for myself, pushing out my frontiers to left and right. I have done everything I wanted. It is good that there should be people like me in this world. But to play this role, one must be old, rich, free, bold, and in good standing at court, but without ever going there.[47]

Soon after his arrival at Ferney, Voltaire met four Jesuit fathers in their little local community of Ornex, and in April he asked Jean-Robert Tronchin for two folding chessboards, with which he could play chess with the Jesuits.[48] Voltaire took a liking to one of the Ornex Jesuits in particular, the 54-year-old Father Antoine Adam, whom he described early in 1759 as 'a pretty decent devil'.[49] Adam was a keen chess player, and no doubt it was mainly to play with him that Voltaire needed his folding chessboards. In 1765 Voltaire invited Adam to move in as his personal priest: 'I have a Jesuit in my house, who says Mass most properly, and who plays chess very well; he's called Adam, and though he is not the First Man, he has merit.'[50] Father Adam stayed for many years as a permanent part of the household, conducting church services, playing chess and conversing with Voltaire.

When he took Ferney, Voltaire was in his mid-sixties, but his energy remained boundless, and he embarked on a two-pronged campaign on behalf of enlightenment and against repression. The first prong took the form of an attack against the forces of superstition and darkness, which he encapsulated in an idiosyncratic personal slogan directed against '*L'Infâme*' or 'The Horror'. In letters to close allies such as d'Alembert and Damilaville, the slogan became '*Écrasez l'Infâme*' ('Crush the Horror'), often abbreviated after 1763 to the virtual password '*Ecrl-Inf*'. Voltaire never defined *L'Infâme*, but his general meaning is clear: his target included all facets of the dark and regressive alliance between the Catholic Church and the French state.

Étienne Noël Damilaville, a forty-year-old tax official, was one of Voltaire's closest and most loyal friends. Born in 1723, he had had a patchy education, and went on to be a soldier. After his discharge, and after a short stint as a lawyer, he went to work for the Finance Ministry (Contrôle Général des Finances); for the past seven years, since 1755, he had been a senior civil servant (*premier commis*) in the office supervising the tax known as the *Vingtième* ('5 Per Cent'). As a poor man, and as an inglorious employee of the state, Damilaville was much less brilliant than Voltaire's brilliant friends. But he was unconditionally on the side of the Enlightenment, and a whole-hearted supporter of Voltaire's campaigns; and he was a man Voltaire loved and trusted.

The conventional picture of Damilaville is pretty unflattering. Melchior Grimm, one of the *philosophes* and the editor of the *Correspondance Littéraire*, found Damilaville's personality as defective as his mind: 'He had neither grace, nor mental wit, and he lacked that worldly *savoir-faire* which makes up for it. He was sad and heavy, and his lack of basic education always showed through. Since he had not done any studies, he had no opinion of his own, and he repeated what he heard others say.'[51] Some modern scholars, such as René Pomeau, closely follow Grimm's disparaging opinion, but they pay too much attention to the *Correspondance Littéraire*, a literary gossip sheet that existed primarily for the spreading of malicious slander, and too little to the facts on the ground.

Damilaville was a close friend and regular drinking and dining companion of Denis Diderot, and he gave him some help with the editing of the *Encyclopédie*, besides contributing two or three articles. No doubt Damilaville was also useful in providing a free and discreet postal service for Diderot's correspondence with his mistress, Sophie Volland, but Diderot's friendship seems to have been genuine: 'I am sincerely glad to have found you', he told him. 'It is one of the happy events of my life.'[52] Damilaville was also a close friend of d'Alembert and Thieriot; several letters addressed to Damilaville were clearly intended to be read by his friends d'Alembert, Damilaville, Diderot and Thieriot, and one of them was explicitly addressed to 'My dear brothers'.[53] If these were his friends, it is hardly likely that Damilaville could have been as dull and dreary as Grimm suggests.

Moreover, Voltaire would simply not have recognised the conventionally disparaging picture of Damilaville that has been imposed on us by Grimm. The conventional view is that Voltaire's closest and most intimate friend was d'Argental, followed in the younger generation by d'Alembert, and that they were in all kinds of ways Voltaire's intellectual equals, as Damilaville was not. And yet it is evident, from the most casual reading of the letters, that of all Voltaire's friends Damilaville was the one whom he loved most deeply and most intensely. Since Voltaire was not stupid, he must have found in Damilaville much that was really worth loving.

One indication of the closeness of the relationship between Voltaire and Damilaville is the sheer volume of their correspondence. To d'Argental, the most frequent addressee of his correspondence, Voltaire wrote some 1,000 letters (though he received far fewer in reply); but their correspondence was spread over sixty years. To Damilaville, Voltaire wrote at least 539 letters, but this correspondence was essentially limited to the eight years 1760–68. In the first half of 1765 Voltaire wrote Damilaville sixty-one letters: that is, an average of one letter every three days. And it was a symptom of Voltaire's sympathy and trust in Damilaville as one of the inner band that he regularly signed off his letters to Damilaville with his battle-cry, *'Écrasez l'Infâme'*.

Some of Voltaire's *philosophe* friends were alarmed that he should be so outspoken in his hostility to oppression, since his letters were always liable to be opened by the authorities, and in any case they often leaked into general circulation. D'Alembert wrote to Voltaire in some concern in May 1761: "*Écrasez l'infâme; écrasez l'infâme!*" That is easily said when one is a hundred leagues from the bastards and the fanatics, when one has an independent income of 100,000 livres, and when one has become independent by reputation and fortune. But a poor devil like me does not tread on the serpents, for fear that they should twist their heads and sting him on the heel.'[54]

The second prong of Voltaire's Enlightenment campaign started in February 1760, when he began work on his *Dictionnaire philosophique portatif*. Voltaire planned this as a brisk, accessible alphabetical guide to Enlightenment thinking and attitudes, and it was his answer to what he saw as the interminable prolixity of the *Encyclopédie*, to which he had by now ceased to contribute. Several years later he was to claim that the great *Encyclopédie* was bound to be harmless because it was both so large and so expensive: 'I should like to know what harm could come from a book which costs 100 écus. A work in twenty folio volumes will never make a revolution; it's the little books costing 30 sous which are to be feared. If the New Testament had cost 1,200 sesterces, the Christian religion would never have been established.'[55]

Never can a 65-year-old have been so busy: doing up Ferney, researching his history of Peter the Great, writing and acting plays, writing his *Dictionnaire Philosophique*, campaigning against *L'Infâme* and, on top of that, the most voluminous letter-writing. Even so, Voltaire also managed to keep up with a wide range of literature, including the latest. In 1759 he encouraged Mme du Deffand to read the Old Testament, which he said was more entertaining than *Tom Jones*; he urged her to learn Italian so that she could read Ariosto; and he suggested she re-read Rabelais, which he used to despise but now enjoyed greatly, despite its excessive vulgarity. He also recommended the writings of Jonathan Swift:

> Let it please God, Madame, for the good I wish you, that there be a faithful copy of the *Tale of a Tub* by Dean Swift! It is a treasure-house of entertainment, of which no one else has any idea. Pascal is only amusing at the expense of the Jesuits; Swift entertains and informs us at the expense of the human race. How I love the English boldness! How I love people who say what they think! People who only half-think are only half alive.[56]

The following year, in September 1760, shortly after the publication in England of the first volume of Laurence Sterne's new novel, he wrote to an Italian acquaintance, in a mixture of French, Italian and English:

'Have you read *Tristram Shandy*? 'Tis a very unaccountable book; an original one. They run mad about it in England.'[57]

Voltaire could not get over how happy he was. 'I had no idea of happiness, until I had my own home, in retirement; but what a retirement! Sometimes I have fifty persons at my table; I leave them with Mme Denis, who does the honours, and I shut myself away. I have built what the Italians would call a *palazzo*, but I only like my study.'[58] The only thing that was missing in the life of Voltaire and Mme Denis was children; but fate almost immediately gave them a surrogate daughter.

24

MLLE CORNEILLE

1760–1763

IN OCTOBER 1760, shortly before they moved to Ferney, Voltaire heard from the poet Jean-Étienne Écouchard Le Brun that there was a teenage girl in Paris who was a descendant of Pierre Corneille, the great tragedian, and that she and her father were living in great poverty. Her name was Marie-Françoise Corneille, and her father, Jean-François Corneille, was a lowly, almost illiterate employee of the postal system, barely surviving on £50 a month. Voltaire decided almost immediately that he would rescue her from poverty, take her into his family, and educate her. Later he would adopt her.

Within days Voltaire made arrangements for her to travel to Ferney. He wrote to Le Brun:

> I am old, I have a niece who loves all the fine arts and who does well in some of them; if the young person of whom you speak wished to accept a decent education from my niece, she would take care of her as of a daughter; I should seek to be a father to her. Part of the education of the young lady would sometimes be to see us act the plays of her grandfather.[1]*

By 16 December Marie-Françoise had already reached Lyon, and was with Jean-Robert Tronchin. 'They will probably introduce her to

---

* At first, Voltaire believed Marie-Françoise was the great Corneille's grand-daughter; he only gradually learned that she was a more distant relative, a first cousin twice removed, from a parallel branch of the family.

Mme de Groslée, who will not fail to feel her tits, according to her laudable custom. It's an honour that she does to all the girls and women introduced to her.'[2] On the same day Voltaire wrote to enquire about a possible tutor for her:

> If you know of some poor man who knows how to read and write, and who may even have a smattering of geography and history, or who is at least capable of learning some, and of teaching the next day what he had learned the day before, we will house him, heat him, launder him, feed him, water him and pay him, but pay him very modestly, for I have ruined myself in building châteaux and churches and theatres.[3]

Four days later Marie-Françoise Corneille arrived, and Voltaire was overjoyed. 'We find her natural, gay and true, with a charming little face, lovely eyes, beautiful skin, a large mouth, rather attractive, with two rows of pearly teeth. If anyone has the pleasure to get his teeth close to hers, I hope it will be a Catholic rather than a Protestant. But on my word of honour, my divine angels, it will not be me: I'm sixty-seven years old.'[4]

Voltaire did not wait for a tutor, however:

> We are taking care of all the parts of her education, until a worthy tutor arrives. She is learning spelling; we make her write, and you can see that she forms her letters well, and that her lines don't go diagonally like some of your Parisiennes. She reads with us at regular hours, and we make sure that she understands the meaning of the words. After her reading, we talk to her about what she has read; and thus we teach her, indirectly, a bit of history. All this happens quite gaily, without the smallest sense of a lesson.[5]

Voltaire and Mme Denis were both delighted with Marie-Françoise:

> We do not cease to give thanks for this treasure we now possess. Her heart seems excellent, and we have every hope that, even if we do not make an intellectual of her, she will become a very lovable person with all the virtues, the graces and the naturalness which make the charm of society. What I like especially about her is her attachment to her father. She has been given a chambermaid, who is delighted to be with her. She is loved by all the servants; everyone competes to serve

her little whims, though her whims are certainly not very demanding. It is too soon to hire any tutors, apart from myself and my niece.
We don't let her get away with bad words or vicious pronunciations.
Habit is everything. I must not leave out the fact that I take her myself
to the parish Mass: we have a duty to give a good example, and we
give it.[6]

From this time on, Voltaire increasingly referred to Mme Denis as
'*maman*'.

Physically, Marie-Françoise was somewhat malformed, since she
suffered from the aftermath of childhood rickets (no doubt owing to
poverty and malnutrition); but it was not until nearly two years later that
Voltaire referred explicitly to the fact, in a letter to Théodore Tronchin:
'Mlle Corneille once had rickets. She sometimes feels the consequences
of this old conformation. Weakness and pain in the hip, vague and rheu-
matic pains in the side near the afflicted hip. In a word, she hobbles and
she suffers. What is to be done?'[7]

Voltaire was enchanted with his new duties as a surrogate father. He
told Mme du Deffand that Marie-Françoise was 'gentle and gay, good,
true, grateful, affectionate without guile but by inclination; she will
have good sense; but as for good taste, she will have to get it where she
can.'[8] 'My most difficult duty', he told d'Argental, 'is teaching grammar
to Mlle Corneille, who has no disposition for this sublime science.'[9]

Voltaire's pleasure at the arrival of Marie-Françoise only added to
his ebullience in all his other newly acquired roles as landowner, mod-
erniser and benefactor. 'Yes, I serve God', he told d'Argental, 'for I love
my country, I go to Mass every Sunday, I am setting up schools, I am
building churches, I am going to set up a hospital, there are no longer
any poor on my estates, despite the efforts of the salt tax inspectors.'[10]
Moreover, he intended to take communion at Easter, with Mme Denis
and Mlle Corneille; 'and you can call me a hypocrite as much as you
like'.[11]

But he never forgot that his happiness depended crucially on his
wealth. He wrote to Jean-Robert Tronchin in January 1761:

My dear correspondent, I was born fairly poor, I have spent my life in
a beggar's trade, as a scribbler on paper, and yet here I am with two
châteaux, two pretty houses, 70,000 livres of income and 200,000 livres
in cash. Sometimes I take all my happiness for a dream. I should find
it quite difficult to say just how I have managed to be the happiest of

men. I just stick to the fact, without reasoning. And to increase my happiness, you should soon receive a partridge pâté with truffles from Angoulême, which I ask you to send on to Les Délices, where we are for some time, because your frightful Geneva plasterers have made fireplaces at Ferney which smoke.[12]

A few days later this partridge pâté, a gift from the marquis d'Argence in Angoulême, arrived safely: 'Thanks to the prudence of your cook, and four fingers of lard placed between the partridge and the crust, your pâté arrived fresh and excellent, and we have been eating it for the past eight days; we have greatly toasted your health, glass in hand.'[13]

By May 1761 Marie-Françoise was starting to show some natural talent for acting small parts in Voltaire's plays.[14] But he soon concluded that the best thing for this charming girl would be to find her a husband. This would require a dowry, and Voltaire hit on a scheme for financing it: he would write an extensive commentary for a new edition of the works of Corneille; he would get it endorsed by the Académie Française; he would publish it in a luxurious and expensive multi-volume edition; and he would get everyone to subscribe to it; and the proceeds would go to Marie-Françoise. He put his plan to Charles Duclos, *secrétaire perpetuel* of the Académie, and three weeks later they approved it.

Voltaire's rationale for the Corneille project was his belief that the great age of French civilisation was the seventeenth century.[15] 'It seems to me that we should regard him as the Greeks regarded Homer, the first in his line, and unique, even with his faults.'[16] Since then, Voltaire believed, there had been a decline into decadence, and he hoped that his commentary would in some sense help to fix the rules of the French language.

Voltaire immediately set about rustling up a list of subscribers:

I trust that the king will head the list. I shall subscribe for six copies [in fact he took 100], and several members of the Académie Française will do as much; I shall tax M. de Brosses for two copies at 40 livres a piece; that's reasonable for an estate which he sold me a bit dear. Our colleagues in the Paris Académie must take more copies than other people.[17]

The king duly put his name down for 200 copies, the Tsarina Elisabeth Petrovna for 200, the Empress Maria Theresa for 100, but Frederick the Great for only six. Yet Voltaire tried to prevent any unduly vulgar marketing of the subscription lists; early in 1763 he urged that Philibert Cramer be discouraged from hawking subscription forms at the theatres and on the promenades, 'as if they were tickets for green oysters'.[18] Nevertheless, the subscription list ended up with 1,176 names, for a total of 4,009 copies.[19]

At first Voltaire planned to confine his commentaries only to the best of Corneille's tragedies, since he thought some of them were really not very good. But he soon found himself dragged by a sense of duty into working on all Corneille's plays, including the bad ones. 'Just think', he told d'Argental: 'I have thirty-two plays to comment on, of which eighteen are unreadable. Pity me, encourage me, don't scold me.'[20] Three weeks later, the number of Corneille's plays which Voltaire thought were 'unbearable and do not deserve to be read', had gone up from eighteen to twenty-two.[21]

And yet Voltaire was sorry for Corneille's personal plight when his plays started to go out of fashion:

He had no consideration, people laughed at him; he went on foot, he arrived at the theatre from his publisher all covered with mud; they hissed his last twelve plays; he could scarcely find actors who deigned to perform them. Don't forget, I was brought up by people who had long known Corneille. My father used to drink with Corneille. He told me that this great man was the most boring mortal he had ever seen, and the one with the lowest conversation. Yet they want commentaries on those works which should never have seen the light of day. All right then, they will have their commentaries, and I shan't complain of my trouble.[22]

By the end of January 1762 just nine months after his first enquiry, the first volume of Voltaire's commentaries went into production.

Voltaire's comments on Corneille were rather harsh, and the final impression was almost as much a denunciation of Corneille's defects as an exposition of his virtues.[23] When the edition appeared in 1764, there was an indignant public outcry in defence of Corneille, and it was over a hundred years, according to René Pomeau, before Corneille's reputation really recovered from Voltaire's critical onslaught.[24] But Voltaire had the satisfaction of knowing that it had been a great commercial success, bringing in £40,000 for Marie-Françoise. Nine years later, in 1773 (when he was seventy-nine), he brought out a second edition, which was half as large again as the first.[25]

Voltaire's health, never good, deteriorated around this time, and he moved back to Les Délices, to be nearer to Théodore Tronchin; but the crisis proved short-lived, as Tronchin related: 'Voltaire's health could not be better. I met him yesterday, between the two bridges over the Rhône, driving a cabriolet, harnessed to a two-year-old pony. I shouted to him through the window: "Old baby, what are you up to?"' Voltaire immediately wrote him an urgent disclaimer: 'I was coming to see you. I had no carriage horses, and I decided to go to see you. Do not go and draw your cruel conclusions, that I am in good health, that I have a body of iron, etc. Do not slander me, but love me.'[26]

By one test Voltaire was not inventing his ill health: at seventy-one, he found he could no longer act in his plays. 'These past few days they wanted me to play the part of an old man in my little theatre, but I found that I was in fact so old and so feeble that I could not even portray a character which should come so naturally to me.'[27] As he wrote to d'Alembert: 'I let Mme Denis lay on meals for twenty-six guests, and put on plays for dukes and presidents and governors, and passers-by whom we shall never see again. Amidst all this hubbub I go to bed, and I shut the door.'[28]

It was soon decided that Marie-Françoise would marry Pierre-Jacques-Claude Dupuits de la Chaux, a 23-year-old cornet of dragoons. This young man was already well known to Voltaire:

A very pleasant gentleman, with charming manners, good-looking, loving, loved, fairly rich. We all agreed, in a moment, without discussion, as if we were arranging a supper party. Yesterday, it seemed that the two parties love one another. If I could, I would hold the marriage tomorrow. There's no point in delaying, life is too short.[29]

The best part of it, for Voltaire, was that Dupuits was a local boy and an orphan, so the married couple could live at Ferney and Voltaire could keep Marie-Françoise near him.

We shall house the two orphans; they love each other passionately, and that cheers me. I wish that Pierre [Corneille] could come back to see all that, and witness Voltaire leading to church the only person left with his name. Mlle Corneille, with her little face, and two dark eyes which are worth a hundred times the last dozen plays of uncle Pierre. Have you seen her? Do you know her? She is a gay child, sensitive, honest, gentle, the best character in the world.[30]

Voltaire sent some money to her father, François Corneille, and tried to see if he could not be found a better job outside Paris, for he did not want Dupuits to have 'a father-in-law who is a little postman trotting along the streets of Paris'.[31] But he was determined that François must at all costs be kept away from the wedding: 'Heaven preserve us! His person, his conversation, his job would not go down well with the family into which Mlle Corneille is marrying. M. le duc de Villars and the other French guests at the ceremony would make nasty jokes at his expense.'[32]

Marie-Françoise Corneille and Pierre-Jacques-Claude Dupuits de la Chaux were married in mid-February 1763, very quietly, for Mme Denis was rather unwell, and Voltaire was suffering from snow-blindness. 'All these things', said Voltaire, 'rather spoiled our little fête.'[33] Nevertheless, 'the two lovers are very happy, the parents [Voltaire and Mme Denis] are enchanted, and apart from the snow, everything is as good as possible.'[34]

Voltaire had great wealth, two chateaux with their estates, great fame and inexhaustible creative energy; and his delightful daughter was now happily married. His personal life had reached a new zenith of contentment.

CAMPAIGNS FOR JUSTICE

1761–1765

VOLTAIRE'S NEW, LARGER THEATRE at Ferney opened in October 1761, and by the new year his theatre entertainments, with their attendant dinners and dances, were becoming increasingly popular. In March 1762 they had a run-through of his play *Cassandre*, in front of 300 people; a few days later, there was another performance, with 200 spectators, followed by a ball. Calvinist Geneva officially disapproved of Voltaire's dramatics, and Geneva preachers would not come themselves; but, as Voltaire exultantly pointed out, they sent their daughters instead.[1] All these people needed refreshments, so Voltaire ordered 'the most enormous cart-load' of wine. 'The *vin ordinaire* will be for the guests, and the better stuff, if you please, for me. A little barrel of this better stuff, containing about 240 pints, will do nicely.'[2] In April, Henri-Louis Lekain of the Comédie Française came to stay and took the lead in *Tancrède* and *Alzire*. By the end of that year (1762) Voltaire's theatre was giving performances every week.

All this was costing a lot of money, so Voltaire decided that the time had come to impose some discipline on his expenditure. 'Mme Denis and Mlle Corneille need some amusements,' he told Jean-Robert Tronchin;

> but I should like to put a bit of order into the pleasures and the affairs of Mme Denis. I have paid all the debts of the household, I have made considerable settlements of every kind on her, I have handed over to her all the income from the Ferney estate, so she should be able to cover all the household expenses with an extra 100 louis per month.[3]

Voltaire's economy drive did not work, as he admitted to Ami Camp: 'I cannot stop the torrent of our expenses, but we shall ruin ourselves if we want.'[4]. In August 1762 he increased Mme Denis's notional monthly allowance from 100 to 120 louis. In future, he said, anything else she ordered would be deducted from her increased allowance. Well, maybe.[5]

Despite the expense, Voltaire was jubilant at the spectacular success and scale of his theatrical performances, as he told d'Argental on 8 March 1762:

> I am exhausted; I have just come from a ball; I can no longer call my head my own. 'A ball, old fool? A ball in your mountains? And for whom have you given it? For the badgers?' Not at all, if you don't mind: for a very fine company of people, for these are the facts.
>
> Perhaps you imagine that we were playing to an audience of primitive provincials; not at all; to people of very refined taste, 300 delighted spectators of every age and condition, gentry and farmers, believers and dandies. They came from Lyon, from Dijon, from Turin. Would you believe that Mlle Corneille won all the votes? How natural she was! Lively! Gay! How she was mistress of the theatre, stamping her foot when she was prompted out of turn! There was one place where the audience forced her to repeat a scene. I played the bailiff and, if I may say so, fit to make them burst out laughing.
>
> But what is one to do with 300 people, in the middle of the snow, at midnight, when the show is over? We had to give them all supper, and then we had to make them dance. It was a pretty well-turned-out party. I was only expecting fifty people. But enough of that, I mustn't boast. We play *Cassandre* in eight or ten days, and afterwards I shall tell you how it went.[6]

Voltaire wrote again to d'Argental about his amateur dramatics two weeks later, on 22 March 1762, and his letter ended with a sardonic throw-away paragraph about a news item that had caught his attention.

> You have perhaps heard of a good Huguenot, whom the *parlement* of Toulouse has had broken on the wheel, for having strangled his own son. This reformed saint thought he had done a good deed, seeing that his son wished to become a Catholic, and he did it to prevent an apostasy. We may not be worth much, but the Huguenots are worse, and in addition they preach against play-acting.[7]

This is Voltaire's first reference to what became famous as the Calas affair, which was one of the most dramatic turning-points in Voltaire's life; it was also a key moment in the history of penal reform in Europe. From his initial throwaway remarks we can tell that Voltaire at first knew few or none of the details of the case and really could not care less. Three days later his attitude had changed totally: he abandoned his mocking, disdainful tone of voice and instead became, first, intensely anxious about the basis for the conviction, and then gradually convinced that Jean Calas had been the victim of a great injustice. One day he was full of self-confidence: supercilious, condescending, uninvolved. Three days later he was anxious, emotional, uncertain and quivering on the edge of horror and indignation.

Very soon he set out to challenge the verdict in the Calas case and in the process found himself launched, at the age of sixty-eight, on a new vocation, as a campaigner for justice. This was not a vocation that he willed or consciously chose; on the contrary, he showed at first every sign of preferring to avoid it. But when he finally responded, he engaged in it with whole-hearted commitment until the end of his life.

Jean Calas was a prosperous cloth merchant who lived with his wife, Anne-Rose Cabibel, over their shop in Toulouse. They were both Protestants, and they had four sons and two daughters. Louis, the third son, and a convert to Catholicism, had left home; Donat, the youngest son, was serving an apprenticeship at Nîmes; and the two daughters, Rosine and Nanette, were away from home, staying with friends. So the family circle, on the evening of 13 October 1761, consisted of Jean Calas and his wife, their two eldest sons, Marc-Antoine (almost twenty-nine) and Pierre (twenty-eight); and their Catholic servant, Jeanne Viguière. There was also a visitor with them at the supper table, young Gaubert Lavaysse, who was a friend of Pierre and the son of a prominent local lawyer.

After supper Marc-Antoine went downstairs, apparently intending to go for a walk; the rest of the family party stayed upstairs for some time talking, until Gaubert Lavaysse said he had to go home; Pierre took a light to show him out. When they got downstairs, they found Marc-Antoine in the shop, dead. A doctor was called; he could do nothing. The Calas family alerted the town authorities, and the magistrate David de Beaudrigue arrived on the scene; he arrested the entire Calas family, on suspicion that they were responsible for the death of Marc-Antoine.

This David de Beaudrigue was a brutal and a hasty man. He assumed, based on gossip overheard that evening on the street, that Jean

Calas, with the help of his family, must have murdered Marc-Antoine, in order to prevent him from converting to Catholicism. His suspicions were intensified when the Calas family changed their story: at first they had said that they found the body of Marc-Antoine lying on the ground; later they said they had found it hanging by a noose between a pair of double doors connecting the shop and the storeroom behind. They said that they had wanted to conceal the fact of suicide, since a suicide would be denied honourable burial, but that then they had decided to tell the truth. It did not look good for them.

We still do not know exactly how and why Marc-Antoine Calas died, but he was almost certainly not killed by his family. His 63-year-old father would have been too weak to do it on his own, and a joint murder by several members of his family is simply unbelievable, not least because the Catholic servant would have had to be part of the conspiracy.

David de Beaudrigue never found any evidence to support his suspicions. But the mainstream assumption at the time was that anyone who was accused must almost certainly be guilty: the purpose of a trial was not to find the truth, but to prove guilt, if possible by confession. The customary trial processes were deliberately rigged against the accused and in favour of state repression. The accused was not allowed any advance notice of the questions, or of the evidence or witnesses against him, and he might even not know the details of the offence he was charged with. He was allowed a lawyer, who could make representations on his behalf, but only outside the court room; he was not permitted to be present at the questioning of the accused, which was held behind closed doors.

Moreover, the second assumption at the time was that on any question affecting Catholics and Protestants, Protestants must be guilty. With the revocation in 1685 of the Edict of Nantes, Louis XIV had re-instituted far-reaching state persecution of Protestants in France. Protestant services of worship were forbidden, male offenders were liable to a life sentence in the galleys, women to life imprisonment, and preachers to execution. The only valid marriages were those sanctified by the Catholic Church, and all new-born children had to be baptised and brought up as Catholics. Protestants were shut out from all sorts of professions, including the law. Protestant families could employ only Catholic servants.

As a result, more than 200,000 French Protestants emigrated, to Holland, Germany, England and Geneva. But the Catholic policy of repression did not drive out Protestantism: in the mid-eighteenth century there were still around 300,000 Protestants in France. Some Protestants were driven by discrimination and persecution to convert to Catholicism; many pretended outwardly to conform and were able to live honourable, even prominent public lives, including in liberal professions such as the law. But many remained Protestant at heart and in private and continued to attend illegal religious services in the remote countryside ('in the desert', as it was known), in permanent danger of imprisonment or execution.

The first phase of the trial of Jean Calas took place before the magistrates, or *capitouls*, of Toulouse, and they immediately enlisted the help of the Catholic Church against the accused. A nine-point summons, or *monitoire*, was posted in every church in Toulouse and read out at Mass on three occasions by the local priest, calling on the (Catholic) faithful to testify against the (Protestant) Calas family. Witnesses were called for, to confirm, 'on the basis of hearsay or otherwise', that Marc-Antoine had been about to convert to Catholicism; that a meeting held in a Protestant house had decided on his death; and that this execution had been carried out on 13 October whether by hanging or strangulation.[8] All this was simply guesswork: the Church had pre-judged the case against Calas and was hoping that someone would provide the evidence.

The *monitoire* failed to produce it. No one could be found with hard evidence (as opposed to rumour and hearsay) that Marc-Antoine intended to convert, and no priest testified that he had done so. Nevertheless, the *capitouls* took Marc-Antoine's conversion for granted and ordered that he be given a Christian burial in Catholic consecrated ground. The Catholic Church then raised the stakes by giving Marc-Antoine a martyr's funeral, accompanied by forty-six clerics and a barefoot procession of the White Penitents, one of several lay Catholic brotherhoods in Toulouse.

The case was now transferred from the *capitouls* to the Toulouse *parlement*, whose judges decided to renew the *monitoire*, this time accompanied by a 'fulmination' – a threat that anyone who withheld the required evidence would be excommunicated. Still no hard evidence was produced. Nevertheless, on 9 March 1762 the court decided, by a narrow majority, that Jean Calas should be broken on the wheel, exposed for two hours, then strangled and thrown on a burning pyre. This punishment, they said, was 'a reparation owed to religion, for the son's happy conversion, which had probably (*vraisemblablement*) been the cause of his death.'[9]

Jean Calas had still not confessed. So before his execution, on 10 March 1762 he was subjected, in the presence of David de Beaudrigue, to two forms of torture. In the first (the *question ordinaire*) his arms and legs were stretched on the rack; in the second (the *question extraordinaire*) he was compelled to drink ten jugs of water, not once but twice. Still he made no confession.

Jean Calas then walked barefoot in a white shirt to the scaffold in the Place Saint-Georges in Toulouse. He was tied face up on the wheel, and his arms and legs were broken with an iron bar. Priests begged him to confess his crime and his sin, but still he did not confess. After two hours he was strangled, and his body burned.

Without any evidence, or any confession from Jean Calas, the judges of the Toulouse *parlement* recoiled from proceeding on the same basis with the trial of the other members of his family. They condemned Pierre to banishment, but they freed Mme Calas, young Gaubert Lavaysse and the servant Jeanne Viguière, but without declaring them innocent. Mme Calas's two daughters were locked up in two different convents, even though they could not possibly have had anything to do with the death of Marc-Antoine. Public opinion in Toulouse was outraged; it had been looking forward to further persecution of the Calas family.

On 25 March, two weeks after the execution of Jean Calas, Voltaire wrote to Cardinal Bernis who, though a Catholic prelate, was a friend and admirer:

> May I beg your eminence to tell me what I should think of the frightful adventure of this Calas, broken at Toulouse for having hanged his son? What they claim here [in Geneva] is that he is totally innocent, and that he called God to witness as he expired. They claim that three judges protested against the sentence. This adventure grips my heart; it casts sadness over my pleasures and corrupts them. We must regard with horror either the *parlement* of Toulouse or the Huguenots.[10]

We do not know what made Voltaire change his mind so suddenly. He certainly talked with a Protestant merchant from Marseille who knew the Calas family well, and his Protestant friends in Geneva may have known something about the case. But what seems to have clinched matters for Voltaire, was a personal interview with 22-year-old Donat Calas, the youngest of Jean Calas's four sons. Donat was an apprentice in Nîmes; when he heard about the tragedy in Toulouse, he went immediately for safety to Protestant Geneva. Three years later Voltaire described his meeting with Donat:

> I had expected to see a roustabout, such as you sometimes find in the country. I saw a child, simple, innocent, of the gentlest and most interesting physiognomy, and who, as he spoke to me, made vain efforts to hold back his tears. I asked him if his father and mother were of a violent character: he told me that they had never beaten a single one of their children, and that there had never been more indulgent or more tender parents. I confess that I needed no more to presume strongly the innocence of the family.[11]

From this moment Voltaire became completely obsessed with the Calas affair: over the next nine months he wrote over 100 letters in whole or in part about the case and about his efforts to challenge the verdict. But if Voltaire now instinctively presumed the innocence of Jean Calas, he needed more information to be sure, and his attempts to get at the facts faced serious obstruction: the processes of a French trial were intensely secret, and the Toulouse authorities stubbornly resisted the release of any information about the procedures of the case. Voltaire soon concluded that publicity would be his best weapon for forcing the authorities to act and the *parlement* to submit. 'If there is anything which can stop the frenzy of fanaticism, it is publicity.'[12]

On enquiry he learned that the death sentence was passed only by a narrow majority of the Toulouse judges. 'There were thirteen of them,' he told d'Argental, 'and five constantly declared Calas innocent. If there had been one more vote in his favour, he would have been acquitted. You may ask why I am so strongly interested in this Calas. It is because I am a man, because I see that all foreigners are indignant at a country which breaks a man on the wheel without any proof.'[13]

By 4 April, Voltaire was categorically asserting his belief in the innocence of Jean Calas. ' My dear brothers,* it is recognised that the judges of Toulouse have broken the most innocent of men. Never since the day of Saint Bartholomew has anything so dishonoured human nature.'[14]†

---

* Voltaire addressed this letter to Étienne-Noël Damilaville. But he starts it with 'My dear brothers', because Damilaville, Jean Le Rond d'Alembert and Nicolas-Claude Thieriot were all close friends, and often passed Voltaire's letters round between them.
† On 24 August 1572, the feast day of Saint Bartholomew, some 3,000 Protestants were massacred in Paris, and the killing continued in the provinces until October. Voltaire was so

On the basis of four legal opinions which he had commissioned he had come to the conclusion that it was quite impossible for Jean Calas, a feeble old man, to have hanged his vigorous young son and that, even with the help of other members of the family, it would have been extremely difficult.*

By 15 May, Voltaire felt sure that the *parlement* now knew that it had made a terrible blunder and wanted at all costs to prevent the truth coming out.[15] But his confidence was shaken when he got a 'very strange letter' from his friend the duc de Villars, expressing complete confidence in the *parlement* and its verdict; he began to fear that there was now a closing of ranks between the *parlement* in Toulouse and the court in Versailles.[16]

Voltaire could see that a serious challenge to the Calas verdict would need a much stronger legal and factual brief. On 5 June he wrote to Jean Ribote-Charron, a young Protestant merchant in Montauban, and asked him to go to Toulouse to dig out the facts. The key question, he said, was: did the Calas family group stay together in the same room after supper or not? Everything depended on this 'great truth'. For if the answer to the question was Yes, then it was impossible that Jean Calas alone could be guilty of the murder of his son.[17]

At home, Voltaire's amateur dramatics were becoming increasingly popular, but they were not really at the centre of his thoughts any more. 'I am at present preoccupied with a more important tragedy,' he told d'Alembert, 'that of a hanged man, of a man broken on the wheel, of a family ruined and scattered, and all for the sake of holy religion. I urge you to cry out loud, and make others cry out. Do you ever see Mme du Deffand and Mme de Luxembourg? Can you stir them up? Farewell my great philosopher, *Écrasez l'Infâme.*'[18]

Voltaire's strategy for his Calas campaign developed on three fronts: delving into the facts of the trial, pulling strings with influential people at court and, finally, mobilising public opinion. Of these, much the most interesting, and surprising, was his declared objective of influencing the authorities through public opinion or, as he put it, making 'a public outcry'. Of course, Voltaire did not understand 'public opinion' in anything like the sense we do today; on the contrary, he rejected the idea that the whole of society at large could have a valid opinion, as he made

---

horrified by his knowledge of the event that he was regularly ill each year on 24 August. See *Letters*, 11381, 30 August 1769.

* Voltaire believed that Jean Calas was sixty-nine. In fact he was sixty-three, having been born on 19 March 1698. See Marc Chassaigne, *L'Affaire Calas*, pp. 16, 23

clear several years later, in the context of a quite different case: 'When I say "the voice of the public", I do not mean that of the population at large, which is almost always absurd; that is not a human voice, it is a cry of brutes; I mean the collective voice of all the decent people who think, and who, over time, reach an infallible judgement.'[19] Voltaire's concept of public opinion was more limited, but still astonishing: he aimed to appeal to the political class as a whole, not just to individual members of it.

Getting the facts proved difficult, because the *parlement* at Toulouse was still totally recalcitrant. 'What do we ask?', Voltaire wrote to d'Argental.

> Nothing more than that justice should not be as dumb as it is blind, that it should speak, and say why it condemned Calas. What horror is this, a secret judgement, a condemnation without explanations! Is there a more execrable tyranny than that of spilling blood on a whim, without giving the least reason? 'It is not the custom', say the judges. Hey, monsters! It must become the custom! You owe an accounting to men for the blood of men. As for me, I do not ask anything more than the publication of the trial procedure. People say that this poor woman [Mme Calas] must first get the documents sent from Toulouse; but where will she get them? Who will open the clerk's den? In any case, it is not just she who interests me, it is the public, it is humanity. It is important for everybody that such decisions should be publicly justified.[20]

In short, Voltaire was by this time primarily motivated no longer by his pity for Jean Calas but by larger principles of state, society and humanity. Later that year he wrote: 'It is in the interest of the state that we discover on which side is the most horrible fanaticism.'[21] And again: 'Please note that the reason which should influence the King's Council to procure the documents is not the memory of Jean Calas, about which the Council cares very little, but the public good; it is humanity that the Council should consider.'[22]

But the *parlement* refused to release the trial records, and Pierre Mariette, one of Voltaire's lawyers, told him that he could do nothing without a summary of the evidence. 'What! Does that mean we cannot demand justice without having the weapons which our enemies deny us? So people can spill innocent blood with impunity, and get away with it, by saying they do not want to say why they spilled it? Ah! *Quelle horreur!*'[23] As for the great and good at court, Voltaire had already knocked on several very important doors, but so far he did not have enough allies to tip the balance.

There remained public opinion. In early July 1762 Voltaire wrote: 'Only the ultimate intervention of the King can force this *parlement* to reveal the truth; we are doing our utmost to secure it; and we believe that a public outcry is the best way to do so.' [24] To that end Voltaire published a pamphlet which he called *Pièces originales* (Original Documents). This purported to be letters from Mme Calas and depositions from her sons Donat and Pierre Calas, giving their version of what happened on 13 October 1761. It also included an ostensible appeal from Donat Calas to the Chancellor and to the King-in-Council, to investigate the case and make the truth known. These documents were, of course, all written by Voltaire himself, and they argued the innocence of Jean Calas and that of his family. But in addition they constituted an indictment of several aspects of the French judicial system – above all, its secrecy – in contrast to the relative openness of the English system.

The *Pièces originales* were widely distributed in Paris, especially to key figures at court: to the duc de Choiseul (the Prime Minister), to the Chancellor, and to Mme de Pompadour (the King's mistress and something of an ally of the *philosophes*). These documents may have marked the turning of the tide of opinion: in July Voltaire claimed that they had had 'a prodigious effect' among leading figures in Paris, and he reported that the duc de La Vallière wanted to present Mme Calas to Mme de Pompadour.[25] Crucially, the Chancellor himself called for a formal review of the Calas case. Voltaire wrote on 20 August:

> The Calas affair is going even better than I dared to hope; yes, the Chancellor has called for the trial record, the whole court is stirred up, and the king is informed. We are working on a reasoned appeal, and it is my barrister at the Council who is in charge of it. So far my campaign against the most barbarous fanaticism has been very successful.[26]

Voltaire was right: in late August Mme de Pompadour wrote a remarkable letter to the duc de Fitzjames, governor of the Limousin:

> You are right, the affair of poor Calas makes one tremble. It seems impossible that he could have committed the crime of which he was accused; it is not in human nature. Yet his judges will not repent. The

king's good heart has really suffered when he heard this strange tale, and the whole of France cries out for revenge. The poor man will be avenged, but not brought back. The people of Toulouse are excitable, and have far more of their kind of religion than they need for being good Christians. May it please God to convert them, and make them more human.[27]

At the end of August, Voltaire's indignation against the *parlement* of Toulouse rose to a new pitch. He wrote to d'Argental: 'I have seen the text of Calas's sentence. The jurisprudence of Toulouse is really very strange, for this sentence does not even say what Jean Calas was accused of. I can only regard the sentence as an assassination carried out in black robes and square hats.'[28]

In September, Voltaire's campaign at last made substantive legal progress, as he told Ribote-Charron in Montauban:

By now they must know in Toulouse, that the widow Calas's request for a review of the case has been accepted, that the *rapporteur* for the case has been named, and that fifteen leading barristers in Paris have signed the opinion which calls for vengeance, that this opinion, and the report of the advocate to the King's Council [Mariette], have been printed, and that this widow, as respectable as she is unfortunate, is not short of help. The little preliminary documents [the *Pièces originales*] which have inspired the public with pity for innocence and indignation at injustice have been translated into English, German and Dutch.[29]

Voltaire was now well on the way to winning. Shortly before the session of the King's Council in early March 1763, Mme Calas surrendered to prison in Versailles. This was customary: a person seeking to overturn a trial verdict had to surrender beforehand, as a sign of readiness to accept a new trial and a new verdict. But all proceeded smoothly: on 7 March 1763 the King's Council in formal session, presided over by the Chancellor, and with three bishops and 100 judges in attendance, acting unanimously, ordered the clerk of the Toulouse *parlement* to submit the record of the trial of Jean Calas, and ordered the Attorney-General of the Toulouse *parlement* to submit the reasons for the verdict.[30] Voltaire was overjoyed. 'This last demand', he told Richelieu, 'is already a sort of reprimand.'[31]

But Voltaire was now turning his attention from the specifics of the case to the systemic malfunctioning of the judicial system in Toulouse. 'I have just learned one of the reasons for the Toulouse verdict which will astonish you,' he told his friend Damilaville. 'These Visigoths have a maxim that four-quarters of a proof, and eight-eighths of a proof, make two complete proofs, and they give to hearsay the weight of quarters and eighths of proof. What do you think of this manner of reasoning and judging. Is it possible that the life of men can depend on such absurd people?'[32]

By now the battle in the Calas affair was virtually over, although the formalities would take another year.[33] The Toulouse *parlement* invented several pretexts to delay handing over the trial records, but they eventually did so, though not until several weeks past the deadline set by the King's Council.

Voltaire now set about using the Calas case as a way of raising much broader issues: the role played by the fanaticism of the Catholic Church, and the pervasive superstition and prejudice of the Catholic population, in bringing in an iniquitous and wholly unproven guilty verdict. In December 1762 Voltaire opened up a new front with a 90-page pamphlet entitled *Traité sur la tolérance* (Treatise on Tolerance). By late January it was taking shape, and Voltaire told Damilaville that he was rather pleased with it: 'My dear brother, we can no longer prevent Jean Calas from being broken, but we can make his judges hated. Look out for a little work on tolerance which will soon appear. There are passages which make one shudder, and others which make one burst out laughing; thank God, intolerance is as absurd as it is horrible.'[34]

The *Traité sur la tolérance* was printed on 13 April 1763, and a small number of copies was circulated privately to key social and political figures, including Mme de Pompadour, the ministers of state, some of the members of the Conseil d'État, as well as to King Frederick and some of the German princes. 'I shall include a circular letter', wrote Voltaire, 'in which I shall beg them to ensure that it is only read by sensible people, and to make sure that their copy does not fall into the hands of a publisher.'[35]

Voltaire's caution was understandable, for with the opening words of the *Traité sur la tolérance* he threw down a challenge to the regime that was brutal in its frankness: 'The murder of Calas, committed in Toulouse with the sword of justice, on 9 March 1762, is one of the most exceptional events which deserve the attention of our age and of posterity.' There followed a recapitulation of the Calas affair and of Voltaire's case against the legal procedures of the Toulouse *parlement*.

If an innocent father of a family is delivered into the hands of error, of passion, or of fanaticism; if the accused has no defence except his own virtue; if the arbiters of his life run no other risk in killing him than that of making a mistake; if they can kill with impunity by a simple decree; then a public outcry is raised, every man feels he is in danger, one can see that no one's life is in safety in the face of a tribunal set up for watching over the life of the citizens, and all voices in unison demand vengeance.[36]

Voltaire's primary thesis in the *Traité sur la tolérance*, apart from the specific innocence of Jean Calas, was that the practices of religious intolerance and the persecution of non-believers were unique to Christianity, whereas all other civilisations, past and present, had been tolerant of religious pluralism. 'I say it with horror, but with truth: it is we Christians who have been persecutors, executioners, assassins! And of whom? Of our own brothers. It is we who have destroyed a hundred cities, with the crucifix or the Bible in our hands, and who have not ceased spilling blood and lighting pyres, from the reign of Constantine until our own day.'[37] And yet Jesus himself did not preach intolerance: 'Almost all the words and actions of Jesus Christ called for gentleness, patience, indulgence. I ask if it is tolerance or intolerance which is the divine law? If you want to resemble Jesus Christ, be martyrs, but not public executioners.'[38]

In contrast to the religious persecution of Protestants in France and other Catholic countries, Voltaire cited the relative toleration towards Catholics in the Protestant countries in Europe: Germany, England, Holland. And he proposed that Protestants should be accorded a similar degree of toleration in France as Catholics enjoyed in England: the protection of natural law, the legal validity of Protestant marriage, security for their children and for themselves, the right of inheritance. Voltaire's recipe for legal toleration was quite restrictive: Protestants would not have equal rights with Catholics, they would not be allowed public temples for worship and they would not be allowed to hold municipal offices or receive public honours. Yet even this very modest suggestion made no headway: the legal position of Protestants remained unchanged for another twenty-four years, until the Edict of Tolerance of 1787, nine years after Voltaire's death and two years before the French Revolution.

Voltaire's second thesis, much more insidious in its implications for the Catholic Church, was his Deistic claim that all civilisations really believe in the same virtuous God. One of the key chapters in the *Traité* is a 'Prayer to God', in which Voltaire addresses 'God of all beings, of all worlds, of all times'. The logical implication of his notion of a universal Deism is not just that Christianity is not the only true religion, but rather that many of the specifically Christian elements of Christian doctrine are not true.

In Geneva the *Traité sur la tolérance* was not formally published until November 1763, and at first Voltaire believed it was going very well. In December he wrote to Gabriel Cramer: 'I can see from the success it has had, and from the approval of the ministers, that if you had run off 4,000 copies, you would still not have printed enough. But this work is not a bird of passage, it seems, it is one for all seasons.'[39] He told d'Argental: 'The duc de Choiseul tells me that he is enchanted with it, and so is Mme de Pompadour.'[40] Voltaire was not exaggerating: he had received a letter from Choiseul, who told him: 'Everyone who has read it, tells himself: we must agree that he is right; I've always thought so myself.'[41]

But even if in private the *Traité* was privately admired by Choiseul and Mme de Pompadour, and even if it quickly became an enormous popular success, it was regarded officially as a dangerous and seditious work. Choiseul, a genuine friend of Voltaire, refused officially to accept a single copy, and the state postal service intercepted all the copies sent from Geneva that it could. Voltaire was not surprised, but he admitted that his tactic, of circulating it at court before releasing it to the public, 'may have done more harm than good'.[42]

Voltaire pretended to Damilaville that he was no longer particularly disturbed by the dangers of state censorship: 'In truth, I do not much mind whether the book is condemned or not. Books survive if they can.'[43] But this was just bravado: in January 1764 he wrote to Mme du Deffand: 'These days, no book can enter France by post without being seized by the officials, who for some time have been building up a rather fine library and who will soon become in every sense men of letters. We no longer even dare send books care of ministers.'[44]

Amidst all these alarms, Damilaville's official position gave him the enormously valuable privilege of free access to the postal system, and he was an indispensable go-between in the distribution of Voltaire's controversial works, including the *Traité sur la tolérance*. On 1 February 1764 Voltaire told Damilaville that if he would 'take a dozen copies, and circulate them with [his] usual prudence to people who are safe and reliable', he would be rendering a great service to honest people.[45]

By March 1764 the storm over the *Traité sur la tolérance* seemed to be dying down.[46] Voltaire wrote to d'Alembert:

Today they are quite disposed to allow this book to get out into the public with a certain discretion, and I should like brother Damilaville to let you have half a dozen copies, which you could give to honest people, who would let it be read by other honest people, and the vine of the Lord would be cultivated. This tolerance is an affair of state, and it is certain that those who are at the head of the kingdom are more tolerant than people have ever been; a new generation is rising which has a horror of fanaticism.[47]

A fortnight later Voltaire was again urging Damilaville to get hold of another twenty-odd copies of the *Traité* from Antoine de Sartine, which he could pass around; but it was too early to think of a Paris edition.[48] A month later, however, Voltaire heard that a pirate edition had come out in Paris, and in June that 'lovely editions' had appeared in Liège and in England.[49]

Voltaire's reference to de Sartine throws a tantalising shaft of light on the internal contradictions of the *ancien régime*. Antoine-Raymond-Jean-Gualbert-Gabriel de Sartine had previously been the chief police officer in Paris; in 1763 he was put in charge of the state publishing directorate (Directeur de la Librairie), and was therefore responsible for controlling book publishing, in line with French censorship policy; in particular, it meant that he would repress all dangerous or seditious books. But Voltaire's reference shows that de Sartine was in fact acting as the undercover depository in Paris for copies of the *Traité sur la tolérance*, imported from Geneva. In other words, the *ancien régime* managed to combine a general system of autocratic repression, in this case of censorship, with flexible and ad hoc practices of collusion with people who were outside the system or even opposed to it.

Sartine was not a unique case. Another official who helped Voltaire in the same way was François-Louis-Claude Marin, previously when he had been the royal censor, and from this year (1763) when he was Secrétaire Général de la Librairie. Later, Voltaire was dismayed when he discovered that Marin was betraying him and playing not just a double but a triple game, selling on one of his forbidden manuscripts to a pirate publisher. But Voltaire's influential friends, such as d'Argental, urged him not to make a fuss because Marin might still be useful, even if he was a double-crosser.

Finally, on 4 June 1764, after long legal palavers, the King's Council decided unanimously to annul the verdict and sentence of the Toulouse *parlement* in the Calas case. 'You can imagine how much the quashing of the Toulouse verdict revives me,' Voltaire told Damilaville. 'There we have fanatical judges confounded, and innocence publicly recognised. But what more can we do? Can we get expenses, damages and interest? Can we bring a suit against Master David [de Beaudrigue]? I can see that it is much easier to break a man than to make reparation. I embrace you tenderly.'[50] And to Cramer he wrote: 'The sentence, by which Calas was broken on the wheel, has been quashed unanimously. But what damages will the family have? If Mme de Pompadour were still alive, the poor widow and her daughters would have a pension.'[51]*

After the quashing of the Toulouse verdict, a new trial had to be held, to reach a new verdict; and when Voltaire heard that the retrial was to be held in the Paris appeals court, he was relieved and delighted.

> A much more interesting thing is that the Calas case has been sent to be heard by the *requêtes de l'hôtel*, that is to say, before the same judges as have quashed the Toulouse verdict. This horrible adventure of Calas has opened many people's eyes. The copies of the *Tolérance* have spread throughout the provinces, where people used to be pretty stupid. The scales are falling from people's eyes, the reign of truth is near. My angels, let us bless God.[52]

By August 1764 Voltaire was reasonably confident that the legal review process would eventually end in a total posthumous rehabilitation for Jean Calas.[53] Final victory was delayed for another six months, but on 9 March 1765 forty senior barristers (*maîtres de requêtes*) recommended the posthumous exoneration and rehabilitation of Jean Calas, and their recommendation was formally enacted by the appeals court (*Hôtel des Requêtes*) on 12 March 1765. This was almost exactly three years after the death sentence passed on Calas by the *parlement* of Toulouse on 9 March 1762.

Voltaire was delighted to report that David de Beaudrigue, the Toulouse *capitoul*, had been stripped of his position, but he now called for a ban on the festival staged each year in Toulouse, in which the Catholics celebrated the massacre of several thousand Protestants on 17 May 1562.[54]† At the same time he urged that Mme Calas and her family should receive financial compensation. Fortunately, Louis XV proved

---

* Mme de Pompadour (1721–1764), mistress of Louis XV, and a friend of the *philosophes*, died on 15 April 1764.
† Ten years before the much bigger and more notorious massacre of Saint Bartholomew, 23–24 August 1572.

generous. On 11 April 1765 he gave the Calas family £39,000 from the royal purse: £12,000 to Mme Calas, £6,000 to each of the daughters, £3,000 to each of the sons and £3,000 to Jeanne Viguière, plus £6,000 for legal and travel expenses.[55] Voltaire wrote to Damilaville: 'I forgot all my ills when I learned of the king's generosity; I felt young and vigorous again.'[56]

Later that month a plan was floated in Paris for making a commemorative print of the Calas family, to be sold for their benefit.[57] The print, by Louis de Carmontelle, shows Mme Calas seated in prison, flanked by her two daughters and her servant, Jeanne Viguière, while Gaubert Lavaysse and Pierre Calas read out the final submission by their lawyer, Elie de Beaumont. Thereafter, Voltaire always kept a copy by his bedside.[58]

The Calas affair was not an isolated event: there were two other similar events that occurred at about the same time and which had much in common. The victims were all Protestants; the cases were all about the persecution of Protestants by the Catholic state and the superstitious tensions between the Catholic and Protestant populations; the cases all took place in the Languedoc, in or near Toulouse, a region with a relatively large Protestant population; and they took place in quick succession within a few months during the winter of 1761 to 1762.

The first case, which occurred just before the execution of Jean Calas and before Voltaire had woken up to the whole question, was that of François Rochette, who was hanged for being a Protestant preacher. The other, where Voltaire did campaign, was that of Pierre-Paul Sirven, a Protestant who, like Calas, was accused of murdering one of his own children but who escaped to Geneva for safety just in time; he was condemned in absentia.

One possible explanation of why these three cases all occurred within a few months of each other in the Languedoc starts from the fact that they all took place towards the end of the Seven Years' War, which was widely perceived as a war between Catholic France and Protestant England. France had suffered a series of major defeats at the hands of the English, and French Catholic opinion may have been especially inflamed against French Protestants, as if they were representatives of an enemy power. At all events, there seems to have been an easing of Catholic–Protestant tensions after the Seven Years' War ended in 1763.

In the case of Pierre-Paul Sirven, Voltaire waited until the Calas affair was over. Then, in September 1766, he launched a campaigning pamphlet, *Avis au public sur les parricides imputés aux Calas et aux Sirven*

(Notice to the Public, on the Parricides imputed to Calas and Sirven),[59] ostensibly a recapitulation of the stories of the Calas and Sirven cases and of the reasons for believing their innocence, but really a broader attack on fanaticism and bad jurisprudence in general. But the most immediate purpose of the pamphlet was to appeal for financial help for the Sirven family, who had been languishing in poverty since their escape from Languedoc four years earlier, in 1762. One important consequence of their condemnation for parricide was that their assets had automatically been confiscated by the authorities. Sirven's assets consisted of £19,000, not counting his salary as a master land-surveyor of £1,500 a year.[60]

Voltaire sent obsequious begging letters, together with the *Avis au public*, to many of his rich, noble and powerful friends, mainly those living outside France: Catherine the Great, Frederick the Great, Frederick of Hesse-Cassel and others.[61] Voltaire's petitions seem to have worked: Catherine the Great and others duly coughed up varying amounts of money for the Sirven cause.

But it took another five years, after interminable foot-dragging in the Languedoc, before the *parlement* in Toulouse was finally compelled to give ground; it quashed the old sentence, yet it stopped short of formally acquitting Sirven. With Voltaire's help Sirven launched a new appeal against this verdict, but it was not until two years later, in November 1771, after the *parlement* which had condemned Sirven in 1764 had been replaced by new judges in a new *parlement*, appointed by the new Chancellor, René-Nicolas-Charles-Augustin de Maupeou (the son of René-Charles de Maupeou), that Pierre-Paul Sirven won a complete victory of rehabilitation, including substantial costs and the restoration of his confiscated property.*

It had been a long struggle for justice. As Voltaire commented after his sensational victory over the archaic French penal justice system: 'It took only two hours to condemn this virtuous family to death, nine years to give them justice'.[62]

Voltaire's conversion to ideals of justice as a result of the Calas affair is obviously admirable, but in the case of his own community at Ferney he was still the paternalist: he made the rules, and he thought he was entitled to do so. 'Everyone gets married here', he told d'Argental on March 1764;

---

* René-Charles de Maupeou (1688–1775) was Vice-Chancellor and Keeper of the Seals from 1763, and Chancellor very briefly in 1768. His son René-Nicolas-Charles-Augustin de Maupeou (1714–1792) was Chancellor from 1768.

we are building houses on every side, we are clearing land where nothing has grown since the Flood, we are sprucing things up, we are fertilising a barbarous country; and if we were absolute masters, we should do even better. I detest feudal anarchy, but I am convinced by my own experience that if the poor masters of the châteaux were less dependent on our masters the governors, they could do as much good to France as the governors sometimes do harm, considering that it is quite natural that a master of his château should regard his vassals as his children.[63]

Moreover, Voltaire evidently had some premonition of political turbulence ahead, for in April 1764 he wrote to Bernard-Louis Chauvelin, French ambassador to Turin: 'Everything that I see sows the seeds of a revolution which will come without fail, but which I shall not have the pleasure to witness. The French arrive late for everything, but they do arrive at last; the light has spread so much from man to man, that there will be an outbreak at the first opportunity, and there will be a fine row; the young are lucky, they will see such beautiful things.'[64]

Voltaire does not explain why the revolution will come, or what kind of revolution it will be; his tantalising words appear abruptly in the letter, without context or explanation. We can only guess. But it is surprising that he should imply that the revolution will be beautiful, for elsewhere his views seem strongly anti-revolutionary, and he appeared to believe strongly in the rights and responsibilities of the powerful in a quasi-feudal order.

The Calas and Sirven cases between them marked a turning-point in Voltaire's life, in his attitudes and in his reputation. Previously he would never have thought of campaigning on behalf of some wretched victim of injustice; from now on he was engaged in a succession of such campaigns. Previously he had not thought much about the principles of justice or the interests of society; from now on he was increasingly interested in justice and social reform. Previously he was famous, mainly among high and literary society, as a literary intellectual; from now on he also became famous, among the common people, as a champion of the downtrodden. And of all the 'human rights' cases that Voltaire took on, the Calas affair stands out, for this was the case in which he set the most astonishing precedent, and which marked Voltaire's name in the popular consciousness. When he finally returned to Paris, thirteen years later, ordinary people in the street referred to him as 'The Man of the Calas'.

DAMILAVILLE

1765

TWO MONTHS BEFORE his final victory in the Calas case Voltaire decided to give up Les Délices, and hand it back to its real owners, the Tronchins; from now on he would live wholly at Ferney. On 12 January 1765 he wrote a formal one-sentence letter of renunciation to Jean-Robert Tronchin: 'I surrender to M. Robert Tronchin the house on the territory of Saint-Jean called Les Délices, with all its outhouses, according to the agreement made between us.'[1]

Voltaire gave varying reasons for his decision. To a protestant pastor in Geneva he implied that he was in a financial squeeze: 'It is true, my dear philosopher, that I am giving up Les Délices, the state of my affairs does not allow me to keep it. I have suffered some little set-back in my fortunes.'[2] Voltaire's income depended, to a considerable extent, on the interest on a large loan to the duke of Württemberg, and the previous summer (July 1764) the duke had suspended all payment of interest on money he owed. Since these payments included £28,000 a year to Voltaire, he could reasonably be said to have 'suffered some little set-back' in his fortunes. By February 1765 Voltaire was telling Richelieu: 'I am getting rid of Les Délices because, having the largest part of my assets dependent on M. le duc de Württemberg, and my affairs with him not being completely settled, I have feared to die of hunger as well as of old age.'[3]

To other people Voltaire gave other reasons for leaving Les Délices: he was getting old and feeble, or he was getting blind. But it seems likely that one of the real reasons was that he was becoming disenchanted with

Geneva and the chronic friction with its political institutions: 'I have lost my taste for Les Délices,' he told d'Argental. 'The troubles of Geneva no longer interest me, and having perceived that I have only one body, I have concluded that I did not need two houses; one is quite enough. After all, there are people who are worth more than me, and who have no house at all.'[4]

In short, the carping criticisms of the Geneva authorities, their disapproval of his amateur dramatic entertainments, and their censorship of his controversial writings were becoming increasingly irksome to Voltaire. No doubt his irritation with the Genevans was reciprocated, for when Voltaire did start proceedings for relinquishing his lease on Les Délices, Jean-Robert Tronchin took a position on the terms of the handover that was at best pernickety, at worst decidedly unfriendly.

As it happened, Jean-Robert was no longer based in Lyon, since he had moved in 1762 from Lyon to Paris, on his appointment by the French government as a tax farmer (*fermier général*). For practical purposes, therefore, he had effectively ceased to be Voltaire's personal banker. For a while longer Voltaire continued to do banking business with Ami Camp, Jean-Robert Tronchin's junior partner in the bank in Lyon; but the personal relationship was not as close, and after a time Voltaire made other arrangements. Voltaire remained on friendly terms with François Tronchin, Jean-Robert's brother, a fellow enthusiast for the theatre and a frequent visitor. But his links with the rest of the Tronchin family were weakened a few months later, at the beginning of 1766, when his doctor, Théodore Tronchin, also left for Paris, to set up a fashionable practice there.

Before Voltaire could give up Les Délices, he had to agree surrender terms with the Tronchins. Voltaire had been disqualified, as a notional Catholic, by the property laws in Protestant Geneva from buying Les Délices himself. It had therefore been bought for him by the Tronchin clan, with money provided by Voltaire and with Jean-Robert Tronchin as the front man and official owner. When the property reverted to the Tronchins, they would reimburse him an agreed proportion of the purchase money.

Unfortunately the Tronchins (or perhaps it was just Jean-Robert) insisted on a formal inventory to assess the state of the property; and they appointed Jean-Louis Labat, a Geneva businessman, to act as their representative in the negotiations. He proved very tiresome, and Voltaire complained about him to François Tronchin:

My dear friend, Mme Denis has been a bit annoyed with M. Labat, who has not accepted any arrangement. M. Labat told our representative that if we have changed chimneypieces of plaster into chimneypieces of marble, we must pay the cost of the plaster. That was not the spirit of our deal. As far as I am concerned, I only need your orders to complete everything to your satisfaction.[5]

Labat was extremely difficult over the state of the house and gardens, even demanding compensation for the large terrace which Voltaire had built; Voltaire later described him as 'more Jew than Calvinist'.[6]

By early February Labat was making Voltaire quite angry, as he told François Tronchin: 'It is difficult to say that a house has deteriorated, when it is worth much more when it is handed back than it was worth before.'[7] Voltaire's architect calculated that the value of the improvements he had made, such as the stables, the outhouses, the attics, the servants' rooms, the new kitchen garden, the rainwater barrels, the water pipes etc., outweighed the value of any deteriorations in a ratio of eight to two. 'This should put a stop to any small desire M. Labat may have had to place us in an embarrassing position.'[8]

Just why the Tronchins should have allowed or encouraged Labat's petty trouble-making is a mystery. Ostensibly they were all friends of Voltaire; they were very prosperous patricians; and Voltaire had spent large amounts of money improving the estate, which they were now on the point of recovering much sooner than they might have expected. And yet it even seemed possible at one point that the Tronchins might resort to lawyers and court proceedings against Voltaire.

Fortunately, on 14 February 1765 François Tronchin (who was to be the new occupier of Les Délices, and would therefore be Voltaire's neighbour) decided to end the conflict: 'My dear friend, no judge or arbitrator will decide between you and my brother. For myself, I can tell you that I am ready, on his behalf, to receive Les Délices in whatever state you think fit to hand it over to me, entrusting myself perfectly and solely to you alone and your good niece.'[9]

From this point on the handover went smoothly. On 21 March Voltaire signed a letter of authorisation for Mme Denis to complete the formalities and to accept £38,000 in letters of credit from Jean-Robert and François Tronchin,[10] and on 2 April 1765 Voltaire left Les Délices for good: 'We have carried to Tournay the few pieces of furniture we could find. But we won't be able to avoid being a bit embarrassed this summer, for Ferney will be crowded right up to the roof.'[11]

Ferney would be crowded because Voltaire ran a very open house and would no longer have Les Délices as an overflow hostel for his visitors. These visitors were of every kind and condition: friends and acquaintances from Geneva and Lausanne; people from further afield (Lyon, Dijon, Turin, Paris); casual passers-by who expected to be fed as well as entertained with a sight of the great man; travellers on the Grand Tour, who increasingly treated Voltaire as an essential stop-over on the Tour; spectators for his tragedies; and in later years troops of soldiers who were billeted on him. As he wrote to Mme du Deffand: 'I happen to live in a part of the country situated right in the middle of Europe. All the passers-by come to my house, I have to deal with Germans, with Englishmen, with Italians, even with Frenchmen, whom I shall never see again.'[12]

In March 1764 he wrote, tongue-in-cheek, to his close friend Étienne-Noël Damilaville: 'Today I had a few Englishmen with me. We were fifteen at table, and I noted with pain that none of us was a Christian, apart from me. This happens every day. It is one of my great griefs. You would not believe how far this cursed *philosophie* has corrupted the world. My brother, *écr l'inf*.'[13]

One of Voltaire's most notable English visitors was James Boswell, the future biographer of Samuel Johnson, who solicited an invitation to Ferney in December 1764, during his travels in Europe on the Grand Tour. Boswell was twenty-four at the time, whereas Voltaire was now seventy, and he left a vivid picture of his encounter with the great man.

He was all brilliance. He gave me continued flashes of wit. I got him to speak English, which he does in a degree that made me now and then start up and cry, 'Upon my soul this is astonishing!' When he talked our language he was animated with the soul of a Briton. He had bold flights. He had humour. He had an extravagance; he had a forcible oddity of style that the most comical of our *dramatis personae* could not have exceeded. He swore bloodily, as was the fashion when he was in England. He hummed a ballad; he repeated nonsense. Then he talked of our Constitution with a noble enthusiasm. I was proud to hear this from the mouth of an illustrious Frenchman.

At last we came upon religion. Then did he rage. The company went to supper. Monsieur de Voltaire and I remained in the drawing room with a great Bible before us; and if ever two mortal men disputed with vehemence, we did. He went too far. His aged frame trembled beneath him. He cried, 'Oh, I am very sick; my head turns round', and he let himself gently fall upon an easy chair. He recovered. I resumed our conversation, but changed the tone. I talked to him serious and earnest. I demanded of him an honest confession of his real sentiments. He expressed his veneration – his love – of the Supreme Being, and his entire resignation to the will of Him who is All-wise. He expressed his desire to resemble the Author of Goodness by being good himself. I was moved; I was sorry. I doubted his sincerity. I called to him with emotion, 'Are you sincere? Are you really sincere?' He answered, 'Before God, I am. I suffer much; not as a Christian – but as a man.'[14]

Boswell wrote Voltaire a thank-you letter from Italy, and Voltaire replied in February 1765 in his best English:

My distempers and my bad eyes do not permit me to answer with that celerity and exactness that my duty and my heart require. You seem solicitous about that pretty thing call'd soul. I do protest you I know nothing of it. Nor whether it is, nor what it is, nor what it shall be. Young scholars and priests know all that perfectly. For my part I am but a very ignorant fellow. Let it be what it will, be assured that my soul has a great regard for your own, and if you should turn aside into our deserts, you shall find me (if alive) ready to show you my respect and obsequiousness.[15]

But Voltaire's eyesight was now becoming somewhat impaired, and with it his ability to recognise people. In July 1765 he wrote to Fyot de La Marche, one of his oldest friends:

I must tell you, my dear and respectable magistrate, that two days before receiving your letter, they came to tell me, in my dirty study, at about two o'clock, that there were, in my little pocket-handkerchief of a salon, a dozen Englishmen and Englishwomen, who had come to dinner. I received them in the English manner (*à l'anglaise*), with little fuss, a few arguments about Shakespeare, some vague small-talk. Then, looking at one of the ladies, insofar as my feeble eyes can look, I said to one of my nieces: 'There is an Englishwoman who looks very like M. le président de la Marche; I could take her for his daughter, if I didn't know that she comes from London.' She overheard my remark, and she told me that she did not come from England, but from Lyon, and that she was your niece. M. de Longecour, whom I had taken for an English officer of dragoons, informed me that he was related to you. I suddenly found I was surrounded by your family. My heart trembled; I forgot my Englishmen and Shakespeare and Milton, and even all the ills which weigh me down.[16]

Since Voltaire's hospitality was so often involuntary, exacted by self-appointed visitors, it is not surprising that his manner of providing it was sometimes brusque and cavalier. 'Mme Denis does the honours,' he told d'Argental, 'and I remain in my room, condemned to suffer, or to scribble on paper. Visits would make me waste my time, so I never pay any. The beauties and grand ladies, the peers, even the governors, have got used to my rudeness. It is not in my power to live any other way, thanks to my old age and my illnesses.'[17]

More often Voltaire was less curmudgeonly than he pretends. That same month he wrote to a friend: 'I am not one of those old men who, unable to have any pleasure themselves, do not want others to have pleasure either. I can't digest, but I want others to have good food; I can no longer act, but I want others to act; in short, I want them to do everything that I can no longer do.'[18] Even here Voltaire was putting on a bit of an act: in practice he took a great interest in his food. He wrote to a friend:

If you could have come here this autumn, I should have tried to provide you with good food, simple rather than delicate. There are dishes which are very traditional and very good. You like them, and I should eat them gladly with you, though I admit that my stomach cannot get used to *nouvelle cuisine*. I can't stand sweetbreads (*ris de veau*) swimming in a salty sauce which rises an inch above the little *ris de veau*. I cannot eat a mince combining poultry (*coq d'Inde*) with hare and rabbit, which they want me to take for a single meat. I do not like pigeon *à la crapaudine*,* nor bread without crust. I drink moderately, and I find very strange people who eat without drinking, and who do not even know what they are eating.

I won't even hide from you that I do not at all like private conversation at table, in which one says what one has done yesterday, to one's neighbour, who couldn't care less. I do not disapprove the saying of grace, but that should be the limit, because if one goes any further there is disagreement, and the company becomes an uproar. As for

---

* Pigeon *à la crapaudine* is a recipe in which the pigeon is spread-eagled like a toad (*crapaud*).

cooks, I cannot bear essence of ham, nor too many morels (*morilles*) or mushrooms, nor too much pepper or nutmeg, with which they disguise dishes which are in themselves very healthy, and which I only wish they wouldn't overdress. A supper without too much elaboration, such as I suggest, gives one hope of a sweet and deep sleep, untroubled by any disagreeable dreams.[19]

Voltaire now decided to build more bedrooms at Ferney, in order to be able to accommodate more guests. This would involve dismantling the theatre at Ferney, but that did not matter so much, because Voltaire was now too old to act, or so he said.

On 21 January 1765 he wrote to Richelieu:

I have the honour to tell you that I am so disgusted with the stage that I have got rid of my own. I have dismantled my theatre, and with it I am making bedrooms and ironing-rooms. I find I am so old that I am giving up the vanities of this world. All that remains is for me to become pious, to be able to die with all possible propriety. I have with me, as I think you know, a Jesuit [Father Adam] who was deprived of his right to perform religious services, as soon as they found out he was living in my profane hovel. His bishop has been badly advised, for he risks making me die without confession, a misfortune for which I shall never be consoled.[20]

Richelieu did not approve of the dismantling of the theatre, and said so. In March, Voltaire wrote to a friend:

If M. le Maréchal de Richelieu regrets my little theatre at Ferney, I regret it too; but when a priest can no longer say Mass, there is no point in having an altar. I am losing my sight, I no longer have any voice, I am condemned to suffer, I am starting my seventy-second year, there is no way of amusing the Genevans. Besides, I no longer write tragedies, nor act in any; and in place of a theatre I am building two wings for the château of Ferney.[21]

But it was the disapproval of d'Argental and his wife that most concerned him. He wrote on 25 February: 'My divine angels, consider, I beg you, that I am, whatever they say, in my seventy-second year, that Mme Denis has started her fifty-sixth, and that at this age you must be possessed (*avoir le diable au corps*) to act in a play. It seems to me that one must know how to grow old, and that the flowers of the spring are not made for the winter.'

This letter ends with a deeply felt reproach, oblique but poignant, to d'Argental for never, ever visiting Voltaire in his exile, either at Les Délices or at Ferney. 'I am having built some new cells for visitors to my convent. If you had ever been able to come to Lyon, and from there to Ferney, I should certainly have preserved my theatre.'[22] It recalls Voltaire's sharp but touching complaint, in an earlier letter he wrote to d'Argental in 1755: 'You only love me as a maker of tragedies; I do not want to be loved like that.'[23] Unfortunately, that is a large part of how and why d'Argental loved Voltaire.

In the spring of 1765 Voltaire became quite anxious about a tightening of censorship in France, which he described as 'a very severe inquisition into books',[24] and he suggested that in future d'Argental should send all packages care of the French Resident in Geneva. 'You can let me know you have sent them, with a simple letter, by post, to Wagnière, without any other envelope.'[25] But he soon discovered that his correspondence had been comprehensively penetrated by the state security services, and he wrote to d'Alembert to warn him:

Most letters are opened by the postal service. Yours have been for a long time. A few months ago you wrote to me: 'What would you say of the ministers who are your protectors, or rather your protégés?', and the passage did not sing their praises. A fortnight later, a minister wrote to me: 'I am not ashamed to be your protégé, but … etc.' This minister appeared to be very irritated. It is also said that people have seen a letter from you to the empress of Russia, in which you said: 'France is like a viper, all of it good, except the head'. They also say that you have written in similar terms to the king of Prussia.[26]

The 'very irritated' minister in question was almost certainly Voltaire's friend the duc de Choiseul, the Prime Minister. The implication is that Choiseul had written to Voltaire to warn him that d'Alembert must in future be more careful about what he wrote.

Voltaire reversed his plans to dismantle his theatre barn, when he heard that Mlle Clairon, the star actress at the Comédie Française, might be coming to Geneva. The main reason for Mlle Clairon's visit was her increasing ill health, and the fact that the doctors were forbidding her to undergo the stress of public performance. Voltaire wrote to d'Alembert in late May: 'People would have me believe that Mlle Clairon may come to consult Tronchin; in that case, I shall have to get my theatre rebuilt; but I have become so old that I can no longer play even the role of an old man.'[27] In late June 1765 he wrote to d'Argental: 'As for Mlle Clairon, it seems decided that, despite the severe injunctions of the doctor, she will perhaps deign to display her talents in our marionette theatre, which Mme Denis has had rebuilt almost despite me.'[28]

By the following month Voltaire's theatre was at least partly restored, but on a much smaller scale: the auditorium now held only twenty-five seats.[29] 'I think I told you that Mme Denis had asked me for a large hall for ironing her washing, and I gave her the theatre auditorium; but after having thought about it deeply, she concluded that it would be better to put up with dirty linen, and perform some plays. She has had the theatre rebuilt, and tomorrow we shall put on *Alzire*, while waiting for Mlle Clairon, who perhaps will never come.'[30] But come she did, at the end of July, and stayed for three weeks; but because of the banging and hammering of the masons who were building the new wings at Ferney, and because she was not in good health, she opted to stay near by in the château of Tournay, which Voltaire had handed over on indefinite loan to his publisher Gabriel Cramer, who used it to give gaudy parties.[31]

In August 1765 Voltaire wrote to d'Argental:

Mlle Clairon will perform in my little theatre at Ferney, which we have restored, as you wanted. This is against the express orders of Dr Tronchin, who says he will not answer for her life if she makes any efforts, and who absolutely insists that she give up acting in tragedies. So she has been obliged to promise him that she would never go back on the stage in Paris, which would put strains on her voice, and require vigorous acting, which would inevitably make her succumb.[32]

Two days later, they put on *Oreste* in Voltaire's rehabilitated theatre, with Mlle Clairon in the lead role. After the show Voltaire hurried back to his study to describe the event: 'I have just come from the play, I have been in heaven for the past two hours. There have been many great talents in France, but none in her line has reached her degree of perfection. I am beside myself. I am sure that she has never made a stronger impression than in my primitive hovel, where I had gathered about 150 people, most of them worthy to hear her.'[33] (Given the tiny size of the restored auditorium, most of the audience must have been standing, or perhaps only a small minority were admitted to the show.)

Mlle Clairon had once been one of the many mistresses of Richelieu, and in a letter to him Voltaire adopted a suggestively leering tone. 'I received Mlle Clairon, as you wished, and as she deserved. She was honoured, and fêted, and serenaded. All that was missing was the little attention with which you honoured her a few years ago; but there is no way that I could be as polite as you. I can assure you that she would have been badly caught out if she had expected the same civilities from me.'[34]

Mlle Clairon's visit inevitably perturbed Voltaire's normal routine, but it also disturbed his ideas on drama and acting.

> Mlle Clairon's stay has a bit upset me. I knew nothing of her merit; I had no idea that acting could be so animated and so perfect. I had become accustomed to the cold declamation of our cold theatres, and I had only ever seen actors reciting verses to other actors, in a little circle surrounded by dandies. Mlle Clairon told me that she had never explored the range of acting which is possible on stage, until M. le comte de Lauraguais had restored, to a fairly ungrateful public, with the gift of his money, the freedom of the theatre and the beauty of the spectacle.[35]

Voltaire harped with increasing frequency on the coldness of theatre in France and on the contrast with the more lively, but yet unbearably vulgar, English theatre. In 1764 he wrote: 'The English, who come here in great numbers, say that all our tragedies are icy; there may be something in it; but theirs are diabolical.'[36] And yet Voltaire knew that he was becoming out of date. In late 1766 he wrote to an acquaintance: 'I am very little suited to decide, in my retirement, whether a play is likely to be successful in Paris. They say that the taste of the public has completely changed. Mine, which hasn't, is too superannuated and out of fashion.'[37]

Voltaire still adhered to the austere seventeenth-century ideals of a noble and high-minded theatre, and yet he was increasingly aware that it lacked vitality. In 1766 he wrote to Thieriot: 'I was becoming tired of always seeing princes with princes, and of hearing nothing but talk of thrones and politics. I thought that one could give a broader scope to the picture of nature, and that with a bit of art one could put on stage the lowest forms of life with the most elevated. This is a very fertile field, which others, more capable than me, will open up.'[38] A few days later he wrote in a similar vein: 'I thought it would be agreeable to put on the same tragic stage, a princess darning her shirts, and people with no shirt at all. It seemed to me that all the conditions of life could be treated without vulgarity.'³⁹ Paradoxically, this was precisely what Shakespeare had done; but when he did it, Voltaire did not like the result.

After Mlle Clairon went back to Paris on 20 August 1765, Étienne-Noël Damilaville came to stay. This was, in fact, the first time that Voltaire and Damilaville had met: for the first five years their friendship was based exclusively on their correspondence. Earlier in the year Damilaville had been suffering from a worryingly obstinate sore throat, and in June Voltaire had invited him to come to Ferney, so as to consult Dr Tronchin. 'Dr Tronchin says you should continue the régime which he prescribed. If it is possible that the care you owe your health should bring you to Geneva, and that I should have the pleasure of embracing you and of opening my heart to you, I should think the end of my life very happy.'⁴⁰

By July, Voltaire was increasingly anxious for Damilaville to visit.

My dear friend, your sore throat worries me a lot. But I should be doubly consoled by the pleasure of embracing you, and by the hope that Tronchin would cure you. My cottage is nothing but a desolate hovel which has been overturned by the masons. But if I could be sure of welcoming you, I should get them to make you a cell in my little convent. You will be lodged, well or ill, my dear friend, and we shall take the greatest care of you.⁴¹

By the end of August 1765 Damilaville had arrived at Ferney, as Voltaire told Thieriot: 'My old friend, the visit of Mlle Clairon, and my health which gets worse by the day, have not allowed me to write to you. I am enjoying the real satisfaction of having M. Damilaville in my hermitage. He is a real philosopher; he's not like Rousseau, who does not even know how to put on the mask of philosophy.'⁴² In September, Voltaire described Damilaville as 'a friend with whom I should like to pass the rest of my life', and he wrote to d'Alembert: 'I love my *philosophe* Damilaville more and more every day; Tronchin has given him a fever to make him better. I hope he will stay a long time in his care, and I really wish you would come and join him.'⁴³

A fortnight later, Damilaville still had not left for Paris. Voltaire wrote to Nicolas-Claude Thieriot:

My old friend, I am starting to be as lazy as you. I was counting on writing to you by M. Damilaville; happily, he has from day to day postponed his return to Paris. Two things charm me in this

M. Damilaville, his reason and his virtue. Why must a man of his merit languish in the tax collector's office of the *Vingtième?* It's a trade which is quite unworthy of him.[44]

But on 8 October 1765, after having been, as Voltaire says, 'for a few months the consolation of my life',[45] Damilaville left Ferney to return to Paris. Voltaire wrote to him in Paris on 16 October:

I passed lovely days with you, my dear brother; I have regrets at your departure, but I also have the sweetness of my memories, and the hope of seeing you again before I die. What would prevent you, for example, from coming back one day? You have won over every heart. I am beginning to read today the Italian book *Of Crimes and Punishments* [by Cesare Beccaria]. One can tell at a glance that it is philosophical; the author is a brother. Adieu, you who will always be mine, adieu, my dear friend, perish the infamous prejudices which dishonour and brutalise human nature, long live reason. Adieu once again.[46]

Damilaville's sore throat still did not get better, and Voltaire wrote to him on 25 November: 'Your sore throat and your loss of weight displease me greatly. You know how interested I am in your well-being and your long-being. Tronchin does not cure everybody. Whatever he does, my dear friend, nature knows more than medicine. Philosophy teaches us to submit to the one and do without the other. That's the position I have adopted.' And in December:

My dear friend, I must tell you: if you are unwell, I am deeply saddened. Tronchin will not cure either you or me. But you will cure yourself by your diet: it is the true medicine in all ordinary cases. It is possible, however, that since the swelling in your throat has not suppurated, the infection (*l'humeur*) may have spread to the blood; in that case you would be obliged to add to your diet some gentle laxatives (*détersifs*). Perhaps a little sage with a bit of milk would do you good. The foods and the drinks which can be used as remedies are the only things which have kept me alive; and I know no doctor who is better than experience.[47]

Damilaville's sore throat did not get better, for it was really cancer of the throat. He lived for another three years and died towards the end of 1768. Voltaire suffered acutely in spirit with him, though his cynical wit never deserted him. In September 1768 he wrote to Mme Denis (who was at that time in Paris):

> I should not be surprised if Tronchin were mistaken on Damilaville. He had condemned Daumart to die in two days, but there he is, for his misfortune, still alive nine years later. When Tronchin is mistaken, he has the glory to be more mistaken than all his colleagues; no one makes greater strides on the road of error; sometimes he hits the mark, but when he goes astray, it is by a hundred leagues.[48]

Charles-Hyacinthe Daumart, a young cousin of Voltaire, had been injured in a riding accident in 1758, when he was seventeen. The following year Théodore Tronchin operated on his legs, and at the time Voltaire thought he had performed 'a miracle'.[49] But after a few weeks Daumart was still limping, and a year later, in 1760, he could no longer walk, even with crutches. In 1761 Voltaire consulted another distinguished doctor, but by now Daumart was confined to his bed and completely paralysed.[50]

Voltaire's comments on the effects of Théodore Tronchin's medical treatment were now becoming increasingly caustic. He wrote to his other niece, Mme Fontaine: 'Daumart has been in bed for the past five months without being able to move. In your case, Tronchin cured you, because he did nothing. But in Daumart's case, he did something, and this poor boy will die of it, or else his life will be worse than death.'[51] A year later Daumart was still totally paralysed, and Voltaire no longer hoped that Théodore Tronchin would be able to help him. By 1763 Daumart was so paralysed that he could no longer move any part of his body and was expected to remain paralysed for the rest of his life.[52]

The rest of Daumart's life was not long, for he died in 1769, at the age of twenty-eight. But the point of the story of the unhappy Daumart is not just that medical science in the eighteenth century was primitive, nor that Théodore Tronchin's reputation may have been inflated, but that Voltaire cared for Daumart throughout his last ten years of sickness and paralysis, and that he was obviously deeply upset by Daumart's sufferings. Here is his testimony to Daumart, in 1764, in a letter to Mme du Deffand, the blind literary hostess, who lived in a fine apartment inside the Convent of Saint Joseph in Paris.

> I agree with you that life is very short, and fairly unhappy; but I must tell you that I have in my house a 23-year-old relative, handsome,

well built, vigorous, and here is what happened to him.

One day while hunting he fell from his horse, he bruised his thigh a bit, they made a little incision, and there he is, paralysed for the rest of his days; not paralysed in part of his body, but so paralysed that he does not have the use of any of his limbs, he cannot raise his head, with the complete certainty that he can never have the least relief; he is accustomed to his state, and he is madly in love with life.

Farewell, Madame, let us bear our life, which is not much, let us not fear death, which is nothing at all, and please believe that my only grief is not to be able to talk with you.[53]

By late November 1768 Voltaire knew that Damilaville's end was near. He told Mme Denis: 'The state of Damilaville overwhelms me with grief. Here is an irreparable loss for people who think. I shall never be consoled.'[54]

On 13 December 1768 Étienne-Noël Damilaville died in great pain, or as Voltaire put it, in 'an abominable trial'.[55] In late January 1769 Voltaire wrote to Thieriot:

I have lost my dear Damilaville, whose firm and courageous friendship had long been my consolation. He never sacrificed his friendship to the malice of those who would impose themselves on the world. He was brave, even with those people on whom his fortune depended. I cannot regret him too much, and my only hope in my last days is to find him again in you.[56]

Voltaire never ceased to mourn Damilaville, and with a lasting intensity that he never expressed for any of his other friends. Eight years after Damilaville's death, in 1776, when he was eighty-two, Voltaire wrote to Denis Diderot, who had never been a close friend of his but who had been one of Damilaville's dearest friends:

I once had a friend, who was also your friend, and who never let me lack my daily bread in my solitude. No one has replaced him, and I am dying of hunger. This friend knew that we [i.e., Voltaire and Diderot] were not so far apart, and that all it needed was a conversation for us to understand each other; but one can't find just anywhere people one can talk to.[57]

BECCARIA
1765–1766

AFTER 1765–66 VOLTAIRE started to direct his critical gaze not just at specific instances where the penal justice system had miscarried but at the defects of the penal justice system itself.

The central problem of the criminal judicial system in France, and in many other European countries, was that the rationale of the criminal law was confused with the rationale of social hierarchy, and both were confused with the rationale of religious dogma. Equality before the law was unknown, both socially and geographically; an offence against a nobleman was more severely punished than an offence against a common person, and some laws only applied to ordinary commoners, not to nobles or churchmen. Moreover, the law in one part of France was likely to be quite different, for traditional reasons, from that in another part. As Voltaire frequently commented, as one travelled across France, the law changed as often as one changed horses.[1]

In 1670 Colbert had made an attempt at a codification of French criminal law; but it was still pervaded by theology and religious bigotry, so that offences against society or one's fellow-man were confused with offences against God, and the punishment of such offences became intertwined with confession to a priest and expiation before God. Criminal prosecution of witches and sorcerers had largely disappeared by the mid-eighteenth century, but these imaginary offences remained on the French statute book until the Revolution. The death penalty, and bodily mutilations, were common punishments, even for many kinds of quite trivial crime, and in France the death penalty came in many versions:

burning alive at the stake, quartering, breaking on the wheel, hanging, strangling and beheading.

Moreover, criminal cases were tried as if they were theological Inquisition cases and depended heavily on the use of torture, ostensibly in order to compel the criminal to reveal his accomplices, in reality to try to force a confession out of him. As we have seen, Jean Calas was condemned to death without any proof of his guilt, and even as they were torturing him to death, the Church-and-state authorities were still attempting to extract a confession out of him. The methods of torture varied from place to place. In Rouen the *question* took the form of a thumb-screw, or even a double thumb-screw, or a vice for crushing a leg; in Brittany the victim's bare feet were slowly pushed towards a fire; in Besançon the 'patient' had his arms tied behind his back and then a rope was fixed to his arms, and he was dragged upwards into the air by a pulley.[2]

Voltaire played a key role in opening up the critique of the defects of the French criminal justice system, and he started to do so systemically from 1765 onwards. But we should not over-simplify. Many earlier political writers in Europe, from Montaigne to Grotius, from Hobbes to Locke, had criticised the defects of various aspects of received judicial practices. In Voltaire's own lifetime a number of powerful critiques of defects in the justice system in France had been published before he really got on to the subject, including by Montesquieu, in his *Lettres persanes* (1721) and his *De l'Esprit des Lois* (1748), and by Helvetius in his *L'Esprit* (1758), as well as by the *encyclopédistes*.

Voltaire himself had made many critical comments, well before 1765, about various aspects of the French judicial system. He was scathing about the practice by which a judge's seat on the bench could be bought and sold, and could be passed down from father to son as a hereditary possession. He was even more scathing about the bizarre French legal calculus which claimed that there could be mathematical fractions of a proof, 'so that four hearsays on one side, and eight popular rumours on the other, add up to two complete proofs, equal to two eyewitnesses.'[3] He had denounced the secrecy of French judicial processes, which was used by the Toulouse *parlement* to obstruct his campaign for the revision of the Calas and Sirven cases. He believed that punishments should be proportional to crimes, and that there should be fewer death penalties. And he systematically contrasted the inquisitorial, priest-ridden, secretive, inconsistent and arbitrary system in France, with the more open, non-clerical and adversarial system in England.[4] In 1763, in the *Traité sur la tolérance*, Voltaire had opened a new social and moral critique, by arguing the connection between impartial justice in the law courts and tolerance and pluralism in society. But it was not until the autumn of 1765, by which time he had launched his campaign on the Sirven scandal, that Voltaire really started to address the systemic problems of the French penal justice system.

This comes out clearly in a key letter written in September 1765 to Élie de Beaumont, who had been his lead lawyer in the Calas case, and who was now re-enlisted in the Sirven case.

> You are undertaking, Sir, a task worthy of you, in trying to reform the criminal jurisprudence. It is certain that the French system sets too little store by the life of men. It is assumed, apparently, that the condemned, if properly confessed, go straight to paradise. England is almost the only place I know where the laws seem designed more for sparing the guilty than for sacrificing the innocent. Everywhere else the criminal procedure is completely arbitrary.
>
> The king of Prussia has made a little code entitled the Code according to Reason, as if our laws were made according to madness. The best usage established in Prussia, as in the whole of Germany, is that no one is executed without the express permission of the sovereign. This custom used formerly to be established in France. But now they break a man on the wheel just like that, at the drop of a hat,* even before the neighbourhood has been informed; and the most pardonable cases slip past the humanity of the sovereign.[5]

Voltaire's interest in the general question of penal reform was further aroused the following month, in October 1765 when, as we saw in Chapter 26, he told Damilaville that he had started reading the Italian book *On Crimes and Punishments*.[6] The author, Cesare Bonesana, marchese de Beccaria, was a young Milanese nobleman, born in 1738, who had studied law at Pavia and then turned to journalism and the study of the French *philosophes*. In 1761, when he was twenty-three, he became friendly with the brothers Pietro and Alessandro Verri, whose home in Milan was a centre of literary and philosophical study and debate. Beccaria was both shy and lazy, and Pietro Verri encouraged him to write his first book, on currency reform, which appeared in 1762; he also played a large part in persuading him, in 1763, when he was just twenty-five, to turn to the study of the principles of penal justice.

By the end of 1763 Beccaria had completed this new book, *Dei delitti*

---

* *de broc en bouche*, literally, 'from the spit to the mouth'.

e delle pene (*On Crimes and Punishments*), advocating a root-and-branch rethink of penal principles on systematic humanitarian, rational and utilitarian lines. It was to prove a landmark in the history of penal reform. The first edition, published anonymously in January 1764, was immediately immensely successful and was quickly followed by a second edition that year and a third in 1765. By 1766 it had been through six editions in Italian. It also attracted international attention, notably among the French *philosophes*.

Considering its pioneering place in the history of penal reform, *On Crimes and Punishments* is a surprisingly short and simple book: it is barely eighty pages long, and its forty-seven chapters are correspondingly brief. Some of Beccaria's key principles are worth summarising, however briefly.

- the law should promote the greatest happiness of the greatest number;
- justice is part of the social contract;
- since the law's only purpose is the preservation of the social contract, it can have no business punishing offences against God: 'What insect will dare to supplement divine justice?'
- punishments should be prescribed by law, not by judges;
- all punishments are unjust if they are more severe than is necessary to preserve the social contract;
- laws should apply equally to all, whether noble or commoner;
- there must be a proportion between crimes and punishments;
- the most serious crimes, deserving the most serious punishments, are those which most damage society;
- if large and small offences carry the same severe punishments, men will not be deterred from large offences;
- the purpose of punishment is not to inflict pain but to deter future offences;
- the accused should be given the time and the means to conduct his defence;
- torture is wrong; for either a man is proved guilty, in which case he does not deserve anything except the punishment prescribed by law; or else he is not proved guilty, in which case there is no basis for torturing him;
- punishment should not be cruel, but it should be prompt and inevitable; the prompter and more certain the punishment, the greater the deterrent effect;

- punishments should be as mild as possible;
- crimes of violence should be punished by corporal penalties; the rich should not be able to avoid it by paying a fine instead; thefts should be punished by fines;
- there is no case for capital punishment, except where a citizen threatens the security of the state.[7]

At the end of his book Beccaria sums up his conclusions in one lapidary sentence: 'In order that any punishment should not be an act of violence committed by one person or many against a private citizen, it is essential that it should be public, prompt, necessary, the minimum possible under the given circumstances, proportionate to the crimes and established by law.'[8]

Not all of Beccaria's ideas were completely new; he openly acknowledged his debt to other writers, notably Montesquieu. Torture was already widely criticised and had been abolished in England, Prussia and Sweden. The principle of proportionality between crime and punishment was frequently recognised. The notion of the social contract as the basis for law could be traced to Hobbes and Rousseau. Many had long urged the importance of clarity in the law and of openness in judicial procedures.

What made Beccaria's book original was its shortness and its simplicity, and the comprehensive coherence of his vision of a non-religious, moderate, open, social utilitarian system of criminal justice. Naturally it provoked furious denunciations from the Church, the lawyers and the defenders of the status quo, but it appealed enormously to the *philosophes* and other modernisers.

Since Voltaire was reading Beccaria's book in the autumn of 1765, he must have been reading it in Italian, presumably in the third edition, eighteen months after the book was first published. Voltaire was normally ultra-quick to pick up the latest literary novelties, and he had already corresponded with Beccaria about his earlier book on monetary reform, soon after its publication in 1762,[9] so it is surprising that it took him so long to get round to the new work, which had for some time been making waves not just in Italy but in several European countries. Perhaps Voltaire had been too busy with his theatre and with Mlle Clairon; perhaps he had been too busy with the Calas and Sirven cases; perhaps he had been too busy with Damilaville. Or perhaps he was just getting on; a few years later he admitted that he no longer read new books.

D'Alembert got hold of *Dei delitti e delle pene* a bit sooner than Voltaire, and in June 1765 he lent a copy to the abbé André Morellet, a friend and fellow *philosophe*, and urged him to translate it into French. Morellet published his translation (incorporating some rearrangement of Beccaria's chapters) in late December 1765, and on 3 January 1766 he sent a copy to Beccaria and invited him to come to France: 'I dare assure you, Sir, that its success is universal. I am particularly charged to convey the thanks and the compliments of M. Diderot, of M. Helvetius and of M. de Buffon. In truth, Sir, if your affairs and your situation allow you to travel to France, you really must come here and receive the thanks and the marks of esteem which you have deserved.'[10] The French translation was even more successful than the original Italian: seven editions in six months. Later that year Beccaria did visit Paris at the invitation of the *philosophes*, but he was so shy, so timid and so homesick, and possibly so love-sick for his young wife at home in Milan, that he returned to Milan as soon as he decently could. Having become famous throughout Europe, he spent the rest of his life in relative obscurity as an academic and civil servant.

Voltaire admired Morellet's translation, and it prompted him to think of writing something about the Beccaria book himself. By September he had finished it, and he published it anonymously as a *Commentaire sur le livre Des délits et des peines, par un avocat de province*.[11] Voltaire's authorship was quickly known, and his *Commentaire* gave substantial new impetus to the international renown of Beccaria. Later in the eighteenth century, in Italy, France, England and Germany, the two books were often published together in the same volume.

If the truth be told, however, Voltaire's is rather an odd little book, which wanders all over the place. In the first place, it is not really a commentary on Beccaria at all, nor does Voltaire follow Beccaria's structure. Where Beccaria is cool, systematic and analytical, Voltaire is polemical, discursive, historical, anecdotal and passionate. The fact is that Voltaire was not particularly suited to systematic and dispassionate analysis, and he had no interest in disguising, behind a cloak of intellectual suavity, his indignation at the barbarities of the French judicial system.

On some important points Voltaire is less radical than Beccaria. Beccaria opposed all use of torture: in the last resort, Voltaire would keep it as a way of discovering the identities of the accomplices of convicted regicides and parricides. Beccaria denied any legitimacy to capital punishment, unless the state was in jeopardy; Voltaire went no further than to argue that the death penalty should be replaced as far as possible by forced labour, and that no execution should be carried out unless explicitly confirmed by the king. On the other hand, Voltaire's *Commentaire* is a powerful complement to *Dei delitti e delle pene*; for whereas Beccaria mainly restricted himself to the discussion of the general principles of a just penal system, Voltaire vigorously attacked some of the worst procedures customary in French judicial practice. Here is a passage from his chapter 'On Criminal Procedure':

> If one day humane laws should soften some over-rigorous practices in France, perhaps they will reform the rules of procedure.
>
> Among the Romans, witnesses were heard publicly, in the presence of the accused, who could reply to them and question them himself. This procedure was noble and frank, it breathed Roman magnanimity. With us, everything takes place in secret. A single judge, with his clerk, hears each witness one after another. The witnesses are, usually, people from the dregs of society, and the judge, shut up with them, can make them say anything he wants. These witnesses are heard a second time, still in secret, which is called 'review' (*récolement*). But if, after this review, they withdraw their testimony, or change it in important respects, they are punished as false witnesses. So that when a simple man, who does not know how to express himself but has an upright heart, and recalls that he has said too much or too little, or that the judge misunderstood him, withdraws what he said for reasons of justice, he is punished as a criminal, and so he is often compelled to stand by his false testimony, simply for fear of being treated as a false witness.[12]

Even before writing his *Commentaire* on Beccaria, and before the final resolution of the Calas case, Voltaire was hard at work finalising one of his most controversial works, his *Dictionnaire philosophique portatif*, which he started to circulate in July 1764. He claimed that it was intended to be a brisker and briefer alternative to the *Encyclopédie*, but its most important characteristic, compared with the *Encyclopédie*, was not just its witty brevity, but its overt anti-clericalism. It did not even attempt a factual survey of knowledge, like the *Encyclopédie*, and the majority of its articles dealt, directly or indirectly, with questions of morality and of society, and in particular with questions relating to Christianity, usually in sceptical or derisory terms. Take, for example, the entry on 'Christianity':

Several scholars have expressed surprise not to find anywhere in the works of the historian Josephus any trace of Jesus Christ. Josephus was of priestly descent, a relative of the queen Mariamne, wife of Herod; he goes in great detail into all the acts of this prince; and yet he does not say a word about the life or death of Jesus; and this historian, who does not hide any of the cruelties of Herod, does not speak of the massacre of the infants.

Or again, the entry on 'Tolerance':

Of all religions, the Christian religion is no doubt the one which should inspire the most tolerance; and yet, up till now, the Christians have been the most intolerant of all men. It would be easy to show how far the Christian religion of today differs from the religion that Jesus practised. If we really look closely, the Catholic religion, apostolic and Roman is, in all its ceremonies and all its doctrines, the opposite of the religion of Jesus. If it were permitted to reason coherently about religion, it is clear that we should all become Jews, because Jesus Christ our Saviour was born a Jew, lived as a Jew and died as a Jew, and he said explicitly that he was accomplishing, that he was fulfilling, the Jewish religion.

Or the entry on 'Torture':

The judge in the criminal court does not regard as a human being a man whom they bring to him haggard, pale, defeated, eyes downcast, the beard long and dirty, covered with the vermin that gnawed at him in his cell. He gives himself the pleasure of applying the great and the little torture, in the presence of a doctor who takes his pulse, up to the point where he could be in danger of death, after which they start again; as they say, 'It helps to pass an hour or two'.

The grave magistrate who has bought, for a certain amount of money, the right to carry out these experiments on his fellow-man, will tell his wife at dinner what happened that morning. The first time Madame was revolted; the second she acquired a taste for it, for after all women are curious; and then the first thing she says to him when he comes home in his judicial robes is: 'My little heart, haven't you had the question applied to anyone today?' The French, who pass, I do not know why, for a very humane people, are astonished that the English, who have had the inhumanity to take from us the whole of Canada, should have given up the pleasure of applying the question.[13]

Voltaire published the *Dictionnaire philosophique* anonymously, in Geneva, in July 1764; it quickly got into trouble with the authorities in several European capitals, and just as quickly became a best-seller. He brought out a second edition that autumn, a new and expanded edition in 1765, with two printings that year, another expanded edition in two volumes, a sixth expanded edition in two volumes in 1767, and yet another edition in two volumes in 1769, reissued twice in 1770, once more in 1773 and twice again in 1776. In parallel, he also launched another analogous dictionary work called *Questions sur l'Encyclopédie*, which he brought out in nine volumes in 1770–72.

Voltaire vigorously and repeatedly denied that he had anything to do with what he describes as 'this abominable little dictionary, a work of Satan',[14] but his denials fooled no one. The French Prime Minister, the duc de Choiseul, wrote to him: 'Why in the devil's name are you agitating so much, you Swiss marmot? No one says anything to you, and certainly no one wants to do you any harm; you disavow the book even though no one has spoken to you about it, so much the better; but you will never persuade me that it is not by you.'[15]

When the Geneva authorities moved to censor the *Dictionnaire*, very shortly after publication, Voltaire at first made light of the matter. He wrote to Damilaville, all wide-eyed innocence: 'It's a work which seems to me pretty strong. I had it bought for me in Geneva, there were only two copies. The consistory of the pedantic priests brought it before the magistrates, so then the booksellers ordered many more copies. The magistrates read it with edification, and the priests were quite astonished to see that something which would have been burned thirty years ago, is today well received by everybody.'[16] In fact, the Geneva authorities brought a prosecution against the book, and in late September it was publicly lacerated and burned by the public executioner. But in private the ruling patricians let Voltaire know that he should not be too worried; they still wanted to be on good terms with him.[17]

Despite the reassurances of Choiseul, Voltaire learned that there was a serious danger that the *Dictionnaire philosophique* might be burned by order of the Paris *parlement*. He wrote to d'Alembert in October 1764: 'I have just learned that storms are brewing against the *Portatif*. The situation is very serious.'[18] The *Portatif* was indeed burned in Paris, in the spring of the following year, 1765, and its condemnation hung like a sword over Voltaire's head for many years to come.

Although Voltaire was extremely critical of many aspects of French judicial practice, he never joined those who opposed all capital punishments. In 1770, when he was seventy-six, Louis Philipon de la Madelaine sent him the text of a 'Discourse on the Necessity and the Means of Suppressing Capital Punishment'.[19] Voltaire agreed that capital punishment should be limited, but his reply was cautious and equivocal:

> Sir: You have sent me a work dictated by humanity and eloquence. It has never been better proved that judges must start by being men, that the punishments of the evil-doers must be useful to society, and that a hanged man is no good to anyone. Undoubtedly, premeditated murderers, parricides, incendiaries, deserve a death whose apparatus must be frightful. I should without regret have condemned Ravaillac to be quartered; but I should not have imposed the same torment on a man who had not wanted, nor been able, to kill his prince, and who must obviously have been mad. It seems to me diabolical to have shot Admiral Byng for not having killed enough Frenchmen.[20]

François Ravaillac's assassination of Henri IV in 1610 was, for Voltaire, a monstrous crime, since it was a mortal blow against the king's attempt to reconcile Catholics and Protestants in France; it therefore deserved the most monstrous punishment. By contrast, it seems from the second half of this passage that Voltaire had now changed his mind about Damiens and his deranged and half-hearted attempt on the life of Louis XV in 1757. At the time he felt nothing but indignant indifference to Damiens's extreme agony; now he was having second thoughts about the utility of imposing those barbaric sufferings on a man who was not responsible for his acts. Voltaire had not moved anything like as far as Beccaria on the question of capital punishment; but to the extent that he had changed his mind, it was partly as a result of having thought about these things over a long life and partly, no doubt, as a result of reading *Dei delitti e delle pene*.

CHEVALIER DE LA BARRE
1765–1768

EVEN BEFORE THE PUBLICATION of Beccaria's *Dei delitti e delle pene*, Voltaire had become convinced that the Calas and Sirven cases were symptoms of general and systemic defects in the French judicial system. This conviction was massively reinforced, in 1766, the year following the rehabilitation of Jean Calas and Voltaire's reading of Beccaria, by the eruption in quick succession of two more major judicial miscarriages: the trial and execution in May 1766 of Thomas Arthur Lally-Tollendal, ostensibly for offences including embezzlement and treason; and the trial and execution in July 1766 of Jean François Lefèvre, chevalier de La Barre, for blasphemy and sacrilege.

Thomas Arthur, Count Lally-Tollendal (1702–66) was a nobleman of Irish descent, whose family had followed James II into exile in France. He pursued a brilliant career as a French army officer, and he was sent to India early in the Seven Years' War to protect the interests of the French India Company (Compagnie Française des Indes) against the English. Voltaire had long known Lally-Tollendal personally, and knew that he was violent, difficult and headstrong; and since Voltaire had invested money in the Compagnie, he had worried at the time that the appointment of 'this Irish hothead' might not be good for the shareholders and might even jeopardise his own income from the company, currently running at some £20,000 a year.[1]

In India, Lally-Tollendal at first had some military successes against the English, but victories soon gave way to defeats. In January 1760 he had to fall back on the French-controlled town of Pondicherry, where he was besieged. There he quarrelled with the local company managers, with his own officers and with the leaders of the town. A year later, in January 1761, the town council decided to capitulate; Lally-Tollendal was taken prisoner by the English, together with over 2,000 officers and men of the French army. In September he was transferred to England.

In his absence everyone blamed Lally-Tollendal for the defeat, and French popular opinion, overheated by the hope of punishing a scapegoat for the French defeat in India, was clamouring for a trial. Lally-Tollendal persuaded the British authorities to let him return to France on parole to defend his honour, and in November 1762 he did return. He was imprisoned in the Bastille, without being questioned, without knowing exactly what he was charged with, or even whether he would be charged. There he languished for the next seventeen months, until the death, early in 1764, of a certain Father Lavaur, formerly father superior of the Jesuits in Pondicherry at the time of the siege. Among his personal effects he left a report cataloguing a series of complaints against Lally-Tollendal, including embezzlement and treason (*lèse-majesté*); its publication prompted the French Attorney-General Omer Joly de Fleury (1715–1810) to bring formal charges.

Joly de Fleury, from a powerful family of parliamentarians, was a die-hard enemy of the Enlightenment and the *philosophes*, and an old opponent of Voltaire. It was he who had pronounced the formal denunciation of *Candide* in February 1759, which he described as a 'scandalous brochure'. In the same year he called for a ban on the printing of the *Encyclopédie*. In 1763 he proposed a *parlement* regulation forbidding inoculation against smallpox. In 1765 he demanded and secured the condemnation by the *parlement* of Voltaire's *Dictionnaire philosophique*. In short, he was an out-and-out reactionary, and Voltaire never missed an opportunity to express his angry derision of this man, whom he described as neither *Homère* ('Homeric') nor *joli* ('pretty') nor *fleuri* ('flowery').

When Lally-Tollendal's trial began in April 1764, he had still not received any documentation of the charges, and he was not allowed to have a lawyer to defend him. Throughout the trial, which lasted two years, Lally-Tollendal protested his innocence and made counter-accusations against his accusers with a violence and intemperance that probably damaged his case. On 6 May 1766 he was sentenced to death for having 'betrayed the interests of the king, of the state, and of the Compagnie des Indes; for abuse of authority, vexations and exactions'.[2] Three days later, after a failed attempt at suicide in prison, Lally-Tollendal was gagged, to prevent him protesting his innocence, and hustled in a garbage cart to the scaffold on the place de la Grève.* The executioner's first blow only sliced open Lally-Tollendal's skull; he did not succeed in beheading him until the second attempt.[3]

Voltaire heard of Lally-Tollendal's execution a few days later, and on 17 May 1766 he wrote to Damilaville: 'I knew Lally-Tollendal for an absurd man, violent, ambitious, capable of pillage and abuse of power; but I should be astonished if he was a traitor.'[4] Ten days later he wrote to another friend: 'I have just been reading up the tragedy of poor Lally. I can easily see that Lally got himself detested by all the officers and all the inhabitants of Pondicherry, but in all the submissions to the trial there is no appearance of embezzlement, nor of treason. There must have been proofs against him which have not been revealed in any of the briefs.'[5]

At the end of May Voltaire wrote again to Damilaville: 'I have seen the briefs for and against the unfortunate Lally-Tollendal. I cannot find anything in them but vague insults; the substance of the charge is apparently in the questioning, which still remains secret. In France no reasons are given for the verdict or sentence, so the public is never informed.'[6] On the same day he wrote to Alexandre d'Hornoy, the lawyer son of his younger niece: 'I do not doubt but that he was legitimately condemned; but I do not see for what. There must have been some embezzlements; yet his numerous enemies do not specify any. Even the term "embezzlement" is not found in the verdict. Please tell me exactly what he was condemned for, and what his assets were. I presume that you will not have any difficulty finding it out from your colleagues.'[7]

In June, Voltaire wrote again to Damilaville:

> As for Lally, I am very sure that he was not a traitor; it was quite impossible for him to have saved Pondicherry. The *parlement* can only have condemned him to death for embezzlement. But it would have been desirable if they had specified what kind of embezzlement he was guilty of. France, once again, is the only country where no reasons are given for verdicts and sentences, just as it is the only country where the right to judge other men can be bought and sold.[8]

Voltaire never succeeded in penetrating the *parlement*'s wall of secrecy; the best he could do was to write up the Lally-Tollendal case

---

* The Place de la Grève in Paris was on the right bank of the Seine, just below the Place de l'Hôtel de Ville. This was the traditional place of execution in Paris. It was also the place where workers would congregate to show that they were ready to be hired for work. Today, of course, to be *en grève* means to be on strike.

and its antecedents, in an updated version of his *Précis du siècle de Louis XV* in 1768, as well as in his *Fragments historiques sur l'Inde* (1773).[9] His handicap, in this case, was that the events had all taken place in a distant part of the world, which was no longer under French control. In the Calas case he had been able to discredit the verdict because he had managed, with the help of lawyers and assiduous friends, to investigate the people and the events in Toulouse on that fateful night, and thus to show, quite independently of the Toulouse *parlement*, that the condemnation of Jean Calas was flawed, unproved, absurd, even impossible. But Pondicherry was far away, and many or most of the key *personae* in the siege of Pondicherry were hostile to Lally-Tollendal.

It is hard to tell whether Voltaire was just irritated at the authoritarian secrecy of the French judicial system or whether he already suspected a major judicial error. Later he came to believe, as he made clear in the *Précis du siècle de Louis XV*, first, that Lally-Tollendal had not been guilty of treason or embezzlement, and second, that the wording of the published verdict was not just misleading but inherently suspicious: it asserted that Lally-Tollendal had 'betrayed the interests' of the king, but it did not say that he was guilty of *lèse-majesté* or high treason. Voltaire felt sure that 'betrayal of interests' was not a recognised legal concept and must be different from outright treason. In other words, the *parlement* had been making up the law as it went along.

By late June 1766 he was becoming distinctly angrier about the Lally-Tollendal case. 'My destiny is not to be happy with the verdicts and sentences of the *parlements*. I cannot get used to sentences of death given without reasons. There is in this jurisprudence an arbitrary barbarity which insults human nature.'[10] Quite independently of whether the Lally-Tollendal verdict could or could not be justified – and he obviously doubted it – Voltaire had reached the point where he rejected the 'arbitrary barbarity' of the French judicial system. But as far as fighting the Lally-Tollendal verdict was concerned, Voltaire had come to a dead end, and he made no further efforts until several years later.

Of all the cases that Voltaire took up, the one that he found most shocking and most moving, because of the contrast between the youth of the victim and the barbarity of the judicial process, was the trial and execution, in Abbeville in Picardy, of the young Jean François Lefèvre, chevalier de La Barre. The offences he was alleged to have committed were: malicious damage to a crucifix; singing anti-religious songs; and showing disrespect to a religious procession. The charges were blasphemy and sacrilege. The verdict was guilty. The sentence was that he should have his tongue torn out, that he should then be beheaded and that his body should be burned on a pyre.

It was on the morning of 9 August 1765, in the middle of the town of Abbeville, that a crucifix on the Pont-Neuf bridge was discovered to have been cut about, perhaps by a sword or a knife. Around the same time a figure of Christ in the cemetery had been soiled with filth. These events stirred up extreme emotions among the God-fearing population. The local bishop, from Amiens, leading a procession of ceremonial apology (*amende honorable*) to the crucifix, declared that the culprits 'deserved the most extreme torments in this world and eternal punishment in the next'. The stage was being set for a highly charged trial.

The two main figures in the investigation, and in the trial that followed, were Charles-Joseph Dumaisniel, sieur de Belleval, a local notable and magistrate, and Nicolas-Pierre Duval de Soicourt, mayor of Abbeville and therefore the chief investigating official in the case. It was Belleval who was mainly responsible for whipping up the judicial investigation, not simply in the line of public duty but essentially for reasons of a personal vendetta.

As a result of his efforts, an enquiry was opened, and it quickly focused on a group of local adolescents, well born but loud, turbulent, very slightly but noisily dissolute, a bit impious and disrespectful of authority. They were frequently heard singing barrack-room songs, vulgar, anti-clerical, bawdy. Some of them had been seen, not long before, passing a religious procession without taking their hats off. In short, they were prominent members of the local youth.

As in the Calas and Sirven affairs, the Church-and-state authorities issued *monitoires* in every parish church summoning the faithful to produce evidence for the prosecution of these crimes. Their initial enquiries produced plenty of hearsay and gossip but no hard evidence against any of the young men.

The chief suspect, and the main target of Belleval's personal vendetta, was Jean François Lefèvre, chevalier de La Barre. He was probably born in 1745, and was therefore nineteen or twenty years old at the time of the events. Voltaire variously says he was sixteen, seventeen, nineteen and twenty-one.

La Barre's dissolute friends and associates included three other young men, all of whom were uncomfortably connected to the investigators: Dumaisniel de Saveuse, the son of Belleval; Jean-François Douville de Maillefer, the son of Duval, the mayor and chief investigating magistrate; and Jacques Marie Bertrand Gaillard d'Étallonde, the son

of the Président de Boëncourt, a senior local judge and Duval's immediate hierarchical superior. Belleval and Duval were able to spirit away
their sons before they were publicly named in the investigation; Gaillard
d'Étallonde was also helped to escape, but not before he had been identified as a possible suspect, along with La Barre.[11]

Gaillard d'Étallonde was born in 1749, and was therefore fifteen or
sixteen at the time of the events. Before he could be arrested, he fled
to Prussia and enlisted in the Prussian army under the pseudonym
Morival; on Voltaire's recommendation, in February 1767 Frederick
located 'Morival', found that he was serving as a military standard-
bearer and soon appointed him an officer.[12]

When the authorities issued their arrest warrants and proceeded to
trial, therefore, they could lay their hands on only two suspects: the chevalier de La Barre and a young friend, Charles François Marcel Moisnel,
sixteen or seventeen years old (Voltaire says he was about fifteen).[13]
After their arrest some evidence emerged that the main perpetrator of
the vandalism on the crucifix on the Pont-Neuf may have been Gaillard
d'Étallonde. Perhaps it was true, but the shadow of the possible guilt of
the absent Gaillard d'Étallonde was used by the prosecution to implicate
his friends and thus to secure the conviction of La Barre.

La Barre was an orphan who had arrived in Abbeville not long
before and was living with his aunt Anne-Marguerite Feydeau, the
abbess of the convent of Villancourt. Mme Feydeau was a worldly and
perhaps an attractive woman, for she had been the object of the pressing attentions of the middle-aged Charles-Joseph de Belleval, the local
magistrate; after the arrival of La Barre, however, she rejected Belleval's advances. Belleval believed that La Barre had displaced him in
the affections of Mme Feydeau and was the cause of his rejection; so he
thought that he could use the scandal of the mutilation of the crucifix
to get his revenge. Belleval pursued a fierce campaign against La Barre,
going from door to door to drum up evidence against him, and invok-
ing the *monitoires* which had been issued in August, with their associated threats of excommunication. By the end of September 1765 he had
secured La Barre's arrest.

As chief investigating magistrate, Duval de Soicourt, mayor of
Abbeville, searched La Barre's room in the convent and discovered
a number of compromising books, including several works of erotic
literature. Most compromising of all, he found a copy of Voltaire's
Dictionnaire philosophique portatif. In the trial the prosecution argued
that the young men had been incited to their crimes by the corrupting

influence of *philosophie* in general and the *Dictionnaire philosophique* in particular.

On 28 February 1766 the court in Abbeville found the chevalier de La Barre guilty and condemned him to have his tongue torn out, to be beheaded and to have his body burned on a pyre; it condemned Gaillard d'Étallonde, in absentia, to have his right hand cut off, to have his tongue torn out and to be burned alive on a pyre; and it condemned the *Dictionnaire philosophique* to be burned on the same pyre as La Barre. La Barre's sentence was slightly less horrendous than Gaillard d'Étallonde's because he was a nobleman and therefore entitled to the privilege of beheading. The court postponed any verdict on young Moisnel.

The sentences could not be carried out, however, until they had been confirmed by the *parlement* in Paris. La Barre and Moisnel were therefore transferred on 12 March to the prison of the Conciergerie in the centre of Paris; there they remained for three months. (It was while they were there, that the Paris *parlement* condemned Lally-Tollendal to death and carried out his execution on 9 May 1766.)

On 4 June, by a majority of fifteen judges to ten, the *parlement* confirmed the sentence on La Barre and Gaillard d'Étallonde, as well as that on the *Dictionnaire philosophique*. The two young men remained in the Conciergerie for another three weeks; during this time various highly placed relatives of Mme Feydeau and La Barre, as well as the bishop of Amiens, appealed to Louis XV for a royal reprieve. The king refused.

On 27 June 1766 La Barre and Moisnel were taken back to Abbeville. Four days later, on 1 July 1766 La Barre's execution took place. First he was tortured: each of his legs was enclosed between two wooden planks, and the executioner hammered thick wooden wedges between the planks and his legs. This torture went on for an hour, during which time Duval insistently demanded a confession: in vain. La Barre was then taken in a cart to the scaffold, wearing a placard reading 'Impious, sacrilegious and hateful blasphemer'. By all accounts, La Barre endured his torments with great fortitude and calmness; he even laughed when he saw, hanging from the gallows, a paper cut-out representing the absent Gaillard d'Étallonde. According to Voltaire, he said, at the foot of the scaffold: 'I did not believe that they could make a gentleman die for such a small thing'.[14] The authorities omitted that part of the sentence requiring the tearing out of La Barre's tongue, and the public executioner – the same who had so recently botched the decapitation of Lally-Tollendal in Paris – proceeded directly to the beheading of

La Barre. This time he achieved it at the first attempt.[15] La Barre's body was burned on the pyre, and with it the copy of Voltaire's *Dictionnaire philosophique*.

Voltaire was slow to hear of the La Barre case, as we can see from a letter he wrote to Damilaville on 23 June 1766, four months after La Barre had been condemned to death:

> My dear friend, I have been told that the *parlement* has not confirmed the verdict condemning the young idiots of Abbeville, and that it wanted to give their relatives the time to get from the king a commutation of the sentence; I hope this news is true. It is not just, to punish idiocy by torments which should only be reserved for great crimes.[16]

Voltaire still hoped that the young men would get off, but he was frightened by the implications of the public condemnation of his *Dictionnaire philosophique*. On 1 July 1766 he wrote to d'Alembert:

> Are you in a position to find out about this young idiot named M. de La Barre, and his companion, whom they so sweetly condemned to lose their fist, their tongue and their life. I have been told that they said, in their interrogation, that they were led to the acts of folly which they committed, by reading the books of the *Encyclopédistes*. I can hardly believe it: idiots do not read, and certainly no *philosophe* would have advised any profanity. This is very serious. Try to get to the bottom of so odious and so dangerous a story.[17]

Voltaire did not yet know quite how serious; for on that very day, 1 July 1766, in Abbeville, La Barre had been executed.

The more Voltaire learned about the case, the more upset he became, and the more frightened for his own safety. He wrote to Damilaville on 7 July 1766: 'My dear brother, my heart is withered, I am cast down. I did not imagine that anyone would blame the silliest and most unrestrained madness on people who only preach wisdom and purity of morals. I am tempted to go and die in some foreign land, where men might be less unjust. I shall be silent, I have too much to say.'[18]

But of course Voltaire was not silent, far from it, for he was becoming increasingly worked up. On the same day he wrote to his younger niece, Mme Fontaine: 'We believe you are informed of the news from Abbeville; we ask you urgently to tell us in the last detail the astonishing adventure of these young people whose heads were so horribly disoriented. Tell us their names, their ages, their employment. Had they any previous outbursts of madness? Is it true that one of them was the nephew of an abbess?'[19]

Given the obduracy with which the Toulouse *parlement* had concealed the facts in the Calas case, it may be imagined that the story behind the trial and execution of La Barre would also have remained a deep and inaccessible secret. Not at all. Within a fortnight of the execution Voltaire was so well informed, at least partly through his great-nephew d'Hornoy, that he was able to recount the gist of the story of Belleval, the abbess and the vendetta, in terms that are recognisably the same as modern scholarship tells today. Perhaps, in the tiny world of the provincial town of Abbeville, the story was almost common knowledge.

Voltaire dressed up the story in the form of an ostensible 900-word letter as if from some anonymous correspondent in Abbeville, and he circulated it to his friends. He wrote to Damilaville on 14 July 1766:

> You will be most astonished, you will shudder, my dear brother, when you read the account that I enclose. Who could believe that the condemnation of five young men of family to the most horrible death could have been the fruit of the love and jealousy of an aged villain of a magistrate of Abbeville? Did you know that several advocates have drafted a memorandum that demonstrated the absurdity of this frightful sentence? Is it possible to get me a copy of this memorandum? Please send a copy of this account to M. de Beaumont.[20]

In some ways the most significant element of this letter was one to which Voltaire drew no overt attention: his address. He was writing it from 'The waters at Rolle in Switzerland'. Since Rolle was a spa a little bit to the north of Ferney but on the same shore of the Lac Léman, he might have gone there for his health. In fact, he was frightened out of his wits by the burning of his *Dictionnaire philosophique* and by the fear that he might now be in serious personal danger from the French authorities, so he had run away to safety in Switzerland.

The more Voltaire looked into the affair, the more scandalous were the problems he discovered. The case, like those against Calas and Sirven, had been based on a highly charged alliance between the bigoted Church–state machine and the superstitious local Catholic population. The factual evidence against La Barre was fragmentary, rumour-based, unreliable, wholly insufficient. The legal basis for the charges of blasphemy and sacrilege was questionable, unsafe, perhaps non-existent; the charges of blasphemy and sacrilege were manifestly out of proportion for the offences alleged; and if there was a legal offence of blasphemy, it almost certainly could not incur the death penalty. Worst of all, the case against the accused had been deliberately whipped up by a local magistrate for reasons of personal grudge against La Barre, quite unrelated to the ostensible charges.

Voltaire wrote to d'Argental:

> I am convinced that the king would have reprieved him if he had known the whole story; but this poor chevalier de La Barre was completely disoriented, no one could defend him, they did not even know how to refute the witnesses who had virtually been suborned by Belleval. Moreover, what is very odd is that there is no specific law for such an offence. It is up to the prudence, or the caprice, of the judge. Is it possible that a majority of five votes can be enough to execute, in the most horrible torments, a young gentleman who was guilty of nothing worse than folly? What more could they have done to him, if he had killed his own father?[21]

Voltaire remained at Rolle for over a month, until he thought the storm had blown over. He dashed briefly back to Ferney in order to welcome and entertain the visiting duke of Brunswick, but this was just a one-day trip; he immediately returned to Rolle and stayed there at least until 16 August.[22]

Voltaire now drafted a much longer narrative, in the form of a twenty-four-page pamphlet entitled: *Relation de la mort du chevalier de La Barre* ('Account of the Death of the Chevalier de La Barre').[23] Once again he concealed his authorship.

In this pamphlet Voltaire explicitly laid out the details of his allegation that Belleval had engineered the investigation of La Barre for reasons of personal envy and sexual jealousy, had pressured witnesses to give evidence against La Barre under threat of excommunication and had pressured the local mayor into holding a trial. Voltaire itemised the evidence of the various witnesses, claiming that all or almost all of it was hearsay, that all or almost all of the offences alleged were of the kind of trivial impiety to which wild youth is often inclined, such as the singing of vulgar songs or disrespect to a religious procession, and that no evidence at all was produced against La Barre implicating him in the vandalism of the crucifix on the Pont-Neuf.

Moreover, he underlined the fact that under French law the offence of blasphemy did not carry the death penalty. 'The legal ordinance of 1666 prescribes a fine for the first offence, a double fine for the second offence etc., and the pillory for the sixth offence.'[24]

In the end, says Voltaire,

there was so little evidence of a substantial offence, that the judges, in their sentence, employed vague and ridiculous terms, like those used by the common people: 'For having sung abominable and execrable songs against the Virgin Mary and all the saints'. Are these terms compatible with the dignity of the bench? An ancient bawdy song is, after all, only a song. It is human blood casually spilt, it is torture, it is the torment of the tongue torn out, the hand cut off, of the body cast into the flames, which is abominable and execrable.

Unfortunately, I have heard several people say that they could not prevent themselves from detesting a sect [i.e., the Catholic Church] which is only sustained by the public executioners. These people wanted to execute, with a torture reserved for poisoners and parricides, mere children accused of having sung ancient blasphemous songs. You could not believe, Sir, how much this event makes our Roman Catholic religion hateful to all foreigners. The judges say that politics forced them to act in this way. What imbecile and barbarous politics! Ah, Sir, what a horrible crime against justice, to pronounce a sentence for political reasons, above all a sentence of death! And what a death!

The sadness and horror which grip me, do not allow me to say any more.[25]

Voltaire's 'sadness and horror' were not assumed; on the contrary, he was so outraged, and so fearful for his own safety, that he was even beginning to think of moving abroad, as he wrote to d'Alembert on 18 July 1766:

Our brother [Damilaville] has no doubt passed on to you the Abbeville story, my dear philosopher. I cannot understand how thinking beings can remain in a country of monkeys, which so often become tigers. As for me, I am ashamed even to be on the frontier. In truth, now is the time to break the connection, and to bear elsewhere the horror we feel. I still have not managed to get hold of the lawyers' memorandum. You have seen it, no doubt, and you have shuddered. What! Monsters in judicial robes put to death children of sixteen years in the most horrible torments! And the nation endures this! Is this the country of *philosophie* and civilisation? No. Even the Inquisition would not have dared do what these Jansenist judges have carried out.[26]

Voltaire continued to think about moving abroad, especially if he could persuade his friends to move with him. When he ran away to Rolle, he had taken with him not just Mme Denis but also his adopted daughter Marie-Françoise Corneille and her husband, Claude Dupuits; it was as if he had gathered all his family around him, ready to flee together at the approach of danger. In mid-August he told Damilaville that he did not know if he would return to Ferney or if he would move instead to Mannheim, seat of his friend Charles Théodore de Sulzbach, the Elector-Palatine; the attractions of Mannheim were that the Elector ran an opulent and entertaining household, including a theatre, and that he owed Voltaire £130,000.[27]

Another option that Voltaire considered, more seriously, was to move to Kleve (or Clèves, in French), one of Frederick the Great's estates in north Germany, near the Rhine and close to the border with the Netherlands. Voltaire wrote to Damilaville on 21 July:

I am not letting myself be got down, my dear brother; but my pain, my anger and my indignation redouble every moment. So little am I letting myself be got down that I shall probably decide to go and finish my days in some country where I could do some good. I shall not be the only one. I am persuaded that the prince who will favour this enterprise [Frederick] would find you a good position, if you wished to join us. I know you have enough courage to follow me, but you probably have commitments which you cannot break. I have already started to take steps; if you back me up, I shall not hesitate.[28]

Then Voltaire had the bright idea of trying to persuade Denis Diderot to join him in Kleve, where he could continue the work of editing his great *Encyclopédie* in safety, an idea that he expanded to a vision of an entire colony of *philosophes*. Voltaire admired Diderot for his learning, his eminence and his commitment, and he referred to him in private by the nickname of Plato; but he and Diderot were not close, and most of the communication between them passed through intermediaries, mainly Damilaville or d'Alembert. But at this juncture of his emotional crisis over the execution of La Barre and the burning of the *Dictionnaire philosophique*, Voltaire wrote directly to Diderot with an emotional appeal to join his projected little colony:

You must see with horror the country in which you have the misfortune to live. You should come to a country where you would have complete liberty not only to print whatever you want but to preach out loud against superstitions that are as infamous as they are bloodstained. You would not be alone, you would have companions and disciples. You could establish a Chair which would be the Chair of Truth. Your library would be transported by water, with only four leagues of overland travel. Finally, you would leave slavery for liberty. If the course we propose satisfies your indignation and pleases your wisdom, just say the word, and we shall try to arrange everything in a manner worthy of you, in the greatest secret, and without compromising you. The country we are proposing is beautiful and close to everything.[29]

Coincidentally, rumours that Voltaire was planning to emigrate were starting to circulate in Paris. Frederick had offered to provide an asylum for the Sirvens, and Voltaire had idly replied that he would be tempted to escort them there. Frederick read Voltaire's letter out loud in the Prussian court, and one of those who heard it was a certain Louis-François Tronchin, son of Théodore Tronchin and secretary of the English ambassador in Berlin. 'The little Tronchin', wrote Voltaire later to Mme du Deffand, 'thought he understood that I would rejoin the king of Prussia. He told his father, his father talked about it in Paris, the newspapers discussed it up and down, and that's how history gets written.* He does not realise that I am seventy-three years old, and that I cannot go out of doors.'[30]

For four months Voltaire went on urging the attractions of his idyllic Kleve colony project, but in vain. His Parisian friends discussed his plan among themselves, but they could not leave Paris; Diderot was the first of the *philosophes* to tell Voltaire that he would not go. Voltaire was dismayed by their reaction: 'It is inexcusable to live under the sword when one could easily secure the triumph of the truth. I cannot understand those who would prefer to crawl to fanaticism in a corner of Paris, when they could crush this monster. What! Couldn't you even find me two zealous disciples? I should only ask three or four years of health and life. My fear is that I may die before I have rendered some service.'[31]

Voltaire did not move to Kleve after all, or to anywhere else; after all, as he never stopped pointing out, he was seventy-two; and he had

---

* Théodore Tronchin had moved to Paris in January that year.

put down quite deep roots of habit and custom at Ferney. Yet the idea of a Utopian colony of *philosophes* was one of those pipedreams he never quite abandoned, and he continued to evoke it with regret several years later.

Voltaire's noisy and eloquent public protests at the illegal barbarity of the trial and execution of the chevalier de La Barre may have had some effect on public opinion, and perhaps even on the legal establishment as well. The court in Abbeville made no attempt to resume the trials of the others accused in the La Barre affair, and young Moisnel was released. Nicolas-Pierre Duval de Soicourt, the mayor of Abbeville and chief investigating magistrate in the case, was dismissed. But La Barre was dead, and Gaillard d'Étallonde, though absent, was still under sentence of a death even more barbaric than that endured by La Barre.

Voltaire was permanently marked in heart and mind by the La Barre case, and he never ceased to evoke it, with pity and anger, as a vivid symptom of so much that was evil in the French judicial system. But after the publication of his *Relation de la mort du chevalier de La Barre*, he did not take any immediate practical steps to attempt to have the trial reopened or the sentence quashed.

The chevalier de La Barre was the last person to be condemned to death in France for blasphemy, but his rehabilitation had to wait for the French Revolution. It was one of the demands of the nobility in their list of political complaints (*cahiers de doléances*) which they submitted to Louis XVI just before the Revolution. After the Revolution it was solemnly granted, but late in the day, by the Convention in 1792.

GENEVA TROUBLES

1765–1768

AS WE SAW IN CHAPTER 26, one of the reasons that Voltaire gave up Les Délices in 1765 and thus shifted his base to Ferney, just outside the frontier of Geneva, was that the political situation inside the republic was becoming increasingly stormy, with growing conflict over the balance of power between the patricians and the rest of the citizenry.

In principle, Geneva was a quasi-democratic republic; in practice, it was an oligarchy dominated by a very small number of hereditary patrician families. The patrician oligarchs were able to control affairs, because the population was divided into four political classes, each of which was subordinate to the class above. At the bottom were the *habitants* (the 'inhabitants'), foreigners who were merely permitted to reside, without any political rights; next above them were the *natifs* (the 'natives'), children of *habitants*, born in Geneva and automatically entitled to live there, but also without any political rights and with quite restricted economic and social rights; next above them were the *bourgeois* ('burghers'), who had been *natifs* but had managed to buy into a more privileged status by paying a substantial fee; and finally, at the top, the *citoyens* ('citizens'), born in Geneva from other 'citizens' or from *bourgeois*. The *bourgeois* and the *citoyens* together accounted for much less than half of the 25,000 population of Geneva, but only they had any political rights, and in addition they also had far-reaching economic and social privileges.

In fact, the system was even more restrictive than this four-tier stratification would suggest. For within the class of 'citizens' there was a tiny group of patrician families which controlled all the real political power in Geneva, through the Council of the Twenty-Five or *Petit Conseil* ('Little Council'). There were two other councils – the Council of 200 and the General Council, which was larger still (up to about 1,500 members) – which were supposed to represent all the *citoyens* and *bourgeois*; and in theory political power in the Republic was meant to be counter-balanced between these three institutions. In reality, the *Petit Conseil* was all-powerful, since it controlled all public appointments as well as the agenda of issues which could be decided, or even discussed, in the lower-level assemblies to which the other 'citizens' and *bourgeois* had access.

This system had evolved from Geneva's history as an immigrant republic. Geneva had grown rich through the absorption of skilled immigrant labour, especially after 1685, when Louis XIV revoked the Edict of Nantes and re-launched full-scale persecution of Protestants in France. The ensuing immigration of Protestants had given added impetus to the prosperity of Geneva, notably in the watchmaking industry. But the old patrician families had no wish to share power with the more recent arrivals, and certainly not with the working class. This hierarchical disequilibrium was reflected in the social geography of Geneva, which still exists today: the patricians lived at the top of the town, in the *rues hautes*, whereas the lesser orders lived lower down, in the *rues basses*.

The system was so patently unfair in its distribution of power and privilege that it was bound to provoke conflict between the haves and the have-nots; and indeed conflict had already broken out several times in recent memory: in 1707, in 1718 and in 1734. On that last occasion, the conflict had become so acute that it was only settled, in 1738, by an outside intervention of mediation by France, Berne and Zurich. But the 'settlement' they imposed did not in fact settle anything, and thereafter the political fermentation between the political orders in Geneva remained endemic.

The fuse for the latest political conflict, which erupted in earnest in 1765, can be traced back to 1762, and to the triangular quarrel between Voltaire, Jean-Jacques Rousseau and the Geneva authorities. In April 1762 Rousseau had published his revolutionary political tract the *Contrat social*, and in May 1762 his educational thesis *Émile*. Both works were denounced by the French and Genevan authorities: the *Contrat social* for being seditious, and *Émile* for being anti-Christian, especially in the chapter known as the *Vicar of Savoie*. Both books were formally condemned; by the *parlement* in Paris, and publicly burned, in early June that year; and immediately afterwards condemned in the same way by the *Petit Conseil* in Geneva, which also issued a warrant for Rousseau's arrest.

Voltaire wrote to d'Alembert later that month:

> Excess of pride and envy has ruined Jean-Jacques, my illustrious *philosophe*. This monster dares to speak of education!, he who would not bring up any of his own sons, and placed them all in an orphanage. I should be sorry if he were hanged, but only out of pure humanity; personally, I can only regard him as Diogenes' dog, or rather as a dog descended from a bastard of that dog. I do not know if he is detested as much in Paris, as by all the honest people of Geneva.[1]

Voltaire's contempt may seem intemperate until we recall that, two years earlier, Rousseau had sent him a celebrated hate-letter:

> I do not like you, Sir; you have done me ills to which I would be most sensitive, to me your disciple and your enthusiast. You have ruined Geneva, in return for the asylum you have received there; you have alienated my fellow citizens from me; it is you who have made it unbearable for me to live in my own country; it is you who will make me die in a foreign country, deprived of all the consolations of the dying. I hate you, finally; you wanted it; but I hate you as a man even more worthy to love you if you had wanted it.[2]

In June 1762 Rousseau riposted to the condemnation by the *Petit Conseil* of his *Contrat social* and *Émile* with a pamphlet defending his works; this pamphlet was itself banned by the *Petit Conseil*. Rousseau then escalated his quarrel with the Geneva authorities, and on 12 May 1763 he publicly and formally renounced his status as a citizen of Geneva.

This prompted a belated series of protests by members of the Geneva citizenry at his mistreatment by the *Petit Conseil*. On 30 June 1763 Voltaire wrote to his friend the duchesse de Saxe-Gotha:

> If your most Serene Highness can be pleased with the little things which show humanity, I shall tell her that Jean-Jacques Rousseau, condemned in the city of Calvin for having depicted a Vicar of Savoie, Jean-Jacques who uncitizened himself from Geneva, has found some citizens who have taken his side. Two hundred people, including two or three clergymen, presented a petition on his behalf to the

magistrate. 'We know well that he is not a Christian', they say, 'but we want him to be our fellow citizen.' That's tolerance for you. God be blessed.[3]

But the *Petit Conseil* did not give way, and the protests continued. Six weeks later Voltaire reported to Damilaville:

Yesterday six hundred persons came, for the third time, to protest in favour of Jean-Jacques against the Council of Geneva, which had dared to condemn the *Vicar of Savoie*. They say that any citizen is permitted to write whatever he wishes about religion, that he cannot be condemned without being heard, and that the rights of men must be respected. People say that all this could end up with an armed uprising. I should not be sorry to see a civil war over the *Vicar of Savoie*.[4]

Still the *Petit Conseil* did not give way, and there was another large demonstration at the end of September. Voltaire wrote to d'Alembert: 'Jean-Jacques has been condemned, because he sided too much with the people against the magistrates. So the people, very gratefully, have sided with Jean-Jacques. Seven hundred citizens went two by two in procession, to protest against the judges.'[5]

The Attorney-General, Jean-Robert Tronchin (not Voltaire's banker, but a cousin by the same name), attempted to justify the actions of the *Petit Conseil* in a pamphlet called *Lettres écrites de la campagne* (Letters Written from the Countryside). From this point on, however, the quarrel between Rousseau and the government of Geneva spilled over into a quarrel between Rousseau and Voltaire, since Rousseau believed (mistakenly) that Voltaire had conspired to engineer his rupture with Geneva; relations between the two *philosophes* soon became irreparable.

At the end of 1764 Rousseau responded to the Attorney-General with a pamphlet of his own, *Lettres écrites de la montagne* (Letters Written from the Mountain), in which he attacked Voltaire personally, by exposing him as the author of the anonymous pamphlet *Sermon des cinquante* (Sermon of the Fifty).[6] Voltaire was acutely sensitive to being identified as the author of the *Sermon des cinquante*, not just because it was scandalously anti-Christian and could get him into trouble, but even more because he had recently started circulating his *Dictionnaire philosophique portatif*, which was destined to be much more popular with readers than the *Sermon des cinquante*, and much more scandalous to the authorities. He wrote to Damilaville in December 1764:

Decent people, and especially my dear brother, should know that Jean-Jacques has written a great book against the tiny (*parvulissime*) republic of Geneva, with the intention of rousing the people against the magistrates. In this book J.-J. accuses me of being the author of the *Sermon des cinquante*. Such a proceeding is certainly not that of a philosopher nor of an honest man. It may be clever, but it isn't honest … Omer [Joly de Fleury, the French Advocate-General] is currently working on an indictment of the *Dictionnaire philosophique*. People keep saying it is by me, but I have nothing to do with it.[7]

In response to Rousseau's accusation Voltaire counter-attacked with a scurrilous pamphlet of his own, *Le Sentiment des citoyens* (The Feeling of the Citizens),[8] in which he denounced Rousseau and, in particular, revealed that Rousseau had abandoned all of the five (illegitimate) children he had had by his companion, Marie-Thérèse Levasseur. This fact was known to very few people, and Voltaire had only recently learned it.

At first the class conflict in Geneva was just between the three top classes: the oligarchs in the *Petit Conseil*, the ordinary *citoyens* and the less privileged *bourgeois*. The ordinary *citoyens* and the *bourgeois* became known as the *Représentants*, because they were representing their claims to a fairer deal; the oligarchs of the *Petit Conseil* were known as the *Négatifs*, because they had recently (in 1763) claimed a veto power (*droit négatif*) over all other institutions.

Inevitably, this conflict of principle could not be confined for long within the upper orders of society. Below them, the artisan class of the *natifs* had an even stronger moral claim for more political and social justice, since they had no political rights and yet constituted over half the population. Sooner or later they too were bound to demand a fairer deal; for the moment, in this year of 1765, the *natifs* were still passive. They started to move the following year, in 1766, and their demands eventually led to an unprecedented outbreak of political violence. (As immigrants, the *habitants* do not seem to have joined the agitation for political rights.)

Of course, once the *natifs* started agitating for better political and economic rights, the *Représentants* had second thoughts: it was one thing for the *citoyens* and *bourgeois* to demand political concessions from the patricians, quite another to share political privilege with the *natifs*. At that point, many of the *Représentants* changed sides, supporting the patricians against the *natifs*.

Voltaire started out instinctively on the side of his friends the patricians; as time went on, he shifted to side with the *Représentants*; and as more time went on, and the *natifs* joined the struggle, he shifted again to side with them. In short, it was a textbook case of the evolution of Voltaire's political thought in a democratic direction. He was not and had never been a principled democrat; but the more he heard the arguments of the rival parties in Geneva, the more democratic his conclusions became. His democratic conclusions were limited to Geneva, however; he still did not become a democrat on grounds of general principle, and he did not apply his Geneva conclusions to Russia, Prussia or France. In this case, as in so many others, he remained eclectic, pragmatic and resistant to systemic thought.

In public, Voltaire insisted that he was not taking sides and would not get involved in the quarrels of the Genevans; and at first this may have been true, at least in intention. But he could not resist the temptation to be helpful; he made repeated efforts to act the part of an initially impartial conciliator, by inviting members of the *Représentants* and of the *Négatifs* to meet socially at the château de Ferney, to talk things over. It was no doubt this process, of repeatedly hearing the arguments of the two sides, which gradually persuaded Voltaire that the *Représentants* had justified claims.

During 1763 and 1764, and most of 1765, Voltaire remained loyal to his oligarchic friends; in January 1765 he wrote: 'the people are insolent, and the *Conseil* is weak.'[9] By mid-October 1765, however, Voltaire had privately swung behind the *Représentants*. He wrote to d'Argental: 'For France, it matters very little whether Geneva should be aristocratic or democratic. I will admit that at present I incline towards democracy, despite my ancient principles, because it seems to me that the magnates have been in the wrong on several points. The twenty-five of the *Petit Conseil* have chosen to take the title of noble lords, and it has gone to their heads.'[10]

But a couple of days later, in a letter to Damilaville, he took a much more uncompromising stand.

> The splits in Geneva will soon break out. It is absolutely necessary that you and your friends should put it about in public that the citizens are in the right against the magistrates; for it is certain that the people only want liberty, and that the magistrature is aiming at absolute power. Is there anything more tyrannical, for example, than to remove the freedom of the press? And how can a people say it is free, when it is not permitted to think in writing? Whoever has the power

in his hands would like to put out the eyes of all those who are subordinate to him. Every village judge would like to be a despot. The madness of domination is an incurable sickness ... Today I am starting to read the Italian book *Of Crimes and Punishments*. At a glance it seems to me philosophical; the author is a brother.[11]

It is perhaps not a complete accident that Voltaire's conversion to the *Représentants* should have happened to coincide with his exposure to Beccaria's work on penal reform. But however that may be, it is clear that he was no longer at heart on the side of his aristocratic friends, and he soon felt obliged to tell them something about the reasons for his change of heart and his hopes for a compromise.

In November 1765 he was sent a pamphlet setting out the demands of the *Représentants*, and he wrote directly to Jacob Tronchin:

Immediately after having read, Sir, the new book in favour of the *Représentants*, the first thing I do is to speak to you about it. It is a collection of bitter complaints. The author is aware how much I am tolerant, impartial and a friend of peace; he must also know how much I am attached to you, to your relatives, to your friends and to the constitution of the government.

If he thought that I would declare myself on the side of the discontented party, and that I should poison open wounds, he does not know me.

I am very far from believing that I could be useful, but I have an idea (mistakenly, perhaps) that it may not be impossible to bring minds together. There have come to my home some citizens who have appeared to combine moderation with enlightenment. Even if such a meeting should serve only to ease bitter feelings, and to encourage a necessary conciliation, that would be a great deal, and nothing but good could come of it. It is not for me to be a conciliator. I simply limit myself to take the liberty of offering a meal where people could listen to each other.[12]

For a while Voltaire continued to observe the most scrupulous self-control in his dealings with the authorities. A week after the previous letter he wrote to Pierre Lullin, Secretary of State of the *Petit Conseil*:

Sir: This morning four citizens let me know that they wished to speak to me; I sent them a carriage; I gave them dinner; and we discussed their business. I must first bear witness that not one of them expressed a single word which could offend the magistrates. I do not believe that it can be impossible to bring minds together, but I admit that conciliation is very difficult. There are questions on which, it seemed to me, they might give way; there are others which need a wiser man than me, and more capable of persuasion.[13]

At first, the patricians notionally accepted Voltaire's efforts to be helpful and impartial. But his efforts at facilitating conciliation made no progress, and by early December 1765 he had had enough. 'My angels, I can confirm that I am tired of wasting my time in trying to pacify the Genevans.'[14]

Voltaire became so impatient with the unreasonable stubbornness of the contestants that he developed some modest proposals of his own for a compromise, and he sent them to d'Argental, to have them shown to lawyers in Paris, as well as to some of the ministers in the French government. At the centre of Voltaire's plan was the rather obvious idea that the leverage of the *Conseil Général* should be increased and the *droit négatif* of the *Petit Conseil* reduced. He proposed that whenever a motion in the *Conseil Général* was supported by 700 – that is, roughly half of the members – it could not simply be blocked by the *Petit Conseil* but must be debated for action. But, as Voltaire commented a little later to d'Argental: 'This number seems too high to the citizens, and too low to the magistrates. As a result, it cannot be far from a fair compromise, since the general assembly almost never has more than 1,300 members at most.'[15]

In addition, Voltaire recommended reforms of the legal system: the patricians had undertaken to publish all the laws governing Geneva but had not done so, and should be required to do so now; moreover, the *Petit Conseil* must give up its practice of imprisonment without trial, simply by administrative fiat.

Voltaire incorporated some of these reform proposals in the short pamphlet *Idées républicaines*, which he wrote at about this time (November 1765). Too much of the pamphlet is devoted to catty attacks on Rousseau's *Contrat social* or to criticisms of Montesquieu's *De l'Espirit des Lois*, but it also contains some unexpectedly radical propositions.

'The civil government is the will of all, carried out by one man or several, by virtue of the laws which all have supported.'

'In a republic worthy of the name, the freedom to publish his thoughts is the natural right of the citizen. That is the law in England, a monarchical country, but where men are freer than elsewhere because they are more enlightened.'

'[In Geneva] they burned this book [the *Contrat social*]. If the book was dangerous, it should have been refuted. To burn a book of argument is to say: "We do not have enough wit to reply to it".'

'There has never been a perfect government, because men have passions. The most tolerable of all is no doubt a republic, because it brings men closest to natural equality.'[16]

For a while Voltaire thought his proposals were making progress, but he deceived himself. The *Petit Conseil* informed him officially that it had no intention of modifying the constitution of Geneva, and, rather than negotiate with the *Représentants*, it called on France to mediate, no doubt on the assumption that the autocrats in Versailles would automatically side with the autocrats in Geneva. Voltaire then declared that he was washing his hands of the conflict, 'when I saw that the Genevans were not seriously interested except in the pre-eminence of their *rues hautes* over the *rues basses*, and were determined to weary the French government to know if the Council of the Twenty-Five has or has not the negative power in every case.'[17]

The French government named as chief mediator Pierre de Buisson, the chevalier de Beauteville, ambassador to Berne; in March 1766 Beauteville arrived in Geneva with an extensive retinue, including ten chefs. He started his mission of mediation in the strangest way: he required the Geneva authorities, including the consistory of the Calvinist clergy, to lift their ban on the opening of a theatre in the town. Such a provision should already have been in force, under the terms of the earlier settlement of 1738. But because it had effectively been blocked by the Calvinist preachers, the local theatre company, which was popular with the people of Geneva, was compelled to perform just outside the territory of Geneva and therefore just out of reach of the Calvinist authorities. With Beauteville's support this theatre company was now able to move into Geneva and perform in the heart of the city.

Voltaire was exultant, especially when, in November that year, the actors scored a big popular success with his tragedy *Olympie*.

The Geneva troupe, which is not totally bad, surpassed itself yesterday with *Olympie*; it has never had such a great success. The crowd watching the show demanded with loud cries that it be put on again the next day. The Genevans have gone mad for *Olympie*, they perform it every day, and at three o'clock in the afternoon all the seats are taken. Everyone has seen *Olympie* except me, for I'm in my bed.[18]

The arrival of the mediators did not calm the political disturbances in Geneva, however; nor did it persuade Voltaire to stop his meddling. In May 1766 he reported, with indignation, an extraordinary example of the quasi-feudal pretensions of the *Petit Conseil*. 'Not long ago the Gentlemen of the Council sent me their property registrar, to demand that I swear my homage-liege to them, in respect of a field I own. I shall certainly make them eat all the hay of that field before I swear homage-liege to them. These people seem to me to have more wig than wit.'[19]

Meanwhile, the *natifs* had decided that the arrival of Beauteville gave them their only chance of a better political deal, and in April they asked him to help them against the patricians; but he sent them packing. They then approached Voltaire for advice, and he helped them draft a memorandum of their demands. But when the *Petit Conseil* found out about Voltaire's intervention on behalf of the *natifs*, they got quite irritated, and Beauteville sent his secretary, Pierre de Taulès, to rebuke him.

I thought I ought to complain to M. de Voltaire, for having once again put in an appearance in the disputes of the Republic. I sent M. de Taulès to Ferney. M. de Voltaire only justified himself by his consternation; he admitted everything with the greatest candour, and ended by personally handing over to M. de Taulès the papers which concerned this little negotiation.

The *Petit Conseil*, all of a tremble, could not be calm until it knew the secret plans of the *natifs*. They had already been several times, seven or eight hundred of them, to Carouge [a suburb just outside Geneva and just inside the territory of Savoie] to debate and coordinate their conduct. Informed that a certain Georges d'Auzière was the principal leader of these movements, the *Petit Conseil* had his papers seized and put the man in prison. It is claimed that the *natifs* hoped to secure political recognition in the republic, and to hold the balance between the magistrates and the *bourgeoisie*; that they had been excited by some of the *Représentants*; and that M. de Voltaire had had the weakness to promise them his protection.[20]

But in reality Beauteville thought that Voltaire's 'absurd and ridiculous behaviour' was more deserving of compassion than anger, considering that he was nearly seventy-three years old, 'and inexpressibly confused'.[21]

By this time, all the different warring parties began to think that Voltaire was on the other side, as he told d'Argental in mid-May.

As for the comedy of Geneva, it is a cold and complicated play which is starting to bore me terribly. The *natifs* say that I take the side of the *bourgeois*; the *bourgeois* fear that I am taking the side of the *natifs*. The *natifs* and the *bourgeois* pretend that I am too deferential to the Council. The Council says that I am too friendly with the *natifs* and the *bourgeois*. I therefore declared to the Council, *bourgeois* and *natifs* that, not being a churchwarden in their parish, it was not appropriate that I should get mixed up in their business, and that I have enough business of my own.[22]

Théodore Tronchin, though far away in Paris, strongly suspected Voltaire of disloyalty, and he went round Paris claiming that Voltaire was on the side of the *Représentants*. Seven months later, in the spring of 1767, Théodore was heard to say to the king that he was no longer Voltaire's friend, on the grounds that Voltaire was siding with the *Représentants*, an assertion that Voltaire described as 'quite ridiculous, especially in the mouth of a doctor'.[23] It was all the more ridiculous, since Voltaire was by now probably at least as much on the side of the *natifs* as on that of the *Représentants*.

But Voltaire soon found himself in the middle of a real-life drama, which had some of the elements of low farce but which threw him into a state of rising panic. This was the drama of Mme Lejeune and the contraband books.

Censorship was more severe in France than in Geneva, so enterprising Parisian booksellers would try by underhand methods to procure from Geneva (and other places) books that could not legally be printed (or sold) in France. Mme Lejeune was the wife of such a Parisian bookseller, and towards the end of 1766 she travelled to Geneva, under the pseudonym of Mme Doiret, to buy some forbidden books. She and her husband were also protégés of the comte d'Argental; d'Argental discreetly supported Lejeune's activities as a bookseller in the distribution of forbidden books, including those by Voltaire, and he allowed Lejeune to claim that he was or had previously been a domestic servant in the d'Argental household. D'Argental wrote to Voltaire to tell him that Mme Lejeune would be coming to Geneva to buy books, and he asked him to help her make her way home. Voltaire naturally agreed, and on 11 December 1766 he wrote to d'Argental:

This honest woman has just arrived, and you can be sure that we have welcomed her in the name of my angels. We immediately sent for her and her luggage from Geneva. We rescued her from the most expensive hostelry in Europe, where she would have been ruined. We shall put her up, and we shall take good care of her. We shall supply a vehicle to conduct her in safety as far as Dijon. The recommendations of my angels are sacred, are they not?[24]

Accordingly, Voltaire lent Mme Lejeune a carriage and horses belonging to Mme Denis and enlisted a local customs inspector called Jeannin, from the tax office at nearby Saconnex, to escort her part of the way. Her three trunks were loaded up, and they set off in the expectation that at the French customs post at Collonges (south-west of Geneva), the trunks would be sealed and Mme Lejeune could proceed in peace. The plan went badly wrong, however, for Jeannin betrayed Mme Lejeune to the French customs officers. The trunks were opened and were found to contain, under a surface covering of old clothes, over eighty forbidden books, including Voltaire's *Dictionnaire philosophique*, and his anti-Christian *Sermon des cinquante*. The customs officials seized the trunks and their contents, as well as the carriage and horses. Mme Lejeune panicked and legged it across country back to Geneva.

Voltaire feared that the mishap at Collonges might be extremely dangerous to him personally, for it had taken place only five months after the execution of La Barre in Abbeville on 1 July 1766, and with it the ceremonial burning of Voltaire's *Dictionnaire philosophique*. But he hoped that it might not prove too dramatic, provided his influential friends could pull the right strings in Paris. He wrote to d'Argental on 23 December 1766:

She took flight through ice and snow through a fearful countryside. We don't know where she is. She has made a really cruel journey. Her flight makes her seem guilty. But of what? She does not know how to read, she was following her husband's orders, she does not know if a book is forbidden or not. I am so sorry for her, I am having her looked for everywhere, I am afraid she may be in prison. There is not a moment to be lost. One word from a *fermier général* to the customs post at Collonges will be enough, but this word is really necessary. You must write immediately.

My worst fear is that the director of the bureau at Collonges may send the papers to the police at Lyon or Paris, and that it could become a criminal affair which could go far.[25]

Four days after his first account of the Lejeune disaster, Voltaire adopted an indignant tone of injured innocence.

Mme Lejeune is in a safe place, she has nothing to fear, she is guilty of nothing. Here is a copy of the letter which I have written today to the vice-chancellor [René-Charles de Maupeou]. We are not asking for favours, we are asking for justice. There is certainly nothing else to be done, unless you would speak to M. Maupeou and make him see the absurdity of the idea that I should sell foreign books, or that I should send fifty or sixty volumes containing ten or twelve different works, that we demand in justice the release of our stolen property. One conversation will be enough. I trust they will not bother the king with this miserable affair.[26]

On 2 January 1767 Voltaire told d'Argental that Mme Lejeune was safe in Switzerland and that he was taking care of her expenses. Towards the end of his letter he told d'Argental that Mme Lejeune had written to him to let him know that she was returning to Paris on horseback. 'You can see how brave she is.'[27]

But early in the new year Voltaire learned that Mme Lejeune had been carrying a note from her husband, signed by him and identifying him as d'Argental's *valet de chambre* and specifying a shopping list of the forbidden books he wanted her to buy. Unfortunately she had mislaid this incriminating evidence while she was in Geneva. By now Voltaire was becoming desperate with anxiety on his own behalf and on 9 January 1767 wrote to Antoine Auget, baron de Montyon, the senior foreign ministry official who was responsible for judging contraband cases.

Sir, it is a great consolation that you should be the judge of my niece, Mme Denis; for as for me, having nothing, I have nothing to lose; I have given everything away. The château that I have built belongs to her; the horses, the carriages, everything belongs to her. It is she whom the Cerberuses of the frontier post are persecuting; we both have the honour to write to you to beg you to free us from the claws of the gate-keepers of hell.

It is absurd to suppose that Mme Denis and I should carry on a trade in foreign books. We have never known any Mme Doiret; there was a Mme Doiret who came to our part of the world in her capacity as an old clothes trader; she bought some clothes from our servants, though we never saw her; she borrowed from them an old cart and some ploughing horses from our farm, which is far from the château; we knew nothing of it until after the arrest.

Far from contravening in any way the laws of the kingdom, I have considerably improved the king's estates on the frontier where I am, clearing waste ground and building eleven houses; and, far from engaging in the least contraband, I have on three occasions armed my vassals and my servants against fraudsters. I am only occupied in serving the king, and I have found in belles-lettres my only recreation at the age of seventy-three years.[28]

It is a pitiful, wretched letter, full of lies and half-truths, pathetic denials and abject snivelling; it is very Voltaire. For if Voltaire was spiritually bold, he was not personally brave at all. In his rising anxiety about the Lejeune case he wrote a torrent of seventeen letters to d'Argental between 11 December 1766 and 2 February 1767. But he got far fewer back, and by 12 January he began to suspect, with distress, fear and anger, that d'Argental was not trying as hard as he might to help him.

You will perhaps be impatient, my adorable angel, to receive so many letters from me; but that's because I am quite upset to receive so few from you. Please forgive, I beg you, the anxieties of Mme Denis, and myself.

You have told us that the ministers had made it a rule never to compromise themselves for their friends, and never to ask favours from each other. It would certainly be a very odious rule, dictated by indifference, weakness and self-satisfied *amour-propre*. I cannot conceive that one can only feel warmth for tragic verses, and not also put some warmth into the concerns which most interest friends like you.

Is it possible, in such an important affair as the one which affects us both, that you never wanted to act?[29]

Coming from Voltaire, who was normally gushingly friendly to d'Argental, these accusations of indifference and neglect come across with great brutality and bear eloquent witness to the intensity of Voltaire's fear. The next day Voltaire wrote d'Argental another long and insistent letter of urgings and complaints on the Lejeune affair; but when he received it, d'Argental wrote coldly cutting comments in the margin.[30]

On the same day, 13 January 1767, Voltaire wrote to Richelieu, suggesting that he might quite suddenly have to escape to Switzerland and openly blaming d'Argental, though without naming him.

> You would be quite astonished at the main reason which could, from one moment to another, force me to make this journey. It is a man whom you know, a man who has been my friend for more than sixty years, a man finally who, by the most extraordinary adventure in the world, has placed me in a strangely embarrassing position; I have compromised myself for him in the most painful manner, but the only thing I can reproach him for is having acted too limply.[31]

Voltaire's fears were intensified when he heard word, in late January, that the Lejeune case might well be referred to the court at Dijon, and he wondered whether he could buy off the customs office by offering to pay them a fine to be negotiated.[32]

Then all of a sudden the sun came out, the clouds evaporated: the Vice-Chancellor, René-Charles de Maupeou, had stifled the Lejeune affair, and Voltaire's worries were at an end. He wrote to d'Argental on 2 February 1767: 'We have learned from [Mme Lejeune] that God is just. We do not yet know the details; but we think that his justice must crush the devils, especially the devil Jeannin. I can breathe again; I shall send no more packets [of books]. I think it is appropriate that I should write a little thank-you note to M. de Montyon.'[33]

When it was all over, Voltaire became quite sheepish about his terrors and his reproaches. He wrote to d'Argental on 6 February 1767:

> Your servant got away with it, my divine angels: the councillors of state, the snows and the illnesses which come with age and the rigours of the climate reduced me to a pitiful state. I consider that of all these scourges, fear is still the worst. It freezes the blood, it gave me a sort of attack of apoplexy. Blessed be the Vice-Chancellor, who has been my main doctor. Without him nothing would have been done. I only had the honour to know him from having played chess with him over

fifty years ago. This time he could have checkmated me with a single word.[34]

Meanwhile, in Geneva, the mediators had totally failed to bring about a negotiated settlement, and by the beginning of January 1767 ambassador Beauteville had abandoned his efforts and had secretly left Geneva; some kind of military pressure by the French was now to be expected. As Voltaire reported a few days later: 'I am patiently waiting for the large army of five or six hundred men which will pretend to besiege Geneva. The only thing the headquarters will really besiege will be Ferney; they will expect to be amused, but they will only find sadness here.'[35]

The political crisis made daily life rather difficult. As Voltaire reported:

> Almost all the shops are closed, and the financial markets too. I have a large part of my assets in Geneva, but all the banks are closed. It so happens that at Tournay and Ferney I have 150 mouths to feed, but you can't keep that going with alexandrine verses and bankruptcies. The ending of almost all trade, which only now happens through smugglers, the terrible expense of foodstuffs, the doubling of guards on the farms, the multiplication of beggars, the looming bankruptcies, none of that is at all poetic. No, no, there won't be war this winter – but while waiting for the war, there is famine here, and the devil everywhere.[36]

The following day, 8 January 1767, the troops arrived. 'There is no longer any communication between Geneva and France. The troops are spread all along the frontier, and by a curious fatality it is we who are being punished for the foolishness of the Genevans. Geneva is the only place where we used to be able to get butcher's meat and all the necessities of life. We are blockaded and we are dying of hunger.'[37] Voltaire added: 'Would you mind, my dear friend, sending on to M. Laleu, in an envelope, my certificate of life, since I am still alive.'[38] (Guillaume-Claude Laleu, the king's secretary, was also Voltaire's personal lawyer in Paris. In order to keep getting the income from his life-rents, Voltaire had every year to provide proof that he was still alive.)

The next day he wrote to the chevalier de Beauteville:

> They have lodged dragoons all around my hen coop known as the

château de Tournay. Maman Denis can no longer have good beef on the table; she has to send to Gex for cow meat. I do not know how we shall manage to get the letters which arrive at the post office in Geneva. Even worse, we shall need a passport from the king to go and fetch cassia [his preferred laxative] from Colladon's [a well-known pharmacy]. Beef and partridges is bad enough, but not to be able to get cassia! It's intolerable![39]

And indeed, Voltaire wrote the same day to the duc de Choiseul, the Prime Minister, to ask for a passport to allow Voltaire's servants to cross the frontier to get supplies from Geneva or Switzerland.

Voltaire's extensive contacts soon proved useful. Even before Choiseul replied to his request for a *laissez-passer*, Pierre-Michel Hennin, the permanent French Resident at Geneva, gave him a limited passport for collecting his post. And Jean-François-René Tabareau, the director of postal services at Lyon, sent him a pair of freshly caught soles; Voltaire's letter of thanks, with its obsequious slithering into new requests, is a marvel.

Sir, we are obliged to you for having perfectly satisfied the taste of one of the mortal sins. Our greed thanks you most warmly for your soles, which were as fresh as if we had eaten them at Marseille. I am embarrassed by your offers; but if you have some agent you could recommend, we should take advantage, Mme Denis and I, of your kindness and go as far as to send you sometimes a little list of our needs. I had just got that far, Sir, when they brought in a shad and two soles, which had just come from you; seriously, the Charterhouse of Ripaille does not eat as well as we. If Mme Denis and I were really impudent, we should beg you to get your supplier to send us this winter, by post, two pieces of poultry twice a week; that would not load him down too much, we would pay the supplier cash, and the postal costs would be taken care of; but really, we dare not be so indiscreet.[40]

But it was not just a question of discretion; it was mainly a question of practicability. By the end of January 1767 Voltaire wrote again to Hennin to explain his difficulties and to ask for more passports.

We have sent to Gex for some butcher's meat, but all they could get was bad cow's meat; our people could not eat it. On two occasions we sent by post to Lyon for rations for one day, but we cannot keep doing it. We used to send to Lyon for provisions by the public carriers, but the carriers stopped running. Our almoner fell dangerously ill at Ornex; we could not get him either a doctor or a surgeon because the carts sent to fetch them could not get through.

We do not complain of the troops; on the contrary, we would wish them to remain permanently at their posts. Not only would they put a brake on the audacity of the smugglers, often numbering as many as fifty or sixty, who cross to the territory of Geneva, and who would soon become highway robbers; but they could prevent the pernicious trade in jewellery and watches made in Geneva, which is prohibited in France but which is mainly sustained by the inhabitants of the province of Gex, almost all of whom have abandoned agriculture to work at home on the manufactures of Geneva.

We have always secured our provisions as far as possible from France, and we would like to go on doing it; but geography does not permit it. We are therefore forced to ask for three passports: for Mr Wagnière, for Mr Faÿ,* and for the postman.[41]

The next day, 30 January, however, he wrote again to Hennin to cancel his request for three passports; for Choiseul had given instructions to the chevalier de Jaucourt, the local French military commander, to provide all-purpose passports for Voltaire and all his household. Voltaire urged Hennin to come and visit him: 'Come, come; *maman* will now be able to feed you well; we shall have good beef, not cow.'[42]

Voltaire's concern to 'prevent the pernicious trade in watches made in Geneva' is doubly ironic. At this stage Voltaire was a vigorous, reforming but still quasi-feudal landowner, and he hated to lose his farmworkers to the Geneva watch industry. But when, three years later, the political troubles in Geneva became so violent that many watchmakers fled the city and sought refuge in the frontier region in France, Voltaire quickly saw a very different opening: he organised the establishment, by the refugees, of a new and remarkably successful watchmaking industry at Ferney, for which he also acted as chief financier and international sales manager.

Despite Choiseul's passports, life at Ferney remained difficult under the blockade. Mme Denis was able to buy meat in Geneva, but she had to get all her other provisions from Lyon, but only by post, since the public carriers were still not operating.[43] As a result, Voltaire cut back on his entertainment of visitors; or at least he said he did:

---

* Louis du Faÿ was *maître d'hôtel* at Ferney.

Mme Denis has been very ill, they bled her twice. As for me, I bear all the burdens of old age. There are no more big suppers, either for her or for me. We eat one pigeon between us at dinner; the Dupuits, the Racle and the La Harpe households dine together with the children. Fortunately, we have closed our doors against the English, the Germans and the Genevans. One must end one's days in retirement; for me the hurly-burly has become unbearable.[44]

But the French troops kept up a perpetual commotion in the château and village: 'I write to you to the sound of the drum. I have here a complete regiment, which has been brought here by the troubles of Geneva. The officers have supper in my house while I am in my bed, and the soldiers have made a fine road, but at the expense of my wheat and my vines; but they won't defend me from the north wind, which will be my despair during the next six months.'[45]

Voltaire's determination to cut back his social life seems to have been rather changeable. In the late summer of 1767 he heard with great distress that Mme d'Argental was seriously ill. But she got better, and a fortnight later Voltaire prepared to hold a party for her recovery. 'We are getting ready to celebrate her convalescence; we shall have a new comedy [his play *Charlot*], and then supper for eighty guests; and then we shall have a ball and fireworks.'[46] A couple of days later he wrote to his great-nephew the judge Alexandre d'Hornoy: 'It is true that there are lots of parties at Ferney, but it is *maman* who takes care of them by herself; she runs the department of good food, spectacles, balls and ruin. As for me, I lead a life of permanent suffering and weakness.'[47]

They had another party on 4 October 1767, the feast day of Saint Francis, Voltaire's saint's day. Voltaire wrote to Damilaville that same evening: 'We have performed *Charlot* again at Ferney, and better than it will ever be played at the Comédie Française. Mme Denis has just given me, in the presence of the Conti regiment and of the whole province, the most agreeable fête I have ever seen.' Although Voltaire did not know it at the time, this turned out to be the last big party at Ferney for a long time. For by the next spring Voltaire and Mme Denis had had a major row, she had left Ferney for Paris and Voltaire had closed his château to all visitors.

In November 1767, ten months after they arrived, the French blockading troops departed. 'Ferney is deserted, for we no longer have any soldiers here. The august powers have decided against the illustrious *Représentants*, and the news of the decision has been even worse received than a new play.'[48] Voltaire elaborated on this judgement six weeks later, in January 1768: 'There is no longer any real disturbance in Geneva, but certainly a lot of ill-will, and many troublesome pamphlets. Everything has remained calm. The two opposing parties have pleaded their cases before their judges; the magistrates have won, but the *Représentants* have not accepted the judgement. People are looking for some means of conciliation.'[49]

The failure of the outside arbitrators was soon apparent on 6 March 1768: 'Tronchin, the Attorney-General of the little republic next door, was assailed yesterday evening in front of his house by 500 people, of whom more than half cried that they wanted to tear him to pieces. The people's commissioners had the greatest difficulty in pulling him from their hands, and they had him guarded all night by fifty *bourgeois*. It is no longer a joke.'[50]

Faced with the violence of the dispossessed, the oligarchs almost immediately offered concessions, both to the *Représentants* and to the *natifs*. Voltaire wrote to Mme Denis on 8 March 1768: 'The Council has surrendered almost everything to the people, who have made peace as victors. It was hardly worth while sending an ambassador and some troops, to leave the mastery to those they wanted to punish.'[51]

Under the peace plan, the *Petit Conseil* would give up the practice of arbitrary arrest, and the *Conseil Général* would have a greater role in the election of the members of the Council of 200, as well as the power to block the election of up to four of the twenty-five members of the *Petit Conseil*. In addition, and perhaps more significantly, the new deal gave some real benefits to the *natifs*: in future they would have the right to full commercial independence as artisans, as well as the right to practise medicine, surgery and pharmacy, and the right to sit on juries. They would also have the right to purchase citizenship of the republic, if in quite limited numbers. On 11 March 1768 this so-called Edict of Conciliation was overwhelmingly adopted in the *Conseil Général*, by 1204 votes to 37; the ultra-*Négatifs* refused to vote it, however, and called it the *Édit des Pistolets* (Edict of the Pistols).[52]

A few days later Voltaire reported that 'everything in Geneva was in a deep peace', and that 'several people, from both sides, are at Ferney, drinking tea together in the greatest friendship. A week ago they were preparing to cut each other's throats. Everything has finished to the satisfaction of the people.'[53]

Despite what Voltaire thought, however, it was not to the satisfaction of the people. Obviously, the patricians had made significant concessions; equally obviously, the balance of power was still heavily skewed in their favour against all other classes of the population. But the really serious problem was the attitude of the *natifs*. Not merely were they not grateful for the unprecedented concessions they had received, but they were deeply dissatisfied that these concessions were not greater and bitterly resentful at their disadvantaged place in society. As so often, it was the beginning of reform that opened the flood-gates of revolution. The Edict of Conciliation turned out to be not a settlement but just a way-station in a long-running saga of conflict between the patricians and the rest. It was the breakdown of this 'settlement' two years later, in February 1770, that paved the way for Voltaire's most extraordinary new incarnation, at the age of seventy-six, as an industrial financier and entrepreneur, and international salesman to the rich and famous on several continents.

THE QUARREL WITH
Mme DENIS

1767–1769

AT THE BEGINNING OF MARCH 1768 Mme Denis abruptly left Voltaire and Ferney and went back to Paris. She and Voltaire had for some time been talking about the idea that she might make a trip to Paris, but in the days immediately preceding her departure they had a running quarrel, which culminated on her last night in Ferney in a violent row – so violent that Mme Denis left on the morning of 1 March without seeing Voltaire or saying goodbye to him.

Voltaire was distraught when he discovered, in the middle of the day, that she had already gone without a word of farewell, and he wrote to her immediately.

No doubt there is a destiny, and often it is really cruel. I went three times to your door, you knocked at mine. I wanted to walk off my pain in the garden. It was ten o'clock, I put the needle at ten o'clock on the solar globe, I was waiting until you should have woken.

I thought that you would be dining at the château, as you had said. None of the servants warned me of anything, they all thought I knew. I called for Father Adam, and we talked until midday. Finally, I asked where you were. Wagnière said to me: 'Eh, what! Don't you know that she left at ten o'clock?' I turned, more dead than alive, to Father Adam. He replied to me like Wagnière: 'I thought you knew!'

I am in despair. I knew that the moment of separation would always have been frightful; but it is even more frightful that you should have left without seeing me.

This is another proof of the persecutions of my destiny. La Harpe is the cause of my unhappiness. Anyone who predicted that La Harpe would have caused me to die a hundred leagues from you would not have been believed. But finally the truth is out. Damilaville went to see Antoine in the rue Hautefeuille, and Antoine said that La Harpe was lying. There, that is the origin of my suffering.

If I die, I shall die all yours, and if I live, my life is yours. I tenderly embrace M. and Mme Dupuits. I love them, I miss them, my heart is pierced.[1]

Voltaire never really explained to his friends the reasons for Mme Denis's departure, and to d'Argental least of all. The nearest he ever got to a credible explanation was that his finances were in a parlous state. 'Mme Denis has gone to Paris to sort out our affairs,' he told a friend, 'which had become rather damaged by suppers for 200 guests, by balls and by plays. I have been like a little duke of Württemberg: I have ruined myself by giving parties.'[2]

If Voltaire's finances were under pressure, it was partly because the duke of Württemberg was failing to keep up the very large payments that he owed. Voltaire had been protesting with increasing agitation, but without success, to the duke's representatives since the previous summer;[3] and it was because of his frustrations on this front that he started to think of turning to his debtors in France, for Richelieu owed him £42,000 and the Guise family over £20,000.[4] He thought that, if Mme Denis went to Paris, she could sort out these problems on the spot; and he thought that she would have special influence in the case of Richelieu, since she had at one time had a liaison with him. '*Maman*, who has lived with him a lot, will find it easier to get him to pay than would a bailiff with a tipstaff. It is true that she is no longer at an age which opens the purses of dukes and peers; but a former liaison is always respected.'[5]

But even if Voltaire had originally persuaded Mme Denis to go to Paris in order to sort out their financial problems, we can be fairly sure that the violent quarrel that precipitated her sudden departure was not about money. For almost immediately after she left for Paris, Voltaire showered money on her and on various members of her family: £20,000 a year for Mme Denis; £2,700 to her sister; £1,800 each for the abbé Mignot, her brother, and for Alexandre d'Hornoy, her nephew; and £1,300 to Marie-Françoise Corneille. Despite Voltaire's feeling of financial embarrassment, he was still enormously wealthy, and even after these new settlements he still expected to keep an income for himself and the Ferney household of £36,000 a year.[6]

On the other hand, the violence of their quarrel, in the days immediately before her departure, may have changed the emotional equation. Jean-Louis Wagnière, Voltaire's secretary, was convinced that Voltaire intended a permanent separation. 'I saw that his mind was made up long ago,' he told Damilaville. 'He wants to live alone; he does not want any visitors, not even his closest friends. He does not want Mme Denis to come back; he wants to sell the estate, to live at Tournay; but he has taken no firm decision. He is very well, and very gay, though sometimes in a bad temper. He works, he amuses himself.'[7]

Voltaire says something similar in a poignant letter, written a fortnight after her departure: 'For the past fifteen years [i.e., ever since he moved to Geneva], I have really only been living by myself, even though I have been the innkeeper of Europe (*l'aubergiste de l'Europe*); finally I am now completely retired, and I shall stay that way, so far as I can see, until the end. At least, that's how I think right now.'[8] Perhaps, at this particular moment, he did not expect or want Mme Denis to return.

Later he changed his mind, and much later Mme Denis offered to return. But the fact that she had taken with her Voltaire's beloved Marie-Françoise and her husband, and the length of time that she stayed away, certainly carry the implications of a separation that might have been permanent. So what was it that transformed a short-term business trip into a deep rupture? Voltaire gives us the answer, in his first letter to Mme Denis: 'La Harpe is the cause of my unhappiness.'[9]

Jean François de La Harpe was an ambitious young writer and a protégé of Voltaire, and with his young and extremely pretty wife he was a frequent visitor to Ferney. Voltaire treated him as a favourite son, and called him 'mon fils'. He also called him 'petit', for he was in fact unusually short of stature.

Unfortunately, La Harpe took to going through Voltaire's manuscripts on the sly, secretly purloining those which he thought he could make use of among the literati in Paris. One of these manuscripts was particularly sensitive to Voltaire, both personally and politically, for it was part of his *Guerre civile de Genève*, a satirical poem in three cantos (later expanded to five), in which Voltaire made mock of many of the protagonists in the recent political troubles in Geneva. Voltaire had circulated the first and the third of these cantos, but he held back the second because it made fun of the Tronchins by name.

In early November 1767 La Harpe made a trip to Paris, and he must have taken with him a copy of the second canto of the *Guerre civile de Genève*, along with other manuscripts he had filched. For in February, 1768, Voltaire heard that the second canto of the *Guerre civile de Genève* was being circulated in Paris, and he immediately suspected La Harpe, as he told Damilaville:

> We have here, my dear friend, a new and very disagreeable trouble that I entrust to you. You know that I had a bit of fun with the ridiculous war in Geneva. I was quite willing to let out two cantos of this little poem, but since the Tronchins were discussed in the second canto, I never gave it to anyone. La Harpe would go into my study every day, and he would ferret about in all my papers. I let him do it; I counted on his discretion, and on his sense of obligation for all I have done for him. As soon as he reached Paris, this second canto was made public.
>
> When he returned here, and I complained of the publication of this second canto, he said nothing and blushed. Knowing that he was accused by the whole household, he went four whole days without daring to speak to me. His wife finally drove him to make his excuses to me, and he said that he had the manuscript from a certain Antoine. This Antoine is a sculptor who lives in the rue Hautefeuille. It is quite certain that I never sent the manuscript to Antoine, since I do not know him. The worst of it is that La Harpe does not seem to feel the dishonesty and turpitude of his actions.[10]

All this while La Harpe still stayed on at Ferney, but without coming clean. On the contrary: 'Instead of repairing the damage he had done me, he wrote, from his bedroom to mine, a very hard letter in which he insulted me without justifying himself.'[11]

Two days later, on 24 February 1768, La Harpe and his wife left Ferney for Paris, but without exchanging any words of farewell or friendship with Voltaire, let alone any expression of regret or remorse. Some time in the next few days Voltaire and Mme Denis must have had their major row, for it was only five days after the departure of La Harpe that Mme Denis also left abruptly for Paris, with Mlle Corneille and her husband, Dupuits. As Voltaire says, it looks as though the row that precipitated their emotional rupture was about La Harpe.

But the row was not primarily about the theft of the second canto of the *Guerre civile de Genève*, but about Voltaire's belief that Mme Denis's relationship with La Harpe had become indecently close. 'I have entirely forgotten the wrong that M. de La Harpe has done me,' he told d'Alembert:

> but it seems to me that he is not familiar with tender and touching expressions. He told you that he had read to Mme Denis the letter which he wrote from his bedroom to mine, and that both of them started weeping; apparently he mistook Mme Denis for his wife; and I do not see how this letter could have drawn tears from my niece. These are his own words:
>
> 'You allege that you had not given it to anyone, I believe you, but what reason would you have for not believing me, when I tell you that it was in Paris that it was given to me? If you were to make damaging complaints against me, you would force me to have some sort of public trial with you.'
>
> He is the cause of my separation from Mme Denis; he is the reason why the last days of my life are deprived of all help; my only consolation is knowing that Mme Denis should be happy in Paris. I am giving her a pension of £20,000, and I have promised her £35,000.[12]

On the same day Voltaire told a similar story to Damilaville.

> He persuaded Mme Denis of his innocence. She was very angry with me for having made her lose, in Mme La Harpe, a complaisant woman who could amuse her during the winter. It is on this subject that Mme Denis treated me very cruelly; but since I forgive La Harpe, you can easily see that I forgive Mme Denis. My life is so different from hers that it is absolutely necessary that she be in Paris, where she has many friends and relatives, and that I should die in solitude.[13]

It is hard to know exactly what has been going on, but it is not too hard to tell what Voltaire thinks has been going on: he believes that Mme Denis has been disloyal to him, siding with La Harpe against him; he may even suspect her of being unfaithful to him in the fullest sense. When he says that Mme Denis and La Harpe were weeping together over La Harpe's letter, when he says that La Harpe mistook Mme Denis for his wife and when he says that Mme Denis regarded La Harpe's wife as a *complaisante*, it seems clear that he believes that Mme Denis and La Harpe have been sharing a wholly improper degree of intimacy.

Inevitably, the rupture led to recriminations and post-mortems between Voltaire and Mme Denis. In one letter to her, Voltaire poured out his pent-up anger.

> The eight-page letter I sent you spelled out my justifiable pain at the cruel ill humour that you inflicted on me several days in a row, and at the dining table, in public. I was deeply pained, and my wound bleeds still, but the sad state you have put me into will never prevent me from rendering what I owe to such a long and such an intimate friendship. Sometimes you let fly barbs which pierce the heart. You have driven me to despair, but you cannot weaken my feelings for you. Think of my age, my weakness, my illness, and forgive me all of them. You will see once more how much I have been wounded, how much I love you and how far I have carried my desire to make you happy.[14]

But if Mme Denis was sometimes ill tempered with Voltaire, it seems clear that Voltaire was quite capable of referring to her in extremely disobliging terms. In August 1760 he had written to a not particularly close acquaintance:

> Mme Denis is a fat pig, Sir, like most of your Parisiennes; they get up at midday; the day passes, they do not know how; they have no time to write, and when they want to write, they can find neither paper, pen, nor ink, so then they have to come and ask me, but now the desire to write disappears. For every ten women, nine are like this. Forgive, Sir, Mme Denis her extreme laziness; she is no less attached to you, but she would rather say it than write it.[15]

But these spats were exceptional. Voltaire went on writing to Mme Denis with great frequency over the next year and a half; he took great pains to ensure that she was comfortably off; and he never ceased to say how much he loved her. When she eventually decided to return, Voltaire was overjoyed. It is possible, therefore, that at the height of their quarrel, and before she left, Voltaire may have wanted shot of her, but that he changed his mind after she left and really wanted her back – provided, of course, that it was on his terms. Inevitably it would be on hers.

One of the strangest things about the rupture between Voltaire and Mme Denis is that he never explained or even discussed it with d'Argental, his oldest and usually his most intimate friend; in fact, he barely alluded to it at all. He wrote to many friends in the days that followed her departure; in several of these letters he mentioned that she was going to Paris, with the explanation that she was going to repair his shattered fortunes. To d'Argental, however, he did not write at all until six weeks later, and even then it was a very curious letter, in which he almost explicitly withheld any explanation of the background of the rupture.

> You ask, my dear angel, that one should open one's heart, and when one has opened it wide, you do not say a word to the usher. I have not talked to you about the adventure of La Harpe, whom I don't think you know, and to whom in any case I do not want to cause any pain, and who never had any intention of harming me, even though he was in the wrong. He is young, he is poor, he is married: he needs help, I did not want to undermine his reputation with you. I want Mme Denis to live happily in Paris, and I wish to die in solitude.[16]

In other words, the 'adventure of La Harpe' was none of d'Argental's business. Voltaire wrote another twelve letters to d'Argental during the next eight months, but in all of them he simply passed over in silence the question of his relationship with Mme Denis. What makes this wall of silence particularly strange is that d'Argental was probably one of the very few people who had been allowed by Voltaire to know the true nature of his liaison with Mme Denis.

Almost the first thing that Voltaire did after Mme Denis's departure was to talk of selling Ferney; the château had been bought in her name, so she would be entitled to all the proceeds of the sale. Within five days of her going he told her that there were potential buyers who could be interested, at the right price, and he urged her to take the opportunity. 'At one o'clock today I received a letter offering to buy Ferney from you, and to pay half in cash, half in *rentes viagères*. All that remains is to settle the price. I suggest that you ask £300,000, but perhaps you should consider whether you would be prepared to go as low as £250,000.'[17] Two days later he told her (perhaps he had only just discovered) that the bidder was Jacob Tronchin, a cousin of Jean-Robert and François and a member of the *Petit Conseil*; and since Jacob was hesitating between Ferney and another property, Voltaire urged her to drop the price to £200,000 or even £180,000.

> You ask what will become of me. I answer that Ferney is odious to me without you. If I sell Ferney, I shall retire in the summer time to

Tournay. But I am thinking more of you than of me. I want you to be happy; I have had my life. I have so far kept all the servants, but I have not left my room. The thermometer has been six degrees below freezing. All the newly planted trees will die. I shall not regret them.[18]

Voltaire's project to sell Ferney can be seen as a practical response to financial difficulties, but it was really a front for deeper questions about the relationship between himself and Mme Denis. For if Mme Denis were to go along with Voltaire's suggestion and agree to sell Ferney, that would be a powerful symbolic indication that she intended her relationship, or at least her life, with Voltaire to be over for good.

In June Voltaire told her that they had missed the chance of selling Ferney to Jacob Tronchin for £200,000, since he had bought another property, but he added: 'As for me, I should leave it tomorrow, if it weren't for the fact that I am kept here by my two centuries.'[19]* In other words, Voltaire was telling Mme Denis that he was working too hard to leave Ferney just yet.

A month later, in July, he raised once again the idea of selling the château; but he was obviously quite half-hearted about it, and by late August Mme Denis told Voltaire that she did not want to sell. For nearly six months she had hesitated, and the fact that she had now decided not to sell strongly suggests, not necessarily that she had opted for life with Voltaire, but at least that she had not decided against it. Voltaire must have been acutely sensitive to these implications.

If Voltaire was depressed by his new solitude, he remained as combative as ever. At Easter 1768, shortly after Mme Denis's departure, he solemnly attended Mass in the church he had built at Ferney and took communion, like the other parishioners. Just before the sermon, however, Voltaire stood up and spoke: he called on the priest to say prayers for the queen, who was at the time very ill, and he informed the congregation that a burglary had been committed in the parish. Wagnière described the scene in a letter to Damilaville: 'I was present at the service, and when I heard him open his mouth to harangue the congregation, my blood froze and I hid myself. This is making a frightful scandal, and is not having the effect that he had hoped.'[20] Quite quickly the rumour mills were putting it about that Voltaire had taken it upon himself to deliver a sermon.

---

* Voltaire was updating and enlarging *Le Siècle de Louis XIV* and working on *Le Précis du Siècle de Louis XV*.

Within a week Voltaire received a written rebuke from Jean-Pierre Biord, the bishop of Annecy: 'If, on the day of your communion, you had not been seen to intervene to preach to the people on the subject of thieving and larceny, which greatly scandalised all those present, then no one would be able to treat as equivocal your public displays of religion.'[21] He said he would like to be able to believe in the sincerity of Voltaire's confession (clearly implying that he did not), and he went on to demand that Voltaire make a public disavowal of his attacks on the Christian religion. Voltaire was unrepentant and protested that he had only been doing his duty as the lord of his estates.[22] But Bishop Biord refused to be fobbed off by Voltaire's evasions, and he returned to the attack. The taking of holy communion, he told Voltaire, required of him a spectacular public recantation; without such a public recantation he would forbid any priest to give him the sacrament in future.

Finding Voltaire recalcitrant, Bishop Biord alerted the authorities in Versailles, and Voltaire soon received a sharp reproof from Louis Phélypeaux, comte de Saint-Florentin, the Minister of the Interior.[23] But Voltaire was determined not to be put down by the bishop, and the following year (1769), at Easter time, he resolved once more to take communion. He knew that Biord would prevent him from taking it in the normal way, so he pretended to be dying, in order to be able to demand that Father Pierre Gros, the local parish priest, give him the last rites in his bed. At first Gros procrastinated and told Voltaire that he must first retract, before a notary, all his bad works. But Voltaire was not to be put off, claiming that he had suffered several attacks of fever and that in such circumstances the law required Gros to give him the last rites.[24]

There was now a prolonged tussle back and forth, in which Gros and various other priests tried to insist that Voltaire could not have absolution, and therefore could not receive communion, without a full recantation of his past impieties and a full declaration of his Catholic faith. Voltaire drafted for them several different statements that were much less than a full declaration of faith but avoided signing any of the texts that they put before him. Eventually, by persistence and evasion and deception and bullying, he wore them down: he demanded and got absolution from a friar, and his 'last rites' from Gros.[25] As he received communion, he said: 'Having my God in my mouth, I declare that I sincerely forgive those who have written calumnies about me to the king, and who have not succeeded in their evil plan.' Having taken his 'last rites', and after all the priests and bystanders had left the room, Voltaire immediately jumped out of bed and went for a walk in the garden with Wagnière.[26]

Voltaire could pride himself on having out-manoeuvred Bishop Biord this time, but he continued to claim, indignantly, that he had only done his public duty by taking communion at Easter. Shortly after Easter 1769 he spilled out his rage to d'Argental: 'I am a better Christian than they are; by taking communion I edify all the inhabitants of my estates and all my neighbours. Not only do I do my own duty, but I also send my Catholic servants regularly to church, and my Protestant servants regularly to the temple, and I employ a schoolmaster to teach the children their catechism. I even have public readings at mealtimes from the history of the Church and the sermons of Massillon.'*[27] Yet even Voltaire's combative vitality had its limits: he did not try the Easter charade again.

Voltaire's claim that he had the sermons of Massillon read aloud at table was actually true, at least on one occasion, but it was only to tease and annoy a clutch of distinguished visitors from the *parlement* of Dijon. According to a visitor who was present, Voltaire had asked permission of the guests to follow 'the custom of the house', and have a sermon read after the soup; and he did not spare them a single syllable of it. But if the Massillon sermon was a totally insincere provocation, the fact that Voltaire had it read aloud at table was not. For in the spring of that year, 1769, he had introduced a regular routine of readings aloud at mealtimes. 'I have myself read to, at dinner and supper, from good books, by very intelligent readers, who are rather my friends than my servants.'[28]

> In our retreat, people have nothing to say to each other; conversation is not kept going by the events of the day. Very few people have in themselves a fund of useful conversation. That is what decided me to have instructive readings during my frugal dinner and my frugal supper, in place of the boredom of saying nothing, or of saying trivial things which leave not a trace.[29]

Left on his own at Ferney, in the spring of 1768, Voltaire battened down the hatches. He wrote to Marie-Élisabeth Fontaine:

> Here I am, all alone with Father Adam, having once had 200 people to supper and put on plays. The hubbub does not suit me; solitude

---

* Jean-Baptiste Massillon (1663–1742), priest, professor of rhetoric and member of the Académie Française, was famous for his sermons. Voltaire genuinely admired Massillon for his eloquence; in 1761 he described him as 'the Racine of the pulpit' (*Letters*, 6593).

becomes me better. I shall put all my papers in order, and that will take time. Ferney is the most beautiful retreat for 50 leagues in any direction. You would not believe how much more beautiful the château and the gardens are now, but I do not receive anyone. Flocks (*volées*) of English turn up, but I shut the door in their face. My taste for solitude has become my dominant passion.[30]

He reflected wryly, in a letter to Mme du Deffand, that his previous hospitality had earned him precious little thanks.

For the past fourteen years I have been the innkeeper of Europe (*l'aubergiste de l'Europe*), and I have wearied of this profession. I have received three or four hundred Englishmen in my home, who are all so in love with their country that almost none of them has remembered me after their departure, apart from a Scottish priest named Brown, who reproached me with going to confession, which is certainly rather hard. I have had in my house French colonels with all their officers for more than a month. They serve the king so well that they have not even had the time to write, either to Mme Denis or to me. I have built a château and a church, and I have spent 500,000 francs on these profane and sacred works. But finally, illustrious debtors, of Paris and Germany, seeing that such magnificence was not suitable for me, thought it appropriate to put me on short commons to make me behave myself (*ont jugé à propos de me retrancher les vivres pour me rendre sage*). All of a sudden, therefore, I almost find myself reduced to plain philosophy.[31]

In July 1768 Voltaire told Mme Denis that he had had the main door of the château double-locked, and was seeing no one.[32] After a while the solitude began to tell on him, and he occasionally invited one or two local acquaintances to supper. But by October 1768 his solitude had become even more lonely, for Father Adam, now his only companion in the château apart from his secretaries, had found a mistress in the village and went to see her every day. Voltaire teased him mercilessly for his love-life and his hypocrisy, and each day at dinner he would get Wagnière to read out loud an act of Molière's comedy *Tartuffe* (a satire on hypocrisy), interjecting mordant comments about people who try to reconcile love and piety.[33]

That autumn Voltaire was also wrestling with the painful knowledge that Damilaville was seriously, probably fatally, ill. In September

Théodore Tronchin gave Voltaire a pessimistic prognosis of Dami-laville's case; Voltaire decided to look on the bright side. 'I should not be surprised if Tronchin were mistaken about Damilaville.'[34] But Tronchin was not mistaken: Damilaville died in great agony in December, of cancer of the throat. Voltaire wrote to d'Alembert: 'I shall regret Dami-laville all my life. I loved the boldness of his soul; I had hoped that at the end he would come and share my retirement. I did not know that he was married and a cuckold. I learn, with astonishment, that he had been separated from his wife for twelve years. He will surely not have left her a large inheritance.'[35] And to Mme Denis: 'I weep bitter tears for Damilaville; nature had made that man for me. I even imagined that he would come and retire to Ferney. Now he is dead; he will never be replaced.'[36]

Voltaire's hopes of getting paid by his Parisian debtors were regu-larly disappointed.[37] In February 1769 Richelieu was still turning a deaf ear to demands for further payment, and nothing had yet been received from the heirs of the Guise family, who were ten years behind in their payments.[38] And yet Voltaire's resources seemed deeper than ever: by the spring of 1769 his allowances to his family and others had risen to £32,000 a year, and in April of that year he told Mme Denis that, once the refinancing of the Württemberg account was settled, as he was sure it would be, she ought to be able to count on *rentes viagères* of nearly £50,000 a year.[39] This seems to imply aggregate income flows to Voltaire, to Mme Denis and to other members of the family of around £98,000 a year.

Nevertheless, Mme Denis's extravagance seems to have been more than a match for Voltaire's generosity. In April 1769 he wrote to Laleu: 'I request you, Sir, with the greatest urgency, to do the impossible, and to transfer £3,000 to Mme Denis. We shall settle up easily, you and I, for the rest, and for the honoraria that I owe you. I have the honour to be, with unbreakable attachment, Sir, your very humble and very obedient servant.'[40]

Voltaire's isolation was all the greater, in that Mme Denis had taken with her Voltaire's beloved adoptive daughter Marie-Françoise Cor-neille, her husband, Claude Dupuits, and their daughter Adélaïde. Their continued absence from Ferney during the rest of 1768 was indirectly symptomatic of the rift between Voltaire and Mme Denis. So when Marie-Françoise and her family returned to Ferney in February 1769, it must have seemed to Voltaire an event vibrant with hope. He wrote to Mme Denis: 'Dupuits, his wife and his little daughter have arrived, and they are well and lively. They are in their estate at Maconnex, in Siberia, surrounded everywhere, like me, with two feet of snow. Our consolation is that in the mountains the snow is eighteen feet deep.'[41]

Negotiations for the return of Mme Denis began soon afterwards; but at first she put forward proposals that implied that she was coming back, but not quite to Ferney. Voltaire was quite upset: 'There is, my dear niece, in your letter of 28 February, a word which pierced my heart. You want an estate half a league from Ferney. The children are coming to dinner today. I embrace you with the greatest tenderness.'[42]

For several more weeks Voltaire and Mme Denis remained at cross-purposes over her future plans. But towards the end of April 1769 she wrote him a letter unusually solicitous for his personal welfare:

> I am worried about your health. I am sure that the type of life you have chosen is not designed to be good for it. You have less need for company than others, I agree, but why sadden yourself deliberately and kill yourself with work without any relaxation other than going to Mass and no recreation apart from Father Adam? You were born gay, nature gave you all her gifts, don't lose your gift of gaiety. You reproach me with having made your house too lively. There was a time when it did not displease you. Yes, there were many people on our theatre days; but would you have preferred us to perform your plays to empty chairs? In the end, I did it for you, thinking that it would please you and relax you. You seem to have changed your way of thinking.
>
> You know, my dear friend, that you obliged and forced me to leave your home. That is what made me leave, with death in my heart. That moment is always with me, it poisons my life, and it seems just as new as on the first day. Yet I reproach you with nothing, for I have never ceased to miss you and love you.[43]

By June Voltaire and Mme Denis were beginning seriously to discuss their future. She suggested that she should move to Geneva. What Voltaire did not know was that Mme Denis was in secret correspondence with Pierre-Michel Hennin, the French Resident in Geneva, with whom she seems to have had a far closer relationship than she could publicly admit. She wrote to Hennin in early August:

> It is a century, Sir, since I had any news from you. My friendship for you cannot accommodate itself to such a long silence. How are you?

How are your affairs? Do you hope to teach reason to a man who has none [Voltaire]? I am currently in great discussions with the boss (*le patron*). The proposition that we put forward, you and I, to let me live in Geneva, has put him in a frightful rage, and has finally brought him to propose that I return to Ferney. He even admitted that he was very bored this past winter, which gave me a certain pleasure. He told me to come when I could. I have not given up the idea of Geneva. You are my only resource, in case I should be too unhappy if I go to Ferney. Do not speak of any of this. Do not doubt the sentiments and the inviolable attachment with which I have the honour to be your friend for life.[44]*

Voltaire rejected the Geneva idea: 'The idea of being separated from you is frightful, and the idea of seeing you in Geneva while I was at Ferney is no less frightful. The best, would be for me to finish my life with you, either at Ferney or in some suburb of Paris.'[45] By now it was almost becoming accepted that she would return to Ferney, though she still kept her options open for a few more weeks. When she finally agreed to rejoin him at Ferney, Voltaire told her: 'Your plans overwhelm me with joy.'[46]

But he went on to object to some of the details of her plans.

The idea of bringing a coachman from Paris makes me shudder. I have only cart-drivers, but they are excellent coachmen on occasion. Your Parisian horses would never want to draw loads of hay. I hear that you no longer have Maton [her lady's maid]. You would be surprised at the *femme de chambre* you could find here, the most adroit, the cleanest, the best seamstress, the most elegant tailor. But a man-about-town (*un monsieur*), a lackey from Paris, would horrify our rustic household. A Parisian lackey who is good for nothing except to stand at the back of a coach is a monster in my eyes. We shall make our arrangements when you have made up your mind.[47]

Inevitably Mme Denis bridled at his terms, and continued to insist on her own.

I feel from your last letter that it would be very difficult for me to

---

* Voltaire was, of course, aware that Mme Denis had long been friendly with Hennin (see *Letters*, 11592). The question was: how friendly?

make plans for my return, since you are not yet decided. You say, my dear friend, that you want me to tell you my conditions. Surely, I should never have imagined that I should talk of conditions to you, but I shall take the liberty to respond.

You say that you have a horror of Parisian lackeys. Nevertheless, I must have a lackey, as well as a lady's maid, for the journey. I would wish, with all my heart, that my sex, my age, my strength and my status could have allowed me to make the journey on foot with a little package on my back. But you surely understand that, whether on foot or on horseback, I must have someone for the journey. Maton is still with me. And yet, if I leave, I shall not take her with me. Here she has her husband and her children, and she could not abandon them. Therefore I should take Agathe, who asks nothing better than to come. I am quite sure, my dear friend, that the *femme de chambre* who lives with you is excellent, but she is accustomed to look after a young man, and there is a furious difference between the condition of a young man and that of an old woman. You can see that that would not be fair or feasible.

As for the coachman, how could I do without him? You tell me not only that there will be no more parties but that I shall have no company. I should certainly be very unhappy to attract a single human being to your home, if it displeases you. But it is an additional reason why I should sometimes be able to look for company elsewhere. At Ferney I should count on leading quite the opposite kind of life to the one I used to lead; that is to say, I should go out often, but I would never invite anyone to your home since it displeases you. You like solitude. For relaxation I would go to visit a dozen persons whom I know and like. Whenever you wanted me, obviously you would always have the preference over them, and I should be only too happy to see you and to hear you.

I should like to ask your kindness, to allow me not to get involved in your household arrangements and to let me have, quite simply, my three servants and my two horses; my lackey to clean my apartment, to polish it, to serve me and to stand behind the coach; my *femme de chambre*; and my coachman to drive me. It seems to me, my dear friend, that those things are not expensive in the country, and that three servants are not too much for a woman of my age. Tell me what you think, but be sure that you are dearer to me than life itself.[48]

Voltaire tried to insist on his terms, but only half-heartedly: he knew he was beaten. But he now proposed new plans:

The easiest and wisest course would be to spend the winter together in Paris and the summer at Ferney. Or perhaps the southern climes of France would suit us. It is with that in mind that I have rearranged a carriage into a kind of sleeping car (*une dormeuse*), where we should be very comfortable. We should be followed by a good wagon, which would contain everything we need. All of that is ready. Hyères in Provence, Montpellier in Languedoc, even Toulouse could have attractions for you; and in the month of May you would come home to a delicious Ferney. All of this is possible, and I shall only do what will please you. The embarrassing and delicate situation I find myself in with M. le duc de Württemberg will require a bit of economy during the first months of our establishment. I have had to give him £100,000 which he owed me. He will pay me back in four years. This affair is good and certain.[49]

And yet almost immediately Voltaire changed his mind, for by now Württemberg's accumulated unpaid debt amounted to £105,600.[50] As a result, Voltaire backed away from his earlier projects for delightful three-month excursions, whether to Paris (as Mme Denis suggested) or to the south (his idea), because he needed to stick around at Ferney in order to nail down the Württemberg re-financing: 'The crisis I am in with the agents of M. de Württemberg will scarcely allow me to get away before the month of November.'[51]

In the middle of September 1769 Mme Denis started to plan her departure from Paris. She told Pierre-Michel Hennin (but not Voltaire): 'Yesterday I received a very pressing letter from the boss (*le patron*) telling me to come. I count on setting off in the first days of October. I beg you to say nothing of this to anyone, I am not even telling *le patron*. I shall then sort things out with the man in question as well as I can.'[52] But on 18 September 1769 Mme Denis did write to Voltaire: 'Whatever happens, I shall have the happiness of embracing you during the month of October. Neither of us should travel later than that.'[53]

By the time Voltaire received this letter, he had finally received some of the revenue assignments he had asked for from Württemberg, and he now reverted to his earlier idea of spending the winter in Toulouse, where he hoped that his long campaign for the exoneration of the Sirvens might at last be entering its final phase.[54] He wrote to Mme Denis: 'You should come home at the end of October; or if you prefer, I would travel to meet you at Lyon and lead you, bags and baggage (*armes et bagages*), to Toulouse, where the winters are very temperate, and you should return in the spring to your lovely dwelling. The *parlement* has become the protector of the Sirvens, and only seeks to expiate the horror of the condemnation of Calas.'[55] But he changed his mind five days later: 'I begin to fear that the Sirven affair may not be finished before St Martin's Day [11 November], and that my health will not allow me to travel to Toulouse, despite the pressing invitations they send me. Could you please go to M. de Laleu [Voltaire's lawyer] and ask for the contract with the prince and princess of Guise. As far as I remember, one can only ask for up to five years of arrears; which is really cruel, since they owe more than ten. If all our affairs go like this, we shall not have enough to put on plays.'[56]

On 28 October 1769 Mme Denis arrived at Ferney, and of course she came with her carriage, her two horses and her three servants. In a letter to d'Alembert, Voltaire alluded laconically, but without comment, to the fact of her arrival: 'Mme Denis, my very dear and very great philosopher, brings me your letter of the 15th. I should have liked even better to talk with you in Paris, but the sad state I am in has not allowed me to travel.'[57] In no other letter does Voltaire refer to her return, and even in this one he makes no reference to his feelings about her or about their reunion.

Three months later Mme Denis wrote to Guillaume-Claude Laleu, Voltaire's lawyer in Paris: 'My uncle is fairly well, for which I have reason to be very glad. I am being patient. He is very pleased with my return, and I do not think that he will suggest another trip to Paris in the near future.'[58]

So Mme Denis tells us that Voltaire is very pleased that she is back, but Voltaire himself does not tell us that he is pleased to have her back; and Mme Denis tells us that she is being patient but not that she is pleased to be back. It is an enigmatic end to an enigmatic separation. And yet we can tell that Voltaire is very glad she has returned, not because he says so but because, in the weeks and months after her return, he becomes more gay and more lively, in word and deed.

WATCHMAKING
AT FERNEY

1770–1776

ONE OF THE CASUALTIES of the running battle between Voltaire and Bishop Biord was that the bishop banned Father Adam from saying Mass, so Voltaire looked around for alternatives. He found them in a small neighbouring community of a dozen Franciscans or Capuchins, some of whom came from time to time to say Mass for him at Ferney.

In recognition of their services Voltaire applied to the duc de Choiseul for a government subsidy for the community.[1] Choiseul generously obliged and arranged a pension for the Franciscans of £600 a year.[2] They commended Voltaire to the head of their order in Rome, Father-General Amatus d'Alamballa, and in February 1770 d'Alamballa notified Voltaire that he would now receive the titles of Spiritual Child, Benefactor and Temporal Father of the order of Saint Francis.

This was the best joke to have come Voltaire's way for years, as he boasted to Mme du Deffand: 'My God, Madame, did you know that I was a Capuchin? Just see how God takes care of his elect, and how grace performs conjuring tricks before reaching the target. The Father-General has sent me my letters patent from Rome.'[3]

When word reached Paris, the French government intervened to put a stop to this tomfoolery, and within weeks Voltaire's brief incarnation as an honorary Franciscan friar was at an end. Nevertheless, he continued on occasion to describe himself as 'Friar François'.[4] He soon had more serious matters on his mind, starting with the eruption of a new wave of political violence in Geneva.

The settlement reached two years earlier, in March 1768, after the

French military blockade, seemed to have patched up the long-standing political quarrels between the warring classes of Geneva. But in mid-1769 the patricians simply revoked that part of the settlement which had given new advantages to the *natifs*, and by early February 1770 violence had broken out again between the haves and the have-nots. Voltaire wrote to his lawyer friend Élie de Beaumont: 'I do not know, my dear Cicero, if the disorders of Geneva will prevent my letter from getting to the post. Yesterday the *bourgeois* killed three *habitants*, and people say that they have killed another four this morning. The whole city is up in arms, everything is in combustion in this wise republic.'[5]

Political conflict in Geneva would have damaging repercussions for Ferney. Its natural geographical relationship was with Geneva, not with the French hinterland, and the French blockade of 1767 had shown how difficult it was to get supplies except from Geneva. At that time Voltaire had had the idea that France in general, and Ferney in particular, would be much better served if the little French fishing village at Versoix, on the shores of Lac Léman and just to the north-east of Geneva, could be developed into a substantial town and trading port. He had put this idea to the French authorities; it was quickly taken up by the Prime Minister, the duc de Choiseul, and construction work was set in train.[6]

In Geneva this project was deeply unwelcome to the ruling classes. Versoix would face them with head-to-head commercial competition and undercut their local trading dominance. More importantly, perhaps, it could also undermine their political dominance at home, since it might offer an alternative haven for those lower-order Genevans who were dissatisfied with the restrictive terms of their existence in Geneva. This political and economic challenge, actively promoted by Voltaire and consciously accepted by the French government, was one of the factors behind the latest wave of political conflict inside Geneva.

As soon as Versoix looked like becoming a reality, a number of dissatisfied *natifs* of Geneva sought to move there. Voltaire reported to Pierre-Michel Hennin, the French Resident: 'When people started to talk of building Versoix, eighteen *natifs* came to bring me their signatures, undertaking to build houses there. I sent their propositions on to M. le duc de Choiseul.'[7] But then he heard that the Geneva authorities were threatening to hang all who tried to withdraw to Versoix. Two days later he wrote: 'They have just cut the throats of those *habitants* who had submitted their names to the Ministry with a view to moving to Versoix. They have killed, among others, an old man of eighty who was walking in the street in his dressing gown. They have wounded, with blows from their rifle butts, a pregnant woman who is likely to die from it. Two thousand *habitants* will leave this den of discord.'[8]

Some of the protesters had already fled Geneva and been given French residence permits, as well as provisional lodging on French territory.[9] And yet they could not move to Versoix because the town had not yet been built, though some progress had been made with the port. They had to look elsewhere, and many of them gravitated to Ferney. Ten days after the outbreak of violence in Geneva, Voltaire reported that sixty families had taken refuge in the neighbourhood, some of them in Ferney itself.[10]

The Genevan patricians tried to persuade the French government not to admit the émigrés from Geneva and sent Philibert Cramer, brother and partner of the publisher Gabriel Cramer, to Paris to discredit them. Voltaire wrote to Choiseul to warn him not to believe anything that Cramer said, for he was afraid that he might tell Choiseul that the emigrants from Geneva were indigent idlers who would become a burden on the French state.

He wrote in the same vein to François de Caire, chief French engineer for the construction of Versoix: 'I beg you urgently, Sir, not to say to M. le duc de Choiseul that the emigrants need money, for then they would only seem to be beggars driven out of their republic, coming here to ask for charity. Cramer counts on passing them off as seditious blackguards who have neither hearth nor home (*ni feu ni lieu*). We must wait. We can find help, and I have an idea which I shall have the honour to communicate to you.' In fact, Choiseul refused to see Philibert Cramer.[11]

Voltaire's 'idea' was that the new arrivals were useful, able-bodied workers and could be employed in the building of Versoix. He even thought of putting some of his own money into it and put his name down for one of the new houses, on condition that it was in a most favoured position. Unfortunately, the French public finances were in difficulties yet again, and there were delays in the building programme. It was to ease these difficulties, in March 1770, that the abbé Terray, the new *Contrôleur-Général* or Finance Minister, confiscated, or at least suspended payment on, a number of government securities, including one category called *rescriptions*, in which Voltaire had invested a large amount of money. Voltaire complained bitterly and repeatedly at this confiscation, not least because, he said, the money he had invested in *rescriptions* was virtually his only freely disposable capital: he had a very large income, but it came essentially from *rente viagère* loans, which would expire with his death.

Pierre-Michel Hennin, the French Resident, sounded out Choiseul to see if there were any way of reimbursing Voltaire, at least in part: 'M. de Voltaire, in the fervour of his first enthusiasm, would have given capital for the construction of Versoix, but unfortunately he has £240,000 in *rescriptions* and very little in cash. He has, however, promised to make some advances. If it were possible to discount his *rescriptions*, we could easily commit him to put up the wherewithal to employ, immediately, a very large number of workers.'[12] Nothing came of this suggestion, and Voltaire never stopped complaining at the confiscation, which he regarded as illegal.

Voltaire now had a better idea. Many of the immigrants from Geneva were skilled craftsmen from the city's large watchmaking industry. So why not set them up in business as independent watchmakers? And since there seemed no prospect that Versoix would be built soon enough to house them, why not set them up in business in Ferney?

Voltaire knew nothing about watches, or industry, or business in general, and he had until very recently been prejudiced, as a land-owner, against manufacturing employment in case it should draw away his peasants from the land. Nevertheless, he pursued his new idea with extraordinary rapidity and dynamism, despite the fact that he was now seventy-six years old.

Voltaire had already dabbled in a little manufacturing venture of a different kind. This was a tiny silk industry, which he had started up during the absence of Mme Denis in Paris, from the cultivation of silk-worms to the production of silk and finally to the weaving of silk stock-ings, of which he sent a pair to the duchesse de Choiseul. By January 1770 Voltaire had converted his theatre into a place for the cultivation of the silkworms.[13]

Voltaire's first reference to 'the manufacture of watches at Ferney' comes in March 1770, shortly after the outbreak of violence in Geneva and the arrival of the first artisan immigrants in Ferney.[14] By early April the Ferney watchmaking industry was up and running, as he told François de Caire:

You will know that I am sending to Monseigneur le duc de Choi-seul a box of watches for Spain, made before my very eyes in less than six weeks, at Ferney, and that we shall have eight or ten more boxes in under three months. What we need is a town, houses, arti-sans, freedom, money, but no fortresses. I salute and embrace my dear commandant.

Friar François, unworthy Capuchin.[15]

Voltaire's vigour in launching his watch industry is all the more remarkable in that his health, never good, at this time went through a bad patch. He wrote for advice to Michel-Philippe Bouvart, the Paris doctor who was looking after Mme d'Argental, to ask whether he thought that goat's milk would help to keep him going. Bouvart did not approve of goat's milk, however, as Voltaire told d'Argental at the end of April: 'I have just received a kind message from M. Bouvart, and I have now given up my goat, my dear angel.'[16]

Although Voltaire frequently asserted his rational belief in freedom of conscience and freedom of trade,[17] his real reflex assumption was that his new enterprise could succeed only with the official patronage of the state. He wrote early in April to the duchesse de Choiseul to ask for her husband's support, without which, he said, his venture would be doomed.

> Just as soon as Choiseul agreed that we could admit emigrants, I immediately invited emigrants into my hovels, and scarcely did they start work but they made enough watches to send a small box to Spain. I throw myself at your feet to beg you to favour this dispatch, so that this parcel shall leave without delay for Cadiz. I am writing passionately to M. de La Ponce [Choiseul's secretary] about this affair, on which depends a trade of £300,000 a year.[18]

Voltaire could not possibly have known at this early stage that his watchmakers would produce sales of £300,000, since they had only just started work at Ferney, and he knew nothing of the trade or its markets. In the event his guess proved an underestimate: in 1775 he said that his watchmakers had total sales of £450,000 or £500,000 a year; in 1776 he put the figure at £500,000–600,000 a year.[19]

These extraordinary results were almost entirely due to Voltaire's personal efforts, for he had reinvented himself in a protean variety of roles: not just the overall manager, co-ordinator and organiser but also the financier, the virtual bank manager, the sponsor, the builder of homes and factory space, the buyer of precious metals and other raw materials and the international sales manager. It is a testimony to the vitality of his mind and the vigour of his spirit.

One of the clues to Voltaire's new-found vitality and vigour comes in a letter he wrote in February 1770 to Gaspard-Henri Schérer, his banker in Lyon: 'I appeal to your kindness, Sir. I should like to have a dozen pints of excellent lavender water; 2 pounds of good sealing wax;

2,000 gilt nails for armchairs; and a barrel of good drinkable wine from the Dauphiné or the Beaujolais. I know nobody to whom I can address these little errands. If you had at hand someone who could take it on, I should be very obliged to you.'[20]

This is the first time for many months, or even years, that Voltaire had written this kind of exuberant shopping list, and it sounds as if the return of Mme Denis had given him a new lease of life. But in addition Voltaire was thoroughly excited by his new watchmaking venture, as he told Pierre-Michel Hennin in April, 1770: 'We have all been ill with a catarrh, which is no good at all for people who are seventy-seven years old. But the prosperity of the hamlet of Ferney has revived me, for I now have about forty workers employed in teaching Europe how to tell the time.'[21]

The best watches had to be made of gold, and often set with precious stones, so one of Voltaire's first tasks was to locate reliable supplies of gold. He wrote to Jean-Joseph, marquis de Laborde, the king's banker:

> I am establishing a considerable manufacture. If it should fail, I should lose only the money which I have lent to it, interest-free. If you could indicate to me some method of procuring Spanish gold, in ingots or coins, you would do me a great service. We should only need about 1,000 louis' worth [£24,000] each year. The workers say that gold is much too expensive in Geneva, and that they lose too much if they melt down gold coins. All this is far from my ordinary occupations, but I have the pleasure of multiplying by ten the inhabitants of my hamlet, to grow wheat where thistles grew before, to attract foreigners and to show the king that I know how to do something else besides writing the *Histoire du siècle de Louis XIV* and a few verses.[22]

After his first enquiry to Laborde, Voltaire turned for his gold requirements to his usual supplier of all and sundry, Gaspard-Henri Schérer. Quite soon he arranged for his leading watchmakers to have drawing rights on his accounts with Schérer in Lyon: 'Dufour & Céret will never draw on you without asking my permission first, and with every letter of credit I shall give you advance notice. I hope the help I am giving them will put them in a position where they can make their manufacture prosper.'[23]

At first Voltaire provided his watchmakers with interest-free finance. 'I have done it purely out of vanity,' he told Mme du Deffand. 'They say that God created the world for his own glory. We must imitate him as far as possible.'[24] But if Voltaire was disinterested, it was partly because he could afford it. His latest financial inventory from Laleu, his Paris lawyer, showed that he had *rentes*, just in Paris, leaving aside his other income from loans to the duke of Württemberg and other German princes, and leaving aside his assets in Lyon and Geneva, of more than £50,000 a year.[25] It seems that the duc de Richelieu, and perhaps the successors of the Guise family, were now paying at least some of the interest they owed.

About the same time Voltaire gave a vivid picture of the turbulent activity in Ferney in a letter to the marquis de Jaucourt, who had previously been billeted on him as a commander of the blockading French troops:

> My very generous and very dear commander, I have established in the hamlet of Ferney a little manufacture of watches. Our theatre auditorium, which you remember, has been transformed into workshops. There, where we once recited verse, we are now melting gold and polishing cogs. We must build new houses for the emigrants. All the workers of Geneva would come here if we were in a position to house them. We must remember that everyone nowadays wants a gold watch, from Peking to Martinique, and that there used to be only three great manufacturing centres, London, Paris and Geneva. Sensitive and tolerant souls will be happy to learn that sixty Huguenots live so well with my parishioners, that it would not be possible to guess that there are two religions here.[26]

In Paris, meanwhile, Voltaire's friends were preparing a little surprise: they planned to commission a life-size statue of him from Jean-Baptiste Pigalle, the famous sculptor. The idea first came from Suzanne Curchod, wife of the rich Protestant banker Jacques Necker and hostess in Paris of a brilliant avant-garde literary salon. On 17 April 1770 she gave a dinner for seventeen *philosophes*, including d'Alembert, Diderot, Grimm, Helvetius, Marmontel, Morellet and Saint-Lambert. She outlined her proposal at the end of the meal, and they enthusiastically endorsed it. The statue was expected to cost between £12,000 and £15,000, including a fee of £10,000 for Pigalle. They had thought of limiting the subscription to men of letters, with the inscription *To the living Voltaire, by men of letters his compatriots*, but then they decided to open the list to anybody, in the hope that the great and the good from all over Europe would want to contribute.[27]

Voltaire was flattered but embarrassed. 'It is not likely, my dear philosopher,' he wrote to d'Alembert, 'that it will be *To the living Voltaire*; it
will be *To the dying Voltaire*, for I am coming to my end. It would not be
bad if Frederick joined the list of subscribers; it would save the generous men of letters some money, of which they do not have much. In any
event, he owes me some reparation.'[28] All the *beau monde* of Paris society
were keen to subscribe, at the standard price of 2 louis each; Frederick
subscribed 200 louis, or £4,800.[29]

When Voltaire heard that Pigalle intended to come to Ferney to
model him in the flesh, he became a bit anxious, as he told Mme Necker.

M. Pigalle is due, they say, to come to model my face. But then, Madam,
I should need to have a face; yet one can scarcely guess where it is. My
eyes are sunk three inches deep; my cheeks are like old parchment
badly stuck on bones which hardly hold together. The few teeth I had
are gone. What I tell you is not coquetterie, it is the simple truth. No
one has ever sculpted a man in such a state. M. Pigalle will think he is
being made fun of, and as for me, I have so much pride that I should
never dare appear in his presence. After all, what does it matter to
posterity if a block of marble looks like one man or like another?[30]

In June Pigalle arrived and spent a week sketching and modelling
Voltaire's head. The modelling sessions were carried out in the open, in
full view of the curious, as Voltaire reported to Mme Necker.

When the people of my village saw Pigalle setting out some of the
instruments of his craft, they said, 'Hey, look, he's going to cut him
open; this will be fun' ('*tiens, tiens, disaient-ils, on va le disséquer, cela
sera drôle*'). It is thus, Madame, as you know, that men are amused by
any spectacle. It is for the same reasons that people go to the mari-
onettes, to the comic opera, to High Mass, to a burial. My statue will
make some philosophers smile.[31]

Within a few days Pigalle had made a preliminary model of Voltaire's
head. 'M. Pigalle has made me speaking and thinking, even though my
age and my illnesses have somewhat deprived me of thought and words.
He even made me smiling; it must be at all the stupidities that one does
every day. He is as good a man as he is an artist. He has the simplicity
of true genius.'[32]

It sounds as if Voltaire was on good form for these modelling sessions;

that is certainly what Pigalle told his friends, after he returned to Paris. But when Voltaire heard, he was indignant, claiming that he was really very ill. 'My dear prophet', he told Grimm, 'M. Pigalle, though the best man in the world, is slandering me most strangely. He goes about saying that I am well, that I am as plump as a monk. I was just trying to be gay in his presence, exercising my smiling muscles (*les muscles buccinateurs*) to be polite to him.'[33]

Voltaire's good humour was spoiled only by the name of Jean-Jacques Rousseau, for Rousseau had insisted on subscribing to the Pigalle statue. Voltaire was enraged and demanded that Rousseau's money be returned to him. D'Alembert eventually managed to persuade him to accept Rousseau's homage with good grace.[34]

A year later Voltaire heard that Pigalle proposed to sculpt him naked. Voltaire wrote to d'Alembert on 18 March 1771: 'Mme Necker has complained bitterly to me that Pigalle wants to make me completely naked. Here is my reply: you decide on my effigy; it is up to you to give me a suit of clothes, if that's what you want. Be sure that, clothed or not, I am all yours.'[35] The question of Voltaire's nudity continued to provoke controversy, but Voltaire insisted that Pigalle, as the artist, must have complete freedom to decide.[36]

In 1776 Pigalle finished his statue of Voltaire, with a pen in one hand and his modesty preserved only by a sheet of parchment. It proved an unloved oddity: there was no agreement where it should be placed, and no one wanted to give it house room, so it stayed in Pigalle's studio. Later it passed to Voltaire's heirs, the family of Mme Denis. In 1806 they gave it to the Académie Française, where it was virtually hidden away, in despised obscurity, for 150 years. It was not finally exhibited in the Louvre until 1962.

In Ferney, meanwhile, the inflow of immigrants was leading to some social friction, both locally and with the Genevois. One such noisy incident took place between one of Voltaire's servants and the guards at the Geneva city gates, and Voltaire complained about it to Pierre-Michel Hennin, the French Resident at Geneva:

> 'Go and get stuffed, go and scratch your arse with the arse of the Resident, you've got bread in your pockets for the French dolts, you come from those French buggers at Ferney, etc., etc.'
>
> Those, Sir, are the very words of the Philippic pronounced today, against Dalloz, errand boy of Ferney, who was carrying not bread for the dolts but a little trout for our supper. These gallantries happen too

often. I have not seen the arse of Dalloz, and I doubt if it is worthy to scratch yours. Frankly, these compliments of the Genevans are getting too strong.[37]

The 'Philippic' quoted by Voltaire came from Sergeant Raisin of the guard at the gate of the city. He was censured for his insults and jailed for three days, but the Geneva authorities sought to take proceedings against Dalloz as well, for refusing to allow the guard to inspect the cart he was driving, and for doing some insulting of his own.[38] Voltaire asked Hennin not to allow Dalloz to be tried before a Geneva magistrate because, as he explained, 'We do not expect any justice from these people'. Hennin promised to administer justice himself. 'You are too good, Sir, and Dalloz is an animal. He still swears that there was some arse in this affair. Mine is in a piteous state. It was not made for being sculpted by Pigalle.'[39]

With the arrival of all the new inhabitants at Ferney the village started to need more tradesmen and better facilities. They got a new butcher, who seemed much better than the old one, and Voltaire made plans to put up a new building to house various merchants 'who will provide the whole region with all the things which cost too much in Geneva'.[40] Towards the end of 1770 the people of Ferney decided they needed a public fountain or drinking trough, and Voltaire passed on their request to Louis-Gaspard Fabry, mayor of Gex.[41] By the following spring the fountain had been built, and Voltaire asked Fabry to impose the costs in proportion to the local property tax. 'The inhabitants demanded the building of the fountain with the greatest insistence, but now some of them are reluctant not merely to pay but even to come to a meeting. The fountain builder is demanding payment. Please send us an official order, which we shall pass on to each individual. If there are some too poor to pay (which we do not believe), we shall pay for them without difficulty.'[42]

Within weeks of the start of the watchmaking enterprise, early in the spring of 1770, Voltaire started to look for customers and markets for his watches. He already knew personally many of the grandest people, both in France and abroad, and he proceeded ruthlessly to milk his contacts. But he soon saw that he would not be able to keep his rapidly growing colony in business by selling watches one by one: he needed markets, agents, representatives.

Early on, he wrote to his friend and fellow member of the Académie Française, Cardinal Bernis, French ambassador to the Vatican in Rome.

'Our watches are very well made, very handsome, very good and cheap. The good work which I beg Your Eminence to undertake is just to deign to look out an honest merchant in Rome, who would agree to be our representative. I answer for it that it would be worth his while. The manufacturers will send him a consignment just as soon as you let us know.'[43]

Bernis did not even bother to reply until seven months later, and then his letter was merely a tissue of languid evasions. 'I have done what I could, my dear colleague, to establish here with confidence the commercial branch for your watchmakers that you suggested. It is just not possible. You can understand that I cannot and must not answer for the good faith of possible agents. This country has no trade.'[44]

Voltaire was angry, and showed it.

I have seen by your silence, about the colony I have built, that you are not helping me at all. I cannot avoid telling you that you have given me infinite pain. I have not deserved this hardness on your part. You seem to have believed that my colony was nothing more than poetic licence. It is, on the contrary, a very real and very substantial colony, composed of three companies, protected by the king, and especially by M. le duc de Choiseul. No other French ambassador has failed to take energetic steps to find us agents in foreign countries. You are the only one, not only who did not have that kindness, but who disdained to reply. What would it have cost you to have got someone to speak a word to the French consul in Rome? May Your Eminence please accept, if he please, the respect and extreme anger of the hermit of Ferney.[45]

In fact, several other ambassadors had been just as unhelpful as Bernis.[46] An exception was Pierre Paul, marquis d'Ossun, French ambassador to Spain, to whom Voltaire was particularly grateful, for Spain was a large potential market, and it was also, of course, the gateway to Cadiz and trade with the Indies.[47]

Voltaire also approached Catherine the Great, and his sales pitch to her was a mixture of obsequiousness, deviousness and cheek. In November 1770 he wrote to her to say that his watchmakers had just finished a watch decorated with diamonds and bearing her portrait, which they trusted she would allow them to send her. It was only in succeeding sentences that he let it emerge that Catherine was expected to pay for this watch, as well as for others which she might like to have to give away as presents. He assured her that the watches from Ferney were half the price of those from London or Paris.[48] Four months later he reported that Catherine had ordered £20,000 worth of watches from Ferney.[49] In June that year he told Catherine that his watchmakers had just sent her an enormous consignment of watches; he suggested that she need only pay half the £40,000 invoice right away; he was sure the watchmakers would be happy to wait a year for the rest.[50] Ten days on, Voltaire reckoned that the value of total recent deliveries to St Petersburg amounted to £60,000.[51]

One reason for the escalation in sales was that, despite Voltaire's claim that his watches were cheaper than those from Paris or London, some of the watches he sent to Catherine were really pretty expensive: a consignment sent in April 1771 included watches costing 80 louis, or £1,920.[52]

Voltaire also looked for sales opportunities in Turkey, which had long been a significant market for watches – so good, in fact, that there was even a little colony of Swiss watchmakers in Constantinople. Voltaire had for some years enthusiastically supported Catherine's military campaigns against the Turks, yet now he had no difficulty in subordinating his political prejudices to his commercial interests. 'I used to be very interested in the troubles of Turkey', he told Richelieu; 'that is to say that I hoped passionately that they would be driven out of Europe. But now I shall come to terms with them, for I have put together a little company which has strong links with Constantinople.' In June 1771 he reported that recent sales to Constantinople had amounted to £30,000.[53]

By the end of 1770 Voltaire had established his main export markets in Spain, Turkey and Russia, a list that he later extended to Holland and Italy. He also explored such exotic markets as Algeria and Tunisia.[54]

At the same time Voltaire worked hard at finding domestic customers for his watches. Having sold some to Louis XV,[55] he then turned to the duc and duchesse de Choiseul and boldly set out his wares.

I take the liberty to importune you, to ask if we could take the extreme liberty to send, from our monastery to Mme la duchesse de Choiseul, the six watches which we have just made at Ferney. We believe they are very pretty and very good, but of course, every author has a good opinion of his own works.

We have thought that, on the occasion of the wedding [of Marie-Antoinette to the dauphin, the future Louis XVI] and the accompanying fêtes, these examples of our manufacture could be given as gifts, either to artists who performed at these fêtes or to persons attached to madame la dauphine. Their cheapness will no doubt please M. l'abbé Terray, since there are two watches which cost only 11 louis each, while the most expensive, decorated with diamonds, is only priced at 46 louis. The one with the portrait of the king in enamel, with diamonds, is only 25, and the one with the portrait of Monseigneur the dauphin, with a hand with diamonds, is only 17. They would all cost well over a third more in Paris.

Friar François, Unworthy Capucin

P.S. The prices are marked on a little piece of parchment attached to the watches; when you want to start one, you must remove a small piece of paper which stops the plate and the balance-wheel.[56]

A price-list from the firm of Dufour & Céret, which Voltaire sent to d'Argental, showed that the watches ranged from 3 louis for a watch in smooth silver, 4 louis for a watch in guilloché silver and 14 louis for a silver repeater watch, up to 42 louis for the best gold repeater watch.[57]

When Voltaire said that his Ferney watches were inexpensive, some of his Paris friends assumed that they must be really very cheap; Voltaire quickly disabused them. 'It is just as impossible, my dear Baron', he told his friend Henri Lambert d'Herbigny, marquis de Thibouville, 'to get a repeater watch for 4 louis as it is to get a sturgeon in Paris for 4 sous; so I seriously advise you to give up the idea.'[58]

By the autumn of 1771 Ferney had spawned four different watch-making companies or partnerships and three smaller enterprises;[59] and as a result of the unexpectedly rapid take-off in sales it was becoming difficult for Voltaire to keep on top of the financial accounting. He wrote to Schérer in November: 'Would you please do me the kindness, Sir, to send me the names of those who have taken Spanish gold from you, for which I am answerable. It is true that we agreed between us that you would not give gold to our dealers except on a note from me, but I am afraid that someone may have taken advantage of your kindness, and it is necessary to put some order into my affairs.'[60]

When the grand Parisian jewellers heard of Voltaire's new watch-making industry, and of the relative cheapness of his high-quality products, a number of them bought up Ferney watches and put their own names on them, with a mark-up which Voltaire reckoned at 50 per cent.[61] In retaliation, Voltaire decided to set up his own sales agency in Paris, to which he appointed Mme Lejeune, notorious for her role in the book-smuggling escapade of December 1766. He told her that Guil-laume-Henri Valentin, one of the master watchmakers, would supply her at cost, and she could sell them at any price she chose and keep the profit.[62]

The arrangement did not work: Mme Lejeune took consignments of Valentin's watches but did not pay for them.[63] So Voltaire did what he should have done from the beginning: he appointed as his Paris repre-sentative the man at the top of his profession, Jean-Antoine Lépine, the king's watchmaker. Lépine set up a business office in a house in Ferney ('at my expense', says Voltaire) and dispatched Joseph Tardy, also one of the king's watchmakers, to manage this Ferney office on a permanent basis.[64]*

But it was not just Mme Lejeune who was not paying. As we saw, Louis XV had agreed in 1770 to take six of the first watches made at Ferney, but three years later he had still not paid for them.[65] 'My colony', Voltaire told d'Alembert, 'had supplied watches decorated with dia-monds for the marriage of M. le Dauphin. They have not been paid for, and the consequences fall on me. What I feel about these fine gentlemen of Paris is indescribable.'[66]

When Voltaire says 'the consequences fall on me', he seems to be assuming not just that the sales operation was his responsibility (which it was) but that he was personally liable to indemnify the watchmak-ers if their consignments were not paid for. This was generous of him, considering that he was also providing interest-free working capital for the watchmakers.

Despite the gruelling demands of his watchmaking industry, Vol-taire continued to write plays throughout the 1770s, as he had always done, but now with little public success. If he was disappointed, he was much revived in June 1772 by the arrival nearby of a local acting troupe at the theatre of La Châtelaine, on the border between Ferney and Geneva. According to his neighbour Mme Louise-Suzanne Gallatin, Voltaire seems to have greatly enjoyed his theatre outings.

> He is very well. Two days ago he went to the playhouse at La Châtelaine. They were putting on *Nanine* [by Voltaire]. The actors had announced that he would be there, and such a large crowd of

---

* Jean-Antoine Lépine was the brother-in-law of Pierre Augustin Caron de Beaumarchais, who started life as a watchmaker, who became famous as a playwright and author of *The Marriage of Figaro*, and who later financed the first posthumous edition of Voltaire's complete works.

people came that more than 300 had to be turned away. Those who stayed had difficulty in seeing him, since they had put gauze round his box. He was pleased with the actors, and he made them come to him, so that he could tell them how to act. We hope to persuade him to go next week as well.[67]

Voltaire went again to La Châtelaine, to see a performance of *Zaïre*, and he told d'Argental that the local actors had been excellent and that their performance had made him weep.[68] He went again in August: another wonderful performance, he said, with a beautiful young actress ('completely new, completely simple, completely naïve'), and she too made him weep. Tears, for Voltaire, were the touchstone of a tragedy.[69]

In September 1772 Henri-Louis Lekain, lead actor at the Comédie Française, came and stayed for a fortnight; he performed six times at La Châtelaine, in three of Voltaire's plays. Voltaire was full of enthusiasm and at one performance was heard to shout out 'Bravo! Bravo!' Lekain, he told d'Alembert, 'has enchanted the whole of Geneva'.[70] When Lekain left Ferney to return to Paris, he wanted to stop off in Lyon to earn some extra money with a few freelance performances, and Voltaire wrote to Richelieu to ask him to let Lekain delay his return to Paris. Richelieu would have none of it.[71] 'M. le maréchal de Richelieu', Voltaire told d'Argental, 'tells me that he will have him put in prison if he is not back in Paris by 4 October. This does not seem to me fair dealing, nor true justice. You had always told me that he could return on the 8th and everyone would have been happy; he could easily reach Paris by 8 October.'[72]

In August 1772 Voltaire was busy writing and rewriting his new tragedy *Les Lois de Minos*, and he hoped that Richelieu would arrange for it to be put on in Bordeaux, if not in Paris. As governor of Guyenne in south-west France, as well as a patron of the Comédie Française, Richelieu was a key figure in the control of public theatre. But d'Alembert brutally disabused him. D'Alembert loathed and despised Richelieu, describing him as 'an ancient doll' and a 'wizened prostitute', and he wrote to tell Voltaire the harsh truth about Richelieu's disloyalty.

He asked Lekain to produce a list of twelve tragedies to be performed at the festivities of the court and at Fontainebleau. Lekain brought him the list, in which he had included, quite rightly, four or five of your pieces. Richelieu crossed them all out, with the exception of *L'Orphelin de la Chine* [The Orphan from China], which he had the kindness to keep. I leave you, my dear master, to make your own reflections on this subject. In truth, I am sorry that you should have been so deceived by a man so vile.[73]

Voltaire was shocked. 'If he is guilty of the little infamy of which you speak,' he replied, 'I admit I am a great dupe; but in my place you would have been just as great a dupe as I. The only lesson I can draw from my deception would be to have no hope in future; but that, they say, is the fate of the damned. The bottom line, however, is that I have feelings; and I will confess that the treachery you tell me of causes me great pain.'[74]

Despite what he now knew of Richelieu's brutal detachment, Voltaire continued to plead with him in his usual tone of servility. 'My hero is committed on his honour to protect my theatrical productions. I shall always count on your indulgence towards me. *Les Lois de Minos* and *Sophonisbe* are spectacles with plenty of action. I therefore reiterate my very humble and very pressing prayer to you, to be kind enough to order our masters the actors to perform these two plays towards the end of your year in office.'[75]

Richelieu simply ignored Voltaire's appeal. D'Argental urged Voltaire not to be so imprudent as to betray any ill humour towards Richelieu but to turn instead to the duc d'Aumont and the duc de Duras, who were due to take over from Richelieu in the new year, as the duty supervisors of the Comédie Française. Voltaire followed his advice, and *Sophonisbe* was duly performed at the Comédie Française in January 1774. It was a flop, hissed and booed, and taken off after four performances.

Voltaire's disappointment with his tragedies was offset by the growth of his watchmaking industry, and an equally rapid growth of the Ferney village and estate.[76]

Florian [the widower of Mme Denis's sister] is beautifying Ferney by bringing here his third wife.* I have built him a little house which is exactly like a pavilion at Marly, but even prettier and cooler. We have four or five houses in this style; we are bringing up a little descendant of Corneille aged twelve [the daughter of Marie-Françoise Corneille], whom we have known since her birth. We are busy encouraging five

---

* Marie-Élisabeth, sister of Mme Denis, fell ill in 1770 and died in February 1771. Her husband, the marquis de Florian, quickly remarried.

or six hundred craftsmen, who will be very useful. That is my situation at the age of eighty, without a word of exaggeration.[77]

The place continued to expand rapidly throughout that year, as witness the following admiring description, the following January, by Paul-Claude Moultou, a Protestant pastor from Geneva:

Ferney is a very fine château, solidly built, with magnificent gardens and terraces. Not a day passes but M. de Voltaire plants more trees, which he looks after himself. The village is composed of about eighty houses, all very well built. The ugliest, seen from the outside, are finer than the most superb of the villages in the Paris region. There are about 800 inhabitants. Three or four of the houses belong to good bourgeois citizens; the rest are for watchmakers, carpenters, artisans of every type. Of these eighty houses, at least sixty belong to M. de Voltaire. He is certainly the creator of that place; he does the most immense good.[78]

The reason why Voltaire was able to build so many houses, according to Moultou, was that his income about this time was in the region of £150,000 a year; since less than half of this was required for the running costs of the household, the remaining £90,000 or so were free for house-building and the development of the estate.[79]

In August 1775 Voltaire boasted: 'The other day we were twelve at table, all of us inhabitants of Ferney, each with his house and his garden. We have several libraries. I may add that, in addition to the *philosophes*, we have a colony of watchmakers who do a trade of about 500,000 francs a year. Right now, we are building a dozen new houses.'[80] By the end of 1775 Voltaire was beginning to sound like a property speculator. 'I am convinced that our property will double in price within a year. It is already starting to be worth much more than before. The simple term "freedom of trade" revives every kind of industry, lifts all hopes, makes the earth more fertile.'[81]

The theatre at La Châtelaine was six miles away, and by 1776 Voltaire was finding it too far to go. He no longer had a theatre of his own, since for the past six years his former theatre in the château of Ferney had been given over to various other activities, such as the manufacture of silk, lace and now watches. So he decided to build a new theatre in a large barn in the village. In fact, Ferney was becoming more of a town than a village and would need a bigger theatre than the one in the château. In any case, Voltaire probably no longer wanted, at his age, to have to put up with large crowds of spectators traipsing through his home.[82]

The plan was that the troupe from La Châtelaine would come and perform in the new Ferney theatre two days a week, and in their own theatre the rest of the time. In July 1776 Henri-Louis Lekain came to stay and gave a number of performances in the new Ferney theatre.[83]

When Voltaire first started his watchmaking enterprise at the beginning of 1770, his immediate assumption was that it would not survive without the patronage of the French government. The duc de Choiseul, the Prime Minister, proved very helpful, as Voltaire gratefully acknowledged. 'My dear angel,' he wrote to d'Argental, 'I was quite wrong to complain of the indifference of the duc de Choiseul to my manufacture. He has been kinder and more considerate than I dared hope.'[84]

Before the end of the year, however, Choiseul suddenly fell from power, and Voltaire feared that the new ministry might be much less friendly; in particular, he worried that the confiscation a year earlier, by the abbé Terray, of his investments known as *rescriptions*, might be an ominous precedent. In the event, the new ministry under Chancellor René-Nicolas-Charles-Augustin de Maupeou, was not particularly unfriendly to the Ferney enterprise, but Voltaire remained anxious, as he told d'Argental: 'My colony, which is no longer protected, causes me acute alarms.'[85]

The protection Voltaire was seeking was protection against taxation. At start-up Voltaire had secured for the watchmakers a general tax exemption, which, like his interest-free loans, may have helped them get going, but it was less easy to justify after they had become financially successful: by 1773 Voltaire was writing that 'the watchmakers whom I set up, at great expense, are doing a prosperous trade.'[86] And though at the start Voltaire had lent money to the watchmakers interest-free, he did not go on doing so indefinitely. In 1776, when some of his leading watchmakers had become very prosperous, he charged interest of 7 per cent, substantially above the normal deposit rate for the time of 4 or 5 per cent.[87]

When the tax farmers heard of the growing prosperity of Ferney's watchmakers, they were bound to try to take their cut. By 1774 they were already sniffing around and provoking panic among the watchmakers. 'Despite the kindnesses of M. Turgot [Finance Minister in the new government], the officials of the new gold assay tax office have been here, upsetting the colony which I set up at such expense, and a hundred fathers of families are close to abandoning me.'[88]

Fortunately Turgot was quite reasonable, and he offered the region of Gex two significant economic concessions: the removal of the high tax on salt, exacted through a private monopoly operated by the tax farmers; and the release of the inhabitants from the traditional *corvée*, or community service labour, mainly for road maintenance.[89] The local inhabitants were delighted by the lifting of the *corvée*; the irony was that the roads at Ferney were suffering from a shortage of labour for road maintenance: 'Two of our labourers are dead, and there are almost no others. We have only watchmakers here.'[90]

Salt in France was a monopoly commodity controlled by the tax farmers, and they kept its price artificially high – much higher than in, say, Geneva. Inevitably the tax farmers were furious at Turgot's proposal to remove their monopoly, and they demanded compensation for loss of revenue. At the same time, the employees of the tax farmers were just as furious at the prospective loss of their jobs, and they engaged in gangster-like intimidation of the local population.[91]

At first, the tax farmers demanded compensation of £50,000 a year; Voltaire offered £15,000; Turgot proposed £30,000.[92] By December, Voltaire decided it was necessary to give way, and on 12 December 1775 he went in person to Gex, to recommend Turgot's figure to a large public meeting of the provincial Estates-General. Pierre-Michel Hennin, French Resident at Geneva, described the event to his minister:

M. de Voltaire thought that some people would oppose the useful project for which he had worked with such zeal, and he resolved to go to the Estates. When he arrived, they made him sit, and everyone gathered round him. He said to them: 'Gentlemen, we have many favours to ask, but I believe that above all we should accept the good offer which has been made to us today, and which we have so long asked for.' He then read a letter from M. Turgot. The representative of the clergy then thanked M. de Voltaire in the most honest manner, for his care for the province, and declared that his order was unanimously in favour of accepting the terms of the decree of the Council; the other orders did the same, they drew up the protocol, and the deputies signed it; they asked M. de Voltaire to help the Estates with his advice on the allocation of the tax [for paying the £30,000] and to continue looking after the interests of the province.

He went out, and as soon as the people gathered in Gex knew that the project had been accepted, there were cries of 'Vive le Roi, Vive M. de Voltaire', they decorated his horses and filled his carriage with

laurels and flowers. He was escorted on horseback by his bourgeoisie from Ferney; and in all the villages where he passed there were
the same acclamations and the same profusion of laurels. This would
have been a really brilliant day for a man indifferent to the happiness
of his fellows or to his own glory, and even more for M. de Voltaire
who, one can say, combines these two sentiments to excess.[93]

Two days later, on Thursday 14 December 1775, Voltaire wrote to
his friend Mme de Saint-Julien:

I have never had a more beautiful story to relate. Everything was
done, everything was written as I wished. A thousand inhabitants of
the region were close by, listening; and they sighed for this moment,
as if for their salvation, despite the £30,000. There was a cry of joy
throughout the whole province.

But you will see that there is no pure joy in this world. For while
we were gently passing our time in thanking M. Turgot, and while
the whole province was busy drinking, the gendarmes of the tax
farmers, whose time runs out on 1 January, had orders to sabotage
us. They marched about in groups of fifty, stopped all the vehicles,
searched all the pockets, forced their way into all the houses and made
every kind of damage there in the name of the king, and made the
peasants buy them off with money. I cannot conceive why the people
did not ring the tocsin against them in all the villages, and why they
were not exterminated. It is very strange that the *ferme générale*, with
only another fortnight left for them to keep their troops here in winter
quarters, should have permitted or even encouraged them in such
criminal excesses. The decent people were very wise and held back
the ordinary folk, who wanted to throw themselves on these brigands,
as if on mad wolves.[94]

This meeting of the Estates-General was a personal triumph for the
81-year-old Voltaire, and when, in recognition of his efforts, the Estates-
General gave Voltaire the honorific title of a *commissionnaire* to advise
them on taxation, it was a spectacular tribute to his moral authority as a
benefactor not just of the inhabitants of his own estates at Ferney but of
the province as a whole.[95] The irony of the situation was that Voltaire,
who had previously argued that the watchmakers needed tax exemption
for the sake of their economic viability, now proposed a progressive tax
regime to finance the salt tax compensation, in which rich watchmakers

would pay more than poor peasants. He wrote to François de Fargès de Polisy, the deputy Finance Minister:

> May I beg you, Sir, in an idle moment, just to ask M. le Contrôleur Général to have a look at this little article, in which I ask on behalf of our Estates-General the favour of leaving them the freedom to allocate the £30,000 for the poor *fermiers généraux*.
>
> The fact is that, in general, agriculture in our canton is a burden on the landowners, and that a man who has no team for ploughing his field, and who hires another man's plough and his labour, loses £12 per acre. A big merchant watchmaker can make £30,000 per year. Is it not right that he should contribute something to help the country that protects him? Everything comes from the earth, no doubt, it produces metals as well as wheat; but a watchmaker does not use 30 sous worth of copper and iron in the movement of a watch which he sells for 50 gold louis. As for the gold from which the case is made, and the diamonds with which it is often decorated, it is well known that our agriculture does not produce them.
>
> We propose, Sir, to charge no more than 6 francs per head for each master watchmaker, and the same from the other merchants and inn-keepers.[96]

Voltaire's phrase that 'everything comes from the earth' was an allusion to the contemporary economic theory that all wealth ultimately derived from the land, and that therefore agriculture should bear the weight of all taxation. It was a convenient theory for those whose income did not derive from the land; but as Voltaire's analysis here demonstrates, it was increasingly absurd and indefensible in the emerging world of industrialisation and international trade.

In the summer of that year (1776) Voltaire reported with satisfaction the increasing prosperity of his colony: 'We currently have eighteen buildings under construction, for a colony which is now doing a trade of five or six hundred thousand francs a year.'[97]

But when Turgot was removed from his position as Contrôleur Général that year, the French tax authorities became increasingly keen to tax Voltaire's watchmaking industry. By October, ten months after the negotiation of the new salt régime, Jacques Necker, the new Finance Minister, was moving to revoke the Ferney watchmakers' general tax exemptions, and to tax them like any Frenchmen. Voltaire assumed that political and national prejudice was at work: Necker was a Protestant financier from Geneva, and Voltaire took it for granted that he must be prejudiced against any competitors of Geneva.[98]

A week later the situation had worsened.

> Our colony of Ferney is not so happy, it is persecuted, almost annihilated. All the craftsmen are going off, one after the other, because M. l'Intendant [the governor of Burgundy] has reimposed the old feudal tax (*la taille*) and the community service labour (*la corvée*). The 500,000 francs that I spent on the houses I built, are just 500,000 francs thrown into the Lake of Geneva. I am in danger of dying as I ought have lived, in the poverty associated with the trade of a man of letters.[99]

The watchmaking colony of Ferney may have felt persecuted, but it was not almost annihilated. The summer of 1776 was perhaps the highwater mark of its prosperity, but watches went on being made there for several decades longer, well into the nineteenth century.

LAST CAMPAIGNS

1770–1778

VOLTAIRE'S FOUR MAJOR BATTLES for justice during the mid-1760s had taken a lot out of him, so when he learned, in 1769, of a new miscarriage of justice, he no longer felt he had the energy to handle it. Not surprisingly: he was seventy-five years old.

The new case was that of a well-to-do farmer called Martin, from the village of Bleurville, near Bar-le-Duc, east of Paris. In 1769 a man was murdered on the highway not far from Martin's house. A footprint on the scene seemed to match one of Martin's shoes. A witness saw the murderer run off. When this witness was confronted with Martin, he did not recognise him. But Martin was quoted as saying: 'Thank God! He did not recognise me!' It was on the strength of these ambiguous but damaging words, but apparently without any other evidence in confirmation, that a local judge condemned Martin to be tortured and then to be put to death by being broken on the wheel. The sentence was carried out that summer. Very shortly afterwards, however, on 26 July 1769 another man, condemned to death for a different crime, confessed just before his execution (also by being broken on the wheel) that it was he who had been guilty of the earlier murder as well.

When Voltaire first heard of the Martin affair, in August 1769, he made some enquiries and soon realised that a grotesque injustice had taken place. But he decided that he could not take it on because he already had too much on his plate.

I am not getting involved in the Martin affair. I have enough with Sirvens, without getting mixed up with Martins as well. I cannot be the Don Quixote of all those who are hanged or broken on the wheel. On every side I see nothing but the most barbarous injustices: Lally-Tollendal and his gag, Sirven, Calas, Martin, the chevalier de La Barre; they sometimes appear before me in my dreams. People seem to believe that our century is merely ridiculous; in fact, it is horrible.[1]

Nevertheless, Voltaire continued his enquiries for several weeks, and it seems possible that these may, indirectly, have had a quasi-campaigning influence on Martin's behalf. At all events, by the following spring, in March 1770, he noted: 'The attorney-general is engaged in rehabilitating Martin. Yet Martin himself is still broken, and his family is still reduced to beggary.'[2]

Later that year, another judicial scandal erupted, as horrific as it was flagrant, and this time Voltaire could not keep quiet. This was the case of François-Joseph Monbailli, of Saint-Omer in northern France, who was accused of having killed his mother. Monbailli and his wife, Anne-Thérèse, lived with Monbailli's widowed mother and slept in a room next to her bedroom. On the morning of 27 July 1770 the mother was found dead. She was widely known to be a heavy drinker of spirits and probably died from a fall, perhaps caused by apoplexy; yet rumour insistently put it about that she had been murdered by Monbailli and his wife.

No meaningful evidence against Monbailli and his wife was produced in the local court of Saint-Omer. As for motive, it was unlikely that they would have killed her in the hope of inheritance, since she left more debts than assets. But popular clamour against Monbailli proved too strong. Monbailli was subjected to torture, both 'ordinary' and 'extraordinary'; he continued to protest his innocence; the prosecution produced no significant evidence against him. Nevertheless, on 9 November 1770 the court of the Council of Arras condemned Monbailli and his wife to death. Ten days later, on 19 November 1770, Monbailli was executed as a parricide: his right hand was cut off, his arms and legs were broken on the wheel and his body was burned on a pyre. The execution of Monbailli's wife was postponed, since she was pregnant.

Voltaire was alerted and persuaded to intervene on behalf of the victims. It was a short, almost effortless campaign, because the prosecution case against Monbailli was so transparently non-existent. Voltaire appealed to the Chancellor, René-Nicolas-Charles-Augustin de Maupeou, and in 1771 published (under his own name, significantly) a ten-page pamphlet called *La Méprise d'Arras* (The Error of Arras), in which he exposed the grotesque absurdity of the trial. The following spring, in May 1772, Mme Monbailli was acquitted and her husband 'rehabilitated'. 'You know the reparation they have made for the error of Arras. But what reparation! The judges should have gone on their knees to beg forgiveness from the widow of that innocent man, and they should have given her a pension of half their assets.'[3]

Voltaire's next campaign was for the liberation of the serfs of Saint-Claude, and he pursued it for the next five years, until he was eighty-one; he got nowhere with it. Saint-Claude is a small town in an area of six parishes in the Jura, not far from Ferney. When France acquired the Franche-Comté from Spain, by the Treaties of Nijmegen in 1678–79, Louis XIV had permitted the inhabitants to keep their traditional economic customs. One of these customs was feudal serfdom, and by a quirk of history it still survived into the eighteenth century in the case of a Benedictine monastery at Saint-Claude. In 1742 the monastery was dissolved and replaced by an open community of some twenty canons of the abbey of Saint-Claude; but the canons continued to enforce their rights of servitude over the local population of some 12,000 people.

The essential principle of the serfdom of Saint-Claude was that all property and the product of all work, and therefore ultimately all the inhabitants, belonged to the canons of Saint-Claude. Anyone who was born in Saint-Claude was a serf; if a man lived in Saint-Claude for a year, he became a serf; if a man or woman from outside married a serf, he or she became a serf; if a man moved away from the area, his 'property' was forfeit; if a son failed to live in his father's house and eat at his father's table throughout the father's life, then at the father's death he would be driven out of the house. In short, as Voltaire repeatedly said, it was a régime of legalised slavery.

Voltaire's intervention on behalf of the serfs of Saint-Claude in 1770 coincided with his involvement that same year with the project to develop Versoix and was in some sense part of his growing preoccupation not just with the welfare and improvement of Ferney and its estate but more broadly with the economic and social development of his region as a whole.

To fight this case, Voltaire recruited his lawyer friend Charles-Frédéric-Gabriel Christin, who had originally come from Saint-Claude and was now Voltaire's bailiff at Ferney. With Christin's help Voltaire wrote two pamphlets and numerous letters appealing for the abolition of serfdom in the Jura, which he sent to the French government. He badgered the duc de Choiseul; he badgered the duchesse de Choiseul. They did not respond.[4]

When the duc de Choiseul fell from power in December 1770, Voltaire did his best to get on good terms with the new key figure in the king's ministry, the new Chancellor, René-Nicolas-Charles-Augustin de Maupeou. He was delighted when Maupeou closed down the *parlements* and sent all the lawyers and judges into exile, replacing them with newly appointed law courts. He conveniently overlooked the fact that Maupeou had come from a long career as a leading judge in the Paris *parlement*, and that it was he who had signed the decree confirming the death sentence on the chevalier de La Barre. Indeed, it was only much later, in 1775, that Voltaire learned just how decisive a role Maupeou had played in 1766, in securing the necessary majority to enforce the death sentence on La Barre.[5]

Voltaire tried to stay on friendly personal terms with the Choiseuls, now exiled to their estate. But the duchesse de Choiseul reacted to Voltaire's worldly adaptability with angry contempt; she wrote to Mme du Deffand: 'How pitiful he is, this Voltaire, how cowardly! He excuses himself, he accuses himself (*il s'excuse, il s'accuse*), he drowns in his own spittle, as a result of having spat when he shouldn't have. He sings a recantation, he blows hot and cold. He does not know what he is doing; he is disgusting and pitiful.'[6]

Voltaire wrote to Mme du Deffand to protest his innocence of any disloyalty to the Choiseuls:

> I do not in the least believe I am failing them, if I detest absurd and bloody pedants. Like the whole of Europe, I loathed the assassins of the chevalier de La Barre, I loathed the assassins of Calas, I loathed the assassins of Sirven, and I loathed the assassins of the comte de Lally-Tollendal [in each case, the old *parlements*]. They have done nothing but evil, and they have produced nothing but evil. You hate the *philosophes*, and I hate the bourgeois tyrants. I have forgiven you your fury against *philosophie*, so forgive me mine against the gang of lawyers.[7]

It was not often that Voltaire allowed his rage to spew out so violently.

With the change of ministry at court, Voltaire returned to his campaign on behalf of the serfs of Saint-Claude. He wrote to Maupeou on the subject, and in 1771 and 1772 he drafted three more formal appeals which he sent to the government. To no avail: Maupeou simply strung him along with soft and soothing words.[8] After Louis XV died, in 1774, Voltaire returned once more to the subject of the serfs of Saint-Claude.

He sent a new appeal to the French government in 1775, and another in 1776, still in vain.[9]

In January 1778, four months before his death, Voltaire wrote to Christin: 'I tremble on every side for our poor dear people of Saint-Claude. I am really afraid that they may be devoured by the Pharisees and publicans. Where will they find refuge? They have no protection, no asylum. I am horrified and discouraged by everything I see. I shall soon die, detesting the persecutors, and loving you.'[10] In 1779, the year after Voltaire died, Louis XVI issued an edict freeing all the serfs in the royal domains, but it did not apply to property belonging to the Church, so the twenty canons of Saint-Claude still retained their feudal rights. The serfs of Saint-Claude were not finally freed until 1789, in the Revolution; their descendants put up a statue of Voltaire in the town, nearly a hundred years later, in 1887, in recognition of his efforts on their behalf.

After 1770 Voltaire did not engage in any new 'human rights' cases, but he did attempt, over the next few years, to resuscitate two of the central cases of the 1760s, those of La Barre and Lally-Tollendal. He was now in his late seventies.

In all of Voltaire's campaigns, the case which had moved him most was that of the nineteen-year-old chevalier de La Barre, executed in 1766 for blasphemy. At the time he had made rather little effort to get the verdict and sentence quashed: he exposed the scandal in his pamphlet *Relation de la mort du chevalier de La Barre*,[11] but it seemed to have no effect, and Voltaire went no further.

Seven years later, however, in 1773, he started a new campaign of rehabilitation; not primarily for the dead La Barre but for La Barre's young friend Gaillard d'Étallonde, who had escaped to Prussia before the trial started and who had been condemned to death in absentia. Gaillard d'Étallonde was now pursuing a successful career as an officer in the Prussian army, but his death sentence meant that he had lost his legal rights in France, and he asked Voltaire to help him. Voltaire persuaded Frederick to give him a year's leave of absence and invited him to come and stay at Ferney, to pursue his case in France. D'Étallonde arrived in Ferney in April 1774 and stayed there for sixteen months, until August 1775.

The main difficulty Voltaire faced, once again, was that the law courts refused to release the trial documents. Eventually he succeeded in accumulating 6,000 pages of trial records, but he came to the conclusion that he could not get the verdict overturned unless he could prove that Belleval and Duval de Soicourt had manipulated the trial and suborned the witnesses.[12] 'Such a trial would last four or five years, would exhaust the purses of the litigants and the patience of the judges, and I should be dead of decrepitude before we should have obtained a judgement which would put things right. The revision of the Calas affair lasted three years; that of Sirven lasted seven years; and I shall probably be dead in six months.'[13] In any case, he probably could not get this verdict overturned unless he also overturned the verdict on La Barre, and that would be even more difficult.

Voltaire wrestled with these difficulties for well over a year. In the summer of 1775 he composed an appeal to the king, ostensibly written by d'Étallonde, under the title *Cri du sang innocent* (Cry of Innocent Blood), which was based in part on the 6,000 pages of the trial records, and in which he denounced the scandal of the 1766 trial.[14] Voltaire was quite nervous about how this pamphlet would go down at court: Louis XV had died the previous year, and one of the first acts of the new king, Louis XVI, had been to recall the old *parlements* which had briefly been exiled by Maupeou. Since it was the old *parlements* which had been responsible for the original verdicts on Lally-Tollendal and La Barre, Voltaire feared that the new ministry might react badly to any appeal against those verdicts. So he released only a handful of copies of the *Cri du sang innocent*, and distributed them privately to a few trusted friends.

In fact, no harm came from the *Cri du sang innocent*, but no good either: the king simply ignored Voltaire's appeal. Twelve years later, in 1787, Gaillard d'Étallonde was offered a deal: he could have his sentence reversed, but the price was a recantation of his offences. D'Étallonde duly obliged and for good measure threw in a denunciation of Voltaire's malign influence on him and on his young friends. In December 1788 his sentence was formally wiped out by the *parlement* of Paris. Voltaire did not witness this abject betrayal, for by that time he had already been dead more than ten years.

In the case of Lally-Tollendal, Voltaire had given up his original campaign for lack of information, and he did not take it up again until he was approached, in 1770, by Lally-Tollendal's nineteen-year-old natural son the chevalier Trophime-Gérard de Lally-Tollendal. Voltaire undertook to help and advise him, but he made almost no headway. It was not until 24 May 1778 that Voltaire heard that Lally-Tollendal's son had been given leave to appeal; but the sentence was not overturned until 1781, and then without rehabilitating Lally-Tollendal.

Voltaire was deeply moved by the news of this breakthrough, which reached him as he was dying in Paris. On 26 May 1778 he wrote young

Lally-Tollendal a touching letter: 'The dying man has been revived by learning this great news; he embraces M. de Lally very tenderly, he sees that the king is the defender of justice; he will die content.'[15] It was the last letter he wrote.

In old age Voltaire largely gave up his individual 'human rights' campaigning, but he made one last effort to grapple with the general problem of penal reform. In February 1777 the *Gazette de Berne* offered a prize of 50 louis for the best essay on the reform of the criminal law. When Voltaire learned of the project, he immediately offered to double the prize money and set to work to compose an essay on the subject himself. He completed his 60-page treatise, entitled *Le Prix de la justice et de l'humanité* (The Prize of Justice and Humanity), towards the end of that year, when he was eighty-three.[16]

In this new work Voltaire returned to many of the ideas familiar in his previous works, but his views on penal reform remained more cautious than, say, those of Beccaria. He went much further than he had done before in condemning torture, but not quite all the way; he went further than he had done before in condemning capital punishment, but not as far as Beccaria. The main characteristics of the essay are typically Voltairean: it is liberal, anecdotal, combative, sceptical, lively, episodic, disputatious, rhetorical and, in the last resort, improvisational. It was more of a tract for prompting questions about the defects in existing legal systems than a comprehensive and systematic programme of reform. Nevertheless, after a quarter of a century, Voltaire was still campaigning for a reform of the French justice system.

≈

In 1776 Henri-Louis Lekain came down from Paris to inaugurate Voltaire's new theatre in Ferney, and on the surface the opening was a great success; but Voltaire did not really enjoy it. It was partly his ill health, which was certainly getting much worse. What was really upsetting him, however, was the increasingly painful contrast between the decline in the popularity of his own rather old-fashioned and formalistic tragedies and the growing fashion in Paris for Shakespeare's plays, a fashion that had recently been stimulated by the publication of the first two volumes of a complete translation of the plays, by Pierre Prime Félicien Le Tourneur.

For most of his life Voltaire had been haunted by Shakespeare's plays, ever since he had first come upon them during his first exile, in

England in 1726–28. Even at that time he had felt a deep ambivalence towards Shakespeare, with a mixture of admiration for his beauties, brilliance and inventiveness, and contempt for his vulgarity and his failure to observe any of the formal rules of dramatic discipline. Fifty years on, the element of contempt had gained the upper hand and by 1776 had hardened into almost hysterical indignation. In July of that year Voltaire wrote to d'Argental to report the arrival of Lekain, but virtually the whole of his letter was devoted to a frothing condemnation of Shakespeare and of the new translations by Le Tourneur.

> I must tell you how upset I am for the honour of the theatre, against a certain Tourneur, who is said to be Secretary of the Office for Publishing (*La Librairie*), but who does not seem to me the Secretary of good taste. Have you read two volumes by this miserable fellow, in which he wants to make us treat Shakespeare as the only model of true tragedy? He calls him 'the god of the theatre'. He sacrifices all Frenchmen, without exception, to his idol, as they used to sacrifice pigs to Ceres in the old days. He does not even deign to mention Corneille and Racine; these two great men are merely wrapped up in the general proscription, without their names even being mentioned.
>
> What is frightful is that this monster has a following in France; and the height of calamity and horror is that it was I who was once the first to speak of this Shakespeare, it was I who was the first to show the French some pearls that I had discovered in his enormous dung-heap.[17]

After talking with Lekain, Voltaire concluded that the Shakespeare situation was even worse than he had thought.

> My dear angel, Lekain tells me that all the youth in Paris are on the side of Le Tourneur, that the scaffolds and brothels of the English stage are taking over the theatre of Racine and the beautiful scenes of Corneille, that nothing grand and decent has been left in Paris by the harlequins from London, and that finally they are going to put on a tragedy in prose, in which there is a company of butchers who will have a marvellous effect. I have seen the end of the reign of reason and taste.[18]

So great was Voltaire's rage that he felt driven, in the summer of 1776, to compose a full-scale denunciation not of Le Tourneur but of

Shakespeare. This was his *Lettre à l'Académie Française*, which he hoped would be read out at a formal session of the Académie. His first draft was so violent that d'Alembert, who was now *secrétaire perpétuel*, had to ask him to soften it.

One of Voltaire's objections was that Shakespeare used crude words on stage. 'My principal intention, and the true aim of my work', he wrote to La Harpe,

> are that the public should be properly informed of the excesses and infamous turpitude of his language. Of course, one cannot say out loud in the Louvre what one says every day so boldly in London: M. d'Alembert will not abase himself by singing out, before the ladies, 'the beast with two backs', 'son of a whore', 'piss', 'deflower', etc. But he can pause at these sacramental words, and by suppressing the word itself, alert the public that he dare not translate Shakespeare in all its energy.[19]

After some cuts and revisions Voltaire's *Lettre* was agreed by the members of the Académie Française and read out by d'Alembert in his little gravelly voice at a formal public session. The *immortels* were so entertained that d'Alembert had to read out several passages more than once; but the English visitors present were not amused, and the king was displeased since he had given his official approval to Le Tourneur's project, and he refused permission for Voltaire's *Lettre* to be printed.[20]

All in all, the episode of the *Lettre à l'Académie Française* was an extraordinary manifestation of Voltaire's fixation with his ideal of rule-based and well-behaved verse drama. But Shakespeare, like Corneille, survived Voltaire's criticisms: his *Hamlet* has been performed more often at the Comédie Française than any of Voltaire's plays.

≈

After Louis XV died, on 10 May 1774, Voltaire started thinking that he might now perhaps be able to return to Paris. Of course, he had alluded to the idea, on and off, on many previous occasions in his long exile near Geneva, but it had almost always been in wistful terms, implying that he knew it was not really possible. But as soon as he heard the news of Louis's death, he began to talk more seriously about going home to Paris, and he wrote to d'Argental almost immediately:

I do not want to die without having the consolation of having seen my angels. It is only my miserable health which can prevent me from making a little trip to Paris. There was a little trouble between me and the late departed [Louis XV], a trouble about which most of the public knew nothing, a verbal trouble, a trouble which leaves no trace behind. It seems to me that I am a sick man who can take the air any-where, without a prescription from the doctors.

And yet I should like it to be secret. I think it is easy to hide in the crowd. There will be so many great ceremonies, so many big troubles, that nobody will think about mine.[21]

Voltaire seems to be implying that his exile had been due to nothing more than a personal difference between him and the late king, and that therefore the death of the king had removed the only political obstacle to his return. He was deceiving himself. The new king regarded Voltaire as a troublesome and perhaps a dangerous individual, and he was worried about the damage that he might do, not even by returning to Paris, but just by dying at his home at Ferney. Two months after his accession, Louis XVI gave instructions that, as soon as Voltaire should die, the authorities should enter his château and seize all his manuscripts and other documents, for the personal attention of the king.

For Pierre-Michel Hennin these instructions were deeply embar-rassing, both personally and politically. During his years as French Resi-dent in Geneva, since 1765, he had been a frequent visitor to Ferney and a warm friend of Voltaire, and he had absolutely no desire to play the part of police bailiff after Voltaire's death. For three months he made no comment on the king's instructions. Then, in October 1774, he wrote a long minute to Bertin, the Foreign Minister, giving a string of reasons why he thought the instructions as they stood were ill advised and prob-ably counter-productive.

First, he said, the authorities would find virtually no unpublished manuscripts. 'Knowing M. de Voltaire's turn of mind as I do, I dare assert that we should not find any of his manuscripts, apart from what-ever he was working on at the moment of his death. For the past many years, scarcely has he started a work, than the first sheets are already at the printer; he told me a hundred times that he had "emptied the sack".' In addition, said Hennin, such an operation would undoubtedly cause a large public scandal, as well as diplomatic friction with King Frederick of Prussia, Empress Catherine of Russia and other princes, when they learned that their private correspondance with Voltaire had simply been confiscated to satisfy the curiosity of Louis XVI.

A year later it seemed that the original instructions had been abandoned, and in the event the king's agitation turned out to have been pointless: when Voltaire died in 1778, in Paris, no attempt was made to seize his letters and other manuscripts at Ferney.[22]

Voltaire soon started to have second thoughts about going back to Paris, on the grounds that he was not yet well enough. 'Ah! My dear angel, my dear angel!' he wrote to d'Argental,

> I must rebuke you. M. de Thibouville, M. de Chabanon, Mme du Deffand, all tell me that I am coming to see you in the spring. Yes, I want to come, but I shall only go to see you, dear angel that you are. I cannot show myself to others than you. I am deaf and blind, or just about. I pass three-quarters of the day in my bed, and the rest beside the fire. I always have to have on my head a large bonnet, without which my brain would be exposed. I take medicine about three times a week, and I speak with great difficulty, having no more teeth, thank God, than I have eyes and ears. Judge, according to this fine portrait, which is quite faithful, if I am in any state to go to Paris in a snowstorm.
>
> I could not avoid going to the Académie, and I should die of cold at the first session. Could I close my door to all the riff-raff of the rascally so-called men of letters, who would have the stupid curiosity to come and look at my skeleton? And then, if I should have the idea, at the age of eighty-one, of dying in your city of Paris, just imagine what embarrassment, what scenes, what absurdity!
>
> So be very careful, my dear angel, not to authorise this frightful rumour that I am coming to see you in the spring. Just say, as I shall say explicitly, that there is no truth in it.[23]

The following year, 1775, any travel plans Voltaire might have had were put on hold when Mme Denis went through a long patch of sickness. She was normally of robust health, and of more than robust appetite. So when she fell ill in April 1775, Voltaire was alarmed: 'Alas! Mme Denis has been in bed for a month, overwhelmed by an inflammation of the chest, and they have twice applied plasters. I am dying quite quietly in my own quarters without plasters and without doctors.'[24] (Voltaire could not resist the temptation to draw attention to his own ailments.)

Mme Louise-Suzanne Gallatin, a neighbour and frequent visitor, gives a touching commentary on Voltaire's sadness at Mme Denis's illness. 'Our friend is well, but at this time he is in great grief, for his niece Mme Denis is very ill. She has been his friend, his companion, he never leaves her, and I am terribly sorry that I am in no position to go and share his grief. But I have news of him twice a day.'[25]

By early May 1775 Mme Denis was still ill but was getting better. Voltaire wrote to Mme Saint-Julien: 'If you come to the furthest limits of Burgundy, you will give life to Mme Denis and me. She is still rather ill, but as for me, I am incurable. You will find the uncle and the niece, each in their own corner of their hospital, and Father Adam in his attic, solely concerned with his breakfast, dinner and supper. Our house is a Lazar-house. Only you could make it bearable.'[26]

Father Adam did not enjoy his attic and his three square meals a day for very much longer. Eighteen months later, in November 1776, Voltaire drove him out, after nearly fourteen years as his resident almoner. Why he did so is not at all clear; in general, Voltaire was an inordinately indulgent and loyal employer. It seems that Adam had a tendency to quarrel with the servants, so perhaps it was Mme Denis who wanted him gone.[27] At all events, Voltaire dismissed him abruptly, and he took refuge in the home of a nearby curé. He was seventy-one years old.

By the middle of May 1775 Mme Denis had recovered, and Voltaire organised a large convalescence party for her. 'I can tell you about the very beautiful and very agreeable fête which our colony gave yesterday for the convalescence of Mme Denis. Not only did we have cavalry and infantry, cannons, kettle-drums, side-drums, trumpets, oboes, clarinets and a table with 200 place-settings in the garden, but very pretty and very short toasts in verse and prose, and all followed by a little comedy.'[28]

By mid-August 1775 Voltaire told Alexandre d'Hornoy, Mme Denis's overweight lawyer nephew, that she now seemed to be quite well, and had completely recovered her appetite: 'Mme Denis has regained all her strength, and she is now managing four meals a day; she could even keep up with you.'[29] Two years later Voltaire reported that Mme Denis had stopped drinking: 'She has recovered her health and will long keep it, because she has become sober (for fear of dying). She is the first woman I have seen exercise any self-control.'[30]

Once Mme Denis had recovered, in August 1775, Voltaire decided to adopt the line that he was perfectly free to go to Paris but that he preferred to stay where he was. For by this time the main obstacle was not Mme Denis's health but Voltaire's. For many years Voltaire had talked constantly of his ailments. This was partly out of self-pity, partly out of self-mockery and partly for the sake of narrative entertainment.

But his ailments were not imaginary. Like many people at that time, Voltaire was often ill, and his illnesses became more frequent and more acute as he got older. In his sixties he complained of hydropsy, colic, scurvy, paralysis, snow-blindness, loss of teeth and deafness, but above all of constipation (*l'article de la garde-robe*), and he made a permanent running bawdy joke of all the many absurd, much-debated, and largely ineffectual remedies for dealing with it, from rhubarb and cassia to goat's milk.

Other people may not always have taken Voltaire's complaints of ill health entirely seriously, because what they noticed, much of the time, was his energy and, above all, his gaiety. Sometimes Voltaire claimed that he was only outwardly cheerful out of politeness. In 1766 he had written to Richelieu: 'I beg my hero's pardon for not writing in my own handwriting, and I beg his pardon again for not writing gaily; but I am ill and sad. I have never been gay except by pretence. Whoever writes tragedies and histories must naturally be serious, however French he may be.'[31]

In 1768 he had written to Jean-François Marmontel: 'My dear friend, the patriarch is still suffering; and if he is satirical in the intervals of his sufferings, he owes his life to the practice of gaiety, which is the best practice. But however much I may put on an appearance of gaiety, deep down I am very sad.'[32]

It is quite likely that Voltaire's gaiety may have been partly assumed for the sake of politeness; after all, he was a writer, and writers spend much of their time not in gaiety but alone. On the other hand, with some people Voltaire genuinely enjoyed company, if they amused and stimulated him, and especially the company of women, particularly if they were young and pretty.

At the end of 1772 an eighteen-year-old girl visited Voltaire in his room, and he fainted three times in succession. This girl was apparently notorious for the freedom of her conduct, and the rumour rapidly spread that Voltaire had passed out trying his luck with her. The story was almost incredible, but the literary world was so excited by the whiff of scandal that even Diderot, who seldom communicated with Voltaire, was moved to write to him. 'Sir and dear master, here they are saying unbelievable things about you. That a young woman should have had the vanity to sleep with the unique man of the century does not surprise me too much, I should even be edified. But you ... I could not believe that sort of madness, it must be just a story. Story or not, reassure us about your health.'[33]

Mme Gallatin was a regular and solicitous visitor to Ferney, and her frequent letters give a lively picture of Voltaire's health and happiness; despite his frequent bouts of illness, the most remarkable feature of her accounts is his gaiety and vitality. Here is her story of a trip Voltaire made to Geneva one day in July 1775.

Our friend is very well. He came one day to Geneva. As there was a jam of carriages at the city gate, he got quite impatient and got down from his carriage and walked as far as the gate-house. As soon as they saw him, everyone wanted to follow; and the crowd was so great that he had difficulty getting through. He had the pleasure of hearing people shout: 'I want to see him too!' All the windows were full of people. I think he was very flattered.[34]

In his late seventies, Voltaire started to suffer from new ailments which were much more serious, including apoplexy, gout and urine retention (*strangurie*). Some of these conditions, such as gout and strangury, were extremely painful and for periods incapacitating; and it may be that his increasingly frequent attacks of strangury were in fact early symptoms of the prostate cancer that eventually killed him. When Voltaire complained of some ailment – whether it was indigestion, snow-blindness, gout, insomnia, apoplexy, constipation, urine retention or piles – he may have been exaggerating, but he was probably not inventing. Sometimes his symptoms were indirectly confirmed by others.

Voltaire's first attack of strangury seems to have occurred in February 1773, when he was seventy-nine. He complained to Gabriel Cramer, his printer, that his urine retention was preventing him from working: 'The old invalid cannot send you anything today, he has been bathed, bled, and dosed for a frightful strangury.'[35]

Voltaire's account was confirmed by Hennin:

M. de Voltaire is rather ill, and I begin to fear for him. Two weeks ago he got up in the middle of the night, when it was very cold, without stockings and without underwear, to light his fire and work. He caught cold, which attacked his bladder, and from there he had a retention of urine. He treated himself in his own way for the next four days, and when they sent for [Dr] Cabanis, he had a high fever, an inflamed strangury; in short, he was in a bad way. Cabanis put him in the bath for four hours, cared for him, his urine returned, and he was a bit better. Whether because he wanted a distraction or because he had something urgent he had to do, he began to work harder than ever. His legs started to swell, he had some indigestion, he cannot sleep, today he has a temperature. If this incident has any bad consequences, he will have been the victim of false medical ideas. At the height of his crisis he purged himself with an enema of soap; since then he has surely dosed himself secretly with many personal remedies; he eats a lot in the evening, in order to sleep. In short, he makes up his own treatments because he is not yet afraid.[36]

In March 1773 Voltaire wrote to Claude-François Passerat, a doctor acquaintance:

You make me love life, Sir, through the interest you deign to take in my ailments. I no longer have a temperature, but I am not getting better. For the last two months I have been suffering from insomnia on top of everything else. I attribute it to the gout, which wanders all over me, sometimes in my feet, sometimes in my knees, sometimes in my hands, and which finds itself everywhere so poorly housed that it does not stay long in any one place. I must endure all this with patience, and thank nature for not having sent me gravel, nor stone, nor apoplexy, nor dysentery, nor gangrene. She has somewhat hardened my ears, but she has not hardened my heart.[37]

Four years later, however, in March 1777, nature did send him a severe attack of apoplexy, as he told Richelieu: 'A few days ago I lost my memory for two days, and I lost it so completely that I could not find any word in the language. Never has nature played such a brutal trick on a member of the Académie Française. It is quite ridiculous that I should endure an apoplexy, considering how thin I am.'[38] Perhaps he had had a mini-stroke.

It is perhaps not surprising, therefore, that for several years Voltaire remained quite ambivalent about the prospect of setting out on a long and stressful journey to Paris. In the middle of 1777, however, he started to have two practical reasons for going. First, he was working on a pair of new tragedies, *Irène* and *Agathocle*, and by October 1777, when they were nearly finished, he began to talk openly of going to Paris in order to see them performed at the Comédie Française.[39]

The second reason was the marriage between Charles Michel, the marquis de Villette, and Reine Philiberte Rouph de Varicourt. She was the teenage daughter of an impoverished local noble family, and so beautiful and so charming that in January, 1776, when she was nineteen, Voltaire decided to take her into his household. He called her *Belle et Bonne* ('Beautiful and Good'), and her affection for him became essential to his happiness.

Villette, by contrast, was a middle-aged libertine, whose disordered life included a scandalous reputation for homosexuality; but Voltaire found him amusing and witty. He had visited Voltaire on previous occasions; but when he arrived at Ferney towards the end of September 1777, he at once fell in love with *Belle et Bonne* and almost immediately decided to marry her. Paris society was scandalised that any well-born young lady should be contaminated by association with the notorious Villette, but Voltaire was delighted by the match and hoped that she would 'convert' Villette to heterosexuality. They were married at Ferney on 19 November, and Voltaire placed a diamond necklace round the neck of his *Belle et Bonne*.

Villette owned a large house in Paris, and by the next day he was already announcing that they should all – that is, he, *Belle et Bonne*, Voltaire and Mme Denis – go to Paris within the next two months.[40] With the new year, the plan took concrete shape: the Comédie Française agreed to stage *Irène* in the spring, and Voltaire prepared for his return to Paris, on a journey from which he was never to return.

TRIUMPH AND DEATH

1778

THE JOURNEY TO PARIS was planned for early February 1778, and for at least a month before Voltaire was quite excited by the prospect. Paul-Claude Moultou, a Protestant pastor from Geneva and a familiar visitor at Ferney, gives a vivid picture of Voltaire's enthusiasm and vitality. 'Voltaire is so infatuated, so taken in by what surrounds him, that he really wants to have this play performed in Paris. Just imagine, my friend, the force of this man: he read, no, he declaimed, the whole of this tragedy to us before supper; after that he had supper with us, he frolicked around like a child until two in the morning, and then he slept seven hours without waking once.'[1]

At the last moment, however, Voltaire hung back. On Tuesday 3 February Mme Denis set out for Paris with Villette and *Belle et Bonne* but without Voltaire. He wrote to d'Argental that morning: 'I am in despair not to be accompanying our travellers. But I have not the strength for one hundred leagues.' Yet in another letter written that same evening, he said that he himself would leave 'on Thursday, or Friday at the latest, for Dijon' – but not, apparently, for Paris.[2]

One theory is that Voltaire was trying to conceal his movements from the French authorities. But that does not seem likely, since he had very recently received reassurances from an impeccable source at Versailles that there was no *lettre de cachet* out against him in the files. 'Some church-goers have put it about that there was against me, in some office or other, a piece of paper that they call *littera sigilli* ("letters of proscription"); I can assure you that there is no such thing.'[3] The most likely explanation is that Voltaire was old and of very uncertain health: when the moment arrived, he was daunted by the prospect of the rigours of a long journey in the depth of winter, and for a day or two he simply vacillated between staying and going.

But only for a day or two. On Thursday 5 February 1778 Voltaire set off for Paris, accompanied by Wagnière and his cook, in his specially adapted sleeping carriage (*la dormeuse*), which was kept warm by a portable stove. On the road Voltaire caught up with Mme Denis and the Villettes, and five days later, on Tuesday 10 February, they all reached Paris and went straight to the Hôtel de Villette, at the corner of the rue de Beaune and the quai des Théatins on the left bank of the Seine (now renamed quai Voltaire).

By one of those wonderful ironies the Hôtel de Villette was a house with which Voltaire had once been intimately familiar over fifty years earlier. At that time it had been the Paris home of the marquis and marquise de Bernières, and Voltaire in his late twenties had rented an apartment from them; he had also enjoyed a love affair with the marquise, Marguerite Madeleine. In 1778, however, Voltaire could probably not have recognised the house itself since it had been substantially modified and enlarged by Villette.

But even before settling into the set of rooms provided for him, Voltaire set out on foot to see his old friend d'Argental, who was now living not far away, on the quai d'Orsay. He evidently cut quite a comical figure, in his long sable fur coat (a present from Catherine the Great), his large old-fashioned wig topped off by a red bonnet and his walking-stick with a handle in the shape of a crow. But if he attracted attention, he was not recognised; he had been away so long, and no one expected to see him. When he found that d'Argental was not at home, Voltaire returned to the rue de Beaune, and there d'Argental soon came to find him. The two old men embraced; it was their first meeting for twenty-eight years, for d'Argental had never once visited Voltaire in his exile.

The day after his arrival the Hôtel de Villette was besieged with visitors and well-wishers from every walk of life. Mme du Deffand, the blind literary hostess, sent her secretary to observe the scene, and he told her that some 300 people called at the Hôtel de Villette that day: the visitors were marshalled by Mme Denis or *Belle et Bonne*, while Voltaire kept to his room, working on revisions of *Irène*. When a new caller was announced, Voltaire would emerge, wearing a dressing gown and night-cap, exchange a few words with the visitor and then withdraw again to his study.

According to Mme Denis, the crowds of visitors kept coming, day after day.

> I have been in such a great agitation since I have been here that I have not had the time to recognise myself. As soon as we arrived, I was obliged to receive the whole of the court and the whole of the town. It started at nine in the morning, and did not stop until ten at night. My uncle would come to the salon several times during the day and from time to time withdraw to his room. It went on like this for ten or twelve days.[4]

In the first few days after his arrival in Paris his visitors included: a ceremonial delegation from the Académie Française on the Thursday; a deputation from the Comédie Française on the Saturday; and visits by the two rival composers, Christoph Willibald Gluck and Nicolas Piccini, in quick succession on the Sunday. They may not have realised that Voltaire had no interest in their music, or any other.

On Monday 16 February he was visited by Benjamin Franklin, the celebrated statesman from the recently founded United States of America. 'He has seen Mr Franklin, who brought his little grandson, and asked the old man [Voltaire] to bless him. The old man gave his blessing in the presence of twenty people, and pronounced these words for a blessing: "*God and Liberty*".'[5]*

The social round did not stop Voltaire from working hard at improving his tragedy *Irène*. Before leaving Ferney, he had been told that the play had been much admired by the Comédie Française actors, and that the duc de Duras had given virtually *carte blanche* for its performance.[6] But many of Voltaire's friends had serious reservations, even if they kept quiet about them; only Condorcet had the courage to spell out to him all the play's shortcomings. Voltaire was shaken, but contrite and submissive: 'I had thought … I had imagined … Unfortunately, I was mistaken … I accept a large part of the truths which you have had the kindness to tell me.'[7] He obediently set about revising the play and said he was sorry the actors at the Comédie Française had been shown what was, he could see now, no more than a first sketch of the play.[8]

In the days immediately after his arrival in Paris, according to Mme du Deffand, he stayed up two nights in succession working at it,[9] and

---

* In the letter Voltaire writes '*Dieu et la Liberté*', but in fact he pronounced the blessing in English.

on the Sunday, five days after arriving, he summoned the actors of the Comédie Française for a first rehearsal at the Hôtel de Villette. Voltaire asked Mme du Deffand to attend the rehearsal, but she declined: 'He invited me; but it will be between eleven o'clock and midday, and as that is often the time when I start to sleep, it is doubtful that I can be there.'

The stresses of work and the hectic social round, coming on top of the strains of the journey, quickly took their toll on Voltaire's failing health. Even Mme du Deffand, for all her blindness, could sense how ill he was. 'He pretends that he will go home this Lent, but I do not think he can; he has pain in his bladder, he has haemorrhoids, and they said yesterday that he was losing his balance; his extreme vivacity sustains him, but it is wearing him out; I should not be astonished if he should die soon.'[10]

On Thursday 12 February Voltaire felt unwell and sent for Dr Théodore Tronchin, now practising in Paris. Tronchin called the next day, but the remedies he prescribed did no good. Five days later, on Tuesday 17 February, Voltaire again appealed to Tronchin for help.

The aged Swiss, whom Monsieur Tronchin had the kindness to come and see at M. de Villette's, wishes to point out that the continuous alternation between strangury and incontinent urination (*diabète*), with a total and complete cessation of peristaltic movement in the entrails, is fairly disagreeable and a bit dangerous. And that a machine so dislocated cannot survive more than a few more days except with the kindness of Monsieur Tronchin. The old invalid would be very glad to be able to talk for a moment with Monsieur Tronchin, before making his farewell.[11]

This time Tronchin did not respond to Voltaire's appeal, and Voltaire wrote to him again the next morning, Wednesday 18 February. 'One is ashamed to importune Monsieur Tronchin for one's little miseries, but the aged traveller from Ferney may well be condemned. The strangury has started again and is now in control; the feet and legs are swollen; otherwise, he would use his legs to come and embrace Monsieur Tronchin at the Palais Royal.'[12]

The day passed, presumably with Voltaire in great pain, but Tronchin did not call. That evening Voltaire wrote to him again.

The aged invalid dares once more to tell his saviour Monsieur Tronchin: that the phlegms (*les glaires*) which sometimes pass by his urethra, get absorbed (*congromelées*) into his entrails, and pass into his blood; that he cannot alleviate the cessation of the peristaltic movement, except by taking the pills of Mme Denis; and that he asks Monsieur Tronchin's permission to go on taking them, and to take a little quinine before meals. He wishes to do nothing without Monsieur Tronchin's advice, and begs him to send word'.[13]

Voltaire's description of his symptoms is obscure, but perhaps his reference to *glaires* was an alarming indication of pus or infection coming from his cancerous prostate or bladder. In those days Tronchin had no means of arriving at such a diagnosis. But it is clear from what he said and wrote at the time that Tronchin was dismissive of Voltaire's ailments, impatient at Voltaire's wilful reluctance to take his advice, and unsympathetic to Voltaire as a human being.

Tronchin's hostility can be traced back to the political conflicts in Geneva in 1770, when Voltaire had gradually sided with the lower orders against the Tronchins and their patrician friends. In any case, all Tronchin's worldly interests lay with the court and the *ancien régime*, not with Voltaire and the *philosophes*. His attitude was eloquently conveyed in the note that he left at the Hôtel de Villette around this time: 'I should very much have liked to say to M. le marquis de Villette, face to face, that M. de Voltaire has been living, since his arrival in Paris, on the capital of his strength and that all his true friends must wish that he should live only on his income. At the rate things are going, his strength will soon be exhausted; and we shall be witnesses, if not accomplices, of the death of M. de Voltaire.'[14]

In short, Tronchin did not wish to take Voltaire's symptoms at all seriously, and he preferred to pretend that his patient was merely suffering from over-exertion. To underline his indifference he passed the text of this grim diagnosis to the *Journal de Paris*, which published it two days later. This was obviously a scandalous violation of the most basic principles of medical ethics, since it implied that Villette would be to blame if anything happened to Voltaire.

The open hostility between Villette and Tronchin was only the most acute manifestation of the poisonous atmosphere now developing in Voltaire's entourage. D'Alembert thought that Voltaire might be dying, and he worried that he could be harassed into submitting to the last rites of a Christian death. At Ferney, Voltaire had his own church and even his own ready-prepared mausoleum; but here in Paris he was much more exposed to the forces of conformity, and he seems to have been afraid that the Church might deny him a respectable burial. On 18 February d'Alembert wrote to Théodore Tronchin to ask him to make sure that Voltaire was kept calm.

> The most important thing you now have to do is to tranquillise him, if it is possible, on his state (real or supposed). Yesterday I passed some time alone with him, and he seemed to me very fearful, not only about his state, but also about the disagreeable consequences that could follow. No doubt you understand me, my dear and illustrious colleague: it is the moral disposition of our old man, above all, which needs your care and your attention.[15]

The Catholic Church could not long be kept at bay. On Friday 20 February, just ten days after Voltaire's arrival in Paris, Voltaire received a creepy-crawly letter from a certain abbé Louis-Laurent Gaultier, requesting an interview. 'Many people, Sir, admire you and write your praises in fine verses and elegant prose. I desire with the deepest part of my heart to be among your admirers. I shall have that advantage, if you wish it, it depends on you, I am sure. There is still time. I should say more if you were to permit me to talk with you. Although the most unworthy of all ministers, I should not say anything unworthy of my ministry.'[16]

Voltaire may have judged, from the tone of the letter, that Gaultier was an insignificant and unsophisticated fellow; and that just as he had got the better of two insignificant churchmen in 1768 and 1769, so now he had a good chance of getting the better of the abbé Gaultier, without having to meet the full demands of the Church. Voltaire breezily agreed to a meeting.

> Your letter, Sir, appears to me that of an honest man, and that is enough to decide me to receive the honour of your visit, on any day and hour that suits you. I am eighty-four years old, and I shall shortly appear before the God who created all the worlds. If you have anything special to tell me, and which is worth the trouble, I shall make it a duty and an honour to receive your visit, despite the sufferings which weigh me down.[17]

Gaultier duly turned up at the Hôtel de Villette the next morning, Saturday 21 February. Little of consequence took place at their short meeting, but Voltaire was relieved to learn that the abbé had come on his own initiative, not as the emissary of his Church superiors. Afterwards

Voltaire commented to Wagnière that Gaultier was 'a good idiot'; presumably he now felt he could count on being able to out-manoeuvre the man at a later meeting.[18]

Voltaire was not in control of events, however. That afternoon, Saturday 21 February, Voltaire conducted a heavy rehearsal of *Irène* which left him exhausted. Four days later, on Wednesday the 25th, while sitting up in bed and dictating to Wagnière, he had a sudden and violent haemorrhage, with blood pouring out of his mouth and nose. Tronchin was called, and this time he came; he bled Voltaire, and the haemorrhage diminished. But Voltaire was still spitting blood, and he continued to spit blood for the next three weeks. The haemorrhage must have shaken Voltaire's confidence, for he wrote to Gaultier again to ask him to come as soon as possible. This time there was no trace of his previous insolence. 'You promised, Sir, to come and hear me, I beg you to be so kind as to give yourself the trouble of coming to see me as soon as you can.'[19]

News of Voltaire's physical deterioration, and of Gaultier's visit, had by this time reached the Church hierarchy. Christophe de Beaumont, the ultra-conservative archbishop of Paris, and one of Voltaire's *bêtes noires* for the past thirty-two years, wrote to Gaultier to commend him for his efforts to bring about the conversion of Voltaire. But he urged him to keep quiet about it, 'for if the project of conversion that you have in mind were to become publicly known, and if word of it reached either M. de Villette, or even M. de Voltaire himself, nothing more would be needed to wreck the good work that you are undertaking.'[20]

The abbé Gaultier did not respond immediately to Voltaire's request; when he did return to the Hôtel de Villette, four days later, on Monday 2 March, he brought with him a prepared text, presumably a formal declaration of Christian faith, and some kind of recantation of Voltaire's anti-Christian writings. Voltaire was not to be caught so easily: he brushed aside Gaultier's text and called in Wagnière to give him pen and paper, so that he could write his own declaration.

> I the undersigned declare that, having been attacked four days ago with a vomiting of blood at the age of eighty-four, and not having been able to drag myself to church, and M. le curé of Saint-Sulpice having kindly added to his good works that of sending to me M. l'abbé Gaultier, priest, I confessed to him, and that if God disposes of me, I die in the holy Catholic religion in which I was born, hoping that the divine mercy will pardon all my faults, and that if I had scandalised the mother Church, I ask pardon from God and from her.[21]

Although Gaultier dismissed this declaration as not meaning any-thing much, he nevertheless gave Voltaire absolution; and he would have proceeded to complete Voltaire's formal reconciliation with the Church by giving him communion, but that Voltaire refused, on the grounds that he was still spitting blood. Gaultier was persuaded to leave the room, and the house.

Voltaire seems to have thought that the essential issue was now settled. With his formal absolution by Gaultier he had secured what he believed would be enough to ensure a 'Christian' burial. But his decla-ration had made no meaningful concessions to the key beliefs of Chris-tianity, and by refusing communion he thought he had prevented any allegations, either by the devout or by the *philosophes*, that he had finally succumbed to the Catholic Church.

Various churchmen continued to yap at Voltaire's heels, most notably Jean-Joseph Faydit de Tersac, the curé of the local parish church of Saint-Sulpice.* On 4 March 1778 Tersac wrote Voltaire an obsequious letter asking for a meeting. But if he thought that he could win Voltaire over by referring to Christian doctrine as 'the sublime philosophy of the Evangelist' or by finessing the question of the divinity of Christ in the phrase 'divine wisdom clothed in our nature', he was mistaken.[22] From now on Voltaire felt that he had no more business to transact with the Church. On Tuesday 3 March, the day after he had given Voltaire absolution, Gaultier returned; he was not admitted. He called again; he was still not admitted. Ten days later he wrote a pathetic letter assuring Voltaire of his deepest good wishes and begging for another meeting. Voltaire replied curtly: 'The master of the house has ordered his door-keeper not to admit any ecclesiastic except M. le curé de Saint-Sulpice; when the invalid has recovered a bit of health, he will have pleasure in receiving M. l'abbé Gaultier.'[23]

Despite Tronchin's recommendation that he rest, Voltaire continued to wear himself out with the preparations for the staging of *Irène*. On Tuesday 10 March he held another rehearsal at the Hôtel de Villette; that night he had another haemorrhage. Five days later, on Sunday 15 March, the actors held a dress rehearsal at the Comédie Française; Vol-taire was too ill to take part, so it was witnessed by Mme Denis.

The first performance of *Irène* was scheduled for the next day, Monday the 16th, but Voltaire was too ill to go. Throughout the evening

---

* Many years earlier Voltaire had described Saint-Sulpice as a 'monument of bad taste' (*Letters*, 1422, 21 August 1740, pp. 322–3).)

he waited impatiently, in a state of extreme excitement and anxiety, for messengers from the theatre, who reported in detail how each act had gone. The play was a triumphant success, but the strain for Voltaire was too much. The next day, and the day after, he was exhausted and received no one.

By the end of the week he had recovered somewhat, and on Saturday 21 March he went sight-seeing in a carriage, his first such outing since his arrival in Paris. But that evening he wrote to Tronchin, complaining of his maladies: 'As I told you, my dear saviour, my vomiting of blood is only one of the symptoms of my illness. The root of it is a stubborn strangury, accompanied by an invincible constipation. That is what makes my feet swell, and which makes me fear a hydropsy which will finish me off, for one day one must finish. Count on it that I shall end my days as a Tronchinian.'[24]

The high point of Voltaire's stay in Paris came on Monday 30 March, with his double apotheosis, at a special session of the Académie Française in the afternoon, followed by the sixth performance of *Irène* at the Comédie Française in the evening. In the early afternoon he left the Hôtel de Villette by carriage for the Académie Française, which at the time was based in the Louvre. In an unprecedented gesture all the academicians present came to greet him at the door, apart from the bishops and other churchmen, who had pointedly stayed away. Voltaire was asked to preside over the meeting and to accept his appointment as the Académie's new director; and Jean Le Rond d'Alembert, as permanent secretary (*secrétaire perpétuel*), read a eulogy in which he compared Voltaire with Racine and Boileau.

After the session Voltaire had to hurry on to the Comédie Française at the Tuileries, for the performance of *Irène*, where the curtain was due to go up at 5.30 p.m. His appearance in the auditorium provoked a tumult of prolonged applause, which delayed the start of the performance for over twenty minutes. When the play started, it was constantly interrupted by cries of adulation for Voltaire. After the play had finished, the curtain was raised again to reveal a bust of Voltaire on a pedestal in the middle of the stage, surrounded by the cast of actors, each of whom in turn placed a wreath on the head of the statue. When Voltaire left the theatre, he was confronted by an enormous crowd, and his carriage horses could only proceed at a walking pace.[25]

A week later, on 6 April, when Voltaire was walking on foot from the Hotel de Villette to the Académie Française, a voice in the crowd called out: 'That's M. de Voltaire; he is the defender of the poor and the oppressed, he saved the family of the Calas and the Sirven.'[26] Madame du Deffand, an old if cynical and increasingly conservative friend of Voltaire, wrote to Horace Walpole: 'The honours which he has received here are unbelievable ... He is followed in the streets by the people, who call him "the man of the Calases (*l'homme aux Calas*)".'[27]

These successive waves of adulation may even have done Voltaire some good physically, for in April and the first week of May he made numerous outings. He attended four working sessions at the Académie Française, partly to discuss his plan for a new dictionary. He went a second time to the Comédie Française, to see a performance of his tragedy *Alzire*. He paid three visits to the duc d'Orléans, whose grand establishment included a private theatre. He attended a meeting at the masonic lodge of the Neuf Sœurs. He went to a ceremonial session at the Académie des Sciences. He called on Mme du Deffand. He called on Suzanne de Livry, one of the mistresses of his youth. He went two or three times to sit for the sculptor Jean-Antoine Houdon.

On 6 April Théodore Tronchin reported to his cousin François Tronchin that Voltaire now seemed full of vigour: 'Your old neighbour is making a frightful uproar here and is well despite his unbelievable fatigues. I have seen some madmen in my life, but I have never seen any as mad as him. He counts on living to at least a hundred. The other day he called on me at half-past seven in the morning; I was still in bed. He stayed for a long time, during which a crowd of 499 people gathered outside my door.'[28]

In fact, two months after arriving in Paris, Voltaire was enjoying life in Paris so much that he even rented a house in the rue de Richelieu. Sometimes he implied that he would divide his time between Ferney in the summer and Paris in the winter, but Théodore Tronchin believed that he intended to make Paris his permanent home. 'He says that he will go home to Ferney after Easter, to arrange his affairs and those of his colony. After that he will come back and settle in Paris. He is buying a house.'[29] Either way, Voltaire seemed to be assuming that he had plenty of life ahead of him.

One reason why Voltaire was thinking of returning to Ferney was that he had left his affairs and his papers in some disorder, and he felt the need to tidy things up. Mme Denis intended to let him go alone, for she had no intention of leaving Paris. But then she was warned that Voltaire must at all costs be stopped from leaving Paris, even briefly, for the authorities might prevent his ever returning. Mme Denis seized on this report as a pretext for getting rid of Wagnière. If it was now unsafe for Voltaire to return to Ferney, even briefly, then someone else had to be sent back to take care of the everyday problems of the estate.

On Sunday 26 April Voltaire and Mme Denis signed over to Wagnière a power of attorney for managing Ferney. Four days later, on Thursday 30 April, Wagnière left Paris, and he reached Ferney on 7 May. The following days and weeks were filled with conscientious letters from Wagnière to Voltaire relating in detail all his loyal services. Wagnière's absence was Voltaire's deepest sadness in the four weeks of life that remained to him; he missed him, and he wanted him back. Nearly a month later, on 25 May, Mme Denis and her nephew Alexandre d'Hornoy agreed to recall Wagnière from Ferney. By then it was too late.

Five months earlier, in October 1777, Voltaire had written to his military friend from Angoulême the marquis d'Argence: 'The trees we have planted remain, and we are leaving. All that I would ask of nature is to let me leave without pain; but it does not seem she will show me that mercy after having made me suffer for nearly eighty-four years. And yet I must still thank her for having given me life.'[30]

Nature did not show Voltaire 'that mercy', however, for he was now not just very sick but dying in increasing pain. At the beginning of May he wrote to Tronchin: 'The old invalid of the quai des Théatins throws himself into the arms of M. Tronchin; he is suffering unbearable pains; he may not have a high temperature, but he has an agitation in the pulse and in the blood which increases all his torments; he has not slept at all for the past fifteen nights; his state is horrible, nothing relieves him, his only hope is in Monsieur Tronchin; he hopes he will have pity on him.'[31]

Despite his sufferings, Voltaire continued to deal in detail with business affairs, as if he expected to be around for quite some time. In the first half of May Voltaire sent Wagnière a series of letters, giving detailed instructions for the management of the estate, or listing the books and papers he was to send to Paris. 'Send my books by the carters. They will arrive when they can. I shall let you know to whom you should address them; but once more, my dear friend, it is you I need most. Come back as soon as you can. I cannot do without you, nor without my books. If you do not come back very soon, I shall set off, dead or alive, to find you.'[32]

On Thursday 7 May Voltaire made his last effort at normal activity, when he went to the Académie Française for another plenary meeting to discuss the plan for a new dictionary. Mme Denis commented: 'My uncle is very well, he goes to the Académie, where he shouts like the very devil. He wants to get them to make a new dictionary; but these gentlemen are balking at it, for they are afraid that it will give them too much trouble.'[33]

Mme Denis must have known that Voltaire was far from being 'very well', but she seems to have been briskly indifferent to the seriousness of his condition. On Saturday 9 May, Voltaire was too ill to attend a new meeting at the Académie Française. The next day he felt a bit better, well enough to go for a walk; but when he got home, he was exhausted and went to bed with a high temperature, which became worse as the evening wore on. When Tronchin was finally called, later that night, he prescribed a pain-killing medicine, which was probably some form of opium. Voltaire may well have taken far more of it than the prescribed doses, for it seems he was in delirium for the next two or three days.

That same Sunday, 10 May, Théodore Tronchin wrote to his cousin François that Voltaire was dying, and his letter eloquently conveyed his deep aversion and contempt for his patient: 'Now that Voltaire is near his end, people are beginning to talk, to evaluate all the damage he has done to society, which even those who are not infinitely severe are comparing to the wars, plagues and famines which for the past several thousand years have desolated the earth.'[34]

In mid-May the Catholic Church made a fresh attempt to drag a valid confession and retraction out of Voltaire. This time the attack was led by Jean-Joseph Faydit de Tersac, the curé de Saint-Sulpice; he told Voltaire's family that he would not give Voltaire a Christian burial unless he first made a full recantation of his anti-Christian sins. But the political authorities were extremely anxious that Voltaire's death should not precipitate a major public scandal, so they pressed the Church to find a way out.

The final compromise, hammered out on Saturday 23 May, a week before Voltaire's death, was grotesque. The curé of Saint-Sulpice could not be compelled to give Voltaire a Christian burial. Yet Voltaire was too ill to be moved while still alive. Therefore he would be allowed to die at the Hôtel de Villette. Once he had died, his corpse would be removed for burial at Ferney. But in order to satisfy everybody's hypocrisy, it would be necessary to pretend, for the purpose of that last journey, that Voltaire was still alive.

Some weeks after Voltaire's death, Théodore Tronchin implied that Voltaire had died in a state of despair and dementia; and his account was subsequently used by Catholic propagandists to claim that Voltaire had been punished by dying in fear of the torments of hell. There is no evidence, however, that Voltaire gave any signs of dementia: great pain, but not madness. On the contrary, his letters, especially those to Wagnière dealing with practical matters, show that his mind remained lucid and rational right up until the end. In the early hours of Sunday 24 May, six days before his death, Voltaire wrote his last letter to Wagnière: 'I am dying, my dear Wagnière, it seems quite difficult that I can avoid it. I am really punished for your departure, for having left Ferney, and for having taken a house in Paris. I embrace you tenderly, my dear friend, and with sadness.'[35]

This was almost the last letter that Voltaire wrote. Two days later, he heard that the young chevalier Trophime-Gérard de Lally-Tollendal, son of Thomas Arthur Lally-Tollendal, had been given permission to appeal against the condemnation of his father, executed in 1766 for embezzlement and treason; and he wrote him a warm note of congratulation. 'The dying man revives on learning this great news; he embraces M. Lally-Tollendal most tenderly; he can see that the king is the defender of justice; he will die content.'[36]

Despite the face-saving compromise already negotiated, Faydit de Tersac and the abbé Gaultier made yet another attempt to extract a declaration of faith out of Voltaire. On Saturday 30 May 1778 they were brought to the bedside of the dying man. When Faydit de Tersac asked him explicitly whether he believed in the divinity of Jesus Christ, Voltaire is said to have replied: 'In the name of God, Sir, do not speak to me any more about that man, and let me die in peace.' Some scholars question the authenticity of this remark, though it is quoted by both Condorcet and the abbé Duvernet. What is not in serious doubt, is that Voltaire did not succumb to the pressure of his Catholic persecutors.[37] He died at eleven o'clock that night.

≈

The agreed plan was that Voltaire's corpse would be taken to Ferney, dressed up as if it were still alive. But this would be a dangerous journey, taking five days or more, and the bishop of Annecy might be able to prevent Voltaire's burial at Ferney. The family therefore decided on different arrangements.

The day after he died, Sunday 31 May, Voltaire's corpse was opened for an autopsy and then embalmed. That evening, after dark, Voltaire's elegant star-spangled carriage, with his body, now fully dressed again, propped up as if he were still alive, set off, followed in a second carriage by Alexandre d'Hornoy, Voltaire's great-nephew. But instead of driving south-east in the direction of Geneva and Ferney, the convoy travelled due east in the direction of the abbey of Scellières near Troyes, in Champagne.

For the abbot of Scellières was Voltaire's nephew, the abbé Alexandre Jean Mignot, and he had decided to use his position to ensure Voltaire's burial in sanctified ground. He had gone on ahead of the funeral cortège, arriving at the abbey on Sunday evening, 31 May. He explained the position to the prior, and he claimed Voltaire's right to Christian burial by producing various certificates which had previously been extracted from Faydit de Tersac and Gaultier. The prior made no difficulty, and when the funeral cortège arrived on Monday 1 June, all was ready for an all-night vigil and for a formal funeral Mass the following day. They were just in time. The following day, the bishop of Troyes, alerted to what had happened, wrote to the prior forbidding him to bury Voltaire, but by then Voltaire was already buried.

There his body remained, in the vault in the centre of the abbey of Scellières, for the next thirteen years, until in 1791 the French revolutionaries decided to canonise Voltaire for their own revolutionary purposes. They had his remains removed from the abbey of Scellières, and they gave it a spectacular reburial on 11 July 1791, in the Panthéon in Paris, with the full works of Revolutionary pomp, twelve white horses and all.

Although Voltaire was not a revolutionary, the revolutionaries nevertheless paid well-judged homage to his achievements. On the catafalque bearing his coffin there were three inscriptions. The first said: 'He avenged Calas, La Barre, Sirven and Monbailli.' The second said: 'Poet, philosopher, historian, he gave a great impetus to the human spirit, and prepared us to be free.' The third said: 'He combated atheists and fanatics. He inspired tolerance. He reclaimed the rights of man against serfdom and feudalism.'[38]

After Voltaire's death the marquis de Condorcet took on the task of editing a new complete edition of Voltaire's works. It was a massive undertaking, lasting ten years (1779–89) and running to seventy volumes; and for the last volume Condorcet appended a biography of Voltaire. Condorcet was one of Voltaire's most admiring disciples, yet, as we saw in an earlier chapter, he could not resist putting in quite strong criticisms of Voltaire's lack of courage and his obsequiousness towards the powerful.

But if Condorcet's *Vie de Voltaire* is interesting and valuable, it is mainly for the light it sheds on the relative importance that Condorcet attached to the different aspects of Voltaire's life. Naturally, Condorcet provides an admiring survey of Voltaire's writings, but he gives his priority to the stories of Voltaire's 'human rights' cases.

'Who would think, in reading these details, that this is the life of a great poet, of a fertile and tireless writer? We have forgotten his literary glory, as he had forgotten it himself. He seemed to recognise only one glory, that of avenging humanity, and rescuing victims of oppression.'[39]

VOLTAIRE'S MOST IMPORTANT CORRESPONDENTS

THIS GLOSSARY IS INTENDED to help the reader identify and situate a few of the people who figure most prominently in Voltaire's correspondence. It does not include all the most important people in Voltaire's life, far from it; only those whose identities may seem most confusing.

Over his life-time, Voltaire wrote to about 1,500 different people, and referred to many more. The final volume of Voltaire's letters in the edition of the Bibliothèque de la Pléiade has a magnificent index, identifying all the people whom he wrote to, as well as all those whom he wrote about; but it runs to 388 pages. It is all too easy to lose track of all these people.

Even on a much smaller scale, it would be easy, tempting and no doubt useful to produce a list of the most significant people in Voltaire's life, with brief annotations and background information. Such a list would have to include his friends, his secretaries, his enemies, his women, the actors at the Comédie Française, the mathematicians who coached him and Émilie du Châtelet, and so on. In particular, it would have to cover several members of Voltaire's family, and especially the family of Mme Denis; and of course many members of the tribe of the Tronchin family in Geneva.

Space does not permit this, however, and compels me to restrict this glossary to a very small number of people where some guidance may be most useful. What makes this list especially necessary, is that quite a number of the people on it have remarkably similar or similar-seeming names, to the point where one can easily get confused as to who is who.

Some of Voltaire's oldest and closest friends were direct contemporaries at the Collège Louis-le-Grand, which Voltaire attended between 1704 and 1711, from the age of ten to the age of seventeen; many of these early friends remained friends for life, and many became distinguished figures on the French scene.

JEAN LE ROND D'ALEMBERT (1717–83), was a brilliant mathematician and physicist, who became a pioneer of the *philosophes* and, though a much younger man, one of Voltaire's closest allies and friends. He ended up as permanent secretary of the Académie Française. D'Alembert was the illegitimate son of a chevalier Destouches, in the French artillery, and the free-living woman of letters Claudine Alexandre Guérin de Tencin, aunt of d'Argental (see below, under d'Argental). By blood, therefore, though not in law, d'Alembert was a virtual cousin of d'Argental. His middle name, Le Rond, came, as was the tradition, from that of the church where he had been abandoned, Saint-Jean-le-Rond; while his surname, d'Alembert, was invented, in place of a legitimate family name.

FRANÇOIS ACHARD JOUMARD TISON, marquis d'Argence (1719–93), was a retired army officer living near Angoulême, who became a literary and philosophical disciple of Voltaire, and visited him twice at Ferney, in 1760 and 1764.

JEAN BAPTISTE DE BOYER, marquis d'Argens (1704–71), was a literary adventurer and journalist, who led a rocambolesque life in various European countries, edited a literary magazine called *Lettres juives*, and wrote a pornographic classic called *Thérèse philosophique* (1748). He and Voltaire corresponded frequently, and he was in Berlin as one of Frederick's chamberlains when Voltaire arrived there in 1750.

Seven members of THE D'ARGENSON FAMILY figure in Voltaire's correspondence, but the most significant were two brothers, both of them prominent public servants, and both politically powerful friends of Voltaire, and more generally of the philosophes and of the *Encyclopédie*.

RENÉ LOUIS DE VOYER DE PAULMY, MARQUIS D'ARGENSON, (1694–1757). He was the same age as Voltaire, though it seems he did not go to the Collège Louis-le-Grand until Voltaire's last two years there, (1709–11). In 1744, he was appointed Foreign Minister, a post he occupied until 1747. He was nick-named 'D'Argenson the Beast'.

MARC PIERRE DE VOYER, COMTE D'ARGENSON, (1696–1764). He was the younger brother by two years, and he was appointed Minister of War in 1743, where he stayed until 1757. He was nick-named 'D'Argenson the Goat'. Voltaire preferred his elder brother.

CHARLES-AUGUSTIN DE FERRIOL, COMTE D'ARGENTAL, (1700–1788), was one of Voltaire's closest friends; over his life-time. Voltaire wrote him more than 1,000 letters, though d'Argental wrote far fewer back. Like Voltaire, d'Argental was educated at the Collège Louis-le-Grand, but since he was six years younger, they may not have known one another at school: Voltaire's first letter to him dates from 1724, when Voltaire was thirty. By profession he became a *conseiller* (senior lawyer) in the parlement de Paris; by inclination he was theatre-mad, and he became a sort of intermediary and adviser for Voltaire with the Comédie Française.

d'Argental's mother was MARIE-ANGÉLIQUE, NÉE GUÉRIN DE TENCIN, daughter of Président de Tencin.

d'Argental's aunt was the notorious courtesan and woman of letters CLAUDINE ALEXANDRE GUÉRIN DE TENCIN (1685–1749). See above, under d'Alembert.

d'Argental's uncle was PIERRE GUÉRIN DE TENCIN (1679–1758), who entered the Catholic Church and became a cardinal.

d'Argental's elder brother, ANTOINE DE FERRIOL DE PONT DE VEYLE (1697–1774) overlapped with Voltaire at Louis-le-Grand; he became a life-long literary dilettante. When Pont de Veyle died, Voltaire wrote to d'Argental: 'I regret your brother, and I love you with all my heart; that is all I can say.'[1]

PIERRE-ROBERT LE CORNIER DE CIDEVILLE, (1693–1776), was with Voltaire at Louis-le-Grand, and over the years he and Voltaire exchanged some 450 letters. He was a great lover of literature; professionally he earned his living as a *conseiller* at the parlement de Rouen.

ÉTIENNE NOËL DAMILAVILLE (1723–68) was a late arrival in Voltaire's life, and a late convert to *philosophie*; but Voltaire probably loved Damilaville more deeply than any other of his friends, and he mourned his early death, from cancer of the throat, more intensely. Their friendship and their correspondence was essentially concentrated in eight short years, from 1760 to 1768, at the height of Voltaire's campaign against *l'Infâme*; in this period Voltaire wrote Damilaville 539 letters.

JEAN HENRI SAMUEL FORMEY (1711–97) was a protestant pastor and literary journalist, whom Voltaire got to know in Berlin, where he was permanent secretary of the Berlin Academy, elected in 1748. Formey was a conservative *philosophe*, too conservative for Voltaire's taste, and Voltaire was too free-thinking for Formey; after Voltaire left Berlin, Formey published a malicious account of Voltaire's peccadilloes, true or false, during his stay there.

JEAN-BAPTISTE NICOLAS DE FORMONT, (?–1758), was a minor poet and *littérateur*, a close friend of Mme du Deffand, and one of Voltaire's literary confidants.

CLAUDE PHILIPPE FYOT DE LA MARCHE, (1694–1768) was a direct contemporary and close friend of Voltaire at Louis le Grand, until May 1711, as we know from a moving sequence of nostalgic letters from Voltaire. He came from a rich and powerful family of *parlementaires*, and he became *premier président* of the *parlement* of Bourgogne. There was apparently a long break in their correspondence, but it resumed in 1755 and continued with great warmth until 1766.

SELECT BIBLIOGRAPHY

THIS BOOK IS NOT INTENDED as a scholarly work for scholars, and the bibliography should not be seen as an implied claim for accreditation to the arcane world of Voltaire scholarship; instead, it is more a sort of record of exploration.

It was only by accident that I embarked, ten years ago, on the subject of Voltaire. My book club had been discussing his *Candide*, and I wondered, on the way home, why it was that Voltaire was so famous and that I knew so little about him. I assumed that I would soon fill in this lacuna, but I discovered, next morning, that there was at that time no biography of Voltaire in print in English and that no biography had been published in English for twenty years; so I decided to investigate the question myself.

My first step was to read *Voltaire en son temps*, the massive work of scholarship by René Pomeau and a team of collaborators, originally published in five volumes in 1985–94, and subsequently reissued in two thick volumes in 1995. It is not an easy read; it suffers from hypertrophy and from the fact that it is a collaborative venture; but it is an impressive work of scholarship, and where Voltaire is the question, it is essential reading.

My second step was to read all 15,284 of Voltaire's letters. I hesitated over this for an absurdly long time: I did not know whether I would have the stamina for such a task, or whether it would repay the effort. My hesitation was symptomatic of my ignorance: I did not realise, first, that this was one of the masterpieces of Western literature, and second, that no one can really know much about Voltaire without reading these letters. From this point on, my investigation of possible source material became more systematic, and so will this bibliography.

There are three main types of reference source for a life of Voltaire: writings by Voltaire; writings by contemporaries; and writings by scholars about Voltaire and his period.

In the first category the most obvious source should be the vast new complete scholarly edition of Voltaire's works, which is in the process of being published by the Voltaire Foundation. But at the time of writing it is not yet complete, and since those volumes which have appeared are not readily available, except at vast expense (£60 – £100 per volume), or only in specialised university libraries, it is not much use to the ordinary reader. When I started researching this book, I asked Blackwell's, one of the world's leading academic booksellers, based in Oxford, home town of the Voltaire Foundation, how many volumes of this splendid new edition they had on their shelves. Answer: none.

Fortunately, the previous complete edition of Voltaire's works, by Louis Moland, is cheaply and readily available on CD-ROM, published by Daniel Boudin (of Tournon-Saint-Martin, France 36220). Of course, it is much less complete, and the edition is a hundred years out of date; but if one wants to track down some of Voltaire's lesser-known works, it is a useful start.

In the case of modern editions of individual works or groups of works by Voltaire, the choice becomes much more circumscribed. There are many, many modern editions of *Candide*, as well as of some others of the *contes*, many in paperback; there are many, many editions of the *Lettres philosophiques*, both in its French and in its English versions, many in paperback; and there are also quite a few modern editions of the *Dictionnaire philosophique*, also in paperback. But there is in print no modern edition of all Voltaire's plays or of his poetry, so if you want to read his plays or his poems, you have to go to the Moland edition or to a university library.

Voltaire's letters

By far the most importance source of information about Voltaire's life comes from his letters. Fortunately, all Voltaire's letters are available in a fine modern thirteen-volume edition in the Bibliothèque de la Pléiade, edited by Frédéric Deloffre and published by Gallimard. This is based on the so-called Definitive Edition, edited in 51 volumes by Theodore Besterman, and published in 1968–77; the main difference between the two is that the Deloffre edition is essentially limited to letters written by Voltaire, whereas the Besterman edition also includes many letters to Voltaire or even between third parties. However, the Deloffre edition has extremely useful explanatory notes, as well as a few of the most significant letters to Voltaire and an absolutely magnificent pair of indexes, tracking all Voltaire's references to people named in his letters or to works of his own or other people.

For anyone wanting to try Voltaire's letters, but daunted by the thirteen volumes of the Pléiade edition, there is a useful selection, entitled *Correspondance choisie*, published by Livre de Poche. It is well done, with helpful notes; the trouble is that, even though it is a pretty thick book, it is still only a small selection of the whole. One of the difficulties with Voltaire's letters is that they are not always easy to date or construe, and this is particularly true of the letters written in Prussia to his friend Mme Bentinck. Besterman's dating of these particular letters, and therefore his interpretation, proved quite unsatisfactory, and anyone interested in this phase of Voltaire's life should certainly read *Voltaire et sa 'grande amie': correspondance complète de Voltaire et de Mme Bentinck*, edited by Deloffre and Cormier, and published by the Fayard/Voltaire Foundation (Oxford, 2003). It is extremely well done, with illuminating notes and explanations.

In the end-notes of this book, for quotation and source-referencing, I have adopted an eclectic approach, based mainly on ease of accessibility. Where I have quoted letters by Voltaire (the vast majority), I have usually taken the quotations from the

Deloffre-Pléiade edition, and I have sourced them to the letter number in this edition (as in: *Letters*, 1234). In the case of the correspondence between Voltaire and Mme Bentinck, I have used the text and the letter-numbering of the Deloffre and Cormier edition. Where I have quoted letters to Voltaire, I have either used the text as given in the notes of the Deloffre-Pléiade edition (as: *Letters*, 1234, and note, p. 1099) or else I have used the text and the letter-numbering in the Besterman Definitive Edition (as: D 5678). Where I have quoted letters between third parties, as for example between Émilie and Richelieu, or between Émilie and d'Argental, or between Émilie and Saint-Lambert, I have sometimes quoted the Besterman edition, sometimes the Moland.

Voltaire's other works

Apart from the thirteen volumes of Voltaire's correspondence, the Pléiade edition also includes three other valuable tomes: *Oeuvres historiques*, which contains most but not all of his historical writings; *Romans et contes*, which is self-explanatory and includes *Candide* and all the other *contes*; and *Mélanges*, which contains a priceless collection of miscellaneous works, including the *Lettres philosophiques* and many of the components of his human rights campaigns. At one time the Pléiade collection also included a volume of an anthology of eighteenth-century French theatre, including a selection of Voltaire's plays, but it seems to have been allowed to go out of print.

Voltaire's contemporaries

There are many writings by his contemporaries which throw light on Voltaire; but they are of variable interest and reliability. The *Mémoires* of Collini are interesting and pretty reliable; the *Mémoires* of Longchamp are interesting and wholly unreliable, but because they are juicy, they are regularly trotted out by all Voltaire biographers.

The very short biography of Voltaire by Condorcet is essential (Jean Antoine Nicolas de Caritat de Condorcet, *Vie de Voltaire*, Quai Voltaire, Paris, 1994), as are the *Discours sur le bonheur* by Émilie du Châtelet (ed. E. Badinter, Rivages Poche, 1997), the essay *On Crimes and Punishments* by Cesare Beccaria, (trans. David Young, Hackett, Indiana,1986) and the letters of Mme de Graffigny, (*Correspondance*, vol. 1, 1716–39, Voltaire Foundation, Oxford, 1985). And then, of course, there are the writings of Diderot, Montesquieu and Rousseau.

Biographical works

Many books have been written about Voltaire's life, but it is surprising, considering the interest of the subject, how few of them make for really good reading; none, so far as I am aware, can stand comparison, for example, with Boswell's *Life of Johnson*. There may be three reasons for this: first, if you want to catch your Boswell, you must catch him young, and for Voltaire it is now too late; second, Voltaire's story was so thoroughly encrusted with the gossip and fabrications of tabloid sensationalism during his lifetime that it has become difficult to scrape off the barnacles; third, and most important, Voltaire was so controversial while he was alive, and so loathed by the ultras of the right wing and the Catholic Church after he was dead, that it took 200 years before anyone in France could take a dispassionate view of him. Indeed, perhaps they still can't.

The most recent substantial biography of Voltaire in English was by the leading scholar Theodore Besterman; but that was forty years ago, and because of Besterman's tendency to bombast and self-importance, it is not an entirely satisfactory read. Since then, the only significant new biography of Voltaire has been *Voltaire en son temps*, in five volumes, subsequently reissued in two thick volumes, by René Pomeau and a team of collaborators, in 1985–94 and 1995.

For those who are interested there is a capacious and very stimulating Voltaire encyclopaedia, called *Inventaire Voltaire*, written and edited by Goulemot, Magnan and Masseau (Gallimard, Paris, 1995): a wonderful bedside book.

At least two biographies of people close to Voltaire are eminently worth reading: Élisabeth Badinter's *Émilie, Émilie,* a parallel study of Émilie du Châtelet and Mme d'Épinay, (Flammarion, Paris, 1983); and Benedetta Craveri's *Madame du Deffand,* (trans. Sibylle Zavriew, Éditions du Seuil, Paris, 1987). Craveri gives a delightful example of Mme du Deffand's mordant wit in her famous exchange with the Cardinal de Polignac. The Cardinal was going on ecstatically about the miraculous story of Saint Denis, after his head had been cut off, how he walked with his head in his hands for a full two miles: '*Ah, Monseigneur,*' said Mme du Deffand, '*Il n'y a que le premier pas qui coûte*'. (It is only the first step that is difficult.)

On the question of Voltaire and his relationship to England and the English, André M. Rousseau's comprehensive study *L'Angleterre et Voltaire* (3 vols, Voltaire Foundation, Oxford, 1976) is essential for underlining how fragmentary is our knowledge and how uncertain the received corpus of myth and legend. By contrast, Boswell's account of his visit to Voltaire at Ferney in Frederick Pottle (ed.) *Boswell on the Grand Tour,* (2 vols, Heinemann, London, 1953–55) is refreshingly down-to-earth and factual.

The *Encyclopédie* has been the subject of many books, and when Frank A. Kafker set out to write a reference book about the contributors to the *Encyclopédie*, he thought it would be a breeze; in the event, it took him many years of toil, but the results are fascinating and indispensable (*The Encyclopedists as Individuals*, Voltaire Foundation, Oxford, 1988, and *The Encyclopedists as a Group*, Voltaire Foundation, Oxford, 1996). Philippe Blom's recent general account of the *Encyclopédie* (Fourth Estate, 2004) is useful. The full text of the *Encyclopédie* is available on CD-ROM (*L'Encyclopédie de Diderot et d'Alembert*, on CD-ROM, Éditions Redon, Marsanne, 1999).

On the Enlightenment in general there are many useful books. Peter Gay's *The Enlightenment* (2 vols, Norton, New York, 1966 & 1969, 1995 & 1996) is stimulating, almost a standard work. Jonathan Israel's *Radical Enlightenment* (Oxford, 2001) is extremely interesting. Robert Darnton's several books in this area – *The Business of Enlightenment* (Belknap Press, Cambridge, MA, 1979); *The Great Cat Massacre* (Basic Books, New York, 1984 and Vintage Books, New York, 1985); *The Kiss of Lamourette* (Faber and Faber, London, 1990); and *The Forbidden Best-sellers of pre-Revolutionary France* (Harper Collins, London, 1996 and 1997) – are all stimulating and very entertaining.

Finally, there is the whole area of Voltaire's pioneering efforts in the field of 'human rights'. In addition to Cesare Beccaria's seminal work *On Crimes and Punishments*, mentioned earlier, there is also Marcello T. Maestro's very interesting *Voltaire and Beccaria as Reformers of Criminal Law* (Columbia University Press, New York, 1942). David D. Bien's *The Calas Affair* (Princeton University Press, Princeton, 1960) is a good modern treatment of the subject, but the key investigative texts are those by Marc Chassaigne: *Le Procès du chevalier de La Barre* (Victor Lecoffre, Paris, 1920) and *L'Affaire Calas* (Perrin et Cie, Paris, 1929).

The following is a list of works consulted and referred to in the text.

WORKS BY VOLTAIRE
Oeuvres historiques, Bibliothèque de la Pléiade, Gallimard, Paris, 1958
Romans et contes, Bibliothèque de la Pléiade, Gallimard, Paris, 1979
Mélanges, Bibliothèque de la Pléiade, Gallimard, Paris, 1981, 1995
Voltaire's Notebooks, ed. Besterman, 2 vols, Institut et Musée Voltaire, Les Délices, Geneva, 1952
Letters concerning the English Nation, World's Classics, Oxford University Press, Oxford, 1994, 1999
Dictionnaire philosophique, Flammarion, Paris, 1964
Œuvres complètes : ed. Louis Moland, Garnier, Paris, 1875, available on CD-ROM, Daniel Boudin, Tournon-Saint-Martin, France 36220

CORRESPONDENCE
Correspondance, Bibliothèque de la Pléiade, Gallimard, 13 vols, Paris, 1977–1992
Complete correspondence, vols 85–135 of *Œuvres complètes de Voltaire*, Definitive Edition, ed. Theodore Besterman, Institut et Musée Voltaire, Geneva, 1968–1977
Correspondance choisie, Classiques Modernes, Livre de Poche, Paris, 1997
Voltaire et sa 'grande amie': Correspondance complète de Voltaire et de Mme Bentinck, ed. F. Deloffie and J. Cormier, Fayard/Voltaire Foundation, Oxford, 2003

OTHER WORKS

Contemporary writings
Jean Antoine Nicolas de Caritat de Condorcet, *Vie de Voltaire*, Quai Voltaire, Paris, 1994
Mme de Graffigny, *Correspondance*, vol 1, 1716–1739, Voltaire Foundation, Oxford, 1985
Mme du Deffand, *Lettres à Voltaire*, Rivages Poche, Paris, 1994
Mme du Châtelet, *Discours sur le bonheur*, ed. E. Badinter, Rivages Poche, 1997
Cosimo Alessandro Collini, *Mémoires,* in *Œuvres complètes*, ed. Louis Moland, Garnier, Paris, 1875, available on CD-ROM
Sebastien Longchamp, *Mémoires,* in *Œuvres complètes*, ed. Louis Moland, Garnier, Paris, 1875, available on CD-ROM

Biographical works
René Pomeau, *Voltaire*, Éditions du Seuil, Paris 1955, 1989, 1994
René Pomeau, ed. *La Politique de Voltaire*, Armand Colin, Paris, 1963, 1994
René Pomeau, *La Religion de Voltaire*, Librairie A.-G. Nizet, Paris, 1969, 1995
René Pomeau et al, *Voltaire en son temps,* 2 vols, Fayard/Voltaire Foundation, Oxford, 1985–94, 1995
Theodore Besterman, *Voltaire*, Longman, London, 1969

A Voltaire encyclopaedia
J. M. Goulemot, A. Magnan and D. Masseau, eds, *Inventaire Voltaire*, Quarto Gallimard, Paris, 1995

Studies

Élisabeth Badinter, *Émilie, Émilie,* Flammarion, Paris, 1983

Benedetta Craveri, *Madame du Deffand,* trans. Sibylle Zavriew, Éditions du Seuil, Paris, 1987

Voltaire and the English

Frederick Pottle, ed., *Boswell on the Grand Tour*, 2 vols, Heinemann, London, 1953–55

André M. Rousseau, *L'Angleterre et Voltaire*, 3 vols, Voltaire Foundation, Oxford, 1976

Haydn Mason, ed. *Voltaire and the English*, Voltaire Foundation, Oxford, 1979

Human rights and penal reform

Marc Chassaigne, *Le Procès du chevalier de La Barre*, Victor Lecoffre, Paris, 1920

Marc Chassaigne, *L'Affaire Calas*, Perrin et Cie, Paris, 1929

Marcello T. Maestro, *Voltaire & Beccaria as Reformers of Criminal Law*, Columbia University Press, New York, 1942

David D. Bien, *The Calas Affair*, Princeton University Press, Princeton, 1960

Michel Foucault, *Discipline and Punish*, trans. A. Sheridan, Penguin, London, 1977, 1991

Cesare Beccaria, trans. David Youngs, *On Crimes and Punishments*, Hackett, Indiana, 1986

The Encyclopédie

L'Encyclopédie de Diderot et d'Alembert, on CD-ROM, Éditions Redon, Marsanne, 1999

Frank A. Kafker, *The Encyclopedists as Individuals*, Voltaire Foundation, Oxford, 1988

Frank A. Kafker, *The Encyclopedists as a Group*, Voltaire Foundation, Oxford, 1996

The Enlightenment

Peter Gay, *Voltaire's Politics*, Yale University Press, New Haven, 1959, 1988

Peter Gay, *The Enlightenment*, 2 vols, Norton, New York, 1966 & 1969, 1995 & 1996

Jonathan Israel, *Radical Enlightenment*, Oxford University Press, Oxford, 2001

Robert Darnton, *The Business of Enlightenment*, Belknap Press, Cambridge, MA, 1979

Robert Darnton, *The Great Cat Massacre*, Basic Books, New York, 1984; Vintage Books, New York, 1985

Robert Darnton, *The Kiss of Lamourette*, Faber and Faber, London, 1990

Robert Darnton, *The Forbidden Best-sellers of Pre-Revolutionary France*, Harper Collins, London, 1996, 1997

LIST OF ILLUSTRATIONS

11b. Condorcet: portrait, French school (Châteaux de Versailles et de Trianon, Versailles. Photo: The Art Archive/Gianni Dagli Orti).

12. Voltaire nude: marble statue by Pigalle, 1776 (Musée du Louvre, Paris. Photo: The Art Archive/Gianni Dagli Orti).

13a. Voltaire and Madame Denis: crayon by Charles Cochin (© Collection of the New-York Historical Society, USA. Photo: Bridgeman Art Library).

13b. Voltaire at the chess table by Jean Huber (Hermitage, St Petersburg, Russia. Photo: The Bridgeman Art Library).

14. Marble bust of Voltaire by Houdon, 1778 (Musée du Louvre, Paris. Photo: Elizabeth Roy).

15. Crowning of Voltaire on the stage of the Théatre Français, 1778: engraving by Gaucher (Mary Evans Picture Library).

16. Thirty-five heads of Voltaire aged eighty-one: etching by Dominique Vivant Denon, c. 1780, after original sketches by Jean Huber, c. 1775 (Photo: Bibliothèque nationale de France, Paris).

Endpapers The quai des Théatins and the Tuileries gardens: detail from the Turgot map of Paris, 1739 (Houghton Library, Harvard University)

NOTES

Note to the Reader
1 Nick Childs, *A Political Academy in Paris, 1724–1731* (Voltaire Foundation, Oxford, 2000), p. 9, note 23, where he quotes Guy Chaussinand-Nogaret, *The French Nobility in the Eighteenth Century* (Cambridge University Press, Cambridge, 1985).

Prologue
1. Condorcet, *Vie de Voltaire*, p. 151.
2. René Pomeau et al., *Voltaire en son temps* (Fayard / Voltaire Foundation, 1985–95).
3. J-M. Goulemot, A. Magnan and D. Masseau (eds), *Inventaire Voltaire* (Quarto Gallimard, Paris, 1995), p. 329.
4. Theodore Besterman (ed.),*The Love Letters, of Voltaire to his Niece* (William Kimber, London, 1958).

1: Youth
1. *Letters,* 2, 8 May 1711.
2. *Letters,* 6, 7 August 1711.
3. These are the facts according to Pomeau et al., *Voltaire en son temps*, vol. I, p. 43. Voltaire's *Letters* to her are addressed to 'Catherine-Olympe du Noyer', and he calls her 'Dear Demoiselle'; so if she was married at the time, he clearly did not know it. According to Besterman's edition of Voltaire's *Letters*, as adapted by Frédéric Deloffre, Pimpette did not marry Winterfeldt until 1716.
4. *Letters,* 7, 25 November 1713.
5. *Letters,* 8, 28 November 1713.
6. *Letters,* 9, 30 November 1713.
7. *Letters,* 10, 2 December 1713.

8. *Letters,* 11, 4 December 1713.

9. *Letters,* 12, 13, 14, 15, 6–16 December 1713.

10. *Letters,* 18, 28 December 1713.

11. *Letters,* 17, 25 December 1713.

12. *Letters,* 20, 20 January 1714.

13. *Letters,* 979, 23 June 1738.

14. *Letters,* 7, 25 November 1713, see note, p. 1354.

2: Comédie Française

1. 'Nos prêtres ne sont pas ce qu'un vain peuple pense, Notre crédulité fait toute leur science.' *Œdipe,* Act IV, scene I, in *Œuvres complètes,* ed. Moland, on CD-ROM.

2. Pierre Milza, *Voltaire* (Perrin, Paris, 2007), p. 335.

3. *Letters,* 29, summer 1716.

4. *Letters,* 23, 11 July 1716.

5. Epître XXXIII, 'Des Vous et des Tu' (1731), in *Œuvres complètes,* ed. Moland.
   Un cœur tendre, un esprit volage,
   Un sein d'albâtre, et de beaux yeux.
   Avec tant d'attraits précieux,
   Hélas! qui n'eût été friponne?
   Tu le fus, objet gracieux;
   Et (que l'Amour me le pardonne!)
   Tu sais que je t'en aimais mieux.

6. *Letters,* 28, summer 1716.

7. *Letters,* 30, summer 1716.

8. *Letters,* 31, September 1716.

9. *Letters,* 34, 21 May 1717.

10. 'La Bastille' (1717), in *Petits Poèmes, Œuvres complètes,* ed. Moland.

11. 'La Bastille' (1717), in *Petits Poèmes, Œuvres complètes,* ed. Moland; *Épitre XVII, à M. de La Faluère de Génonville,* in *Œuvres complètes,* ed. Moland.

12. *Letters,* 35, 15 April 1718; *Letters,* 36, 2 May 1718.

13. *Letters,* 36, 2 May 1718.

14. *Letters,* 37, 19 May 1718; *Letters,* 39, 4 July 1718.

15. *Letters,* 43, March 1719.

16. *Lettres écrites en 1719,* in *Œuvres complètes,* ed. Moland.

3: Money, and the shortage of it

1. *Letters,* 45, spring 1719.

2. *Letters,* 44, spring, 1719.

3. *Letters,* 46, 20 June 1719.

4. *Letters,* 47, June 1719.

5. *Letters,* 68, June 1722.

6. *Letters,* 157, 25 October 1724.

7. *Letters,* 49, July 1719.

8. *Letters,* 269, 1 June 1731.

9. *Letters,* 48, July 1719.

10. *Letters*, 46, 20 June 1719.

11. *Letters*, 12673, 28 January 1772.

4: Friends and lovers

1. *Letters*, 64, April 1722.

2. *Letters*, 65, 28 May 1722.

3. *Letters*, 66, June 1722.

4. *Letters*, 68, June 1722.

5. *Letters*, 71, 1 July 1722.

6. *Letters*, 88, 5 December 1722.

7. *Letters*, 115, 20 October 1723; *Letters*, 117, 30 October 1723.

8. *Letters*, 71, 1 July 1722.

9. *Letters*, 138, 140, 141, 143, 144, August – September 1724, notes, p. 1401.

10. *Letters*, 146, 26 September 1724.

11. *Letters*, 146, 149, 150, 153, 155, 26 September – 25 October 1724.

12. *Letters*, 155, 20 October 1724.

13. *Letters*, 66, June 1722; *Letters*, 70, June, 1722.

14. *Letters*, 58, 15 October 1721.

15. *Letters*, 90, 19 December 1722; *Letters*, 91, 25 December 1722; *Letters*, 101, 10 June 1723; *Letters*, 92, 27 December 1722; *Letters*, 107, 17 July 1723.

16. *Letters*, 73, July 1722, note, p. 1382.

17. *Letters*, 77, 11–18 September 1722.

18. *Letters*, 78, 2 October 1722.

19. *Letters*, 76, 8 September 1722; *Letters*, 78, 2 October 1722.

20. *Letters*, 79, 7 October 1722.

21. *Letters*, 104, 28 June 1723.

22. *Letters*, 87, 5 December 1722.

23. *Letters*, 85, 1 December 1722.

24. *Letters*, 86, 4 December 1722; and note 3, p. 1386.

25. *Letters*, 93, 3 January 1723.

26. *Letters*, 128, 22 March 1724.

27. *Letters*, 131, 20 July 1724.

28. *Letters*, 106, 15 July 1723; *Letters*, 111, 24 September 1723.

29. *Letters*, 117, 30 October 1723.

30. *Letters*, 120, 5 December 1723.

31. *Letters*, 120, 5 December 1723.

5: *La Henriade*

1. *Letters*, 121, 15 December 1723.

2. *Letters*, 184, December 1725.

3. *Letters*, 131, 20 July 1724.

4. *Letters*, 67, June 1722; *Letters*, 106, 15 July 1723, *Letters*, 108, 5 August 1723.

5. *Letters*, 112, 8 October 1723; *Letters*, 134, 4 August 1724; *Letters*, 141, 24 August 1724.

6. *Letters*, 101, 10 June 1723.

7. *Letters*, 142, September 1724.

8. *Letters*, 145, 20 September 1724.
9. *Letters*, 145, 20 September 1724; *Letters*, 150, 5 October 1724.
10. *Letters*, 155, 20 October 1724.
11. *Letters*, 123, 20 December 1723.
12. *Letters*, 138, 17 August 1724.
13. *Letters*, 138, 17 August 1724.
14. *Letters*, 140, 21 August 1724.
15. *Letters*, 141, 24 August 1724; *Letters*, 143, 10 September 1724.
16. *Letters*, 141, 24 August 1724.
17. *Letters*, 152, 10 October 1724.
18. *Letters*, 143, 10 September 1724.
19. *Letters*, 148, 28 September 1724.
20. *Letters*, 160, March 1725.
21. *Letters*, 173, 23 July 1725.
22. *Letters*, 170, 27 June 1725.
23. *Letters*, 170, 27 June 1725.
24. *Letters*, 169, 21 June 1725.
25. *Letters*, 171, 27 June 1725.
26. *Letters*, 168, 4 June 1725.
27. *Letters*, 182, 13 November 1725.
28. *Letters*, 172, 3 July 1725.
29. *Letters*, 175, 20 August 1725; *Letters*, 179, 17 October 1725.
30. *Letters*, 130, 20 July 1724.
31. *Letters*, 437, 15 September 1733; *Letters*, 517, 1 November 1734.

6: From the Court to the Bastille

1. *Letters*, 100, 7 June 1723.
2. *Letters*, 129, 10 July 1724.
3. *Letters*, 177, 17 September 1725.
4. *Letters*, 177, 17 September 1725.
5. *Letters*, 179, 17 October 1725.
6. *Letters*, 180, 17 October 1725.
7. *Letters*, 180, 17 October 1725.
8. *Letters*, 182, 13 November 1725.
9. *Letters*, 186, 20 April 1726.
10. Montesquieu, *Spicilège* (Bouquins Robert Laffont, Paris, 1991), para. 773.
11. *Letters*, 186, 20 April 1726.
12. *Letters*, 192, 1 May 1726.
13. *Letters*, 184, probably summer 1725.
14. *Letters*, 178, 6 October 1725.
15. *Letters*, 189, 30 April 1726.
16. *Letters*, 191, 1 May 1726.
17. *Letters*, 193, 5 May 1726.
18. *Letters*, 193, 5 May 1726.

7: In England

1. *Letters*, 199, 26 October 1726.
2. *Letters*, 199, 26 October 1726.
3. *Letters*, 196, 12 August 1726.
4. *Letters*, 200, 27 October 1726.
5. *Letters*, 199, 26 October 1726.
6. From Voltaire's *An Essay upon the Civil Wars of France* (December 1727).
7. A. M. Rousseau, *L'Angleterre et Voltaire* (Voltaire Foundation, Oxford, 1976), p. 64.
8. A. M. Rousseau, *L'Angleterre et Voltaire*, p. 113.
9. Voltaire, *Letters concerning the English Nation*, ed. Nicolas Cronk (Oxford, 1999) p. 87.
10. From William Chetwood, *A General History of the Stage* (London, 1749), quoted in Voltaire, *Letters concerning the English Nation*.
11. From *The Letters of John Gay* (Oxford University Press, Oxford, 1966), quoted in Voltaire, *Letters concerning the English Nation*, ed. Nicolas Cronk, pp. xi–xii.
12. Rousseau, *L'Angleterre et Voltaire*, p. 46, note 17.
13. *Letters*, 201, 13 February 1727.
14. *Letters*, 208, 14 December 1727; *Letters*, 213, March 1728.
15. Voltaire, *Letters concerning the English Nation*, pp. 9–10.
16. Rousseau, *L'Angleterre et Voltaire*, p. 153.

8: Return to France

1. *Letters*, 223, February 1729.
2. *Letters*, 201, 13 February 1727.
3. *Letters*, 241, September 1729.
4. *Letters*, 241, September 1729.
5. Quoted in Pomeau et al., *Voltaire en son temps*, vol. I, p. 108.
6. Voltaire, *Histoire de Charles XII* (Garnier Flammarion, Paris, 1968).
7. *Letters*, 264, 16 February 1731.
8. *Letters*, 348, 25 August 1732.
9. *Letters*, 333, 25 June 1732.
10. *Letters*, 246, 15 August 1730.
11. *Letters*, 274, 26 July 1731.
12. *Letters*, 279, August 1731; *Letters*, 281, 3 September 1731.
13. *Letters*, 285, 27 September 1731.
14. *Letters*, 328, 26 May 1732.
15. *Letters*, 293, December 1731; *Letters*, 299, 26 December 1731.
16. *Letters*, 329, 29 May 1732.
17. *Letters*, 321, 18 April 1732.
18. *Letters*, 379, 27 January 1733.
19. *Letters*, 352, 12 September 1732.
20. *Letters*, 347, 23 August 1732.
21. *Letters*, 351, 3 September 1732.
22. *Letters*, 367, 19 December 1732.
23. *Letters*, 379, 27 January 1733.

24. *Letters*, 378, 27 January 1733.
25. *Letters*, 380, 24 February 1733.
26. *Letters*, 404, 15 May 1733.

9: *Lettres Philosophiques*

1. Condorcet, *Vie de Voltaire* (Quai Voltaire, Paris, 1994), p. 46.
2. *Letters*, 421, 24 July 1733.
3. Harcourt Brown, 'The Composition of the *Letters concerning the English Nation*', in *The Age of Enlightenment* (Edinburgh and London, 1967).
4. See *Voltaire's Notebooks*, ed. T. Besterman (Geneva, 1952).
5. J. Patrick Lee, 'The Unexamined Premise: Voltaire, John Lockman and the Myth of the English *Letters*', in *Studies on Voltaire and the Eighteenth century*, vol. 10 (2001); pp. 240–70.
6. *Letters*, 199, 26 October 1726.
7. *Letters*, 290, 21 November 1731.
8. *Letters*, 307, 3 February 1732; *Letters*, 326, 13May 1732; *Letters*, 337, 9 July 1732; *Letters*, 352, 12 September 1732.
9. Voltaire, *Letters concerning the English Nation*, p. 30.
10. Voltaire, *Lettres philosophiques*, letter XV, 'On Attraction'; *Essay on Epic Poetry*, 2nd ed. (1727); *Éléments de la Philosophie de Newton* (1738).
11. *Letters*, 355, 30 October 1732.
12. *Letters*, 356, 3 November 1732.
13. *Letters*, 357, 12 November 1732.
14. *Letters*, 360, 20 November 1732.
15. *Letters*, 366, 15 December 1732.
16. *Letters*, 369, 20 December 1732.
17. *Letters*, 363, 6 December 1732.
18. *Letters*, 365, 15 December 1732.
19. Voltaire, *Letters concerning the English Nation*, Chapter XIII.
20. *Letters*, 376, 4 January 1733.
21. *Letters*, 378, 27 January 1733.
22. *Letters*, 380, 24 February 1733.
23. *Letters*, 388, 1 April 1733.
24. *Letters*, 394, 12 April 1733; *Letters*, 411, 10 June 1733.
25. *Letters*, 430, 15 August 1733.
26. *Letters*, 423, 26 July 1733.
27. *Letters*, 415, 3 July 1733.
28. *Letters*, 424, 27 July 1733.

10: Voltaire and Emilie

1. *Letters*, 2520, 26 October 1749.
2. 'Portrait de feu Madame la marquise du Châtelet, par Madame du Deffand', in *Correspondence Littéraire*, (March 1777).
3. Voltaire, *Éloge historique de la marquise du Châtelet* (1752) and *Mémoires pour servir à la vie de Monsieur de Voltaire*.
4. *Letters*, 401, 6 May 1733.

5. *Letters*, 415, 3 July 1733.

6. *Letters*, 419, July 1733.

7. *Letters*, 431, 29 August 1733.

8. *Letters*, 442, 11 October 1733.

9. *Letters*, 460, 27 December 1733.

10. *Letters*, 439, 28 September 1733.

11. Voltaire, *Complete Correspondence*, Besterman edn, D 700, January(?) 1734.

12. Voltaire, *Complete Correspondence*, Besterman edn, D 698, January(?) 1734, and D 707, January(?) 1734.

13. *Épitre XXXIX, à Mme du Châtelet sur sa liaison avec Maupertuis*, in *Œuvres complètes*, ed. Moland.

14. *Letters*, 410, 1 June 1733.

15. *Letters*, 465, 1 February 1734.

16. *Letters*, 430, 15 August 1733.

17. *Letters*, 482, 8 May 1734.

18. *Letters*, 423, 26 July 1733.

19. *Letters*, 410, 1 June 1733.

20. *Letters*, 414, 1 July 1733.

21. *Letters*, 470, 31 March 1734.

22. Pomeau et al., *Voltaire en son temps*, vol. I, p. 261; Voltaire, *Complete Correspondence*, Besterman edn, D 741, 12 May 1734.

23. *Letters*, 10422, 7 December 1767.

24. *Letters*, 473, 24 April 1734.

25. *Letters*, 474, 24 April 1734.

26. *Letters*, 483, 8 May 1734.

11: Émilie comes and goes

1. *Letters*, 488, 23 May 1734.

2. *Letters*, 486 23 May 1734.

3. *Letters*, 490, May 1734.

4. Voltaire, *Letters concerning the English Nation*, Letter X.

5. *Letters*, 491, 1 June 1734.

6. *Letters*, 491, 1 June 1734; *Letters*, 492, 5 June 1734; *Letters*, 493, 5 June 1734.

7. *Letters*, 505, August 1734.

8. Voltaire, *Complete Correspondence*, Besterman edn, D 730, 7 June 1734.

9. Voltaire, *Complete Correspondence*, Besterman edn, D 755, 12 May 1734.

10. Voltaire, *Complete Correspondence*, Besterman edn, D 770, July 1734.

11. *Letters*, 507, August 1734.

12. 'Correspondence de Mme du Châtelet, August 1734', D 778, in *Œuvres complètes*, ed. Moland.

13. Voltaire, *Complete Correspondence*, Besterman edn, D 782, 6 September 1734.

14. *Letters*, 514, October 1734.

15. *Letters*, 516, October 1734.

16. Voltaire, *Complete Correspondence*, Besterman edn, D 797, 23 October 1734.

17. *Letters*, 523 and 524, December 1734.

18. *Letters*, 518, 1 November 1734.

19. *Letters*, 528, December 1734.
20. Voltaire, *Complete Correspondence*, Besterman edn, D 823, 3 January 1735.
21. Voltaire, *Complete Correspondence*, Besterman edn, D 820, 24 December 1734.
22. Voltaire, *Complete Correspondence*, Besterman edn, D 842, 2 March 1735.
23. *Letters*, 548, 31 March 1735.
24. *Letters*, 558, 6 May 1735.
25. *Letters*, 559, 6 May 1735.
26. Voltaire, *Complete Correspondence*, Besterman edn, D 871, 21 May 1735.
27. Voltaire, *Complete Correspondence*, Besterman edn, D 872, 22 May 1735.
28. Voltaire, *Complete Correspondence*, Besterman edn, D 874, 30 May 1735.
29. Voltaire, *Complete Correspondence*, Besterman edn, D 876, 15 June 1735.
30. *Letters*, 580, 15 August 1735.
31. *Letters*, 569, 26 June 1735.
32. *Letters*, 570, 30 June 1735.
33. *Letters*, 603, 3 November 1735.
34. *Letters*, 603, 3 November 1735.
35. *Letters*, 575, 15 July 1735; *Letters*, 578, 4 August 1735; *Letters*, 597, 4 August 1735; and note p. 1569, *Portrait de Voltaire*.
36. *Letters*, 578, 4 August 1735.
37. *Letters*, 466, 14 February 1734.
38. *Letters*, 577, 3 August 1735.
39. *Letters*, 590, 11 September 1735.
40. *Letters*, 568, 25 June 1735.
41. *Letters*, 868, 25 July 1737.
42. *Letters*, 648, 10 February 1736; *Letters*, 649, 10 February 1736; *Letters*, 720, 16 July 1736.
43. Voltaire, *Complete Correspondence*, Besterman edn, D 900, August 1735.
44. Voltaire, *Complete Correspondence*, Besterman edn, D 912, 15 September 1735.
45. Voltaire, *Complete Correspondence*, Besterman edn, D 921, 3 October 1735.
46. Voltaire, *Complete Correspondence*, Besterman edn, D 917, 22 September 1735.
47. *Letters*, 570, 30 June 1735.
48. Voltaire, *Complete Correspondence*, Besterman edn, D 955, 1 December 1735.
49. *Letters*, 6044, 20 June 1760.
50. *Letters*, 765, 18 October 1736.

12: The intellectual love-nest

1. *Letters*, 603, 3 November 1735.
2. *Le Mondain,* in *Œuvres complètes*, ed. Moland.
3. *Letters*, 724, 5 August 1736.
4. *Letters*, 638, 25 January 1736.
5. *Letters*, 615, 8 December 1735.
6. *Letters*, 623, 28 December 1735.
7. *Letters*, 644, 6 February 1736.
8. *Letters*, 659, 26 February 1736.
9. *Letters*, 664, 8 March 1736.
10. *Letters*, 673, 21 March 1736.

11. *Letters*, 681, 12 April 1736.
12. *Letters*, 688, 20 April 1736.
13. Letter 676, 25 March 1736.
14. *Letters*, 705, 20 June 1736.
15. *Letters*, 689, 1 May 1736.
16. *Letters*, 695, 30 May 1736, and note p. 1620.
17. *Letters*, 718, 5 July 1736.
18. *Letters*, 719, July 1736.
19. *Letters*, 736, 31 August 1736.
20. *Letters*, 739, 5 September 1736.
21. *Letters*, 752, 25 September 1736.
22. *Letters*, 719, July 1736.
23. Correspondence, Frederick the Great, 8 August 1736, in *Œuvres complètes*, ed. Moland.
24. *Letters*, 737, 1 September 1736.
25. *Letters*, 655, 22 February 1736.
26. *Letters*, 655, 22 February 1736.
27. *Letters*, 766, 18 October 1736.
28. *Letters*, 770, 21 October 1736.
29. *Letters*, 781, 6 November 1736.
30. *Letters*, 787, 17 November 1736.
31. *Letters*, 797, 30 November 1736.
32. *Letters*, 792, 24 November 1736.
33. *Letters*, 801, 9 December 1736.
34. *Letters*, 792, 24 November 1736; *Letters*, 794, 26 November 1736; *Letters*, 795, 27 November 1736; *Letters*, 797, 30 November 1736.
35. Correspondence, Mme du Châtelet, in *Œuvres complètes*, ed. Moland.
36. *Letters*, 816, 17 January 1737.
37. *Letters*, 808, 1 January 1737.
38. *Letters*, 811, 15 January 1737.
39. *Letters*, 824, 18 February 1737.
40. *Letters*, 827, 20 February 1737.
41. *Letters*, 829, 1 March 1737.
42. *Letters*, 941, 3 April 1738; *Letters*, 946, 29 April 1738.
43. *Letters*, 833, 834, 835, 836, 837, 838, 18–30 March 1737.
44. *Letters*, 843, 20 April 1737.
45. *Letters*, 853, 5 June 1737.
46. *Letters*, 855, 10 June 1737.
47. *Letters*, 839, 30 March 1737.
48. *Letters*, 845, 25 April 1737; *Letters*, 852, 1 June 1737.
49. *Letters*, 848, 17 May 1737; *Letters*, 858, 20 June 1737.
50. *Letters*, 860, 23 June 1737; *Letters*, 861, 27 June 1737.
51. *Letters*, 862, 29 June 1737; *Letters*, 863, 6 July 1737.
52. *Letters*, 876, 14 September 1737; *Letters*, 866, 13 July 1737.
53. *Letters*, 869, 30 July 1737; *Letters*, 874, 17 August 1737.
54. *Letters*, 865, 10 July 1737.

55. *Letters*, 868, 25 July 1737.
56. *Letters*, 876, 14 September 1737.
57. *Letters*, 877, 20 September 1737.
58. Voltaire, *Complete Correspondence*, Besterman edn, D 1402, 12 December 1737.
59. *Letters*, 902 and 903, 23 December 1737.
60. *Letters*, 1081, 27 December 1738; *Letters*, 1082, 29 December 1738.
61. *Letters*, 2145, 1746.
62. *Letters*, 961, 18 May 1738.
63. *Letters*, 977, 21 June 1738.
64. *Letters*, 984, 3 July 1738.
65. *Letters*, 921, 25 January 1738.
66. *Letters*, 949, 3 May 1738.
67. *Letters*, 964, 22 May 1738; *Letters*, 972, 15 June 1738.
68. *Letters*, 979, 23 June 1738; *Letters*, 824, 18 February 1737.
69. *Letters*, 912, 10 January 1738; *Letters*, 959, 14 May 1738.
70. *Letters*, 967, 5 June 1738; *Letters*, 974, 17 June 1738

13: Ordeal of Mme de Graffigny

1. *Letters*, 883, 26 October 1737.
2. *Letters*, 886, 3 November 1737.
3. *Letters*, 894, 6 December 1737.
4. *Letters*, 904, 23 December 1737.
5. *Letters*, 909, 4 January 1738.
6. Voltaire, *Complete Correspondence*, Besterman edn, D 1498, 10 May 1738.
7. *Letters*, 974, 17 June 1738.
8. *Letters*, 983, 1 July 1738.
9. *Letters*, 1014, 8 August 1738; *Letters*, 1015, 8 August 1738; *Letters*, 1017, 11 August 1738; *Letters*, 1025, 1 September 1738; *Letters*, 1042, 30 October 1738; *Letters*, 1039, 27 October 1738; *Letters*, 1012, 7 August 1738.
10. *Letters*, 1033, 20 October 1738.
11. Correspondence de Mme de Graffigny (Oxford, 1985), letter 60, 4 December 1738.
12. Correspondence de Mme de Graffigny, letter 61, 5 December 1738.
13. Correspondence de Mme de Graffigny, letter 63, 12 December 1738.
14. Correspondence de Mme de Graffigny, letter 62, 9 December 1738.
15. Correspondence de Mme de Graffigny, letter 63, 12 December 1738.
16. Correspondence de Mme de Graffigny, letter 63, 12 December 1738.
17. Correspondence de Mme de Graffigny, letter 66, 22 December 1738.
18. Correspondence de Mme de Graffigny, letter 70, 1 January 1738.
19. Correspondence de Mme de Graffigny, letter 73, 8 January 1738; letter 74, 10 January 1738.
20. Correspondence de Mme de Graffigny, letter 75, 12 January 1738.
21. Correspondence de Mme de Graffigny, letter 75, 12 January 1738.
22. Correspondence de Mme de Graffigny, letter 78, 17 January 1738.
23. Correspondence de Mme de Graffigny, letter 79, 19 January 1738.

24. The key phrase in his letter is: 'Le chant de *Jeanne* me paraît charmant', but that is all he says on the subject. By contrast, in the next paragraph he thanks her for sending him *extracts* of Voltaire's *Vie de Molière*.

25. Pomeau et al. *Voltaire en son temps*, vol. I, p. 361.

26. Correspondence de Mme de Graffigny, letter 80, 19 January–8 February 1738.

27. Correspondence de Mme de Graffigny, letter 86, 2 February 1738.

28. Correspondence de Mme de Graffigny, letter 87, 5 February 1738.

29. Correspondence de Mme de Graffigny, letter 89, 9 February 1738.

30. Correspondence de Mme de Graffigny, letter 90, 11 February 1738.

31. Correspondence de Mme de Graffigny, letter 91, 12 February 1738.

32. *Letters*, 1105, 12 January 1739.

14: Émilie's court case

1. *Letters*, 1091, 2 January 1739.

2. *Letters*, 1094, 6 January 1739; *Letters*, 1104, 10 January 1739; *Letters*, 1095, 7 January 1739; *Letters*, 1130, 26 January 1739; *Letters*, 1118, 18 January 1739.

3. *Letters*, 1153, 9 February 1739.

4. *Letters*, 1159, 12 February 1739.

5. *Letters*, 1171, 21 February 1739.

6. *Letters*, 1213, 25 March 1739.

7. *Letters*, 1039, 27 October 1738; *Letters*, 1082, 29 December 1738.

8. Voltaire, *Complete Ccorrespondence*, Besterman edn, D 1738, 3 January 1739.

9. *Letters*, 1206, 17 March 1739; *Letters*, 1228, 15 April 1739.

10. Jacques Hillairet, *Dictionnaire historique des rues de Paris* (Editions de Minuit, Paris, 1985), vol. II, p. 456.

11. Jacques Hillairet, *Dictionnaire historique des rues de Paris* vol. II, p. 456.

12. *Letters*, 1244, 7 May 1739.

13. *Letters*, 1255, June 1739.

14. *Letters*, 1279, 20 August 1739.

15. *Letters*, 1288, 28 September 1739.

16. *Letters*, 1094, 6 January 1739.

17. *Letters*, 1142, 30 January 1739.

18. *Letters*, 1282, 5 September 1739; *Letters*, 1350, 12 March 1740.

19. *Letters*, 1385, 15 June 1740.

20. *Letters*, 1392, 24 June 1740.

21. *Letters*, 1326, 24 January 1740; *Letters*, 1329, 30 January 1740.

22. *Letters*, 879, 12 October 1737.

23. *Letters*, 913, 15 January 1738.

24. *Letters*, 915, 22 January 1738.

25. *Letters*, 935, 8 March 1738.

26. *Letters*, 1372, 1 June 1740.

27. *Letters*, 845, 25 April 1737.

28. *Letters*, 913, 15 January 1738.

29. *Letters*, 945, 25 April 1738.

30. *Letters*, 1387, 18 June 1740.

31. Voltaire, *Complete Correspondence*, Besterman edn, D 2207, 18 May 1740.

32. *Letters*, 1406, 10 July 1740.
33. Voltaire, *Complete Correspondence*, Besterman edn, D 2278, 29 July 1740.
34. Voltaire, *Complete Correspondence*, Besterman edn, D 2281, 2 August 1740.
35. *Letters*, 1428, 1 September 1740.
36. Voltaire, *Complete Correspondence*, Besterman edn, D 2308, 6 September 1740.
37. Voltaire, *Mémoires pour servir à la vie de M. de Voltaire,* in *Œuvres complètes*, ed. Moland.
38. *Letters*, 1430, 14 September 1740.
39. *Letters*, 1458, 2 November 1740.
40. *Letters*, 1452, 25 October 1740.
41. *Letters*, 1460, 4 November 1740.
42. Voltaire, *Complete Correspondence*, Besterman edn, D 2364, 14 November 1740.
43. Voltaire, *Complete Correspondence*, Besterman edn, D 2365, 23 November 1740.
44. *Letters*, 1470, 1 December 1740.
45. *Letters*, 1469, 1 December 1740; *Letters*, 1473, 15 December 1740.
46. *Letters*, 1476, 31 December 1740.
47. *Letters*, 1486, 19 January 1741.
48. *Letters*, 1520, 6 April 1741.
49. Voltaire, *Complete Correspondence*, Besterman edn, D 1591, August 1738 (or 17 February 1739?).
50. Voltaire, *Complete Correspondence*, Besterman edn, D 2390, 24 December 1740.
51. *Letters*, 1473, 15 December 1740.

15: Mission to Potsdam

1. *Letters*, 1338, 16 February 1740.
2. *Letters*, 1517, 1 April 1741.
3. *Letters*, 1528, 5 May 1741.
4. *Letters*, 1549, 11 July 1741.
5. Voltaire, *Mémoires pour servir à la vie de M. de Voltaire,* in *Œuvres complètes*, ed. Moland.
6. *Letters*, 1526, 2 May 1741.
7. *Letters*, 1534, 27 May 1741.
8. *Letters*, 1542, 19 June 1741.
9. *Letters*, 1609, 30 June 1742.
10. *Letters*, 1622, 10 September 1742.
11. Voltaire, *Complete Correspondence*, Besterman edn, D 2658, 18 September 1742.
12. *Letters*, 1666, February 1743.
13. *Letters*, 1667, February 1743.
14. Voltaire, *Complete Correspondence*, Besterman edn, D 2762, 21 May 1743.
15. *Letters*, 1662 and 1663, 1 February 1743.
16. Voltaire, *Mémoires pour servir à la vie de M. de Voltaire,* in *Œuvres complètes*, ed.Moland.
17. *Letters*, 1680, March 1743, and note p. 1515.
18. *Letters*, 1680, March 1743.
19. *Letters*, 1683, 4 April 1743.
20. *Letters*, 1690, 5 June 1743.

21. *Letters*, 1693, 15 June 1743; *Letters*, 1697, 28 June 1743.
22. *Letters*, 1700, 5 July 1743.
23. *Letters*, 1703, 15 July 1743.
24. *Letters*, 1705, 21 July 1743.
25. *Letters*, 1725, 3 September 1743.
26. *Letters*, 1729, 10 September 1743.
27. Voltaire, *Complete Correspondence*, Besterman edn, D 2815, 20 August 1743.
28. *Letters*, 1737, 5 October 1743.
29. Voltaire, *Complete Correspondence*, Besterman edn, D 2860, 10 October 1743.
30. *Letters*, 1743, 16 October 1743.
31. *Letters*, 1740, 8 October 1743.
32. Voltaire, *Complete Correspondence*, Besterman edn, D 2855, 7 October 1743.
33. *Letters*, 1748, 4 November 1743.
34. *Letters*, 1753, 12 November 1743.
35. Voltaire, *Complete Correspondence*, Besterman edn, D 2883, 13 November 1743.
36. Pomeau et al., *Voltaire en son temps,* vol. I, p. 438.

16: Voltaire at Court again

1. Voltaire, *Complete Correspondence*, Besterman edn, D 2904, ?January 1744.
2. *Letters*, 1792, 14 March 1744.
3. *Letters*, 1785, 21 February 1744.
4. *Letters*, 1802, 18 April 1744.
5. *Letters*, 1805, 24 April 1744.
6. *Letters*, 1828, 18 June 1744.
7. *Letters*, 1835, 18 July 1744.
8. *Letters*, 1837, 27 July 1744.
9. *Letters*, 1838, 4 August 1744.
10. *Letters*, 1883, 31 January 1745.
11. Voltaire, *Œuvres Complètes*, ed. Moland.
12. *Letters*, 1885, 25 February 1745.
13. *Letters*, 1885, 25 February 1745.
14. *Letters*, 1889, 5 March 1745.
15. *Letters*, 1898, 1 April 1745.
16. *Letters*, 1899, 3 April 1745.
17. *Letters*, 2188, 24 December 1746.
18. *Letters*, 2174, 14 November 1746.
19. *Letters*, 1887, February/March 1745.
20. *Letters*, 1901, 5 April 1745.
21. *Letters*, 1896, 28 March 1745.
22. *Letters*, 1906, April 1745.
23. *Letters*, 1951, 22 June 1745.
24. *Letters*, 1910, 20 April 1745.
25. *Letters*, 1911, 29 April 1745; *Letters*, 1913, 1 May 1745.
26. Voltaire, *Œuvres Historiques*, *Précis du Siècle de Louis XV* (Édition de la Pléiade, Paris) p. 1377.
27. Voltaire, *Œuvres Historiques*, *Précis du Siècle de Louis XV*, p. 1377.

28. Voltaire, *Œuvres Historiques, Précis du Siècle de Louis XV*, p. 1381.

29. Voltaire, *Œuvres Historiques, Précis du Siècle de Louis XV*, p. 1387.

30. *Letters*, 1926, 29 May 1745.

31. *Letters*, 1926, 29 May 1745; *Letters*, 1942, 16 June 1745.

32. *Letters*, 1946, 18 June 1745; *Letters*, 1964, 7 July 1745.

33. *Letters*, 1956, 27 June 1745.

34. Voltaire, *Complete Correspondence*, Besterman edn, D 3308, 8 January 1746.

35. *Letters*, 2111, 1 May 1746.

36. *Letters*, 2027, 15 December 1745.

37. *Letters*, 1997, 1 October 1745.

38. *Letters*, 1347, 2 March 1740; *Letters*, 1608, June 1742.

39. *Letters*, 2012, 21 October 1745.

40. *Letters*, 2009, 20 October 1745; *Letters*, 2014, 23 October 1745.

41. *Letters*, 2085, 18 March 1746.

42. *Letters*, 1985, 18 August 1745.

43. Theodore Besterman, *Voltaire* (London, 1969), p. 261.

44. *Letters*, 2022, 19 November 1745; *Letters*, 2024, 2 December 1745.

45. *Letters*, 2029, December 1745; *Letters*, 2019, November 1745.

46. *Letters*, 2031, 27 December 1745.

47. *Letters*, 2035, 1745–6.

48. *Letters*, 2054, 1745–6.

49. *Letters*, 2086, 20 March 1746.

50. *Letters*, 2103, 19 April 1746.

51. *Letters*, 2109, 26 April 1746, and note p. 1665; *Letters*, 2111, 1 May 1746.

52. Montesquieu, *Pensées*, no. 896: 'It would be shameful for the Académie that Voltaire should be a member; but one day it will be shameful if he was not a member.'

53. *Letters*, 2124, 16 May 1746.

17: End of a relationship

1. *Letters*, 2111, 1 May 1746.

2. *Letters*, 2058, January 1746.

3. *Letters*, 2170, 15 October 1746.

4. *Letters*, 2045, 1745–6.

5. *Letters*, 2049, 1745–6.

6. *Letters*, 2080, 7 March 1746.

7. *Letters*, 2146, 1746.

8. *Letters*, 2235, July–August, 1747.

9. *Letters*, 2020, November 1745.

10. Voltaire, *Complete Correspondence*, Besterman edn, D 3561, 14 August 1747.

11. Voltaire, *Complete Correspondence*, Besterman edn, D 3579, 16 October 1747.

12. Voltaire, *Complete Correspondence*, Besterman edn, D 3685, 1748?

13. *Letters*, 2146, 1746.

14. *Letters*, 2080, 7 March 1746.

15. *Letters*, 2170, 15 October 1746.

16. *Letters*, 2147, 1746.

17. Robert Mauzi, *L'Idée du bonheur au XVIIIe siècle* (Paris, 1960).
18. Mme du Châtelet, *Discours sur le bonheur* (Paris, 1997), p. 60–61, 65–67, 70.
19. *Letters*, 2169, 22 September 1746.
20. *Letters*, 2169, 22 September 1746, note p. 168.
21. S.G.Longchamp, *Mémoires*, in Voltaire, *Œuvres complètes*, ed. Moland.
22. Voltaire, *Complete Correspondence*, Besterman edn, D 3562, 15 August 1747.
23. Voltaire, *Complete Correspondence*, Besterman edn, D 3565, 20 August 1747.
24. Voltaire, *Complete Correspondence*, Besterman edn, D 3567, 27 August 1747.
25. Voltaire, *Complete Correspondence*, Besterman edn, D 3569, 30 August 1747.
26. *Letters*, 2239, 25 August 1747.
27. *Letters*, 2246, September/October 1747.
28. Longchamp, *Mémoires*, Chapter V, in *Œuvres complètes*, ed. Moland.
29. Quoted in Pomeau et al, *Voltaire en sontemps*, vol. I, p. 532.
29. *Letters*, 2280, 15 February 1748; *Letters*, 2285, 1 March 1748.

18: Death of Émilie

1. *Letters*, 2290, April 1748.
2. *Letters*, 2271, 1 February 1748.
3. *Letters*, 2283, 25 February 1748.
4. *Letters*, 2289, 3 April 1748.
5. Voltaire, *Complete Correspondence*, Besterman edn D 3644, 1 May 1748.
6. Voltaire, *Complete Correspondence*, Besterman edn D 3640, April/May 1748.
7. Voltaire, *Complete Correspondence*, Besterman edn D 3642, April/May 1748.
8. *Letters*, 2292, 29 April 1748.
9. Voltaire, *Complete Correspondence*, Besterman edn D 3648, 9 May 1748.
10. Voltaire, *Complete Correspondence*, Besterman edn D 3652, 23 May 1748.
11. *Letters*, 2272, 1 February 1748; *Letters*, 2278, 15 February 1748; *Letters*, 2285, 1 March 1748; *Letters*, 2287, 20 March 1748; *Letters*, 2289, 3 April 1748; *Letters*, 2292, 29 April 1748.
12. *Letters*, 2295, 22 May 1748; *Letters*, 2311, 1748; 'je ne pourrai vous voir aujourd'hui'.
13. *Letters*, 2318, 27 July 1748.
14. *Letters*, 2321, 8 August 1748; *Letters*, 2324, 15 August 1748.
15. Voltaire, *Complete Correspondence*, Besterman edn D 3687, July 1748.
16. Voltaire, *Complete Correspondence*, Besterman edn D 3738, 30 August 1748.
17. *Letters*, 2345, 4 October 1748.
18. *Letters*, 2461, 29 July 1749.
19. *Letters*, 2340, 26 September 1748.
20. *Letters*, 2326, August/September 1748; *Letters*, 2327, 1748; *Letters*, 2328, 1748; *Letters*, 2329, 1748; *Letters*, 2330, 1748.
21. *Letters*, 2341, 26 September 1748.
22. *Letters*, 2350, 10 October 1748.
23. *Letters*, 2365, 30 October 1748.
24. *Letters*, 2378, 12 December 1748.
25. Voltaire, *Complete Correspondence*, Besterman edn, D 3815, 30 November 1748.
26. *Letters*, 2391, 29 December 1748.

27. Voltaire, *Complete Correspondence*, Besterman edn D 3869, 15 February 1749.
28. *Letters*, 2388, 27 December 1748; *Letters*, 2391, 29 December 1748.
29. *Letters*, 2395, 4 January 1749; *Letters*, 2396, 5 January 1749.
30. *Letters*, 2399, 13 January, 1749.
31. *Letters*, 2437, 2 May 1749.
32. *Letters*, 10591, 1 March 1768.
33. *Letters*, 2403, 18 January 1749.
34. Voltaire, *Romans et contes, pot-pourri*, vol. XIII (Éditions de La Pléiade, Paris), p. 464 (first published in 1765); Voltaire, *Mélanges, La Défense de mon oncle, de l'inceste* (Éditions de La Pléiade, Paris), p. 1156, (first published in 1767).
35. *Letters*, 2406, 26 January 1749.
36. Voltaire, *Complete Correspondence*, Besterman edn, D 3933 and 3934, 24 May 1749.
37. Voltaire, *Complete Correspondence*, Besterman edn, D 3846, 13 January 1749.
38. *Letters*, 2398, 11 January 1749.
39. Voltaire, *Complete Correspondence*, Besterman edn D 3912, 21 April 1749.
40. Voltaire, *Complete Correspondence*, Besterman edn D 3877, 24 February 1749.
41. Voltaire, *Complete Correspondence*, Besterman edn D 3880, February/March 1749.
42. Voltaire, *Complete Correspondence*, Besterman edn D 3899, March/April 1749.
43. *Letters*, 2435, 25 April 1749.
44. *Letters*, 2446, 10 June 1749.
45. *Letters*, 2462, 30 July 1749.
46. Voltaire, *Complete Correspondence*, Besterman edn D 3936, 25 May 1749.
47. Voltaire, *Complete Correspondence*, Besterman edn D 3938, 7 June 1749.
48. Voltaire, *Complete Correspondence*, Besterman edn D 3942, 10 June 1749.
49. *Letters*, 2460, 28 July 1749.
50. Voltaire, *Complete Correspondence*, Besterman edn D 3960, July 1749.
51. Voltaire, *Complete Correspondence*, Besterman edn D 4002, 31 August 1749.
52. *Letters*, 2479, 28 August 1749. *Les Saisons* was eventually published in 1769.
53. *Letters*, 2481 and 2482, 29 August 1749.
54. *Letters*, 2463, 12 August 1749. Despite its revisions, the new tragedy was not put on at the Comédie Française until February 1752.
55. *Letters*, 2476, 23 August 1749.
56. Voltaire, *Complete Correspondence*, Besterman edn D 4012, 5 September 1749.
57. *Letters*, 2484, 31 August 1749.
58. *Letters*, 2487, 4 September 1749.
59. *Letters*, 2494, 10 September 1749.
60. *Letters*, 2492, 10 September 1749.
61. *Letters*, 2493, 10 September 1749.
62. *Letters*, 2533 and 2534, 15 November 1749.
63. *Letters*, 2204, 30 March 1747.
64. *Letters*, 2534, 15 November 1749.
65. *Letters*, 2497, 17 September 1749; *Letters*, 2499, 21 September 1749.
66. *Letters*, 2501, 23 September 1749.
67. *Letters*, 2509, 8 October 1749.

68. *Letters*, 2508, 5 October 1749.
69. *Letters*, 2520, 26 October 1749.
70. *Letters*, 2514, 15 October 1749.
71. *Letters*, 2513, 14 October 1749.
72. *Letters*, 2500, 23 September 1749.

19: Voltaire in Prussia

1. *Letters*, 2926, 14 September 1751.
2. *Letters*, 2926, 14 September 1751.
3. *Letters*, 2183, 13 December 1746.
4. *Letters*, 2513, 14 October 1749; *Letters*, 2514, 15 October 1749.
5. *Letters*, 2493, 10 September 1749.
6. *Letters*, 2501, 23 September 1749.
7. *Letters*, 2520, 26 October 1749.
8. *Letters*, 2549, 1 January 1750.
9. Pomeau et al., *Voltaire en son temps*, vol. I, p. 612.
10. *Letters*, 2590, 21 April 1750.
11. *Letters*, 3123, 27 January 1752.
12. *Letters*, 2601, 19 May 1750.
13. *Letters*, 2637, 28 August 1750.
14. *Letters*, 2593, 8 May 1750.
15. Voltaire, *Complete Correspondence*, Besterman edn, D 4149, 24 May 1750.
16. *Letters*, 2612, 26 June 1750.
17. *Letters*, 2619, 24 July 1750.
18. *Letters*, 2618, 24 July 1750.
19. *Letters*, 2613, 26 June 1750, and note p. 1198.
20. *Letters*, 983, 1 July 1738; *Letters*, 1955, 25 June 1745; *Letters*, 2111, 1 May 1746.
21. Voltaire, *Complete Correspondence*, Besterman edn, D 14891, 28 March 1768.
22. *Letters*, 2622, 7 August 1750.
23. *Letters*, 2618, 24 July 1750.
24. *Letters*, 2631, 21 August 1750.
25. René Pomeau et al., *La Religion de Voltaire* (Nizet, Paris, 1995), p. 282; see also Deloffre and Cormier, *Voltaire et sa 'grande amie'*, (Voltaire Foundation, Oxford, 2003), p. 102; and Henri de Catt, *Mes Entretiens avec Frédéric le Grand*.
26. *Letters*, 3014, February 1752, D 4666. Many of Voltaire's letters to Mme Bentinck are undated, so the chronology is uncertain; I follow the dating, and the letter numbering, of Deloffre and Cormier, *Voltaire et sa 'grande amie'*;this one is Deloffre and Cormier, letter 167, February 1752.
27. *Letters*, 2624, 7 August 1750.
28. *Letters*, 2625, 7 August 1750.
29. *Letters*, 2633, 23 August 1750, p. 1206, note; Voltaire, *Complete Correspondence*, Besterman edn, D 4195, 23 August 1750.
30. *Letters*, 2635, 25 August 1750.
31. Voltaire, *Complete Correspondence*, Besterman edn, D 4539, 6 August 1751.
32. *Letters*, 2637, 28 August 1750
33. *Letters*, 2627, 14 August 1750.

34. *Letters*, 2650, 14 September 1750; *Letters*, 2673, 27 October 1750; *Letters*, 2699, 28 November 1750; *Letters*, 2701, 8 December 1750.

35. *Letters*, 2745, 9 January 1751.

36. *Letters*, 2682, 9 November 1750.

37. *Letters*, 241, September 1729.

38. Voltaire, *Complete Correspondence*, Besterman edn, D 4303, 19 December 1750.

39. *Letters*, 2782, 19 February 1751.

40. *Letters*, 2694, 21 November 1750, D 4276; Deloffre and Cormier, letter 30.

41. *Letters*, 2676, early December 1750, D 4253; Deloffre and Cormier, letter 34.

42. *Letters*, 3307, 20 December 1750, D 5016; Deloffre and Cormier, letter 36.

43. *Letters*, 2694, 21 November 1750, D 4276; Deloffre and Cormier, letter 30; and *Letters*, 2655, 8 January 1751, D 4227; Deloffre and Cormier, letter 44.

44. *Letters*, 3022, January 1751, D 4674; Deloffre and Cormier, letter 66; and *Letters*, 3066, January 1751, D 4718; Deloffre and Cormier, letter 48.

45. *Letters*, 2844, 7 March 1751, D 4465; Deloffre and Cormier, letter 76.

46. Besterman, *Voltaire*, p. 312.

47. *Letters*, 2721, 9 August 1751, D 4315; Deloffre and Cormier, letter 109.

48. *Letters*, 2896, 19 August 1751, D 4527; Deloffre and Cormier, letter 112.

49. *Letters*, 2922, 2 September 1751.

50. *Letters*, 3258, 24 July 1752.

51. Voltaire, *Complete Correspondence*, Besterman edn, D 4400, 24 February 1751.

52. *Letters*, 2791, 25 February 1751; *Letters*, 2793, 27 February 1751.

53. *Letters*, 2795, 28 February 1751.

54. *Letters*, 2839, 4 May 1751.

55. *Letters*, 2662, 5 October 1750.

56. *Letters*, 2641, 1 September 1750.

57. *Letters*, 2762, 31 January 1751.

58. *Letters*, 2826, 13 April 1751.

59. *Letters*, 2895, 20 July 1751.

60. *Letters*, 2909, 17 August 1751.

61. *Letters*, 2818, June 1751.

62. *Letters*, 2919, 31 August 1751.

63. *Letters*, 2911, 24 August 1751.

64. *Letters*, 2899, July/August 1751.

65. *Letters*, 2639, end-September 1751.

66. *Letters*, 2971, 14 December 1751; *Letters*, 2973, December 1751.

67. *Letters*, 3211, 31 May 1752.

68. Voltaire, *Le Siècle de Louis XIV*, in *Œuvres Historiques* (Édition de la Pléiade), p. 614.

69. *Letters*, 3168, 18 March 1752.

70. *Letters*, 3190, 15 April 1752.

71. *Letters*, 2969, 8 December 1751; *Letters*, 3298, 5 September 1752.

72. *Letters*, 3253, 18 July 1752.

73. Voltaire, *Sermon des cinquante* and *Poème sur la loi naturelle* in *Mélanges* (Édition de la Pléiade), pp. 253 and 287.

74. Voltaire, *Complete Correspondence*, Besterman edn, D 5052–5057, October–November, 1752.
75. *Letters*, 3326, 9 October 1752.
76. *Letters*, 2639, 31 August 1750 (or September 1751); *Letters*, 2960, 22 November 1751.
77. *Letters*, 3328, 12 October 1752.
78. *Letters*, 3310, 18 September 1752.
79. *Letters*, 3346, 15 November 1752.
80. *Letters*, 3353, 17 November 1752.
81. Voltaire, *Histoire du Docteur Akakia*, in *Mélanges*, p. 289.
82. *Letters*, 3429, 28 January 1753.
83. *Letters*, 3420, 17 January 1753.
84. *Letters*, 3270, 5 August 1752.
85. *Letters*, 3448, 26 February 1753.
86. Voltaire, *Complete Correspondence*, Besterman edn, D 5232, 15 March 1753.

20: Humiliation at Frankfurt

1. *Letters*, 3483, 4 June 1753; 3489, 7 June 1753.
2. *Letters*, 3548, 5 August 1753.
3. *Letters*, 3551, 11 August 1753.
4. *Letters*, 3565, 3 September 1753.
5. *Letters*, 3568, 8 September 1753.
6. *Letters*, 3592, 14 October 1753.
7. *Letters*, 3594, 22 October 1753.
8. *Letters*, 3658, 27 January 1754; *Letters*, 3667, 5 February 1754.
9. Voltaire, *Complete Correspondence*, Besterman edn D 4012, 5 September 1749.
10. *Letters*, 3658, 27 January 1754.
11. *Letters*, 3706, 3 March 1754; *Letters*, 3711, 10 March 1754.
12. *Letters*, 3715, 12 March 1754.
13. *Letters*, 3739, 30 March 1754.
14. *Letters*, 3751, 12 April 1754.

21 Sentence of exile

1. *Letters*, 3856, 29 August 1754.
2. *Letters*, 3900, 18 November 1754
3. *Letters*, 3919, 9 December 1754.
4. Pomeau et al., *Voltaire en son temps*, vol. I, p. 113.
5. *Letters*, 3926, 15 December, 1754.
6. *Letters*, 3929, 16 December 1754.
7. *Letters*, 3694, 24 February 1754.
8. *Letters*, 4104, 18 June 1755.
9. *Letters*, 4052, 8 April 1755.
10. *Letters*, 4074, 16 May 1755.
11. *Letters*, 4301, 23 December 1755.
12. *Letters*, 3968, 23 January 1755.
13. *Letters*, 3970, 23 January 1755.

14. *Letters*, 4018, 27 February 1755.
15. *Letters*, 4027, 8 March 1755.
16. *Letters*, 4030, 17 March 1755.
17. *Letters*, 4040, 28 March 1755.
18. *Letters*, 4051, 5 April 1755.
19. *Letters*, 4061, 18 April 1755.
20. *Letters*, 4071, 7 May 1755.
21. *Letters*, 4085, 26 May 1755.
22. *Letters*, 4163, 16 August 1755.
23. *Letters*, 4048, 2 April 1755; *Letters*, 4246, 5 November 1755.
24. *Letters*, 4153, 8 August 1755.
25. *Letters*, 4163, 16 August 1755.
26. *Letters*, 4221, 1 October 1755.
27. *Letters*, 4224, 10 October 1755, and note, p. 1382.
28. *Letters*, 4410, 17 March 1756.
29. *Letters*, 4032, 24 March 1755.
30. *Letters*, 4046, 2 April 1755.
31. *Letters*, 4047, 2 April 1755.
32. *Letters*, 4056, 14 April 1755.
33. *Letters*, 4132, 30 July 1755.
34. *Letters*, 4164, 17 August 1755.
35. *Letters*, 4145, 4 August 1755.
36. *Letters*, 4468, 23 May 1756.
37. *Letters*, 4326, 8 January 1756.
38. *Letters*, 4409, 17 March 1756.
39. *Letters*, 4491, 19 June 1756.
40. *Letters*, 5101, 22 March 1758.
41. *Letters*, 4735, 20 March 1757.
42. *Letters*, 4443, 16 April 1756; *Letters*, 4629, 8 December 1756.
43. *Letters*, 4568, 20 September 1756.
44. *Letters*, 4734, 20 March 1757.

22: *Encyclopédie*

1. Voltaire, *Dictionnaire philosophique* (Flammarion, Paris, 1997).
2. *Letters*, 4305, 26 December 1755; *Letters*, 4643, 22 December 1756; *Letters*, 3791, 6 June 1754.
3. *Letters*, 4282, 9 December 1755.
4. *Letters*, 4265, 24 November 1755; *Letters*, 4269, 30 November 1755.
5. *Letters*, 4286, 10 December 1755.
6. *Letters*, 4473, 27 May 1756.
7. *Letters*, 4601, 1 November 1756; *Letters*, 4605, 3 November 1756; *Letters*, 4614, 20 November 1756; *Letters*, 4630, 8 December 1756.
8. *Letters*, 4621, 28 November 1756.
9. Voltaire, *Précis du siècle de Louis XV*, p. 1527-8, in *Oeuvres Historiques* (Édition de la Pléiade).
10. *Letters*, 4660, 13 January 1757.

11. *Letters*, 4666, 16 January 1757.

12. Voltaire, *Histoire du parlement de Paris*, p. 105.

13. Voltaire, *Histoire du parlement de Paris*, p. 106–107.

14. *Letters*, 4684, 6 February 1757 and note p. 1528.

15. *Letters*, 4493, 20 June 1756.

16. *Letters*, 4640, 20 December 1756; *Letters*, 4654, 2 January 1757, and note p. 1494; *Letters*, 4781, 26 May 1757; *Letters*, 9558, 4 August 1766.

17. *Letters*, 4678, 1 February 1757; *Letters*, 4682, 4 February 1757; *Letters*, 4900, 26 October 1757; *Letters*, 4945, 2 December 1757; *Letters*, 5109, 7 April 1758.

18. Voltaire, *Candide ou l'optimisme*, chapter XXIII, in *Romans et contes* (Édition de la Pléiade).

19. *Letters*, 4683, 6 February 1757; *Letters*, 4712, 3 March 1757.

20. *Letters*, 5761, 22 November 1759; *Letters*, 5927, 25 March 1760; *Letters*, 6330, 17 November 1760.

21. *Letters*, 4831, 7 August 1757.

22. *Letters*, 4738, 26 March 1757; *Letters*, 4777, 20 May 1757.

23. *Letters*, 4965, 12 December 1757; *Letters*, 4985, 29 December 1757; *Letters*, 5062, 25 February 1758; and René Pomeau et al., *La Religion de Voltaire* (Librairie Nizet, Saint-Genough, 1995), p. 307.

24. *Letters*, 5446, 12 March 1759.

25. *Letters*, 5441, 10 March 1759.

26. Voltaire, *Candide ou l'optimisme*, chapter XXX, in *Romans et contes* (Édition de la Pléiade).

23: Ferney

1. *Letters*, 5287, 9 December 1758.

2. Pomeau et al., *Voltaire en son temps,* vol. I, p. 891.

3. *Letters*, 5271, 18 November 1758, and note, p. 1261; *Letters*, 5288, 10 December 1758; *Letters*, 5333, 5 January 1759.

4. *Letters*, 5224, 23 September 1758, and note, p. 1243.

5. *Letters*, 5400, 15 February 1759; *Letters*, 5539, 23 May 1759; *Letters*, 5554, 3 June 1759; *Letters*, 5619, 15 August 1759.

6. *Letters*, 5539, 23 May 1759; *Letters*, 5619, 15 August 1759.

7. *Letters*, 5390, 11 February 1759; *Letters*, 5393, 12 February 1759; *Letters*, 5435, 9 March 1759; *Letters*, 5552, 2 June 1759; *Letters*, 5553, 3 June 1759; *Letters*, 5555, 3 June 1759; *Letters*, 5580, 29 June 1759.

8. *Letters*, 12103, 19 December 1770, note, p. 1306.

9. *Letters*, 5272, 18 November 1758.

10. *Letters*, 5295, 16 December 1758; *Letters*, 5309, 25 December 1758; *Letters*, 5311, 25 December 1758; *Letters*, 5312, 25 December 1758; *Letters*, 5323, 29 December 1758; *Letters*, 5331, 3 January 1759; *Letters*, 6471, 30 January 1761.

11. *Letters*, 5663, 17 September 1759; *Letters*, 5744, 1 December 1759; *Letters*, 5832, 7 January 1760.

12. *Letters*, 5301, 19 December 1758; *Letters*, 5288, 10 December 1758; *Letters*, 5321, 29 December 1758; *Letters*, 5349, 17 January 1759.

13. *Letters*, 6542; Pomeau et al., *Voltaire en son temps,* vol. II, p. 34.

14. *Letters*, 5595, 16 July 1759; *Letters*, 5503, 16 April 1759; *Letters*, 5505, 17 April 1759; *Letters*, 5515, 2 May 1759; *Letters*, 5522, 7 May 1759; *Letters*, 5618, 14 August 1759.
15. *Letters*, 5522, 7 May 1759.
16. *Letters*, 5534, 20 May 1759.
17. *Letters*, 5546, 18 May 1759.
18. *Letters*, 5596, 20 July 1759.
19. *Letters*, 5610, 2 August 1759.
20. *Letters*, 5698, 6 October 1759.
21. *Letters*, 5524, 10 May 1759.
22. *Letters*, 5529, 16 May 1759.
23. *Letters*, 5610, 2 August 1759.
24. *Letters*, 5665, 21 September 1759.
25. *Letters*, 5703, 12 October 1759.
26. *Letters*, 5688, September 1759, and note, p. 1418.
27. *Letters*, 5573, 18 June 1759.
28. *Letters*, 5494, 6 April 1759, and note, p. 1346.
29. *Letters*, 5615, 10 August 1759.
30. *Letters*, 5721, 22 October 1759.
31. *Letters*, 5724, 24 October 1759.
32. *Letters*, 5733, 5 November 1759, *Letters*, 5734, 5 November 1759.
33. *Letters*, 6225, 22 September 1760.
34. *Letters*, 5493, 5 April 1759.
35. *Letters*, 6221, 20 September 1760.
36. *Letters*, 6212, 16 September 1760.
37. *Letters*, 6248, 1 October 1760.
38. *Letters*, 6255, 8 October 1760.
39. *Letters*, 6261, 10 October 1760.
40. *Letters*, 5967, 25 April 1760.
41. *Letters*, 6247, September 1760.
42. *Letters*, 6835, 3 October 1761.
43. *Letters*, 6797, 14 September 1761.
44. *Letters*, 5659, September 1759.
45. *Letters*, 5704, 13 October 1759.
46. *Letters*, 5968, 25 April 1760.
47. *Letters*, 6281, 22 October 1760.
48. *Letters*, 5488, 2 April 1759.
49. *Letters*, 5353, 20 January 1759.
50. *Letters*, 8676, 21 January 1765; *Letters*, 8760, 14 March 1765.
51. Melchior Grimm, *Correspondance Littéraire*, 15 December 1768; quoted in Frank A. Kafker, *The Encyclopaedists as Individuals* (Voltaire Foundation, Oxford, 1988), p. 85.
52. Denis Diderot, *Correspondence*, quoted in *The Encyclopaedists as Individuals*, p. 86.
53. *Letters*, 7112, 4 April 1762.
54. *Letters*, 6627, 31 May 1761, and note, p. 1315.

55. *Letters*, 9376, 5 April 1766.
56. *Letters*, 5704, 13 October 1759.
57. *Letters*, 6206, September 1760.
58. *Letters*, 6544, 19 March 1761.

24: Mlle Corneille

1. *Letters*, 6311, 5 November 1760.
2. *Letters*, 6376, 16 December 1760.
3. *Letters*, 6377, 16 December 1760.
4. *Letters*, 6387, 22 December 1760.
5. *Letters*, 6412, 2 January 1761.
6. *Letters*, 6439, 15 January 1761.
7. *Letters*, 7344, September 1762.
8. *Letters*, 6532, 6 March 1761.
9. *Letters*, 6465, 26 January 1761.
10. *Letters*, 6470, 30 January 1761.
11. *Letters*, 6507, 16 February 1761.
12. *Letters*, 6456, 21 January 1761.
13. *Letters*, 6518, 24 February 1761.
14. *Letters*, 6849, 11 October 1761.
15. *Letters*, 6840, 7 October 1761.
16. *Letters*, 6601, 1 May 1761.
17. *Letters*, 6754, 18 August 1761; *Letters*, 6674, 26 June 1761.
18. *Letters*, 7590, 15 February 1763.
19. Pomeau et al., *Voltaire en son temps,* vol. II, p. 93.
20. *Letters*, 6785, 7 September 1761.
21. *Letters*, 6825, 28 September 1761.
22. *Letters*, 6791, 10 September 1761.
23. Pomeau et al., *Voltaire en son temps,* vol. II, p. 94.
24. Pomeau et al., *Voltaire en son temps,* vol. II, p. 94–95.
25. *Letters*, 8305, 14 May 1764; *Letters*, 13121, 22 January 1773; *Letters*, 13539, 15 December 1773.
26. *Letters*, 8369, 22 June 1764, and note, p. 1399.
27. *Letters*, 8446, 10 August 1764.
28. *Letters*, 8467, 7 September 1764; *Letters*, 8468, 7 September 1764.
29. *Letters*, 7532, 25 January 1763.
30. *Letters*, 7540, 26 January 1763.
31. *Letters*, 7539, 26 January 1763.
32. *Letters*, 7551, 29 January 1763.
33. *Letters*, 7590, 15 February 1763.
34. *Letters*, 7583, 13 February 1763.

25: Campaigns for justice

1. *Letters*, 7103, 29 March 1762.
2. *Letters*, 7108, 2 April 1762.
3. *Letters*, 6999, 10 January 1762.

4. *Letters*, 7157, 28 May 1762.
5. *Letters*, 7289, 9 August 1762.
6. *Letters*, 7082, 8 March 1762.
7. *Letters*, 7094, 22 March 1762.
8. See David D. Bien, *The Calas Affair* (Princeton University Press, Princeton, 1960), pp. 15–17.
9. Pomeau et al., *Voltaire en son temps,* vol. II, p. 119 ; Marc Chassaigne, *L'Affaire Calas* (Perrin & Cie, Paris 1929).
10. *Letters*, 7096, 25 March 1762.
11. *Letters*, 8738, 1 March 1765.
12. *Letters*, 7116, 15 April 1762.
13. *Letters*, 7099, 27 March 1762.
14. *Letters*, 7112, 4 April 1762.
15. *Letters*, 7135, 15 May 1762.
16. *Letters*, 7162, May-June 1762, and note, p. 1488.
17. *Letters*, 7170, 5 June 1762.
18. *Letters*, 7244, 12 July 1762.
19. Voltaire, *La Méprise d'Arras* (1771), in *Oeuvres Complètes*, ed. Moland.
20. *Letters*, 7227, 5 July 1772.
21. *Letters*, 7237, 8 July 1762.
22. *Letters*, 7268, 28 July 1762.
23. *Letters*, 7232, 8 July 1762.
24. *Letters*, 7238, 9 July 1762.
25. *Letters*, 7246, 14 July 1762.
26. *Letters*, 7306, 20 August 1762.
27. *Letters*, 7316, 27 August 1762, and note, p. 1532.
28. *Letters*, 7318, 29 August 1762.
29. *Letters*, 7351, 20 September 1762.
30. *Letters*, 7656, 12 March 1763; *Letters*, 7678, 16 March 1763.
31. *Letters*, 7699, 30 March 1763.
32. *Letters*, 7687, 23 March 1763; *Letters*, 7862, 6 August 1763.
33. *Letters*, 7662, 14 March 1763.
34. *Letters*, 7536, 24 January 1763.
35. *Letters*, 7709, 3 April 1763.
36. Voltaire, *Traité sur la tolérance*, in *Mélanges,* p. 563.
37. Voltaire, *Traité sur la tolérance*, in *Mélanges,* p. 599.
38. Voltaire, *Traité sur la tolérance*, in *Mélanges,* pp. 616, 618.
39. *Letters*, 8042, 15 December 1763.
40. *Letters*, 8015, 4 December 1763.
41. *Letters*, 8020, 6 December 1763, and note, p. 1297.
42. *Letters*, 8071, 31 December 1763.
43. *Letters*, 7814, 23 June 1763.
44. *Letters*, 8095, 6 January 1764.
45. *Letters*, 8144, 1 February 1764.
46. *Letters*, 8240, 21 March 1764.
47. *Letters*, 8196, 1 March 1764.

48. *Letters*, 8231, 16 March 1764.
49. *Letters*, 8265, 15 April 1764; *Letters*, 8357, 18 June 1764.
50. *Letters*, 8346, 11 June 1764.
51. *Letters*, 8341, 7 or 8 June 1764. For Voltaire's regret at Mme de Pompadour's death on 15 April, see *Letters*, 8280, 23 April 1764.
52. *Letters*, 8354, 17 June 1764.
53. *Letters*, 8441, 6 August 1764.
54. *Letters*, 8761, 15 March 1765; *Letters*, 8776, 18 March 1765.
55. *Letters*, 8341, 7 or 8 June 1764, and note, p. 1392; *Letters*, 8830, 13 April 1765, and note, p. 1202.
56. *Letters*, 8837, 17 April 1765.
57. *Letters*, 8851, 29 April 1765.
58. *Letters*, 9412, 9 May 1766.
59. Voltaire, *Avis au public*, in *Mélanges,* pp. 809–29; and in *L'Affaire Calas* (Gallimard, Paris, 1996), pp. 204–30.
60. *Letters*, 8841, 19 April 1765.
61. *Letters*, 9474, 21 June 1766; *Letters*, 9475, 21 June 1766; *Letters*, 9476, 21 June 1766; *Letters*, 9529, 22 July 1766.
62. *Letters*, 12617, 6 December 1771.
63. *Letters*, 8220, 14 March 1764.
64. *Letters*, 8253, 2 April 1764.

26: Damilaville

1. *Letters*, 8656, 12 January 1765.
2. *Letters*, 8690, 28 January 1765.
3. *Letters*, 8737, 27 February 1765.
4. *Letters*, 8715, 9 February 1765.
5. *Letters*, 8705, 3 February 1765.
6. *Letters*, 8728, 20 February 1765.
7. *Letters*, 8709, 4 February 1765.
8. *Letters*, 8722, 14 February 1765.
9. *Letters*, 8722, 14 February 1765, and note, pp. 1498–9.
10. *Letters*, 8785, 21 March 1765.
11. *Letters*, 8815, 2 April 1765.
12. *Letters*, 8337, 4 June 1764.
13. *Letters*, 8215, 11 March 1764.
14. Frederick Pottle (ed.), *Boswell on the Grand Tour* (Heinemann, London, 1953), vol. 1, pp. 285–6.
15. *Letters*, 8719, 11 February 1765.
16. *Letters*, 9041, 3 July 1765.
17. *Letters*, 9158, 26 October 1765.
18. *Letters*, 9137, 4 October 1765.
19. *Letters*, 9102, 6 September 1765.
20. *Letters*, 8676, 21 January 1765.
21. *Letters*, 8763, 15 March 1765.
22. *Letters*, 8730, 25 February 1765.

23. *Letters*, 4211, 20 September 1755.

24. *Letters*, 8878, 20 May 1765.

25. *Letters*, 9042, 6 July 1765.

26. *Letters*, 9043, 8 July 1765.

27. *Letters*, 8887, 27 May 1765.

28. *Letters*, 8918, 25 June 1765.

29. *Letters*, 9043, 8 July 1765, and note, p. 1241.

30. *Letters*, 9044, 8 July 1765.

31. *Letters*, 9055, 25 July 1765; *Letters*, 9070, August 1765, and note, p. 1250.

32. *Letters*, 9066, 12 August 1765.

33. *Letters*, 9069, 14 August 1765.

34. *Letters*, 9082, 23 August 1765.

35. *Letters*, 9097, 1 September 1765; see Chapter 23 above and *Letters*, 5494, 6 April 1759, and note, p. 1346.

36. *Letters*, 8178, 22 February 1764.

37. *Letters*, 9809, 1766–77.

38. *Letters*, 9781, 19 December 1766.

39. *Letters*, 9788, 22 December 1766.

40. *Letters*, 8915, 22 June 1765.

41. *Letters*, 9040, 3 July 1765.

42. *Letters*, 9092, 30 August 1765.

43. *Letters*, 9111, 18 September 1765; *Letters*, 9119, 22 September 1765.

44. *Letters*, 9138, 4 October 1765.

45. *Letters*, 9141, 8 October 1765.

46. *Letters*, 9150, 16 October 1765; *Of Crimes and Punishments* (*Dei delitti e delle pene*), by Cesare Beccaria, was first published in 1764.

47. *Letters*, 9222, 9 December 1765.

48. *Letters*, 10893, 5 September 1768.

49. *Letters*, 5502, 15 April 1759.

50. *Letters*, 5517, 5 May 1759; *Letters*, 6012, 28 May 1760; *Letters*, 6427, 11 January 1761; *Letters*, 6491, 5 February 1761; *Letters* 6523, 27 February 1761.

51. *Letters*, 6523, 27 February 1761.

52. *Letters*, 7428, 28 November 1762; *Letters*, 7541, 26 January 1763; *Letters*, 8222, 14 March 1764.

53. *Letters*, 8303, 9 May 1764.

54. *Letters*, 11002, 29 November 1768.

55. *Letters*, 11020, 16 December 1768.

56. *Letters*, 11083, 27 January 1769.

57. *Letters*, 14818, 8 December 1776.

27: Beccaria

1. *Letters*, 11517, 20 December 1769.

2. See Marcello T. Maestro, *Voltaire and Beccaria as Reformers of Criminal Law* (Columbia University Press, New York, 1942), p. 11.

3. *Letters*, 7862, 6 August 1763.

4. Maestro, *Voltaire and Beccaria as Reformers of Criminal Law*, pp. 34–50.

5. *Letters*, 9125, 26 September 1765.
6. *Letters*, 9150, 16 October 1765.
7. Cesare Beccaria, *On Crimes and Punishments*, trans. David Young (Indianapolis: Hackett, 1986).
8. Beccaria, *On Crimes and Punishments*, p. 81.
9. *Letters*, 7217; Beccaria: *Del disordine e de' rimedii delle monete nello stato di Milano nell'anno 1762* (1762).
10. Quoted in Maestro, *Voltaire and Beccaria as Reformers of Criminal Law*, pp. 68–9.
11. Voltaire, *Commentaire sur le livre 'Des délits et des peines'*, in *Mélanges*, pp 769–807; also in *L'Affaire Calas*, pp. 235–84.
12. Voltaire, *Commentaire sur le livre 'Des délits et des peines'*, in *Mélanges*, pp. 802–06.
13. Voltaire, *Dictionnaire philosophique* (Flammarion, Paris, 1964).
14. *Letters*, 8401, 16 July 1764.
15. *Letters*, 8541, 29 October 1764, and note, p. 1449; *Letters*, 8551.
16. *Letters*, 8489, 24 September 1764.
17. *Letters*, 8615, 23 December 1764.
18. *Letters*, 8498, 1 October 1764; see also: *Letters*, 8524, 8525 and 8527, all 19 October 1764.
19. Louis Philipon de la Madelaine, *Discours sur la nécessité et les moyens de supprimer les peines capitales* (1770).
20. *Letters*, 12129, 28 December 1770.

28: Chevalier de La Barre

1. *Letters*, 5878, 15 February 1760.
2. Voltaire, *Fragments historiques sur l'Inde, sur le général Lally et sur le comte de Morangiés* (Geneva, 1773).
3. Pomeau et al., *Voltaire en son temps,* vol. II, p. 471–2.
4. *Letters*, 9422, 17 May 1766.
5. *Letters*, 9439, 29 May 1766.
6. *Letters*, 9441, 30 May 1766.
7. *Letters*, 9442, 30 May 1766.
8. *Letters*, 9460, 13 June 1766.
9. Voltaire, *Précis du siècle de Louis XV*, in *Œuvres historiques*, pp. 1499–1506; Voltaire, *Fragments historiques sur l'Inde*, Chapters XVIII and XIX.
10. *Letters*, 9478, 22 June 1766.
11. *Letters*, 9512, 14 July 1766, and note, pp. 1390–1. These details are from Voltaire's early 'letter' account. Pomeau confirms that Dumaisniel de Saveuse was a suspect and son of Belleval; he does not mention Douville de Maillefer, except in an endnote.
12. *Letters*, 9936, 10 February 1767, and note, pp. 1512–3; ('soon': either April 1767 or April 1768); *Letters*, 10061, 5 April 1767, and note, pp. 1556–7; *Letters*. 10088, 16 April 1767.
13. Marc Chassaigne, *Le Procès du chevalier de La Barre* (Victor Lecoffre, Paris, 1920), p. 141.
14. Voltaire, *Relation de la mort du chevalier de La Barre*, in *Mélanges*, p. 765.
15. Pomeau et al., *Voltaire en son temps,* vol. II pp. 241–8.

16. *Letters*, 9480, 23 June 1766.

17. *Letters*, 9487, 1 July 1766.

18. *Letters*, 9499, 7 July 1766.

19. *Letters*, 9501, 7 July 1766.

20. *Letters*, 9512, 14 July 1766, and note, pp. 1390–1.

21. *Letters*, 9513, 14 July 1766.

22. *Letters*, 9569, 11 August 1766; *Letters*, 9578, 16 August 1766; *Letters*, 9583, 20 August 1766.

23. Voltaire, *Relation de la mort du chevalier de La Barre*, in *Mélanges*, pp. 755–67.

24. Voltaire, *Relation de la mort du chevalier de La Barre*, in *Mélanges*, p. 762.

25. Voltaire, *Relation de la mort du chevalier de La Barre*, in *Mélanges*, pp. 763, 766–7.

26. *Letters*, 9524, 18 July 1766.

27. *Letters*, 9578, 16 August 1766.

28. *Letters*, 9528, 21 July 1766.

29. *Letters*, 9535, 23 July 1766.

30. *Letters*, 9650, 24 September 1766.

31. *Letters*, 9591, 25 August 1766.

29: Geneva Troubles

1. *Letters*, 7193, 17 June 1762.

2. *Letters*, 6054, 23 June 1760, and note, p. 1560.

3. *Letters*, 7818, 30 June 1763.

4. *Letters*, 7889, 21 August 1763.

5. *Letters*, 7935, 28 September 1763.

6. Voltaire, *Sermon des cinquante*, in *Mélanges*, p. 253.

7. *Letters*, 8629, 31 December 1764.

8. Voltaire, *Le Sentiment des citoyens*, in *Mélanges*, p. 715.

9. *Letters*, 8646, 10 January 1765.

10. *Letters*, 9147, 14 October 1765.

11. *Letters*, 9150, 16 October 1765.

12. *Letters*, 9174, 13 November 1765.

13. *Letters*, 9191, 21 November 1765.

14. *Letters*, 9211, 2 November 1765.

15. *Letters*, 9200, 27 November 1765.

16. Voltaire, *Idées républicaines*, in *Mélanges*, p. 503.

17. *Letters*, 9268, 10 January 1766.

18. *Letters*, 9697, 3 November 1766; *Letters*, 9704, 5 November 1766.

19. *Letters*, 9405, 1 May 1766.

20. *Letters*, 9408, 4 May 1766, and note, p. 1364.

21. *Letters*, 9408, 4 May 1766, and note, p. 1364.

22. *Letters*, 9417, 12 May 1766.

23. *Letters*, 10059, 3 April 1767.

24. *Letters*, 9765, 11 December 1766.

25. *Letters*, 9795, 23 December 1766.

26. *Letters*, 9798, 27 December 1766.

27. *Letters*, 9813, 2 January 1767.

28. *Letters*, 9837, 9 January 1767.
29. *Letters*, 9844, 12 January 1767.
30. *Letters*, 9850, 13 January 1767, and note, pp. 1490–91.
31. *Letters*, 9849, 13 January 1767.
32. *Letters*, 9883, 25 January 1767.
33. *Letters*, 9907, 2 February 1767.
34. *Letters*, 9921, 6 February 1767.
35. *Letters*, 9829, 7 January 1767.
36. *Letters*, 9777, 17 December 1766; *Letters*, 9779, 19 December 1766; *Letters*, 9787, 22 December 1766; *Letters*, 9808, December 1766.
37. *Letters*, 9831, 8 January 1767.
38. *Letters*, 9831, 8 January 1767.
39. *Letters*, 9835, 9 January 1767.
40. *Letters*, 9874, 20 January 1767.
41. *Letters*, 9895, 29 January 1767.
42. *Letters*, 9902, 30 January 1767.
43. *Letters*, 10048, 27 March 1767.
44. *Letters*, 10045, 24 March 1767.
45. *Letters*, 10313, 18 September 1767; *Letters*, 10333, 30 September 1767.
46. *Letters*, 10292, 2 September 1767.
47. *Letters*, 10297, 4 September 1767.
48. *Letters*, 10410, 30 November 1767.
49. *Letters*, 10486, 8 January 1768.
50. *Letters*, 10607, 6 March 1768.
51. *Letters*, 10613, 8 March 1768.
52. Voltaire, *Correspondence choisie*, note, p. 925; Peter Gay, *Voltaire's Politics* (Yale University Press, New Haven, 1988), p. 231.
53. *Letters*, 10619, 15 March 1768; *Letters*, 10620, 15 March 1768.

30: The quarrel with Mme Denis

1. *Letters*, 10589, 1 March 1768, at two in the afternoon, and note, pp. 1251–2.
2. *Letters*, 10627, 17 March 1768; *Letters*, 10629, 18 March 1768.
3. *Letters*, 10373, 27 October 1767.
4. *Letters*, 10422, 7 December 1767.
5. *Letters*, 10591, 1 March 1768.
6. *Letters*, 10724, 25 April 1768.
7. *Letters*, 10640, 22 March 1768, and note, pp. 1265–1267.
8. *Letters*, 10660, 30 March 1768; see also *Letters*, 10617, 14 March 1768; and *Letters*, 10645, 23 March 1768.
9. *Letters*, 10589, 1 March 1768, and note, pp. 1251–2.
10. *Letters*, 10575, 19 February 1768.
11. *Letters*, 10606, 5 March 1768; see also *Letters*, 10585, 1 March 1768; and *Letters*, 10607, 6 March 1768.
12. *Letters*, 10690, 11 April 1768.
13. *Letters*, 10694, 11 April 1768.
14. *Letters*, 10675, 4 April 1768.

15. *Letters*, 6145, 13 August 1760.

16. *Letters*, 10707, 16 April 1768.

17. *Letters*, 10610, 6 March 1768.

18. *Letters*, 10613, 8 March 1768.

19. *Letters*, 10807, 24 June 1768.

20. *Letters*, 10703, 15 April 1768, and note, p. 1284.

21. *Letters*, 10703, 15 April 1768, and note, pp. 1283–5.

22. *Letters*, 10703, 15 April 1768.

23. *Letters*, 10806, 23 June 1768.

24. *Letters*, 11153, 30 March 1769.

25. *Letters*, 11142, 19 March 1769, and note, p. 1432; *Letters*, 11144, 24 March 1769, and note, p. 1433; *Letters*, 11153, 30 March 1769, and note, p. 1447; *Letters*, 11167, 4 April 1769; *Letters*, 11180, 15 April 1769, and note, pp. 1447–9; *Letters*, 11186, 17 April 1769; *Letters*, 11187, 20 April 1769; *Letters*, 11233, 23 May 1769; *Letters*, 11234, 24 May 1769; *Letters*, 11256, 15 June 1769.

26. Pomeau et al., *Voltaire en son temps,* vol. II, p. 326.

27. *Letters*, 11233, 23 May 1769.

28. *Letters*, 11126, 8 March 1769.

29. *Letters*, 11407, 11 September 1769.

30. *Letters*, 10620, 15 March 1768.

31. *Letters*, 10660, 30 March 1768.

32. *Letters*, 10842, 11 July 1768; *Letters*, 10877, 24 August 1768.

33. *Letters*, 10929, 6 October 1768, and note, p. 1356.

34. *Letters*, 10893, 5 September 1768.

35. *Letters*, 11029, 23 December 1768.

36. *Letters*, 11030, 23 December 1768.

37. *Letters*, 10808, 24 June 1768.

38. *Letters*, 11114, 27 February 1769.

39. *Letters*, 11123, 4 March 1769.

40. *Letters*, 11164, 3 April 1769.

41. *Letters*, 11114, 27 February 1769.

42. *Letters*, 11124, 7 March 1769.

43. *Letters*, 11192, 26 April 1769, and note, p. 1454.

44. *Letters*, 11351, 9 August 1769, and note, pp. 1506–7.

45. *Letters*, 11261, 19 June 1769.

46. *Letters*, 11308, 17 July 1769; *Letters*, 11332, 31 July 1769.

47. *Letters*, 11332, 31 July 1769.

48. *Letters*, 11365, 16 August 1769, and note, pp. 1511–2.

49. *Letters*, 11365, 16 August 1769.

50. *Letters*, 11363, 15 August 1769.

51. *Letters*, 11370, 18 August 1769.

52. *Letters*, 11413, 16 September 1769, and note, p. 1530.

53. *Letters*, 11423, 20 September 1769, and note, p. 1534.

54. *Letters*, 11420, 19 September 1769.

55. *Letters*, 11423, 20 September 1769.

56. *Letters*, 11428, 25 September 1769.

57. *Letters*, 11462, 28 October 1769.

58. *Letters*, 11575, 3 February 1770, and note, p. 1134.

31: Watchmaking at Ferney

1. *Letters*, 11483, 20 November 1769.

2. *Letters*, 11500, 8 December 1769.

3. *Letters*, 11607, 21 February 1770.

4. See, for example, *Letters*, 11582, 9 February 1770; *Letters*, 11591, 16 February 1770; and *Letters*, 11596, 18 February 1770.

5. *Letters*, 11591, 16 February 1770.

6. *Letters*, 9933, 10 February 1767.

7. *Letters*, 11592, 16 February 1770.

8. *Letters*, 11599, 19 February 1770; *Letters*, 11605, 21 February 1770, *Letters*, 11607, 21 February 1770.

9. *Letters*, 11606, 21 February 1770.

10. *Letters*, 11615, 25 February 1770.

11. *Letters*, 11642, 12 March 1770; *Letters*, 11643, 12 March 1770, *Letters*, 11654, 16 March 1770, and note, p. 1156.

12. *Letters*, 11652, 16 March 1770, and note, pp. 1155–6.

13. *Letters*, 11550, 17 January 1770.

14. *Letters*, 11650, March 1770.

15. *Letters*, 11690, 9 April 1770.

16. *Letters*, 11627, 5 March 1770; *Letters*, 11720, 30 April 1770.

17. *Letters*, 11857, 16 July 1770; *Letters*, 14402, 23 December 1775.

18. *Letters*, 11691, 9 April 1770.

19. *Letters*, 14237, 11 August 1775; *Letters*, 14274, 5 September 1775; *Letters*, 14659, 12 June 1776.

20. *Letters*, 11601, 19 February 1770.

21. *Letters*, 11708, 24 April 1770.

22. *Letters*, 11702, 16 April 1770.

23. *Letters*, 11749, 21 May 1770; *Letters*, 11796, 20 June 1770; *Letters*, 11861, 20 July 1770.

24. *Letters*, 12003, 21 October 1770.

25. *Letters*, 11575, 3 February 1770.

26. *Letters*, 11723, April-May 1770.

27. Pomeau et al., *Voltaire en son temps,* vol. II, pp. 348–9.

28. *Letters*, 11714, 27 April 1770, and note, p. 1178.

29. *Letters*, 11729, 5 May 1770.

30. *Letters*, 11748, 21 May 1770.

31. *Letters*, 11793, 19 June 1770.

32. *Letters*, 11797, 22 June 1770.

33. *Letters*, 11867, 22 July 1770; *Letters*, 11871, 23 July 1770.

34. *Letters*, 11801, 25 June 1770; *Letters*, 11840, 9 July 1770, and note, pp. 1219–20; *Letters*, 11871, 23 July 1770.

35. *Letters*, 12317, 18 March 1771.

36. *Letters*, 12604, 1 December 1771.

37. *Letters*, 11785, 16 June 1770; *Letters*, 11787, 17 June 1770.
38. *Letters*, 11785, 16 June 1770, and note, p. 1203.
39. *Letters*, 11789, 17 June 1770; *Letters*, 11791, 18 June 1770.
40. *Letters*, 11884, 30 July 1770; *Letters*, 11903, 15 August 1770.
41. *Letters*, 12048, 19 November 1770; *Letters*, 12078, 6 December 1770.
42. *Letters*, 12414, 11 June 1771.
43. *Letters*, 11737, 11 May 1770.
44. *Letters*, 12126, 28 December 1770, and note, p. 1315.
45. *Letters*, 12126, 28 December 1770.
46. *Letters*, 11867, 22 July 1770.
47. *Letters*, 11859, 16 July 1770; *Letters*, 11917, 20 August 1770; *Letters*, 11924, 24 August 1770.
48. *Letters*, 12029, 9 November 1770.
49. *Letters*, 12292, 6 March 1771.
50. *Letters*, 12433, 19 June 1771.
51. *Letters*, 12439, 29 June 1771.
52. *Letters*, 12364, 30 April 1771.
53. *Letters*, 11904, 15 August 1770, and note, p. 1241; *Letters*, 12439, 29 June 1771.
54. *Letters*, 12210, 14 January 1771; *Letters*, 12381, 9 May 1771; *Letters*, 12430, 17 June 1771; *Letters*, 11966, 26 September 1770.
55. *Letters*, 11783, 12 June 1770; *Letters*, 11842, 11 July 1770.
56. *Letters*, 11738, 11 May 1770.
57. *Letters*, 11746, 21 May 1770; *Letters*, 11761, 4 June 1770, and note, p. 1194.
58. *Letters*, 12379, 8 May 1771.
59. *Letters*, 12520, 20 September 1771.
60. *Letters*, 12574, 9 November 1771.
61. *Letters*, 12430, 17 June 1771; *Letters*, 12520, 20 September 1771; *Letters*, 13893, 14 October 1774.
62. *Letters*, 12664, 19 January 1772; *Letters*, 12700, 19 February 1772.
63. *Letters*, 13108, 11 January 1773.
64. *Letters*, 13478, 25 October 1773; *Letters*, 13596, 17 January 1774; *Letters*, 13791, 27 June 1774.
65. *Letters*, 13289, 15 May 1773.
66. *Letters*, 13296, 19 May 1773; *Letters*, 13327, 4 June 1773.
67. *Letters*, 12831, 17 June 1772, and note, p. 1580.
68. *Letters*, 12852, 6 July 1772; *Letters*, 12853, 8 July 1772.
69. *Letters*, 12912, 28 August 1772.
70. *Letters*, 12931, 16 September 1772, and note, p. 951.
71. *Letters*, 12938, 21 September 1772; *Letters*, 12945, 29 September 1772; *Letters*, 12952, 2 October 1772.
72. *Letters*, 12956, 5 October 1772.
73. *Letters*, 13169, 19 February 1773, and note, pp. 1041–2.
74. *Letters*, 13296, 19 May 1773, and note, pp. 1087–8.
75. *Letters*, 13327, 4 June 1773.

76. *Letters*, 14745, 3 October 1776; *Letters*, 14746, 4 October 1776; *Letters*, 14766, 30 October 1766; *Letters*, 14771, 3 November 1776; *Letters*, 14783, 13 November 1776; *Letters*, 14785, 15 November 1776; *Letters*, 14821, 10 December 1776.
77. *Letters*, 13902, 24 October 1774.
78. *Letters*, 13998, 6 January 1775, and note, p. 852.
79. Pomeau et al., *Voltaire en son temps,* vol. II, pp. 456–7, and Voltaire, *Correspondence*, Moultou to Meister, D 19217.
80. *Letters*, 14237, 11 August 1775.
81. *Letters*, 14402, 23 December 1775.
82. *Letters*, 14561, 23 March 1776, and note, p. 1111.
83. *Letters*, 14561, 23 March 1776, and note, p. 1111.
84. *Letters*, 11727, 4 May 1770.
85. *Letters*, 12540, 11 October 1771.
86. *Letters*, 13331, 7 June 1773.
87. *Letters*, 14666, 20 June 1776, and note, p. 1162.
88. *Letters*, 13888, 10 October 1774.
89. *Letters*, 14257, 28 August 1775; *Letters*, 14265, 31 August 1775; *Letters*, 14313, 8 October 1775.
90. *Letters*, 13246, 12 April 1773.
91. *Letters*, 14262, 31 August 1775; *Letters*, 14306, 3 October 1775.
92. *Letters*, 14313, 8 October 1775; *Letters*, 14316, 10 October 1775; *Letters*, 14340, 6 November 1775, and note, p. 1011.
93. *Letters*, 14392, 15 December 1775, and note, pp. 1032–1033.
94. *Letters*, 14389, 14 December 1775.
95. *Letters*, 14432, 4 January 1776; and note, pp. 1048–9.
96. *Letters*, 14488, 9 February 1776.
97. *Letters*, 14659, 12 June 1776.
98. *Letters*, 14766, 30 October 1776.
99. *Letters*, 14752, 11 October 1776.

32: Last campaigns

1. *Letters*, 11381, 30 August 1769; *Letters*, 11393, 4 September 1769; *Letters*, 11517, 20 December 1769.
2. *Letters*, 11624, 3 March 1770.
3. *Letters*, 12784, 4 May 1772.
4. Voltaire, *Au Roi en son conseil*, and *Nouvelle Requête* (1770), in Voltaire, *Œuvres complètes*, ed. Moland.
5. *Letters*, 14102, 16 April 1775.
6. *Letters*, 12337, 5 April 1771, and note, p. 1378.
7. *Letters*, 12372, 5 May 1771.
8. *Letters*, 12378, 8 May 1771, and note, p. 1397; Voltaire, *La Coutume de Franche-Comté* (1771), and *Supplique des serfs* (1772) and *La Voix du curé* (1772), in *Œuvres complètes*, ed. Moland.
9. Voltaire, *Extrait d'un mémoire* (1775) and *Supplique à M. Turgot* (1776), in Voltaire, *Œuvres complètes*, ed. Moland.
10. *Letters*, 15153, 13 January 1778.

11. Voltaire, *Relation de la mort du chevalier de La Barre*, in *Mélanges*, pp. 755–68.
12. *Letters*, 14004, 16 January 1775.
13. *Letters*, 14006, 16 January 1775.
14. Voltaire, *Cri du sang innocent*, in *L'Affaire Calas* (Gallimard), pp. 341–50.
15. *Letters*, 15284, 26 May 1778.
16. Voltaire, *Le Prix de la justice et de l'humanité*, in *Œuvres complètes*, ed. Moland.
17. *Letters*, 14682, 19 July 1776.
18. *Letters*, 14691, 30 July 1776.
19. *Letters*, 14706, 15 August 1776.
20. *Letters*, 12501, 4 September 1771; *Letters*, 14714, 3 September 1776, and note, p. 1186.
21. *Letters*, 13740, 18 May 1774.
22. *Letters*, 13904, 26 October 1774, and note, pp. 1312–6; Pomeau et al., *Voltaire en son temps,* vol. II, pp. 438–9; Jean Goulemot, André Magnan and Didier Masseau (eds), *Inventaire Voltaire* (Gallimard, Paris, 1995), p. 631.
23. *Letters*, 13982, 30 December 1774.
24. *Letters*, 14089, 7 April 1775.
25. *Letters*, 14089, 7 April 1775, and note, pp. 903–4.
26. *Letters*, 14131, 5 May 1775.
27. *Letters*, 10680, 6 April 1768.
28. *Letters*, 14152, 19 May 1775.
29. *Letters*, 14240, 15 August 1775.
30. *Letters*, 14886, 17 February 1777.
31. *Letters*, 9582, 19 August 1766.
32. *Letters*, 10999, 28 November 1768.
33. *Letters*, 13079, 21 December 1772, and note, p. 1008; *Letters*, 13257, 20 April 1773, and note, p. 1073.
34. *Letters*, 14221, 29 July 1775, and note, p. 959.
35. *Letters*, 13168, 16 February 1773.
36. *Letters*, 13162, 12 February 1773, and note, p. 1038.
37. *Letters*, 13215, 26 March 1773.
38. *Letters*, 14912, 28 March 1777.
39. *Letters*, 14754, 18 October 1776; *Letters*, 14766, 30 October 1776.
40. Pomeau et al., *Voltaire en son temps,* vol. II, p. 559.

33: Triumph and Death

1. *Letters*, 15146, 1 January 1778, and note, p. 299.
2. *Letters*, 15176, 3 February 1778; *Letters*, 15176, 3 February 1778.
3. *Letters*, 15175, 2 February 1778.
4. *Letters*, 15250, 10 April 1778, and note, p. 351.
5. *Letters*, 15189, 17 February 1778.
6. *Letters*, 15145, 1 January 1778, and note, p. 298.
7. *Letters*, 15151, 12 January 1778.
8. *Letters*, 15155, 14 January 1778.
9. *Letters*, 15187, 16 February 1778, and note, p. 321.
10. *Letters*, 15187, 16 February 1778, and note, p. 321.

11. *Letters*, 15189, 17 February 1778.
12. *Letters*, 15191, 18 February 1778.
13. *Letters*, 15192, 18 February 1778.
14. *Letters*, 15192, 18 February 1778, and note, p. 322.
15. *Letters*, 15192, 18 February 1778, and note, p. 323.
16. *Letters*, 15203, 20 February 1778, and note, p. 326.
17. *Letters*, 15203, 20 February 1778.
18. Pomeau et al., *Voltaire en son temps,* vol. II, p. 579.
19. *Letters*, 15212, 26 February 1778.
20. *Letters*, 15214, 27 February 1778, and note, p. 330.
21. Pomeau et al., *Voltaire en son temps,* vol. II, p. 583.
22. *Letters*, 15217, 4 March 1778, and note, pp. 332–3.
23. *Letters*, 15221, 15 March 1778, and note, pp. 334–5.
24. *Letters*, 15230, 21 March 1778.
25. Pomeau et al., *Voltaire en son temps,* vol. II, p. 599.
26. Pomeau et al., *Voltaire en son temps,* vol. II, p. 604.
27. Pomeau et al., *Voltaire en son temps,* vol. II, p. 738.
28. *Letters*, 15259, 22 April 1778, and note, p. 353.
29. *Letters*, 15259, 22 April 1778, and note, p. 353.
30. *Letters*, 15077, 30 October 1777.
31. *Letters*, 15264, April-May 1778.
32. *Letters*, 15269, 10 May 1778; *Letters*, 15268, 7 May 1778.
33. *Letters*, 15267, 7 May 1778, and note, p. 357.
34. *Letters*, 15270, 10 May 1778, and note, p. 359.
35. *Letters*, 15283, 24 May 1778.
36. *Letters*, 15284, 26 May 1778.
37. Condorcet, *Vie de Voltaire* (Quai Voltaire, Paris, 1994), p. 147; Pomeau et al., *Voltaire en son temps,* vol. II, p. 624.
38. Quoted in Goulemot, Magnan and Masseau (eds), *Inventaire Voltaire.*
39. Condorcet, *Vie de Voltaire*, p. 132.

Voltaire's most important correspondents

1. Letters 13868, September 14, 1774.

INDEX